Acclaim for Francis Parkman
&
The Francis Parkman Reader

"[Parkman] wrote history as well as it has ever been written in America.... It is sufficient proof of the enduring vitality of Parkman's work that controversy still arises about its author. What all critics admit is that Parkman was superbly equipped with the tools of his trade: a talent for research and evaluation, and literary skill.... It is good to have a selection of his major writings made available to the general reader."

—New York Times Book Review

"Morison gives us a true labor of love.... Parkman was the ideal historian. He knew the shape and the look and the feel of the land about which he wrote. He was never content with dusty manuscripts.... [His] is the sort of writing that makes history irresistible."

—Christian Science Monitor

"There is no denying Parkman's command of an immense amount of material and his prowess at storytelling." *—Washington Post Book World*

"[Parkman's narratives] are as moving as the tribulations and defiances of Milton's Satan. It is the spiritual conflict in the author, as well as his reading of history as a war between two basic types of personality, which gives Parkman's work its power. The archetypal struggle gives it epic character. The personal conflict gives it the intricacy and ambiguity of a psychological novel." **—Kenneth Rexroth,** *The Nation*

"Francis Parkman's history [is one of] the two greatest works produced about the cultural experience of this country." **—Jed Perl**

"An excellent epitomization of the majestic *France and England in North America*. Morison [is] an unusually sensitive editor.... [*The Francis Parkman Reader*] conveys much of the sweep of the whole and reminds us most enjoyably that in Parkman's mastery of the grand style he stands very close to Edward Gibbon." *—New Yorker*

"Parkman was a master of narrative history, with a sense of style and gift of portraiture based upon a thorough knowledge of the terrain and exhaustive and scrupulous research. . . . A great craftsman still casts a spell." **—Richard B. Morris,** coeditor of *The Spirit of 'Seventy-Six*

"[Parkman] sought by creative imagination to bring the past to life. He tried to imbue himself with the spirit of the time, events, and people he described, to become a sharer in the crises and adventures of which he wrote." **—C. Vann Woodward**

"Marked by literary power and painstaking research, [his work] stands the test of time surprisingly well. . . . Here is Parkman presented so attractively that the general reader should turn once more to the greatest of our historians." *—Library Journal*

"A judicious selection and a rich sampling. . . . [Morison's] penetrating introduction is the best and most accurate appraisal of Parkman and his works in print. . . . Parkman combined literary workmanship, exacting scholarship, imagination, and understanding of human nature in a work of art. . . . [An] attractive, readable, and authoritative book. It is a fitting tribute to one of America's greatest historians."

—American Historical Review

"Parkman's history is the lives of men and women, and his genius consisted of his mastery of the skill that all dramatists and all good novelists must have. . . . Morison has handsomely served those who know Parkman well, and even more notably the multitude who will know him only through this book, on whose justness they can so confidently rely." **—Bernard DeVoto,** *New England Quarterly*

"Parkman is one of the greatest historians that the English-speaking world has produced. His *France and England in North America* is a magnificent epic. . . . The soundness of his work is amazing. . . . He had a rare sensitivity and imagination, and was a very gifted and skilled literary artist. His style is vivid, picturesque, and fluent, without being self-conscious. . . . He reconstructed the past, not as a dead thing but as a living reality." *—Saturday Review*

The Francis Parkman Reader

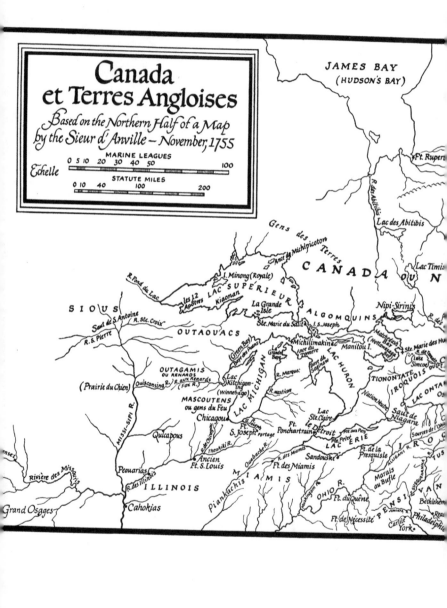

Canada
et Terres Angloises

Based on the Northern Half of a Map by the Sieur d'Anville — November, 1755

Echelle

MARINE LEAGUES
0 5 10 20 30 40 50   100

STATUTE MILES
0 10   40   100   200

JAMES BAY
(HUDSON'S BAY)

Ft. Rupert

R. des Abitibis

Lac des Abitibis

Lac Timis

CANADA OU N

Gens des Terres

Ance de Michipicoton

I. Minong (Royale)

R. Fond du Lac

les 12 Apôtres

Kioonan

LAC SUPERIEUR

La Grande Isle

ALGOMQUINS

Nipi-Sirinis

R. de

SIOUS

Sault de S. Antoine

R. Ste. Croix

Ste. Marie du Saut

I. S. Joseph

OUTAOUACS

R. S. Pierre

Matchedeck (Nottawasaga)

Ste. Marie des Hur (Lake Simcoe) du F

Green Bay Baye des Puans

Michilimakinac Ance du Tonnerre

Manitou I.

OUTAGAMIS OU RENARDS R. aux Renards (Fox R.)

Lac Kitchigami (Winnebago)

Grande Baye

R. Marque

Baye du Saguinam

TIONONTATE

IROQUOIS

(Prairie du Chien)

Quisconsing R.

Nation Neutre

LAC ONTA

MASCOUTENS ou gens du Feu

R. mestion

Sault de Niagara

MISSI-SIPI R.

Chicagou

Lac Ste. Claire

Ft. le Detroit

Ance aux Peau

Os

IROQ

Qulcapous

S. Joseph portage

Ft. S. Joseph

Pt. Pelce

LAC ERIE

US

Theakiki R.

Pontchartrain

Ft. de la Presquisle

Sandouské

ALLIGANI R.

Sources de l'Ohio

Riviere des Miss

Peouarias

Ancien Ft. S. Louis

M I A M I S

Ft. des Miamis

Marais au Buffe

R. des Illinois

Piankachis R.

R. des Miamis

PENSI

VAN

nses

Grand Osages

ILLINOIS

OHIO R.

Ft. duQuêne

Bethlehem

JUNIATA

Cahokias

Ft. de Nécessité

Carlise

Philadelphi

York

Real

Francis Parkman

THE
Francis Parkman
READER

SELECTED AND EDITED
WITH AN INTRODUCTION
AND NOTES BY

Samuel Eliot Morison

Illustrated with Maps

DA CAPO PRESS • NEW YORK

Library of Congress Cataloging-in-Publication Data

Parkman, Francis, 1823–1893.
    [Parkman reader]
    The Francis Parkman reader / selected and edited with an introduction
and notes by Samuel Eliot Morison.—1st Da Capo Press ed.
        p.   cm.
    Originally published: Boston: Little, Brown, 1955.
    Includes bibliographical references (p.   ) and index.
    ISBN 0-306-80823-4 (alk. paper)
    1. Canada—History—To 1763 (New France) 2. United States—History—
Colonial period, ca. 1600–1775. I. Morison, Samuel Eliot, 1887–1976. II.
Title.
F1030.P245   1998
971.01—dc21   97-42967
                                                                      CIP

First Da Capo Press edition 1998

This Da Capo Press paperback edition of *The Francis Parkman Reader* is an
unabridged republication of the edition originally published under the title
The Parkman Reader in Boston in 1955. It is reprinted by permission of
Little, Brown and Company.

Published by Da Capo Press, Inc.
A Subsidiary of Plenum Publishing Corporation
233 Spring Street, New York, N.Y. 10013

Manufactured in the United States of America

To my beloved wife
PRISCILLA BARTON MORISON
this volume is
devotedly dedicated

Preface

The purpose of this Reader is to present the public with selections from the works of Francis Parkman, who is universally admitted to be one of the greatest — if not the greatest — historians that the New World has produced. He combined depth and accuracy of research, literary skill, and sensitivity, both to natural beauty and to the human heart, as few historians of any age or country have done. Yet all his works are now out of print. His writings have been such a joy and inspiration to me and to countless others that, in the hope of sharing this pleasure with new readers, I have made these selections from his multivolumed series on *France and England in North America.*

My principles of selection and editing have been these:

1. Whole chapters, or groups of chapters, have been selected rather than short extracts and brief passages, in order to enable the reader to follow a story from start to finish.

2. Parkman's text has been scrupulously respected. The only changes made are typographical, such as giving the modern spelling for certain place names, and printing ships' names in italics. The actual "copy" sent to the printer has been taken from pages of the Frontenac or the Centenary Edition, both of which incorporate the last author's revisions.

3. Many of Parkman's footnotes, including almost all the bibliographical ones, have been deleted, because most of them are of little interest to general readers, and students who wish to check his sources may easily find the notes in the various editions of Parkman's works. The French, British and Canadian documents to which Parkman refers may be consulted in the longhand copies that he had made, which he bequeathed to the Massachusetts Historical Society in Boston. The editor

has added a number of notes of his own, including corrections of statements by Parkman that have been proved to be inaccurate or misleading by research during the sixty-odd years since his death — and they are remarkably few; and he has also provided a few introductory or connecting paragraphs. All these additions by the editor are printed in square brackets to distinguish them from Parkman's own notes.

4. In making the selection, which amounts to perhaps one seventh of *France and England in North America*, I have chosen chapters which, in my judgment, have the greater interest for present-day readers, and at the same time have best stood the test of time for accuracy. The "Native Tribes" introduction to *The Jesuits* is included, despite the fact that it was written before the scientific study of the American Indian began, both because it incorporates much of Parkman's personal experience, and because it is, in a sense, the key to all his work. He started with the forest and the Indians and worked from them to the French and the English in North America.

As an historian, Parkman was almost entirely self-taught. Industrious in searching out new material, and skillful in its interpretation, he was equal to any of the professionally trained historians of a later generation; and he had what most of them lacked — a sense of style. His unusual combination of superlative skill in the three qualities that make good historical literature — research, evaluation and literary presentation — besides the fascination of his chosen field, have caused the works of Parkman to endure longer than those of any other American historian of his era. This was very well said by M. Ægidius Fauteux, a Canadian archivist, in his address at the Parkman Centenary in 1923:

Si Parkman n'a pas vielli, si les lauriers reverdissent sur sa tête avec un fraîcheur toujours nouvelle, c'est que son œuvre est jeune de la jeunesse immortelle de l'art. Tout en ne négligeant rien de la méthode scientifique, sans laquelle l'historien risquerait de manquer au premier de ses devoirs, l'exactitude, il a su en dérober le rébarbatif appareil sous l'éclat de la forme. A la sècheresse du fait, il a superposé la magie du style. L'érudit se double chez lui d'un artiste. Toute son histoire est traversée d'un large souffle qui la soutient et qui l'anime: le don de vie.

That is it — the gift of vitality. Parkman's work is forever young, "with the immortal youth of art"; his men and women are alive; they feel, think and act within the framework of a living nature. Documents are, to be sure, the basis of his History; but to him documents were not facts; rather, the symbols of events, which the historian must recreate for his readers. In Parkman's prose the forests ever murmur, the rapids perpetually foam and roar; the people have parts and passions. Like that "sylvan historian" of Keats's *Ode on a Grecian Urn*, he caught the spirit of an age and fixed it for all time, "forever panting and forever young."

Among those who have helped me in this compilation, I owe special thanks to my wife, who accompanied me to the "Parkman country," and has delighted me by deciding to build a cottage on a headland near the spot where Chief Asticou welcomed Père Biard; to Mr. Richard W. Hale, curator of Canadian History in the Harvard College Library; to the Reverend Honorius Provost, Archivist of the Grand Séminaire, Université Laval, Quebec; to Professor Marshall Smelser of the University of Nôtre Dame; to Mrs. John F. Perkins, granddaughter of the historian; and to Miss Antha E. Card, my secretary, who has carried the major part of the burden of preparing the text.

SAMUEL ELIOT MORISON

"GOOD HOPE"
NORTHEAST HARBOR, MAINE
June, 1954

Contents

Preface   ix

Editor's Introduction   3

I   The Native Tribes   25
     1. The Algonquins   25
     2. The Hurons   28
     3. The Huron-Iroquois Family   38
     4. Social and Political Organization   41
     5. The Iroquois   44
     6. Religion and Superstitions   52

II   Verrazano, Cartier and Roberval   65

III   LaRoche, Champlain: St. Croix   86

IV   Lescarbot, Port Royal and Poutrincourt   102
     1. Marc Lescarbot Winters at Port Royal   102
     2. Poutrincourt and the Jesuits   112
     3. Madame de Guercheville   115

V   The Colonies at Port Royal and Mount Desert   119
     1. Biard and Biencourt at Port Royal   119
     2. La Saussaye's Settlement on Mount Desert   125
     3. The Ruin of French Acadia   131

VI   Champlain in Canada   135
      1. The Founding of Quebec   135
      2. The Expedition to Lake Champlain   143
      3. The Death of Champlain   151

VII   Isaac Jogues   153

VIII The Martyrdom of Father Jogues   169

IX   The Heroes of the Long Saut   174

X   Marriage and Population   184

XI   The New Home   193

XII   Canadian Feudalism   200

XIII The Rulers of Canada   211

XIV   Trade and Industry   224

XV   Priests and People   239

XVI   Morals and Manners   255

XVII Canadian Absolutism   266

XVIII The Success of La Salle   271

XIX   St. Louis of the Illinois   283

XX   La Salle Painted by Himself   292

XXI   La Salle's Last Expedition   300
      1. A Wretched Voyage   300
      2. Ashore and Abandoned   306

XXII St. Louis of Texas   312

XXIII Death of La Salle, End of the Colony   327

XXIV King William's War on the New England Frontier   336

XXV	The Death of Frontenac	345
XXVI	The Founding of Detroit	351
XXVII	Queen Anne's War	360
XXVIII	The Sack of Deerfield	371
XXIX	A Mad Scheme	391
XXX	Louisbourg Besieged	405
XXXI	Louisbourg Taken	420
XXXII	Ticonderoga	434
XXXIII	James Wolfe	452
XXXIV	Wolfe at Quebec	458
XXXV	The Heights of Abraham	481
XXXVI	The Fall of Quebec	504
	Bibliography	519
	Index	527

List of Maps

The Discoveries of La Salle, from Joutel's *Voyages de Sieur LaSale* 275

Siege of Louisbourg, 1745 409

The Town and Fort of Carillon at Ticonderoga, from Jefferys 442–443

Siege of Quebec, 1759 473

Canada et Terres Angloises, from D'Anville's *Canada, Louisiane et Terres Angloises* At Front

Editor's Introduction

In his introduction to *Montcalm and Wolfe* (1884), last volume but one of *France and England in North America* to appear, Parkman wrote:

> The plan of the work was formed in early youth; and though various causes have long delayed its execution, it has always been kept in view. Meanwhile, I have visited and examined every spot where events of any importance in connection with the contest took place, and have observed with attention such scenes and persons as might help to illustrate those I meant to describe. In short, the subject has been studied as much from life and in the open air as at the library table.

Early youth is correct! Francis Parkman conceived the plan of writing the history of the struggle between France and England in the New World during his sophomore year at Harvard College, when he was eighteen years old. He prepared for it, not only by the conventional means of reading and research but, as he says, "from life and in the open air." He persisted in his plan, through long, dark years of suffering, until some measure of health returned; and he had the satisfaction to see the last of his volumes in print, forty-one years after the first had appeared.

To know what manner of man this historian was, and the surroundings in which he worked, there is no better description than that of his friend the Reverend Henri-Raymond Casgrain, "l'Abbé Casgrain" as he was known throughout French Canada. This account of his visit to Parkman in 1871, when he was forty-seven years old and at the height of his strength and achievement, is translated from

the Memoirs that the Abbé wrote in 1898–99. It is here printed for
the first time, by the kind permission of his heirs.[1]

*   *   *

In the month of May 1871, I was climbing the steps of the peristyle
of the Revere House in Boston,[2] admiring the two fine couchant lions
on each side of the staircase, when my attention was distracted by a
stranger who advanced toward me, and smilingly bade me welcome.
I recognized instantly my old friend Mr. Francis Parkman. For several
years we had corresponded without having seen one another. . . .
I begged him to come to my hotel parlor, where we talked for some
time.

"You intend," he said, "to stay several days in Boston. So I shall
take you with me to Jamaica Plain, my summer residence where I
have been installed for some weeks with my family. You will meet
my sister who keeps house for me and takes care of my two children,
Grace and Catherine, both in the flower of their age. My carriage will
convey us to my house in a short time. Jamaica Plain is only four miles
from Boston, and not far from Harvard University, which I shall
insist that you visit. I shall introduce you to some of the most celebrated professors, and you will be in the center of the intellectual
aristocracy of our country."

Mr. Parkman's phaëton, which he drove himself, was waiting at
the door of the hotel. The route that we followed in leaving Boston
is adorned with luxurious villas, half concealed at their entrance by
richly wooded grounds, with foliage in all the freshness of early
spring. One may say that all is artificial; even the soil is so sterile that
it has to be covered with good loam, or literally, with fertilizer, to
produce anything. The jest has passed into a proverb that in Massachusetts nature is so ungrateful that the farmers have to carry a file
in their pockets to sharpen the teeth of their animals, to give them a
chance to crop a bit of grass! You would not believe it in seeing on
every side magnificent gardens created by millions of money. That is
what Mr. Parkman has done for his property at Jamaica Plain.

---

[1] Incorporated in them is a shorter account of the same visit, which the Abbé
printed as *Francis Parkman*, and which is reprinted in his *Oeuvres Complètes*
(Quebec 1885) II 294–335.

[2] The Revere House stood on the south side of Bowdoin Square, on the site
of the headquarters of the City Fire Department. It was separated by a then
narrow Cambridge Street from the mansion built by Parkman's grandfather, which
was the historian's home from 1838 to his marriage.

The cottage which he then inhabited on the edge of a little pond was modest compared with the princely châteaux which surrounded it. He has since had it rebuilt.[3] Miss Mary Parkman and her two nieces [4] awaited us on the verandah. Their welcome was both warm and graceful. American politeness has the naturalness and ease of French courtesy, but with less exuberance and marks of demonstration.

The interior of the cottage corresponded to the exterior; everything was comfortable, but no display of luxury. What I most observed, and comes back to me when my thought returns to that American home, was the perfume of flowers spread through all the rooms. Everywhere there were very beautiful bouquets, or rather bunches, composed principally of rhododendrons of the most delicate rose tints.

Mr. Parkman was not only an eminent historian, he was also a horticulturist of high distinction. His favorite flower was the rose; he had collected, they say, a thousand different varieties. At the annual shows in Boston, he often won the first prizes. I have at my hand a charming little volume composed by him, *The Book of Roses,* which he sent me as a souvenir. It is the fruit of several years of study and of personal experience.

He told me himself how he had happened to take up this avocation. During a buffalo hunt in the Rocky Mountains, when he was still young, he had contracted, as a consequence of his exhaustion and the intemperate climate, a malady of which he has never been cured. He explained the nature of it to me in one of his letters, of 26 January 1872:—

"According to the 'Medical Faculty' — as the newspapers say — the trouble comes from an abnormal state or partial paralysis of certain arteries of the brain. Whatever it is, it is a nuisance of the first order, and a school of patience by which Job himself might have profited." To which he added pleasantly, "However, Providence permitting I will spite the devil yet."

During the acute crisis of this malady, the sensation that he felt was

[3] Parkman's cottage on Jamaica Pond was enlarged and practically rebuilt shortly after this visit. After his death the property was purchased by the Commonwealth to round out the parkway that extends from Back Bay to Franklin Park. A new road, named the Francis Parkman Drive, has been run through the site of the historian's rose garden, and a monument to his memory, erected by his friends, is on the site of the house.

[4] This was either Mary Bigelow, Parkman's sister-in-law, who undertook to look after the little girls, or Eliza Parkman, the historian's sister. His own sister Mary died in 1866. The two nieces were Parkman's daughters Grace, later Mrs. Charles P. Coffin, and Katherine, later Mrs. J. Templeman Coolidge, Jr.

that of a weight of several hundred pounds pressing on his head. His sight was extremely affected by it, and he almost lost the use of his eyes. All mental effort was forbidden, he had to look for distractions in the country, and what agreed with him best was the cultivation of his garden, which he first oversaw while remaining seated near his employes. When his strength began to return, he tried to work with his own hands, while seated for the most part of the time in a folding chair. In this position he would cut his plants and the edges of his flower beds, or weed the ground nearby. . . .

At the time of my stay at Jamaica Plain, his health had obviously improved. He had for some time resumed his historical work, and was continuing the series of works on Canada which he had begun. After *The Jesuits in North America* came *The Discovery of the Great West,* and next successively *The Old Régime; Frontenac; Montcalm and Wolfe;* and *A Half Century of Conflict,* forming, with the *Pioneers* (1865) and *The Conspiracy of Pontiac* (1851), the most learned history of the French régime in Canada that we possess. Many years elapsed before he succeeded in finishing this great work.

When one reflects on the state of health in which he almost always lived, one finds it difficult to conceive the amount of energy and perseverance which he had to employ in order to succeed.

And what of his appearance? He was the ideal type of Yankee, tall, thin, but with big bones. His face was smooth-shaven, its features well sculptured; small, tired eyes under a fine forehead radiating intelligence. His expression, normally serious and meditative, lighted up easily with a fugitive smile. The tone of his voice was nasal, like that of New Englanders; his speech hesitating in conversation; it would seem that he was searching for words.[5] There was nothing to suggest a writer with the imaginative and brilliant style that one admires in his books. His discourse had quite another charm, that of a high intelligence served by a vast extent of knowledge. His bearing was fairly alert, although one observed that his legs were weak. He did not seem too fatigued in conducting me to see what would interest me most, at Boston, Cambridge and Harvard. . . .

---

[5] In his little booklet *Francis Parkman* of 1872, p. 41, the Abbé adds: "The features of his face resemble one of those remarkable types that Leonardo da Vinci loved to paint: a harmonious combination of intelligence, *finesse* and energy; large forehead, finely sculptured nose, strong and prominent chin." Bostonians visiting Venice were struck by the resemblance of Verrochio's head of Bartolommeo Colleoni to Parkman, and several friends brought him photographs of the famous equestrian statue. Parkman felt much flattered by the comparison!

My stay in Boston confirmed my conviction of the immense services that Mr. Parkman has rendered to our country by his historical works. A natural sympathy and interest is connected with this writer, who has so nobly avenged the odious calumnies that had been invented to sully the name and character of our ancestors.

*   *   *

With this picture of the active historian in mind, let us go back to the beginning. Francis Parkman was born in Boston on September 16, 1823. The Parkmans, who had come to New England in the early Puritan migration, had risen from obscurity to fame through the familiar means of commerce and the Congregational Church. Frank, as his friends called him, was related to half the families who constituted Boston society in the Federalist era. His grandfather, Samuel Parkman, who had become wealthy by shipping and foreign commerce, owned the trapezoid of land stretching back from Bowdoin Square to Staniford Street. Most of it was garden; the three-story mansion house stood on the narrow end, facing the square; and among the nearby smaller houses were two or three inhabited by some of the merchant's many children.

Of these, the Reverend Francis Parkman, minister of the New North Church in Hanover Street,[6] is the only one that interests us; for his eldest son and namesake was the future historian. Frank had three younger sisters, one of whom, Eliza, acted as his hostess and amanuensis in later life; and a much younger brother, John Eliot, who went to sea and joined the United States Navy in the Civil War.[7]

Frank was so high-strung a child that at the age of eight he was "put out to grass" with his maternal grandfather Samuel Hall, a merchant who lived in the neighboring town of Medford. The Hall property abutted a rough, rocky, wooded tract of some three thou-

[6] Their meetinghouse was eventually purchased by the Catholic Archdiocese of Boston, and as St. Stephen's Church maintains the severe dignity of Bulfinch's architecture.

[7] He also had a half-sister Sarah, daughter of the Reverend Francis Parkman by an earlier marriage, and Mary, who died unmarried in 1866. His sister Caroline married the Reverend John Cordner, minister of a Unitarian Church in Montreal; their daughter still (1954) lives in the historian's house at 50 Chestnut Street, Boston. John E. Parkman joined the Navy as Captain's Clerk (corresponding in rank to Ensign) in 1862, and had sundry adventures during the Civil War; he was appointed Commodore's Secretary to Commodore R. N. Stembel USN of the Pacific Fleet in 1871, and at the close of that year was killed in a shipboard accident. The name of the historian's mother was Caroline Hall.

sand acres which even the early Puritans had been unable to farm; it is now a state reservation known as the Middlesex Fells, crisscrossed by trails and bridle paths. There young Parkman spent his holidays, and many other days when he should have been at school, roaming the forest, collecting birds' eggs, trapping squirrels, shooting with bow and arrow, and conjuring up Redskins. Here he acquired his lifelong love of the woods and of natural history. Every Saturday, to his great displeasure, his reverend father drove out to fetch him home to keep the Sabbath; but he usually managed to smuggle into the Boston house a few dead birds or a rat or chipmunk, which he stealthily stuffed between services during the tedious hours of the Puritan Sunday.

After four years of rustication, Frank was considered sufficiently robust to stand the rough-and-tumble of a Boston school, the famous Chauncy Hall. There the masters developed their pupils' sense of English style by requiring frequent translations of Virgil and Homer into idiomatic English. There, too, Frank first learned French, which stood him in good stead throughout his life, and he became an enthusiastic reader of Walter Scott and Lord Byron. His parents were now living in the Bowdoin Square mansion built by his grandfather.

In 1840, just before his seventeenth birthday, Francis Parkman entered Harvard College, of which Josiah Quincy was then President. Henry W. Longfellow was lecturing on French and Spanish literature; John W. Webster (who nine years later murdered Frank's uncle George) taught chemistry, and Edward T. Channing headed what would now be called the "English Department"; but "Potty" Channing, as the boys called him, was a completely undepartmentalized character with a genius for teaching good speaking and writing; among his pupils were Emerson and Thoreau. The studies of Harvard undergraduates were mostly prescribed. Freshmen and Sophomores took Latin, Greek, mathematics, natural and ancient history, English rhetoric, chemistry, metaphysics and one modern language; Juniors read Æschylus, Terence and Plautus, wrote Greek and Latin prose, went on with their chosen modern language, studied the Calculus, and received a few smatterings of philosophy. Juniors also studied the then famous work by William Smyth, professor at the English Cambridge, called *Lectures on Modern History, from the Irruption of the Northern Nations to the Close of the American Revolution*. They could, if they chose, attend the lectures of Professor Jared Sparks on the American Revolution; and Frank Parkman evidently did, since he received highest honors in history, and dedicated his *Pontiac* to Mr. Sparks. Formidable as this undergraduate curriculum sounds, it actually made very easy demands on a student's time, and boys like Parkman who had outside interests had plenty of opportunities to exercise them.

In the summer of freshman year, Frank made his first journey through the northern New England woods. That seems to have confirmed the love of the wilderness which he had acquired in childhood. "I had a taste for the woods and the Indians," he wrote to Casgrain, over forty years later, "and it was this that turned my attention to forest themes. At one time I thought of writing the history of the Indians, with the Iroquois as a central point; but on reflection I preferred the French colonies as equally suiting my purpose, while offering at once more unity and more variety, as well as more interest to civilized readers." [8] It was early in his sophomore year, when he was only eighteen, that the two influences, academic and outdoors, became "crystallized into a plan of writing the story of what was then known as the 'Old French War,' that is, the war that ended in the conquest of Canada. . . . My theme fascinated me, and I was haunted with wilderness images day and night." Before long he "enlarged the plan to include the whole course of the American conflict between France and England, or, in other words, the history of the American forest." [9]

In college with Parkman, although not all in his Class of 1844, were an unusual number of boys who later became famous: Benjamin Apthorp Gould the astronomer (who roomed with him freshman year); Daniel Denison Slade (who went on one of his summer hikes); J. C. Bancroft Davis of the Geneva Tribunal; Colonel Thomas Wentworth Higginson; Stephen H. Phillips, Minister of Foreign Affairs in the Kingdom of Hawaii; William Morris Hunt, the painter; William A. Richardson, a future Secretary of the Treasury, and William Crowninshield Endicott, a future Secretary of War; Horace Gray, a future Justice of the Supreme Court; George F. Hoar, United States Senator from Massachusetts; and three who became great scholars: Francis James Child, Charles Eliot Norton and George Martin Lane. Frank knew them all and liked most of them. He was distinctly "one of the boys"; member of several short-lived undergraduate clubs, of the then literary Institute of 1770, and the ever convivial Hasty Pudding, of which he was president. Handsome and well dressed, he was a favorite with the young ladies at Mr. Papanti's Boston assemblies, but

[8] To Casgrain, 23 Oct. 1887; signed draft of letter, in Harvard College Library.
[9] Autobiography in 2 *Proceedings* Massachusetts Historical Society VIII 351-52, notes; Sedgwick's *Life of Parkman* pp. 30-31.

fell in love with an accomplished horsewoman, a high-spirited beauty of Keene, New Hampshire. She resisted his ardent wooing and eventually married someone else.

What distinguished Frank from his fellows in those pre-athletic days was his zest for outdoor life. He would study in the early morning by candlelight in order to spend the sunlit hours out of doors, walking earnestly and briskly with a rifle on his shoulder — and he became a dead shot with the rifle, disdaining, like Westerners, a "scatter-gun." He was the principal patron of the crude college gymnasium, and the admired "strong man" of his class. His pace and endurance on the vacation tours in the northern forest exhausted his companions, few of whom ever went with him twice; he thought nothing of sleeping outdoors without a blanket, harassed by black flies and "no-see-'ems," and living off the country on trout and moose meat. But he kept a journal of each summer's excursion which proves that, at seventeen or eighteen, he was already well on his way to being a master of English style.

In these excursions, and in his daily regimen, Parkman pushed himself too hard. Late in life he once attributed his accumulation of physical ills to the three days and nights spent in the woods during continual rain, after his spruce-bark canoe fell apart in the rapids of the Magalloway.[10] On another occasion (as Casgrain has already told us) he said that hardships on his Far Western journey of 1846 were responsible. But in his autobiography he admits that his Spartan and ill-advised efforts to cure "conditions of the nervous system abnormal . . . from infancy" were responsible.[11] It is fairly certain that the nervous disorder, which troubled Parkman for at least forty years, was derived not from one or another accident or overstrain on his outings, but from the relentless driving of his physical powers from his eighteenth until his twenty-seventh year. His symptoms form a now recognizable pattern of neurosis. Consciously or unconsciously, he created a "struggle situation." Given his worship of manliness and contempt for weakness, he could be content with no less than mastery of "the enemy," as he personified the terrible headaches, the insomnia and the semiblindness.[12]

A comparison with Theodore Roosevelt, born thirty-five years later

[10] To Casgrain, 1889, *Le Canada français* XXIX 795. The story of this trip is told in the 1842 Journal.

[11] 2 *Proceedings* Mass. Hist. Soc. VIII 352.

[12] This is the conclusion of the most recent scholar to study Parkman's case, Prof. Wilbur R. Jacobs.

than Parkman, is relevant. Roosevelt as a boy suffered from poor eye-sight and asthma, and endeavored to overcome them by "the strenuous life"; but his weakness was not nearly as serious as Parkman's, and in his day there were physicians who knew what to do about it. So "T.R." became in almost every respect a healthy and vigorous man. Parkman either disregarded medical advice, or had none until it was too late; his method of being tough with himself merely made matters worse. Thus he was denied the balanced sort of life, partly literary, partly of action, that Roosevelt achieved; but by the most severe self-discipline and denial he was able to carry on his writing. It is also worth noting that by the time "T.R." entered Harvard, college athletics were going full swing, much as today; it had become "the thing" for college men to play ball games, run, leap and wrestle, row races, go camping, big-game hunting and all that; whilst in Parkman's youth such activities for a college student were almost unheard of, and Frank found it diffi-cult to recruit friends for his forest adventures. Consequently he had to fight the opinions and desires of his parents and older friends; and his urge to justify himself, by proving a success at his chosen tasks, in turn reacted on his health. Roosevelt recognized a certain affinity with Parkman, to whom he dedicated his *Winning of the West;* and Parkman, one may guess, envied the robust health which permitted his young admirer to enter public life and at the same time to shoot, hunt, fight, and write books. But the parallel must not be pushed too far. Parkman was neither egoist nor extrovert, but a man dedicated to one pursuit — his history; all else was secondary. Unlike Theodore Roosevelt (and also unlike Henry Adams), Parkman had no quarrel with his education, and he refused to be discouraged when the public refrained from buying his first book of history.

Parkman's first physical breakdown occurred shortly after the beginning of his senior year. His parents then persuaded him to make the grand tour of Europe; but Frank, although well provided with money, made about the most unconventional grand tour possible. In mid-November 1843, just turned twenty, he sailed as the only passenger on board a Mediterranean fruiter barque, the *Nautilus* of Boston. The passage interested him very little, and he was never tempted to write of sea voyages and discoveries. At Gibraltar he left this vessel and made his way by steamer to Malta, Syracuse, Messina and Palermo. There he procured a guide, three mules, provisions and a portable stove for a tour of western Sicily. In this manner, spending nights in fleabitten *alberghi* but catered to by the faithful Luighi, he reversed the course followed by the United States Seventh Army a century later, visiting Agrigento, Selinunte, Marsala, Trápani and Segesta. His journal of this tour is as fascinating as those of the northern woods. Note these two passages:

> The church of the Benedictines [in Messina] is the noblest edifice I have seen. This and others not unlike it have impressed me with new ideas of the Catholic religion. Not exactly, for I reverenced it before as the religion of brave and great men — but now I honor it for itself. They are mistaken who sneer at its ceremonies as a mere mechanical farce: they have a powerful and salutary effect on the mind. Those who have witnessed the services in this Benedictine church, and deny what I say, must either be singularly stupid and insensible by nature, or rendered so by prejudice.
>
> *Saturday.* I recall what I said of the beauty of the Sicilian women — so far, at least, as concerns those of high rank. This is a holy day. They are all abroad, in carriages and on foot. One passed me in the church of the Capuchin convent, with the black eye, the warm rich cheek, and the bright glance that belong to southern climates, and are beautiful beyond all else.[13]

At Naples Frank had the good fortune to encounter the Reverend Theodore Parker, then thirty-three years old, a left-wing Unitarian minister but a wise and intelligent cicerone. Together they attended the carnival and the puppet shows, and climbed Vesuvius; with Mrs. Parker they drove by six-horse diligence to Rome, saw all the sights, and were presented to Pope Gregory XVI. Frank's classmate Hunt, the artist, also turned up, and together they wandered over the Alban Hills. In Sicily, as we have seen, Frank had been impressed by the Catholic Church; and as the execution of his life plan required some knowledge of that Church and her ways, he took the original step (which shocked the Reverend Mr. Parker) of joining a retreat in the Passionist Fathers' monastery at Rome. This experience naturally did not afford him a very profound insight into the Catholic mind; but it did help him to understand French Canada, just as his later sojourn among the Sioux helped him to understand Red Indians; and he used to say with a smile that he found the Sioux more congenial than the monks. They tried to convert him but made not the slightest dent. Young Parkman, brought up a Unitarian, became what he called a "reverent agnostic," and so remained.

[13] Mason Wade *Journals of Francis Parkman* I 138-9.

After Easter, the youth continued his grand tour as far as Scotland. He returned home by steam packet, just in time to pass his examinations and take part in the festivities of Class Day and Commencement, 1844. As one of the first twenty scholars in his class of sixty-two, he was given a Commencement part — "Romance in America" — and was taken into Phi Beta Kappa.

If Parkman's parents hoped to restore Frank's health by this tour, they were rewarded; but if they expected to woo him from love of the forest to the more reputable fields of scholarship, they were disappointed. Europe fascinated him, but only as a background to America. There was no chance of his becoming an American scholar rooted in Europe, like his college friend Charles Eliot Norton; none whatever of his turning out to be a Miniver Cheevy, or one of those faint and futile expatriates described by Henry James. All his life Parkman had nothing but contempt for "a way of life whose natural fruit is that pallid and emasculate scholarship of which New England has had too many examples." [14]

After another summer tour, in the Berkshires, he entered Harvard Law School at the earnest request of his father, who still hoped that "Frank would settle down." He consoled himself by the thought that knowledge of the law would help him in studying and writing history, and undoubtedly it did. And in the summer of 1845 he extended his travels to the Great Lakes, in order to obtain both visual and documentary material for the first book that he planned to write, *Pontiac's Rebellion*.

It is difficult nowadays to imagine the disappointment among Parkman's friends and well wishers when he announced that his life work was to be the story of the conflict between France and England in North America. The subject seemed odd for a cultivated gentleman to take up. The proper thing, at that time, was Ancient History, or something Spanish. As Barrett Wendell recalled, the New England historians "were generally held by the local public opinion of their time rather more profoundly respectable than anything else on earth." Washington Irving, the senior American historian, had written his *Columbus* and *Conquest of Granada;* Mr. Prescott followed suit with *Ferdinand and Isabella* and *The Conquest of Mexico;* Mr. Ticknor was about to publish his *History of Spanish Literature,* and Mr. Eliot had produced the first volume of his *History of Liberty,* starting with

[14] 2 *Proceedings* Mass. Hist. Soc. VIII 353.

Rome. Those were subjects that proved their authors to be scholars. Mr. Bancroft, to be sure, had already produced three volumes of his *History of the Colonization of the United States*, but he wrote in the Whig tradition, almost as a sequel to Macaulay — and, anyway, he had left literature temporarily, for Democratic politics. What possible interest could there be for any cultivated reader in the crude struggles of Redskins with almost equally barbarous French and English colonists in the wilderness? Nobody, it seems, except Mr. Sparks and the Reverend Mr. Ellis, a local historian, encouraged Parkman's ambition; yet he persisted. And, by the time he was through, there was no question but that North American colonial history was a "respectable" and "scholarly" subject. The trouble was, to get young men to write about anything else!

Research for *Pontiac* was begun by Parkman even as an undergraduate; most of the available source materials were gathered in his law-school years, but he did not follow the life of the typical scholar. "For the student there is, in its season, no better place than the saddle, and no better companion than the rifle or the oar," he wrote late in life.[15] A jockey brought a string of untrained horses to Boston; Parkman and his friends helped to break them, and he perfected his horsemanship by learning to perform circus stunts while riding bareback. That was a form of exercise that stood him in good stead; nobody but an accomplished equestrian could have survived his sojourn with the Sioux.

He had plenty of fun, too. There is extant a letter of his, describing a "Class of '44 old-fashioned supper," in the fall of that year, which broke up after 1 A.M. with a smashing of empty bottles against the Washington Elm, followed by "a War-dance with scalp-yells in the middle of the Common."

Parkman first broke into print with some blood-and-thunder tales in the *Knickerbocker Magazine* in 1845, based on his own experiences in the northern woods. And then, suddenly, a great opportunity opened. Reading for his law degree, which he took in 1846, had severely strained his eyes. A cousin, Quincy A. Shaw, about to leave on a hunting expedition in the Far West, invited Frank to come along. He promptly accepted, since for him it was a heaven-sent opportunity to observe a new frontier and to see Indians in their primitive state. He

[15] 2 *Proceedings* Mass. Hist. Soc. VIII 353. Parkman loved rowing but he never took to sailing, probably because bright sun and reflections hurt his eyes, and because sailing does not require continuous physical exertion.

walked and rode through Pennsylvania, calling on the celebrated Mr. Schoolcraft for Indian lore; then dropped down the Ohio by sternwheeler and exulted at his first sight of the Father of the Waters, whose descent by La Salle he would chronicle, years later. At St. Louis he presented letters of introduction to the Chouteaus, leaders in that center of the fur industry; and through them he engaged Henry Chatillon, an expert Rocky Mountain trapper, as guide. In May 1846 the young men jumped off from Independence on the Oregon Trail. The story of their adventures is told in Parkman's famous book of that name, and even better in the original journals which Mr. Wade has printed.

This journey to the Black Hills had a profound effect, for good and ill, on Parkman's career. Owing to the fortunate circumstance of Chatillon's wife being an Oglala Sioux, the tribe of Sitting Bull and Crazy Horse, Parkman was able to join a roving band of their warriors and to stay with them for weeks. This gave him the unique opportunity of observing Indians who in many respects resembled the Iroquois, and who were still in the wild and primitive state that Champlain and LaSalle had found their forebears. On the other hand, the experience almost killed him. The burning sun of the high plains injured his eyes; and by sharing the strange diet of the Sioux, prepared in their filthy manner, he suffered a severe attack of dysentery. Nevertheless he kept on, scorning to show any weakness; even participating in mounted buffalo hunts over rough and rocky ground when he was so weak that only firmness of will kept him in the saddle.

The result of this culmination of imprudent overdoing was a complete nervous breakdown — a state that to Parkman, of all people, was intolerable and humiliating. For weeks after returning home, he was deprived of the use of his eyes; he passed sleepless nights in great pain. Yet his determination was such that under these conditions he wrote the account of his Western adventures that has become a classic, *The Oregon Trail*. It was all written literally in the dark, for his eyes could not stand the light. One of his sisters or Quincy Shaw would read the rough notes aloud to the author, who composed while tramping his father's garret in Bowdoin Square; then, with closed eyes, he dictated it to one of these devoted amanuenses; someone else even had to read the proof.

The Oregon Trail and its author have found detractors in recent years because Parkman was not interested in the American westward migration, in the thick of which he found himself; so he has been labeled a "Boston Brahmin," a "Harvard snob," "Federalist oligarch," "Proper Bostonian," and victim of "Anglo-Saxon superiority complex." Now, although any attempt to label, ticket or otherwise account for an individual like Francis Parkman is vain, and although nobody properly described by one of the above labels even thought of doing as he did, there is no doubt that he was a gentleman; and, even in the best sense of a much-abused word, an aristocrat. "My political faith," he wrote in 1875, "lies between two vicious extremes, democracy and absolute authority, each of which I detest, the more because it tends to react into the other." [16] Like most gentlemen, he disliked equally the newly rich and democrats of the envious and pushing type; but like a true sportsman he loved primitive people like Indians and trappers and rough-and-ready white folk who were not trying to put on airs.

Although, on his tour of Europe, he had received the cringing obsequiousness then accorded to traveling gentlemen, he much preferred the rude, independent Yankee tavernkeepers whom he encountered in his American travels, and greatly preferred the ordinary run of American country people to the smirking and bowing European peasants.[17] Some of the Western pioneers whom he met he summed up as "a very good set of men, chiefly Missourians"; others as "finelooking fellows, with an air of frankness, generosity and even courtesy." [18] But others whom he encountered — the ancestors apparently of Steinbeck's "Okies" — he described as "rude and intrusive" and "mean-looking fellows." It is true that Parkman was not interested in the westward movement; it was simply not his dish. He went West to hunt buffalo, view the scenery and study the Indians — which is what he did. Everyone praises Parkman for seeing through that eighteenth-century myth of the Noble Savage; why, then, scold him for not supporting the nineteenth-century myth of the Noble Democrat, or the twentieth-century myth of the Noble Western Pioneer? His guide Chatillon once remarked that "gentlemen of the right sort" could stand hardship better than ordinary people; and if Parkman had not been that kind of gentleman, he could never have surmounted his

[16] To Casgrain 9 May 1875, *Le Canada français* XXIX 696.
[17] See esp. Wade ed. *Journals* I 255 ff on the 1844 trip which came immediately after his European tour. Note his pleasure over a landlord who talked back, and his contempt for the Bostonian who imitated English dress and manners, and wrote "Cosmopolite" as his profession in a hotel register.
[18] *Journals* II 436–8.

physical infirmities and we should have had no great history from his pen.

The greater part of 1847–48 was spent by Parkman in search of health at the spa of Brattleboro, Vermont, in New York City, and with a specialist on Staten Island. Under the most trying circumstances — using his eyes for a minute, resting a minute, and not reading for more than an hour a day; hiring a schoolgirl who did not know French to read aloud French documents to him — he managed to finish *Pontiac* early in 1851, and that year it came out. He had to pay for having the book set up and stereotyped, and it was not an immediate success. The reason he published first this, the concluding volume of his series, was that he had already put in a great deal of work on the subject, and feared lest it be his last. But for his indomitable will, it doubtless would have been. "In achievement I expect to fail," he wrote to his cousin and confidante, Mary Eliot Parkman, "but I shall never recoil from endeavor."

In 1850, when he was almost twenty-seven years old, believing that his health was on the way to complete recovery, Parkman wooed and won Catherine Bigelow, daughter of an eminent Boston physician. Of this marriage he wrote, after his wife's death, "Looking for peace and rest, I found happiness."[19] After the Rev. Francis Parkman's death in 1852 they bought the cottage at Jamaica Pond described by Abbé Casgrain; and for several years they were very happy. Two daughters and a son were born. For several hours a day Mrs. Parkman and her sister Mary Bigelow would read aloud copies of documents from the foreign archives, or take down the historian's dictation for his one novel, *Vassall Morton*. An awful novel it was, and difficult for the young wife to take; since the hero was obviously her husband, and the heroine the high-spirited Amazon from Keene who had been his first love. Mrs. Parkman must have been blessed with a sense of humor, and an unusually strong conviction of marital security.

Suddenly darkness descended. The little boy died in 1857, and within a year his mother followed him to the grave. "The enemy," as Parkman called his malady, moved in on him. He feared lest he go mad. He journeyed to Paris to consult Dr. Brown-Séquard; but that famous eye specialist could do little for him. What he probably needed was a neurologist, but none there were until much later.

To Jamaica Plain he returned in 1859, where his sister Eliza kept

19 Doughty "Parkman's Dark Years," *Harvard Library Bulletin* IV (1950) 61.

house for him and his two little girls, in summer, and for him and his widowed mother at 8 Walnut Street, Boston, in winter. His malady was now complicated by arthritis in both knees, so that he could no longer walk; reading and writing were out of the question. It was then that he turned to horticulture for solace and an occupation. He could supervise the gardeners, and even do a little raking and weeding himself, from a wheeled chair; and this hobby he turned into a second profession. It used to be a joke in Boston that visiting Englishmen and Frenchmen asked to be presented to Mr. Parkman the historian, while the first person whom visitors from the Netherlands wished to see was Mr. Parkman the horticulturist.

It was not until 1862 that Parkman's "power of mental application was in the smallest degree restored," as he later recalled. Up to then, "several bushels of historical MSS," copies which he had ordered from European archives, "and fragments of abortive chapters have been packed under lock and key, to bide their time."[20] Now he began to break them out; and when *Pioneers* appeared in 1865, the first volume (except the abortive novel) since *Pontiac*, it was a signal that the harvest was coming in, ripe and full. Indeed, he felt so well in 1863 that he almost screwed up his courage to propose marriage to Ida, the daughter of Louis Agassiz; but a young cavalry officer, Major Henry Higginson, got ahead of him.

The summer home at Jamaica Plain was kept up; and for a winter residence he moved, after his mother's death, to 50 Chestnut Street, Boston. Although he could have had any of the sunny rooms in the house, he characteristically chose one on the top floor with a northern exposure, toward his beloved Canadian forests. Through the sixty years since his death, in the occupation of his niece Miss Cordner, this room has been kept exactly as he left it. Souvenirs of the Oregon Trail, photographs of Chatillon and of the Colleoni statue, are on the walls; and the wire frame which he used to guide his pencil when he could not use his eyes is in the desk drawer. In late spring the family, now consisting of Parkman, his sister Eliza and the two little girls, moved to Jamaica Plain; and after the younger daughter married J. Templeman Coolidge Jr., who acquired the old Benning Wentworth mansion at Little Harbor, New Hampshire, the historian passed a few weeks of each summer with them; he had a room looking out on the harbor and Leach's Island, which he bought for his daughter. Five times, between 1868 and 1887, he visited France in search of documents; and every

[20] Letter of 4 April 1862 to Mary Parkman, Doughty p. 73.

other year he made an excursion to the scenes he was writing about, from western Canada to Louisiana and Florida.

It is probable that the extreme difficulties under which Parkman worked, having most of his sources read aloud to him, and either dictating his text or writing it in the dark by means of his wire frame, enhanced the quality of the product. His own impressions of northern woods and western rivers, the data in ancient chronicles and Jesuit Relations, the reports of French and English officials, were distilled in the crucible of his powerful and creative mind. It can hardly be a coincidence that both leading stylists among American historians, Parkman and Prescott, overcame the handicap of partial blindness; and, out of the semidarkness in which they worked, wove a tapestry of brilliant prose.

Although Parkman once wrote that he "loathed the drudgery of historical research," I for one find the statement hard to believe, because he never employed a research assistant, and his relish over the discovery of new source material, which complicated and lengthened his task, was obvious. He revised his text again and again, and was scrupulously accurate in checking his quotations with the sources.

It was very irksome to Parkman to be a mere spectator of the Civil War, in which several friends and classmates lost their lives, and to be unable to take part in public affairs. The demagoguery and corruption of the postwar era was a grievous disappointment to him, as to Henry Adams. He seems to have expected that war would purge the Republic of its grossness and restore the rule of an educated elite.

Except for an occasional article or review in *The Nation* or *North American* or in horticultural journals, Parkman confined his writing to the History. As each volume rolled from the press — *Pioneers* (1865), *Jesuits* (1867), *Great West* (1869), *Old Régime* (1874), *Frontenac* (1877), *Montcalm and Wolfe* (1884) and, finally, *Half-Century of Conflict* (1892), his fame increased. Yet his health was never fully restored. Even when his eyes were functioning fairly well, arthritis or water on the knee compelled him to walk with two canes. In 1889 he wrote that he had been getting only two or three hours' sleep in the twenty-four for the last five years.[21] The two last works were the only ones of which he was able to write a part with his own hand.

It must not be supposed that his works had universal acclaim. American, British and British Canadian reviewers were generally enthusiastic; but many French Canadians, accustomed to view their history

[21] *Le Canada français* XXIX 795.

through rose-colored glasses as a romantic lost cause, began to attack Parkman after *The Old Régime* appeared in 1874. He had expected that they would. In the preface to that work he wrote, "Some of the results here reached are of a character which I regret, since they cannot be agreeable to persons for whom I have a very cordial regard. The conclusions drawn from the facts may be a matter of opinion, but it will be remembered that the facts themselves can be overthrown only by overthrowing the evidence on which they rest, or bringing forward counter-evidence of equal or greater strength; and neither task will be found an easy one." His research in Paris had brought out many incidents of clerical politics in Canada which had long been forgotten, and which the French Canadians thought should have been left in a pious oblivion.

Parkman did not attempt to conceal his indignation at Jesuit intrigues against La Salle and Frontenac. His friend Margry, after reading what he wrote, or was about to write, on the subject, begged him to remember the good that the Jesuits had done in Canada during the infancy of the colony, when it was neglected by the French government; and added this warning, "Watch yourself, my friend; for the honor of the historian is to elevate himself above the preoccupations of his era, of his party, even of his country." [22] Let the reader decide for himself whether or not Parkman followed this good advice.

Moreover, besides the theme of French heroism, piety and tenacity, of which French Canadians were proud, there was another theme running through his work that they could not be expected to accept. That was the antithesis: English liberty vs. French absolutism, Protestant freedom vs. Catholic authority, with victory to the forces of light and progress.

Nevertheless, many French Canadians have appreciated Parkman's services to their people, and have been willing to overlook his theories because of the charm of his narrative and his fidelity to historic truth. It was proposed, and apparently decided, that the Université Laval confer on him an honorary degree. The news leaked out in Quebec and provoked such a fury of opposition that the University authorities were frightened and wrote to Parkman that he could not have it. But an honorary degree was conferred on him next year (1879) by McGill University.

[22] "Surveillez-vous donc, mon ami: car l'honneur de l'Historien, c'est de s'élever au-dessus des préoccupations de son temps, de son parti, de son pays même." To Parkman 16 Sept. 1873, ms. in Mass. Hist. Soc.

When *Montcalm and Wolfe* appeared a new outcry arose, on account of Parkman's treatment of the expulsion of the Acadians. He did not attempt to justify that unfortunate act, but he did point out that equally to blame with the English were the French priests and other emissaries who kept the Acadians and Indians stirred up to a point where they became a menace to the English settlers, and then let them down. No French Canadian, however, could regard the expulsion as anything but indefensible and wholly abominable. Even Abbé Casgrain entered the lists against Parkman, arguing that he had ignored or supressed the real reason for removing the Acadians, the greed of New England Yankees for their land. Parkman was not indifferent to these clerical attacks on his integrity; but Stoic that he was, he gave no sign of being wounded; and he answered his critics in kind, by reviewing Casgrain's *Pélérinage au pays d'Evangeline* in the New York *Nation*. And friendship outlasted the dispute. Shortly after, their correspondence was resumed, and continued to the day of Parkman's death.

The historian was never a severe and lonely man, detached from time and place, pontifical or sacerdotal, living in a past world of his imagination, as he has sometimes been described. He was no reformer or protagonist of "every good cause" like many Bostonians of his class; but he had plenty of compatriots who were neither liberals nor reformers and who agreed with him in deploring the tendencies of the times. He read Godkin's New York *Nation*, voted mugwump, and occasionally reviewed a book or wrote an article pointing out the sins of democracy for the *North American Review*. He liked people, loved to have his friends in to dinner or in the afternoon, and even dined out as much as his health permitted, although he could not stand crowds. Unlike most American men of letters of his generation, he never cultivated the English nobility or the French noblesse, unless they had documents pertaining to his theme. He saw to it that his daughters were properly presented to society, and both were happily married in 1880. He attended his college class functions regularly, belonged to the Saturday Club (that mutual-appreciation society of the New England literati), as well as to the Historical Society and other organizations enjoyed by elderly Bostonians. He helped to organize the convivial St. Botolph Club on the model of London's Savage and New York's Century, served for six years as its president and took part in its jovial gatherings, from which Edward Everett Hale vainly endeavored to banish alcoholic beverages. He was one of the founders of the Archæological Institute of America and took a lively interest in its work, directed by the Bandeliers, in the American Southwest. He served faithfully as Overseer of Harvard College and Fellow of the Corporation for many years, and on numerous committees. One who knew him well said that "there was always about his eyes and mouth an expression of kindly, alert interest in what was doing, which did away with the notion of severity." [23] He was, essentially, a simple, uncomplicated person, with a direct approach to everyone and everything; kindly, with a whimsical sense of humor, and naturally sociable; but he had dedicated his life to a great literary task, and that always came first.

Perhaps the best test of an author's humanity is his attitude toward small children. Parkman loved to have his grandchildren and their friends about him, especially at Little Harbor where they ran wild, playing and shrieking; but he never complained of the noise, and for their amusement he made up stories about personified animals. A collection of china cats became endowed with life as he and the children handled them together, and letters were produced, supposedly from errant family felines who had gone hunting and never returned.

Want of money never troubled Parkman after his early married life — when it troubled him a good deal, as he and his wife started housekeeping with a total annual income of slightly over four hundred dollars. From his grandfather and father, who died in 1852, he inherited enough to live according to his simple tastes, until his books began to bring in royalties; but he received very little net from his writings, because the profits from one volume went toward copying documents for the next, or for travel. He regarded his inheritance as a trust, which conferred on him the obligation to make all the return he could to his country, in the form of historical literature. Owing in part to his independent means, and perhaps even more to his frugal manner of living, Parkman was never tempted to teach history, or even to go on the lecture circuit, as almost all the New England literati of his day were forced to do. However, when the Bussey Institution, the agricultural department of Harvard University, was opened in 1871 on one of the country estates adjoining Parkman's Jamaica Pond cottage, he was prevailed upon to accept the appointment of Professor of Horticulture, with a salary of two thousand dollars a year. The catalogue announced that the following year, after the freshmen had been

---

[23] Barrett Wendell's Memoir.

indoctrinated, he would give a course on plant propagation and the management of hothouses, nurseries, flower and fruit gardens. But even the light duties of the first year, supervising the building of greenhouses and planting, in what later became the Arnold Arboretum, so fatigued the historian that he resigned the chair before giving any formal instruction.

A good example of Parkman's practical side is the *affaire Margry*. That crotchety French archivist had under lock and key a mass of documents about La Salle and French exploration of the Far West, and would let nobody see them until and unless he could get funds for publication. The French government was not interested; and Parkman's friends, whom he had solicited for subscriptions, were too badly hit by the fire of 1871 to come through. But he did not despair. By writing dozens of letters a day, stirring up the Wisconsin and other Western historical societies, and playing on the idea that these documents were essential to the history of the Great West, he enlisted the support of several Congressmen, notably the future President James M. Garfield, and actually procured an appropriation of ten thousand dollars. That, however, was not the end of it. Mr. Spofford, the Librarian of Congress, appointed paymaster, hated to see the money go, and easily persuaded himself that Margry was cheating; the two exchanged furious letters and Parkman had to calm them down. Eventually the six volumes of Margry's *Découvertes et établissements des français dans l'ouest et dans le sud de l'Amérique* were published. All Parkman got out of them was a few new facts for revising his volume on the Discovery of the Mississippi.

In the summer of 1892, with the publication of *Half-Century of Conflict*, the last gap in the series was filled; the last voussoir fell into its planned place in the great arch. Yet, even then, the indefatigable historian carried on. Some new documents on the amusing rivalries between La Tour and d'Aunay in L'Acadie, and the absurd attempts of Governor Winthrop to play international politics, persuaded him to write fifty new pages on "The Feudal Chiefs of Acadia" for a new edition of *The Old Régime*, and this he saw through the press. He was about to begin a complete revision of the entire series when, in 1893, he suffered successive attacks of pleurisy and phlebitis. From both he recovered, and on his seventieth birthday, in September, he received many friends at his cottage. It was a warm and lovely autumn that tempted him to linger on in the country; but one day in early November, after returning from a short row on Jamaica Pond, he suffered a sudden and severe attack of peritonitis. For three days more the heroic historian struggled to live, but on the 8th he breathed his last.

He was buried from King's Chapel, the Westminster Abbey for unchurched Bostonians. Harvard University held in his honor a commemorative service at which addresses were made by President Eliot, Justin Winsor and John Fiske. The last-named then well said, "Of all American historians" Parkman was "the most deeply and peculiarly American," yet "at the same time the broadest and most cosmopolitan"; that his History of France and England in the New World was "a book for all mankind and for all time."

CHAPTER I

The Native Tribes

[This appeared in 1867, as Parkman's Introduction to *The Jesuits in North America*.]

[PARKMAN had already written some general remarks on the North American Indians, in *Pontiac* — as a result of his experience with the Sioux, and his early readings; but he had since learned much more about them, especially from L. H. Morgan *The League of the Iroquois* and E. G. Squier *Aboriginal Monuments of the State of New York*. He did not get the chapter ready in time for *Pioneers of France*, the first volume to appear after *Pontiac*; but as he intended it to supersede his earlier remarks on the Indians, and to be a general introduction to the series, the editor has placed it first.]

1. *The Algonquins* [1]

America, when it became known to Europeans, was, as it had long been, a scene of wide-spread revolution. North and south, tribe was giving place to tribe, language to language; for the Indian, hopelessly unchanging in respect to individual and social development, was, as regarded tribal relations and local haunts, mutable as the wind. In Canada and the northern section of the United States, the elements of change were especially active. The Indian population which, in 1535, Cartier found at Montreal and Quebec, had disappeared at the opening of the next century, and another race had succeeded, in language and customs widely different; while, in the region now forming the State of New York, a power was rising to a ferocious vitality, which, but for

[1] The word *Algonquin* is here used in its broadest signification. It was originally applied to a group of tribes north of the river St. Lawrence. The difference of language between the original Algonquins and the Abenakis of New England, the Ojibwas of the Great Lakes, or the Illinois of the West corresponded to the difference between French and Italian, or Italian and Spanish. Each of these languages, again, had its dialects, like those of different provinces of France.

the presence of Europeans, would probably have subjected, absorbed, or exterminated every other Indian community east of the Mississippi and north of the Ohio.

The vast tract of wilderness from the Mississippi to the Atlantic, and from the Carolinas to Hudson's Bay, was divided between two great families of tribes, distinguished by a radical difference of language. A part of Virginia and of Pennsylvania, New Jersey, southeastern New York, New England, New Brunswick, Nova Scotia, and Lower Canada were occupied, so far as occupied at all, by tribes speaking various Algonquin languages and dialects. They extended, moreover, along the shores of the Upper Lakes, and into the dreary northern wastes beyond. They held Wisconsin, Michigan, Illinois, and Indiana, and detached bands ranged the lonely hunting-ground of Kentucky.

Like a great island in the midst of the Algonquins lay the country of tribes speaking the generic tongue of the Iroquois. The true Iroquois, or Five Nations, extended through Central New York, from the Hudson to the Genesee. Southward lay the Andastes, on and near the Susquehanna; westward, the Eries, along the southern shore of Lake Erie, and the Neutral Nation, along its northern shore from Niagara towards the Detroit; while the towns of the Hurons lay near the lake to which they have left their name.

Of the Algonquin populations, the densest, despite a recent epidemic which had swept them off by thousands, was in New England. Here were Mohicans, Pequots, Narragansetts, Wampanoags, Massachusetts, Penacooks, thorns in the side of the Puritan. On the whole, these savages were favorable specimens of the Algonquin stock, belonging to that section of it which tilled the soil, and was thus in some measure spared the extremes of misery and degradation to which the wandering hunter tribes were often reduced. They owed much, also, to the bounty of the sea, and hence they tended towards the coast; which, before the epidemic, Champlain and Smith had seen at many points studded with wigwams and waving with harvests of maize. Fear, too, drove them eastward; for the Iroquois pursued them with an inveterate enmity. Some paid yearly tribute to their tyrants, while others were still subject to their inroads, flying in terror at the sound of the Mohawk war-cry. Westward, the population thinned rapidly; northward, it soon disappeared. Northern New Hampshire, the whole of Vermont, and western Massachusetts had no human tenants but the roving hunter or prowling warrior.

We have said that this group of tribes was relatively very populous;

yet it is more than doubtful whether all of them united, had union been possible, could have mustered eight thousand fighting men. To speak further of them is needless, for they were not within the scope of the Jesuit labors. The heresy of heresies had planted itself among them; and it was for the apostle Eliot, not the Jesuit, to assay their conversion.

Landing at Boston, three years before a solitude, let the traveller push northward, pass the river Piscataqua and the Penacooks, and cross the river Saco. Here, a change of dialect would indicate a different tribe, or group of tribes. These were the Abenakis, found chiefly along the course of the Kennebec and other rivers, on whose banks they raised their rude harvests, and whose streams they ascended to hunt the moose and bear in the forest desert of northern Maine, or descended to fish in the neighboring sea.

Crossing the Penobscot, one found a visible descent in the scale of humanity. Eastern Maine and the whole of New Brunswick were occupied by a race called Etchemins, to whom agriculture was unknown, though the sea, prolific of fish, lobsters, and seals, greatly lightened their miseries. The Souriquois, or Micmacs of Nova Scotia, closely resembled them in habits and condition. From Nova Scotia to the St. Lawrence, there was no population worthy of the name. From the Gulf of St. Lawrence to Lake Ontario, the southern border of the great river had no tenants but hunters. Northward, between the St. Lawrence and Hudson's Bay, roamed the scattered hordes of the Papinachois, Bersiamites, and others, included by the French under the general name of Montagnais. When, in spring, the French trading-ships arrived and anchored in the port of Tadoussac, they gathered from far and near, toiling painfully through the desolation of forests, mustering by hundreds at the point of traffic, and setting up their bark wigwams along the strand of that wild harbor. They were of the lowest Algonquin type. Their ordinary sustenance was derived from the chase; though often, goaded by deadly famine, they would subsist on roots, the bark and buds of trees, or the foulest offal; and in extremity, even cannibalism was not rare among them.

Ascending the St. Lawrence, it was seldom that the sight of a human form gave relief to the loneliness, until, at Quebec, the roar of Champlain's cannon from the verge of the cliff announced that the savage prologue of the American drama was drawing to a close, and that the civilization of Europe was advancing on the scene. Ascending farther, all was solitude, except at Three Rivers, a noted place of trade, where a few Algonquins of the tribe called Atticamegues might possibly be seen. The fear of the Iroquois was everywhere; and as the voyager passed some wooded point, or thicket-covered island, the whistling of a stone-headed arrow proclaimed, perhaps, the presence of these fierce marauders. At Montreal there was no human life, save during a brief space in early summer, when the shore swarmed with savages, who had come to the yearly trade from the great communities of the interior. To-day there were dances, songs, and feastings; to-morrow all again was solitude, and the Ottawa was covered with the canoes of the returning warriors.

Along this stream, a main route of traffic, the silence of the wilderness was broken only by the splash of the passing paddle. To the north of the river there was indeed a small Algonquin band, called *La Petite Nation*, together with one or two other feeble communities; but they dwelt far from the banks, through fear of the ubiquitous Iroquois. It was nearly three hundred miles, by the windings of the stream, before one reached that Algonquin tribe, *La Nation de l'Isle*, who occupied the great island of the Allumettes. Then, after many a day of lonely travel, the voyager found a savage welcome among the Nipissings, on the lake which bears their name; and then circling west and south for a hundred and fifty miles of solitude, he reached for the first time a people speaking a dialect of the Iroquois tongue. Here all was changed. Populous towns, rude fortifications, and an extensive, though barbarous tillage, indicated a people far in advance of the famished wanderers of the Saguenay, or their less abject kindred of New England. These were the Hurons, of whom the modern Wyandots are a remnant. Both in themselves and as a type of their generic stock they demand more than a passing notice.

2. *The Hurons*

More than two centuries have elapsed since the Hurons vanished from their ancient seats, and the settlers of this rude solitude stand perplexed and wondering over the relics of a lost people. In the damp shadow of what seems a virgin forest, the axe and plough bring strange secrets to light, — huge pits, close packed with skeletons and disjointed bones, mixed with weapons, copper kettles, beads, and trinkets. Not even the straggling Algonquins, who linger about the scene of Huron prosperity, can tell their origin. Yet on ancient worm-eaten pages, between covers of begrimed parchment, the daily life of this ruined community, its firesides, its festivals, its funeral rites, are painted with a minute and vivid fidelity.

The ancient country of the Hurons is now the northern and eastern portion of Simcoe County, Canada West, and is embraced within the peninsula formed by the Nottawassaga and Matchedash Bays of Lake Huron, the river Severn, and Lake Simcoe. Its area was small, — its population comparatively large. In the year 1639 the Jesuits made an enumeration of all its villages, dwellings, and families. The result showed thirty-two villages and hamlets, with seven hundred dwellings, about four thousand families, and twelve thousand adult persons, or a total population of at least twenty thousand.

The region whose boundaries we have given was an alternation of meadows and deep forests, interlaced with footpaths leading from town to town. Of these towns, some were fortified, but the greater number were open and defenceless. They were of a construction common to all tribes of Iroquois lineage, and peculiar to them. Nothing similar exists at the present day.[2] They covered a space of from one to ten acres, the dwellings clustered together with little or no pretension to order. In general, these singular structures were about thirty or thirty-five feet in length, breadth, and height; but many were much larger, and a few were of prodigious length. In some of the villages there were dwellings two hundred and forty feet long, though in breadth and height they did not much exceed the others. In shape they were much like an arbor overarching a garden-walk. Their frame was of tall and strong saplings, planted in a double row to form the two sides of the house, bent till they met, and lashed together at the top. To these other poles were bound transversely, and the whole was covered with large sheets of the bark of the oak, elm, spruce, or white cedar, overlapping like the shingles of a roof, upon which, for their better security, split poles were made fast with cords of linden bark. At the crown of the arch, along the entire length of the house, an opening a foot wide was left for the admission of light and the escape of smoke. At each end was a close porch of similar construction; and here were stored casks of bark, filled with smoked fish, Indian corn, and other stores not liable to injury from frost. Within, on both sides, were wide scaffolds, four feet from the floor, and extending the entire

---

[2] The permanent bark villages of the Dahcotah of the St. Peter's are the nearest modern approach to the Huron towns. The whole Huron country abounds with evidences of having been occupied by a numerous population.

length of the house, like the seats of a colossal omnibus. These were formed of thick sheets of bark, supported by posts and transverse poles, and covered with mats and skins. Here, in summer, was the sleeping-place of the inmates, and the space beneath served for storage of their firewood. The fires were on the ground, in a line down the middle of the house. Each sufficed for two families, who, in winter, slept closely packed around them. Above, just under the vaulted roof, were a great number of poles, like the perches of a hen-roost; and here were suspended weapons, clothing, skins, and ornaments. Here, too, in harvest time, the squaws hung the ears of unshelled corn, till the rude abode, through all its length, seemed decked with a golden tapestry. In general, however, its only lining was a thick coating of soot from the smoke of fires with neither draught, chimney, nor window. So pungent was the smoke that it produced inflammation of the eyes, attended in old age with frequent blindness. Another annoyance was the fleas; and a third, the unbridled and unruly children. Privacy there was none. The house was one chamber, sometimes lodging more than twenty families.[3]

He who entered on a winter night beheld a strange spectacle: the vista of fires lighting the smoky concave; the bronzed groups encircling each, — cooking, eating, gambling, or amusing themselves with idle badinage; shrivelled squaws, hideous with threescore years of hardship; grisly old warriors, scarred with Iroquois war-clubs; young aspirants, whose honors were yet to be won; damsels gay with ochre and wampum; restless children pellmell with restless dogs. Now a tongue of resinous flame painted each wild feature in vivid light; now the fitful gleam expired, and the group vanished from sight, as their nation has vanished from history.

The fortified towns of the Hurons were all on the side exposed to Iroquois incursions. The fortifications of all this family of tribes were, like their dwellings, in essential points alike. A situation was chosen favorable to defence, — the bank of a lake, the crown of a difficult hill, or a high point of land in the fork of confluent rivers. A ditch, several feet deep, was dug around the village, and the earth thrown up on the inside. Trees were then felled by alternate process of burning and hacking the burnt part with stone hatchets, and by similar means were

[3] The Iroquois preserved this mode of building, in all essential points, down to a recent period. They usually framed the sides of their houses on rows of upright posts, arched with separate poles for the roof. The Hurons, no doubt, did the same in their larger structures. For a door, there was a sheet of bark hung on wooden hinges, or suspended by cords from above.

cut into lengths to form palisades. These were planted on the embankment, in one, two, three, or four concentric rows, — those of each row inclining towards those of the other rows until they intersected. The whole was lined within, to the height of a man, with heavy sheets of bark; and at the top, where the palisades crossed, was a gallery of timber for the defenders, together with wooden gutters, by which streams of water could be poured down on fires kindled by the enemy. Magazines of stones, and rude ladders for mounting the rampart, completed the provision for defence. The forts of the Iroquois were stronger and more elaborate than those of the Hurons; and to this day large districts in New York are marked with frequent remains of their ditches and embankments.

Among these tribes there was no individual ownership of land, but each family had for the time exclusive right to as much as it saw fit to cultivate. The clearing process — a most toilsome one — consisted in hacking off branches, pulling them together with brushwood around the foot of the standing trunks, and setting fire to the whole. The squaws, working with their hoes of wood and bone among the charred stumps, sowed their corn, beans, pumpkins, tobacco, sunflowers, and Huron hemp. No manure was used; but at intervals of from ten to thirty years, when the soil was exhausted and firewood distant, the village was abandoned and a new one built.

There was little game in the Huron country; and here, as among the Iroquois, the staple of food was Indian corn, cooked without salt in a variety of forms, each more odious than the last. Venison was a luxury found only at feasts; dog-flesh was in high esteem; and, in some of the towns, captive bears were fattened for festive occasions. These tribes were far less improvident than the roving Algonquins, and stores of provision were laid up against a season of want. Their main stock of corn was buried in *caches*, or deep holes in the earth, either within or without the houses.

In respect to the arts of life, all these stationary tribes were in advance of the wandering hunters of the North. The women made a species of earthen pot for cooking, but these were supplanted by the copper kettles of the French traders. They wove rush mats with no little skill. They spun twine from hemp, by the primitive process of rolling it on their thighs; and of this twine they made nets. They extracted oil from fish and from the seeds of the sunflower, — the latter, apparently, only for the purposes of the toilet. They pounded their maize in huge mortars of wood, hollowed by alternate burnings and scrapings. Their stone axes, spear and arrow heads, and bone fish-hooks, were fast giving place to the iron of the French; but they had not laid aside their shields of raw bison-hide, or of wood overlaid with plaited and twisted thongs of skin. They still used, too, their primitive breast-plates and greaves of twigs interwoven with cordage. The masterpiece of Huron handiwork, however, was the birch canoe, in the construction of which the Algonquins were no less skilful. The Iroquois in the absence of the birch were forced to use the bark of the elm, which was greatly inferior both in lightness and strength. Of pipes, than which nothing was more important in their eyes, the Hurons made a great variety, — some of baked clay, others of various kinds of stone, carved by the men, during their long periods of monotonous leisure, often with great skill and ingenuity. But their most mysterious fabric was wampum. This was at once their currency, their ornament, their pen, ink, and parchment; and its use was by no means confined to tribes of the Iroquois stock. It consisted of elongated beads, white and purple, made from the inner part of certain shells. It is not easy to conceive how, with their rude implements, the Indians contrived to shape and perforate this intractable material. The art soon fell into disuse, however; for wampum better than their own was brought them by the traders, besides abundant imitations in glass and porcelain. Strung into necklaces, or wrought into collars, belts, and bracelets, it was the favorite decoration of the Indian girls at festivals and dances. It served also a graver purpose. No compact, no speech, or clause for a speech, to the representative of another nation, had any force, unless confirmed by the delivery of a string or belt of wampum. The belts, on occasions of importance, were wrought into significant devices, suggestive of the substance of the compact or speech, and designed as aids to memory. To one or more old men of the nation was assigned the honorable, but very onerous, charge of keepers of the wampum, — in other words, of the national records; and it was for them to remember and interpret the meaning of the belts. The figures on wampum-belts were, for the most part, simply mnemonic. So also were those carved on wooden tablets, or painted on bark and skin, to preserve in memory the songs of war, hunting, or magic. The Hurons had, however, in common with other tribes, a system of rude pictures and arbitrary signs, by which they could convey to each other, with tolerable precision, information touching the ordinary subjects of Indian interest.

Their dress was chiefly of skins, cured with smoke after the well-known Indian mode. That of the women, according to the Jesuits, was more modest than that "of our most pious ladies of France." The young girls on festal occasions must be excepted from this commendation, as they wore merely a kilt from the waist to the knee, besides the wampum decorations of the breast and arms. Their long black hair, gathered behind the neck, was decorated with discs of native copper, or gay pendants made in France, and now occasionally unearthed in numbers from their graves. The men, in summer, were nearly naked, — those of a kindred tribe wholly so, with the sole exception of their moccasins. In winter they were clad in tunics and leggins of skin, and at all seasons, on occasions of ceremony, were wrapped from head to foot in robes of beaver or otter furs, sometimes of the greatest value. On the inner side, these robes were decorated with painted figures and devices, or embroidered with the dyed quills of the Canada hedgehog. In this art of embroidery, however, the Hurons were equalled or surpassed by some of the Algonquin tribes. They wore their hair after a variety of grotesque and startling fashions. With some, it was loose on one side, and tight braided on the other; with others, close shaved, leaving one or more long and cherished locks; while, with others again, it bristled in a ridge across the crown, like the back of a hyena.[4] When in full dress, they were painted with ochre, white clay, soot, and the red juice of certain berries. They practised tattooing, sometimes covering the whole body with indelible devices. When of such extent, the process was very severe; and though no murmur escaped the sufferer, he sometimes died from its effects.

Female life among the Hurons had no bright side. It was a youth of license, an age of drudgery. Despite an organization which, while it perhaps made them less sensible of pain, certainly made them less susceptible of passion, than the higher races of men, the Hurons were notoriously dissolute, far exceeding in this respect the wandering and starving Algonquins. Marriage existed among them, and polygamy was exceptional; but divorce took place at the will or caprice of either party. A practice also prevailed of temporary or experimental marriage, lasting a day, a week, or more. The seal of the compact was merely the acceptance of a gift of wampum made by the suitor to the object of his desire or his whim. These gifts were never returned on the dissolution of the connection; and as an attractive and enterprising damsel might, and often did, make twenty such marriages before her

[4] See Le Jeune, *Relation*, 1633, 35. "Quelles hures!" exclaimed some astonished Frenchman. Hence the name, *Hurons*.

final establishment, she thus collected a wealth of wampum with which to adorn herself for the village dances.[5] This provisional matrimony was no bar to a license boundless and apparently universal, unattended with loss of reputation on either side. Every instinct of native delicacy quickly vanished under the influence of Huron domestic life; eight or ten families, and often more, crowded into one undivided house, where privacy was impossible, and where strangers were free to enter at all hours of the day or night.

Once a mother, and married with a reasonable permanency, the Huron woman from a wanton became a drudge. In March and April she gathered the year's supply of firewood. Then came sowing, tilling, and harvesting, smoking fish, dressing skins, making cordage and clothing, preparing food. On the march it was she who bore the burden; for, in the words of Champlain, "their women were their mules." The natural effect followed. In every Huron town were shrivelled hags, hideous and despised, who in vindictiveness, ferocity, and cruelty far exceeded the men.

To the men fell the task of building the houses, and making weapons, pipes, and canoes. For the rest, their home-life was a life of leisure and amusement. The summer and autumn were their seasons of serious employment, — of war, hunting, fishing, and trade. There was an established system of traffic between the Hurons and the Algonquins of the Ottawa and Lake Nipissing: the Hurons exchanging wampum, fishing-nets, and corn for fish and furs. From various relics found in their graves, it may be inferred that they also traded with tribes of the Upper Lakes, as well as with tribes far southward, towards the Gulf of Mexico. Each branch of traffic was the monopoly of the family or clan by whom it was opened. They might, if they could, punish interlopers, by stripping them of all they possessed, unless the latter had succeeded in reaching home with the fruits of their trade, — in which case the outraged monopolists had no further right of redress, and could not attempt it without a breaking of the public peace, and exposure to the authorized vengeance of the other party. Their

[5] "Some girls spend their youth thus, having had more than twenty husbands, who are by no means the only ones who have the enjoyment of the belle, married though these men be; for when night falls the young girls run about from one lodge to another, as also do the young men who have them as they please, yet without any violence, leaving the decision to the women. The husband does the like to his neighboring woman; no jealousy arising on that account, and no disgrace or infamy incurred, that being the custom of the country." [Trans. by editor of passage Parkman quotes from Champlain's *Voyages*, 1619 ed. This will be found in the Champlain Society ed. of his *Works* III 138–9.]

fisheries, too, were regulated by customs having the force of laws. These pursuits, with their hunting, — in which they were aided by a wolfish breed of dogs unable to bark, — consumed the autumn and early winter; but before the new year the greater part of the men were gathered in their villages.

Now followed their festal season; for it was the season of idleness for the men, and of leisure for the women. Feasts, gambling, smoking, and dancing filled the vacant hours. Like other Indians, the Hurons were desperate gamblers, staking their all, — ornaments, clothing, canoes, pipes, weapons, and wives. One of their principal games was played with plum-stones, or wooden lozenges, black on one side and white on the other. These were tossed up in a wooden bowl, by striking it sharply upon the ground, and the players betted on the black or white. Sometimes a village challenged a neighboring village. The game was played in one of the houses. Strong poles were extended from side to side, and on these sat or perched the company, party facing party, while two players struck the bowl on the ground between. Bets ran high; and Brébeuf relates that once in midwinter, with the snow nearly three feet deep, the men of his village returned from a gambling visit bereft of their leggins, and barefoot, yet in excellent humor. Ludicrous as it may appear, these games were often medical prescriptions, and designed as a cure of the sick.

Their feasts and dances were of various character, social, medical, and mystical or religious. Some of their feasts were on a scale of extravagant profusion. A vain or ambitious host threw all his substance into one entertainment, inviting the whole village, and perhaps several neighboring villages also. In the winter of 1635 there was a feast at the village of Contarrea, where thirty kettles were on the fires, and twenty deer and four bears were served up. The invitation was simple. The messenger addressed the desired guest with the concise summons, "Come and eat"; and to refuse was a grave offence. He took his dish and spoon, and repaired to the scene of festivity. Each, as he entered, greeted his host with the guttural ejaculation, *Ho!* and ranged himself with the rest, squatted on the earthen floor or on the platform along the sides of the house. The kettles were slung over the fires in the midst. First, there was a long prelude of lugubrious singing. Then the host, who took no share in the feast, proclaimed in a loud voice the contents of each kettle in turn, and at each announcement the company responded in unison, *Ho!* The attendant squaws filled with their ladles the bowls of all the guests. There was talking, laughing, jesting, singing, and smoking; and at times the entertainment was protracted through the day.

When the feast had a medical or mystic character, it was indispensable that each guest should devour the whole of the portion given him, however enormous. Should he fail, the host would be outraged, the community shocked, and the spirits roused to vengeance. Disaster would befall the nation, — death, perhaps, the individual. In some cases, the imagined efficacy of the feast was proportioned to the rapidity with which the viands were despatched. Prizes of tobacco were offered to the most rapid feeder; and the spectacle then became truly porcine. These *festins à manger tout* were much dreaded by many of the Hurons, who, however, were never known to decline them.

Invitation to a dance was no less concise than to a feast. Sometimes a crier proclaimed the approaching festivity through the village. The house was crowded. Old men, old women, and children thronged the platforms, or clung to the poles which supported the sides and roof. Fires were raked out, and the earthen floor cleared. Two chiefs sang at the top of their voices, keeping time to their song with tortoise-shell rattles. The men danced with great violence and gesticulation; the women, with a much more measured action. The former were nearly divested of clothing, — in mystical dances, sometimes wholly so; and, from a superstitious motive, this was now and then the case with the women. Both, however, were abundantly decorated with paint, oil, beads, wampum, trinkets, and feathers.

Religious festivals, councils, the entertainment of an envoy, the inauguration of a chief, were all occasions of festivity, in which social pleasure was joined with matter of grave import, and which at times gathered nearly all the nation into one great and harmonious concourse. Warlike expeditions, too, were always preceded by feasting, at which the warriors vaunted the fame of their ancestors, and their own past and prospective exploits. A hideous scene of feasting followed the torture of a prisoner. Like the torture itself, it was, among the Hurons, partly an act of vengeance, and partly a religious rite. If the victim had shown courage, the heart was first roasted, cut into small pieces, and given to the young men and boys, who devoured it to increase their own courage. The body was then divided, thrown into the kettles, and eaten by the assembly, the head being the portion of the chief. Many of the Hurons joined in the feast with reluctance and horror, while others took pleasure in it. This was the only form of cannibalism among them, since, unlike the wandering Algonquins, they were rarely under the desperation of extreme famine.

A great knowledge of simples for the cure of disease is popularly ascribed to the Indian. Here, however, as elsewhere, his knowledge is in fact scanty. He rarely reasons from cause to effect, or from effect to cause. Disease, in his belief, is the result of sorcery, the agency of spirits or supernatural influences, undefined and indefinable. The Indian doctor was a conjurer, and his remedies were to the last degree preposterous, ridiculous, or revolting. The well-known Indian sweating-bath is the most prominent of the few means of cure based on agencies simply physical; and this, with all the other natural remedies, was applied, not by the professed doctor, but by the sufferer himself, or his friends.

The Indian doctor beat, shook, and pinched his patient, howled, whooped, rattled a tortoise-shell at his ear to expel the evil spirit, bit him till blood flowed, and then displayed in triumph a small piece of wood, bone, or iron, which he had hidden in his mouth, and which he affirmed was the source of the disease, now happily removed.[6] Sometimes he prescribed a dance, feast, or game; and the whole village bestirred themselves to fulfil the injunction to the letter. They gambled away their all; they gorged themselves like vultures; they danced or played ball naked among the snowdrifts from morning till night. At a medical feast, some strange or unusual act was commonly enjoined as vital to the patient's cure: as, for example, the departing guest, in place of the customary monosyllable of thanks, was required to greet his host with an ugly grimace. Sometimes, by prescription, half the village would throng into the house where the patient lay, led by old women disguised with the heads and skins of bears, and beating with sticks on sheets of dry bark. Here the assembly danced and whooped for hours together, with a din to which a civilized patient would promptly have succumbed. Sometimes the doctor wrought himself into a prophetic fury, raving through the length and breadth of the dwelling, snatching firebrands and flinging them about him, to the terror of the squaws, with whom, in their combustible tenements, fire was a constant bugbear.

[6] The Indians had many simple applications for wounds, said to have been very efficacious; but the purity of their blood, owing to the absence from their diet of condiments and stimulants, as well as to their active habits, aided the remedy. In general, they were remarkably exempt from disease or deformity, though often seriously injured by alternations of hunger and excess. The Hurons sometimes died from the effects of their *festins à manger tout.*

Among the Hurons and kindred tribes, disease was frequently ascribed to some hidden wish ungratified. Hence the patient was overwhelmed with gifts, in the hope that in their multiplicity the desideratum might be supplied. Kettles, skins, awls, pipes, wampum, fish-hooks, weapons, objects of every conceivable variety, were piled before him by a host of charitable contributors; and if, as often happened, a dream, the Indian oracle, had revealed to the sick man the secret of his cure, his demands were never refused, however extravagant, idle, nauseous, or abominable. Hence it is no matter of wonder that sudden illness and sudden cures were frequent among the Hurons. The patient reaped profit, and the doctor both profit and honor.

3. The Huron-Iroquois Family

And now, before entering upon the very curious subject of Indian social and tribal organization, it may be well briefly to observe the position and prominent distinctive features of the various communities speaking dialects of the generic tongue of the Iroquois. In this remarkable family of tribes occur the fullest developments of Indian character, and the most conspicuous examples of Indian intelligence. If the higher traits popularly ascribed to the race are not to be found here, they are to be found nowhere. A palpable proof of the superiority of this stock is afforded in the size of the Iroquois and Huron brains. In average internal capacity of the cranium, they surpass, with few and doubtful exceptions, all other aborigines of North and South America, not excepting the civilized races of Mexico and Peru.[7]

In the woody valleys of the Blue Mountains, south of the Nottawassaga Bay of Lake Huron, and two days' journey west of the frontier Huron towns, lay the nine villages of the Tobacco Nation, or Tionnontates. In manners, as in language, they closely resembled the Hurons. Of old they were their enemies, but were now at peace with them, and about the year 1640 became their close confederates. Indeed, in the ruin which befell that hapless people, the Tionnontates alone retained a tribal organization; and their descendants, with a trifling exception, are to this day the sole inheritors of the Huron or Wyandot name. Expatriated and wandering, they held for generations a paramount influence among the Western tribes. In their original seats

---

[7] [Modern ethnologists do not regard these data on the size of brain cavities as significant.]

among the Blue Mountains, they offered an example extremely rare among Indians, of a tribe raising a crop for the market; for they traded in tobacco largely with other tribes. Their Huron confederates, keen traders, would not suffer them to pass through their country to traffic with the French, preferring to secure for themselves the advantage of bartering with them in French goods at an enormous profit.

Journeying southward five days from the Tionnontate towns, the forest traveller reached the border villages of the Attiwandarons, or Neutral Nation. As early as 1626, they were visited by the Franciscan friar, La Roche Dallion, who reports a numerous population in twenty-eight towns, besides many small hamlets. Their country, about forty leagues in extent, embraced wide and fertile districts on the north shore of Lake Erie, and their frontier extended eastward across the Niagara, where they had three or four outlying towns. Their name of "Neutrals" was due to their neutrality in the war between the Hurons and the Iroquois proper. The hostile warriors, meeting in a Neutral cabin, were forced to keep the peace, though, once in the open air, the truce was at an end. Yet this people were abundantly ferocious, and, while holding a pacific attitude betwixt their warring kindred, waged deadly strife with the Mascoutins, an Algonquin horde beyond Lake Michigan. Indeed, it was but recently that they had been at blows with seventeen Algonquin tribes. They burned female prisoners, a practice unknown to the Hurons. Their country was full of game, and they were bold and active hunters. In form and stature they surpassed even the Hurons, whom they resembled in their mode of life, and from whose language their own, though radically similar, was dialectically distinct. Their licentiousness was even more open and shameless; and they stood alone in the extravagance of some of their usages. They kept their dead in their houses till they became insupportable; then scraped the flesh from the bones, and displayed them in rows along the walls, there to remain till the periodical Feast of the Dead, or general burial. In summer, the men wore no clothing whatever, but were usually tattooed from head to foot with powdered charcoal.

The sagacious Hurons refused them a passage through their country to the French; and the Neutrals apparently had not sense or reflection enough to take the easy and direct route of Lake Ontario, — which was probably open to them, though closed against the Hurons by Iroquois enmity. Thus the former made excellent profit by exchanging French goods at high rates for the valuable furs of the Neutrals.

Southward and eastward of Lake Erie dwelt a kindred people, the Eries, or "Nation of the Cat." Little besides their existence is known of them. They seem to have occupied southwestern New York, as far east as the Genesee, the frontier of the Senecas, and in habits and language to have resembled the Hurons. They were noted warriors, fought with poisoned arrows, and were long a terror to the neighboring Iroquois.

On the Lower Susquehanna dwelt the formidable tribe called by the French Andastes. Little is known of them, beyond their general resemblance to their kindred, in language, habits, and character. Fierce and resolute warriors, they long made head against the Iroquois of New York, and were vanquished at last more by disease than by the tomahawk.[8]

In central New York, stretching east and west from the Hudson to the Genesee, lay that redoubted people who have lent their name to the tribal family of the Iroquois, and stamped it indelibly on the early pages of American history. Among all the barbarous nations of the continent, the Iroquois of New York stand paramount. Elements which among other tribes were crude, confused, and embryotic were among them systematized and concreted into an established polity. The Iroquois was the Indian of Indians. A thorough savage, yet a finished and developed savage, he is perhaps an example of the highest elevation which man can reach without emerging from his primitive condition of the hunter. A geographical position, commanding on one hand the portal of the Great Lakes, and on the other the sources of the streams flowing both to the Atlantic and the Mississippi, gave the ambitious and aggressive confederates advantages which they perfectly understood, and by which they profited to the utmost. Patient and politic as they were ferocious, they were not only conquerors of their own race, but the powerful allies and the dreaded foes of the French and English colonies, flattered and caressed by both, yet too sagacious to give themselves without reserve to either. Their organization and their history evince their intrinsic superiority. Even their traditionary lore, amid its wild puerilities, shows at times the stamp of an energy and force in striking contrast with the flimsy creations of Algonquin fancy. That the Iroquois, left under their institutions to work out their destiny undisturbed, would ever have developed a civilization of their own, I do not believe. These institu-

---

[8] The research of Mr. Shea has shown their identity with the *Susquehannocks* of the English, and the *Minquas* of the Dutch.

tions, however, are sufficiently characteristic and curious, and we shall soon have occasion to observe them.[9]

4. *Social and Political Organization*

In Indian social organization, a problem at once suggests itself. In these communities, comparatively populous, how could spirits so fierce, and in many respects so ungoverned, live together in peace, without law and without enforced authority? Yet there were towns where savages lived together in thousands, with a harmony which civilization might envy. This was in good measure due to peculiarities of Indian character and habits. This intractable race were, in certain external respects, the most pliant and complaisant of mankind. The early missionaries were charmed by the docile acquiescence with which their dogmas were received; but they soon discovered that their facile auditors neither believed nor understood that to which they had so promptly assented. They assented from a kind of courtesy, which, while it vexed the priests, tended greatly to keep the Indians in mutual accord. That well-known self-control, which, originating in a form of pride, covered the savage nature of the man with a veil, opaque, though thin, contributed not a little to the same end. Though vain, arrogant, boastful, and vindictive, the Indian bore abuse and sarcasm with an astonishing patience. Though greedy and grasping, he was lavish without stint, and would give away his all to soothe the manes of a departed relative, gain influence and applause, or ingratiate himself with his neighbors. In his dread of public opinion, he rivalled some of his civilized successors.

[9] The name *Iroquois* is French. Charlevoix says, "It was formed from the term *hiro*, which means, 'I have spoken,' with which these savages end all their speeches, just as the Romans did with their *dixi;* and of *koué*, which is a cry either of distress or of joy according to the intonation." Their true name is *Hodenosaunee*, or "People of the Long House," because their confederacy of five distinct nations, ranged in a line along central New York, was likened to one of the long bark houses already described, with five fires and five families. The following are the true names of the Five Nations, with their French and English synonyms.

	English.	French.
Ganeagaono,	Mohawk,	Agnier.
Onayotekaono,	Oneida,	Onneyut.
Onundagaono,	Onondaga,	Onnontagué.
Gweugwehono,	Cayuga,	Goyogouin.
Nundawaono,	Seneca,	Tsonnontouans.

All Indians, and especially these populous and stationary tribes, had their code of courtesy, whose requirements were rigid and exact; nor might any infringe it without the ban of public censure. Indian nature, inflexible and unmalleable, was peculiarly under the control of custom. Established usage took the place of law, — was, in fact, a sort of common law, with no tribunal to expound or enforce it. In these wild democracies, — democracies in spirit, though not in form, — a respect for native superiority, and a willingness to yield to it, were always conspicuous. All were prompt to aid each other in distress, and a neighborly spirit was often exhibited among them. When a young woman was permanently married, the other women of the village supplied her with firewood for the year, each contributing an armful. When one or more families were without shelter, the men of the village joined in building them a house. In return, the recipients of the favor gave a feast, if they could; if not, their thanks were sufficient. Among the Iroquois and Hurons — and doubtless among the kindred tribes — there were marked distinctions of noble and base, prosperous and poor; yet while there was food in the village, the meanest and the poorest need not suffer want. He had but to enter the nearest house, and seat himself by the fire, when, without a word on either side, food was placed before him by the women.

Contrary to the received opinion, these Indians, like others of their race, when living in communities, were of a very social disposition. Besides their incessant dances and feasts, great and small, they were continually visiting, spending most of their time in their neighbors' houses, chatting, joking, bantering one another with witticisms, sharp, broad, and in no sense delicate, yet always taken in good part. Every village had its adepts in these wordy tournaments, while the shrill laugh of young squaws, untaught to blush, echoed each hardy jest or rough sarcasm.

In the organization of the savage communities of the continent, one feature, more or less conspicuous, continually appears. Each nation or tribe — to adopt the names by which these communities are usually known — is subdivided into several clans. These clans are not locally separate, but are mingled throughout the nation. All the members of each clan are, or are assumed to be, intimately joined in consanguinity. Hence it is held an abomination for two persons of the same clan to intermarry; and hence, again, it follows that every family must contain members of at least two clans. Each clan has its name, as the clan of the Hawk, of the Wolf, or of the Tortoise; and each has for its emblem the figure of the beast, bird, reptile, plant, or other object, from which its name is derived. This emblem, called *totem* by the Algonquins, is often tattooed on the clansman's body, or rudely painted over the entrance of his lodge. The child belongs, in most cases, to the clan, not of the father, but of the mother. In other words, descent, not of the *totem* alone, but of all rank, titles, and possessions, is through the female. The son of a chief can never be a chief by hereditary title, though he may become so by force of personal influence or achievement. Neither can he inherit from his father so much as a tobacco-pipe. All possessions alike pass of right to the brothers of the chief, or to the sons of his sisters, since these are all sprung from a common mother. This rule of descent was noticed by Champlain among the Hurons in 1615. That excellent observer refers it to an origin which is doubtless its true one. The child may not be the son of his reputed father, but must be the son of his mother, — a consideration of more than ordinary force in an Indian community.

This system of clanship, with the rule of descent usually belonging to it, was of very wide prevalence. Indeed, it is more than probable that close observation would have detected it in every tribe east of the Mississippi; while there is positive evidence of its existence in by far the greater number. It is found also among the Dahcotah and other tribes west of the Mississippi; and there is reason to believe it universally prevalent as far as the Rocky Mountains, and even beyond them. The fact that with most of these hordes there is little property worth transmission, and that the most influential becomes chief, with little regard to inheritance, has blinded casual observers to the existence of this curious system.

It was found in full development among the Creeks, Choctaws, Cherokees, and other Southern tribes, including that remarkable people, the Natchez, who, judged by their religious and political institutions, seem a detached offshoot of the Toltec family. It is no less conspicuous among the roving Algonquins of the extreme North, where the number of *totems* is almost countless. Everywhere it formed the foundation of the polity of all the tribes, where a polity could be said to exist.

The Franciscans and Jesuits, close students of the languages and superstitions of the Indians, were by no means so zealous to analyze their organization and government. In the middle of the seventeenth century the Hurons as a nation had ceased to exist, and their political portraiture, as handed down to us, is careless and unfinished. Yet some decisive features are plainly shown. The Huron nation was a confederacy of four distinct contiguous nations, afterwards increased to five by the addition of the Tionnontates. It was divided into clans; it was governed by chiefs, whose office was hereditary through the female; the power of these chiefs, though great, was wholly of a persuasive or advisory character; there were two principal chiefs, one for peace, the other for war; there were chiefs assigned to special national functions, as the charge of the great Feast of the Dead, the direction of trading voyages to other nations, etc.; there were numerous other chiefs, equal in rank, but very unequal in influence, since the measure of their influence depended on the measure of their personal ability; each nation of the confederacy had a separate organization, but at certain periods grand councils of the united nations were held, at which were present, not chiefs only, but also a great concourse of the people; and at these and other councils the chiefs and principal men voted on proposed measures by means of small sticks or reeds, the opinion of the plurality ruling.

5. The Iroquois

The Iroquois were a people far more conspicuous in history, and their institutions are not yet extinct. In early and recent times, they have been closely studied, and no little light has been cast upon a subject as difficult and obscure as it is curious. By comparing the statements of observers, old and new, the character of their singular organization becomes sufficiently clear.[10]

Both reason and tradition point to the conclusion, that the Iroquois formed originally one undivided people. Sundered, like countless other tribes, by dissension, caprice, or the necessities of the hunter life, they separated into five distinct nations, cantoned from east to west along the centre of New York, in the following order: Mohawks, Oneidas, Onondagas, Cayugas, Senecas. There was discord among them; wars followed, and they lived in mutual fear, each ensconced in

[10] Among modern students of Iroquois institutions, a place far in advance of all others is due to Lewis H. Morgan, himself an Iroquois by adoption, and intimate with the race from boyhood. His work, *The League of the Iroquois*, is a production of most thorough and able research, conducted under peculiar advantages, and with the aid of an efficient co-laborer, Hasanoanda (Ely S. Parker), an educated and highly intelligent Iroquois of the Seneca nation. [Morgan is now regarded as classic.] None of the old writers are so satisfactory as Lafitau.

its palisaded villages. At length, says tradition, a celestial being, incarnate on earth, counselled them to compose their strife and unite in a league of defence and aggression. Another personage, wholly mortal, yet wonderfully endowed, a renowned warrior and a mighty magician, stands, with his hair of writhing snakes, grotesquely conspicuous through the dim light of tradition at this birth of Iroquois nationality. This was Atotarho, a chief of the Onondagas; and from this honored source has sprung a long line of chieftains, heirs not to the blood alone, but to the name of their great predecessor. A few years since, there lived in Onondaga Hollow a handsome Indian boy on whom the dwindled remnant of the nation looked with pride as their destined Atotarho. With earthly and celestial aid the league was consummated, and through all the land the forests trembled at the name of the Iroquois.

The Iroquois people were divided into eight clans. When the original stock was sundered into five parts, each of these clans was also sundered into five parts; and as, by the principle already indicated, the clans were intimately mingled in every village, hamlet, and cabin, each one of the five nations had its portion of each of the eight clans.[11] When the league was formed, these separate portions readily resumed their ancient tie of fraternity. Thus, of the Turtle clan, all the members became brothers again, — nominal members of one family, whether Mohawks, Oneidas, Onondagas, Cayugas, or Senecas; and so, too, of the remaining clans. All the Iroquois, irrespective of nationality, were therefore divided into eight families, each tracing its descent to a common mother, and each designated by its distinctive emblem or *totem*. This connection of clan or family was exceedingly strong, and by it the five nations of the league were linked together as by an eightfold chain.

The clans were by no means equal in numbers, influence, or honor. So marked were the distinctions among them, that some of the early writers recognize only the three most conspicuous, — those of the Tortoise, the Bear, and the Wolf. To some of the clans, in each nation, belonged the right of giving a chief to the nation and to the league. Others had the right of giving three, or, in one case, four chiefs; while others could give none. As Indian clanship was but an extension of the family relation, these chiefs were, in a certain sense, hereditary; but the law of inheritance, though binding, was extremely elastic, and

[11] The eight clans of the Iroquois were as follows: Wolf, Bear, Beaver, Tortoise, Deer, Snipe, Heron, Hawk.

capable of stretching to the farthest limits of the clan. The chief was almost invariably succeeded by a near relative, always through the female, — as a brother by the same mother, or a nephew by the sister's side. But if these were manifestly unfit, they were passed over, and a chief was chosen at a council of the clan from among remoter kindred. In these cases, the successor is said to have been nominated by the matron of the late chief's household. Be this as it may, the choice was never adverse to the popular inclination. The new chief was "raised up," or installed, by a formal council of the sachems of the league; and on entering upon his office, he dropped his own name, and assumed that which, since the formation of the league, had belonged to this especial chieftainship.

The number of these principal chiefs, or, as they have been called by way of distinction, *sachems,* varied in the several nations from eight to fourteen. The sachems of the five nations, fifty in all, assembled in council, formed the government of the confederacy. All met as equals, but a peculiar dignity was ever attached to the Atotarho of the Onondagas.

There was a class of subordinate chiefs, in no sense hereditary, but rising to office by address, ability, or valor. Yet the rank was clearly defined, and the new chief installed at a formal council. This class embodied, as might be supposed, the best talent of the nation, and the most prominent warriors and orators of the Iroquois have belonged to it. In its character and functions, however, it was purely civil. Like the sachems, these chiefs held their councils, and exercised an influence proportionate to their number and abilities.

There was another council, between which and that of the subordinate chiefs the line of demarcation seems not to have been very definite. The Jesuit Lafitau calls it "the senate." Familiar with the Iroquois at the height of their prosperity, he describes it as the central and controlling power, so far, at least, as the separate nations were concerned. In its character it was essentially popular, but popular in the best sense, and one which can find its application only in a small community. Any man took part in it whose age and experience qualified him to do so. It was merely the gathered wisdom of the nation. Lafitau compares it to the Roman Senate, in the early and rude age of the Republic, and affirms that it loses nothing by the comparison. He thus describes it: "It is a greasy assemblage, sitting *sur leur derrière,* crouched like apes, their knees as high as their ears, or lying, some on their bellies, some on their backs, each with a pipe in his mouth, discussing affairs of state with as much coolness and gravity as the Spanish Junta or the Grand Council of Venice."

The young warriors had also their councils; so, too, had the women; and the opinions and wishes of each were represented by means of deputies before the "senate," or council of the old men, as well as before the grand confederate council of the sachems.

The government of this unique republic resided wholly in councils. By councils all questions were settled, all regulations established, — social, political, military, and religious. The war-path, the chase, the council-fire, — in these was the life of the Iroquois; and it is hard to say to which of the three he was most devoted.

The great council of the fifty sachems formed, as we have seen, the government of the league. Whenever a subject arose before any of the nations, of importance enough to demand its assembling, the sachems of that nation might summon their colleagues by means of runners, bearing messages and belts of wampum. The usual place of meeting was the valley of Onondaga, the political as well as geographical centre of the confederacy. Thither, if the matter were one of deep and general interest, not the sachems alone, but the greater part of the population, gathered from east and west, swarming in the hospitable lodges of the town, or bivouacked by thousands in the surrounding fields and forests. While the sachems deliberated in the council-house, the chiefs and old men, the warriors, and often the women, were holding their respective councils apart; and their opinions, laid by their deputies before the council of sachems, were never without influence on its decisions.

The utmost order and deliberation reigned in the council, with rigorous adherence to the Indian notions of parliamentary propriety. The conference opened with an address to the spirits, or the chief of all the spirits. There was no heat in debate. No speaker interrupted another. Each gave his opinion in turn, supporting it with what reason or rhetoric he could command, — but not until he had stated the subject of discussion in full, to prove that he understood it, repeating also the arguments, *pro* and *con*, of previous speakers. Thus their debates were excessively prolix; and the consumption of tobacco was immoderate. The result, however, was a thorough sifting of the matter in hand; while the practised astuteness of these savage politicians was a marvel to their civilized contemporaries. "It is by a most subtle policy," says Lafitau, "that they have taken the ascendant over the other nations, divided and overcome the most warlike, made themselves a terror to the most remote, and now hold a peaceful neutrality between the French and English, courted and feared by both."

Unlike the Hurons, they required an entire unanimity in their decisions. The ease and frequency with which a requisition seemingly so difficult was fulfilled afford a striking illustration of Indian nature, — on one side, so stubborn, tenacious, and impracticable; on the other, so pliant and acquiescent. An explanation of this harmony is to be found also in an intense spirit of nationality; for never since the days of Sparta were individual life and national life more completely fused into one.

The sachems of the league were likewise, as we have seen, sachems of their respective nations; yet they rarely spoke in the councils of the subordinate chiefs and old men, except to present subjects of discussion. Their influence in these councils was, however, great, and even paramount; for they commonly succeeded in securing to their interest some of the most dexterous and influential of the conclave, through whom, while they themselves remained in the background, they managed the debates.

There was a class of men among the Iroquois always put forward on public occasions to speak the mind of the nation or defend its interests. Nearly all of them were of the number of the subordinate chiefs. Nature and training had fitted them for public speaking, and they were deeply versed in the history and traditions of the league. They were in fact professed orators, high in honor and influence among the people. To a huge stock of conventional metaphors, the use of which required nothing but practice, they often added an astute intellect, an astonishing memory, and an eloquence which deserved the name.

In one particular, the training of these savage politicians was never surpassed. They had no art of writing to record events, or preserve the stipulations of treaties. Memory, therefore, was tasked to the utmost, and developed to an extraordinary degree. They had various devices for aiding it, such as bundles of sticks, and that system of signs, emblems, and rude pictures which they shared with other tribes. Their famous wampum-belts were so many mnemonic signs, each standing for some act, speech, treaty, or clause of a treaty. These represented the public archives, and were divided among various custodians, each charged with the memory and interpretation of those assigned to him. The meaning of the belts was from time to time expounded in their councils. In conferences with them, nothing more astonished the French, Dutch, and English officials than the precision with which, before replying to their addresses, the Indian orators repeated them point by point.

It was only in rare cases that crime among the Iroquois or Hurons was punished by public authority. Murder, the most heinous offence, except witchcraft, recognized among them, was rare. If the slayer and the slain were of the same household or clan, the affair was regarded as a family quarrel, to be settled by the immediate kin on both sides. This, under the pressure of public opinion, was commonly effected without bloodshed, by presents given in atonement. But if the murderer and his victim were of different clans or different nations, still more, if the slain was a foreigner, the whole community became interested to prevent the discord or the war which might arise. All directed their efforts, not to bring the murderer to punishment, but to satisfy the injured parties by a vicarious atonement. To this end, contributions were made and presents collected. Their number and value were determined by established usage. Among the Hurons, thirty presents of very considerable value were the price of a man's life. That of a woman's was fixed at forty, by reason of her weakness, and because on her depended the continuance and increase of the population. This was when the slain belonged to the nations. If of a foreign tribe, his death demanded a higher compensation, since it involved the danger of war. These presents were offered in solemn council, with prescibed formalities. The relatives of the slain might refuse them, if they chose, and in this case the murderer was given them as a slave; but they might by no means kill him, since in so doing they would incur public censure, and be compelled in their turn to make atonement. Besides the principal gifts, there was a great number of less value, all symbolical, and each delivered with a set form of words: as, "By this we wash out the blood of the slain: By this we cleanse his wound: By this we clothe his corpse with a new shirt: By this we place food on his grave;" and so, in endless prolixity, through particulars without number.

The Hurons were notorious thieves; and perhaps the Iroquois were not much better, though the contrary has been asserted. Among both, the robbed was permitted not only to retake his property by force, if he could, but to strip the robber of all he had. This apparently acted as a restraint in favor only of the strong, leaving the weak a prey to the plunderer; but here the tie of family and clan intervened to aid him. Relatives and clansmen espoused the quarrel of him who could not right himself.

Witches, with whom the Hurons and Iroquois were grievously infested, were objects of utter abomination to both, and any one might kill them at any time. If any person was guilty of treason, or by his character and conduct made himself dangerous or obnoxious to the public, the council of chiefs and old men held a secret session on his case, condemned him to death, and appointed some young man to kill him. The executioner, watching his opportunity, brained or stabbed him unawares, usually in the dark porch of one of the houses. Acting by authority, he could not be held answerable; and the relatives of the slain had no redress, even if they desired it. The council, however, commonly obviated all difficulty in advance, by charging the culprit with witchcraft, thus alienating his best friends.

The military organization of the Iroquois was exceedingly imperfect and derived all its efficiency from their civil union and their personal prowess. There were two hereditary war-chiefs, both belonging to the Senecas; but, except on occasions of unusual importance, it does not appear that they took a very active part in the conduct of wars. The Iroquois lived in a state of chronic warfare with nearly all the surrounding tribes, except a few from whom they exacted tribute. Any man of sufficient personal credit might raise a war-party when he chose. He proclaimed his purpose through the village, sang his war-songs, struck his hatchet into the war-post, and danced the war-dance. Any who chose joined him; and the party usually took up their march at once, with a little parched corn-meal and maple-sugar as their sole provision. On great occasions, there was concert of action, — the various parties meeting at a rendezvous, and pursuing the march together. The leaders of war-parties, like the orators, belonged, in nearly all cases, to the class of subordinate chiefs. The Iroquois had a discipline suited to the dark and tangled forests where they fought. Here they were a terrible foe: in an open country, against a trained European force, they were, despite their ferocious valor, far less formidable.

In observing this singular organization, one is struck by the incongruity of its spirit and its form. A body of hereditary oligarchs was the head of the nation, yet the nation was essentially democratic. Not that the Iroquois were levellers. None were more prompt to acknowledge superiority and defer to it, whether established by usage and prescription, or the result of personal endowment. Yet each man, whether of high or low degree, had a voice in the conduct of affairs, and was never for a moment divorced from his wild spirit of independence. Where there was no property worthy the name, authority had no fulcrum and no hold. The constant aim of sachems and chiefs was to exercise it without seeming to do so. They had no insignia of office. They were no richer than others; indeed, they were often poorer, spending their substance in largesses and bribes to strengthen their influence. They hunted and fished for subsistence; they were as foul, greasy, and unsavory as the rest; yet in them, withal, was often seen a native dignity of bearing, which ochre and bear's grease could not hide, and which comported well with their strong, symmetrical, and sometimes majestic proportions.

To the institutions, traditions, rites, usages, and festivals of the league the Iroquois was inseparably wedded. He clung to them with Indian tenacity; and he clings to them still. His political fabric was one of ancient ideas and practices, crystallized into regular and enduring forms. In its component parts it has nothing peculiar to itself. All its elements are found in other tribes; most of them belong to the whole Indian race. Undoubtedly there was a distinct and definite effort of legislation; but Iroquois legislation invented nothing. Like all sound legislation, it built of materials already prepared. It organized the chaotic past, and gave concrete forms to Indian nature itself. The people have dwindled and decayed; but, banded by its ties of clan and kin, the league, in feeble miniature, still subsists, and the degenerate Iroquois looks back with a mournful pride to the glory of the past.

Would the Iroquois, left undisturbed to work out their own destiny, ever have emerged from the savage state? Advanced as they were beyond most other American tribes, there is no indication whatever of a tendency to overpass the confines of a wild hunter and warrior life. They were inveterately attached to it, impracticable conservatists of barbarism, and in ferocity and cruelty they matched the worst of their race. Nor did the power of expansion apparently belonging to their system ever produce much result. Between the years 1712 and 1715, the Tuscaroras, a kindred people, were admitted into the league as a sixth nation; but they were never admitted on equal terms. Long after, in the period of their decline, several other tribes were announced as new members of the league; but these admissions never took effect. The Iroquois were always reluctant to receive other tribes, or parts of tribes, collectively, into the precincts of the "Long House." Yet they constantly practised a system of adoptions, from which, though cruel and savage, they drew great advantages. Their prisoners of war, when they had burned and butchered as many of them as would serve to sate their own ire and that of their women, were divided — man by man, woman by woman, and child by child, — adopted into different families and clans, and thus incorporated into the nation. It was by this means, and this alone, that they could offset the losses of their incessant wars. Early in the eighteenth century, and even long before, a vast proportion of their population consisted of adopted prisoners.[12]

It remains to speak of the religious and superstitious ideas which so deeply influenced Indian life.

6. Religion and Superstitions

The religious belief of the North-American Indians seems, on a first view, anomalous and contradictory. It certainly is so, if we adopt the popular impression. Romance, Poetry, and Rhetoric point, on the one hand, to the august conception of a one all-ruling Deity, a Great Spirit, omniscient and omnipresent; and we are called to admire the untutored intellect which could conceive a thought too vast for Socrates and Plato. On the other hand, we find a chaos of regrading, ridiculous, and incoherent superstitions. A closer examination will show that the contradiction is more apparent than real. We will begin with the lowest forms of Indian belief, and thence trace it upward to the highest conceptions to which the unassisted mind of the savage attained.

To the Indian, the material world is sentient and intelligent. Birds, beasts, and reptiles have ears for human prayers, and are endowed with an influence on human destiny. A mysterious and inexplicable power resides in inanimate things. They, too, can listen to the voice of man, and influence his life for evil or for good. Lakes, rivers, and waterfalls

[12] The Iroquois were at the height of their prosperity about the year 1650. Morgan reckons their number at this time at 25,000 souls; but this is far too high an estimate. The author of the *Relation* of 1660 makes their whole number of warriors 2,200. Le Mercier, in the *Relation* of 1665, says, 2,350. In the Journal of Greenhalgh, an Englishman who visited them in 1677, their warriors are set down at 2,150. Du Chesneau, in 1681, estimates them at 2,000; De la Barre, in 1684, at 2,600, they having been strengthened by adoptions. A memoir addressed to the Marquis de Seignelay, in 1687, again makes them 2,000. These estimates imply a total population of ten or twelve thousand. As the anonymous writer of the *Relation* of 1660 remarked: "It is marvellous that so few should make so great a havoc, and strike such terror into so many tribes."

are sometimes the dwelling-place of spirits; but more frequently they are themselves living beings, to be propitiated by prayers and offerings. The lake has a soul; and so has the river, and the cataract. Each can hear the words of men, and each can be pleased or offended. In the silence of a forest, the gloom of a deep ravine, resides a living mystery, indefinite, but redoubtable. Through all the works of Nature or of man, nothing exists, however seemingly trivial, that may not be endowed with a secret power for blessing or for bane.

Men and animals are closely akin. Each species of animal has its great archetype, its progenitor or king, who is supposed to exist somewhere, prodigious in size, though in shape and nature like his subjects. A belief prevails, vague, but perfectly apparent, that men themselves owe their first parentage to beasts, birds, or reptiles, — as bears, wolves, tortoises, or cranes; and the names of the totemic clans, borrowed in nearly every case from animals, are the reflection of this idea.

An Indian hunter was always anxious to propitiate the animals he sought to kill. He has often been known to address a wounded bear in a long harangue of apology. The bones of the beaver were treated with especial tenderness, and carefully kept from the dogs, lest the spirit of the dead beaver, or his surviving brethren, should take offence. This solicitude was not confined to animals, but extended to inanimate things. A remarkable example occurred among the Hurons, a people comparatively advanced, who, to propitiate their fishing-nets and persuade them to do their office with effect, married them every year to two young girls of the tribe, with a ceremony far more formal than that observed in the case of mere human wedlock. The fish, too, no less than the nets, must be propitiated; and to this end they were addressed every evening from the fishing-camp by one of the party chosen for that function, who exhorted them to take courage and be caught, assuring them that the utmost respect should be shown to their bones. The harangue, which took place after the evening meal, was made in solemn form; and while it lasted, the whole party, except the speaker, were required to lie on their backs, silent and motionless, around the fire.

Besides ascribing life and intelligence to the material world, animate and inanimate, the Indian believes in supernatural existences, known among the Algonquins as *Manitous*, and among the Iroquois and Hurons as *Okies* or *Otkons*. These words comprehend all forms of supernatural being, from the highest to the lowest, with the exception, possibly, of certain diminutive fairies or hobgoblins, and certain giants and anomalous monsters, which appear under various forms, grotesque and horrible, in the Indian fireside legends. There are local manitous of streams, rocks, mountains, cataracts, and forests. The conception of these beings betrays, for the most part, a striking poverty of imagination. In nearly every case, when they reveal themselves to mortal sight, they bear the semblance of beasts, reptiles, or birds, in shapes unusual or distorted. There are other manitous without local habitation, some good, some evil, countless in number and indefinite in attributes. They fill the world, and control the destinies of men, — that is to say, of Indians; for the primitive Indian holds that the white man lives under a spiritual rule distinct from that which governs his own fate. These beings, also, appear for the most part in the shape of animals. Sometimes, however, they assume human proportions; but more frequently they take the form of stones, which, being broken, are found full of living blood and flesh.

Each primitive Indian has his guardian manitou, to whom he looks for counsel, guidance, and protection. These spiritual allies are gained by the following process. At the age of fourteen or fifteen, the Indian boy blackens his face, retires to some solitary place, and remains for days without food. Superstitious expectancy and the exhaustion of abstinence rarely fail of their results. His sleep is haunted by visions, and the form which first or most often appears is that of his guardian manitou, — a beast, a bird, a fish, a serpent, or some other object, animate or inanimate. An eagle or a bear is the vision of a destined warrior; a wolf, of a successful hunter; while a serpent foreshadows the future medicine-man, or, according to others, portends disaster. The young Indian thenceforth wears about his person the object revealed in his dream, or some portion of it, — as a bone, a feather, a snake-skin, or a tuft of hair. This, in the modern language of the forest and prairie, is known as his "medicine." The Indian yields to it a sort of worship, propitiates it with offerings of tobacco, thanks it in prosperity, and upbraids it in disaster. If his medicine fails to bring the desired success, he will sometimes discard it and adopt another. The superstition now becomes mere fetich-worship, since the Indian regards the mysterious object which he carries about him rather as an embodiment than as a representative of a supernatural power.

Indian belief recognizes also another and very different class of beings. Besides the giants and monsters of legendary lore, other conceptions may be discerned, more or less distinct, and of a character partly mythical. Of these the most conspicuous is that remarkable personage of Algonquin tradition, called Manabozho, Messou, Michabou, Nanabush, or the Great Hare. As each species of animal has its archetype or king, so, among the Algonquins, Manabozho is king of all these animal kings. Tradition is diverse as to his origin. According to the most current belief, his father was the West-Wind, and his mother a great-granddaughter of the moon. His character is worthy of such a parentage. Sometimes he is a wolf, a bird, or a gigantic hare, surrounded by a court of quadrupeds; sometimes he appears in human shape, majestic in stature and wondrous in endowment, — a mighty magician, a destroyer of serpents and evil manitous; sometimes he is a vain and treacherous imp, full of childish whims and petty trickery, the butt and victim of men, beasts, and spirits. His powers of transformation are without limit; his curiosity and malice are insatiable; and of the numberless legends of which he is the hero, the greater part are as trivial as they are incoherent. It does not appear that Manabozho was ever an object of worship; yet, despite his absurdity, tradition declares him to be chief among the manitous, in short, the "Great Spirit." It was he who restored the world, submerged by a deluge. He was hunting in company with a certain wolf, who was his brother, or, by other accounts, his grandson, when his quadruped relative fell through the ice of a frozen lake, and was at once devoured by certain serpents lurking in the depths of the waters. Manabozho, intent on revenge, transformed himself into the stump of a tree, and by this artifice surprised and slew the king of the serpents, as he basked with his followers in the noontide sun. The serpents, who were all manitous, caused, in their rage, the waters of the lake to deluge the earth. Manabozho climbed a tree, which, in answer to his entreaties, grew as the flood rose around it, and thus saved him from the vengeance of the evil spirits. Submerged to the neck, he looked abroad on the waste of waters, and at length descried the bird known as the loon, to whom he appealed for aid in the task of restoring the world. The loon dived in search of a little mud, as material for reconstruction, but could not reach the bottom. A musk-rat made the same attempt, but soon reappeared floating on his back, and apparently dead. Manabozho, however, on searching his paws, discovered in one of them a particle of the desired mud, and of this, together with the body of the loon, created the world anew.

There are various forms of this tradition, in some of which Manabozho appears, not as the restorer, but as the creator of the world, forming mankind from the carcasses of beasts, birds, and fishes. Other stories represent him as marrying a female musk-rat, by whom he became the progenitor of the human race.

Searching for some higher conception of supernatural existence, we find, among a portion of the primitive Algonquins, traces of a vague belief in a spirit dimly shadowed forth under the name of Atahocan, to whom it does not appear that any attributes were ascribed or any worship offered, and of whom the Indians professed to know nothing whatever; but there is no evidence that this belief extended beyond certain tribes of the Lower St. Lawrence. Others saw a supreme manitou in the Sun. The Algonquins believed also in a malignant manitou, in whom the early missionaries failed not to recognize the Devil, but who was far less dreaded than his wife. She wore a robe made of the hair of her victims, for she was the cause of death; and she it was whom, by yelling, drumming, and stamping, they sought to drive away from the sick. Sometimes, at night, she was seen by some terrified squaw in the forest, in shape like a flame of fire; and when the vision was announced to the circle crouched around the lodge-fire, they burned a fragment of meat to appease the female fiend.

The East, the West, the North, and the South were vaguely personified as spirits or manitous. Some of the winds, too, were personal existences. The West-Wind, as we have seen, was father of Manabozho. There was a Summer-Maker and a Winter-Maker; and the Indians tried to keep the latter at bay by throwing firebrands into the air.

When we turn from the Algonquin family of tribes to that of the Iroquois, we find another cosmogony, and other conceptions of spiritual existence. While the earth was as yet a waste of waters, there was, according to Iroquois and Huron traditions, a heaven with lakes, streams, plains, and forests, inhabited by animals, by spirits, and, as some affirm, by human beings. Here a certain female spirit, named Ataentsic, was once chasing a bear, which, slipping through a hole, fell down to the earth. Ataentsic's dog followed, when she herself, struck with despair, jumped after them. Others declare that she was kicked out of heaven by the spirit, her husband, for an amour with a man; while others, again, hold the belief that she fell in the attempt to gather for her husband the medicinal leaves of a certain tree. Be this as it may, the animals swimming in the watery waste below saw her falling, and hastily met in council to determine what should be done. The case was referred to the beaver. The beaver commended it to the judgment of the tortoise, who thereupon called on the other animals to dive, bring up mud, and place it on his back. Thus was formed a floating island, on which Ataentsic fell; and here, being pregnant, she was soon delivered of a daughter, who in turn bore two boys, whose paternity is unexplained. They were called Taouscaron and Jouskeha, and presently fell to blows, Jouskeha killing his brother with the horn of a stag. The back of the tortoise grew into a world full of verdure and life; and Jouskeha, with his grandmother, Ataentsic, ruled over its destinies.

He is the Sun; she is the Moon. He is beneficent; but she is malignant, like the female demon of the Algonquins. They have a bark house, made like those of the Iroquois, at the end of the earth, and they often come to feasts and dances in the Indian villages. Jouskeha raises corn for himself, and makes plentiful harvests for mankind. Sometimes he is seen, thin as a skeleton, with a spike of shrivelled corn in his hand, or greedily gnawing a human limb; and then the Indians know that a grievous famine awaits them. He constantly interposes between mankind and the malice of his wicked grandmother, whom, at times, he soundly cudgels. It was he who made lakes and streams: for once the earth was parched and barren, all the water being gathered under the armpit of a colossal frog; but Jouskeha pierced the armpit, and let out the water. No prayers were offered to him, his benevolent nature rendering them superfluous.

The early writers call Jouskeha the creator of the world, and speak of him as corresponding to the vague Algonquin deity, Atahocan. Another deity appears in Iroquois mythology, with equal claims to be regarded as supreme. He is called Areskoui, or Agreskoui, and his most prominent attributes are those of a god of war. He was often invoked, and the flesh of animals and of captive enemies was burned in his honor. Like Jouskeha, he was identified with the sun; and he is perhaps to be regarded as the same being, under different attributes. Among the Iroquois proper, or Five Nations, there was also a divinity called Tarenyowagon, or Teharonhiawagon, whose place and character it is very difficult to determine. In some traditions he appears as the son of Jouskeha. He had a prodigious influence; for it was he who spoke to men in dreams. The Five Nations recognized still another superhuman personage, — plainly a deified chief or hero. This was Taounyawatha, or Hiawatha, said to be a divinely appointed messenger, who made his abode on earth for the political and social instruction of the chosen race, and whose counterpart is to be found in the traditions of the Peruvians, Mexicans, and other primitive nations.[13]

Close examination makes it evident that the primitive Indian's idea of a Supreme Being was a conception no higher than might have been expected. The moment he began to contemplate this object of his faith, and sought to clothe it with attributes, it became finite, and commonly ridiculous. The Creator of the World stood on the level of a barbarous and degraded humanity, while a natural tendency became apparent to look beyond him to other powers sharing his dominion. The Indian belief, if developed, would have developed into a system of polytheism.

In the primitive Indian's conception of a God the idea of moral good has no part. His deity does not dispense justice for this world or the next, but leaves mankind under the power of subordinate spirits, who fill and control the universe. Nor is the good and evil of these inferior beings a moral good and evil. The good spirit is the spirit that gives good luck, and ministers to the necessities and desires of mankind: the evil spirit is simply a malicious agent of disease, death, and mischance.

In no Indian language could the early missionaries find a word to express the idea of God. *Manitou* and *Oki* meant anything endowed with supernatural powers, from a snake-skin, or a greasy Indian conjurer, up to Manabozho and Jouskeha. The priests were forced to use a circumlocution, — "The Great Chief of Men," or "He who lives in the Sky." Yet it should seem that the idea of a supreme controlling spirit might naturally arise from the peculiar character of Indian belief. The idea that each race of animals has its archetype or chief would easily suggest the existence of a supreme chief of the spirits or of the human race, — a conception imperfectly shadowed forth in Manabozho. The Jesuit missionaries seized this advantage. "If each sort of animal has its king," they urged, "so, too, have men; and as man is above all the animals, so is the spirit that rules over men the master of all the other spirits." The Indian mind readily accepted the idea, and tribes in no sense Christian quickly rose to the belief in one con-

---

[13] For the tradition of Hiawatha, see Clark, *History of Onondaga*, i. 21. It will also be found in Schoolcraft's *Notes on the Iroquois*, and in his *History, Condition and Prospects of Indian Tribes*. [These were the sources of Longfellow's *Song of Hiawatha*, which appeared in 1855. Parkman was a friend of Longfellow; but he did not mention this poem, as he regarded it as a sentimental throwback to the "Noble Savage" concept.]

trolling spirit. The Great Spirit became a distinct existence, a pervading power in the universe, and a dispenser of justice. Many tribes now pray to him, though still clinging obstinately to their ancient superstitions; and with some, as the heathen portion of the modern Iroquois, he is clothed with attributes of moral good.[14]

The primitive Indian believed in the immortality of the soul, but he did not always believe in a state of future reward and punishment. Nor, when such a belief existed, was the good to be rewarded a moral good, or the evil to be punished a moral evil. Skilful hunters, brave warriors, men of influence and consideration, went, after death, to the happy hunting-ground; while the slothful, the cowardly, and the weak were doomed to eat serpents and ashes in dreary regions of mist and darkness. In the general belief, however, there was but one land of shades for all alike. The spirits, in form and feature as they had been in life, wended their way through dark forests to the villages of the dead, subsisting on bark and rotten wood. On arriving, they sat all day in the crouching posture of the sick, and, when night came, hunted the shades of animals, with the shades of bows and arrows, among the shades of trees and rocks: for all things, animate and inanimate, were alike immortal, and all passed together to the gloomy country of the dead.

The belief respecting the land of souls varied greatly in different tribes and different individuals. Among the Hurons there were those

---

[14] In studying the writers of the last and of the present century, it is to be remembered that their observations were made upon savages who had been for generations in contact, immediate or otherwise, with the doctrines of Christianity. Many observers have interpreted the religious ideas of the Indians after preconceived ideas of their own; and it may safely be affirmed that an Indian will respond with a grunt of acquiescence to any question whatever touching his spiritual state. [My friend Dr. John O. Brew tells me that they will do more than that now; they will give you a lecture on their religion!] By far the most close and accurate observers of Indian superstition were the French and Italian Jesuits of the first half of the seventeenth century. Their opportunities were unrivalled; and they used them in a spirit of faithful inquiry, accumulating facts, and leaving theory to their successors. Of recent American writers, no one has given so much attention to the subject as Mr. Schoolcraft; but, in view of his opportunities and his zeal, his results are most unsatisfactory. The work in six large quarto volumes, *History, Condition, and Prospects of Indian Tribes*, published by Government under his editorship, includes the substance of most of his previous writings. It is a singularly crude and illiterate production, stuffed with blunders and contradictions, giving evidence on every page of a striking unfitness either for historical or philosophical inquiry, and taxing to the utmost the patience of those who would extract what is valuable in it from its oceans of pedantic verbiage.

who held that departed spirits pursued their journey through the sky, along the Milky Way, while the souls of dogs took another route, by certain constellations, known as the "Way of the Dogs."

At intervals of ten or twelve years, the Hurons, the Neutrals, and other kindred tribes, were accustomed to collect the bones of their dead, and deposit them, with great ceremony, in a common place of burial. The whole nation was sometimes assembled at this solemnity; and hundreds of corpses, brought from their temporary resting-places, were inhumed in one capacious pit. From this hour the immortality of their souls began. They took wing, as some affirmed, in the shape of pigeons; while the greater number declared that they journeyed on foot, and in their own likeness, to the land of shades, bearing with them the ghosts of the wampum-belts, beaver-skins, bows, arrows, pipes, kettles, beads, and rings buried with them in the common grave.[15] But as the spirits of the old and of children are too feeble for the march, they are forced to stay behind, lingering near their earthly villages, where the living often hear the shutting of their invisible cabin-doors, and the weak voices of the disembodied children driving birds from their corn-fields. An endless variety of incoherent fancies is connected with the Indian idea of a future life. They commonly owe their origin to dreams, often to the dreams of those in extreme sickness, who, on awakening, supposed that they had visited the other world, and related to the wondering bystanders what they had seen.

The Indian land of souls is not always a region of shadows and gloom. The Hurons sometimes represented the souls of their dead — those of their dogs included — as dancing joyously in the presence of Ataentsic and Jouskeha. According to some Algonquin traditions, heaven was a scene of endless festivity, the ghosts dancing to the sound of the rattle and the drum, and greeting with hospitable welcome the occasional visitor from the living world: for the spirit-land was not far off, and roving hunters sometimes passed its confines unawares.

Most of the traditions agree, however, that the spirits, on their journey heavenward, were beset with difficulties and perils. There was a swift river which must be crossed on a log that shook beneath their feet, while a ferocious dog opposed their passage, and drove many

[15] The practice of burying treasures with the dead is not peculiar to the North American aborigines. Thus, the London *Times* of Oct. 28, 1865, describing the funeral rites of Lord Palmerston, says: "As the words, 'Dust to dust, ashes to ashes,' were pronounced, the chief mourner, as a last precious offering to the dead, threw into the grave several diamond and gold rings."

into the abyss. This river was full of sturgeon and other fish, which the ghosts speared for their subsistence. Beyond was a narrow path between moving rocks, which each instant crashed together, grinding to atoms the less nimble of the pilgrims who essayed to pass. The Hurons believed that a personage named Oscotarach, or the Head-Piercer, dwelt in a bark house beside the path, and that it was his office to remove the brains from the heads of all who went by, as a necessary preparation for immortality. This singular idea is found also in some Algonquin traditions, according to which, however, the brain is afterwards restored to its owner.

Dreams were to the Indian a universal oracle. They revealed to him his guardian spirit, taught him the cure of his diseases, warned him of the devices of sorcerers, guided him to the lurking-places of his enemy or the haunts of game, and unfolded the secrets of good and evil destiny. The dream was a mysterious and inexorable power, whose least behests must be obeyed to the letter, — a source, in every Indian town, of endless mischief and abomination. There were professed dreamers, and professed interpreters of dreams. One of the most noted festivals among the Hurons and Iroquois was the Dream Feast, a scene of frenzy, where the actors counterfeited madness, and the town was like a bedlam turned loose. Each pretended to have dreamed of something necessary to his welfare, and rushed from house to house, demanding of all he met to guess his secret requirement and satisfy it.

Believing that the whole material world was instinct with powers to influence and control his fate; that good and evil spirits, and existences nameless and indefinable, filled all Nature; that a pervading sorcery was above, below, and around him, and that issues of life and death might be controlled by instruments the most unnoticeable and seemingly the most feeble, — the Indian lived in perpetual fear. The turning of a leaf, the crawling of an insect, the cry of a bird, the creaking of a bough, might be to him the mystic signal of weal or woe.

An Indian community swarmed with sorcerers, medicine-men, and diviners, whose functions were often united in the same person. The sorcerer, by charms, magic songs, magic feasts, and the beating of his drum, had power over the spirits and those occult influences inherent in animals and inanimate things. He could call to him the souls of his enemies. They appeared before him in the form of stones. He chopped and bruised them with his hatchet; blood and flesh issued forth; and the intended victim, however distant, languished and died. Like the sorcerer of the Middle Ages, he made images of those he wished to destroy, and, muttering incantations, punctured them with an awl, whereupon the persons represented sickened and pined away.

The Indian doctor relied far more on magic than on natural remedies. Dreams, beating of the drum, songs, magic feasts and dances, and howling to frighten the female demon from his patient were his ordinary methods of cure.

The prophet, or diviner, had various means of reading the secrets of futurity, such as the flight of birds, and the movements of water and fire. There was a peculiar practice of divination very general in the Algonquin family of tribes, among some of whom it still subsists. A small, conical lodge was made by planting poles in a circle, lashing the tops together at the height of about seven feet from the ground, and closely covering them with hides. The prophet crawled in, and closed the aperture after him. He then beat his drum and sang his magic songs to summon the spirits, whose weak, shrill voices were soon heard, mingled with his lugubrious chanting; while at intervals the juggler paused to interpret their communications to the attentive crowd seated on the ground without. During the whole scene, the lodge swayed to and fro with a violence which has astonished many a civilized beholder, and which some of the Jesuits explain by the ready solution of a genuine diabolic intervention.

The sorcerers, medicine-men, and diviners did not usually exercise the function of priests. Each man sacrificed for himself to the powers he wished to propitiate, whether his guardian spirit, the spirits of animals, or the other beings of his belief. The most common offering was tobacco, thrown into the fire or water; scraps of meat were sometimes burned to the manitous; and, on a few rare occasions of public solemnity, a white dog, the mystic animal of many tribes, was tied to the end of an upright pole, as a sacrifice to some superior spirit, or to the sun, with which the superior spirits were constantly confounded by the primitive Indian. In recent times, when Judaism and Christianity have modified his religious ideas, it has been, and still is, the practice to sacrifice dogs to the Great Spirit. On these public occasions, the sacrificial function is discharged by chiefs, or by warriors appointed for the purpose.

Among the Hurons and Iroquois, and indeed all the stationary tribes, there was an incredible number of mystic ceremonies, extravagant, puerile, and often disgusting, designed for the cure of the sick or for the general weal of the community. Most of their observances seem originally to have been dictated by dreams, and transmitted as a sacred heritage from generation to generation. They consisted in an endless variety of dances, masqueradings, and nondescript orgies; and a scrupulous adherence to all the traditional forms was held to be of the last moment, as the slightest failure in this respect might entail serious calamities. If children were seen in their play imitating any of these mysteries, they were grimly rebuked and punished. In many tribes secret magical societies existed, and still exist, into which members are initiated with peculiar ceremonies. These associations are greatly respected and feared. They have charms for love, war, and private revenge, and exert a great, and often a very mischievous influence. The societies of the Metai and the Wabeno, among the Northern Algonquins, are conspicuous examples; while other societies of similar character have, for a century, been known to exist among the Dahcotah.

A notice of the superstitious ideas of the Indians would be imperfect without a reference to the traditionary tales through which these ideas are handed down from father to son. Some of these tales can be traced back to the period of the earliest intercourse with Europeans. One at least of those recorded by the first missionaries, on the Lower St. Lawrence, is still current among the tribes of the Upper Lakes. Many of them are curious combinations of beliefs seriously entertained with strokes intended for humor and drollery, which never fail to awaken peals of laughter in the lodge-circle. Giants, dwarfs, cannibals, spirits, beasts, birds, and anomalous monsters, transformations, tricks, and sorcery form the staple of the story. Some of the Iroquois tales embody conceptions which, however preposterous, are of a bold and striking character; but those of the Algonquins are, to an incredible degree, flimsy, silly, and meaningless; nor are those of the Dahcotah tribes much better. In respect to this wigwam lore, there is a curious superstition of very wide prevalence. The tales must not be told in summer; since at that season, when all Nature is full of life, the spirits are awake, and, hearing what is said of them, may take offence; whereas in winter they are fast sealed up in snow and ice, and no longer capable of listening.[16]

[16] The prevalence of this fancy among the Algonquins in the remote parts of Canada is well established. The writer found it also among the extreme western bands of the Dahcotah. He tried, in the month of July, to persuade an old chief, a noted story-teller, to tell him some of the tales; but, though abundantly loquacious in respect to his own adventures, and even his dreams, the Indian obstinately refused, saying that winter was the time for the tales, and that it was bad to tell them in summer.

It is obvious that the Indian mind has never seriously occupied itself with any of the higher themes of thought. The beings of its belief are not impersonations of the forces of Nature, the courses of human destiny, or the movements of human intellect, will, and passion. In the midst of Nature, the Indian knew nothing of her laws. His perpetual reference of her phenomena to occult agencies forestalled inquiry and precluded inductive reasoning. If the wind blew with violence, it was because the water-lizard, which makes the wind, had crawled out of his pool; if the lightning was sharp and frequent, it was because the young of the thunder-bird were restless in their nest; if a blight fell upon the corn, it was because the Corn Spirit was angry; and if the beavers were shy and difficult to catch, it was because they had taken offence at seeing the bones of one of their race thrown to a dog. Well, and even highly developed, in a few instances, — I allude especially to the Iroquois, — with respect to certain points of material concernment, the mind of the Indian in other respects was and is almost hopelessly stagnant. The very traits that raise him above the servile races are hostile to the kind and degree of civilization which those races so easily attain. His intractable spirit of independence, and the pride which forbids him to be an imitator, reinforce but too strongly that savage lethargy of mind from which it is so hard to rouse him. No race, perhaps, ever offered greater difficulties to those laboring for its improvement.

To sum up the results of this examination, the primitive Indian was as savage in his religion as in his life. He was divided between fetich-worship and that next degree of religious development which consists in the worship of deities embodied in the human form. His conception of their attributes was such as might have been expected. His gods were no whit better than himself. Even when he borrows from Christianity the idea of a Supreme and Universal Spirit, his tendency is to reduce Him to a local habitation and a bodily shape; and this tendency disappears only in tribes that have been long in contact with civilized white men. The primitive Indian, yielding his untutored homage to One All-pervading and Omnipotent Spirit, is a dream of poets, rhetoricians and sentimentalists.

CHAPTER II

Verrazano, Cartier and Roberval
1504–1543

[*Pioneers of France in the New World*, PART II, CHAPTER I]

When America was first made known to Europe, the part assumed by France on the borders of that new world was peculiar, and is little recognized. While the Spaniard roamed sea and land, burning for achievement, red-hot with bigotry and avarice, and while England, with soberer steps and a less dazzling result, followed in the path of discovery and gold-hunting, it was from France that those barbarous shores first learned to serve the ends of peaceful commercial industry.

A French writer, however, advances a more ambitious claim. In the year 1488, four years before the first voyage of Columbus, America, he maintains was found by Frenchmen. Cousin, a navigator of Dieppe, being at sea off the African coast, was forced westward, it is said, by winds and currents to within sight of an unknown shore, where he presently descried the mouth of a great river. On board his ship was one Pinzon, whose conduct became so mutinous that, on his return to Dieppe, Cousin made complaint to the magistracy, who thereupon dismissed the offender from the maritime service of the town. Pinzon went to Spain, became known to Columbus, told him the discovery, and joined him on his voyage of 1492.[1]

To leave this cloudland of tradition, and approach the confines of recorded history. The Normans, offspring of an ancestry of con-

---

[1] [This story is an unverified myth of a later date, as is the one that French fishermen were on the Grand Bank of Newfoundland before Cabot or Columbus. Newfoundland was probably discovered in 1500 by Gaspar Cortereal, and the Portuguese were much more active along the North American coast before 1525 than were the French. As early as 1521 they had a fishing station on Cape Breton Island, probably at Ingonish, and spent a winter there, but were discouraged by the severity of the climate. The fishermen from Brittany, after whom the Cape is named, later supplanted the Portuguese on that coast.]

querors, — the Bretons, that stubborn, hardy, unchanging race, who, among Druid monuments changeless as themselves, still cling with Celtic obstinacy to the thoughts and habits of the past, — the Basques, that primeval people, older than history, — all frequented from a very early date the cod-banks of Newfoundland. There is some reason to believe that this fishery existed before the voyage of Cabot, in 1497; there is strong evidence that it began as early as the year 1504; and it is well established that, in 1517, fifty Castilian, French, and Portuguese vessels were engaged in it at once; while in 1527, on the third of August, eleven sail of Norman, one of Breton, and two of Portuguese fishermen were to be found in the Bay of St. John.

From this time forth, the Newfoundland fishery was never abandoned. French, English, Spanish, and Portuguese made resort to the Banks, always jealous, often quarrelling, but still drawing up treasure from those exhaustless mines, and bearing home bountiful provision against the season of Lent.

On this dim verge of the known world there were other perils than those of the waves. The rocks and shores of those sequestered seas had, so thought the voyagers, other tenants than the seal, the walrus, and the screaming sea-fowl, the bears which stole away their fish before their eyes, and the wild natives dressed in seal-skins. Griffins — so ran the story — infested the mountains of Labrador. Two islands, north of Newfoundland, were given over to the fiends from whom they derived their name, the Isles of Demons. An old map pictures their occupants at length, — devils rampant, with wings, horns, and tail. The passing voyager heard the din of their infernal orgies, and woe to the sailor or the fisherman who ventured alone into the haunted woods. "True it is," writes the old cosmographer Thevet, "and I myself have heard it, not from one, but from a great number of the sailors and pilots with whom I have made many voyages, that, when they passed this way, they heard in the air, on the tops and about the masts, a great clamor of men's voices, confused and inarticulate, such as you may hear from the crowd at a fair or market-place; whereupon they well knew that the Isle of Demons was not far off." And he adds, that he himself, when among the Indians, had seen them so tormented by these infernal persecutors, that they would fall into his arms for relief; on which, repeating a passage of the Gospel of St. John, he had driven the imps of darkness to a speedy exodus. They are comely to look upon, he further tells us; yet, by reason of their malice, that island is of late abandoned, and all who dwelt there have fled for refuge to the main.

While French fishermen plied their trade along these gloomy coasts, the French government spent its energies on a different field. The vitality of the kingdom was wasted in Italian wars. Milan and Naples offered a more tempting prize than the wilds of Baccalaos. Eager for glory and for plunder, a swarm of restless nobles followed their knight-errant King, the would-be paladin, who, misshapen in body and fantastic in mind, had yet the power to raise a storm which the lapse of generations could not quell. Under Charles VIII and his successor, war and intrigue ruled the day; and in the whirl of Italian politics there was no leisure to think of a new world.

Yet private enterprise was not quite benumbed. In 1506, one Denis of Honfleur explored the Gulf of St. Lawrence; two years later, Aubert of Dieppe followed on his track; and in 1518, the Baron de Léry made an abortive attempt at settlement on Sable Island, where the cattle left by him remained and multiplied.

The crown passed at length to Francis of Angoulême. There were in his nature seeds of nobleness, — seeds destined to bear little fruit. Chivalry and honor were always on his lips; but Francis I, a forsworn gentleman, a despotic king, vainglorious, selfish, sunk in debaucheries, was but the type of an era which retained the forms of the Middle Age without its soul, and added to a still prevailing barbarism the pestilential vices which hung fog-like around the dawn of civilization. Yet he esteemed arts and letters, and, still more, coveted the *éclat* which they could give. The light which was beginning to pierce the feudal darkness gathered its rays around his throne. Italy was rewarding the robbers who preyed on her with the treasures of her knowledge and her culture; and Italian genius, of whatever stamp, found ready patronage at the hands of Francis. Among artists, philosophers, and men of letters enrolled in his service stands the humbler name of a Florentine navigator, John Verrazano.

He was born of an ancient family, which could boast names eminent in Florentine history, and of which the last survivor died in 1819. He has been called a pirate, and he was such in the same sense in which Drake, Hawkins, and other valiant sea-rovers of his own and later times, merited the name; that is to say, he would plunder and kill a Spaniard on the high seas without waiting for a declaration of war.

The wealth of the Indies was pouring into the coffers of Charles V, and the exploits of Cortés had given new lustre to his crown. Francis I begrudged his hated rival the glories and profits of the New World. He would fain have his share of the prize; and Verrazano, with four

ships, was despatched to seek out a passage westward to the rich kingdom of Cathay.

Some doubt has of late been cast on the reality of this voyage of
Verrazano, and evidence, mainly negative in kind, has been adduced
to prove the story of it a fabrication; but the difficulties of incredulity
appear greater than those of belief, and no ordinary degree of scepticism
is required to reject the evidence that the narrative is essentially true.[2]

Towards the end of the year 1523, his four ships sailed from Dieppe;
but a storm fell upon him, and, with two of the vessels, he ran back in
distress to a port of Brittany. What became of the other two does not
appear. Neither is it clear why, after a preliminary cruise against the
Spaniards, he pursued his voyage with one vessel alone, a caravel called
the *Dauphine*. With her he made for Madeira, and, on the 17th of
January, 1524, set sail from a barren islet in its neighborhood, and bore
away for the unknown world. In forty-nine days they neared a low
shore, not far from the site of Wilmington in North Carolina, "a newe
land," exclaims the voyager, "never before seen of any man, either
auncient or moderne." Verrazano steered southward in search of a harbor, and, finding none, turned northward again. Presently he sent a
boat ashore. The inhabitants, who had fled at first, soon came down to
the strand in wonder and admiration, pointing out a landing-place, and
making gestures of friendship. "These people," says Verrazano, "goe
altogether naked, except only certain skinnes of beastes like unto
marterns [martens], which they fasten onto a narrowe girdle made of
grasse. They are of colour russet, and not much unlike the Saracens,
their hayre blacke, thicke, and not very long, which they tye togeather
in a knot behinde, and weare it like a taile."

He describes the shore as consisting of small low hillocks of fine sand,
intersected by creeks and inlets, and beyond these a country "full of
Palme [pine?] trees, Bay trees, and high Cypresse trees, and many other
sortes of trees, vnknowne in Europe, which yeeld most sweete sauours,
farre from the shore." Still advancing northward, Verrazano sent a boat
for a supply of water. The surf ran high, and the crew could not land;
but an adventurous young sailor jumped overboard and swam shore-
ward with a gift of beads and trinkets for the Indians, who stood

[2] [There is no longer any question of the authenticity of Verrazano's Voyage,
hence Parkman's paragraph and long note examining the "historic doubts" of
Buckingham Smith are omitted. Parkman's quotations are from the Hakluyt translation of the now lost original. A good recent account of his voyage is Jacques
Habert *When New York was Called Angoulême* (New York: Transocean Press
1949).]

watching him. His heart failed as he drew near; he flung his gift among them, turned, and struck out for the boat. The surf dashed him back, flinging him with violence on the beach among the recipients of his bounty, who seized him by the arms and legs, and, while he called lustily for aid, answered him with outcries designed to allay his terrors. Next they kindled a great fire, — doubtless to roast and devour him before the eyes of his comrades, gazing in horror from their boat. On the contrary, they carefully warmed him, and were trying to dry his clothes, when, recovering from his bewilderment, he betrayed a strong desire to escape to his friends; whereupon, "with great love, clapping him fast about, with many embracings," they led him to the shore, and stood watching till he had reached the boat.

It only remained to requite this kindness, and an opportunity soon occurred; for, coasting the shores of Virginia or Maryland, a party went on shore and found an old woman, a young girl, and several children, hiding with great terror in the grass. Having, by various blandishments, gained their confidence, they carried off one of the children as a curiosity, and, since the girl was comely, would fain have taken her also, but desisted by reason of her continual screaming.

Verrazano's next resting-place was the Bay of New York. Rowing up in his boat through the Narrows, under the steep heights of Staten Island, he saw the harbor within dotted with canoes of the feathered natives, coming from the shore to welcome him. But what most engaged the eyes of the white man were the fancied signs of mineral wealth in the neighboring hills.

Following the shores of Long Island, they came to an island, which may have been Block Island, and thence to a harbor, which was probably that of Newport. Here they stayed fifteen days, most courteously received by the inhabitants. Among others appeared two chiefs, gorgeously arrayed in painted deer-skins, — kings, as Verrazano calls them, with attendant gentlemen; while a party of squaws in a canoe, kept by their jealous lords at a safe distance from the caravel, figure in the narrative as the queen and her maids. The Indian wardrobe had been taxed to its utmost to do the strangers honor, — copper bracelets, lynx-skins, raccoon-skins, and faces bedaubed with gaudy colors.

Again they spread their sails, and on the 5th of May bade farewell to the primitive hospitalities of Newport, steered along the rugged coasts of New England, and surveyed, ill pleased, the surf-beaten rocks, the pine-tree and the fir, the shadows and the gloom of mighty forests. Here man and nature alike were savage and repellent. Perhaps some plundering straggler from the fishing-banks, some man-stealer like the Portuguese Cortereal, or some kidnapper of children and ravisher of squaws like themselves, had warned the denizens of the woods to beware of the worshippers of Christ. Their only intercourse was in the way of trade. From the brink of the rocks which overhung the sea the Indians would let down a cord to the boat below, demand fish-hooks, knives, and steel, in barter for their furs, and, their bargain made, salute the voyagers with unseemly gestures of derision and scorn. The French once ventured ashore; but a war-whoop and a shower of arrows sent them back to their boats.

Verrazano coasted the seaboard of Maine, and sailed northward as far as Newfoundland, whence, provisions failing, he steered for France. He had not found a passage to Cathay, but he had explored the American coast from the thirty-fourth degree to the fiftieth, and at various points had penetrated several leagues into the country. On the 8th of July, he wrote from Dieppe to the King the earliest description known to exist of the shores of the United States.

Great was the joy that hailed his arrival, and great were the hopes of emolument and wealth from the new-found shores. The merchants of Lyons were in a flush of expectation. For himself, he was earnest to return, plant a colony, and bring the heathen tribes within the pale of the Church. But the time was inauspicious. The year of his voyage was to France a year of disasters, — defeat in Italy, the loss of Milan, the death of the heroic Bayard; and, while Verrazano was writing his narrative at Dieppe, the traitor Bourbon was invading Provence. Preparation, too, was soon on foot for the expedition which, a few months later, ended in the captivity of Francis on the field of Pavia. Without a king, without an army, without money, convulsed within, and threatened from without, France after that humiliation was in no condition to renew her Transatlantic enterprise.

Henceforth few traces remain of the fortunes of Verrazano. Ramusio affirms, that, on another voyage, he was killed and eaten by savages, in sight of his followers; and a late writer hazards the conjecture that this voyage, if made at all, was made in the service of Henry VIII of England. But a Spanish writer affirms that, in 1527, he was hanged at Puerto del Pico as a pirate, and this assertion is fully confirmed by authentic documents recently brought to light.

The fickle-minded King, always ardent at the outset of an enterprise and always flagging before its close, divided, moreover, between the smiles of his mistresses and the assaults of his enemies, might probably have dismissed the New World from his thoughts. But among the favorites of his youth was a high-spirited young noble, Philippe de Brion-Chabot, the partner of his joustings and tennis-playing, his gaming and gallantries. He still stood high in the royal favor, and, after the treacherous escape of Francis from captivity, held the office of Admiral of France. When the kingdom had rallied in some measure from its calamities, he conceived the purpose of following up the path which Verrazano had opened.

The ancient town of St. Malo — thrust out like a buttress into the sea, strange and grim of aspect, breathing war from its walls and battlements of ragged stone, a stronghold of privateers, the home of a race whose intractable and defiant independence neither time nor change has subdued — has been for centuries a nursery of hardy mariners. Among the earliest and most eminent on its list stands the name of Jacques Cartier. His portrait hangs in the town-hall of St. Malo, — bold, keen features bespeaking a spirit not apt to quail before the wrath of man or of the elements. In him Chabot found a fit agent of his design, if, indeed, its suggestion is not due to the Breton navigator.[3]

Sailing from St. Malo on the 20th of April, 1534, Cartier steered for Newfoundland, passed through the Straits of Belle Isle, entered the Gulf of Chaleurs, planted a cross at Gaspé, and, never doubting that he was on the high road to Cathay, advanced up the St. Lawrence till he saw the shores of Anticosti. But autumnal storms were gathering. The voyagers took counsel together, turned their prows eastward, and bore away for France, carrying thither, as a sample of the natural products of the New World, two young Indians, lured into their clutches by an act of villainous treachery. The voyage was a mere reconnoissance.

The spirit of discovery was awakened. A passage to India could be found, and a new France built up beyond the Atlantic. Mingled with such views of interest and ambition was another motive scarcely less potent. The heresy of Luther was convulsing Germany, and the deeper heresy of Calvin infecting France. Devout Catholics, kindling with redoubled zeal, would fain requite the Church for her losses in the Old World by winning to her fold the infidels of the New. But, in pursuing an end at once so pious and so politic, Francis I was setting at naught the supreme Pontiff himself, since, by the preposterous bull of Alexander VI, all America had been given to the Spaniards.

In October, 1534, Cartier received from Chabot another commission, and, in spite of secret but bitter opposition from jealous traders of St.

[3] Cartier was at this time forty years of age, having been born in December 1494.

Malo, he prepared for a second voyage. Three vessels, the largest not above a hundred and twenty tons, were placed at his disposal, and Claude de Pontbriand, Charles de la Pommeraye, and other gentlemen of birth, enrolled themselves for the adventure. On the 16th of May, 1535, officers and sailors assembled in the cathedral of St. Malo, where, after confession and mass, they received the parting blessing of the bishop. Three days later they set sail. The dingy walls of the rude old seaport, and the white rocks that line the neighboring shores of Brittany, faded from their sight, and soon they were tossing in a furious tempest. The scattered ships escaped the danger, and, reuniting at the Straits of Belle Isle, steered westward along the coast of Labrador, till they reached a small bay opposite the island of Anticosti. Cartier called it the Bay of St. Lawrence, — a name afterwards extended to the entire gulf, and to the great river above.[4]

To ascend this great river, and tempt the hazards of its intricate navigation with no better pilots than the two young Indians kidnapped the year before, was a venture of no light risk. But skill or fortune prevailed; and, on the first of September, the voyagers reached in safety the gorge of the gloomy Saguenay, with its towering cliffs and sullen depth of waters. Passing the Isle aux Coudres, and the lofty promontory of Cape Tourmente, they came to anchor in a quiet channel between the northern shore and the margin of a richly wooded island, where the trees were so thickly hung with grapes that Cartier named it the Island of Bacchus.[5]

Indians came swarming from the shores, paddled their canoes about the ships, and clambered to the decks to gaze in bewilderment at the novel scene, and listen to the story of their travelled countrymen, marvellous in their ears as a visit to another planet. Cartier received them kindly, listened to the long harangue of the great chief Donnacona, regaled him with bread and wine; and, when relieved at length of his guests, set forth in a boat to explore the river above.

As he drew near the opening of the channel, the Hochelaga again spread before him the broad expanse of its waters. A mighty promontory,

[4] Cartier calls the St. Lawrence the "River of Hochelaga," or "the great river of Canada." He confines the name *Canada* to a district extending from the Isle aux Coudres in the St. Lawrence to a point at some distance above the site of Quebec. The country below, he adds, was called by the Indians *Saguenay*, and that above, *Hochelaga*. . . . The name of Canada . . . is, without doubt, not Spanish, but Indian. In the vocabulary of the language of Hochelaga, appended to the journal of Cartier's second voyage, *Canada* is set down as the word for a town or village. . . . It bears the same meaning in the Mohawk tongue.

[5] Now Ile d'Orléans.

rugged and bare, thrust its scarped front into the surging current. Here, clothed in the majesty of solitude, breathing the stern poetry of the wilderness, rose the cliffs now rich with heroic memories, where the fiery Count Frontenac cast defiance at his foes, where Wolfe, Montcalm, and Montgomery fell. As yet, all was a nameless barbarism, and a cluster of wigwams held the site of the rock-built city of Quebec.[6] Its name was Stadaconé, and it owned the sway of the royal Donnacona.

Cartier set out to visit this greasy potentate; ascended the river St. Charles, by him called the St. Croix, landed, crossed the meadows, climbed the rocks, threaded the forest, and emerged upon a squalid hamlet of bark cabins. When, having satisfied their curiosity, he and his party were rowing for the ships, a friendly interruption met them at the mouth of the St. Charles. An old chief harangued them from the bank, men, boys, and children screeched welcome from the meadow, and a troop of hilarious squaws danced knee-deep in the water. The gift of a few strings of beads completed their delight and redoubled their agility; and, from the distance of a mile, their shrill songs of jubilation still reached the ears of the receding Frenchmen.

The hamlet of Stadaconé, with its king, Donnacona, and its naked lords and princes, was not the metropolis of this forest state, since a town far greater — so the Indians averred — stood by the brink of the river, many days' journey above. It was called Hochelaga, and the great river itself, with a wide reach of adjacent country, had borrowed its name. Thither, with his two young Indians as guides, Cartier resolved to go; but misgivings seized the guides as the time drew near, while Donnacona and his tribesmen, jealous of the plan, set themselves to thwart it. The Breton captain turned a deaf ear to their dissuasions; on which, failing to touch his reason, they appealed to his fears.

One morning, as the ships still lay at anchor, the French beheld three Indian devils descending in a canoe towards them, dressed in black and white dog-skins, with faces black as ink, and horns long as a man's arm. Thus arrayed, they drifted by, while the principal fiend, with fixed eyes, as of one piercing the secrets of futurity, uttered in a loud voice a long harangue. Then they paddled for the shore; and no sooner did they reach it than each fell flat like a dead man in the bottom of the canoe. Aid, however, was at hand; for Donnacona and his tribesmen, rushing pell-mell from the adjacent woods, raised the swooning masqueraders, and, with shrill clamors, bore them in their arms within the sheltering thickets. Here, for a full half-hour, the French could hear them ha-

[6] On ground now covered by the suburbs of St. Roque and St. John.

ranguing in solemn conclave. Then the two young Indians whom Cartier had brought back from France came out of the bushes, enacting a pantomime of amazement and terror, clasping their hands, and calling on Christ and the Virgin; whereupon Cartier, shouting from the vessel, asked what was the matter. They replied, that the god Coudouagny had sent to warn the French against all attempts to ascend the great river, since, should they persist, snows, tempests, and drifting ice would requite their rashness with inevitable ruin. The French replied that Coudouagny was a fool; that he could not hurt those who believed in Christ; and that they might tell this to his three messengers. The assembled Indians, with little reverence for their deity, pretended great contentment at this assurance, and danced for joy along the beach.

Cartier now made ready to depart. And, first, he caused the two larger vessels to be towed for safe harborage within the mouth of the St. Charles. With the smallest, a galleon of forty tons, and two open boats, carrying in all fifty sailors, besides Pontbriand, La Pommeraye, and other gentlemen, he set out for Hochelaga.

Slowly gliding on their way by walls of verdure brightened in the autumnal sun, they saw forests festooned with grape-vines, and waters alive with wild-fowl; they heard the song of the blackbird, the thrush, and, as they fondly thought, the nightingale. The galleon grounded; they left her, and, advancing with the boats alone, on the second of October neared the goal of their hopes, the mysterious Hochelaga.

Just below where now are seen the quays and storehouses of Montreal, a thousand Indians thronged the shore, wild with delight, dancing, singing, crowding about the strangers, and showering into the boats their gifts of fish and maize; and, as it grew dark, fires lighted up the night, while, far and near, the French could see the excited savages leaping and rejoicing by the blaze.

At dawn of day, marshalled and accoutred, they marched for Hochelaga. An Indian path led them through the forest which covered the site of Montreal. The morning air was chill and sharp, the leaves were changing hue, and beneath the oaks the ground was thickly strewn with acorns. They soon met an Indian chief with a party of tribesmen, or, as the old narrative has it, "one of the principal lords of the said city," attended with a numerous retinue. Greeting them after the concise courtesy of the forest, he led them to a fire kindled by the side of the path for their comfort and refreshment, seated them on the ground, and made them a long harangue, receiving in requital of his eloquence two hatchets, two knives, and a crucifix, the last of which he was invited to kiss. This done, they resumed their march, and presently came upon open fields, covered far and near with the ripened maize, its leaves rustling, and its yellow grains gleaming between the parting husks. Before them, wrapped in forests painted by the early frosts, rose the ridgy back of the Mountain of Montreal, and below, encompassed with its corn-fields, lay the Indian town. Nothing was visible but its encircling palisades. They were of trunks of trees, set in a triple row. The outer and inner ranges inclined till they met and crossed near the summit, while the upright row between them, aided by transverse braces, gave to the whole an abundant strength. Within were galleries for the defenders, rude ladders to mount them, and magazines of stones to throw down on the heads of assailants. It was a mode of fortification practised by all the tribes speaking dialects of the Iroquois.

The voyagers entered the narrow portal. Within, they saw some fifty of those large oblong dwellings so familiar in after years to the eyes of the Jesuit apostles in Iroquois and Huron forests. They were about fifty yards in length, and twelve or fifteen wide, framed of sapling poles closely covered with sheets of bark, and each containing several fires and several families. In the midst of the town was an open area, or public square, a stone's throw in width. Here Cartier and his followers stopped, while the surrounding houses of bark disgorged their inmates, — swarms of children, and young women and old, their infants in their arms. They crowded about the visitors, crying for delight, touching their beards, feeling their faces, and holding up the screeching infants to be touched in turn. The marvellous visitors, strange in hue, strange in attire, with moustached lip and bearded chin, with arquebuse, halberd, helmet, and cuirass, seemed rather demigods than men.

Due time having been allowed for this exuberance of feminine rapture, the warriors interposed, banished the women and children to a distance, and squatted on the ground around the French, row within row of swarthy forms and eager faces, "as if," says Cartier, "we were going to act a play." Then appeared a troop of women, each bringing a mat, with which they carpeted the bare earth for the behoof of their guests. The latter being seated, the chief of the nation was borne before them on a deer-skin by a number of his tribesmen, a bedridden old savage, paralyzed and helpless, squalid as the rest in his attire, and distinguished only by a red fillet, inwrought with the dyed quills of the Canada porcupine, encircling his lank black hair. They placed him on the ground at Cartier's feet and made signs of welcome for him, while he pointed feebly to his powerless limbs, and implored the healing touch from the hand of the French chief. Cartier complied, and received in acknowledgment the red fillet of his grateful patient. Then from surrounding dwellings appeared a woeful throng, the sick, the lame, the blind, the maimed, the decrepit, brought or led forth and placed on the earth before the perplexed commander, "as if," he says, "a god had come down to cure them." His skill in medicine being far behind the emergency, he pronounced over his petitioners a portion of the Gospel of St. John, made the sign of the cross, and uttered a prayer, not for their bodies only, but for their miserable souls. Next he read the passion of the Saviour, to which, though comprehending not a word, his audience listened with grave attention. Then came a distribution of presents. The squaws and children were recalled, and, with the warriors, placed in separate groups. Knives and hatchets were given to the men, and beads to the women, while pewter rings and images of the *Agnus Dei* were flung among the troop of children, whence ensued a vigorous scramble in the square of Hochelaga. Now the French trumpeters pressed their trumpets to their lips, and blew a blast that filled the air with warlike din and the hearts of the hearers with amazement and delight. Bidding their hosts farewell, the visitors formed their ranks and defiled through the gate once more, despite the efforts of a crowd of women, who, with clamorous hospitality, beset them with gifts of fish, beans, corn, and other viands of uninviting aspect, which the Frenchmen courteously declined.

A troop of Indians followed, and guided them to the top of the neighboring mountain. Cartier called it *Mont Royal*, Montreal; and hence the name of the busy city which now holds the site of the vanished Hochelaga. Stadaconé and Hochelaga, Quebec and Montreal, in the sixteenth century as in the nineteenth, were the centres of Canadian population.

From the summit, that noble prospect met his eye which at this day is the delight of tourists, but strangely changed, since, first of white men, the Breton voyager gazed upon it. Tower and dome and spire, congregated roofs, white sail, and gliding steamer, animate its vast expanse with varied life. Cartier saw a different scene. East, west, and south, the mantling forest was over all, and the broad blue ribbon of the great river glistened amid a realm of verdure. Beyond, to the bounds of Mexico, stretched a leafy desert, and the vast hive of industry, the mighty battle-ground of later centuries, lay sunk in savage torpor, wrapped in illimitable woods.

The French re-embarked, bade farewell to Hochelaga, retraced their lonely course down the St. Lawrence, and reached Stadaconé in safety. On the bank of the St. Charles, their companions had built in their absence a fort of palisades, and the ships, hauled up the little stream, lay moored before it. Here the self-exiled company were soon besieged by the rigors of the Canadian winter. The rocks, the shores, the pine-trees, the solid floor of the frozen river, all alike were blanketed in snow beneath the keen cold rays of the dazzling sun. The drifts rose above the sides of their ships; masts, spars, and cordage were thick with glittering incrustations and sparkling rows of icicles; a frosty armor, four inches thick, encased the bulwarks. Yet, in the bitterest weather, the neighboring Indians, "hardy," says the journal, "as so many beasts," came daily to the fort, wading, half-naked, waist-deep through the snow. At length, their friendship began to abate; their visits grew less frequent, and during December had wholly ceased, when a calamity fell upon the French.

A malignant scurvy broke out among them. Man after man went down before the hideous disease, till twenty-five were dead, and only three or four were left in health. The sound were too few to attend the sick, and the wretched sufferers lay in helpless despair, dreaming of the sun and the vines of France. The ground, hard as flint, defied their feeble efforts, and, unable to bury their dead, they hid them in snowdrifts. Cartier appealed to the saints; but they turned a deaf ear. Then he nailed against a tree an image of the Virgin, and on a Sunday summoned forth his woe-begone followers, who, haggard, reeling, bloated with their maladies, moved in procession to the spot, and, kneeling in the snow, sang litanies and psalms of David. That day died Philippe Rougemont, of Amboise, aged twenty-two years. The Holy Virgin deigned no other response.

There was fear that the Indians, learning their misery, might finish the work that scurvy had begun. None of them, therefore, were allowed to approach the fort; and when a party of savages lingered within hearing, Cartier forced his invalid garrison to beat with sticks and stones against the walls, that their dangerous neighbors, deluded by the clatter, might think them engaged in hard labor. These objects of their fear proved, however, the instruments of their salvation. Cartier, walking one day near the river, met an Indian, who not long before had been prostrate, like many of his fellows, with the scurvy, but who was now, to all appearance, in high health and spirits. What agency had wrought this marvellous recovery? According to the Indian, it was a certain evergreen, called by him *ameda*,[7] a decoction of the leaves of which was sovereign against the disease. The experiment was tried. The sick men drank copiously of the healing draught, — so copiously indeed that in six days they drank a tree as large as a French oak. Thus vigorously assailed, the distemper relaxed its hold, and health and hope began to revisit the hapless company.

When this winter of misery had worn away, and the ships were thawed from their icy fetters, Cartier prepared to return. He had made notable discoveries; but these were as nothing to the tales of wonder that had reached his ear, — of a land of gold and rubies, of a nation white like the French, of men who lived without food, and of others to whom Nature had granted but one leg. Should he stake his credit on these marvels? It were better that they who had recounted them to him should, with their own lips, recount them also to the King, and to this end he resolved that Donnacona and his chiefs should go with him to court. He lured them therefore to the fort, and led them into an ambuscade of sailors, who, seizing the astonished guests, hurried them on board the ships. Having accomplished this treachery, the voyagers proceeded to plant the emblem of Christianity. The cross was raised, the fleur-de-lis planted near it, and, spreading their sails, they steered for home. It was the 16th of July, 1536, when Cartier again cast anchor under the walls of St. Malo.

A rigorous climate, a savage people, a fatal disease, and a soil barren of gold were the allurements of New France. Nor were the times auspicious for a renewal of the enterprise. Charles V, flushed with his African triumphs, challenged the Most Christian King to single combat. The war flamed forth with renewed fury, and ten years elapsed before a hollow truce varnished the hate of the royal rivals with a thin pretence of courtesy. Peace returned; but Francis I was sinking to his ignominious grave, under the scourge of his favorite goddess, and Chabot, patron of the former voyages, was in disgrace.

Meanwhile the ominous adventure of New France had found a champion in the person of Jean François de la Roque, Sieur de Roberval, a nobleman of Picardy. Though a man of high account in his own province, his past honors paled before the splendor of the titles said to have been now conferred on him, — Lord of Norembega, Viceroy and Lieutenant-General in Canada, Hochelaga, Saguenay, Newfoundland,

[7] The wonderful tree seems to have been a spruce, or, more probably, an arbor-vitae.

Belle Isle, Carpunt, Labrador, the Great Bay, and Baccalaos.[8] To this windy gift of ink and parchment was added a solid grant from the royal treasury, with which five vessels were procured and equipped; and to Cartier was given the post of Captain-General. "We have resolved," says Francis, "to send him again to the lands of Canada and Hochelaga, which form the extremity of Asia towards the west." His commission declares the objects of the enterprise to be discovery, settlement, and the conversion of the Indians, who are described as "men without knowledge of God or use of reason," — a pious design, held doubtless in full sincerity by the royal profligate, now, in his decline, a fervent champion of the Faith and a strenuous tormentor of heretics. The machinery of conversion was of a character somewhat questionable, since Cartier and Roberval were empowered to ransack the prisons for thieves, robbers, and other malefactors, to complete their crews and strengthen the colony. "Whereas," says the King, "we have undertaken this voyage for the honor of God our Creator, desiring with all our heart to do that which shall be agreeable to Him, it is our will to perform a compassionate and meritorious work towards criminals and malefactors, to the end that they may acknowledge the Creator, return thanks to Him, and mend their lives. Therefore we have resolved to cause to be delivered to our aforesaid lieutenant (Roberval), such and so many of the aforesaid criminals and malefactors detained in our prisons as may seem to him useful and necessary to be carried to the aforesaid countries." Of the expected profits of the voyage the adventurers were to have one third and the King another, while the remainder was to be reserved towards defraying expenses.

With respect to Donnacona and his tribesmen, basely kidnapped at Stadaconé, their souls had been better cared for than their bodies; for, having been duly baptized, they all died within a year or two, to the great detriment, as it proved, of the expedition.

[8] [Norumbega, a word of Indian origin, was applied by the French to most of the present New England, more especially to Maine, where some of the early maps place a fabulous Indian metropolis of that name on the Penobscot. (Sigmund Diamond "Norumbega: New England Xanadu" *American Neptune* XI 98–107.) The name Labrador was originally attached to Greenland, named after João Fernandes, a *lavrador* (farmer) of Terceira, who rediscovered it in 1500 or 1501. The name was later transferred to the present Labrador. (S. E. Morison *Portuguese Voyages to America in the 15th Century* pp. 51–68.) Belle Isle and Carpunt are the strait and island between the present Labrador and Newfoundland. The Great Bay meant the Gulf of St. Lawrence. Baccalaos, the Basque and Portuguese name for codfish, was applied by the Portuguese to Newfoundland.]

Meanwhile, from beyond the Pyrenees, the Most Catholic King, with alarmed and jealous eye, watched the preparations of his Most Christian enemy. America, in his eyes, was one vast province of Spain, to be vigilantly guarded against the intruding foreigner. To what end were men mustered, and ships fitted out in the Breton seaports? Was it for colonization, and if so, where? Was it in Southern Florida, or on the frozen shores of Baccalaos, of which Breton cod-fishers claimed the discovery? Or would the French build forts on the Bahamas, whence they could waylay the gold ships in the Bahama Channel? Or was the expedition destined against the Spanish settlements of the islands or the Main? Reinforcements were despatched in haste, and a spy was sent to France, who, passing from port to port, Quimper, St. Malo, Brest, Morlaix, came back freighted with exaggerated tales of preparation. The Council of the Indies was called. "The French are bound for Baccalaos," — such was the substance of their report; "your Majesty will do well to send two caravels to watch their movements, and a force to take possession of the said country. And since there is no other money to pay for it, the gold from Peru, now at Panama, might be used to that end." The Cardinal of Seville thought lightly of the danger, and prophesied that the French would reap nothing from their enterprise but disappointment and loss. The King of Portugal, sole acknowledged partner with Spain in the ownership of the New World, was invited by the Spanish ambassador to take part in an expedition against the encroaching French. "They can do no harm at Baccalaos," was the cold reply; "and so," adds the indignant ambassador, "this King would say if they should come and take him here at Lisbon; such is the softness they show here on the one hand, while, on the other, they wish to give law to the whole world."

The five ships, occasions of this turmoil and alarm, had lain at St. Malo waiting for cannon and munitions from Normandy and Champagne. They waited in vain, and as the King's orders were stringent against delay, it was resolved that Cartier should sail at once, leaving Roberval to follow with additional ships when the expected supplies arrived.

On the 23rd of May, 1541, the Breton captain again spread his canvas for New France, and, passing in safety the tempestuous Atlantic, the fog-banks of Newfoundland, the island rocks clouded with screaming sea-fowl, and the forests breathing piny odors from the shore, cast anchor again beneath the cliffs of Quebec. Canoes came out from shore filled with feathered savages inquiring for their kidnapped chiefs,

"Donnacona," replied Cartier, "is dead"; but he added the politic falsehood, that the others had married in France, and lived in state, like great lords. The Indians pretended to be satisfied; but it was soon apparent that they looked askance on the perfidious strangers.

Cartier pursued his course, sailed three leagues and a half up the St. Lawrence, and anchored off the mouth of the River of Cap Rouge. It was late in August, and the leafy landscape sweltered in the sun. The Frenchmen landed, picked up quartz crystals on the shore and thought them diamonds, climbed the steep promontory, drank at the spring near the top, looked abroad on the wooded slopes beyond the little river, waded through the tall grass of the meadow, found a quarry of slate, and gathered scales of a yellow mineral which glistened like gold, then returned to their boats, crossed to the south shore of the St. Lawrence, and, languid with the heat, rested in the shade of forests laced with an entanglement of grape-vines.

Now their task began, and while some cleared off the woods and sowed turnip-seed, others cut a zigzag road up the height, and others built two forts, one at the summit, and one on the shore below. The forts finished, the Vicomte de Beaupré took command, while Cartier went with two boats to explore the rapids above Hochelaga. When at length he returned, the autumn was far advanced; and with the gloom of a Canadian November came distrust, foreboding, and homesickness. Roberval had not appeared; the Indians kept jealously aloof; the motley colony was sullen as the dull, raw air around it. There was disgust and ire at Charlesbourg-Royal, for so the place was called.

Meanwhile, unexpected delays had detained the impatient Roberval; nor was it until the 16th of April, 1542, that, with three ships and two hundred colonists, he set sail from Rochelle. When, on the 8th of June, he entered the harbor of St. John, he found seventeen fishing-vessels lying there at anchor. Soon after, he descried three other sail rounding the entrance of the haven, and, with anger and amazement, recognized the ships of Jacques Cartier. That voyager had broken up his colony and abandoned New France. What motives had prompted a desertion little consonant with the resolute spirit of the man it is impossible to say, — whether sickness within, or Indian enemies without, disgust with an enterprise whose unripened fruits had proved so hard and bitter, or discontent at finding himself reduced to a post of subordination in a country which he had discovered and where he had commanded. The Viceroy ordered him to return; but Cartier escaped with his vessels under cover of night, and made sail for France, carrying with him as trophies a few quartz diamonds from Cap Rouge, and grains of sham gold from the neighboring slate ledges. Thus closed the third Canadian voyage of this notable explorer. His discoveries had gained for him a patent of nobility, and he owned the seigniorial mansion of Limoilu, a rude structure of stone still standing. Here, and in the neighboring town of St. Malo, where also he had a house, he seems to have lived for many years.

Roberval once more set sail, steering northward to the Straits of Belle Isle and the dreaded Isles of Demons. And here an incident befell which the all-believing Thevet records in manifest good faith, and which, stripped of the adornments of superstition and a love of the marvellous, has without doubt a nucleus of truth. I give the tale as I find it.

The Viceroy's company was of a mixed complexion. There were nobles, officers, soldiers, sailors, adventurers, with women too, and children. Of the women, some were of birth and station, and among them a damsel called Marguerite, a niece of Roberval himself. In the ship was a young gentleman who had embarked for love of her. His love was too well requited; and the stern Viceroy, scandalized and enraged at a passion which scorned concealment and set shame at defiance, cast anchor by the haunted island, landed his indiscreet relative, gave her four arquebuses for defence, and, with an old Norman nurse named Bastienne, who had pandered to the lovers, left her to her fate. Her gallant threw himself into the surf, and by desperate effort gained the shore, with two more guns and a supply of ammunition.

The ship weighed anchor, receded, vanished, and they were left alone. Yet not so, for the demon lords of the island beset them day and night, raging around their hut with a confused and hungry clamoring, striving to force the frail barrier. The lovers had repented of their sin, though not abandoned it, and Heaven was on their side. The saints vouchsafed their aid, and the offended Virgin, relenting, held before them her protecting shield. In the form of beasts or other shapes abominably and unutterably hideous, the brood of hell, howling in baffled fury, tore at the branches of the sylvan dwelling; but a celestial hand was ever interposed, and there was a viewless barrier which they might not pass. Marguerite became pregnant. Here was a double prize, two souls in one, mother and child. The fiends grew frantic, but all in vain. She stood undaunted amid these horrors; but her lover, dismayed and heartbroken, sickened and died. Her child soon followed; then the old Norman nurse found her unhallowed rest in that accursed soil, and

Marguerite was left alone. Neither her reason nor her courage failed. When the demons assailed her, she shot at them with her gun, but they answered with hellish merriment, and thenceforth she placed her trust in Heaven alone. There were foes around her of the upper, no less than of the nether world. Of these, the bears were the most redoubtable; yet, being vulnerable to mortal weapons, she killed three of them, all, says the story, "as white as an egg."

It was two years and five months from her landing on the island, when, far out at sea, the crew of a small fishing-craft saw a column of smoke curling upward from the haunted shore. Was it a device of the fiends to lure them to their ruin? They thought so, and kept aloof. But misgiving seized them. They warily drew near, and descried a female figure in wild attire waving signals from the strand. Thus at length was Marguerite rescued and restored to her native France, where, a few years later, the cosmographer Thevet met her at Natron in Perigord, and heard the tale of wonder from her own lips.

Having left his offending niece to the devils and bears of the Isles of Demons, Roberval held his course up the St. Lawrence, and dropped anchor before the heights of Cap Rouge. His company landed; there were bivouacs along the strand, a hubbub of pick and spade, axe, saw, and hammer; and soon in the wilderness uprose a goodly structure, half barrack, half castle, with two towers, two spacious halls, a kitchen, chambers, store-rooms, workshops, cellars, garrets, a well, an oven, and two water-mills. Roberval named it France-Roy, and it stood on that bold acclivity where Cartier had before intrenched himself, the St. Lawrence in front, and on the right the River of Cap Rouge. Here all the colony housed under the same roof, like one of the experimental communities of recent days, — officers, soldiers, nobles, artisans, laborers, and convicts, with the women and children in whom lay the future hope of New France.

Experience and forecast had both been wanting. There were storehouses, but no stores; mills, but no grist; an ample oven, and a dearth of bread. It was only when two of the ships had sailed for France that they took account of their provision and discovered its lamentable shortcoming. Winter and famine followed. They bought fish from the Indians, and dug roots and boiled them in whale-oil. Disease broke out, and, before spring, killed one third of the colony. The rest would have quarrelled, mutinied, and otherwise aggravated their inevitable woes, but disorder was dangerous under the iron rule of the inexorable Roberval. Michel Gaillon was detected in a petty theft, and hanged. Jean de

Nantes, for a more venial offence, was kept in irons. The quarrels of men and the scolding of women were alike requited at the whipping-post, "by which means," quaintly says the narrative, "they lived in peace."

Thevet, while calling himself the intimate friend of the Viceroy, gives a darker coloring to his story. He says that, forced to unceasing labor, and chafed by arbitrary rules, some of the soldiers fell under Roberval's displeasure, and six of them, formerly his favorites, were hanged in one day. Others were banished to an island, and there kept in fetters; while, for various light offences, several, both men and women, were shot. Even the Indians were moved to pity, and wept at the sight of their woes.

And here, midway, our guide deserts us, the ancient narrative is broken, and the latter part is lost, leaving us to divine as we may the future of the ill-starred colony. That it did not long survive is certain. The King, in great need of Roberval, sent Cartier to bring him home, and this voyage seems to have taken place in the summer of 1543. It is said that, in after years, the Viceroy essayed to repossess himself of his Transatlantic domain, and lost his life in the attempt. Thevet, on the other hand, with ample means of learning the truth, affirms that Roberval was slain at night, near the Church of the Innocents, in the heart of Paris.[9]

[9] [The contemporary narratives of Cartier's three voyages and of Roberval's voyage, which Parkman used in a variety of editions, were collected by H. P. Biggar and published, as *The Voyages of Jacques Cartier*, in *Publications* of the Public Archives of Canada No. 11 (Ottawa 1924); and in No. 14 of the same series (Ottawa 1930). Dr. Biggar published *A Collection of Documents Relating to Cartier and Roberval*, including many that were unknown to Parkman. The most important of these (pp. 275–9) is the report by a Spanish spy on the Third Voyage, which was found in the Imperial Archives at Vienna in 1910. This report shows that the Third Voyage was a much larger enterprise than Parkman or anyone else had suspected. Cartier and Roberval had in all ten ships varying from 70 to 110 tons' burden, each provided with a chaplain, two pilots, an average of 40 sailors, and a barber. Roberval had command of 300 soldiers, 60 masons and carpenters, and 20 workmen, 20 horses, and a number of live cattle. The provisions included 1500 swine and 800 beef in pickle, 100 tuns of grain, part of it seed corn; 200 tuns of wine and 100 of cider, and other stores in proportion. The total complement was 800 to 900 people.

The same document clears up the reasons for the "unexpected delays" that "detained the impatient Roberval." While waiting for his ammunition and other supplies to arrive, his crews became mutinous; so, in the summer of 1542, he put to sea and, in conjunction with a notorious pirate named Bidoux, captured a number of English ships in the chops of the Channel. Henry VIII, who was at peace with Francis I, complained, and Roberval's departure was further delayed. These newly found documents also enable us to trace the conclusion of Roberval's

With him closes the prelude of the French-American drama. Tempestuous years and a reign of blood and fire were in store for France. The religious wars begot the hapless colony of Florida, but for more than half a century they left New France a desert. Order rose at length out of the sanguinary chaos; the zeal of discovery and the spirit of commercial enterprise once more awoke, while, closely following, more potent than they, moved the black-robed forces of the Roman Catholic reaction.

---

voyage where Thevet "deserts us." On 6 June 1543, Roberval started up the St. Lawrence with 70 men in 8 boats to discover the "Kingdom of Saguenay," leaving 30 men in charge of Fort France-Roy. He returned, after losing several men by drowning, and failing to find gold or silver. The King sent out a ship to rescue Roberval in the summer of 1643, probably under Cartier's command; both were back in France that autumn. Thevet, recording the disappointment when it was found that Cartier's "diamonds" were quartz crystals, wrote that the phrase "a Canada diamond" became a byword for anything that glittered but was not gold.]

CHAPTER III

La Roche, Champlain: St. Croix
1542–1605

[Pioneers of France in the New World, PART II, CHAPTERS II AND III]

Years rolled on. France, long tossed among the surges of civil commotion, plunged at last into a gulf of fratricidal war. Blazing hamlets, sacked cities, fields steaming with slaughter, profaned altars, and ravished maidens, marked the track of the tornado. There was little room for schemes of foreign enterprise. Yet, far aloof from siege and battle, the fishermen of the western ports still plied their craft on the Banks of Newfoundland. Humanity, morality, decency, might be forgotten, but codfish must still be had for the use of the faithful in Lent and on fast days. Still the wandering Eskimos saw the Norman and Breton sails hovering around some lonely headland, or anchored in fleets in the harbor of St. John; and still, through salt spray and driving mist, the fishermen dragged up the riches of the sea.

In January and February, 1545, about two vessels a day sailed from French ports for Newfoundland. In 1565, Pedro Menendez complains that the French "rule despotically" in those parts. In 1578, there were 150 French fishing-vessels there, besides 200 of other nations, Spanish, Portuguese, and English. Added to these were twenty or thirty Biscayan whalers. In 1607, there was an old French fisherman at Canseau who had voyaged to these seas for forty-two successive years.

But if the wilderness of ocean had its treasures, so too had the wilderness of woods. It needed but a few knives, beads, and trinkets, and the Indians would throng to the shore burdened with the spoils of their winter hunting. Fishermen threw up their old vocation for the more lucrative trade in bear-skins and beaver-skins. They built rude huts along the shores of Anticosti, where, at that day, the bison, it is said, could be seen wallowing in the sands.[1] They outraged the Indians; they quarrelled with each other; and this infancy of the Canadian fur-trade showed rich promise of the disorders which marked its riper growth. Others, meanwhile, were ranging the gulf in search of walrus tusks; and, the year after the battle of Ivry, St. Malo sent out a fleet of small craft in quest of this new prize.

In all the western seaports, merchants and adventurers turned their eyes towards America; not, like the Spaniards, seeking treasures of silver and gold, but the more modest gains of codfish and train-oil, beaver-skins and marine ivory. St. Malo was conspicuous above them all. The rugged Bretons loved the perils of the sea, and saw with a jealous eye every attempt to shackle their activity on this its favorite field. When in 1588 Jacques Noël and Estienne Chaton — the former a nephew of Cartier and the latter pretending to be so — gained a monopoly of the American fur-trade for twelve years, such a clamor rose within the walls of St. Malo that the obnoxious grant was promptly revoked.

But soon a power was in the field against which all St. Malo might clamor in vain. A Catholic nobleman of Brittany, the Marquis de la Roche, bargained with the King to colonize New France. On his part, he was to receive a monopoly of the trade, and a profusion of worthless titles and empty privileges. He was declared Lieutenant-General of Canada, Hochelaga, Newfoundland, Labrador, and the countries adjacent, with sovereign power within his vast and ill-defined domain. He could levy troops, declare war and peace, make laws, punish or pardon at will, build cities, forts, and castles, and grant out lands in fiefs, seigniories, counties, viscounties, and baronies. Thus was effete and cumbrous feudalism to make a lodgement in the New World. It was a scheme of high-sounding promise, but in performance less than contemptible. La Roche ransacked the prisons, and, gathering thence a gang of thieves and desperadoes, embarked them in a small vessel, and set sail to plant Christianity and civilization in the West. Suns rose and set, and the wretched bark, deep freighted with brutality and vice, held on her course. She was so small that the convicts, leaning over her side, could wash their hands in the water. At length, on the gray horizon they described a long, gray line of ridgy sand. It was Sable Island, off the coast of Nova Scotia. A wreck lay stranded on the beach, and the surf broke ominously over the long, submerged

[1] Thevet says that he had himself seen them. Perhaps he confounds them with the moose.

arms of sand, stretched far out into the sea on the right hand and on the left.

Here La Roche landed the convicts, forty in number, while, with his more trusty followers, he sailed to explore the neighboring coasts, and choose a site for the capital of his new dominion, to which, in due time, he proposed to remove the prisoners. But suddenly a tempest from the west assailed him. The frail vessel was forced to run before the gale, which, howling on her track, drove her off the coast, and chased her back towards France.

Meanwhile the convicts watched in suspense for the returning sail. Days passed, weeks passed, and still they strained their eyes in vain across the waste of ocean. La Roche had left them to their fate. Rueful and desperate, they wandered among the sandhills, through the stunted whortleberry bushes, the rank sand-grass, and the tangled cranberry vines which filled the hollows. Not a tree was to be seen; but they built huts of the fragments of the wreck. For food they caught fish in the surrounding sea, and hunted the cattle which ran wild about the island, — sprung, perhaps, from those left here eighty years before by the Baron de Léry. They killed seals, trapped black foxes, and clothed themselves in their skins. Their native instincts clung to them in their exile. As if not content with inevitable miseries, they quarrelled and murdered one another. Season after season dragged on. Five years elapsed, and, of the forty, only twelve were left alive. Sand, sea, and sky, — there was little else around them; though, to break the dead monotony, the walrus would sometimes rear his half-human face and glistening sides on the reefs and sand-bars. At length, on the far verge of the watery desert, they descried a sail. She stood on towards the island; a boat's crew landed on the beach, and the exiles were once more among their countrymen.

When La Roche returned to France, the fate of his followers sat heavy on his mind. But the day of his prosperity was gone. A host of enemies rose against him and his privileges, and it is said that the Duc de Mercœur seized him and threw him into prison. In time, however, he gained a hearing of the King; and the Norman pilot, Chefdhôtel, was despatched to bring the outcasts home.

He reached Sable Island in September, 1603, and brought back to France eleven survivors, whose names are still preserved. When they arrived, Henry IV summoned them into his presence. They stood before him, says an old writer, like river-gods of yore; for from head to foot they were clothed in shaggy skins, and beards of prodigious length hung from their swarthy faces. They had accumulated, on their island, a quantity of valuable furs. Of these Chefdhôtel had robbed them; but the pilot was forced to disgorge his prey, and, with the aid of a bounty from the King, they were enabled to embark on their own account in the Canadian trade. To their leader, fortune was less kind. Broken by disaster and imprisonment, La Roche died miserably.

In the mean time, on the ruin of his enterprise, a new one had been begun. Pontgravé, a merchant of St. Malo, leagued himself with Chauvin, a captain of the navy, who had influence at court. A patent was granted to them, with the condition that they should colonize the country. But their only thought was to enrich themselves.

At Tadoussac, at the mouth of the Saguenay, under the shadow of savage and inaccessible rocks, feathered with pines, firs, and birch-trees, they built a cluster of wooden huts and store-houses. Here they left sixteen men to gather the expected harvest of furs. Before the winter was over, several of them were dead, and the rest scattered through the woods, living on the charity of the Indians.

But a new era had dawned on France. Exhausted with thirty years of conflict, she had sunk at last to a repose, uneasy and disturbed, yet the harbinger of recovery. The rugged soldier whom, for the weal of France and of mankind, Providence had cast to the troubled surface of affairs, was throned in the Louvre, composing the strife of factions and the quarrels of his mistresses. The bear-hunting prince of the Pyrenees wore the crown of France; and to this day, as one gazes on the time-worn front of the Tuileries, above all other memories rises the small, strong figure, the brow wrinkled with cares of love and war, the bristling moustache, the grizzled beard, the bold, vigorous, and withal somewhat odd features of the mountaineer of Béarn. To few has human liberty owed so deep a gratitude or so deep a grudge. He cared little for creeds or dogmas. Impressible, quick in sympathy, his grim lip lighted often with a smile, and his war-worn cheek was no stranger to a tear. He forgave his enemies and forgot his friends. Many loved him; none but fools trusted him. Mingled of mortal good and ill, frailty and force, of all the kings who for two centuries and more sat on the throne of France Henry IV alone was a man.

Art, industry, and commerce, so long crushed and overborne, were stirring into renewed life, and a crowd of adventurous men, nurtured in war and incapable of repose, must seek employment for their restless energies in fields of peaceful enterprise.

Two small, quaint vessels, not larger than the fishing-craft of

Gloucester and Marblehead, — one was of twelve, the other of fifteen tons, — held their way across the Atlantic, passed the tempestuous headlands of Newfoundland and the St. Lawrence, and, with adventurous knight-errantry, glided deep into the heart of the Canadian wilderness. On board of one of them was the Breton merchant, Pontgravé, and with him a man of spirit widely different, a Catholic of good family, — Samuel de Champlain, born in 1567 at the small seaport of Brouage on the Bay of Biscay. His father was a captain in the royal navy, where he himself seems also to have served, though during the war he had fought for the King in Brittany, under the banners of D'Aumont, St. Luc, and Brissac. His purse was small, his merit great; and Henry IV out of his own slender revenues had given him a pension to maintain him near his person. But rest was penance to him. The war in Brittany was over. The rebellious Duc de Mercœur was reduced to obedience, and the royal army disbanded. Champlain, his occupation gone, conceived a design consonant with his adventurous nature. He would visit the West Indies, and bring back to the King a report of those regions of mystery whence Spanish jealousy excluded foreigners, and where every intruding Frenchman was threatened with death. Here much knowledge was to be won and much peril to be met. The joint attraction was resistless.

The Spaniards, allies of the vanquished Leaguers, were about to evacuate Blavet, their last stronghold in Brittany. Thither Champlain repaired; and here he found an uncle, who had charge of the French fleet destined to take on board the Spanish garrison. Champlain embarked with them, and, reaching Cadiz, succeeded, with the aid of his relative, who had just accepted the post of Pilot-General of the Spanish marine, in gaining command of one of the ships about to sail for the West Indies under Don Francisco Colombo.

At Dieppe there is a curious old manuscript, in clear, decisive, and somewhat formal handwriting of the sixteenth century, garnished with sixty-one colored pictures, in a style of art which a child of ten might emulate. Here one may see ports, harbors, islands, and rivers, adorned with portraitures of birds, beasts, and fishes thereto pertaining. Here are Indian feasts and dances; Indians flogged by priests for not going to mass; Indians burned alive for heresy, six in one fire; Indians working the silver mines. Here, too, are descriptions of natural objects, each with its illustrative sketch, some drawn from life and some from memory, — as, for example, a chameleon with two legs; others from hearsay, among which is the portrait of the griffin said to haunt certain districts of Mexico, — a monster with the wings of a bat, the head of an eagle, and the tail of an alligator.

This is Champlain's journal, written and illustrated by his own hand, in that defiance of perspective and absolute independence of the canons of art which mark the earliest efforts of the pencil.

A true hero, after the chivalrous mediæval type, his character was dashed largely with the spirit of romance. Though earnest, sagacious, and penetrating, he leaned to the marvellous; and the faith which was the life of his hard career was somewhat prone to overstep the bounds of reason and invade the domain of fancy. Hence the erratic character of some of his exploits, and hence his simple faith in the Mexican griffin.

His West-Indian adventure occupied him more than two years. He visited the principal ports of the islands, made plans and sketches of them all, after his fashion, and then, landing at Vera Cruz, journeyed inland to the city of Mexico. On his return he made his way to Panama. Here, more than two centuries and a half ago, his bold and active mind conceived the plan of a ship-canal across the isthmus, "by which," he says, "the voyage to the South Sea would be shortened by more than fifteen hundred leagues."[2]

On reaching France he repaired to court, and it may have been at this time that a royal patent raised him to the rank of the untitled nobility. He soon wearied of the antechambers of the Louvre. It was here, however, that his destiny awaited him, and the work of his life was unfolded. Aymar de Chastes, Commander of the Order of St. John and Governor of Dieppe, a gray-haired veteran of the civil wars, wished to mark his closing days with some notable achievement for France and the Church. To no man was the King more deeply indebted. In his darkest hour, when the hosts of the League were gathering round him, when friends were falling off, and the Parisians, exulting in his certain ruin, were hiring the windows of the Rue St. Antoine to see him led to the Bastille, De Chastes, without condition or reserve, gave up to him the town and castle of Dieppe. Thus he was enabled to fight beneath its walls the

[2] [Champlain's *Bref Discours* of his voyage to the West Indies is printed with English translation in Vol. I of the best and most modern edition of Champlain's *Works*, edited for the Champlain Society by H. P. Biggar (Toronto 1922). The illustrations are in the same edition's *Portfolio of Plates and Maps*. Parkman used a copy of the original manuscript, which is now in the John Carter Brown Library of Providence, R. I. Dr. Biggar's monograph *Early Trading Companies of New France to 1629* (Toronto 1901) contains many data on minor enterprises of this period not known to Parkman.]

battle of Arques, the first in the series of successes which secured his triumph; and he had been heard to say that to this friend in his adversity he owed his own salvation and that of France.

De Chastes was one of those men who, amid the strife of factions and rage of rival fanaticisms, make reason and patriotism their watchwords, and stand on the firm ground of a strong and resolute moderation. He had resisted the madness of Leaguer and Huguenot alike; yet, though a foe of the League, the old soldier was a devout Catholic, and it seemed in his eyes a noble consummation of his life to plant the cross and the fleur-de-lis in the wilderness of New France. Chauvin had just died, after wasting the lives of a score or more of men in a second and a third attempt to establish the fur-trade at Tadoussac. De Chastes came to court to beg a patent of Henry IV; "and," says his friend Champlain, "though his head was crowned with gray hairs as with years, he resolved to proceed to New France in person, and dedicate the rest of his days to the service of God and his King."

The patent, costing nothing, was readily granted; and De Chastes, to meet the expenses of the enterprise, and forestall the jealousies which his monopoly would awaken among the keen merchants of the western ports, formed a company with the more prominent of them. Pontgravé, who had some knowledge of the country, was chosen to make a preliminary exploration.

This was the time when Champlain, fresh from the West Indies, appeared at court. De Chastes knew him well. Young, ardent, yet ripe in experience, a skilful seaman and a practised soldier, he above all others was a man for the enterprise. He had many conferences with the veteran, under whom he had served in the royal fleet off the coast of Brittany. De Chastes urged him to accept a post in his new company; and Champlain, nothing loath, consented, provided always that permission should be had from the King, "to whom," he says, "I was bound no less by birth than by the pension with which his Majesty honored me." To the King, therefore, De Chastes repaired. The needful consent was gained, and, armed with a letter to Pontgravé, Champlain set out for Honfleur. Here he found his destined companion, and embarking with him, as we have seen, they spread their sails for the west.

Like specks on the broad bosom of the waters, the two pygmy vessels held their course up the lonely St. Lawrence. They passed abandoned Tadoussac, the channel of Orleans, and the gleaming cataract of Montmorenci; the tenantless rock of Quebec, the wide Lake of St. Peter and its crowded archipelago, till now the mountain reared before them its rounded shoulder above the forest-plain of Montreal. All was solitude. Hochelaga had vanished; and of the savage population that Cartier had found here, sixty-eight years before, no trace remained. In its place were a few wandering Algonquins, of different tongue and lineage. In a skiff, with a few Indians, Champlain essayed to pass the rapids of St. Louis. Oars, paddles, and poles alike proved vain against the foaming surges, and he was forced to return. On the deck of his vessel, the Indians drew rude plans of the river above, with its chain of rapids, its lakes and cataracts; and the baffled explorer turned his prow homeward, the objects of his mission accomplished, but his own adventurous curiosity unsated. When the voyagers reached Havre de Grace, a grievous blow awaited them. The Commander de Chastes was dead.[3]

His mantle fell upon Pierre du Guast, Sieur de Monts, gentleman in ordinary of the King's chamber, and Governor of Pons. Undaunted by the fate of La Roche, this nobleman petitioned the king for leave to colonize La Cadie, or Acadie,[4] a region defined as extending from the fortieth to the forty-sixth degree of north latitude, or from Philadelphia to beyond Montreal. The King's minister, Sully, as he himself tells us, opposed the plan, on the ground that the colonization of this northern wilderness would never repay the outlay; but De Monts gained his point. He was made Lieutenant-General in Acadia, with viceregal powers; and withered Feudalism, with her antique forms and tinselled follies, was again to seek a new home among the rocks and pine-trees of Nova Scotia. The foundation of the enterprise was a monopoly of the fur-trade, and in its favor all past grants were unceremoniously annulled. St. Malo, Rouen, Dieppe, and Rochelle greeted the announcement with unavailing outcries. Patents granted and revoked, monopolies decreed and extinguished, had involved the unhappy traders in ceaseless embarrassment. De Monts, however, preserved De Chastes's old company, and enlarged it, — thus making the chief malcontents sharers

[3] Champlain, *Des Sauvages* (1604). [This, too, is printed with translation in the Champlain Society edition, Vol. I.] Champlain's Indian informants gave him very confused accounts.

[4] The word is said to be derived from the Indian *Aquoddiauke*, or *Aquoddie*, supposed to mean the fish called a pollock. The Bay of Passamaquoddy, "Great Pollock Water," if we may accept the same authority, derives its name from the same origin. This derivation is doubtful. The Micmac word, *Quoddy, Kady,* or *Cadie,* means simply a place or region, and is properly used in conjunction with some other noun; as, for example, *Katakady,* the Place of Eels; *Sunakady* (Sunacadie), the Place of Cranberries; *Pestumoquoddy* (Passamaquoddy), the Place of Pollocks.

in his exclusive rights, and converting them from enemies into partners.

A clause in his commission empowered him to impress idlers and vagabonds as material for his colony, — an ominous provision of which he largely availed himself. His company was strangely incongruous. The best and the meanest of France were crowded together in his two ships. Here were thieves and ruffians dragged on board by force; and here were many volunteers of condition and character, with Baron de Poutrincourt and the indefatigable Champlain. Here, too, were Catholic priests and Huguenot ministers; for though De Monts was a Calvinist, the Church, as usual, displayed her banner in the van of the enterprise, and he was forced to promise that he would cause the Indians to be instructed in the dogmas of Rome.

De Monts, with one of his vessels, sailed from Havre de Grace on the seventh of April, 1604. Pontgravé, with stores for the colony, was to follow in a few days.

Scarcely were they at sea, when ministers and priests fell first to discussion, then to quarrelling, then to blows. "I have seen our *curé* and the minister," says Champlain, "fall to with their fists on questions of faith. I cannot say which had the more pluck, or which hit the harder; but I know that the minister sometimes complained to the Sieur de Monts that he had been beaten. This was their way of settling points of controversy. I leave you to judge if it was a pleasant thing to see."

Sagard, the Franciscan friar, relates with horror, that, after their destination was reached, a priest and a minister happening to die at the same time, the crew buried them both in one grave, to see if they would lie peaceably together.

De Monts, who had been to the St. Lawrence with Chauvin, and learned to dread its rigorous winters, steered for a more southern, and, as he flattered himself, a milder region. The first land seen was Cap la Hêve, on the southern coast of Nova Scotia. Four days later, they entered a small bay, where, to their surprise, they saw a vessel lying at anchor. Here was a piece of good luck. The stranger was a fur-trader, pursuing her traffic in defiance, or more probably in ignorance, of De Mont's monopoly. The latter, as empowered by his patent, made prize of ship and cargo, consoling the commander, one Rossignol, by giving his name to the scene of his misfortune. It is now called Liverpool Harbor.

In an adjacent harbor, called by them Port Mouton, because a sheep here leaped overboard, they waited nearly a month for Pontgravé's store-ship. At length, to their great relief, she appeared, laden with the spoils of four Basque fur-traders, captured at Canseau. The supplies delivered, Pontgravé sailed for Tadoussac to trade with the Indians, while De Monts, followed by his prize, proceeded on his voyage.

He doubled Cape Sable, and entered St. Mary's Bay, where he lay two weeks, sending boats' crews to explore the adjacent coasts. A party one day went on shore to stroll through the forest, and among them was Nicolas Aubry, a priest from Paris, who, tiring of the scholastic haunts of the Rue de la Sorbonne and the Rue d'Enfer, had persisted, despite the remonstrance of his friends, in joining the expedition. Thirsty with a long walk, under the sun of June, through the tangled and rock-encumbered woods, he stopped to drink at a brook, laying his sword beside him on the grass. On rejoining his companions, he found that he had forgotten it; and turning back in search of it, more skilled in the devious windings of the Quartier Latin than in the intricacies of the Acadian forest, he soon lost his way. His comrades, alarmed, waited for a time, and then ranged the woods, shouting his name to the echoing solitudes. Trumpets were sounded, and cannon fired from the ships, but the priest did not appear. All now looked askance on a certain Huguenot, with whom Aubry had often quarrelled on questions of faith, and who was now accused of having killed him. In vain he denied the charge. Aubry was given up for dead, and the ship sailed from St. Mary's Bay; while the wretched priest roamed to and fro, famished and despairing, or, couched on the rocky soil, in the troubled sleep of exhaustion, dreamed, perhaps, as the wind swept moaning through the pines, that he heard once more the organ roll through the columned arches of Sainte Geneviève.

The voyagers proceeded to explore the Bay of Fundy, which De Monts called La Baye Françoise. Their first notable discovery was that of Annapolis Harbor. A small inlet invited them. They entered, when suddenly the narrow strait dilated into a broad and tranquil basin, compassed by sunny hills, wrapped in woodland verdure, and alive with waterfalls. Poutrincourt was delighted with the scene. The fancy seized him of removing thither from France with his family; and, to this end, he asked a grant of the place from De Monts, who by his patent had nearly half the continent in his gift. The grant was made, and Poutrincourt called his new domain Port Royal.

Thence they sailed round the head of the Bay of Fundy, coasted its northern shore, visited and named the river St. John, and anchored at last in Passamaquoddy Bay.

The untiring Champlain, exploring, surveying, sounding, had made charts of all the principal roads and harbors;[5] and now, pursuing his research, he entered a river which he calls La Rivière des Etechemins, from the name of the tribe of whom the present Passamaquoddy Indians are descendants. Near its mouth he found an islet, fenced round with rocks and shoals, and called it St. Croix, a name now borne by the river itself. With singular infelicity this spot was chosen as the site of the new colony. It commanded the river, and was well fitted for defence: these were its only merits; yet cannon were landed on it, a battery was planted on a detached rock at one end, and a fort begun on a rising ground at the other.

At St. Mary's Bay the voyagers thought they had found traces of iron and silver; and Champdoré, the pilot, was now sent back to pursue the search. As he and his men lay at anchor, fishing, not far from land, one of them heard a strange sound, like a weak human voice; and, looking towards the shore, they saw a small black object in motion, apparently a hat waved on the end of a stick. Rowing in haste to the spot, they found the priest Aubry. For sixteen days he had wandered in the woods, sustaining life on berries and wild fruits; and when, haggard and emaciated, a shadow of his former self, Champdoré carried him back to St. Croix, he was greeted as a man risen from the grave.

In 1783 the river St. Croix, by treaty, was made the boundary between Maine and New Brunswick. But which was the true St. Croix? In 1798, the point was settled. De Mont's island was found; and, painfully searching among the sand, the sedge, and the matted whortleberry bushes, the commissioners could trace the foundations of buildings long crumbled into dust; for the wilderness had resumed its sway, and silence and solitude brooded once more over this ancient resting-place of civilization.[6]

But while the commissioner bends over a moss-grown stone, it is for us to trace back the dim vista of the centuries to the life, the zeal, the energy, of which this stone is the poor memorial. The rock-fenced islet was covered with cedars, and when the tide was out the shoals around were dark with the swash of sea-weed, where, in their leisure moments, the Frenchmen, we are told, amused themselves with detaching the limpets from the stones, as a savory addition to their fare. But there was little leisure at St. Croix. Soldiers, sailors, and artisans betook

[5] See Champlain, *Voyages* (1613), where the charts are published. [This, too, is printed with translation in the Champlain Society edition, Vol. I.]

[6] [The modern name is Dochet Island. Recent excavations there are described in *Old-Time New England* XLIV (1954) 93–9.]

themselves to their task. Before the winter closed in, the northern end of the island was covered with buildings, surrounding a square, where a solitary tree had been left standing. On the right was a spacious house, well built, and surmounted by one of those enormous roofs characteristic of the time. This was the lodging of De Monts. Behind it, and near the water, was a long, covered gallery, for labor or amusement in foul weather. Champlain and the Sieur d'Orville, aided by the servants of the latter, built a house for themselves nearly opposite that of De Monts; and the remainder of the square was occupied by storehouses, a magazine, workshops, lodgings for gentlemen and artisans, and a barrack for the Swiss soldiers, the whole enclosed with a palisade. Adjacent there was an attempt at a garden, under the auspices of Champlain; but nothing would grow in the sandy soil. There was a cemetery, too, and a small rustic chapel on a projecting point of rock. Such was the "Habitation de l'Isle Saincte-Croix," as set forth by Champlain in quaint plans and drawings, in that musty little quarto of 1613, sold by Jean Berjon, at the sign of the Flying Horse, Rue St. Jean de Beauvais.

Their labors over, Poutrincourt set sail for France, proposing to return and take possession of his domain of Port Royal. Seventy-nine men remained at St. Croix. Here was De Monts, feudal lord of half a continent in virtue of two potent syllables, "Henri," scrawled on parchment by the rugged hand of the Béarnais. Here were gentlemen of birth and breeding, Champlain, D'Orville, Beaumont, Sourin, La Motte, Boulay, and Fougeray; here also were the pugnacious *curé* and his fellow priests, with the Huguenot ministers, objects of their unceasing ire. The rest were laborers, artisans, and soldiers, all in the pay of the company, and some of them forced into its service.

Poutrincourt's receding sails vanished between the water and the sky. The exiles were left to their solitude. From the Spanish settlements northward to the pole, there was no domestic hearth, no lodgement of civilized men, save one weak band of Frenchmen, clinging, as it were for life, to the fringe of the vast and savage continent. The gray and sullen autumn sank upon the waste, and the bleak wind howled down the St. Croix, and swept the forest bare. Then the whirling snow powdered the vast sweep of desolate woodland, and shrouded in white the gloomy green of pine-clad mountains. Ice in sheets, or broken masses, swept by their island with the ebbing and flowing tide, often debarring all access to the main, and cutting off their supplies of wood and water. A belt of cedars, indeed, hedged the island; but De Monts had ordered them to be spared, that the north wind might spend something of its force with whistling through their shaggy boughs. Cider and wine froze in the casks, and were served out by the pound. As they crowded round their half-fed fires, shivering in the icy currents that pierced their rude tenements, many sank into a desperate apathy.

Soon the scurvy broke out, and raged with a fearful malignity. Of the seventy-nine, thirty-five died before spring, and many more were brought to the verge of death. In vain they sought that marvellous tree which had relieved the followers of Cartier. Their little cemetery was peopled with nearly half their number, and the rest, bloated and disfigured with the relentless malady, thought more of escaping from their woes than of building up a Transatlantic empire. Yet among them there was one, at least, who, amid languor and defection, held to his purpose with indomitable tenacity; and where Champlain was present, there was no room for despair.

Spring came at last, and, with the breaking up of the ice, the melting of the snow, and the clamors of the returning wild-fowl, the spirits and the health of the woe-begone company began to revive. But to misery succeeded anxiety and suspense. Where was the succor from France? Were they abandoned to their fate like the wretched exiles of La Roche? In a happy hour, they saw an approaching sail. Pontgravé, with forty men, cast anchor before their island on the sixteenth of June; and they hailed him as the condemned hails the messenger of his pardon.

Weary of St. Croix, De Monts resolved to seek out a more auspicious site, on which to rear the capital of his wilderness dominion. During the preceding September, Champlain had ranged the westward coast in a pinnace, visited and named the island of Mount Desert, and entered the mouth of the river Penobscot, called by him the Pemetigoet, or Pentegoet, and previously known to fur-traders and fishermen as the Norumbega, a name which it shared with all the adjacent region.[7] Now, embarking a second time, in a bark of fifteen tons, with De Monts, several gentlemen, twenty sailors, and an Indian with his squaw, he set forth on the eighteenth of June on a second voyage of discovery. They coasted the strangely indented shores of Maine, with its reefs and surf-washed islands, rocky headlands, and deep embosomed bays, passed Mount Desert and the Penobscot, explored the mouths of the Kennebec, crossed Casco Bay, and descried the distant peaks of the White Mountains. The ninth of July brought them to Saco Bay. They were now within the limits of a group of tribes who were called by

[7] [See chap. ii note 8.]

the French the Armouchiquois, and who included those whom the English afterwards called the Massachusetts. They differed in habits as well as in language from the Etechemins and Micmacs of Acadia, for they were tillers of the soil, and around their wigwams were fields of maize, beans, pumpkins, squashes, tobacco, and the so-called Jerusalem artichoke. Near Prout's Neck, more than eighty of them ran down to the shore to meet the strangers, dancing and yelping to show their joy. They had a fort of palisades on a rising ground by the Saco, for they were at deadly war with their neighbors towards the east.

On the twelfth, the French resumed their voyage, and, like some adventurous party of pleasure, held their course by the beaches of York and Wells, Portsmouth Harbor, the Isles of Shoals, Rye Beach, and Hampton Beach, till, on the fifteenth, they descried the dim outline of Cape Ann. Champlain called it Cap aux Isles, from the three adjacent islands, and in a subsequent voyage he gave the name of Beauport to the neighboring harbor of Gloucester. Thence steering southward and westward, they entered Massachusetts Bay, gave the name of Rivière du Guast to a river flowing into it, probably the Charles; passed the islands of Boston Harbor, which Champlain describes as covered with trees, and were met on the way by great numbers of canoes filled with astonished Indians. On Sunday, the seventeenth, they passed Point Allerton and Nantasket Beach, coasted the shores of Cohasset, Scituate, and Marshfield, and anchored for the night near Brant Point. On the morning of the eighteenth, a head wind forced them to take shelter in Port St. Louis, for so they called the harbor of Plymouth, where the Pilgrims made their memorable landing fifteen years later. Indian wigwams and garden patches lined the shore. A troop of the inhabitants came down to the beach and danced; while others, who had been fishing, approached in their canoes, came on board the vessel, and showed Champlain their fish-hooks, consisting of a barbed bone lashed at an acute angle to a slip of wood.

From Plymouth the party circled round the bay, doubled Cape Cod, called by Champlain Cap Blanc, from its glistening white sands, and steered southward to Nauset Harbor, which, by reason of its shoals and sand-bars, they named Port Mallebarre. Here their prosperity deserted them. A party of sailors went behind the sand-banks to find fresh water at a spring, when an Indian snatched a kettle from one of them, and its owner, pursuing, fell, pierced with arrows by the robber's comrades. The French in the vessel opened fire. Champlain's arquebuse burst, and was near killing him, while the Indians, swift as deer, quickly gained the woods. Several of the tribe chanced to be on board the vessel, but flung themselves with such alacrity into the water that only one was caught. They bound him hand and foot, but soon after humanely set him at liberty.

Champlain, who we are told "delighted marvellously in these enterprises," had busied himself throughout the voyage with taking observations, making charts, and studying the wonders of land and sea. The "horse-foot crab" seems to have awakened his special curiosity, and he describes it with amusing exactness. Of the human tenants of the New England coast he has also left the first precise and trustworthy account. They were clearly more numerous than when the Puritans landed at Plymouth, since in the interval a pestilence made great havoc among them. But Champlain's most conspicuous merit lies in the light that he threw into the dark places of American geography, and the order that he brought out of the chaos of American cartography; for it was a result of this and the rest of his voyages that precision and clearness began at last to supplant the vagueness, confusion, and contradiction of the earlier map-makers.

At Nauset Harbor provisions began to fail, and steering for St. Croix the voyagers reached that ill-starred island on the third of August.[8] De Monts had found no spot to his liking. He now bethought him of that inland harbor of Port Royal which he had granted to Poutrincourt, and thither he resolved to remove. Stores, utensils, even portions of the buildings, were placed on board the vessels, carried across the Bay of Fundy, and landed at the chosen spot. It was on the north side of the

[8] [Parkman was not much interested in Champlain's course along the New England coast, which can best be traced by the footnotes in the Champlain Society ed. of his *Works*, and in notes to W. L. Grant ed. *Voyages of Samuel de Champlain* (Original Narratives of American History) 1907, chaps. iii–ix, xii–xv. His most remarkable feat of navigation was to sail up the Kennebec River and through the back passage from Bath to Boothbay, a difficult feat for sailing craft at any time. President Charles W. Eliot of Harvard established this by following Champlain's course in his own yacht. Marshall H. Saville has a detailed account of "Champlain and his Landings at Cape Ann, 1605–06," in *Proceedings* American Antiquarian Society n.s. XVIII (1933) 447–69. Several names that Champlain gave to points on the Nova Scotia, New Brunswick and New England coasts have stuck — notably La Hève, Port Mouton, Capes Negro, Sable and Fourchu, St. Mary Bay, the Grand and Petit Passage, St. John and St. Croix Rivers, Grand and Petit Manan, Mount Desert, Isle Haute, Malabar (transferred from Nauset to Monomoy), and perhaps Roque Island (Isle au Perroquets). All Champlain's charts and drawings contained in his original works are reproduced in the Champlain Society edition; a manuscript general chart by him of Nouvelle France, dated 1607, in the Library of Congress, is reproduced in Fite and Freeman *A Book of Old Maps* (1926) No. 29.]

basin opposite Goat Island, and a little below the mouth of the river Annapolis, called by the French the Equille, and, afterwards, the Dauphin. The axe-men began their task; the dense forest was cleared away, and the buildings of the infant colony soon rose in its place.

But while De Monts and his company were struggling against despair at St. Croix, the enemies of his monopoly were busy at Paris; and, by a ship from France, he was warned that prompt measures were needed to thwart their machinations. Therefore he set sail, leaving Pontgravé to command at Port Royal; while Champlain, Champdoré, and others, undaunted by the past, volunteered for a second winter in the wilderness.

CHAPTER IV

Lescarbot, Port Royal and Poutrincourt
1605–1617

[*Pioneers of France in the New World*, PART II, CHAPTERS IV, V]

1. *Marc Lescarbot Winters at Port Royal*

Evil reports of a churlish wilderness, a pitiless climate, disease, misery, and death, had heralded the arrival of De Monts. The outlay had been great, the returns small; and when he reached Paris, he found his friends cold, his enemies active and keen. Poutrincourt, however, was still full of zeal; and, though his private affairs urgently called for his presence in France, he resolved, at no small sacrifice, to go in person to Acadia. He had, moreover, a friend who proved an invaluable ally. This was Marc Lescarbot, "avocat en Parlement," who had been roughly handled by fortune, and was in the mood for such a venture, being desirous, as he tells us, "to fly from a corrupt world," in which he had just lost a lawsuit. Unlike De Monts. Poutrincourt, and others of his associates, he was not within the pale of the *noblesse*, belonging to the class of "gens de robe," which stood at the head of the *bourgeoisie*, and which, in its higher grades, formed within itself a virtual nobility. Lescarbot was no common man, — not that his abundant gift of verse-making was likely to avail much in the woods of New France, nor yet his classic lore, dashed with a little harmless pedantry, born not of the man, but of the times; but his zeal, his good sense, the vigor of his understanding, and the breadth of his views, were as conspicuous as his quick wit and his lively fancy. One of the best, as well as earliest, records of the early settlement of North America is due to his pen; and it has been said, with a certain degree of truth, that he was no less able to build up a colony than to write its history. He professed himself a Catholic, but his Catholicity sat lightly on him; and he might have passed for one of those amphibious religionists who in the civil wars were called "Les Politiques."

De Monts and Poutrincourt bestirred themselves to find a priest, since the foes of the enterprise had been loud in lamentation that the spiritual welfare of the Indians had been slighted. But it was Holy Week. All the priests were, or professed to be, busy with exercises and confessions, and not one could be found to undertake the mission of Acadia. They were more successful in engaging mechanics and laborers for the voyage. These were paid a portion of their wages in advance, and were sent in a body to Rochelle, consigned to two merchants of that port, members of the company. De Monts and Poutrincourt went thither by post. Lescarbot soon followed, and no sooner reached Rochelle than he penned and printed his *Adieu à la France*, a poem which gained for him some credit.

More serious matters awaited him, however, than this dalliance with the Muse. Rochelle was the centre and citadel of Calvinism, — a town of austere and grim aspect, divided, like Cisatlantic communities of later growth, betwixt trade and religion, and, in the interest of both, exacting a deportment of discreet and well-ordered sobriety. "One must walk a strait path here," says Lescarbot, "unless he would hear from the mayor or the ministers." But the mechanics sent from Paris, flush of money, and lodged together in the quarter of St. Nicolas, made day and night hideous with riot, and their employers found not a few of them in the hands of the police. Their ship, bearing the inauspicious name of the *Jonas*, lay anchored in the stream, her cargo on board, when a sudden gale blew her adrift. She struck on a pier, then grounded on the flats, bilged, careened, and settled in the mud. Her captain, who was ashore, with Poutrincourt, Lescarbot, and others, hastened aboard, and the pumps were set in motion; while all Rochelle, we are told, came to gaze from the ramparts, with faces of condolence, but at heart well pleased with the disaster. The ship and her cargo were saved, but she must be emptied, repaired, and reladen. Thus a month was lost; at length, on the 13th of May, 1606, the disorderly crew were all brought on board, and the *Jonas* put to sea. Poutrincourt and Lescarbot had charge of the expedition, De Monts remaining in France.

Lescarbot describes his emotions at finding himself on an element so deficient in solidity, with only a two-inch plank between him and death. Off the Azores, they spoke a supposed pirate. For the rest, they beguiled the voyage by harpooning porpoises, dancing on deck in calm weather, and fishing for cod on the Grand Bank. They were two months on their way; and when, fevered with eagerness to reach land, they listened hourly for the welcome cry, they were involved in impenetrable fogs. Suddenly the mists parted, the sun shone forth, and streamed fair and bright over the fresh hills and forests of the New World, in near view before them. But the black rocks lay between, lashed by the snow-white breakers. "Thus," writes Lescarbot, "doth a man sometimes seek the land as one doth his beloved, who sometimes repulseth her sweetheart very rudely. Finally, upon Saturday, the 15th of July, about two o'clock in the afternoon, the sky began to salute us as it were with cannon-shots, shedding tears, as being sorry to have kept us so long in pain; . . . but, whilst we followed on our course, there came from the land odors incomparable for sweetness, brought with a warm wind so abundantly that all the Orient parts could not produce greater abundance. We did stretch out our hands as it were to take them, so palpable were they, which I have admired a thousand times since." [1]

It was noon on the 27th when the *Jonas* passed the rocky gateway of Port Royal Basin, and Lescarbot gazed with delight and wonder on the calm expanse of sunny waters, with its amphitheatre of woody hills, wherein he saw the future asylum of distressed merit and impoverished industry. Slowly, before a favoring breeze, they held their course towards the head of the harbor, which narrowed as they advanced; but all was solitude, — no moving sail, no sign of human presence. At length, on their left, nestling in deep forests, they saw the wooden walls and roofs of the infant colony. Then appeared a birch canoe, cautiously coming towards them, guided by an old Indian. Then a Frenchman, arquebuse in hand, came down to the shore; and then, from the wooden bastion, sprang the smoke of a saluting shot. The ship replied; the trumpets lent their voices to the din, and the forests and the hills gave back unwonted echoes. The voyagers landed, and found the colony of Port Royal dwindled to two solitary Frenchmen.

These soon told their story. The preceding winter had been one of much suffering, though by no means the counterpart of the woful experience of St. Croix. But when the spring had passed, the summer far advanced, and still no tidings of De Monts had come, Pontgravé grew deeply anxious. To maintain themselves without supplies and succor was impossible. He caused two small vessels to be built, and set out in search of some of the French vessels on the fishing-stations. This was

[1] [Lescarbot *Histoire de la Nouvelle France* came out in 1609 with a supplement in 1612. The best edition is the one edited with a translation by W. L. Grant for the Champlain Society (3 vols., 1907–14). The translation called *Nova Francia* quoted by Parkman is a partial one made by Pierre Erondelle for *Purchas His Pilgrimes* (1625).]

but twelve days before the arrival of the ship *Jonas*. Two men had bravely offered themselves to stay behind and guard the buildings, guns, and munitions; and an old Indian chief named Membertou, a fast friend of the French, and still a redoubted warrior, we are told, though reputed to number more than a hundred years, proved a stanch ally. When the ship approached, the two guardians were at dinner in their room at the fort. Membertou, always on the watch, saw the advancing sail, and, shouting from the gate, roused them from their repast. In doubt who the new-comers might be, one ran to the shore with his gun, while the other repaired to the platform where four cannon were mounted, in the valorous resolve to show fight should the strangers prove to be enemies. Happily this redundancy of mettle proved needless. He saw the white flag fluttering at the masthead, and joyfully fired his pieces as a salute.

The voyagers landed, and eagerly surveyed their new home. Some wandered through the buildings; some visited the cluster of Indian wigwams hard by; some roamed in the forest and over the meadows that bordered the neighboring river. The deserted fort now swarmed with life; and, the better to celebrate their prosperous arrival, Poutrincourt placed a hogs-head of wine in the courtyard at the discretion of his followers, whose hilarity, in consequence, became exuberant. Nor was it diminished when Pontgravé's vessels were seen entering the harbor. A boat sent by Poutrincourt, more than a week before, to explore the coasts, had met them near Cape Sable, and they joyfully returned to Port Royal.

Pontgravé, however, soon sailed for France in the *Jonas*, hoping on his way to seize certain contraband fur-traders, reported to be at Canseau and Cape Breton. Poutrincourt and Champlain, bent on finding a better site for their settlement in a more southern latitude, set out on a voyage of discovery, in an ill-built vessel of eighteen tons, while Lescarbot remained in charge of Port Royal. They had little for their pains but danger, hardship, and mishap. The autumn gales cut short their exploration; and, after visiting Gloucester Harbor, doubling Monomoy Point, and advancing as far as the neighborhood of Hyannis, on the southeast coast of Massachusetts, they turned back, somewhat disgusted with their errand. Along the eastern verge of Cape Cod they found the shore thickly studded with the wigwams of a race who were less hunters than tillers of the soil. At Chatham Harbor — called by them Port Fortuné — five of the company, who, contrary to orders, had remained on shore all night, were assailed, as they slept around their fire, by a shower of arrows from four hundred Indians. Two were killed outright, while the survivors fled for their boat, bristling like porcupines with the feathered missiles, — a scene oddly portrayed by the untutored pencil of Champlain. He and Poutrincourt, with eight men, hearing the war-whoops and the cries for aid, sprang up from sleep, snatched their weapons, pulled ashore in their shirts, and charged the yelling multitude, who fled before their spectral assailants, and vanished in the woods. "Thus," observes Lescarbot, "did thirty-five thousand Midianites fly before Gideon and his three hundred." The French buried their dead comrades; but, as they chanted their funeral hymn, the Indians, at a safe distance on a neighboring hill, were dancing in glee and triumph, and mocking them with unseemly gestures; and no sooner had the party re-embarked, than they dug up the dead bodies, burnt them, and arrayed themselves in their shirts. Little pleased with the country or its inhabitants, the voyagers turned their prow towards Port Royal, though not until, by a treacherous device, they had lured some of their late assailants within their reach, killed them, and cut off their heads as trophies. Near Mount Desert, on a stormy night, their rudder broke, and they had a hair-breadth escape from destruction. The chief object of their voyage, that of discovering a site for their colony under a more southern sky, had failed. Pontgravé's son had his hand blown off by the bursting of his gun; several of their number had been killed; others were sick or wounded; and thus, on the 14th of November, with somewhat downcast visages, they guided their helpless vessel with a pair of oars to the landing at Port Royal.

"I will not," says Lescarbot, "compare their perils to those of Ulysses, nor yet of Æneas, lest thereby I should sully our holy enterprise with things impure."

He and his followers had been expecting them with great anxiety. His alert and buoyant spirit had conceived a plan for enlivening the courage of the company, a little dashed of late by misgivings and forebodings. Accordingly, as Poutrincourt, Champlain, and their weather-beaten crew approached the wooden gateway of Port Royal, Neptune issued forth, followed by his tritons, who greeted the voyagers in good French verse, written in all haste for the occasion by Lescarbot. And, as they entered, they beheld, blazoned over the arch, the arms of France, circled with laurels, and flanked by the scutcheons of De Monts and Poutrincourt.[2]

---

[2] Lescarbot, *Muses de la Nouvelle France*, where the programme is given, and the speeches of Neptune and the tritons in full [Reprinted with a translation by

The ingenious author of these devices had busied himself, during the absence of his associates, in more serious labors for the welfare of the colony. He explored the low borders of the river Équille, or Annapolis. Here, in the solitude, he saw great meadows, where the moose, with their young, were grazing, and where at times the rank grass was beaten to a pulp by the trampling of their hoofs. He burned the grass, and sowed crops of wheat, rye, and barley in its stead. His appearance gave so little promise of personal vigor, that some of the party assured him that he would never see France again, and warned him to husband his strength; but he knew himself better, and set at naught these comforting monitions. He was the most diligent of workers. He made gardens near the fort, where, in his zeal, he plied the hoe with his own hands late into the moonlight evenings. The priests, of whom at the outset there had been no lack, had all succumbed to the scurvy at St. Croix; and Lescarbot, so far as a layman might, essayed to supply their place, reading on Sundays from the Scriptures, and adding expositions of his own after a fashion not remarkable for rigorous Catholicity. Of an evening, when not engrossed with his garden, he was reading or writing in his room, perhaps preparing the material of that *History of New France* in which, despite the versatility of his busy brain, his good sense and capacity are clearly made manifest.

Now, however, when the whole company were reassembled, Lescarbot found associates more congenial than the rude soldiers, mechanics, and laborers who gathered at night around the blazing logs in their rude hall. Port Royal was a quadrangle of wooden buildings, enclosing a spacious court. At the southeast corner was the arched gateway, whence a path, a few paces in length, led to the water. It was flanked by a sort of bastion of palisades, while at the southwest corner was another bastion, on which four cannon were mounted. On the east side of the quadrangle was a range of magazines and storehouses; on the west were quarters for the men; on the north, a dining-hall and lodgings for the principal persons of the company; while on the south, or water side, were the kitchen, the forge, and the oven. Except the garden-patches and the cemetery, the adjacent ground was thickly studded with the stumps of the newly felled trees.

Most bountiful provision had been made for the temporal wants of

Harriette T. Richardson as *The Theatre of Neptune in New France* (Boston: 1927). Owing largely to the devoted labors of Mrs. Richardson, the French *habitation* of Port Royal, as depicted by Champlain, has been restored full scale; it is situated near Annapolis Royal, Nova Scotia. See C. W. Jefferys' account of it in *Canadian Hist. Rev.* Dec. 1939.]

the colonists, and Lescarbot is profuse in praise of the liberality of De Monts and two merchants of Rochelle, who had freighted the ship *Jonas*. Of wine, in particular, the supply was so generous, that every man in Port Royal was served with three pints daily.

The principal persons of the colony sat, fifteen in number, at Poutrincourt's table, which, by an ingenious device of Champlain, was always well furnished. He formed the fifteen into a new order, christened "L'Ordre de Bon-Temps." Each was Grand Master in turn, holding office for one day. It was his function to cater for the company; and, as it became a point of honor to fill the post with credit, the prospective Grand Master was usually busy, for several days before coming to his dignity, in hunting, fishing, or bartering provisions with the Indians. Thus did Poutrincourt's table groan beneath all the luxuries of the winter forest, — flesh of moose, caribou, and deer, beaver, otter, and hare, bears and wild-cats; with ducks, geese, grouse, and plover; sturgeon, too, and trout, and fish innumerable, speared through the ice of the Équille, or drawn from the depths of the neighboring bay. "And," says Lescarbot, in closing his bill of fare, "whatever our gourmands at home may think, we found as good cheer at Port Royal as they at their Rue aux Ours in Paris, and that, too, at a cheaper rate." For the preparation of this manifold provision, the Grand Master was also answerable; since, during his day of office, he was autocrat of the kitchen.

Nor did this bounteous repast lack a solemn and befitting ceremonial. When the hour had struck, — after the manner of our fathers they dined at noon, — the Grand Master entered the hall, a napkin on his shoulder, his staff of office in his hand, and the collar of the Order — valued by Lescarbot at four crowns — about his neck. The brotherhood followed, each bearing a dish. The invited guests were Indian chiefs, of whom old Membertou was daily present, seated at table with the French, who took pleasure in this red-skin companionship. Those of humbler degree, warriors, squaws, and children, sat on the floor or crouched together in the corners of the hall, eagerly waiting their portion of biscuit or of bread, a novel and much coveted luxury. Being always treated with kindness, they became fond of the French, who often followed them on their moose-hunts, and shared their winter bivouac.

At the evening meal there was less of form and circumstance; and when the winter night closed in, when the flame crackled and the sparks streamed up the wide-throated chimney, and the founders of New

France with their tawny allies were gathered around the blaze, then did the Grand Master resign the collar and the staff to the successor of his honors, and, with jovial courtesy, pledge him in a cup of wine. Thus these ingenious Frenchmen beguiled the winter of their exile.

It was an unusually mild winter. Until January, they wore no warmer garment than their doublets. They made hunting and fishing parties, in which the Indians, whose lodges were always to be seen under the friendly shelter of the buildings, failed not to bear part. "I remember," says Lescarbot, "that on the fourteenth of January, of a Sunday afternoon, we amused ourselves with singing and music on the river Équille; and that in the same month we went to see the wheat-fields two leagues from the fort, and dined merrily in the sunshine."

Good spirits and good cheer saved them in great measure from the scurvy; and though towards the end of winter severe cold set in, yet only four men died. The snow thawed at last, and as patches of the black and oozy soil began to appear, they saw the grain of their last autumn's sowing already piercing the mould. The forced inaction of the winter was over. The carpenters built a water-mill on the stream now called Allen's River; others enclosed fields and laid out gardens; others, again, with scoop-nets and baskets, caught the herrings and ale-wives as they ran up the innumerable rivulets. The leaders of the colony set a contagious example of activity. Poutrincourt forgot the prejudices of his noble birth, and went himself into the woods to gather turpentine from the pines, which he converted into tar by a process of his own invention; while Lescarbot, eager to test the qualities of the soil, was again, hoe in hand, at work all day in his garden.

All seemed full of promise; but alas for the bright hope that kindled the manly heart of Champlain and the earnest spirit of the vivacious advocate! A sudden blight fell on them, and their rising prosperity withered to the ground. On a morning, late in spring, as the French were at breakfast, the ever watchful Membertou came in with news of an approaching sail. They hastened to the shore; but the vision of the centenarian sagamore put them all to shame. They could see nothing. At length their doubts were resolved. A small vessel stood on towards them, and anchored before the fort. She was commanded by one Chevalier, a young man from St. Malo, and was freighted with disastrous tidings. De Monts's monopoly was rescinded. The life of the enterprise was stopped, and the establishment at Port Royal could no longer be supported; for its expense was great, the body of the colony being laborers in the pay of the company. Nor was the annulling of the patent the full extent of the disaster: for, during the last summer, the Dutch had found their way to the St. Lawrence, and carried away a rich harvest of furs, while other interloping traders had plied a busy traffic along the coasts, and, in the excess of their avidity, dug up the bodies of buried Indians to rob them of their funeral robes.

It was to the merchants and fishermen of the Norman, Breton, and Biscayan ports, exasperated at their exclusion from a lucrative trade, and at the confiscations which had sometimes followed their attempts to engage in it, that this sudden blow was due. Money had been used freely at court, and the monopoly, unjustly granted, had been more unjustly withdrawn. De Monts and his company, who had spent 100,000 livres, were allowed 6000 in requital, to be collected, if possible, from the fur-traders in the form of a tax.

Chevalier, captain of the ill-omened bark, was entertained with a hospitality little deserved, since, having been intrusted with sundry hams, fruits, spices, sweetmeats, jellies, and other dainties, sent by the generous De Monts to his friends of New France, he with his crew had devoured them on the voyage, alleging that, in their belief, the inmates of Port Royal would all be dead before their arrival.

Choice there was none, and Port Royal must be abandoned. Built on a false basis, sustained only by the fleeting favor of a government, the generous enterprise had come to naught. Yet Poutrincourt, who in virtue of his grant from De Monts owned the place, bravely resolved that, come what might, he would see the adventure to an end, even should it involve emigration with his family to the wilderness. Meanwhile, he began the dreary task of abandonment, sending boat-loads of men and stores to Canseau, where lay the ship *Jonas,* eking out her diminished profits by fishing for cod.

Membertou was full of grief at the departure of his friends. He had built a palisaded village not far from Port Royal, and here were mustered some 400 of his warriors for a foray into the country of the Armouchiquois, dwellers along the coasts of Massachusetts, New Hampshire, and Western Maine. One of his tribesmen had been killed by a chief from the Saco, and he was bent on revenge. He proved himself a sturdy beggar, pursuing Poutrincourt with daily petitions, — now for a bushel of beans, now for a basket of bread, and now for a barrel of wine to regale his greasy crew. Membertou's long life had not been one of repose. In deeds of blood and treachery he had no rival in the Acadian forest; and, as his old age was beset with enemies, his alliance with the French had a foundation of policy no less than of affection. In right of his rank of Sagamore, he claimed perfect equality both with Poutrincourt and with the King, laying his shrivelled fore-fingers together in token of friendship between peers. Calumny did not spare him; and a rival chief intimated to the French, that, under cover of a war with the Armouchiquois, the crafty veteran meant to seize and plunder Port Royal. Precautions, therefore, were taken; but they were seemingly needless; for, their feasts and dances over, the warriors launched their birchen flotilla and set out. After an absence of six weeks they reappeared with howls of victory, and their exploits were commemorated in French verse by the muse of the indefatigable Lescarbot.

With a heavy heart the advocate bade farewell to the dwellings, the cornfields, the gardens, and all the dawning prosperity of Port Royal, and sailed for Canseau in a small vessel on the 30th of July. Poutrincourt and Champlain remained behind, for the former was resolved to learn before his departure the results of his agricultural labors. Reaching a harbor on the southern coast of Nova Scotia, six leagues west of Canseau, Lescarbot found a fishing-vessel commanded and owned by an old Basque, named Savalet, who for forty-two successive years had carried to France his annual cargo of codfish. He was in great glee at the success of his present venture, reckoning his profits at 10,000 francs. The Indians, however, annoyed him beyond measure, boarding him from their canoes as his fishing-boats came alongside, and helping themselves at will to his halibut and cod. At Canseau — a harbor near the strait now bearing the name — the ship *Jonas* still lay, her hold well stored with fish; and here, on the 27th of August, Lescarbot was re-joined by Poutrincourt and Champlain, who had come from Port Royal in an open boat. For a few days, they amused themselves with gathering raspberries on the islands; then they spread their sails for France, and early in October, 1607, anchored in the harbor of St. Malo.

First of Europeans, they had essayed to found an agricultural colony in the New World.[3] The leaders of the enterprise had acted less as merchants than as citizens; and the fur-trading monopoly, odious in itself, had been used as the instrument of a large and generous design. There was a radical defect, however, in their scheme of settlement. Excepting a few of the leaders, those engaged in it had not chosen a home in the wilderness of New France, but were mere hirelings, without wives or families, and careless of the welfare of the colony. The

[3] [An obvious slip for "North America, north of Mexico," as the Spaniards had already founded several hundred agricultural colonies.]

life which should have pervaded all the members was confined to the heads alone. In one respect, however, the enterprise of De Monts was truer in principle than the Roman Catholic colonization of Canada, on the one hand, or the Puritan colonization of Massachusetts, on the other, for it did not attempt to enforce religious exclusion.

Towards the fickle and bloodthirsty race who claimed the lordship of the forests, these colonists, excepting only in the treacherous slaughter at Port Fortuné, bore themselves in a spirit of kindness contrasting brightly with the rapacious cruelty of the Spaniards and the harshness of the English settlers. When the last boat-load left Port Royal, the shore resounded with lamentation; and nothing could console the afflicted savages but reiterated promises of a speedy return.

2. *Poutrincourt and the Jesuits*

Poutrincourt, we have seen, owned Port Royal in virtue of a grant from De Monts. The ardent and adventurous baron was in evil case, involved in litigation and low in purse; but nothing could damp his zeal. Acadia must become a new France, and he, Poutrincourt, must be its father. He gained from the King a confirmation of his grant, and, to supply the lack of his own weakened resources, associated with himself one Robin, a man of family and wealth. This did not save him from a host of delays and vexations; and it was not until the spring of 1610 that he found himself in a condition to embark on his new and doubtful venture.

Meanwhile an influence, of sinister omen as he thought, had begun to act upon his schemes. The Jesuits were strong at court. One of their number, the famous Father Coton, was confessor to Henry IV, and, on matters of this world as of the next, was ever whispering at the facile ear of the renegade King. New France offered a fresh field of action to the indefatigable Society of Jesus, and Coton urged upon the royal convert, that, for the saving of souls, some of its members should be attached to the proposed enterprise. The King, profoundly indifferent in matters of religion, saw no evil in a proposal which at least promised to place the Atlantic betwixt him and some of those busy friends whom at heart he deeply mistrusted. Other influences, too, seconded the confessor. Devout ladies of the court, and the Queen herself, supplying the lack of virtue with an overflowing piety, burned, we are assured, with a holy zeal for snatching the tribes of the West from the bondage of Satan. Therefore it was insisted that the projected colony should combine the spiritual with the temporal character, — or, in other words, that Poutrincourt should take Jesuits with him. Pierre Biard, Professor of Theology at Lyons, was named for the mission, and repaired in haste to Bordeaux, the port of embarkation, where he found no vessel, and no sign of preparation; and here, in wrath and discomfiture, he remained for a whole year.

That Poutrincourt was a good Catholic appears from a letter to the Pope, written for him in Latin by Lescarbot, asking a blessing on his enterprise, and assuring his Holiness that one of his grand objects was the saving of souls. But, like other good citizens, he belonged to the national party in the Church, — those liberal Catholics, who, side by side with the Huguenots, had made head against the League, with its Spanish allies, and placed Henry IV upon the throne. The Jesuits, an order Spanish in origin and policy, determined champions of ultramontane principles, the sword and shield of the Papacy in its broadest pretensions to spiritual and temporal sway, were to him, as to others of his party, objects of deep dislike and distrust. He feared them in his colony, evaded what he dared not refuse, left Biard waiting in solitude at Bordeaux, and sought to postpone the evil day by assuring Father Coton that, though Port Royal was at present in no state to receive the missionaries, preparation should be made to entertain them the next year after a befitting fashion.

Poutrincourt owned the barony of St. Just in Champagne, inherited a few years before from his mother. Hence, early in February, 1610, he set out in a boat loaded to the gunwales with provisions, furniture, goods, and munitions for Port Royal, descended the rivers Aube and Seine, and reached Dieppe safely with his charge.[4] Here his ship was awaiting him; and on the 26th of February he set sail, giving the slip to the indignant Jesuit at Bordeaux.

The tedium of a long passage was unpleasantly broken by a mutiny among the crew. It was suppressed, however, and Poutrincourt entered at length the familiar basin of Port Royal. The buildings were still standing, whole and sound save a partial falling in of the roofs. Even furniture was found untouched in the deserted chambers. The centenarian Membertou was still alive, his leathern, wrinkled visage beaming with welcome.

[4] Lescarbot, *Relation Dernière* (1612) p. 6. This is a pamphlet of 39 pages, containing matters not included in the larger work.

Poutrincourt set himself without delay to the task of Christianizing New France, in an access of zeal which his desire of proving that Jesuit aid was superfluous may be supposed largely to have reinforced. He had a priest with him, one La Flêche, whom he urged to the pious work. No time was lost. Membertou first was catechised, confessed his sins, and renounced the Devil, whom we are told he had faithfully served during a hundred and ten years. His squaws, his children, his grandchildren, and his entire clan were next won over. It was in June, the day of St. John the Baptist, when the naked proselytes, twenty-one in number, were gathered on the shore at Port Royal. Here was the priest in the vestments of his office; here were gentlemen in gay attire, soldiers, laborers, lackeys, all the infant colony. The converts kneeled; the sacred rite was finished, *Te Deum* was sung, and the roar of cannon proclaimed this triumph over the powers of darkness. Membertou was named Henri, after the King; his principal squaw, Marie, after the Queen. One of his sons received the name of the Pope, another that of the Dauphin; his daughter was called Marguerite, after the divorced Marguerite de Valois, and, in like manner, the rest of the squalid company exchanged their barbaric appellatives for the names of princes, nobles, and ladies of rank.

The fame of this *chef-d'œuvre* of Christian piety, as Lescarbot gravely calls it, spread far and wide through the forest, whose denizens, — partly out of a notion that the rite would bring good luck, partly to please the French, and partly to share in the good cheer with which the apostolic efforts of Father La Flêche had been sagaciously seconded — came flocking to enroll themselves under the banners of the Faith. Their zeal ran high. They would take no refusal. Membertou was for war on all who would not turn Christian. A living skeleton was seen crawling from hut to hut in search of the priest and his saving waters; while another neophyte, at the point of death, asked anxiously whether, in the realms of bliss to which he was bound, pies were to be had comparable to those with which the French regaled him.

A formal register of baptisms was drawn up to be carried to France in the returning ship, of which Poutrincourt's son, Biencourt, a spirited youth of eighteen, was to take charge. He sailed in July, his father keeping him company as far as Port la Hêve, whence, bidding the young man farewell, he attempted to return in an open boat to Port Royal. A north wind blew him out to sea; and for six days he was out of sight of land, subsisting on rain-water wrung from the boat's sail, and on a few wild-fowl which he had shot on an island. Five weeks passed before he could rejoin his colonists, who, despairing of his safety, were about to choose a new chief.

Meanwhile, young Biencourt, speeding on his way, heard dire news from a fisherman on the Grand Bank. The knife of Ravaillac had done its work. Henry IV was dead.

3. Madame de Guercheville

There is an ancient street in Paris, where a great thoroughfare contracts to a narrow pass, the Rue de la Ferronnerie. Tall buildings overshadow it, packed from pavement to tiles with human life, and from the dingy front of one of them the sculptured head of a man looks down on the throng that ceaselessly defiles beneath. On the 14th of May, 1610, a ponderous coach, studded with fleurs-de-lis and rich with gilding, rolled along this street. In it was a small man, well advanced in life, whose profile once seen could not be forgotten, — a hooked nose, a protruding chin, a brow full of wrinkles, grizzled hair, a short, grizzled beard, and stiff, gray moustaches, bristling like a cat's. One would have thought him some whiskered satyr, grim from the rack of tumultuous years; but his alert, upright port bespoke unshaken vigor, and his clear eye was full of buoyant life. Following on the footway strode a tall, strong, and somewhat corpulent man, with sinister, deep-set eyes and a red beard, his arm and shoulder covered with his cloak. In the throat of the thoroughfare, where the sculptured image of Henry IV still guards the spot, a collision of two carts stopped the coach. Ravaillac quickened his pace. In an instant he was at the door. With his cloak dropped from his shoulders, and a long knife in his hand, he set his foot upon a guardstone, thrust his head and shoulders into the coach, and with frantic force stabbed thrice at the King's heart. A broken exclamation, a gasping convulsion, — and then the grim visage drooped on the bleeding breast. Henry breathed his last, and the hope of Europe died with him.

The omens were sinister for Old France and for New. Marie de Medicis, "cette grosse banquière," coarse scion of a bad stock, false wife and faithless queen, paramour of an intriguing foreigner, tool of the Jesuits and of Spain, was Regent in the minority of her imbecile son. The Huguenots drooped, the national party collapsed, the vigorous hand of Sully was felt no more, and the treasure gathered for a vast and beneficent enterprise became the instrument of despotism

and the prey of corruption. Under such dark auspicies, young Biencourt entered the thronged chambers of the Louvre.

He gained audience of the Queen, and displayed his list of baptisms;
while the ever present Jesuits failed not to seize him by the button,
assuring him, not only that the late King had deeply at heart the
establishment of their Society in Acadia, but that to this end he had
made them a grant of 2000 livres a year. The Jesuits had found an ally
and the intended mission a friend at court, whose story and whose
character are too striking to pass unnoticed.

This was a lady of honor to the Queen, Antoinette de Pons, Marquise
de Guercheville, once renowned for grace and beauty, and not less
conspicuous for qualities rare in the unbridled court of Henry's predecessor, where her youth had been passed. When the civil war was
at its height, the royal heart, leaping with insatiable restlessness from
battle to battle, from mistress to mistress, had found a brief repose in
the affections of his Corisande, famed in tradition and romance; but
Corisande was suddenly abandoned, and the young widow, Madame
de Guercheville, became the load-star of his erratic fancy. It was an
evil hour for the Béarnais. Henry sheathed in rusty steel, battling for
his crown and his life, and Henry robed in royalty and throned
triumphant in the Louvre, alike urged their suit in vain. Unused to
defeat, the King's passion rose higher for the obstacle that barred it.
On one occasion he was met with an answer not unworthy of record:—

"Sire, my rank, perhaps, is not high enough to permit me to be
your wife, but my heart is too high to permit me to be your mistress."

She left the court and retired to her château of La Roche-Guyon, on
the Seine, ten leagues below Paris, where, fond of magnificence, she
is said to have lived in much expense and splendor. The indefatigable
King, haunted by her memory, made a hunting-party in the neighboring forests; and, as evening drew near, separating himself from his
courtiers, he sent a gentleman of his train to ask of Madame de
Guercheville the shelter of her roof. The reply conveyed a dutiful
acknowledgment of the honor, and an offer of the best entertainment
within her power. It was night when Henry, with his little band of
horsemen, approached the château, where lights were burning in
every window, after a fashion of the day on occasions of welcome
to an honored guest. Pages stood in the gateway, each with a blazing
torch; and here, too, were gentlemen of the neighborhood, gathered
to greet their sovereign. Madame de Guercheville came forth, followed
by the women of her household; and when the King, unprepared for

so benign a welcome, giddy with love and hope, saw her radiant in pearls and more radiant yet in a beauty enhanced by the wavy torch-light and the surrounding shadows, he scarcely dared trust his senses:—

"Que vois-je, madame; est-ce bien vous, et suis-je ce roi méprisé?" [5]

He gave her his hand, and she led him within the château, where, at the door of the apartment destined for him, she left him, with a graceful reverence. The King, nowise disconcerted, did not doubt that she had gone to give orders for his entertainment, when an attendant came to tell him that she had descended to the courtyard and called for her coach. Thither he hastened in alarm:—

"What! am I driving you from your house?"

"Sire," replied Madame de Guercheville, "where a king is, he should be the sole master; but, for my part, I like to preserve some little authority wherever I may be."

With another deep reverence, she entered her coach and disappeared, seeking shelter under the roof of a friend, some two leagues off, and leaving the baffled King to such consolation as he might find in a magnificent repast, bereft of the presence of the hostess.

Henry could admire the virtue which he could not vanquish; and, long after, on his marriage, he acknowledged his sense of her worth by begging her to accept an honorable post near the person of the Queen.

"Madame," he said, presenting her to Marie de Medicis, "I give you a lady of honor who is a lady of honor indeed."

Some twenty years had passed since the adventure of La Roche-Guyon. Madame de Guercheville had outlived the charms which had attracted her royal suitor, but the virtue which repelled him was reinforced by a devotion no less uncompromising. A rosary in her hand and a Jesuit at her side, she realized the utmost wishes of the subtle fathers who had moulded and who guided her. She readily took fire when they told her of the benighted souls of New France, and the wrongs of Father Biard kindled her utmost indignation. She declared herself the protectress of the American missions; and the only difficulty, as a Jesuit writer tells us, was to restrain her zeal within reasonable bounds.

She had two illustrious coadjutors. The first was the jealous Queen, whose unbridled rage and vulgar clamor had made the Louvre a hell. The second was Henriette d'Entragues, Marquise de Verneuil, the crafty and capricious siren who had awakened these conjugal tempests.

[5] ["What do I see, Madam; is this really you, and am I that scorned king?"]

To this singular coalition were joined many other ladies of the court; for the pious flame, fanned by the Jesuits, spread through hall and boudoir, and fair votaries of the Loves and Graces found it a more grateful task to win heaven for the heathen than to merit it for themselves.

Young Biencourt saw it vain to resist. Biard must go with him in the returning ship, and also another Jesuit, Enemond Masse. The two fathers repaired to Dieppe, wafted on the wind of court favor, which they never doubted would bear them to their journey's end. Not so, however. Poutrincourt and his associates, in the dearth of their own resources, had bargained with two Huguenot merchants of Dieppe, Du Jardin and Du Quesne, to equip and load the vessel, in consideration of their becoming partners in the expected profits. Their indignation was extreme when they saw the intended passengers. They declared that they would not aid in building up a colony for the profit of the King of Spain, nor risk their money in a venture where Jesuits were allowed to intermeddle; and they closed with a flat refusal to receive them on board, unless, they added with patriotic sarcasm, the Queen would direct them to transport the whole order beyond sea. Biard and Masse insisted, on which the merchants demanded reimbursement for their outlay, as they would have no further concern in the business.

Biard communicated with Father Coton, Father Coton with Madame de Guercheville. No more was needed. The zealous lady of honor, "indignant," says Biard, "to see the efforts of hell prevail," and resolved "that Satan should not remain master of the field," set on foot a subscription, and raised an ample fund within the precincts of the court. Biard, in the name of the "Province of France of the Order of Jesus," bought out the interest of the two merchants for 3800 livres, thus constituting the Jesuits equal partners in business with their enemies. Nor was this all; for, out of the ample proceeds of the subscription, he lent to the needy associates a further sum of 737 livres, and advanced 1225 more to complete the outfit of the ship. Well pleased, the triumphant priests now embarked, and friend and foe set sail together on the 26th of January, 1611.[6]

[6] It is noteworthy that the first contract of the French Jesuits in America relates to a partnership to carry on the fur trade. [Père Biard's *Relation* is reprinted with translation in R. G. Thwaites ed. of Jesuit *Relations* III, IV 8-167; and a translation of the *Relation* — the above-mentioned letters and other material — is in Alexander Brown *Genesis of the United States* (1890) II 700-29.]

CHAPTER V

The Colonies at Port Royal and Mount Desert

[Pioneers of France in the New World, PART II, CHAPTERS VI, VII AND VIII]

1. *Biard and Biencourt at Port Royal*

The voyage was one of inordinate length, — beset, too, with ice-bergs, larger and taller, according to the Jesuit voyagers, than the Church of Notre Dame; but on the day of Pentecost their ship, *The Grace of God*, anchored before Port Royal. Then first were seen in the wilderness of New France the close black cap, the close black robe, of the Jesuit father, and the features seamed with study and thought and discipline. Then first did this mighty Proteus, this many-colored Society of Jesus, enter upon that rude field of toil and woe, where, in after years, the devoted zeal of its apostles was to lend dignity to their order and do honor to humanity.

Few were the regions of the known world to which the potent brotherhood had not stretched the vast network of its influence. Jesuits had disputed in theology with the bonzes of Japan, and taught astronomy to the mandarins of China; had wrought prodigies of sudden conversion among the followers of Brahma, preached the papal supremacy to Abyssinian schismatics, carried the cross among the savages of Caffraria, wrought reputed miracles in Brazil, and gathered the tribes of Paraguay beneath their paternal sway. And now, with the aid of the Virgin and her votary at court, they would build another empire among the tribes of New France. The omens were sinister and the outset was unpropitious. The Society was destined to reap few laurels from the brief apostleship of Biard and Masse.

When the voyagers landed, they found at Port Royal a band of half-famished men, eagerly expecting their succor. The voyage of four months had, however, nearly exhausted their own very moderate stock of provisions, and the mutual congratulations of the old colonists and the new were damped by a vision of starvation. A friction, too, speedily declared itself between the spiritual and the temporal powers. Pontgravé's son, then trading on the coast, had exasperated the Indians by an outrage on one of their women, and, dreading the wrath of Poutrincourt, had fled to the woods. Biard saw fit to take his part, remonstrated for him with vehemence, gained his pardon, received his confession, and absolved him. The Jesuit says that he was treated with great consideration by Poutrincourt, and that he should be forever beholden to him. The latter, however, chafed at Biard's interference.

"Father," he said, "I know my duty, and I beg you will leave me to do it. I, with my sword, have hopes of paradise, as well as you with your breviary. Show me my path to heaven. I will show you yours on earth."

He soon set sail for France, leaving his son Biencourt in charge. This hardy young sailor, of ability and character beyond his years, had, on his visit to court, received the post of Vice-Admiral in the seas of New France, and in this capacity had a certain authority over the trading-vessels of St. Malo and Rochelle, several of which were upon the coast. To compel the recognition of this authority, and also to purchase provisions, he set out along with Biard in a boat filled with armed followers. His first collision was with young Pontgravé, who with a few men had built a trading-hut on the St. John, where he proposed to winter. Meeting with resistance, Biencourt took the whole party prisoners, in spite of the remonstrances of Biard. Next, proceeding along the coast, he levied tribute on four or five traders wintering at St. Croix, and, continuing his course to the Kennebec, found the Indians of that region greatly enraged at the conduct of certain English adventurers, who three or four years before had, as they said, set dogs upon them and otherwise maltreated them. These were the colonists under Popham and Gilbert, who in 1607 and 1608 made an abortive attempt to settle near the mouth of the river. Nothing now was left of them but their deserted fort. The neighboring Indians were Abenakis, one of the tribes included by the French under the general name of Armouchiquois. Their disposition was doubtful, and it needed all the coolness of young Biencourt to avoid a fatal collision. On one occasion a curious incident took place. The French met six canoes full of warriors descending the Kennebec, and, as neither party trusted the other, the two encamped on opposite banks of the river. In the evening the Indians began to sing and dance. Biard suspected these proceedings to be an invocation of the Devil, and "in order," he says, "to thwart this accursed tyrant, I made our people sing a few church hymns, such as the *Salve*, the *Ave Maris Stella*, and others. But being once in train, and getting to the end of their spiritual songs, they fell to singing such others as they knew, and when these gave out they took to mimicking the dancing and singing of the Armouchiquois on the other side of the water; and as Frenchmen are naturally good mimics, they did it so well that the Armouchiquois stopped to listen; at which our people stopped too; and then the Indians began again. You would have laughed to hear them, for they were like two choirs answering each other in concert, and you would hardly have known the real Armouchiquois from the sham ones."

Before the capture of young Pontgravé, Biard made him a visit at his camp, six leagues up the St. John. Pontgravé's men were sailors from St. Malo, between whom and the other Frenchmen there was much ill blood. Biard had hardly entered the river when he saw the evening sky crimsoned with the dancing fires of a superb aurora borealis, and he and his attendants marvelled what evil thing the prodigy might portend. Their Indian companions said that it was a sign of war. In fact, the night after they had joined Pontgravé a furious quarrel broke out in the camp, with abundant shouting, gesticulating, and swearing; and, says the father, "I do not doubt that an accursed band of furious and sanguinary spirits were hovering about us all night, expecting every moment to see a horrible massacre of the few Christians in those parts; but the goodness of God bridled their malice. No blood was shed, and on the next day the squall ended in a fine calm."

He did not like the Indians, whom he describes as "lazy, gluttonous, irreligious, treacherous, cruel, and licentious." He makes an exception in favor of Membertou, whom he calls "the greatest, most renowned, and most redoubted savage that ever lived in the memory of man," and especially commends him for contenting himself with but one wife, hardly a superlative merit in a centenarian. Biard taught him to say the Lord's Prayer, though at the petition, "Give us this day our daily bread," the chief remonstrated, saying, "If I ask for nothing but bread, I shall get no fish or moose-meat." His protracted career was now drawing to a close, and, being brought to the settlement in a dying state, he was placed in Biard's bed and attended by the two Jesuits. He was as remarkable in person as in character, for he was bearded like a Frenchman. Though, alone among La Flèche's converts, the Faith seemed to have left some impression upon him, he insisted on being buried with his heathen forefathers, but was persuaded to forego a wish fatal to his salvation, and slept at last in consecrated ground.

Another of the scanty fruits of the mission was a little girl on the point of death, whom Biard had asked her parents to give him for baptism. "Take her and keep her, if you like," was the reply, "for she is no better than a dead dog." "We accepted the offer," says Biard, "in order to show them the difference between Christianity and their impiety; and after giving her what care we could, together with some instruction, we baptized her. We named her after Madame the Marquise de Guercheville, in gratitude for the benefits we have received from that lady, who can now rejoice that her name is already in heaven; for, a few days after baptism, the chosen soul flew to that place of glory."

Biard's greatest difficulty was with the Micmac language. Young Biencourt was his best interpreter, and on common occasions served him well; but the moment that religion was in question he was, as it were, stricken dumb, — the reason being that the language was totally without abstract terms. Biard resolutely set himself to the study of it, — a hard and thorny path, on which he made small progress, and often went astray. Seated, pencil in hand, before some Indian squatting on the floor, whom with the bribe of a mouldy biscuit he had lured into the hut, he plied him with questions which he often neither would nor could answer. What was the Indian word for *Faith, Hope, Charity, Sacrament, Baptism, Eucharist, Trinity, Incarnation?* The perplexed savage, willing to amuse himself, and impelled, as Biard thinks, by the Devil, gave him scurrilous and unseemly phrases as the equivalent of things holy, which, studiously incorporated into the father's Indian catechism, produced on his pupils an effect the reverse of that intended. Biard's colleague, Masse, was equally zealous, and still less fortunate. He tried a forest life among the Indians with signal ill success. Hard fare, smoke, filth, the scolding of squaws, and the cries of children reduced him to a forlorn condition of body and mind, wore him to a skeleton, and sent him back to Port Royal without a single convert.

The dark months wore slowly on. A band of half-famished men gathered about the huge fires of their barn-like hall, moody, sullen, and quarrelsome. Discord was here in the black robe of the Jesuit and the brown capote of the rival trader. The position of the wretched little colony may well provoke reflection. Here lay the shaggy continent, from Florida to the Pole, outstretched in savage slumber along the sea, the stern domain of Nature, — or, to adopt the ready solution of the Jesuits, a realm of the powers of night, blasted beneath the sceptre of hell. On the banks of James River was a nest of woe-begone Englishmen, a handful of Dutch fur-traders at the mouth of the Hudson,[1] and a few shivering Frenchmen among the snow-drifts of Acadia; while deep within the wild monotony of desolation, on the icy verge of the great northern river, the hand of Champlain upheld the fleur-de-lis on the rock of Quebec. These were the advance guard, the forlorn hope of civilization, messengers of promise to a desert continent. Yet, unconscious of their high function, not content with inevitable woes, they were rent by petty jealousies and miserable feuds; while each of these detached fragments of rival nationalities, scarcely able to maintain its own wretched existence on a few square miles, begrudged to the others the smallest share in a domain which all the nations of Europe could hardly have sufficed to fill.

One evening, as the forlorn tenants of Port Royal sat together disconsolate, Biard was seized with a spirit of prophecy. He called upon Biencourt to serve out the little of wine that remained, — a proposal which met with high favor from the company present, though apparently with none from the youthful Vice-Admiral. The wine was ordered, however, and, as an unwonted cheer ran round the circle, the Jesuit announced that an inward voice told him how, within a month, they should see a ship from France. In truth, they saw one within a week. On the 23rd of January, 1612, arrived a small vessel laden with a moderate store of provisions and abundant seeds of future strife.

This was the expected succor sent by Poutrincourt. A series of ruinous voyages had exhausted his resources; but he had staked all on the success of the colony, had even brought his family to Acadia, and he would not leave them and his companions to perish. His credit was gone; his hopes were dashed; yet assistance was proffered, and, in his extremity, he was forced to accept it. It came from Madame de Guercheville and her Jesuit advisers. She offered to buy the interest

1 [Victor H. Paltsits, in *Proceedings* American Antiquarian Society n.s. XXXIV (1924) 39–65, has proved that the alleged four houses which Parkman believed were on Manhattan in 1613 were mythical. The first Dutch settlement was Fort Orange (Albany) in 1624, and there was no permanent settlement on Manhattan before 1626.]

of a thousand crowns in the enterprise. The ill-omened succor could not be refused; but this was not all. The zealous protectress of the missions obtained from De Monts, whose fortunes, like those of Poutrincourt, had ebbed low, a transfer of all his claims to the lands of Acadia; while the young King, Louis the Thirteenth, was persuaded to give her, in addition, a new grant of all the territory of North America, from the St. Lawrence to Florida. Thus did Madame de Guercheville, or in other words, the Jesuits who used her name as a cover, become proprietors of the greater part of the future United States and British Provinces. The English colony of Virginia and the Dutch trading-houses of New York were included within the limits of this destined Northern Paraguay; while Port Royal, the seigniory of the unfortunate Poutrincourt, was encompassed, like a petty island, by the vast domain of the Society of Jesus. They could not deprive him of it, since his title had been confirmed by the late King, but they flattered themselves, to borrow their own language, that he would be "confined as in a prison." His grant, however, had been vaguely worded, and, while they held him restricted to an insignificant patch of ground, he claimed lordship over a wide and indefinite territory. Here was argument for endless strife. Other interests, too, were adverse. Poutrincourt, in his discouragement, had abandoned his plan of liberal colonization, and now thought of nothing but beaver-skins. He wished to make a trading-post; the Jesuits wished to make a mission.

When the vessel anchored before Port Royal, Biencourt, with disgust and anger, saw another Jesuit landed at the pier. This was Gilbert du Thet, a lay brother, versed in affairs of this world, who had come out as representative and administrator of Madame de Guercheville. Poutrincourt, also, had his agent on board; and, without the loss of a day, the two began to quarrel. A truce ensued; then a smothered feud, pervading the whole colony, and ending in a notable explosion. The Jesuits, chafing under the sway of Biencourt, had withdrawn without ceremony, and betaken themselves to the vessel, intending to sail for France. Biencourt, exasperated at such a breach of discipline, and fearing their representations at court, ordered them to return, adding that, since the Queen had commended them to his especial care, he could not, in conscience, lose sight of them. The indignant fathers excommunicated him. On this, the sagamore Louis, son of the grisly convert Membertou, begged leave to kill them; but Biencourt would not countenance this summary mode of relieving his embarrassment. He again, in the King's name, ordered the clerical mutineers to return to the fort. Biard declared that he would not, threatened to excommunicate any who should lay hand on him, and called the Vice-Admiral a robber. His wrath, however, soon cooled; he yielded to necessity, and came quietly ashore, where, for the next three months, neither he nor his colleagues would say mass, or perform any office of religion. At length a change came over him; he made advances of peace, prayed that the past might be forgotten, said mass again, and closed with a petition that Brother du Thet might be allowed to go to France in a trading vessel then on the coast. His petition being granted, he wrote to Poutrincourt a letter overflowing with praises of his son; and, charged with this missive, Du Thet set sail.

2. *La Saussaye's Settlement on Mount Desert*

Pending these squabbles, the Jesuits at home were far from idle. Bent on ridding themselves of Poutrincourt, they seized, in satisfaction of debts due them, all the cargo of his returning vessel, and involved him in a network of litigation. If we accept his own statements in a letter to his friend Lescarbot, he was outrageously misused, and indeed defrauded, by his clerical copartners, who at length had him thrown into prison. Here, exasperated, weary, sick of Acadia, and anxious for the wretched exiles who looked to him for succor, the unfortunate man fell ill. Regaining his liberty, he again addressed himself with what strength remained to the forlorn task of sending relief to his son and his comrades.

Scarcely had Brother Gilbert du Thet arrived in France, when Madame de Guercheville and her Jesuits, strong in court favor and in the charity of wealthy penitents, prepared to take possession of their empire beyond sea. Contributions were asked, and not in vain; for the sagacious fathers, mindful of every spring of influence, had deeply studied the mazes of feminine psychology, and then, as now, were favorite confessors of the fair. It was on the 12th of March, 1613, that the *Mayflower* of the Jesuits sailed from Honfleur for the shores of New England. She was the *Jonas*, formerly in the service of De Monts, a small craft bearing forty-eight sailors and colonists, including two Jesuits, Father Quentin and Brother Du Thet. She carried horses, too, and goats, and was abundantly stored with all things needful by the pious munificence of her patrons. A courtier named La Saussaye was chief of the colony, Captain Charles Fleury commanded the ship, and, as she winged her way across the Atlantic, benedictions hovered over her from lordly halls and perfumed chambers.

On the 16th of May, La Saussaye touched at La Hêve, where he heard mass, planted a cross, and displayed the scutcheon of Madame de Guercheville. Thence, passing on to Port Royal, he found Biard, Masse, their servant-boy, an apothecary, and one man beside. Biencourt and his followers were scattered about the woods and shores, digging the tuberous roots called ground-nuts, catching alewives in the brooks, and by similar expedients sustaining their miserable existence. Taking the two Jesuits on board, the voyagers steered for the Penobscot. A fog rose upon the sea. They sailed to and fro, groping their way in blindness, straining their eyes through the mist, and trembling each instant lest they should descry the black outline of some deadly reef and the ghostly death-dance of the breakers. But Heaven heard their prayers. At night they could see the stars. The sun rose resplendent on a laughing sea, and his morning beams streamed fair and full on the wild heights of the island of Mount Desert. They entered a bay that stretched inland between iron-bound shores, and gave it the name of St. Sauveur. It is now called Frenchman's Bay. They saw a coast-line of weather-beaten crags set thick with spruce and fir, the surf-washed cliffs of Great Head and Schooner Head, the rocky front of Newport Mountain, patched with ragged woods, the arid domes of Dry Mountain and Green Mountain, the round bristly backs of the Porcupine Islands, and the waving outline of the Gouldsborough Hills.[2]

La Saussaye cast anchor not far from Schooner Head, and here he lay till evening. The jet-black shade betwixt crags and sea, the pines along the cliff, pencilled against the fiery sunset, the dreamy slumber of distant mountains bathed in shadowy purple, — such is the scene that in this our day greets the wandering artist, the roving collegian bivouacked on the shore, or the pilgrim from stifled cities renewing his jaded strength in the mighty life of Nature. Perhaps they then greeted the adventurous Frenchmen. There was peace on the wilderness and peace on the sea; but none in this missionary bark, pioneer of Christianity and civilization. A rabble of angry sailors clamored on

[2] [Since Parkman wrote, the wilder parts of Mt. Desert have become the Acadia National Park, and the mountains, unfortunately, have been renamed. Newport is now called Champlain; Dry has become Mount Dorr; and Green, Mount Cadillac.]

her deck, ready to mutiny over the terms of their engagement. Should the time of their stay be reckoned from their landing at La Hêve, or from their anchoring at Mount Desert? Fleury, the naval commander, took their part. Sailor, courtier, and priest gave tongue together in vociferous debate. Poutrincourt was far away, a ruined man, and the intractable Vice-Admiral had ceased from troubling; yet not the less were the omens of the pious enterprise sinister and dark. The company, however, went ashore, raised a cross, and heard mass.

At a distance in the woods they saw the signal smoke of Indians, whom Biard lost no time in visiting. Some of them were from a village on the shore, three leagues westward. They urged the French to go with them to their wigwams. The astute savages had learned already how to deal with a Jesuit.

"Our great chief, Asticou, is there. He wishes for baptism. He is very sick. He will die unbaptized. He will burn in hell, and it will be all your fault."

This was enough. Biard embarked in a canoe, and they paddled him to the spot, where he found the great chief, Asticou, in his wigwam, with a heavy cold in the head. Disappointed of his charitable purpose, the priest consoled himself with observing the beauties of the neighboring shore, which seemed to him better fitted than St. Sauveur for the intended settlement. It was a gentle slope, descending to the water, covered with tall grass, and backed by rocky hills. It looked southeast upon a harbor where a fleet might ride at anchor, sheltered from the gales by a cluster of islands.[3]

The ship was brought to the spot, and the colonists disembarked. First they planted a cross; then they began their labors, and with their labors their quarrels. La Saussaye, zealous for agriculture, wished to break ground and raise crops immediately; the rest opposed him, wishing first to be housed and fortified. Fleury demanded that the ship should be unladen, and La Saussaye would not consent. Debate ran high, when suddenly all was harmony, and the disputants were friends once more in the pacification of a common danger.

Far out at sea, beyond the islands that sheltered their harbor, they saw an approaching sail; and as she drew near, straining their anxious eyes, they could descry the red flags that streamed from her masthead

[3] [Fernald Point on the western entrance of Somes Sound, the fiord that almost bisects Mt. Desert, can be certainly identified as the seat of St. Sauveur by the two springs on the beach mentioned by Biard. Across the Sound, on Manchester Point, was the village of Chief Asticou, whose name has since been attached to the eastern side of the nearby Northeast Harbor.]

and her stern; then the black muzzles of her cannon, — they counted seven on a side; then the throng of men upon her decks. The wind was brisk and fair; all her sails were set; she came on, writes a spectator, more swiftly than an arrow.

Six years before, in 1607, the ships of Captain Newport had conveyed to the banks of James River the first vital germ of English colonization on the continent. Noble and wealthy speculators, with Hispaniola, Mexico, and Peru for their inspiration, had combined to gather the fancied golden harvest of Virginia, received a charter from the Crown, and taken possession of their El Dorado. From tavern, gaming-house, and brothel was drawn the staple of the colony, — ruined gentlemen, prodigal sons, disreputable retainers, debauched tradesmen. Yet it would be foul slander to affirm that the founders of Virginia were all of this stamp; for among the riotous crew were men of worth, and, above them all, a hero disguised by the homeliest of names. Again and again, in direst woe and jeopardy, the infant settlement owed its life to the heart and hand of John Smith.

Several years had elapsed since Newport's voyage; and the colony, depleted by famine, disease, and an Indian war, had been recruited by fresh emigration, when one Samuel Argall arrived at Jamestown, captain of an illicit trading-vessel. He was a man of ability and force, — one of those compounds of craft and daring in which the age was fruitful; for the rest, unscrupulous and grasping. In the spring of 1613 he achieved a characteristic exploit, — the abduction of Pocahontas, that most interesting of young squaws, or, to borrow the style of the day, of Indian princesses. Sailing up the Potomac he lured her on board his ship, and then carried off the benefactress of the colony a prisoner to Jamestown. Here a young man of family, Rolfe, became enamoured of her, married her with more than ordinary ceremony, and thus secured a firm alliance between her tribesmen and the English.

Meanwhile Argall had set forth on another enterprise. With a ship of 130 tons, carrying fourteen guns and sixty men, he sailed in May for islands off the coast of Maine to fish, as he says, for cod. He had a more important errand; for Sir Thomas Dale, Governor of Virgina, had commissioned him to expel the French from any settlement they might have made within the limits of King James's patents. Thick fogs involved him; and when the weather cleared he found himself not far from the Bay of Penobscot. Canoes came out from shore; the Indians climbed the ship's side, and, as they gained the deck, greeted the astonished English with an odd pantomime of bows and flourishes, which, in the belief of the latter, could have been learned from none but Frenchmen. By signs, too, and by often repeating the word *Norman*, — by which they always designated the French, — they betrayed the presence of the latter. Argall questioned them as well as his total ignorance of their language would permit, and learned, by signs, the position and number of the colonists. Clearly they were no match for him. Assuring the Indians that the Normans were his friends, and that he longed to see them, he retained one of the visitors as a guide, dismissed the rest with presents, and shaped his course for Mount Desert.

Now the wild heights rose in view; now the English could see the masts of a small ship anchored in the sound; and now, as they rounded the islands, four white tents were visible on the grassy slope between the water and the woods. They were a gift from the Queen to Madame de Guercheville and her missionaries. Argall's men prepared for fight, while their Indian guide, amazed, broke into a howl of lamentation.

On shore all was confusion. Bailleul, the pilot, went to reconnoitre, and ended by hiding among the islands. La Saussaye lost presence of mind, and did nothing for defence. La Motte, his lieutenant, with Captain Fleury, an ensign, a sergeant, the Jesuit Du Thet, and a few of the bravest men, hastened on board the vessel, but had no time to cast loose her cables. Argall bore down on them, with a furious din of drums and trumpets, showed his broadside, and replied to their hail with a volley of cannon and musket shot. "Fire! Fire!" screamed Fleury. But there was no gunner to obey, till Du Thet seized and applied the match. "The cannon made as much noise as the enemy's," writes Biard; but, as the inexperienced artillerist forgot to aim the piece, no other result ensued. Another storm of musketry, and Brother Gilbert du Thet rolled helpless on the deck.

The French ship was mute. The English plied her for a time with shot, then lowered a boat and boarded. Under the awnings which covered her, dead and wounded men lay strewn about her deck, and among them the brave lay brother, smothering in his blood. He had his wish; for, on leaving France, he had prayed with uplifted hands that he might not return, but perish in that holy enterprise. Like the Order of which he was a humble member, he was a compound of qualities in appearance contradictory. La Motte, sword in hand, showed fight to the last, and won the esteem of his captors.

The English landed without meeting any show of resistance, and ranged at will among the tents, the piles of baggage and stores, and the buildings and defences newly begun. Argall asked for the commander, but La Saussaye had fled to the woods. The crafty Englishman seized his chests, caused the locks to be picked, searched till he found the royal letters and commissions, withdrew them, replaced everything else as he had found it, and again closed the lids. In the morning, La Saussaye, between the English and starvation, preferred the former, and issued from his hiding-place. Argall received him with studious courtesy. That country, he said, belonged to his master, King James. Doubtless they had authority from their own sovereign for thus encroaching upon it; and, for his part, he was prepared to yield all respect to the commissions of the King of France, that the peace between the two nations might not be disturbed. Therefore he prayed that the commissions might be shown to him. La Saussaye opened his chests. The royal signature was nowhere to be found. At this, Argall's courtesy was changed to wrath. He denounced the Frenchmen as robbers and pirates who deserved the gallows, removed their property on board his ship, and spent the afternoon in dividing it among his followers. The disconsolate French remained on the scene of their woes, where the greedy sailors as they came ashore would snatch from them, now a cloak, now a hat, and now a doublet, till the unfortunate colonists were left half naked. In other respects the English treated their captives well, — except two of them, whom they flogged; and Argall, whom Biard, after recounting his knavery, calls "a gentleman of noble courage," having gained his point, returned to his former courtesy.

But how to dispose of the prisoners? Fifteen of them, including La Saussaye and the Jesuit Masse, were turned adrift in an open boat, at the mercy of the wilderness and the sea. Nearly all were landsmen; but while their unpractised hands were struggling with the oars, they were joined among the islands by the fugitive pilot and his boat's crew. Worn and half starved, the united bands made their perilous way eastward, stopping from time to time to hear mass, make a procession, or catch codfish. Thus sustained in the spirit and in the flesh, cheered too by the Indians, who proved fast friends in need, they crossed the Bay of Fundy, doubled Cape Sable, and followed the southern coast of Nova Scotia, till they happily fell in with two French trading-vessels, which bore them in safety to St. Malo.[4]

[4] [For a more favorable view of Argall than Parkman's, see Charles M. Andrews *The Colonial Period of American History* (1934) I 148–9. Richard W. Hale *The Story of Bar Harbor* (1949) goes into the local aspects.]

3. *The Ruin of French Acadia*

"Praised be God, behold two thirds of our company safe in France, telling their strange adventures to their relatives and friends. And now you will wish to know what befell the rest of us." Thus writes Father Biard, who with his companions in misfortune, fourteen in all, prisoners on board Argall's ship and the prize, were borne captive to Virginia. Old Point Comfort was reached at length, the site of Fortress Monroe; Hampton Roads, renowned in our day for the sea-fight of the Titans; Sewell's Point; the Rip Raps; Newport News, — all household words in the ears of this generation. Now, far on their right, buried in the damp shade of immemorial verdure, lay, untrodden and voiceless, the fields where stretched the leaguering lines of Washington, where the lilies of France floated beside the banners of the new-born republic, and where in later years embattled treason confronted the manhood of an outraged nation. And now before them they could descry the masts of small craft at anchor, a cluster of rude dwellings fresh from the axe, scattered tenements, and fields green with tobacco.

Throughout the voyage the prisoners had been soothed with flattering tales of the benignity of the Governor of Virginia, Sir Thomas Dale; of his love of the French, and his respect for the memory of Henry IV, to whom, they were told, he was much beholden for countenance and favor. On their landing at Jamestown, this consoling picture was reversed. The Governor fumed and blustered, talked of halter and gallows, and declared that he would hang them all. In vain Argall remonstrated, urging that he had pledged his word for their lives. Dale, outraged by their invasion of British territory, was deaf to all appeals; till Argall, driven to extremity, displayed the stolen commissions, and proclaimed his stratagem, of which the French themselves had to that moment been ignorant. As they were accredited by their government, their lives at least were safe. Yet the wrath of Sir Thomas Dale still burned high. He summoned his council, and they resolved promptly to wipe off all stain of French intrusion from shores which King James claimed as his own.

Their action was utterly unauthorized. The two kingdoms were at peace. James I, by the patents of 1606, had granted all North America, from the thirty-fourth to the forty-fifth degree of latitude, to the two companies of London and Plymouth, — Virginia being assigned to the former, while to the latter were given Maine and Acadia, with adjacent regions. Over these, though as yet the claimants had not taken possession of them, the authorities of Virginia had no color of jurisdiction. England claimed all North America, in virtue of the discovery of Cabot; and Sir Thomas Dale became the self-constituted champion of British rights, not the less zealous that his championship promised a harvest of booty.

Argall's ship, the captured ship of La Saussaye, and another smaller vessel, were at once equipped and despatched on their errand of havoc. Argall commanded; and Biard, with Quentin and several others of the prisoners, were embarked with him. They shaped their course first for Mount Desert. Here they landed, levelled La Saussaye's unfinished defences, cut down the French cross, and planted one of their own in its place. Next they sought out the island of St. Croix, seized a quantity of salt, and razed to the ground all that remained of the dilapidated buildings of De Monts. They crossed the Bay of Fundy to Port Royal, guided, says Biard, by an Indian chief, — an improbable assertion, since the natives of these coasts hated the English as much as they loved the French, and now well knew the designs of the former. The unfortunate settlement was tenantless. Biencourt, with some of his men, was on a visit to neighboring bands of Indians, while the rest were reaping in the fields on the river, two leagues above the fort. Succor from Poutrincourt had arrived during the summer. The magazines were by no means empty, and there were cattle, horses, and hogs in adjacent fields and enclosures. Exulting at their good fortune, Argall's men butchered or carried off the animals, ransacked the buildings, plundered them even to the locks and bolts of the doors, and then laid the whole in ashes; "and may it please the Lord," adds the pious Biard, "that the sins therein committed may likewise have been consumed in that burning."

Having demolished Port Royal, the marauders went in boats up the river to the fields where the reapers were at work. These fled, and took refuge behind the ridge of a hill, whence they gazed helplessly on the destruction of their harvest. Biard approached them, and, according to the declaration of Poutrincourt made and attested before the Admiralty of Guienne, tried to persuade them to desert his son, Biencourt, and take service with Argall. The reply of one of the men gave little encouragement for further parley:—

"Begone, or I will split your head with this hatchet."

*   *   *

His work done, and, as he thought, the French settlements of Acadia effectually blotted out, Argall set sail for Virginia on the 13th of November. Scarcely was he at sea when a storm scattered the vessels. Of the smallest of the three nothing was ever heard. Argall, severely buffeted, reached his port in safety, having first, it is said, compelled the Dutch at Manhattan to acknowledge for a time the sovereignty of King James.[5] The captured ship of La Saussaye, with Biard and his colleague Quentin on board, was forced to yield to the fury of the western gales, and bear away for the Azores. To Biard the change of destination was not unwelcome. He stood in fear of the truculent Governor of Virginia, and his tempest-rocked slumbers were haunted with unpleasant visions of a rope's end. It seems that some of the French at Port Royal, disappointed in their hope of hanging him, had commended him to Sir Thomas Dale as a proper subject for the gallows, drawing up a paper, signed by six of them, and containing allegations of a nature well fitted to kindle the wrath of that vehement official.

Biard was sent to Dover and thence to Calais, returning, perhaps, to the tranquil honors of his chair of theology at Lyons. La Saussaye, La Motte, Fleury, and other prisoners were at various times sent from Virginia to England, and ultimately to France. Madame de Guercheville, her pious designs crushed in the bud, seems to have gained no further satisfaction than the restoration of the vessel. The French ambassador complained of the outrage, but answer was postponed; and, in the troubled state of France, the matter appears to have been dropped.

Argall, whose violent and crafty character was offset by a gallant bearing and various traits of martial virtue, became Deputy-Governor of Virginia, and, under a military code, ruled the colony with a rod of iron. He enforced the observance of Sunday with an edifying rigor. Those who absented themselves from church were, for the first offence, imprisoned for the night, and reduced to slavery for a week; for the second offence, enslaved a month; and for the third, a year. Nor was he less strenuous in his devotion to mammon. He enriched himself by extortion and wholesale peculation; and his audacious dexterity, aided by the countenance of the Earl of Warwick, who is said to have had a trading connection with him, thwarted all the efforts of the company to bring him to account. In 1623, he was knighted by the hand of King James.

Early in the spring following the English attack, Poutrincourt came

5 [This statement is now generally regarded as a myth; see Paltsits *op. cit.* p. 43.]

to Port Royal. He found the place in ashes, and his unfortunate son, with the men under his command, wandering houseless in the forests. They had passed a winter of extreme misery, sustaining their wretched existence with roots, the buds of trees, and lichens peeled from the rocks.

Despairing of his enterprise, Poutrincourt returned to France. In the next year, 1615, during the civil disturbances which followed the marriage of the King, command was given him of the royal forces destined for the attack on Méry; and here, happier in his death than in his life, he fell, sword in hand.

In spite of their reverses, the French kept hold on Acadia.[6] Biencourt, partially at least, rebuilt Port Royal; while winter after winter the smoke of fur traders' huts curled into the still, sharp air of these frosty wilds, till at length, with happier auspices, plans of settlement were resumed.

Rude hands strangled the "Northern Paraguay" in its birth. Its beginnings had been feeble, but behind were the forces of a mighty organization, at once devoted and ambitious, enthusiastic and calculating. Seven years later the *Mayflower* landed her emigrants at Plymouth. What would have been the issues had the zeal of the pious lady of honor preoccupied New England with a Jesuit colony?

In an obscure stroke of lawless violence began the strife of France and England, Protestantism and Rome, which for a century and a half shook the struggling communities of North America, and closed at last in the memorable triumph on the Plains of Abraham.

[6] According to Biard, more than 500 French vessels sailed annually, at this time, to America, for the whale and cod fishery and the fur-trade. [This, as Biggar shows, is an exaggeration.]

CHAPTER VI

Champlain in Canada
1608–1635

[*Pioneers of France in the New World*, PART II, CHAPTERS IX, X AND PART OF XVII]

1. *The Founding of Quebec*

A lonely ship sailed up the St. Lawrence. The white whales floundering in the Bay of Tadoussac, and the wild duck diving as the foaming prow drew near, — there was no life but these in all that watery solitude, twenty miles from shore to shore. The ship was from Honfleur, and was commanded by Samuel de Champlain. He was the Æneas of a destined people, and in her womb lay the embryo life of Canada.

De Monts, after his exclusive privilege of trade was revoked and his Acadian enterprise ruined, had, as we have seen, abandoned it to Poutrincourt. Perhaps would it have been well for him had he abandoned with it all Transatlantic enterprises; but the passion for discovery and the noble ambition of founding colonies had taken possession of his mind. These, rather than a mere hope of gain, seem to have been his controlling motives; yet the profits of the fur-trade were vital to the new designs he was meditating, to meet the heavy outlay they demanded, and he solicited and obtained a fresh monopoly of the traffic for one year.

Champlain was, at the time, in Paris; but his unquiet thoughts turned westward. He was enamoured of the New World, whose rugged charms had seized his fancy and his heart; and as explorers of Arctic seas have pined in their repose for polar ice and snow, so did his restless thoughts revert to the fog-wrapped coasts, the piny odors of forests, the noise of waters, the sharp and piercing sunlight, so dear to his remembrance. He longed to unveil the mystery of that boundless wilderness, and plant the Catholic faith and the power of France amid its ancient barbarism.

Five years before, he had explored the St. Lawrence as far as the rapids above Montreal. On its banks, as he thought, was the true site for a settlement, — a fortified post, whence, as from a secure basis, the waters of the vast interior might be traced back towards their sources, and a western route discovered to China and Japan. For the fur-trade, too, the innumerable streams that descended to the great river might all be closed against foreign intrusion by a single fort at some commanding point, and made tributary to a rich and permanent commerce; while — and this was nearer to his heart, for he had often been heard to say that the saving of a soul was worth more than the conquest of an empire — countless savage tribes, in the bondage of Satan, might by the same avenues be reached and redeemed.

De Monts embraced his views; and fitting out two ships, gave command of one to the elder Pontgravé, of the other to Champlain. The former was to trade with the Indians and bring back the cargo of furs which, it was hoped, would meet the expense of the voyage. To Champlain fell the harder task of settlement and exploration.

Pontgravé, laden with goods for the Indian trade of Tadoussac, sailed from Honfleur on the 5th of April, 1608. Champlain, with men, arms, and stores for the colony, followed, eight days later. On the 15th of May he was on the Grand Bank; on the 30th he passed Gaspé, and on the 3rd of June neared Tadoussac. No living thing was to be seen. He anchored, lowered a boat, and rowed into the port, round the rocky point at the southeast, then, from the fury of its winds and currents, called La Pointe de Tous les Diables.[1] There was life enough within, and more than he cared to find. In the still anchorage under the cliffs lay Pontgravé's vessel, and at her side another ship, which proved to be a Basque fur-trader.

Pontgravé, arriving a few days before, had found himself anticipated by the Basques, who were busied in a brisk trade with bands of Indians cabined along the borders of the cove. He displayed the royal letters, and commanded a cessation of the prohibited traffic; but the Basques proved refractory, declared that they would trade in spite of the King, fired on Pontgravé with cannon and musketry, wounded him and two of his men, and killed a third. They then boarded his vessel, and carried away all his cannon, small arms, and ammunition, saying that they would restore them when they had finished their trade and were ready to return home.

Champlain found his comrade on shore, in a disabled condition.

[1] Champlain *Les Voyages* (1613), p. 166. Also called La Pointe aux Rochers.

The Basques, though still strong enough to make fight, were alarmed for the consequences of their conduct, and anxious to come to terms. A peace, therefore, was signed on board their vessel; all differences were referred to the judgment of the French courts, harmony was restored, and the choleric strangers betook themselves to catching whales.

This port of Tadoussac was long the centre of the Canadian fur-trade. A desolation of barren mountains closes round it, betwixt whose ribs of rugged granite, bristling with savins, birches, and firs, the Saguenay rolls its gloomy waters from the northern wilderness. Centuries of civilization have not tamed the wildness of the place; and still, in grim repose, the mountains hold their guard around the wave-less lake that glistens in their shadow, and doubles, in its sullen mirror, crag, precipice, and forest.

Near the brink of the cove or harbor where the vessels lay, and a little below the mouth of a brook which formed one of the outlets of this small lake, stood the remains of the wooden barrack built by Chauvin eight years before. Above the brook were the lodges of an Indian camp, — stacks of poles covered with birch-bark. They belonged to an Algonquin horde, called *Montagnais*, denizens of surrounding wilds, and gatherers of their only harvest, — skins of the moose, caribou, and bear; fur of the beaver, marten, otter, fox, wild-cat, and lynx. Nor was this all, for there were intermediate traders betwixt the French and the shivering bands who roamed the weary stretch of stunted forest between the head-waters of the Saguenay and Hudson's Bay. Indefatigable canoe-men, in their birchen vessels, light as egg-shells, they threaded the devious tracks of countless rippling streams, shady by-ways of the forest, where the wild duck scarcely finds depth to swim; then descended to their mart along those scenes of picturesque yet dreary grandeur which steam has made familiar to modern tourists. With slowly moving paddles, they glided beneath the cliff whose shaggy brows frown across the zenith, and whose base the deep waves wash with a hoarse and hollow cadence; and they passed the sepulchral Bay of the Trinity, dark as the tide of Acheron, — a sanctuary of solitude and silence: depths which, as the fable runs, no sounding line can fathom, and heights at whose dizzy verge the wheeling eagle seems a speck.[2]

Peace being established with the Basques, and the wounded Pont-

---

[2] Bouchette estimates the height of these cliffs at 1800 feet. They overhang the river and bay. The scene is one of the most remarkable on the continent.

gravé busied, as far as might be, in transferring to the hold of his ship the rich lading of the Indian canoes, Champlain spread his sails, and again held his course up the St. Lawrence. Far to the south, in sun and shadow, slumbered the woody mountains whence fell the countless springs of the St. John, behind tenantless shores, now white with glimmering villages, — La Chenaie, Granville, Kamouraska, St. Roche, St. Jean, Vincelot, Berthier. But on the north the jealous wilderness still asserts its sway, crowding to the river's verge its walls, domes, and towers of granite; and, to this hour, its solitude is scarcely broken.

Above the point of the Island of Orleans, a constriction of the vast channel narrows it to less than a mile, with the green heights of Point Levi on one side, and on the other the cliffs of Quebec.[3] Here, a small stream, the St. Charles, enters the St. Lawrence, and in the angle betwixt them rises the promontory, on two sides a natural fortress. Between the cliffs and the river lay a strand covered with walnuts and other trees. From this strand, by a rough passage gullied downward from the place where Prescott Gate now guards the way, one might climb the heights to the broken plateau above, now burdened with its ponderous load of churches, convents, dwellings, ramparts, and batteries. Thence, by a gradual ascent, the rock sloped upward to its highest summit, Cape Diamond,[4] looking down on the St. Lawrence from a height of 350 feet. Here the citadel now stands; then the fierce sun fell on the bald, baking rock, with its crisped mosses and parched lichens. Two centuries and a half have quickened the solitude with swarming life, covered the deep bosom of the river with barge and steamer and gliding sail, and reared cities and villages on the site of forests; but nothing can destroy the surpassing grandeur of the scene.

On the strand between the water and the cliffs Champlain's axemen fell to their work. They were pioneers of an advancing host, — advancing, it is true, with feeble and uncertain progress, — priests, soldiers, peasants, feudal scutcheons, royal insignia: not the Middle Age, but engendered of it by the stronger life of modern centralization, sharply stamped with a parental likeness, heir to parental weakness and parental force.

---

[3] The origin of this name has been disputed, but there is no good ground to doubt its Indian origin, which is distinctly affirmed by Champlain and Lescarbot. Charlevoix derives it from the Algonquin word *Quebeio* or *Quelibec*, signifying a narrowing or contracting. A half-breed Algonquin told Garneau that the word *Québec*, or *Ouabec*, means a strait.

[4] Champlain calls Cape Diamond Mont du Gas (Guast), from the family name of De Monts. He gave the name Cape Diamond to Pointe à Puiseaux.

In a few weeks a pile of wooden buildings rose on the brink of the St. Lawrence, on or near the site of the market-place of the Lower Town of Quebec. The pencil of Champlain, always regardless of proportion and perspective, has preserved its likeness. A strong wooden wall, surmounted by a gallery loopholed for musketry, enclosed three buildings, containing quarters for himself and his men, together with a courtyard, from one side of which rose a tall dove-cot, like a belfry. A moat surrounded the whole, and two or three small cannon were planted on salient platforms towards the river. There was a large storehouse near at hand, and a part of the adajcent ground was laid out as a garden.

In this garden Champlain was one morning directing his laborers, when Têtu, his pilot, approached him with an anxious countenance, and muttered a request to speak with him in private. Champlain assenting, they withdrew to the neighboring woods, when the pilot disburdened himself of his secret. One Antoine Natel, a locksmith, smitten by conscience or fear, had revealed to him a conspiracy to murder his commander and deliver Quebec into the hands of the Basques and Spaniards then at Tadoussac. Another locksmith, named Duval, was author of the plot, and, with the aid of three accomplices, had befooled or frightened nearly all the company into taking part in it. Each was assured that he should make his fortune, and all were mutually pledged to poniard the first betrayer of the secret. The critical point of their enterprise was the killing of Champlain. Some were for strangling him, some for raising a false alarm in the night and shooting him as he came out from his quarters.

Having heard the pilot's story, Champlain, remaining in the woods, desired his informant to find Antoine Natel, and bring him to the spot. Natel soon appeared, trembling with excitement and fear, and a close examination left no doubt of the truth of his statement. A small vessel, built by Pontgravé at Tadoussac, had lately arrived, and orders were now given that it should anchor close at hand. On board was a young man in whom confidence could be placed. Champlain sent him two bottles of wine, with a direction to tell the four ringleaders that they had been given him by his Basque friends at Tadoussac, and to invite them to share the good cheer. They came aboard in the evening, and were seized and secured. "Voyla donc mes galants bien estonnez," writes Champlain.

It was ten o'clock, and most of the men on shore were asleep. They were wakened suddenly, and told of the discovery of the plot and the arrest of the ringleaders. Pardon was then promised them, and they were dismissed again to their beds, greatly relieved; for they had lived in trepidation, each fearing the other. Duval's body, swinging from a gibbet, gave wholesome warning to those he had seduced; and his head was displayed on a pike, from the highest roof of the buildings, food for birds and a lesson to sedition. His three accomplices were carried by Pontgravé to France, where they made their atonement in the galleys.

It was on the 18th of September that Pontgravé set sail, leaving Champlain with 28 men to hold Quebec through the winter. Three weeks later, and shores and hills glowed with gay prognostics of approaching desolation, — the yellow and scarlet of the maples, the deep purple of the ash, the garnet hue of young oaks, the crimson of the tupelo at the water's edge, and the golden plumage of birch saplings in the fissures of the cliff. It was a short-lived beauty. The forest dropped its festal robes. Shrivelled and faded, they rustled to the earth. The crystal air and laughing sun of October passed away, and November sank upon the shivering waste, chill and sombre as the tomb.

A roving band of Montagnais had built their huts near the buildings, and were busying themselves with their autumn eel-fishery, on which they greatly relied to sustain their miserable lives through the winter. Their slimy harvest being gathered, and duly smoked and dried, they gave it for safe-keeping to Champlain, and set out to hunt beavers. It was deep in the winter before they came back, reclaimed their eels, built their birch cabins again, and disposed themselves for a life of ease, until famine or their enemies should put an end to their enjoyments. These were by no means without alloy. While, gorged with food, they lay dozing on piles of branches in their smoky huts, where, through the crevices of the thin birch bark, streamed in a cold capable at times of congealing mercury, their slumbers were beset with nightmare visions of Iroquois forays, scalpings, butcherings, and burnings. As dreams were their oracles, the camp was wild with fright. They sent out no scouts and placed no guard; but, with each repetition of these nocturnal terrors, they came flocking in a body to beg admission within the fort. The women and children were allowed to enter the yard and remain during the night, while anxious fathers and jealous husbands shivered in the darkness without.

On one occasion, a group of wretched beings was seen on the farther bank of the St. Lawrence, like wild animals driven by famine to the borders of the settler's clearing. The river was full of drifting ice, and there was no crossing without risk of life. The Indians, in their desperation, made the attempt; and midway their canoes were ground to atoms among the tossing masses. Agile as wild-cats, they all leaped upon a huge raft of ice, the squaws carrying their children on their shoulders, a feat at which Champlain marvelled when he saw their starved and emaciated condition. Here they began a wail of despair; when happily the pressure of other masses thrust the sheet of ice against the northern shore. They landed and soon made their appearance at the fort, worn to skeletons and horrible to look upon. The French gave them food, which they devoured with a frenzied avidity, and, unappeased, fell upon a dead dog left on the snow by Champlain for two months past as a bait for foxes. They broke this carrion into fragments, and thawed and devoured it, to the disgust of the spectators, who tried vainly to prevent them.

This was but a severe access of the periodical famine which, during the winter, was a normal condition of the Algonquin tribes of Acadia and the Lower St. Lawrence, who, unlike the cognate tribes of New England, never tilled the soil, or made any reasonable provision against the time of need.

One would gladly know how the founders of Quebec spent the long hours of their first winter; but on this point the only man among them, perhaps, who could write, has not thought it necessary to enlarge. He himself beguiled his leisure with trapping foxes, or hanging a dead dog from a tree and watching the hungry martens in their efforts to reach it. Towards the close of winter, all found abundant employment in nursing themselves or their neighbors, for the inevitable scurvy broke out with virulence. At the middle of May, only eight men of the twenty-eight were alive, and of these half were suffering from disease.

This wintry purgatory wore away; the icy stalactites that hung from the cliffs fell crashing to the earth; the clamor of the wild geese was heard; the bluebirds appeared in the naked woods; the water-willows were covered with their soft caterpillar-like blossoms; the twigs of the swamp maple were flushed with ruddy bloom; the ash hung out its black tufts; the shad-bush seemed a wreath of snow; the white stars of the bloodroot gleamed among dank, fallen leaves; and in the young grass of the wet meadows the marsh-marigolds shone like spots of gold.

Great was the joy of Champlain when, on the 5th of June, he saw a sailboat rounding the Point of Orleans, betokening that the spring had brought with it the longed-for succors. A son-in-law of Pontgravé, named Marais, was on board, and he reported that Pontgravé was then at Tadoussac, where he had lately arrived. Thither Champlain hastened, to take counsel with his comrade. His constitution or his courage had defied the scurvy. They met, and it was determined betwixt them, that, while Pontgravé remained in charge of Quebec, Champlain should enter at once on his long-meditated explorations, by which, like La Salle seventy years later, he had good hope of finding a way to China.

But there was a lion in the path. The Indian tribes, to whom peace was unknown, infested with their scalping parties the streams and pathways of the forest, and increased tenfold its inseparable risks. The after career of Champlain gives abundant proof that he was more than indifferent to all such chances; yet now an expedient for evading them offered itself, so consonant with his instincts that he was glad to accept it.

During the last autumn, a young chief from the banks of the then unknown Ottawa had been at Quebec; and, amazed at what he saw, he had begged Champlain to join him in the spring against his enemies. These enemies were a formidable race of savages, — the Iroquois, or Five Confederate Nations, who dwelt in fortified villages within limits now embraced by the State of New York, and who were a terror to all the surrounding forests. They were deadly foes of their kindred the Hurons, who dwelt on the lake which bears their name, and were allies of Algonquin bands on the Ottawa. All alike were tillers of the soil, living at ease when compared with the famished Algonquins of the Lower St. Lawrence.

By joining these Hurons and Algonquins against their Iroquois enemies, Champlain might make himself the indispensable ally and leader of the tribes of Canada, and at the same time fight his way to discovery in regions which otherwise were barred against him. From first to last it was the policy of France in America to mingle in Indian politics, hold the balance of power between adverse tribes, and envelop in the network of her power and diplomacy the remotest hordes of the wilderness. Of this policy the Father of New France may perhaps be held to have set a rash and premature example. Yet while he was apparently following the dictates of his own adventurous spirit, it became evident, a few years later, that under his thirst for discovery and spirit of knight-errantry lay a consistent and deliberate purpose. That it had already assumed a definite shape is not likely; but his after course makes it plain that, in embroiling himself and his colony with the most formidable savages on the continent, he was by no means acting so recklessly as at first sight would appear.

2. *The Expedition to Lake Champlain*

It was past the middle of June, and the expected warriors from the upper country had not come, — a delay which seems to have given Champlain little concern, for, without waiting longer, he set out with no better allies than a band of Montagnais. But, as he moved up the St. Lawrence, he saw, thickly clustered in the bordering forest, the lodges of an Indian camp, and, landing, found his Huron and Algonquin allies. Few of them had ever seen a white man, and they surrounded the steel-clad strangers in speechless wonder. Champlain asked for their chief, and the staring throng moved with him toward a lodge where sat, not one chief, but two; for each band had its own. There were feasting, smoking, and speeches; and, the needful ceremony over, all descended together to Quebec; for the strangers were bent on seeing those wonders of architecture, the fame of which had pierced the recesses of their forests.

On their arrival, they feasted their eyes and glutted their appetites; yelped consternation at the sharp explosions of the arquebuse and the roar of the cannon; pitched their camps, and bedecked themselves for their war-dance. In the still night, their fire glared against the black and jagged cliff, and the fierce red light fell on tawny limbs convulsed with frenzied gestures and ferocious stampings; on contorted visages, hideous with paint; on brandished weapons, stone war-clubs, stone hatchets, and stone-pointed lances; while the drum kept up its hollow boom, and the air was split with mingled yells.

The war-feast followed, and then all embarked together. Champlain was in a small shallop, carrying, besides himself, eleven men of Pontgravé's party, including his son-in-law Marais and the pilot La Routte. They were armed with the arquebuse, — a matchlock or firelock somewhat like the modern carbine, and from its shortness not ill suited for use in the forest. On the 28th of June they spread their sails and held their course against the current, while around them the river was alive with canoes, and hundreds of naked arms plied the paddle with a steady, measured sweep. They crossed the Lake of St. Peter, threaded the devious channels among its many islands, and reached at last the mouth of the Rivière des Iroquois, since called the Richelieu, or the St.

John.[5] Here, probably on the site of the town of Sorel, the leisurely warriors encamped for two days, hunted, fished, and took their ease, regaling their allies with venison and wild-fowl. They quarrelled, too; three fourths of their number seceded, took to their canoes in dudgeon, and paddled towards their homes, while the rest pursued their course up the broad and placid stream.

Walls of verdure stretched on left and right. Now, aloft in the lonely air rose the cliffs of Belœil, and now, before them, framed in circling forests, the Basin of Chambly spread its tranquil mirror, glittering in the sun. The shallop outsailed the canoes. Champlain, leaving his allies behind, crossed the basin and tried to pursue his course; but, as he listened in the stillness, the unwelcome noise of rapids reached his ear, and, by glimpses through the dark foliage of the Islets of St. John he could see the gleam of snowy foam and the flash of hurrying waters. Leaving the boat by the shore in charge of four men, he went with Marais, La Routte, and five others, to explore the wild before him. They pushed their way through the damps and shadows of the wood, through thickets and tangled vines, over mossy rocks and mouldering logs. Still the hoarse surging of the rapids followed them; and when, parting the screen of foliage, they looked out upon the river, they saw it thick set with rocks where, plunging over ledges, gurgling under drift-logs, darting along clefts, and boiling in chasms, the angry waters filled the solitude with monotonous ravings.

Champlain retraced his steps. He had learned the value of an Indian's word. His allies had promised him that his boat could pass unobstructed throughout the whole journey. "It afflicted me," he says, "and troubled me exceedingly to be obliged to return without having seen so great a lake, full of fair islands and bordered with the fine countries which they had described to me."

When he reached the boat, he found the whole savage crew gathered at the spot. He mildly rebuked their bad faith, but added, that, though they had deceived him, he, as far as might be, would fulfil his pledge. To this end, he directed Marais, with the boat and the greater part of the men, to return to Quebec, while he, with two who offered to follow him, should proceed in the Indian canoes.

The warriors lifted their canoes from the water, and bore them on their shoulders half a league through the forest to the smoother stream above. Here the chiefs made a muster of their forces, count-

[5] Also called the Chambly, the St. Louis, and the Sorel.

ing twenty-four canoes and sixty warriors. All embarked again, and advanced once more, by marsh, meadow, forest, and scattered islands, — then full of game, for it was an uninhabited land, the war-path and battle-ground of hostile tribes. The warriors observed a certain system in their advance. Some were in front as a vanguard; others formed the main body; while an equal number were in the forests on the flanks and rear, hunting for the subsistence of the whole; for, though they had a provision of parched maize pounded into meal, they kept it for use when, from the vicinity of the enemy, hunting should become impossible.

Late in the day they landed and drew up their canoes, ranging them closely, side by side. Some stripped sheets of bark, to cover their camp sheds; others gathered wood, the forest being full of dead, dry trees; others felled the living trees, for a barricade. They seem to have had steel axes, obtained by barter from the French; for in less than two hours they had made a strong defensive work, in the form of a half-circle, open on the river side, where their canoes lay on the strand, and large enough to enclose all their huts and sheds.[6] Some of their number had gone forward as scouts, and, returning, reported no signs of an enemy. This was the extent of their precaution, for they placed no guard, but all, in full security, stretched themselves to sleep, — a vicious custom from which the lazy warrior of the forest rarely departs.

They had not forgotten, however, to consult their oracle. The medicine-man pitched his magic lodge in the woods, formed a small stack of poles, planted in a circle and brought together at the tops like stacked muskets. Over these he placed the filthy deer-skins which served him for a robe, and, creeping in at a narrow opening, hid himself from view. Crouched in a ball upon the earth, he invoked the spirits in mumbling inarticulate tones; while his naked auditory, squatted on the ground like apes, listened in wonder and awe. Suddenly, the lodge moved, rocking with violence to and fro, — by the power of the spirits, as the Indians thought, while Champlain could plainly see the tawny fist of the medicine-man shaking the poles. They begged him to keep a watchful eye on the peak of the lodge, whence fire and smoke would presently issue; but with the best efforts of his vision, he

---

[6] Such extempore works of defence are still used among some tribes of the remote West. The author has twice seen them, made of trees piled together as described by Champlain, probably by war parties of the Crow or Snake Indians. Champlain is very minute in his description of the march and encampment.

discovered none. Meanwhile the medicine-man was seized with such convulsions, that, when his divination was over, his naked body streamed with perspiration. In loud, clear tones, and in an unknown tongue, he invoked the spirit, who was understood to be present in the form of a stone, and whose feeble and squeaking accents were heard at intervals, like the wail of a young puppy.

In this manner they consulted the spirit — as Champlain thinks, the Devil — at all their camps. His replies, for the most part, seem to have given them great content; yet they took other measures, of which the military advantages were less questionable. The principal chief gathered bundles of sticks, and, without wasting his breath, stuck them in the earth in a certain order, calling each by the name of some warrior, a few taller than the rest representing the subordinate chiefs. Thus was indicated the position which each was to hold in the expected battle. All gathered round and attentively studied the sticks, ranged like a child's wooden soldiers, or the pieces on a chessboard; then, with no further instruction, they formed their ranks, broke them, and reformed them again and again with excellent alacrity and skill.

Again the canoes advanced, the river widening as they went. Great islands appeared, leagues in extent, — Isle à la Motte, Long Island, Grande Isle; channels where ships might float and broad reaches of water stretched between them, and Champlain entered the lake which preserves his name to posterity. Cumberland Head was passed, and from the opening of the great channel between Grande Isle and the main he could look forth on the wilderness sea. Edged with woods, the tranquil flood spread southward beyond the sight. Far on the left rose the forest ridges of the Green Mountains, and on the right the Adirondacks, — haunts in these later years of amateur sportsmen from the counting-room or college halls. Then the Iroquois made them their hunting-ground; and beyond, in the valleys of the Mohawk, the Onondaga, and the Genesee, stretched the long line of their five cantons and palisaded towns.

At night they encamped again. The scene is a familiar one to many a tourist; and perhaps, standing at sunset on the peaceful strand, Champlain saw what a roving student of this generation has seen on those same shores, at that same hour, — the glow of the vanished sun behind the western mountains, darkly piled in mist and shadow along the sky; near at hand, the dead pine, mighty in decay, stretching its ragged arms athwart the burning heaven, the crow perched on its top like an image carved in jet; and aloft, the nighthawk, circling in his flight, and, with a strange whirring sound, diving through the air each moment for the insects he makes his prey.

The progress of the party was becoming dangerous. They changed their mode of advance and moved only in the night. All day they lay close in the depth of the forest, sleeping, lounging, smoking tobacco of their own raising, and beguiling the hours, no doubt, with the shallow banter and obscene jesting with which knots of Indians are wont to amuse their leisure. At twilight they embarked again, paddling their cautious way till the eastern sky began to redden. Their goal was the rocky promontory where Fort Ticonderoga was long afterward built. Thence, they would pass the outlet of Lake George, and launch their canoes again on that Como of the wilderness, whose waters, limpid as a fountain-head, stretched far southward between their flanking mountains. Landing at the future site of Fort William Henry, they would carry their canoes through the forest to the river Hudson, and, descending it, attack perhaps some outlying town of the Mohawks. In the next century this chain of lakes and rivers became the grand highway of savage and civilized war, linked to memories of momentous conflicts.

The allies were spared so long a progress. On the morning of the 29th of July, after paddling all night, they hid as usual in the forest on the western shore, apparently between Crown Point and Ticonderoga. The warriors stretched themselves to their slumbers, and Champlain, after walking till nine or ten o'clock through the surrounding woods, returned to take his repose on a pile of spruce-boughs. Sleeping, he dreamed a dream, wherein he beheld the Iroquois drowning in the lake; and, trying to rescue them, he was told by his Algonquin friends that they were good for nothing, and had better be left to their fate. For some time past he had been beset every morning by his superstitious allies, eager to learn about his dreams; and, to this moment, his unbroken slumbers had failed to furnish the desired prognostics. The announcement of this auspicious vision filled the crowd with joy, and at nightfall they embarked, flushed with anticipated victories.

It was ten o'clock in the evening, when, near a projecting point of land, which was probably Ticonderoga, they descried dark objects in motion on the lake before them. These were a flotilla of Iroquois canoes, heavier and slower than theirs, for they were made of oak bark.[7] Each

---

[7] Champlain (1613), 232. Probably a mistake; the Iroquois canoes were usually of elm bark. The paper-birch was used wherever it could be had, being incomparably the best material. All the tribes, from the mouth of the Saco northward

party saw the other, and the mingled war-cries pealed over the darkened water. The Iroquois, who were near the shore, having no stomach for an aquatic battle, landed, and, making night hideous with their clamors, began to barricade themselves. Champlain could see them in the woods, laboring like beavers, hacking down trees with iron axes taken from the Canadian tribes in war, and with stone hatchets of their own making. The allies remained on the lake, a bowshot from the hostile barricade, their canoes made fast together by poles lashed across. All night they danced with as much vigor as the frailty of their vessels would permit, their throats making amends for the enforced restraint of their limbs. It was agreed on both sides that the fight should be deferred till daybreak; but meanwhile a commerce of abuse, sarcasm, menace, and boasting gave unceasing exercise to the lungs and fancy of the combatants, — "much," says Champlain, "like the besiegers and besieged in a beleaguered town."

As the day approached, he and his two followers put on the light armor of the time. Champlain wore the doublet and long hose then in vogue. Over the doublet he buckled on a breastplate, and probably a back-piece, while his thighs were protected by cuisses of steel, and his head by a plumed casque. Across his shoulder hung the strap of his bandoleer, or ammunition-box; at his side was his sword, and in his hand his arquebuse. Such was the equipment of this ancient Indian-fighter, whose exploits date eleven years before the landing of the Puritans at Plymouth, and sixty-six years before King Philip's War.

Each of the three Frenchmen was in a separate canoe, and as it grew light, they kept themselves hidden, either by lying at the bottom, or covering themselves with an Indian robe. The canoes approached the shore, and all landed without opposition at some distance from the Iroquois, whom they presently could see filing out of their barricade, — tall, strong men, some two hundred in number, the boldest and fiercest warriors of North America. They advanced through the forest with a steadiness which excited the admiration of Champlain. Among them could be seen three chiefs, made conspicuous by their tall plumes. Some bore shields of wood and hide, and some were covered with a kind of armor made of tough twigs interlaced with a vegetable fibre supposed by Champlain to be cotton.

---

and eastward, and along the entire northern portion of the valley of the St. Lawrence and the Great Lakes, used the birch. The best substitutes were elm and spruce. The birch bark, from its laminated texture, could be peeled at any time, the others only when the sap was in motion.

The allies, growing anxious, called with loud cries for their champion, and opened their ranks that he might pass to the front. He did so, and, advancing before his red companions in arms, stood revealed to the gaze of the Iroquois, who, beholding the warlike apparition in their path, stared in mute amazement. "I looked at them," says Champlain, "and they looked at me. When I saw them getting ready to shoot their arrows at us, I levelled my arquebuse, which I had loaded with four balls, and aimed straight at one of the three chiefs. The shot brought down two, and wounded another. On this, our Indians set up such a yelling that one could not have heard a thunder-clap, and all the while the arrows flew thick on both sides. The Iroquois were greatly astonished and frightened to see two of their men killed so quickly, in spite of their arrow-proof armor. As I was reloading, one of my companions fired a shot from the woods, which so increased their astonishment that, seeing their chiefs dead, they abandoned the field and fled into the depth of the forest." The allies dashed after them. Some of the Iroquois were killed, and more were taken. Camp, canoes, provisions, all were abandoned, and many weapons flung down in the panic flight. The victory was complete.[8]

At night, the victors led out one of the prisoners, told him that he was to die by fire, and ordered him to sing his death-song if he dared. Then they began the torture, and presently scalped their victim alive, when Champlain, sickening at the sight, begged leave to shoot him. They refused, and he turned away in anger and disgust; on which they called him back and told him to do as he pleased. He turned again, and a shot from his arquebuse put the wretch out of misery.

The scene filled him with horror; but a few months later, on the Place de la Grève at Paris, he might have witnessed tortures equally revolting and equally vindictive, inflicted on the regicide Ravaillac by the sentence of grave and learned judges.

The allies made a prompt retreat from the scene of their triumph. Three or four days brought them to the mouth of the Richelieu. Here they separated; the Hurons and Algonquins made for the Ottawa, their homeward route, each with a share of prisoners for future torments. At parting, they invited Champlain to visit their towns and aid them again in their wars, an invitation which this paladin of the woods failed not to accept.

[8] [The site of this small but decisive battle is marked by a tablet on the shore of Lake Champlain just below Fort Ticonderoga.]

The companions now remaining to him were the Montagnais. In their camp on the Richelieu, one of them dreamed that a war party of Iroquois was close upon them; on which, in a torrent of rain, they left their huts, paddled in dismay to the islands above the Lake of St. Peter, and hid themselves all night in the rushes. In the morning they took heart, emerged from their hiding-places, descended to Quebec, and went thence to Tadoussac, whither Champlain accompanied them. Here the squaws, stark naked, swam out to the canoes to receive the heads of the dead Iroquois, and, hanging them from their necks, danced in triumph along the shore. One of the heads and a pair of arms were then bestowed on Champlain, — touching memorials of gratitude, which, however, he was by no means to keep for himself, but to present to the King.

Thus did New France rush into collision with the redoubted warriors of the Five Nations. Here was the beginning, and in some measure doubtless the cause, of a long suite of murderous conflicts, bearing havoc and flame to generations yet unborn. Champlain had invaded the tiger's den; and now, in smothered fury, the patient savage would lie biding his day of blood.

[Champlain, after making two round voyages to France and founding a trading post at the site of Montreal, organized a new company to exploit the Canadian fur trade. In 1615, with a Récollet friar (one of four whom he had induced to come out as missionaries), and Indian guides, he pushed up the Ottawa River, portaged to Lake Nipissing, discovered Lake Huron, made a treaty with the Hurons, and joined one of their war parties against the Iroquois. After an unsuccessful attack on a fortified town of the Onondagas, a few miles south of Lake Oneida, he returned to Quebec. The total French population of that town in 1617 did not exceed 60 people; it was still, in Parkman's words, "half trading factory, half mission."

In 1628 Cardinal Richelieu gave Canada a new deal. He formed the Company of New France (also called the Hundred Associates) and conferred upon it the whole of French America from Florida to the Arctic Circle, with a complete commercial monopoly. The Company, on its part, was required to import four thousand immigrants, all Catholic Frenchmen, into Canada by the year 1643. During the short Anglo-French War of 1628–29, Quebec, defended only by Champlain and sixteen men, surrendered to the Kirkes; but at the end of the war it was given back to France in return for the French King's paying to Charles I the sum of about $240,000 still due for the dowry of his

Queen. Champlain resumed command at Quebec in 1633 on behalf of the Company.]

3. *The Death of Champlain*

Two years passed. The mission of the Hurons was established, and here the indomitable Brébeuf, with a band worthy of him, toiled amid miseries and perils as fearful as ever shook the constancy of man; while Champlain at Quebec, in a life uneventful, yet harassing and laborious, was busied in the round of cares which his post involved.

Christmas Day, 1635, was a dark day in the annals of New France. In a chamber of the fort, breathless and cold, lay the hardy frame which war, the wilderness and the sea had buffeted so long in vain. After two months and a half of illness, Champlain, stricken with paralysis, at the age of sixty-eight, was dead. His last cares were for his colony and the succor of its suffering families. Jesuits, officers, soldiers, traders, and the few settlers of Quebec followed his remains to the church; Le Jeune pronounced his eulogy, and the feeble community built a tomb to his honor.

The colony could ill spare him. For twenty-seven years he had labored hard and ceaselessly for its welfare, sacrificing fortune, repose, and domestic peace to a cause embraced with enthusiasm and pursued with intrepid persistency. His character belonged partly to the past, partly to the present. The *preux chevalier*, the crusader, the romance-loving explorer, the curious, knowledge-seeking traveller, the practical navigator, all claimed their share in him. His views, though far beyond those of the mean spirits around him, belonged to his age and his creed. He was less statesman than soldier. He leaned to the most direct and boldest policy, and one of his last acts was to petition Richelieu for men and munitions for repressing that standing menace to the colony, the Iroquois. His dauntless courage was matched by an unwearied patience, proved by life-long vexations, and not wholly subdued even by the saintly follies of his wife. He is charged with credulity, from which few of his age were free, and which in all ages has been the foible of earnest and generous natures, too ardent to criticise, and too honorable to doubt the honor of others. Perhaps the heretic might have liked him more if the Jesuit had liked him less. The adventurous explorer of Lake Huron, the bold invader of the Iroquois, befits but indifferently the monastic sobrieties of the fort of Quebec, and his sombre environment of priests. Yet Champlain was no formalist, nor was his an empty zeal. A soldier from his youth, in an age of unbridled license, his life had answered to his maxims; and when a generation had passed after his visit to the Hurons, their elders remembered with astonishment the continence of the great French war-chief. . . .

With the life of the faithful soldier closes the opening of New France. Heroes of another stamp succeed; and it remains to tell the story of their devoted lives, their faults, follies, and virtues.

CHAPTER VII

Isaac Jogues
1641–1644

The waters of the St. Lawrence rolled through a virgin wilderness, where, in the vastness of the lonely woodlands, civilized man found a precarious harborage at three points only, — at Quebec, at Montreal, and at Three Rivers. Here and in the scattered missions was the whole of New France, — a population of some 300 souls in all. And now, over these miserable settlements, rose a war-cloud of frightful portent.

It was thirty-two years since Champlain had first attacked the Iroquois. They had nursed their wrath for more than a generation, and at length their hour was come. The Dutch traders at Fort Orange, now Albany, had supplied them with firearms. The Mohawks, the most easterly of the Iroquois nations, had, among their seven or eight hundred warriors, no less than 300 armed with the arquebuse, a weapon somewhat like the modern carbine. They were masters of the thunderbolts which, in the hands of Champlain, had struck terror into their hearts.

We have surveyed in the introductory chapter the character and organization of this ferocious people, — their confederacy of five nations, bound together by a peculiar tie of clanship; their chiefs, half hereditary, half elective; their government, an oligarchy in form and a democracy in spirit; their minds, thoroughly savage, yet marked here and there with traits of a vigorous development. The war which they had long waged with the Hurons was carried on by the Senecas and the other Western nations of their league; while the conduct of hostilities against the French and their Indian allies in Lower Canada was left to the Mohawks. In parties of from ten to a hundred or more, they would leave their towns on the river Mohawk, descend Lake Champlain and the river Richelieu, lie in ambush on the banks of the St. Lawrence, and attack the passing boats or canoes. Sometimes they hovered about the fortifications of Quebec and Three Rivers, killing stragglers, or luring armed parties into ambuscades. They followed like hounds on the trail of travellers and hunters; broke in upon unguarded camps at midnight; and lay in wait, for days and weeks, to intercept the Huron traders on their yearly descent to Quebec. Had they joined to their ferocious courage the discipline and the military knowledge that belong to civilization, they could easily have blotted out New France from the map, and made the banks of the St. Lawrence once more a solitude; but though the most formidable of savages, they were savages only.

In the early morning of the 2nd of August, 1642, twelve Huron canoes were moving slowly along the northern shore of the expansion of the St. Lawrence known as the Lake of St. Peter. There were on board about forty persons, including four Frenchmen, one of them being the Jesuit, Isaac Jogues, whom we have already followed on his missionary journey to the towns of the Tobacco Nation. In the interval he had not been idle. During the last autumn (1641) he, with Father Charles Raymbault, had passed along the shore of Lake Huron northward, entered the strait through which Lake Superior discharges itself, pushed on as far as the Sault Sainte Marie, and preached the Faith to two thousand Ojibwas and other Algonquins there assembled. He was now on his return from a far more perilous errand. The Huron mission was in a state of destitution. There was need of clothing for the priests, of vessels for the altars, of bread and wine for the eucharist, of writing materials, — in short, of everything; and early in the summer of the present year Jogues had descended to Three Rivers and Quebec, with the Huron traders, to procure the necessary supplies. He had accomplished his task, and was on his way back to the mission. With him were a few Huron converts and among them a noted Christian chief, Eustache Ahatsistari. Others of the party were in course of instruction for baptism; but the greater part were heathen, whose canoes were deeply laden with the proceeds of their bargains with the French fur-traders.

Jogues sat in one of the leading canoes. He was born at Orleans in 1607, and was thirty-five years of age. His oval face and the delicate mould of his features indicated a modest, thoughtful, and refined nature. He was constitutionally timid, with a sensitive conscience and great religious susceptibilities. He was a finished scholar, and might have gained a literary reputation; but he had chosen another career, and one for which he seemed but ill fitted. Physically, however, he was well matched with his work; for, though his frame was slight, he was so active that none of the Indians could surpass him in running.

With him were two young men, René Goupil and Guillaume Couture, *donnés* of the mission, — that is to say, laymen who, from a religious motive and without pay, had attached themselves to the service of the Jesuits. Goupil had formerly entered upon the Jesuit novitiate at Paris, but failing health had obliged him to leave it. As soon as he was able, he came to Canada, offered his services to the Superior of the mission, was employed for a time in the humblest offices, and afterwards became an attendant at the hospital. At length, to his delight, he received permission to go up to the Hurons, where the surgical skill which he had acquired was greatly needed; and he was now on his way thither. His companion, Couture, was a man of intelligence and vigor, and of character equally disinterested. Both were, like Jogues, in the foremost canoes; while the fourth Frenchman was with the unconverted Hurons, in the rear.

The twelve canoes had reached the western end of the Lake of St. Peter, where it is filled with innumerable islands. The forest was close on their right; they kept near the shore to avoid the current; and the shallow water before them was covered with a dense growth of tall bulrushes. Suddenly the silence was frightfully broken. The war-whoop rose from among the rushes, mingled with the reports of guns and the whistling of bullets; and several Iroquois canoes, filled with warriors, pushed out from their concealment, and bore down upon Jogues and his companions. The Hurons in the rear were seized with a shameful panic. They leaped ashore; left canoes, baggage, and weapons, and fled into the woods. The French and the Christian Hurons made fight for a time; but when they saw another fleet of canoes approaching from the opposite shores or islands, they lost heart, and those escaped who could. Goupil was seized amid triumphant yells, as were also several of the Huron converts. Jogues sprang into the bulrushes, and might have escaped; but when he saw Goupil and the neophytes in the clutches of the Iroquois, he had no heart to abandon them, but came out from his hiding-place, and gave himself up to the astonished victors. A few of them had remained to guard the prisoners; the rest were chasing the fugitives. Jogues mastered his agony, and began to baptize those of the captive converts who needed baptism.

Couture had eluded pursuit; but when he thought of Jogues and of what perhaps awaited him, he resolved to share his fate, and, turning, retraced his steps. As he approached, five Iroquois ran forward to meet him; and one of them snapped his gun at his breast, but it missed fire. In his confusion and excitement, Couture fired his own piece, and laid the savage dead. The remaining four sprang upon him, stripped off all his clothing, tore away his finger-nails with their teeth, gnawed his fingers with the fury of famished dogs, and thrust a sword through one of his hands. Jogues broke from his guards, and, rushing to his friend, threw his arms about his neck. The Iroquois dragged him away, beat him with their fists and war-clubs till he was senseless, and, when he revived, lacerated his fingers with their teeth, as they had done those of Couture. Then they turned upon Goupil, and treated him with the same ferocity. The Huron prisoners were left for the present unharmed. More of them were brought in every moment, till at length the number of captives amounted in all to twenty-two, while three Hurons had been killed in the fight and pursuit. The Iroquois, about seventy in number, now embarked with their prey; but not until they had knocked on the head an old Huron, whom Jogues, with his mangled hands, had just baptized, and who refused to leave the place. Then, under a burning sun, they crossed to the spot on which the town of Sorel now stands, at the mouth of the river Richelieu, where they encamped.

Their course was southward, up the river Richelieu and Lake Champlain; thence, by way of Lake George, to the Mohawk towns. The pain and fever of their wounds, and the clouds of mosquitoes, which they could not drive off, left the prisoners no peace by day nor sleep by night. On the eighth day, they learned that a large Iroquois war-party, on their way to Canada, were near at hand; and they soon approached their camp, on a small island near the southern end of Lake Champlain. The warriors, two hundred in number, saluted their victorious countrymen with volleys from their guns; then, armed with clubs and thorny sticks, ranged themselves in two lines, between which the captives were compelled to pass up the side of a rocky hill. On the way, they were beaten with such fury that Jogues, who was last in the line, fell powerless, drenched in blood and half dead. As the chief man among the French captives, he fared the worst. His hands were again mangled, and fire applied to his body; while the Huron chief, Eustache, was subjected to tortures even more atrocious. When, at night, the exhausted sufferers tried to rest, the young warriors came to lacerate their wounds and pull out their hair and beards.

In the morning they resumed their journey. And now the lake narrowed to the semblance of a tranquil river. Before them was a woody mountain, close on their right a rocky promontory, and between these flowed a stream, the outlet of Lake George. On those rocks, more than a hundred years after, rose the ramparts of Ticonderoga. They landed, shouldered their canoes and baggage, took their way through the woods, passed the spot where the fierce Highlanders and the dauntless regiments of England breasted in vain the storm and lead and fire, and soon reached the shore where Abercrombie landed and Lord Howe fell. First of white men, Jogues and his companions gazed on the romantic lake that bears the name, not of its gentle discoverer, but of the dull Hanoverian king. Like a fair Naiad of the wilderness, it slumbered between the guardian mountains that breathe from crag and forest the stern poetry of war. But all then was solitude; and the clang of trumpets, the roar of cannon, and the deadly crack of the rifle had never as yet awakened their angry echoes.[1]

Again the canoes were launched, and the wild flotilla glided on its way, — now in the shadow of the heights, now on the broad expanse, now among the devious channels of the narrows, beset with woody islets, where the hot air was redolent of the pine, the spruce, and the cedar, — till they neared that tragic shore, where, in the following century, New-England rustics baffled the soldiers of Dieskau, where Montcalm planted his batteries, where the red cross waved so long amid the smoke, and where at length the summer night was hideous with carnage, and an honored name was stained with a memory of blood.

The Iroquois landed at or near the future site of Fort William Henry, left their canoes, and, with their prisoners, began their march for the nearest Mohawk town. Each bore his share of the plunder. Even Jogues, though his lacerated hands were in a frightful condition and his body covered with bruises, was forced to stagger on with the rest under a heavy load. He with his fellow-prisoners, and indeed the whole party, were half starved, subsisting chiefly on wild berries. They crossed the upper Hudson, and in thirteen days after leaving the St. Lawrence neared the wretched goal of their pilgrimage, — a palisaded town, standing on a hill by the banks of the river Mohawk.

The whoops of the victors announced their approach, and the savage hive sent forth its swarms. They thronged the side of the hill, the old

---

[1] Lake George, according to Jogues, was called by the Mohawks *Andiatarocte*, or "Place where the lake closes." I have seen an old Latin map on which the name "Horiconi" is set down as belonging to a neighboring tribe. This seems to be only a misprint for "Iroquoi," or "Iroquois." In 1646 the lake was named "Lac St. Sacrement."

and the young, each with a stick, or a slender iron rod, bought from the Dutchmen on the Hudson. They ranged themselves in a double line, reaching upward to the entrance of the town; and through this "narrow road of Paradise," as Jogues calls it, the captives were led in single file, — Couture in front, after him a half-score of Hurons, then Goupil, then the remaining Hurons, and at last Jogues. As they passed, they were saluted with yells, screeches, and a tempest of blows. One, heavier than the others, knocked Jogues's breath from his body, and stretched him on the ground; but it was death to lie there, and, regaining his feet, he staggered on with the rest. When they reached the town, the blows ceased, and they were all placed on a scaffold, or high platform, in the middle of the place. The three Frenchmen had fared the worst, and were frightfully disfigured. Goupil, especially, was streaming with blood, and livid with bruises from head to foot.

They were allowed a few minutes to recover their breath, undisturbed, except by the hootings and gibes of the mob below. Then a chief called out, "Come, let us caress these Frenchmen!" — and the crowd, knife in hand, began to mount the scaffold. They ordered a Christian Algonquin woman, a prisoner among them, to cut off Jogues's left thumb, which she did; and a thumb of Goupil was also severed, a clam-shell being used as the instrument, in order to increase the pain. It is needless to specify further the tortures to which they were subjected, all designed to cause the greatest possible suffering without endangering life. At night, they were removed from the scaffold and placed in one of the houses, each stretched on his back, with his limbs extended, and his ankles and wrists bound fast to stakes driven into the earthen floor. The children now profited by the examples of their parents, and amused themselves by placing live coals and red-hot ashes on the naked bodies of the prisoners, who, bound fast, and covered with wounds and bruises which made every movement a torture, were sometimes unable to shake them off.

In the morning, they were again placed on the scaffold, where, during this and the two following days, they remained exposed to the taunts of the crowd. Then they were led in triumph to the second Mohawk town, and afterwards to the third,[2] suffering at each a repetition of cruelties, the detail of which would be as monotonous as revolting.

---

[2] The Mohawks had but three towns. The first, and the lowest on the river, was Osseruenon; the second, two miles above, was Andagaron; and the third, Teonontogen. They all seem to have been fortified in the Iroquois manner, and their united population was 3500, or somewhat more.

In a house in the town of Teonontogen, Jogues was hung by the wrists between two of the upright poles which supported the structure, in such a manner that he remained for some fifteen minutes, in extreme torture, until, as he was on the point of swooning, an Indian, with an impulse for pity, cut the cords and released him. While they were in this town, four fresh Huron prisoners, just taken, were brought in, and placed on the scaffold with the rest. Jogues, in the midst of his pain and exhaustion, took the opportunity to convert them. An ear of green corn was thrown to him for food, and he discovered a few rain-drops clinging to the husks. With these he baptized two of the Hurons. The remaining two received baptism soon after from a brook which the prisoners crossed on the way to another town.

Couture, though he had incensed the Indians by killing one of their warriors, had gained their admiration by his bravery; and, after torturing him most savagely, they adopted him into one of their families, in place of a dead relative. Thenceforth he was compara-tively safe. Jogues and Goupil were less fortunate. Three of the Hurons had been burned to death, and they expected to share their fate. A council was held to pronounce their doom; but dissensions arose, and no result was reached. They were led back to the first village, where they remained, racked with suspense and half dead with ex-haustion. Jogues, however, lost no opportunity to baptize dying infants, while Goupil taught children to make the sign of the cross. On one occasion, he made the sign on the forehead of a child, grandson of an Indian in whose lodge they lived. The superstition of the old savage was aroused. Some Dutchmen had told him that the sign of the cross came from the Devil, and would cause mischief. He thought that Goupil was bewitching the child; and, resolving to rid himself of so dangerous a guest, applied for aid to two young braves. Jogues and Goupil, clad in their squalid garb of tattered skins, were soon after walking together in the forest that adjoined the town, consoling them-selves with prayer, and mutually exhorting each other to suffer pa-tiently for the sake of Christ and the Virgin, when, as they were returning, reciting their rosaries, they met the two young Indians, and read in their sullen visages an augury of ill. The Indians joined them, and accompanied them to the entrance of the town, where one of the two, suddenly drawing a hatchet from beneath his blanket, struck it into the head of Goupil, who fell, murmuring the name of Christ. Jogues dropped on his knees, and, bowing his head in prayer, awaited the blow, when the murderer ordered him to get up and go home. He obeyed, but not until he had given absolution to his still breathing friend, and presently saw the lifeless body dragged through the town amid hootings and rejoicings.

Jogues passed a night of anguish and desolation, and in the morning, reckless of life, set forth in search of Goupil's remains. "Where are you going so fast?" demanded the old Indian, his master. "Do you not see those fierce young braves, who are watching to kill you?" Jogues persisted, and the old man asked another Indian to go with him as a protector. The corpse had been flung into a neighboring ravine, at the bottom of which ran a torrent; and here, with the Indian's help, Jogues found it, stripped naked, and gnawed by dogs. He dragged it into the water, and covered it with stones to save it from further mutilation, resolving to return alone on the following day and secretly bury it. But with the night there came a storm; and when, in the gray of the morning, Jogues descended to the brink of the stream, he found it a rolling, turbid flood, and the body was nowhere to be seen. Had the Indians or the torrent borne it away? Jogues waded into the cold current: it was the first of October; he sounded it with his feet and with his stick; he searched the rocks, the thicket, the forest; but all in vain. Then, crouched by the pitiless stream, he mingled his tears with its waters, and, in a voice broken with groans, chanted the service of the dead.

The Indians, it proved, and not the flood, had robbed him of the remains of his friend. Early in the spring, when the snows were melting in the woods, he was told by Mohawk children that the body was lying, where it had been flung, in a lonely spot lower down the stream. He went to seek it; found the scattered bones, stripped by the foxes and the birds; and, tenderly gathering them up, hid them in a hollow tree, hoping that a day might come when he could give them a Christian burial in consecrated ground.

After the murder of Goupil, Jogues's life hung by a hair. He lived in hourly expectation of the tomahawk, and would have welcomed it as a boon. By signs and words, he was warned that his hour was near; but, as he never shunned his fate, it fled from him, and each day, with renewed astonishment, he found himself still among the living.

Late in the autumn, a party of the Indians set forth on their yearly deer-hunt, and Jogues was ordered to go with them. Shivering and half-famished, he followed them through the chill November forest, and shared their wild bivouac in the depths of the wintry desolation. The game they took was devoted to Areskoui, their god, and eaten in his honor. Jogues would not taste the meat offered to a demon; and thus he starved in the midst of plenty. At night, when the kettle was slung, and the savage crew made merry around their fire, he crouched in a corner of the hut, gnawed by hunger, and pierced to the bone with cold. They thought his presence unpropitious to their hunting, and the women especially hated him. His demeanor at once astonished and incensed his masters. He brought them firewood, like a squaw; he did their bidding without a murmur, and patiently bore their abuse; but when they mocked at his God, and laughed at his devotions, their slave assumed an air and tone of authority, and sternly rebuked them.

He would sometimes escape from "this Babylon," as he calls the hut, and wander in the forest, telling his beads and repeating passages of Scripture. In a remote and lonely spot, he cut the bark in the form of a cross from the trunk of a great tree; and here he made his prayers. This living martyr, half clad in shaggy furs, kneeling on the snow among the icicled rocks and beneath the gloomy pines, bowing in adoration before the emblem of the faith in which was his only consolation and his only hope, is alike a theme for the pen and a subject for the pencil.

The Indians at last grew tired of him, and sent him back to the village. Here he remained till the middle of March, baptizing infants and trying to convert adults. He told them of the sun, moon, planets, and stars. They listened with interest; but when from astronomy he passed to theology, he spent his breath in vain. In March, the old man with whom he lived set forth for his spring fishing, taking with him his squaw and several children. Jogues also was of the party. They repaired to a lake, perhaps Lake Saratoga, four days distant. Here they subsisted for some time on frogs, the entrails of fish, and other garbage. Jogues passed his days in the forest, repeating his prayers, and carving the name of Jesus on trees, as a terror to the demons of the wilderness. A messenger at length arrived from the town; and on the following day, under the pretence that signs of an enemy had been seen, the party broke up their camp, and returned home in hot haste. The messenger had brought tidings that a war-party, which had gone out against the French, had been defeated and destroyed, and that the whole population were clamoring to appease their grief by torturing Jogues to death. This was the true cause of the sudden and mysterious return; but when they reached the town, other tidings had arrived. The missing warriors were safe, and on their way home in triumph with a large number of prisoners. Again Jogues's life was spared; but he was forced to witness the torture and butchery of the converts and allies of the French. Existence became unendurable to him, and he longed to die. War-parties were continually going out. Should they be defeated and cut off, he would pay the forfeit at the stake; and if they came back, as they usually did, with booty and prisoners, he was doomed to see his countrymen and their Indian friends mangled, burned, and devoured.

Jogues had shown no disposition to escape, and great liberty was therefore allowed him. He went from town to town, giving absolution to the Christian captives, and converting and baptizing the heathen. On one occasion, he baptized a woman in the midst of the fire, under pretence of lifting a cup of water to her parched lips. There was no lack of objects for his zeal. A single war-party returned from the Huron country with nearly a hundred prisoners, who were distributed among the Iroquois towns, and the greater part burned. Of the children of the Mohawks and their neighbors, he had baptized, before August, about seventy; insomuch that he began to regard his captivity as a Providential interposition for the saving of souls.

At the end of July, he went with a party of Indians to a fishing-place on the Hudson, about twenty miles below Fort Orange. While here, he learned that another war-party had lately returned with prisoners, two of whom had been burned to death at Osseruenon. On this, his conscience smote him that he had not remained in the town to give the sufferers absolution or baptism; and he begged leave of the old woman who had him in charge to return at the first opportunity. A canoe soon after went up the river with some of the Iroquois, and he was allowed to go in it. When they reached Rensselaerswyck, the Indians landed to trade with the Dutch, and took Jogues with them.

The centre of this rude little settlement was Fort Orange, a miserable structure of logs, standing on a spot now within the limits of the city of Albany. It contained several houses and other buildings; and behind it was a small church, recently erected, and serving as the abode of the pastor, Dominie Megapolensis, known in our day as the writer of an interesting though short account of the Mohawks. Some twenty-five or thirty houses, roughly built of boards and roofed with thatch, were scattered at intervals on or near the borders of the Hudson, above and below the fort. Their inhabitants, about a hundred in number, were for the most part rude Dutch farmers, tenants of Van Rensselaer, the patroon, or lord of the manor. They raised wheat, of which they made beer, and oats, with which they fed their numerous horses. They traded, too, with the Indians, who profited greatly by the competition among them, receiving guns, knives, axes, kettles, cloth, and beads, at moderate rates, in exchange for their furs. The Dutch were on excellent terms with their red neighbors, met them in the forest without the least fear, and sometimes intermarried with them. They had known of Jogues's captivity, and, to their great honor, had made efforts for his release, offering for that purpose goods to a considerable value, but without effect.

At Fort Orange, Jogues heard startling news. The Indians of the village where he lived were, he was told, enraged against him, and determined to burn him. About the first of July, a war-party had set out for Canada, and one of the warriors had offered to Jogues to be the bearer of a letter from him to the French commander at Three Rivers, thinking probably to gain some advantage under cover of a parley. Jogues knew that the French would be on their guard; and he felt it his duty to lose no opportunity of informing them as to the state of affairs among the Iroquois. A Dutchman gave him a piece of paper; and he wrote a letter, in a jargon of Latin, French, and Huron, warning his countrymen to be on their guard, as war-parties were constantly going out, and they could hope for no respite from attack until late in the autumn. When the Iroquois reached the mouth of the river Richelieu, where a small fort had been built by the French the preceding summer, the messenger asked for a parley, and gave Jogues's letter to the commander of the post, who, after reading it, turned his cannon on the savages. They fled in dismay, leaving behind them their baggage and some of their guns; and returning home in a fury, charged Jogues with having caused their discomfiture. Jogues had expected this result, and was prepared to meet it; but several of the principal Dutch settlers, and among them Van Curler, who had made the previous attempt to rescue him, urged that his death was certain if he returned to the Indian town, and advised him to make his escape. In the Hudson, opposite the settlement, lay a small Dutch vessel nearly ready to sail. Van Curler offered him a passage in her to Bordeaux or Rochelle, — representing that the opportunity was too good to be lost, and making light of the prisoner's objection that a connivance in his escape on the part of the Dutch would excite the resentment of the Indians against them. Jogues thanked him warmly; but, to his amazement, asked for a night to consider the matter, and take counsel of God in prayer.

He spent the night in great agitation, tossed by doubt, and full of anxiety lest his self-love should beguile him from his duty. Was it not possible that the Indians might spare his life, and that, by a timely drop of water, he might still rescue souls from torturing devils and eternal fires of perdition? On the other hand, would he not, by remaining to meet a fate almost inevitable, incur the guilt of suicide? And even should he escape torture and death, could he hope that the Indians would again permit him to instruct and baptize their prisoners? Of his French companions, one, Goupil, was dead; while Couture had urged Jogues to flight, saying that he would then follow his example, but that, so long as the Father remained a prisoner, he, Couture, would share his fate. Before morning, Jogues had made his decision. God, he thought, would be better pleased should he embrace the opportunity given him. He went to find his Dutch friends, and, with a profusion of thanks, accepted their offer. They told him that a boat should be left for him on the shore, and that he must watch his time, and escape in it to the vessel, where he would be safe.

He and his Indian masters were lodged together in a large building, like a barn, belonging to a Dutch farmer. It was a hundred feet long, and had no partition of any kind. At one end the farmer kept his cattle; at the other he slept with his wife, a Mohawk squaw, and his children, while his Indian guests lay on the floor in the middle. As he is described as one of the principal persons of the colony, it is clear that the civilization of Rensselaerswyck was not high.

In the evening, Jogues, in such a manner as not to excite the suspicion of the Indians, went out to reconnoitre. There was a fence around the house, and, as he was passing it, a large dog belonging to the farmer flew at him, and bit him very severely in the leg. The Dutchman, hearing the noise, came out with a light, led Jogues back into the building, and bandaged his wound. He seemed to have some suspicion of the prisoner's design; for, fearful perhaps that his escape might exasperate the Indians, he made fast the door in such a manner that it could not readily be opened. Jogues now lay down among the Indians, who, rolled in their blankets, were stretched around him. He was fevered with excitement; and the agitation of his mind, joined to the pain of his wound, kept him awake all night. About dawn, while the Indians were still asleep, a laborer in the employ of the farmer came in with a lantern, and Jogues, who spoke no Dutch, gave him to understand by signs that he needed his help and guidance. The man was disposed to aid him, silently led the way out, quieted the dogs, and showed him the path to the river. It was more than half a mile distant, and the way was rough and broken. Jogues was greatly exhausted, and his wounded limb gave him such pain that he walked with the utmost difficulty. When he reached the shore, the day was breaking, and he found, to his dismay, that the ebb of the tide had left the boat high and dry. He shouted to the vessel, but no one heard him. His desperation gave him strength; and, by working the boat to and fro, he pushed it at length, little by little, into the water, entered it, and rowed to the vessel. The Dutch sailors received him kindly, and hid him in the bottom of the hold, placing a large box over the hatchway.

He remained two days, half stifled, in this foul lurking-place, while the Indians, furious at his escape, ransacked the settlement in vain to find him. They came off to the vessel, and so terrified the officers that Jogues was sent on shore at night, and led to the fort. Here he was hidden in the garret of a house occupied by a miserly old man, to whose charge he was consigned. Food was sent to him; but, as his host appropriated the larger part to himself, Jogues was nearly starved. There was a compartment of his garret, separated from the rest by a partition of boards. Here the old Dutchman, who, like many others of the settlers, carried on a trade with the Mohawks, kept a quantity of goods for that purpose; and hither he often brought his customers. The boards of the partition had shrunk, leaving wide crevices; and Jogues could plainly see the Indians, as they passed between him and the light. They, on their part, might as easily have seen him, if he had not, when he heard them entering the house, hidden himself behind some barrels in the corner; where he would sometimes remain crouched for hours, in a constrained and painful posture, half suffocated with heat, and afraid to move a limb. His wounded leg began to show dangerous symptoms; but he was relieved by the care of a Dutch surgeon of the fort. The minister, Megapolensis, also visited him, and did all in his power for the comfort of his Catholic brother, with whom he seems to have been well pleased, and whom he calls "a very learned scholar."

When Jogues had remained for six weeks in this hiding-place, his Dutch friends succeeded in satisfying his Indian masters by the payment of a large ransom. A vessel from Manhattan, now New York, soon after brought up an order from the Director-General, Kieft, that he should be sent to him. Accordingly he was placed in a small vessel, which carried him down the Hudson. The Dutch on board treated him with great kindness; and, to do him honor, they named after him one of the islands in the river. At Manhattan he found a dilapidated fort, garrisoned by sixty soldiers, and containing a stone church and the Director-General's house, together with storehouses and barracks. Near it were ranges of small houses, occupied chiefly by mechanics and laborers; while the dwellings of the remaining colonists, numbering in all four or five hundred, were scattered here and there on the island and the neighboring shores. The settlers were of different sects and nations, but chiefly Dutch Calvinists. Kieft told his guest that eighteen different languages were spoken at Manhattan. The colonists were in the midst of a bloody Indian war, brought on by their own besotted cruelty; and while Jogues was at the fort, some forty of the Dutch-men were killed on the neighboring farms, and many barns and houses burned.

The Director-General, with a humanity that was far from usual with him, exchanged Jogues's squalid and savage dress for a suit of Dutch cloth, and gave him passage in a small vessel which was then about to sail. The voyage was rough and tedious; and the passenger slept on deck or on a coil of ropes, suffering greatly from cold, and often drenched by the waves that broke over the vessel's side. At length she reached Falmouth, on the southern coast of England, when all the crew went ashore for a carouse, leaving Jogues alone on board. A boat presently came alongside with a gang of desperadoes, who boarded her, and rifled her of everything valuable, threatened Jogues with a pistol, and robbed him of his hat and coat. He obtained some assistance from the crew of a French ship in the harbor, and, on the day before Christmas, took passage in a small coal vessel for the neigh-boring coast of Brittany. In the following afternoon he was set on shore a little to the north of Brest, and, seeing a peasant's cottage not far off, he approached it, and asked the way to the nearest church. The peasant and his wife, as the narrative gravely tells us, mistook him, by reason of his modest deportment, for some poor but pious Irishman, and asked him to share their supper, after finishing his devotions, — an invitation which Jogues, half famished as he was, gladly accepted. He reached the church in time for the early mass, and with an unutterable joy knelt before the altar, and renewed the communion of which he had been deprived so long. When he returned to the cottage, the attention of his hosts was at once attracted to his mutilated and dis-torted hands. They asked with amazement how he could have received such injuries; and when they heard the story of his tortures, their surprise and veneration knew no bounds. Two young girls, their daughters, begged him to accept all they had to give, — a handful of sous; while the peasant made known the character of his new guest to his neighbors. A trader from Rennes brought a horse to the door, and offered the use of it to Jogues, to carry him to the Jesuit College in that town. He gratefully accepted it; and, on the morning of the 5th of January, 1644, reached his destination.

He dismounted, and knocked at the door of the college. The porter opened it, and saw a man wearing on his head an old woolen nightcap, and in an attire little better than that of a beggar. Jogues asked to see the Rector; but the porter answered, coldly, that the Rector was busied in the Sacristy. Jogues begged him to say that a man was at the door with news from Canada. The missions of Canada were at this time an object of primal interest to the Jesuits, and above all to the Jesuits of France. A letter from Jogues, written during his captivity, had already reached France, as had also the Jesuit *Relation* of 1643, which contained a long account of his capture; and he had no doubt been an engrossing theme of conversation in every house of the French Jesuits. The Father Rector was putting on his vestments to say mass; but when he heard that a poor man from Canada had asked for him at the door, he postponed the service, and went to meet him. Jogues, without discovering himself, gave him a letter from the Dutch Director-General attesting his character. The Rector, without reading it, began to question him as to the affairs of Canada, and at length asked him if he knew Father Jogues.

"I knew him very well," was the reply.

"The Iroquois have taken him," pursued the Rector. "Is he dead? Have they murdered him?"

"No," answered Jogues; "he is alive and at liberty, and I am he." And he fell on his knees to ask his Superior's blessing.

That night was a night of jubilation and thanksgiving in the college of Rennes.

Jogues became a centre of curiosity and reverence. He was summoned to Paris. The Queen, Anne of Austria, wished to see him; and when the persecuted slave of the Mohawks was conducted into her presence, she kissed his mutilated hands, while the ladies of the Court thronged around to do him homage. We are told, and no doubt with truth, that these honors were unwelcome to the modest and single-hearted missionary, who thought only of returning to his work of converting the Indians. A priest with any deformity of body is debarred from saying mass. The teeth and knives of the Iroquois had inflicted an injury worse than the torturers imagined, for they had robbed Jogues of the privilege which was the chief consolation of his life; but the Pope, by a special dispensation, restored it to him, and with the opening spring he sailed again for Canada.

CHAPTER VIII

The Martyrdom of Father Jogues
1645–1646

[The Jesuits in North America, CHAPTER XX in part]

It was the Mohawks who had made war on the French and their Indian allies on the lower St. Lawrence. They claimed, as against the other Iroquois, a certain right of domain to all this region; and though the warriors of the four upper nations had sometimes poached on the Mohawk preserve, by murdering both French and Indians at Montreal, they employed their energies for the most part in attacks on the Hurons, the Upper Algonquins, and other tribes of the interior. These attacks still continued, unaffected by the peace with the Mohawks. Imperfect, however, as the treaty was, it was invaluable, could it but be kept inviolate; and to this end Montmagny, the Jesuits, and all the colony anxiously turned their thoughts.

It was to hold the Mohawks to their faith that Couture had bravely gone back to winter among them; but an agent of more acknowledged weight was needed, and Father Isaac Jogues was chosen. No white man, Couture excepted, knew their language and their character so well. His errand was half political, half religious; for not only was he to be the bearer of gifts, wampum-belts, and messages from the Governor, but he was also to found a new mission, christened in advance with a prophetic name, — the Mission of the Martyrs.

For two years past, Jogues had been at Montreal; and it was here that he received the order of his Superior to proceed to the Mohawk towns. At first, nature asserted itself, and he recoiled involuntarily at the thought of the horrors of which his scarred body and his mutilated hands were a living memento. It was a transient weakness; and he prepared to depart with more than willingness, giving thanks to Heaven that he had been found worthy to suffer and to die for the saving of souls and the greater glory of God.

He felt a presentiment that his death was near, and wrote to a friend, "I shall go, and shall not return." An Algonquin convert gave him sage advice. "Say nothing about the Faith at first, for there is nothing so repulsive, in the beginning, as our doctrine, which seems to destroy everything that men hold dear; and as your long cassock preaches, as well as your lips, you had better put on a short coat." Jogues, therefore, exchanged the uniform of Loyola for a civilian's doublet and hose; "for," observes his Superior, "one should be all things to all men, that he may gain them all to Jesus Christ." It would be well if the application of the maxim had always been as harmless.

Jogues left Three Rivers about the middle of May, with the Sieur Bourdon, engineer to the Governor, two Algonquins with gifts to confirm the peace, and four Mohawks as guides and escort. He passed the Richelieu and Lake Champlain, well-remembered scenes of former miseries, and reached the foot of Lake George on the eve of Corpus Christi. Hence he called the lake "Lac St. Sacrement;" and this name it preserved, until, a century after, an ambitious Irishman, in compliment to the sovereign from whom he sought advancement, gave it the name it bears.

From Lake George they crossed on foot to the Hudson, where, being greatly fatigued by their heavy loads of gifts, they borrowed canoes at an Iroquois fishing-station, and descended to Fort Orange. Here Jogues met the Dutch friends to whom he owed his life, and who now kindly welcomed and entertained him. After a few days he left them, and ascended the river Mohawk to the first Mohawk town. Crowds gathered from the neighboring towns to gaze on the man whom they had known as a scorned and abused slave, and who now appeared among them as the ambassador of a power which hitherto, indeed, they had despised, but which in their present mood they were willing to propitiate.

There was a council in one of the lodges; and while his crowded auditory smoked their pipes, Jogues stood in the midst, and harangued them. He offered in due form the gifts of the Governor, with the wampum belts and their messages of peace, while at every pause his words were echoed by a unanimous grunt of applause from the attentive concourse. Peace speeches were made in return; and all was harmony. When, however, the Algonquin deputies stood before the council, they and their gifts were coldly received. The old hate, maintained by traditions of mutual atrocity, burned fiercely under a thin semblance of peace; and though no outbreak took place, the prospect of the future was very ominous.

The business of the embassy was scarcely finished, when the Mohawks counselled Jogues and his companions to go home with all despatch, saying that if they waited longer, they might meet on the way warriors of of the four upper nations, who would inevitably kill the two Algonquin deputies, if not the French also. Jogues, therefore, set out on his return; but not until, despite the advice of the Indian convert, he had made the round of the houses, confessed and instructed a few Christian prisoners still remaining here, and baptized several dying Mohawks. Then he and his party crossed through the forest to the southern extremity of Lake George, made bark canoes, and descended to Fort Richelieu, where they arrived on the twenty-seventh of June.

His political errand was accomplished. Now, should he return to the Mohawks, or should the Mission of the Martyrs be for a time abandoned? Lalemant, who had succeeded Vimont as Superior of the missions, held a council at Quebec with three other Jesuits, of whom Jogues was one, and it was determined, that, unless some new contingency should arise, he should remain for the winter at Montreal. This was in July. Soon after, the plan was changed, for reasons which do not appear, and Jogues received orders to repair to his dangerous post. He set out on the 24th of August, accompanied by a young Frenchman named Lalande, and three or four Hurons. On the way they met Indians who warned them of a change of feeling in the Mohawk towns, and the Hurons, alarmed, refused to go farther. Jogues, naturally perhaps the most timid man of the party, had no thought of drawing back, and pursued his journey with his young companion, who, like other *donnés* of the missions, was scarcely behind the Jesuits themselves in devoted enthusiasm.

The reported change of feeling had indeed taken place; and the occasion of it was characteristic. On his previous visit to the Mohawks, Jogues, meaning to return, had left in their charge a small chest or box. From the first they were distrustful, suspecting that it contained some secret mischief. He therefore opened it, and showed them the contents, which were a few personal necessaries; and having thus, as he thought, reassured them, locked the box, and left it in their keeping. The Huron prisoners in the town attempted to make favor with their Iroquois enemies by abusing their French friends, — declaring them to be sorcerers, who had bewitched, by their charms and mummeries, the whole Huron nation, and caused drought, famine, pestilence, and a host of insupportable miseries. Thereupon, the suspicions of the Mohawks against the box revived with double force; and they were convinced that famine, the pest, or some malignant spirit was shut up in it, waiting the moment to issue forth and destroy them. There was sickness in the town, and caterpillars were eating their corn: this was ascribed to the sorceries of the Jesuit. Still they were divided in opinion. Some stood firm for the French; others were furious against them. Among the Mohawks, three clans or families were predominant, if indeed they did not compose the entire nation, — the clans of the Bear, the Tortoise, and the Wolf. Though, by the nature of their constitution, it was scarcely possible that these clans should come to blows, so intimately were they bound together by ties of blood, yet they were often divided on points of interest or policy and on this occasion the Bear raged against the French, and howled for war, while the Tortoise and the Wolf still clung to the treaty. Among savages, with no government except the intermittent one of councils, the party of action and violence must always prevail. The Bear chiefs sang their war-songs, and, followed by the young men of their own clan, and by such others as they had infected with their frenzy, set forth, in two bands, on the war-path.

The warriors of one of these bands were making their way through the forests between the Mohawk and Lake George, when they met Jogues and Lalande. They seized them, stripped them, and led them in triumph to their town. Here a savage crowd surrounded them, beating them with sticks and with their fists. One of them cut thin strips of flesh from the back and arms of Jogues, saying, as he did so, "Let us see if this white flesh is the flesh of an oki." — "I am a man like yourselves," replied Jogues; "but I do not fear death or torture. I do not know why you would kill me. I come here to confirm the peace and show you the way to heaven, and you treat me like a dog." — "You shall die to-morrow," cried the rabble. "Take courage, we shall not burn you. We shall strike you both with a hatchet, and place your heads on the palisade, that your brothers may see you when we take them prisoners." The clans of the Wolf and the Tortoise still raised their voices in behalf of the captive Frenchmen; but the fury of the minority swept all before it.

In the evening, — it was the 18th of October — Jogues, smarting with his wounds and bruises, was sitting in one of the lodges, when an

Indian entered, and asked him to a feast. To refuse would have been an offence. He arose and followed the savage, who led him to the lodge of the Bear chief. Jogues bent his head to enter, when another Indian, standing concealed within, at the side of the doorway, struck at him with a hatchet. An Iroquois, called by the French Le Berger, who seems to have followed in order to defend him, bravely held out his arm to ward off the blow; but the hatchet cut through it, and sank into the missionary's brain. He fell at the feet of his murderer, who at once finished the work by hacking off his head. Lalande was left in suspense all night, and in the morning was killed in a similar manner. The bodies of the two Frenchmen were then thrown into the Mohawk, and their heads displayed on the points of the palisade which enclosed the town.

Thus died Isaac Jogues, one of the purest examples of Roman Catholic virtue which this Western continent has seen. The priests, his associates, praise his humility, and tell us that it reached the point of self-contempt, — a crowning virtue in their eyes; that he regarded himself as nothing, and lived solely to do the will of God as uttered by the lips of his Superiors. They add that, when left to the guidance of his own judgment, his self-distrust made him very slow of decision, but that when acting under orders he knew neither hesitation nor fear. With all his gentleness, he had a certain warmth of vivacity of temperament; and we have seen how, during his first captivity, while humbly submitting to every caprice of his tyrants and appearing to rejoice in abasement, a derisive word against his faith would change the lamb into the lion, and the lips that seemed so tame would speak in sharp, bold tones of menace and reproof.

CHAPTER IX

The Heroes of the Long Saut
1660–1661

[*The Old Regime in Canada*, CHAPTER VI]

Canada had writhed for twenty years, with little respite, under the scourge of Iroquois war. During a great part of this dark period the entire French population was less than three thousand. What, then, saved them from destruction? In the first place, the settlements were grouped around three fortified posts, — Quebec, Three Rivers, and Montreal, — which in time of danger gave asylum to the fugitive inhabitants. Again, their assailants were continually distracted by other wars, and never, except at a few spasmodic intervals, were fully in earnest to destroy the French colony. Canada was indispensable to them. The four upper nations of the league soon became dependent on her for supplies; and all the nations alike appear, at a very early period, to have conceived the policy on which they afterwards distinctly acted, of balancing the rival settlements of the Hudson and the St. Lawrence, the one against the other. They would torture, but not kill. It was but rarely that, in fits of fury, they struck their hatchets at the brain; and thus the bleeding and gasping colony lingered on in torment.

The seneschal of New France, son of the governor Lauson, was surprised and killed on the island of Orleans, along with seven companions. About the same time, the same fate befell the son of Godefroy, one of the chief inhabitants of Quebec. Outside the fortifications there was no safety for a moment. A universal terror seized the people. A comet appeared above Quebec, and they saw in it a herald of destruction. Their excited imaginations turned natural phenomena into portents and prodigies. A blazing canoe sailed across the sky; confused cries and lamentations were heard in the air; and a voice of thunder sounded from mid-heaven. The Jesuits despaired for their scattered and persecuted flocks. "Everywhere," writes their superior, "we see infants to be saved for heaven, sick and dying to be baptized, adults to be instructed; but everywhere we see the Iroquois. They haunt us like persecuting goblins. They kill our new-made Christians in our arms. If they meet us on the river, they kill us. If they find us in the huts of our Indians, they burn us and them together." And he appeals urgently for troops to destroy them, as a holy work inspired by God, and needful for his service.

Canada was still a mission, and the influence of the Church was paramount and pervading. At Quebec, as at Montreal, the war with the Iroquois was regarded as a war with the hosts of Satan. Of the settlers' cabins scattered along the shores above and below Quebec, many were provided with small iron cannon, made probably by blacksmiths in the colony; but they had also other protectors. In each was an image of the Virgin or some patron saint; and every morning the pious settler knelt before the shrine to beg the protection of a celestial hand in his perilous labors of the forest or the farm.

When, in the summer of 1658, the young Vicomte d'Argenson came to assume the thankless task of governing the colony, the Iroquois war was at its height. On the day after his arrival, he was washing his hands before seating himself at dinner in the hall of the Château St. Louis, when cries of alarm were heard, and he was told that the Iroquois were close at hand. In fact, they were so near that their war-whoops and the screams of their victims could plainly be heard. Argenson left his guests, and, with such a following as he could muster at the moment, hastened to the rescue; but the assailants were too nimble for him. The forests, which grew at that time around Quebec, favored them both in attack and in retreat. After a year or two of experience, he wrote urgently to the court for troops. He adds that, what with the demands of the harvest and the unmilitary character of many of the settlers, the colony could not furnish more than a hundred men for offensive operations. A vigorous, aggressive war, he insists, is absolutely necessary, and this not only to save the colony, but to save the only true faith; "for," to borrow his own words, "it is this colony alone which has the honor to be in the communion of the Holy Church. . . . "

In May, 1660, a party of French Algonquins captured a Wolf, or Mohegan, Indian, naturalized among the Iroquois, brought him to Quebec, and burned him there with their usual atrocity of torture.

A modern Catholic writer says that the Jesuits could not save him; but this is not so. Their influence over the consciences of the colonists was at that time unbounded, and their direct political power was very great. A protest on their part, and that of the newly arrived bishop, who was in their interest, could not have failed of effect. The truth was, they did not care to prevent the torture of prisoners of war, — not solely out of that spirit of compliance with the savage humor of Indian allies which stains so often the pages of French American history, but also, and perhaps chiefly, from motives purely religious. Torture, in their eyes, seems to have been a blessing in disguise. They thought it good for the soul, and in case of obduracy the surest way of salvation. "We have very rarely indeed," writes one of them, "seen the burning of an Iroquois without feeling sure that he was on the path to paradise; and we never knew one of them to be surely on the path to paradise without seeing him pass through this fiery punishment." So they let the Wolf burn; but first, having instructed him after their fashion, they baptized him, and his savage soul flew to heaven out of the fire. "Is it not," pursues the same writer, "a marvel to see a wolf changed at one stroke into a lamb, and enter into the fold of Christ, which he came to ravage?"

Before he died, he requited their spiritual cares with a startling secret. He told them that 800 Iroquois warriors were encamped below Montreal; that 400 more, who had wintered on the Ottawa, were on the point of joining them; and that the united force would swoop upon Quebec, kill the governor, lay waste the town, and then attack Three Rivers and Montreal. This time, at least, the Iroquois were in deadly earnest. Quebec was wild with terror. The Ursulines and the nuns of the Hôtel Dieu took refuge in the strong and extensive building which the Jesuits had just finished, opposite the Parish Church. Its walls and palisades made it easy of defence; and in its yards and court were lodged the terrified Hurons, as well as the fugitive inhabitants of the neighboring settlements. Others found asylum in the fort, and others in the convent of the Ursulines, which, in place of nuns, was occupied by twenty-four soldiers, who fortified it with redoubts, and barricaded the doors and windows. Similar measures of defence were taken at the Hôtel Dieu, and the streets of the Lower Town were strongly barricaded. Everybody was in arms, and the *Qui vive* of the sentries and patrols resounded all night.

Several days passed, and no Iroquois appeared. The refugees took heart, and began to return to their deserted farms and dwellings. Among the rest was a family consisting of an old woman, her daughter, her son-in-law, and four small children, living near St. Anne, some twenty miles below Quebec. On reaching home, the old woman and the man went to their work in the fields, while the mother and children remained in the house. Here they were pounced upon and captured by eight renegade Hurons, Iroquois by adoption, who placed them in their large canoe, and paddled up the river with their prize. It was Saturday, a day dedicated to the Virgin; and the captive mother prayed to her for aid, "feeling," writes a Jesuit, "a full conviction that, in passing before Quebec on a Saturday, she would be delivered by the power of this Queen of Heaven." In fact, as the marauders and their captives glided in the darkness of night by Point Levi, under the shadow of the shore, they were greeted with a volley of musketry from the bushes, and a band of French and Algonquins dashed into the water to seize them. Five of the eight were taken, and the rest shot or drowned. The governor had heard of the descent at St. Anne, and despatched a party to lie in ambush for the authors of it. The Jesuits, it is needless to say, saw a miracle in the result. The Virgin had answered the prayer of her votary, — "though it is true," observes the father who records the marvel, "that, in the volley, she received a mortal wound." The same shot struck the infant in her arms. The prisoners were taken to Quebec, where four of them were tortured with even more ferocity than had been shown in the case of the unfortunate Wolf. Being questioned, they confirmed his story, and expressed great surprise that the Iroquois had not come, adding that they must have stopped to attack Montreal or Three Rivers. Again all was terror, and again days passed and no enemy appeared. Had the dying converts, so charitably despatched to heaven through fire, sought an unhallowed consolation in scaring the abettors of their torture with a lie? Not at all. Bating a slight exaggeration, they had told the truth. Where, then, were the Iroquois? As one small point of steel disarms the lightning of its terrors, so did the heroism of a few intrepid youths divert this storm of war, and save Canada from a possible ruin.

In the preceding April, before the designs of the Iroquois were known, a young officer named Daulac, commandant of the garrison of Montreal, asked leave of Maisonneuve, the governor, to lead a party of volunteers against the enemy. His plan was bold to desperation. It was known that Iroquois warriors in great numbers had wintered among the forests of the Ottawa. Daulac proposed to waylay them on their descent of the river, and fight them without regard to disparity of force. The settlers of Montreal had hitherto acted solely on the defensive, for their numbers had been too small for aggressive war. Of late their strength had been somewhat increased, and Maisonneuve, judging that a display of enterprise and boldness might act as a check on the audacity of the enemy, at length gave his consent.

Adam Daulac, or Dollard, Sieur des Ormeaux, was a young man of good family, who had come to the colony three years before, at the age of twenty-two. He had held some military command in France, though in what rank does not appear. It was said that he had been involved in some affair which made him anxious to wipe out the memory of the past by a noteworthy exploit; and he had been busy for some time among the young men of Montreal, inviting them to join him in the enterprise he meditated. Sixteen of them caught his spirit, struck hands with him, and pledged their word. They bound themselves by oath to accept no quarter; and, having Maisonneuve's consent, they made their wills, confessed, and received the sacraments. As they knelt for the last time before the altar in the chapel of the Hôtel Dieu, that sturdy little population of pious Indian-fighters gazed on them with enthusiasm, not unmixed with an envy which had in it nothing ignoble. Some of the chief men of Montreal, with the brave Charles Le Moyne at their head, begged them to wait till the spring sowing was over, that they might join them; but Daulac refused. He was jealous of the glory and the danger, and he wished to command, which he could not have done had Le Moyne been present.

The spirit of the enterprise was purely medieval. The enthusiasm of honor, the enthusiasm of adventure, and the enthusiasm of faith were its motive forces. Daulac was a knight of the early crusades among the forests and savages of the New World. Yet the incidents of this exotic heroism are definite and clear as a tale of yesterday. The names, ages, and occupations of the seventeen young men may still be read on the ancient register of the parish of Montreal; and the notarial acts of that year, preserved in the records of the city, contain minute accounts of such property as each of them possessed. The three eldest were of twenty-eight, thirty, and thirty-one years respectively. The age of the rest varied from twenty-one to twenty-seven. They were of various callings, — soldiers, armorers, locksmiths, lime-burners, or settlers without trades. The greater number had come to the colony as part of the reinforcement brought by Maisonneuve in 1653.

After a solemn farewell, they embarked in several canoes well supplied with arms and ammunition. They were very indifferent canoe-men; and it is said that they lost a week in vain attempts to pass the swift current of St. Anne, at the head of the island of Montreal. At length they were more successful, and entering the mouth of the Ottawa, crossed the Lake of Two Mountains, and slowly advanced against the current.

Meanwhile, forty warriors of that remnant of the Hurons who, in spite of Iroquois persecutions, still lingered at Quebec, had set out on a war-party, led by the brave and wily Etienne Annahotaha, their most noted chief. They stopped by the way at Three Rivers, where they found a band of Christian Algonquins under a chief named Mituvemeg. Annahotaha challenged him to a trial of courage, and it was agreed that they should meet at Montreal, where they were likely to find a speedy opportunity of putting their mettle to the test. Thither, accordingly, they repaired, the Algonquin with three followers, and the Huron with thirty-nine.

It was not long before they learned of the departure of Daulac and his companions. "For," observes the honest Dollier de Casson, "the principal fault of our Frenchmen is to talk too much." The wish seized them to share the adventure, and to that end the Huron chief asked the governor for a letter to Daulac, to serve as credentials. Maisonneuve hesitated. His faith in Huron valor was not great, and he feared the proposed alliance. Nevertheless, he at length yielded so far as to give Annahotaha a letter, in which Daulac was told to accept or reject the proffered reinforcement as he should see fit. The Hurons and Algonquins now embarked, and paddled in pursuit of the seventeen Frenchmen.

They meanwhile had passed with difficulty the swift current at Carillon, and about the first of May reached the foot of the more formidable rapid called the Long Saut, where a tumult of waters, foaming among ledges and boulders, barred the onward way. It was needless to go farther. The Iroquois were sure to pass the Saut, and could be fought here as well as elsewhere. Just below the rapid, where the forests sloped gently to the shore, among the bushes and stumps of the rough clearing made in constructing it, stood a palisade fort, the work of an Algonquin war-party in the past autumn. It was a mere enclosure of trunks of small trees planted in a circle, and was already runinous. Such as it was, the Frenchmen took possession of it. Their first care, one would think, should have been to repair and strengthen it; but this they seem not to have done, — possibly, in the exaltation of their minds, they scorned such precaution. They made their fires, and slung their kettles on the neighboring shore; and here they were soon joined by the Hurons and Algonquins. Daulac, it seems, made no objection to their company, and they all bivouacked together. Morning and noon and night they prayed in three different tongues; and when at sunset the long reach of forests on the farther shore basked peacefully in the level rays, the rapids joined their hoarse music to the notes of their evening hymn.

In a day or two their scouts came in with tidings that two Iroquois canoes were coming down the Saut. Daulac had time to set his men in ambush among the bushes at a point where he thought the strangers likely to land. He judged aright. The canoes, bearing five Iroquois, approached, and were met by a volley fired with such precipitation that one or more of them escaped the shot, fled into the forest, and told their mischance to their main body, 200 in number, on the river above. A fleet of canoes suddenly appeared, bounding down the rapids, filled with warriors eager for revenge. The allies had barely time to escape to their fort, leaving their kettles still slung over the fires. The Iroquois made a hasty and desultory attack, and were quickly repulsed. They next opened a parley, hoping, no doubt, to gain some advantage by surprise. Failing in this, they set themselves, after their custom on such occasions, to building a rude fort of their own in the neighboring forest.

This gave the French a breathing-time, and they used it for strengthening their defences. Being provided with tools, they planted a row of stakes within their palisade, to form a double fence, and filled the intervening space with earth and stones to the height of a man, leaving some twenty loop-holes, at each of which three marksmen were stationed. Their work was still unfinished when the Iroquois were upon them again. They had broken to pieces the birch canoes of the French and their allies, and, kindling the bark, rushed up to pile it blazing against the palisade; but so brisk and steady a fire met them that they recoiled, and at last gave way. They came on again, and again were driven back, leaving many of their number on the ground, — among them the principal chief of the Senecas. Some of the French dashed out, and, covered by the fire of their comrades, hacked off his head, and stuck it on the palisade, while the Iroquois howled in a frenzy of helpless rage. They tried another attack, and were beaten off a third time.

This dashed their spirits, and they sent a canoe to call to their aid five hundred of their warriors who were mustered near the mouth of the Richelieu. These were the allies whom, but for this untoward check, they were on their way to join for a combined attack on Quebec, Three Rivers, and Montreal. It was maddening to see their grand project thwarted by a few French and Indians ensconced in a paltry redoubt, scarcely better than a cattle pen; but they were forced to digest the affront as best they might.

Meanwhile, crouched behind trees and logs, they beset the fort, harassing its defenders day and night with a spattering fire and a constant menace of attack. Thus five days passed. Hunger, thirst, and want of sleep wrought fatally on the strength of the French and their allies, who, pent up together in their narrow prison, fought and prayed by turns. Deprived as they were of water, they could not swallow the crushed Indian corn, or "hominy," which was their only food. Some of them, under cover of a brisk fire, ran down to the river and filled such small vessels as they had; but this pittance only tantalized their thirst. They dug a hole in the fort, and were rewarded at last by a little muddy water oozing through the clay.

Among the assailants were a number of Hurons, adopted by the Iroquois and fighting on their side. These renegades now shouted to their countrymen in the fort, telling them that a fresh army was close at hand; that they would soon be attacked by seven or eight hundred warriors; and that their only hope was in joining the Iroquois, who would receive them as friends. Annahotaha's followers, half dead with thirst and famine, listened to their seducers, took the bait, and, one, two, or three at a time, climbed the palisade and ran over to the enemy, amid the hootings and execrations of those whom they deserted. Their chief stood firm; and when he saw his nephew, La Mouche, join the other fugitives, he fired his pistol at him in a rage. The four Algonquins, who had no mercy to hope for, stood fast, with the courage of despair.

On the fifth day an uproar of unearthly yells from seven hundred savage throats, mingled with a clattering salute of musketry, told the Frenchmen that the expected reinforcement had come; and soon, in the forest and on the clearing, a crowd of warriors mustered for the attack. Knowing from the Huron deserters the weakness of their enemy, they had no doubt of an easy victory. They advanced cautiously, as was usual with the Iroquois before their blood was up, screeching, leaping from side to side, and firing as they came on; but the French were at their posts, and every loophole darted its tongue of fire. Besides muskets, they had heavy musketoons of large calibre, which, scattering scraps of lead and iron among the throng of savages, often maimed several of them at one discharge. The Iroquois, astonished at the persistent vigor of the defence, fell back discomfited. The fire of the French, who were themselves completely under cover, had told upon them with deadly effect. Three days more wore away in a series of futile attacks, made with little concert or vigor; and during all this time Daulac and his men, reeling with exhaustion, fought and prayed as before, sure of a martyr's reward.

The uncertain, vacillating temper common to all Indians now began to declare itself. Some of the Iroquois were for going home. Others revolted at the thought, and declared that it would be an eternal disgrace to lose so many men at the hands of so paltry an enemy, and yet fail to take revenge. It was resolved to make a general assault, and volunteers were called for to lead the attack. After the custom on such occasions, bundles of small sticks were thrown upon the ground, and those picked them up who dared, thus accepting the gage of battle, and enrolling themselves in the forlorn hope. No precaution was neglected. Large and heavy shields four or five feet high were made by lashing together three split logs with the aid of cross-bars, Covering themselves with these mantelets, the chosen band advanced, followed by the motley throng of warriors. In spite of a brisk fire, they reached the palisade, and, crouching below the range of shot; hewed furiously with their hatchets to cut their way through. The rest followed close, and swarmed like angry hornets around the little fort, hacking and tearing to get in.

Daulac had crammed a large musketoon with powder, and plugged up the muzzle. Lighting the fuse inserted in it, he tried to throw it over the barrier, to burst like a grenade among the crowd of savages without; but it struck the ragged top of one of the palisades, fell back among the Frenchmen and exploded, killing and wounding several of them, and nearly blinding others. In the confusion that followed, the Iroquois got possession of the loopholes, and, thrusting in their guns, fired on those within. In a moment more they had torn a breach in the palisade; but nerved with the energy of desperation, Daulac and his followers sprang to defend it. Another breach was made, and then another. Daulac was struck dead, but the survivors kept up the fight. With a sword or a hatchet in one hand and a knife in the other, they threw themselves against the throng of enemies, striking and stabbing with the fury of madmen; till the Iroquois, despairing of taking them alive, fired volley after volley and shot them down. All was over, and a burst of triumphant yells proclaimed the dear-bought victory.

Searching the pile of corpses, the victors found four Frenchmen still breathing. Three had scarcely a spark of life, and as no time was to be lost, they burned them on the spot. The fourth, less fortunate, seemed likely to survive, and they reserved him for future torments. As for the Huron deserters, their cowardice profited them little. The Iroquois, regardless of their promises, fell upon them, burned some at once, and carried the rest to their villages for a similar fate. Five of the number had the good fortune to escape; and it was from them, aided by admissions made long afterwards by the Iroquois themselves, that the French of Canada derived all their knowledge of this glorious disaster.

To the colony it proved a salvation. The Iroquois had had fighting enough. If seventeen Frenchmen, four Algonquins, and one Huron, behind a picket fence, could hold 700 warriors at bay so long, what might they expect from many such, fighting behind walls of stone? For that year they thought no more of capturing Quebec and Montreal, but went home dejected and amazed, to howl over their losses, and nurse their dashed courage for a day of vengeance.

CHAPTER X

Marriage and Population
1661–1673

[*The Old Regime in Canada*, CHAPTER XVI]

[PREVIOUS CHAPTERS TOLD of the coming of Bishop Laval, the "Father of the Canadian Church," and his relations with the governors, most of whom were bent to his will; of the end of the Company régime and the inauguration of royal government for Canada in 1665 with the Marquis de Tracy as the first lieutenant general of King Louis XIV. He brought out with him two hundred soldiers of the Carignan-Salières Regiment, and before the end of 1665 some two thousand colonists had been landed at Quebec at the royal charge. Tracy in 1667 led his soldiers on a successful punitive expedition against the Mohawks, at the end of which that formidable tribe sued for peace and asked for Jesuit missionaries. The last chapter describes the efforts of the French authorities to organize new industries in Canada.]

The peopling of Canada was due in the main to the King. Before the accession of Louis XIV the entire population — priests, nuns, traders, and settlers — did not exceed twenty-five hundred; but scarcely had he reached his majority when the shipment of men to the colony was systematically begun. Even in Argenson's time, loads of emigrants sent out by the Crown were landed every year at Quebec. The Sulpitians of Montreal also brought over colonists to people their seigneurial estate; the same was true on a small scale of one or two other proprietors, and once at least the company sent a considerable number: yet the government was the chief agent of emigration. Colbert did the work, and the King paid for it.

In 1661, Laval wrote to the cardinals of the Propaganda that during the past two years the King had spent 200,000 livres on the colony; that since 1659 he had sent out 300 men a year; and that he had promised to send an equal number every summer during ten years. These men were sent by squads in merchant-ships, each one of which was required to carry a certain number. In many instances, emigrants were bound on their arrival to enter into the service of colonists already established. In this case the employer paid them wages, and after a term of three years they became settlers themselves.[1]

The destined emigrants were collected by agents in the provinces, conducted to Dieppe or Rochelle, and thence embarked. At first men were sent from Rochelle itself, and its neighborhood; but Laval remonstrated, declaring that he wanted none from that ancient stronghold of heresy. The people of Rochelle, indeed, found no favor in Canada. Another writer describes them as "persons of little conscience, and almost no religion," — adding that the Normans, Percherons, Picards, and peasants of the neighborhood of Paris are docile, industrious, and far more pious. "It is important," he concludes, "in beginning a new colony, to sow good seed." It was, accordingly, from the northwestern provinces that most of the emigrants were drawn. They seem in the main to have been a decent peasantry, though writers who from their position should have been well informed have denounced them in unmeasured terms.[2] Some of them could read and write, and some brought with them a little money.

Talon was constantly begging for more men, till Louis XIV at length took alarm. Colbert replied to the over-zealous intendant that the King did not think it expedient to depopulate France in order to people Canada; that he wanted men for his armies; and that the colony must rely chiefly on increase from within. Still the shipments did not cease; and, even while tempering the ardor of his agent, the King gave another proof how much he had the growth of Canada at heart.[3]

[1] Marie de l'Incarnation, letter of 18 August 1664. These *engagés* were sometimes also brought over by private persons.

[2] "Une foule d'aventuriers, ramassés au hazard en France, presque tous de la lie du peuple, la plupart oberés de dettes ou chargés de crimes," etc. (La Tour *Vie de Laval*). Mère Marie de l'Incarnation, after speaking of the emigrants as of a very mixed character, says that it would have been far better to send a few who were good Christians, rather than so many who give so much trouble. Le Clerc, on the other hand, is emphatic in praise, calling the early colonists "très honnêtes gens, ayant de la probité, de la droiture, et de la religion. . . . L'on a examiné et choisi les habitants, et renvoyé en France les personnes vicieuses."

[3] The King had sent out more emigrants than he had promised, to judge from the census reports during the years 1666, 1667 and 1668. The total population for

The regiment of Carignan-Salières had been ordered home, with the exception of four companies kept in garrison, and a considerable number discharged in order to become settlers. Of those who returned, six companies were a year or two later sent back, discharged in their turn, and converted into colonists. Neither men nor officers were positively constrained to remain in Canada; but the officers were told that if they wished to please his Majesty this was the way to do so; and both they and the men were stimulated by promises and rewards. Fifteen hundred livres were given to La Motte, because he had married in the country and meant to remain there. Six thousand livres were assigned to other officers because they had followed, or were about to follow, La Motte's example; and 12,000 were set apart to be distributed to the soldiers under similar conditions. Each soldier who consented to remain and settle was promised a grant of land and a hundred livres in money; or, if he preferred it, fifty livres with provisions for a year. This military colonization had a strong and lasting influence on the character of the Canadian people.

But if the colony was to grow from within, the new settlers must have wives. For some years past the Sulpitians had sent out young women for the supply of Montreal; and the King, on a larger scale, continued the benevolent work. Girls for the colony were taken from the hospitals of Paris and of Lyons, which were not so much hospitals for the sick as houses of refuge for the poor. Mother Mary writes in 1665 that a hundred had come that summer, and were nearly all provided with husbands, and that two hundred more were to come next year. The case was urgent, for the demand was great. Complaints, however, were soon heard that women from cities made indifferent partners; and peasant girls, healthy, strong, and accustomed to field-work, were demanded in their place. Peasant girls were therefore sent; but this was not all. Officers as well as men wanted wives; and Talon asked for a consignment of young ladies. His request was promptly answered. In 1667, he writes: "They send us eighty-four girls from Dieppe and twenty-five from Rochelle; among them are fifteen or twenty of pretty good birth; several of them are really *demoiselles*, and tolerably well brought up." They complained of neglect and hardship during the voyage. "I shall do what I can to soothe their discontent," adds the intendant; "for

---

those years is 3418, 4312, and 5870 respectively. A small part of this growth may be set down to emigration not under government auspices, and a large part to natural increase — which was enormous at this time, from causes which will soon appear.

if they write to their correspondents at home how ill they have been treated, it would be an obstacle to your plan of sending us next year a number of select young ladies."

Three years later we find him asking for three or four more in behalf of certain bachelor officers. The response surpassed his utmost wishes; and he wrote again: "It is not expedient to send more *demoiselles*. I have had this year fifteen of them, instead of the four I asked for."

As regards peasant girls, the supply rarely equalled the demand. Count Frontenac, Courcelle's successor complained of the scarcity: "If a hundred and fifty girls and as many servants," he says, "had been sent out this year, they would all have found husbands and masters within a month."

The character of these candidates for matrimony has not escaped the pen of slander. The caustic La Hontan, writing fifteen or twenty years after, draws the following sketch of the mothers of Canada: "After the regiment of Carignan was disbanded, ships were sent out freighted with girls of indifferent virtue, under the direction of a few pious old duennas, who divided them into three classes. These vestals were, so to speak, piled one on the other in three different halls, where the bridegrooms chose their brides as a butcher chooses his sheep out of the midst of the flock. There was wherewith to content the most fantastical in these three harems; for here were to be seen the tall and the short, the blond and the brown, the plump and the lean; everybody, in short, found a shoe to fit him. At the end of a fortnight not one was left. I am told that the plumpest were taken first, because it was thought that, being less active, they were more likely to keep at home, and that they could resist the winter cold better. Those who wanted a wife applied to the directresses, to whom they were obliged to make known their possessions and means of livelihood before taking from one of the three classes the girl whom they found most to their liking. The marriage was concluded forthwith, with the help of a priest and a notary; and the next day the governor-general caused the couple to be presented with an ox, a cow, a pair of swine, a pair of fowls, two barrels of salted meat, and eleven crowns in money." [4]

As regards the character of the girls, there can be no doubt that this amusing sketch is, in the main, maliciously untrue. Since the colony began, it had been the practice to send back to France women of the

[4] La Hontan *Nouveaux Voyages* I 11 (1709).

class alluded to by La Hontan, as soon as they became notorious. Those who were not taken from institutions of charity usually belonged to the families of peasants overburdened with children, and glad to find the chance of establishing them. How some of them were obtained appears from a letter of Colbert to Harlay, Archbishop of Rouen. "As in the parishes about Rouen," he writes, "fifty or sixty girls might be found who would be very glad to go to Canada to be married, I beg you to employ your credit and authority with the curés of thirty or forty of these parishes, to try to find in each of them one or two girls disposed to go voluntarily for the sake of a settlement in life."

Mistakes nevertheless occurred. "Along with the honest people," complains Mother Mary, "comes a great deal of *canaille* of both sexes, who cause a great deal of scandal." After some of the young women had been married at Quebec, it was found that they had husbands at home. The priests became cautious in tying the matrimonial knot, and Colbert thereupon ordered that each girl should provide herself with a certificate from the curé or magistrate of her parish to the effect that she was free to marry. Nor was the practical intendant unmindful of other precautions to smooth the path to the desired goal. "The girls destined for this country," he writes, "besides being strong and healthy, ought to be entirely free from any natural blemish or anything personally repulsive."

Thus qualified canonically and physically, the annual consignment of young women was shipped to Quebec, in charge of a matron employed and paid by the King. Her task was not an easy one, for the troop under her care was apt to consist of what Mother Mary in a moment of unwonted levity calls "mixed goods." [5] On one occasion the office was undertaken by the pious widow of Jean Bourdon. Her flock of 150 girls, says Mother Mary, "gave her no little trouble on the voyage, for they are of all sorts, and some of them are very rude and hard to manage." Madame Bourdon was not daunted. She not only saw her charge distributed and married, but she continued to receive and care for the subsequent ship-loads as they arrived summer after summer. She was indeed chief among the pious duennas of whom La Hontan irreverently speaks. Marguerite Bourgeoys did the same good offices for the young women sent to Montreal. Here the "King's girls," as they were called, were all lodged together in a house to

---

[5] "Une marchandise mêlée." The total number of girls sent from 1665 to 1673 inclusive was about 1000.

which the suitors repaired to make their selection. "I was obliged to live there myself," writes the excellent nun, "because families were to be formed;" that is to say, because it was she who superintended these extemporized unions. Meanwhile she taught the girls their catechism, and, more fortunate than Madame Bourdon, inspired them with a confidence and affection which they retained long after.

At Quebec, where the matrimonial market was on a large scale, a more ample bazaar was needed. That the girls were assorted into three classes, each penned up for selection in a separate hall, is a statement probable enough in itself, but resting on no better authority than that of La Hontan. Be this as it may, they were submitted together to the inspection of the suitor; and the awkward young peasant or the rugged soldier of Carignan was required to choose a bride without delay from among the anxious candidates. They, on their part, were permitted to reject any applicant who displeased them; and the first question, we are told, which most of them asked was whether the suitor had a house and a farm.

Great as was the call for wives, it was thought prudent to stimulate it. The new settler was at once enticed and driven into wedlock. Bounties were offered on early marriages. Twenty livres were given to each youth who married before the age of twenty, and to each girl who married before the age of sixteen. This, which was called the "King's gift," was exclusive of the dowry given by him to every girl brought over by his orders. The dowry varied greatly in form and value; but, according to Mother Mary, it was sometimes a house with provisions for eight months. More often it was fifty livres in household supplies, besides a barrel or two of salted meat. The royal solicitude extended also to the children of colonists already established. "I pray you," writes Colbert to Talon, "to commend it to the consideration of the whole people, that their prosperity, their subsistence, and all that is dear to them depend on a general resolution, never to be departed from, to marry youths at eighteen or nineteen years and girls at fourteen or fifteen; since abundance can never come to them except through the abundance of men." This counsel was followed by appropriate action. Any father of a family who, without showing good cause, neglected to marry his children when they had reached the ages of twenty and sixteen was fined; and each father thus delinquent was required to present himself every six months to the local authorities to declare what reason, if any, he had for such delay. Orders were issued, a little before the arrival of the yearly ships from

France, that all single men should marry within a fortnight after the landing of the prospective brides. No mercy was shown to the obdurate bachelor. Talon issued an order forbidding unmarried men to hunt, fish, trade with the Indians, or go into the woods under any pretence whatsoever. In short, they were made as miserable as possible. Colbert goes further. He writes to the intendant, "Those who may seem to have absolutely renounced marriage should be made to bear additional burdens, and be excluded from all honors; it would be well even to add some marks of infamy." The success of these measures was complete. "No sooner," says Mother Mary, "have the vessels arrived than the young men go to get wives; and, by reason of the great number, they are married by thirties at a time." Throughout the length and breadth of Canada, Hymen, if not Cupid, was whipped into a frenzy of activity. Dollier de Casson tells us of a widow who was married afresh before her late husband was buried.

Nor was the fatherly care of the King confined to the humbler classes of his colonists. He wished to form a Canadian *noblesse*, to which end early marriages were thought needful among officers and others of the better sort. The progress of such marriages was carefully watched and reported by the intendant. We have seen the reward bestowed upon La Motte for taking to himself a wife, and the money set apart for the brother officers who imitated him. In his despatch of October, 1667, the intendant announces that two captains are already married to two damsels of the country; that a lieutenant has espoused a daughter of the governor of Three Rivers; and that "four ensigns are in treaty with their mistresses, and are already half engaged." The paternal care of government, one would think, could scarcely go further.

It did, however, go further. Bounties were offered on children. The King, in council, passed a decree "that in future all inhabitants of the said country of Canada who shall have living children to the number of ten, born in lawful wedlock, not being priests, monks, or nuns, shall each be paid out of the moneys sent by his Majesty to the said country a pension of three hundred livres a year, and those who shall have twelve children, a pension of four hundred livres; and that, to this effect, they shall be required to declare the number of their children every year in the months of June or July to the intendant of justice, police, and finance, established in the said country, who, having verified the same, shall order the payment of said pensions, one-half in cash, and the other half at the end of each year." [6] This was applicable to all. Colbert had before offered a reward, intended specially for the better class, of 1200 livres to those who had fifteen children, and 800 to those who had ten.

These wise encouragements, as the worthy Faillon calls them, were crowned with the desired result. A despatch of Talon in 1670 informs the minister that most of the young women sent out last summer are pregnant already; and in 1671 he announces that from 600 to 700 children have been born in the colony during the year, — a prodigious number in view of the small population. The climate was supposed to be particularly favorable to the health of women, which is somewhat surprising in view of recent American experience. "The first reflection I have to make," says Dollier de Casson, "is on the advantage that women have in this place [Montreal] over men; for though the cold is very wholesome to both sexes, it is incomparably more so to the female, who is almost immortal here." Her fecundity matched her longevity, and was the admiration of Talon and his successors, accustomed as they were to the scanty families of France.

Why, with this great natural increase joined to an immigration which, though greatly diminishing, did not entirely cease, was there not a corresponding increase in the population of the colony? Why, more than half a century after the King took Canada in charge, did the census show a total of less than 25,000 souls? [7] The reasons will appear hereafter.

It is a peculiarity of Canadian immigration, at this its most flourishing epoch, that it was mainly an immigration of single men and single women. The cases in which entire families came over were comparatively few. The new settler was found by the King, sent over by the King, and supplied by the King with a wife, a farm and sometimes with a house. Well did Louis XIV earn the title of Father of New

[6] It was thought at this time that the Indians, mingled with the French, might become a valuable part of the population. The reproductive qualities of Indian women, therefore, became an object of Talon's attention, and he reports that they impair their fertility by nursing their children longer than is necessary; "but," he adds, "this obstacle to the speedy building up of the colony can be overcome by a police regulation."

[7] [According to the colonial censuses reported in Guy Frégault La Civilisation de la Nouvelle France (1944) p. 39, Canada had a population of 18,119 in 1713; 37,716 in 1734; and 55,009 in 1754. The 1713 figures apparently do not include about 2000 Acadians.]

France. But the royal zeal was spasmodic. The King was diverted to other cares; and soon after the outbreak of the Dutch war in 1672 the regular despatch of emigrants to Canada well-nigh ceased — though the practice of disbanding soldiers in the colony, giving them lands, and turning them into settlers, was continued in some degree, even to the last.

CHAPTER XI

The New Home
1665–1672

[The Old Régime in Canada, CHAPTER XVII]

We have seen the settler landed and married; let us follow him to his new home. At the end of Talon's administration, the head of the colony — that is to say, the island of Montreal and the borders of the Richelieu — was the seat of a peculiar colonization, the chief object of which was to protect the rest of Canada against Iroquois incursions. The lands along the Richelieu, from its mouth to a point above Chambly, were divided in large seigneurial grants among several officers of the regiment of Carignan, who in their turn granted out the land to the soldiers, reserving a sufficient portion as their own. The officer thus became a kind of feudal chief, and the whole settlement a permanent military cantonment admirably suited to the object in view. The disbanded soldier was practically a soldier still, but he was also a farmer and a landholder.

Talon had recommended this plan as being in accordance with the example of the Romans. "The practice of that politic and martial people," he wrote, "may, in my opinion, be wisely adopted in a country a thousand leagues distant from its monarch. And as the peace and harmony of peoples depend above all things on their fidelity to their sovereign, our first kings, better statesmen than is commonly supposed, introduced into newly conquered countries men of war, of approved trust, in order at once to hold the inhabitants to their duty within, and repel the enemy from without."

The troops were accordingly discharged, and settled not alone on the Richelieu, but also along the St. Lawrence, between Lake St. Peter and Montreal, as well as at some other points. The Sulpitians, feudal owners of Montreal, adopted a similar policy, and surrounded their island with a border of fiefs large and small, granted partly to officers and partly to humbler settlers, bold, hardy, and practised in bush-fighting. Thus a line of sentinels was posted around their entire shore, ready to give the alarm whenever an enemy appeared. About Quebec the settlements, covered as they were by those above, were for the most part of a more pacific character.

To return to the Richelieu. The towns and villages which have since grown upon its banks and along the adjacent shores of the St. Lawrence owe their names to these officers of Carignan, ancient lords of the soil, — Sorel, Chambly, Saint Ours, Contrecœur, Varennes, Verchères. Yet let it not be supposed that villages sprang up at once. The military seigneur, valiant and poor as Walter the Penniless, was in no condition to work such magic. His personal possessions usually consisted of little but his sword and the money which the King had paid him for marrying a wife. A domain varying from half a league to six leagues in front on the river, and from half a league to two leagues in depth, had been freely given him. When he had distributed a part of it in allotments to the soldiers, a variety of tasks awaited him, — to clear and cultivate his land; to build his seigneurial mansion, often a log hut;[1] to build a fort; to build a chapel; and to build a mill. To do all this at once was impossible. Chambly, the chief proprietor on the Richelieu, was better able than the others to meet the exigency. He built himself a good house, where, with cattle and sheep furnished by the King, he lived in reasonable comfort. The King's fort, close at hand, spared him and his tenants the necessity of building one for themselves, and furnished, no doubt, a mill, a chapel, and a chaplain. His brother officers, Sorel excepted, were less fortunate. They and their tenants were forced to provide defence as well as shelter. Their houses were all built together, and surrounded by a palisade, so as to form a little fortified village.

---

[1] [Like other nineteenth-century historians, Parkman supposed that the earliest settlers in North America, whether French, English or Dutch, built themselves log cabins. He had seen them as a youth on the New Hampshire-Quebec border, and assumed that such houses had been built from the first. This has been definitely disproved by Harold R. Shurtleff in *The Log Cabin Myth* (Cambridge 1939), but his references to Acadia and Quebec are few. Wilfred Jury *Sainte Marie Among the Hurons* (Toronto 1954), who has been reconstructing that mission, points out, on pages 38–39, quoting Mère Marie de l'Incarnation, that all the houses in Quebec, except two or three, were of a construction called *columbage pierotté*. This was a frame construction using short logs and clay to fill in between the posts and studs. He quotes Ramsay Traquair *The Cottages of Quebec* (Montreal, 1926) as an authority. Log construction for houses was introduced by the Swedes on the Delaware before 1640, and gradually spread along the North American frontier; but exactly when it reached Canada, and from what source, has not yet been ascertained.]

The ever-active benevolence of the King had aided them in the task, for the soldiers were still maintained by him while clearing the lands and building the houses destined to be their own; nor was it till this work was done that the provident government despatched them to Quebec with orders to bring back wives. The settler, thus lodged and wedded, was required on his part to aid in clearing lands for those who should come after him.[2]

It was chiefly in the more exposed parts of the colony that the houses were gathered together in palisaded villages, thus forcing the settler to walk or paddle some distance to his farm. He naturally preferred to build when he could on the front of his farm itself, near the river, which supplied the place of a road. As the grants of land were very narrow, his house was not far from that of his next neighbor; and thus a line of dwellings was ranged along the shore, forming what in local language was called a *côte*, — a use of the word peculiar to Canada, where it still prevails.

The impoverished seigneur rarely built a chapel. Most of the early Canadian churches were built with funds furnished by the seminaries of Quebec or of Montreal, aided by contributions of material and labor from the parishioners. Meanwhile mass was said in some house of the neighborhood by a missionary priest, paddling his canoe from village to village, or from *côte* to *côte*.

The mill was an object of the last importance. It was built of stone and pierced with loopholes, to serve as a blockhouse in case of attack. The great mill at Montreal was one of the chief defences of the place. It was at once the duty and the right of the seigneur to supply his tenants, or rather vassals, with this essential requisite; and they on their part were required to grind their grain at his mill, leaving the fourteenth part in payment. But for many years there was not a seigneury in Canada where this fraction would pay the wages of a miller; and, except the ecclesiastical corporations, there were few seigneurs who could pay the cost of building. The first settlers were usually forced to grind for themselves after the tedious fashion of the Indians.

Talon, in his capacity of counsellor, friend, and father to all Canada, arranged the new settlements near Quebec in the manner which he

---

[2] This applied to civil and military settlers alike. The established settler was allowed four years to clear two arpents of land for a newcomer. The soldiers were maintained by the King during a year, while preparing their farms and houses. Talon asked, in 1670, that two more years be given them.

judged best, and which he meant to serve as an example to the rest of the colony. It was his aim to concentrate population around this point, so that, should an enemy appear, the sound of a cannon-shot from the Château St. Louis might summon a numerous body of defenders to this the common point of rendezvous. He bought a tract of land near Quebec, laid it out, and settled it as a model seigneury, hoping, as he says, to kindle a spirit of emulation among the newmade seigneurs to whom he had granted lands from the King. He also laid out at the royal cost three villages in the immediate neighborhood, planning them with great care, and peopling them partly with families newly arrived, partly with soldiers, and partly with old settlers, in order that the newcomers might take lessons from the experience of these veterans. That each village might be complete in itself, he furnished it as well as he could with the needful carpenter, mason, blacksmith, and shoemaker. These inland villages, called respectively Bourg Royal, Bourg la Reine, and Bourg Talon, did not prove very thrifty. Wherever the settlers were allowed to choose for themselves, they ranged their dwellings along the watercourses. With the exception of Talon's villages, one could have seen nearly every house in Canada, by paddling a canoe up the St. Lawrence and the Richelieu. The settlements formed long thin lines on the edges of the rivers, — a convenient arrangement, but one very unfavorable to defence, to ecclesiastical control, and to strong government. The King soon discovered this; and repeated orders were sent to concentrate the inhabitants and form Canada into villages, instead of *côtes*. To do so would have involved a general revocation of grants and abandonment of houses and clearings, — a measure too arbitrary and too wasteful, even for Louis XIV, and one extremely difficult to enforce. Canada persisted in attenuating herself, and the royal will was foiled.

As you ascended the St. Lawrence, the first harboring place of civilization was Tadoussac, at the mouth of the Saguenay, where the company had its trading station, where its agents ruled supreme, and where, in early summer, all was alive with canoes and wigwams, and troops of Montagnais savages, bringing their furs to market. Leave Tadoussac behind, and, embarked in a sail-boat or a canoe, follow the northern coast. Far on the left, twenty miles away, the southern shore lies pale and dim, and mountain ranges wave their faint outline along the sky. You pass the beetling rocks of Mal Bay,[3] a solitude but for the bark hut of some wandering Indian beneath the cliff, the Eboule-

[3] [The same as Murray Bay.]

ments with their wild romantic gorge and foaming waterfalls, and the Bay of St. Paul with its broad valley and its woody mountains, rich with hidden stores of iron. Vast piles of savage verdure border the mighty stream, till at length the mountain of Cape Tourmente upheaves its huge bulk from the bosom of the water, shadowed by lowering clouds, and dark with forests. Just beyond, begin the settlements of Laval's vast seigneury of Beaupré, which had not been forgotten in the distribution of emigrants, and which, in 1667, contained more inhabitants than Quebec itself.[4] The ribbon of rich meadow land that borders that beautiful shore was yellow with wheat in harvest time; and on the woody slopes behind, the frequent clearings and the solid little dwellings of logs continued for a long distance to relieve the sameness of the forest. After passing the cataract of Montmorenci, there was another settlement, much smaller, at Beauport, the seigneury of the ex-physician Giffard, one of the earliest proprietors in Canada. The neighboring shores of the Island of Orleans were also edged with houses and clearings. The promontory of Quebec now towered full in sight, crowned with church, fort, château, convents, and seminary. There was little else on the rock. Priests, nuns, government officials, and soldiers were the denizens of the Upper Town; while commerce and the trades were cabined along the strand beneath. From the gallery of the château, you might toss a pebble far down on their shingled roofs. In the midst of them was the magazine of the company, with its two round towers and two projecting wings. It was here that all the beaver-skins of the colony were collected, assorted, and shipped for France. The so-called Château St. Louis was an indifferent wooden structure planted on a site truly superb, — above the Lower Town, above the river, above the ships, gazing abroad on a majestic panorama of waters, forests, and mountains. Behind it was the area of the fort, of which it formed one side. The governor lived in the château, and soldiers were on guard night and day in the fort. At some little distance was the convent of the Ursulines, ugly but substantial, where Mother Mary of the Incarnation ruled her pupils and her nuns; and a little farther on, towards the right, was the Hôtel Dieu. Between them were the massive buildings of the Jesuits, then as now facing the

[4] The census of 1667 gives to Quebec only 448 souls; Côte de Beaupré, 656; Beauport, 123; Ile d'Orléans, 529; other settlements included under the government of Quebec, 1011; Côte de Lauzon (south shore), 113; Trois Rivières and its dependencies, 666; Montreal, 766. Both Beaupré and Ile d'Orléans belonged at this time to the bishop. According to Juchereau, there were 70 houses at Quebec about the time of Tracy's arrival.

principal square. At one side was their church, newly finished; and opposite, across the square, stood and still stands the great church of Notre Dame. Behind the church was Laval's seminary, with the extensive enclosures belonging to it. The *sénéchaussée* or court-house, the tavern of one Jacques Boisdon on the square near the church, and a few houses along the line of what is now St. Louis Street comprised nearly all the civil part of the Upper Town. The ecclesiastical buildings were of stone, and the church of Notre Dame and the Jesuit College were marvels of size and solidity in view of the poverty and weakness of the colony.[5]

Proceeding upward along the north shore of the St. Lawrence, one found a cluster of houses at Cap Rouge, and, farther on, the frequent rude beginnings of a seigneury. The settlements thickened on approaching Three Rivers, a fur-trading hamlet enclosed with a square palisade. Above this place, a line of incipient seigneuries bordered the river, most of them granted to officers, — Laubia, a captain; Labadie, a sergeant; Moras, an ensign; Berthier, a captain; Raudin, an ensign; La Valterie, a lieutenant. Under their auspices, settlers, military and civilian, were ranging themselves along the shore, and ugly gaps in the forest thickly set with stumps bore witness to their toils. These settlements rapidly extended, till in a few years a chain of houses and clearings reached with little interruption from Quebec to Montreal. Such was the fruit of Tracy's chastisement of the Mohawks, and the influx of immigrants that followed.

As you approached Montreal, the fortified mill built by the Sulpitians at Point aux Trembles towered above the woods; and soon after the newly built chapel of the Infant Jesus. More settlements followed, till at length the great fortified mill of Montreal rose in sight; then the long row of compact wooden houses, the Hôtel Dieu, and the rough masonry of the Seminary of St. Sulpice. Beyond the town, the clearings continued at intervals till you reached Lake St. Louis, where young Cavelier de la Salle had laid out his seigneury of La Chine, and abandoned it to begin his hard career of western exploration. Above the island of Montreal, the wilderness was broken only by a solitary trading station on the neighboring Isle Pérot.

Now cross Lake St. Louis, shoot the rapids of La Chine, and follow

[5] The first stone of Notre Dame de Québec was laid in September 1647, and the first mass was said in it on the 24th of December 1650. The side walls still remain as part of the present structure. The Jesuit College was also begun in 1647. The walls and roof were finished in 1649. The church connected with it, since destroyed, was begun in 1666.

the southern shore downward. Here the seigneuries of Longueuil, Boucherville, Varennes, Verchères, and Contrecœur were already begun. From the fort of Sorel one could visit the military seigneuries along the Richelieu or descend towards Quebec, passing on the way those of Lussaudière, Becancour, Lotbinière, and others still in a shapeless infancy. Even far below Quebec, at St. Anne de la Pocatière, River Ouelle, and other points, cabins and clearings greeted the eye of the passing canoeman.

For a year or two the settler's initiation was a rough one; but when he had a few acres under tillage he could support himself and his family on the produce, aided by hunting, if he knew how to use a gun, and by the bountiful profusion of eels which the St. Lawrence never failed to yield in their season, and which, smoked or salted, supplied his larder for months. In winter he hewed timber, sawed planks, or split shingles for the market of Quebec, obtaining in return such necessaries as he required. With thrift and hard work he was sure of comfort at last; but the former habits of the military settlers and of many of the others were not favorable to a routine of dogged industry. The sameness and solitude of their new life often became insufferable; nor, married as they had been, was the domestic hearth likely to supply much consolation. Yet, thrifty or not, they multiplied apace. "A poor man," says Mother Mary, "will have eight children and more, who run about in winter with bare heads and bare feet, and a little jacket on their backs, live on nothing but bread and eels, and on that grow fat and stout." With such treatment the weaker sort died, but the strong survived; and out of this rugged nursing sprang the hardy Canadian race of bush-rangers and bush-fighters.

CHAPTER XII

Canadian Feudalism
1663–1763

[The Old Regime in Canada, CHAPTER XVIII]

Canadian society was beginning to form itself, and at its base was the feudal tenure. European feudalism was the indigenous and natural growth of political and social conditions which preceded it. Canadian feudalism was an offshoot of the feudalism of France, modified by the lapse of centuries, and further modified by the royal will.

In France, as in the rest of Europe, the system had lost its vitality. The warrior-nobles who placed Hugh Capet on the throne, and began the feudal monarchy, formed an aristocratic republic; and the King was one of their number, whom they chose to be their chief. But through the struggles and vicissitudes of many succeeding reigns royalty had waxed and oligarchy had waned. The fact had changed, and the theory had changed with it. The King, once powerless among a host of turbulent nobles, was now a king indeed. Once a chief, because his equals had made him so, he was now the anointed of the Lord. This triumph of royalty had culminated in Louis XIV. The stormy energies and bold individualism of the old feudal nobles had ceased to exist. They who had held his predecessors in awe had become his obsequious servants. He no longer feared his nobles: he prized them as gorgeous decorations of his court and satellites of his royal person.

It was Richelieu who first planted feudalism in Canada, by the charter of the Company of the Hundred Associates, 1627. The King would preserve it there, because with its teeth drawn he was fond of it, and because, as the feudal tenure prevailed in Old France, it was natural that it should prevail also in the New. But he continued as Richelieu had begun, and moulded it to the form that pleased him. Nothing was left which could threaten his absolute and undivided authority over the colony. In France, a multitude of privileges and prescriptions still clung, despite its fall, about the ancient ruling class. Few of these were allowed to cross the Atlantic, while the old lingering abuses, which had made the system odious, were at the same time lopped away. Thus retrenched, Canadian feudalism was made to serve a double end, — to produce a faint and harmless reflection of French aristocracy, and simply and practically to supply agencies for distributing land among the settlers.

The nature of the precautions which it was held to require appear in the plan of administration which Talon and Tracy laid before the minister. They urge that, in view of the distance from France, special care ought to be taken to prevent changes and revolutions, aristocratic or otherwise, in the colony, whereby in time sovereign jurisdictions might grow up, as formerly occurred in various parts of France. And in respect to grants already made an inquiry was ordered, to ascertain "if seigneurs in distributing lands to their vassals have exacted any conditions injurious to the rights of the Crown and the subjection due solely to the King." In the same view the seigneur was denied any voice whatever in the direction of government; and it is scarcely necessary to say that the essential feature of feudalism in the day of its vitality, the requirement of military service by the lord from the vassal, was utterly unknown in Canada. The royal governor called out the militia whenever he saw fit, and set over it what officers he pleased.

The seigneur was usually the immediate vassal of the Crown, from which he had received his land gratuitously. In a few cases he made grants to other seigneurs inferior in the feudal scale, and they, his vassals, granted in turn to their vassals, — the *habitants*, or cultivators of the soil.[1] Sometimes the *habitant* held directly of the Crown, in which case there was no step between the highest and lowest degrees of the feudal scale. The seigneur held by the tenure of faith and homage, the *habitant* by the inferior tenure *en censive*. Faith and homage were rendered to the Crown or other feudal superior whenever the seigneury changed hands, or, in the case of seigneuries held by corporations, after long stated intervals. The following is an example, drawn from the early days of the colony, of the performance of this ceremony by the owner of a fief to the seigneur who had granted it to him. It is that of Jean Guion, vassal of Giffard, seigneur of Beauport.

[1] Most of the seigneuries of Canada were simple fiefs; but there were some exceptions. In 1671 the King, as a mark of honor to Talon, erected his Seigneurie des Islets into a barony; and it was soon afterwards made an earldom (comté).

The act recounts how, in presence of a notary, Guion presented himself at the principal door of the manor-house of Beauport; how, having knocked, one Boullé, farmer of Giffard, opened the door, and in reply to Guion's question if the seigneur was at home, replied that he was not, but that he, Boullé, was empowered to receive acknowledgments of faith and homage from the vassals in his name. "After the which reply," proceeds the act, "the said Guion, being at the principal door, placed himself on his knees on the ground, with head bare, and without sword or spurs, and said three times these words: 'Monsieur de Beauport, Monsieur de Beauport, Monsieur de Beauport! I bring you the faith and homage which I am bound to bring you on account of my fief Du Buisson, which I hold as a man of faith of your seigneury of Beauport, declaring that I offer to pay my seigneurial and feudal dues in their season, and demanding of you to accept me in faith and homage as aforesaid.' "

The following instance is the more common one of a seigneur holding directly of the Crown. It is widely separated from the first in point of time, having occurred a year after the army of Wolfe entered Quebec.

Philippe Noël had lately died, and Jean Noël, his son, inherited his seigneury of Tilly and Bonsecours. To make the title good, faith and homage must be renewed. Jean Noël was under the bitter necessity of rendering this duty to General Murray, governor for the King of Great Britain. The form is the same as in the case of Guion, more than a century before. Noël repairs to the Government House at Quebec, and knocks at the door. A servant opens it. Noël asks if the governor is there. The servant replies that he is. Murray, informed of the visitor's object, comes to the door, and Noël then and there, "without sword or spurs, with bare head, and one knee on the ground," repeats the acknowledgment of faith and homage for his seigneury. He was compelled, however, to add a detested innovation, — the oath of fidelity to his Britannic Majesty, coupled with a pledge to keep his vassals in obedience to the new sovereign.

The seigneur was a proprietor holding that relation to the feudal superior which, in its pristine character, has been truly described as servile in form, proud and bold in spirit. But in Canada this bold spirit was very far from being strengthened by the changes which the policy of the Crown had introduced into the system. The reservation of mines and minerals, oaks for the royal navy, roadways, and a site (if needed) for royal forts and magazines, had in it nothing extraordinary. The great difference between the position of the Canadian seigneur and that of the vassal proprietor of the Middle Ages lay in the extent and nature of the control which the Crown and its officers held over him. A decree of the King, an edict of the council, or an ordinance of the intendant, might at any moment change old conditions, impose new ones, interfere between the lord of the manor and his grantees, and modify or annul his bargains, past or present. He was never sure whether or not the government would let him alone; and against its most arbitrary intervention he had no remedy.

One condition was imposed on him which may be said to form the distinctive feature of Canadian feudalism, — that of clearing his land within a limited time on pain of forfeiting it. The object was the excellent one of preventing the lands of the colony from lying waste. As the seigneur was often the penniless owner of a domain three or four leagues wide and proportionably deep, he could not clear it all himself, and was therefore under the necessity of placing the greater part in the hands of those who could. But he was forbidden to sell any part of it which he had not cleared. He must grant it without price, on condition of a small perpetual rent; and this brings us to the cultivator of the soil, the *censitaire*, the broad base of the feudal pyramid.[2]

The tenure *en censive*, by which the *censitaire* held of the seigneur, consisted in the obligation to make annual payments in money, produce, or both. In Canada these payments, known as *cens et rente*, were strangely diverse in amount and kind; but in all the early period of the colony they were almost ludicrously small. A common charge at Montreal was half a sou and half a pint of wheat for each arpent. The rate usually fluctuated in the early times between half a sou and two sous; so that a farm of 160 arpents would pay from four to sixteen francs, of which a part would be in money and the rest in live capons, wheat, eggs, or all three together, in pursuance of contracts as amusing in their precision as they are bewildering in their variety. Live capons, estimated at twenty sous each, though sometimes not worth ten, form a conspicuous feature in these agreements; so that on payday the seigneur's barnyard presented an animated scene. Later in the history of the colony grants were at somewhat higher rates. Payment was commonly made on St. Martin's day, when there was a general muster of

[2] The greater part of the grants made by the old Company of New France were resumed by the Crown for neglect to occupy and improve the land, which was granted out anew under the administration of Talon.

tenants at the seigneurial mansion, with a prodigious consumption of tobacco and a corresponding retail of neighborhood gossip, joined to the outcries of the captive fowls bundled together for delivery, with legs tied, but throats at full liberty.

A more considerable but a very uncertain source of income to the seigneur were the *lods et ventes*, or mutation fines. The land of the *censitaire* passed freely to his heirs; but if he sold it, a twelfth part of the purchase-money must be paid to the seigneur. The seigneur, on his part, was equally liable to pay a mutation fine to his feudal superior if he sold his seigneury; and for him the amount was larger, — being a *quint*, or a fifth of the price received, of which, however, the greater part was deducted for immediate payment. This heavy charge, constituting as it did a tax on all improvements, was a principal cause of the abolition of the feudal tenure in 1854.

The obligation of clearing his land and living on it was laid on seigneur and *censitaire* alike; but the latter was under a variety of other obligations to the former, partly imposed by custom and partly established by agreement when the grant was made. To grind his grain at the seigneur's mill, bake his bread in the seigneur's oven, work for him one or more days in the year, and give him one fish in every eleven, for the privilege of fishing in the river before his farm, — these were the most annoying of the conditions to which the *censitaire* was liable. Few of them were enforced with much regularity. That of baking in the seigneur's oven was rarely carried into effect, though occasionally used for purposes of extortion. It is here that the royal government appears in its true character, so far as concerns its relations with Canada, — that of a well-meaning despotism. It continually intervened between *censitaire* and seigneur, on the principle that "as his Majesty gives the land for nothing, he can make what conditions he pleases, and change them when he pleases."

These interventions were usually favorable to the *censitaire*. On one occasion an intendant reported to the minister, that in his opinion all rents ought to be reduced to one sou and one live capon for every arpent of front, equal in most cases to forty superficial arpents. Everything, he remarks, ought to be brought down to the level of the first grants "made in days of innocence," — a happy period which he does not attempt to define. The minister replies that the diversity of the rent is, in fact, vexatious, and that for his part he is disposed to abolish it altogether. Neither he nor the intendant gives the slightest hint of any compensation to the seigneur.

Though these radical measures were not executed, many changes were decreed from time to time in the relations between seigneur and *censitaire*, — sometimes as a simple act of sovereign power, and sometimes on the ground that the grants had been made with conditions not recognized by the *Coutume de Paris*. This was the code of law assigned to Canada; but most of the contracts between seigneur and *censitaire* had been agreed upon in good faith by men who knew as much of the *Coutume de Paris* as of the Capitularies of Charlemagne, and their conditions had remained in force unchallenged for generations. These interventions of government sometimes contradicted one another, and often proved a dead letter. They are more or less active through the whole period of the French rule.

The seigneur had judicial powers, which, however, were carefully curbed and controlled. His jurisdiction, when exercised at all, extended in most cases only to trivial causes. He very rarely had a prison, and seems never to have abused it. The dignity of a seigneurial gallows with *high justice* or jurisdiction over heinous offences was granted only in three or four instances.

Four arpents in front by forty in depth were the ordinary dimension of a grant *en censive*. These ribbons of land, nearly a mile and a half long, with one end on the river and the other on the uplands behind, usually combined the advantages of meadows for cultivation, and forests for timber and firewood. So long as the *censitaire* brought in on Saint Martin's day his yearly capons and his yearly handful of copper, his title against the seigneur was perfect. There are farms in Canada which have passed from father to son for two hundred years. The condition of the cultivator was incomparably better than that of the French peasant, crushed by taxes, and oppressed by feudal burdens far heavier than those of Canada. In fact, the Canadian settler scorned the name of peasant, and then, as now, was always called the *habitant*. The government held him in wardship, watched over him, interfered with him, but did not oppress him or allow others to oppress him. Canada was not governed to the profit of a class; and if the King wished to create a Canadian *noblesse*, he took care that it should not bear hard on the country.

Under a genuine feudalism, the ownership of land conferred nobility; but all this was changed. The King and not the soil was now the parent of honor. France swarmed with landless nobles, while *roturier* landholders grew daily more numerous. In Canada half the seigneuries were in *roturier* or plebeian hands, and in course of time some of them came into possession of persons on very humble degrees of the social scale. A seigneury could be bought and sold, and a trader or a thrifty *habitant* might, and often did, become the buyer.[3] If the Canadian noble was always a seigneur, it is far from being true that the Canadian seigneur was always a noble.

In France, it will be remembered, nobility did not in itself imply a title. Besides its titled leaders, it had its rank and file, numerous enough to form a considerable army. Under the later Bourbons, the penniless young nobles were, in fact, enrolled into regiments, — turbulent, difficult to control, obeying officers of high rank, but scorning all others, and conspicuous by a fiery and impetuous valor which on more than one occasion turned the tide of victory. The *gentilhomme*, or untitled noble, had a distinctive character of his own, — gallant, punctilious, vain; skilled in social and sometimes in literary and artistic accomplishments, but usually ignorant of most things except the handling of his rapier. Yet there were striking exceptions; and to say of him, as has been said, that "he knew nothing but how to get himself killed," is hardly just to a body which has produced some of the best writers and thinkers of France. Sometimes the origin of his nobility was lost in the mists of time; sometimes he owed it to a patent from the King. In either case, the line of demarcation between him and the classes below him was perfectly distinct; and in this lies an essential difference between the French *noblesse* and the English gentry, a class not separated from others by a definite barrier. The French *noblesse*, unlike the English gentry, constituted a caste.

The *gentilhomme* had no vocation for emigrating. He liked the army and he liked the court. If he could not be of it, it was something to live in its shadow. The life of a backwoods settler had no charm for him. He was not used to labor; and he could not trade, at least in retail, without becoming liable to forfeit his nobility. When Talon came to Canada, there were but four noble families in the colony.[4] Young nobles in abundance came out with Tracy; but they went home with him. Where, then, should be found the material of a Canadian *noblesse?* First, in the regiment of Carignan, of which most of the

---

[3] In 1712, the engineer Catalogne made a very long and elaborate report on the condition of Canada, with a full account of all the seigneurial estates. Of 91 seigneuries, fiefs and baronies described by him, 10 belonged to merchants, 12 to husbandmen, and 2 to masters of small river craft. The rest belonged to religious corporations, members of the council, judges, officials of the Crown, widows, and discharged officers or their sons.

[4] Repentigny, Tilly, Potherie and Ailleboust.

officers were *gentilshommes*; secondly, in the issue of patents of nobility to a few of the more prominent colonists. Tracy asked for four such patents; Talon asked for five more; and such requests were repeated at intervals by succeeding governors and intendants, in behalf of those who had gained their favor by merit or otherwise. Money smoothed the path to advancement, so far had *noblesse* already fallen from its old estate. Thus Jacques Le Ber, the merchant, who had long kept a shop at Montreal, got himself made a "gentleman" for 6000 livres.

All Canada soon became infatuated with *noblesse;* and country and town, merchant and seigneur, vied with each other for the quality of *gentilhomme*. If they could not get it, they often pretended to have it, and aped its ways with the zeal of Monsieur Jourdain himself. "Everybody here," writes the intendant Meules, "calls himself *Esquire*, and ends with thinking himself a gentleman." Successive intendants repeat this complaint. The case was worst with *roturiers* who had acquired seigneuries. Thus Noël Langlois was a good carpenter till he became owner of a seigneury, on which he grew lazy and affected to play the gentleman. The real *gentilshommes*, as well as the spurious, had their full share of official stricture. The governor Denonville speaks of them thus: "Several of them have come out this year with their wives, who are very much cast down; but they play the fine lady, nevertheless. I had much rather see good peasants; it would be a pleasure to me to give aid to such, knowing, as I should, that within two years their families would have the means of living at ease; for it is certain that a peasant who can and will work is well off in this country, while our nobles with nothing to do can never be anything but beggars. Still they ought not to be driven off or abandoned. The question is how to maintain them."

The intendant Duchesneau writes to the same effect: "Many of our *gentilshommes*, officers, and other owners of seigneuries, lead what in France is called the life of a country gentleman, and spend most of their time in hunting and fishing. As their requirements in food and clothing are greater than those of the simple *habitants*, and as they do not devote themselves to improving their land, they mix themselves up in trade, run in debt on all hands, incite their young *habitants* to range the woods, and send their own children there to trade for furs in the Indian villages and in the depths of the forest, in spite of the prohibition of his Majesty. Yet, with all this, they are in miserable poverty."

Their condition, indeed, was often deplorable. "It is pitiful," says the intendant Champigny, "to see their children, of which they have great numbers, passing all summer with nothing on them but a shirt, and their wives and daughters working in the fields." In another letter he asks aid from the King for Repentigny with his thirteen children, and for Tilly with his fifteen. "We must give them some corn at once," he says, "or they will starve." These were two of the original four noble families of Canada. The family of Ailleboust, another of the four, is described as equally destitute. "Pride and sloth," says the same intendant, "are the great faults of the people of Canada, and especially of the nobles and those who pretend to be such. I pray you grant no more letters of nobility, unless you want to multiply beggars."

The governor Denonville is still more emphatic: "Above all things, Monseigneur, permit me to say that the nobles of this new country are everything that is most beggarly, and that to increase their number is to increase the number of do-nothings. A new country requires hard workers, who will handle the axe and mattock. The sons of our councillors are no more industrious than the nobles; and their only resource is to take to the woods, trade a little with the Indians, and, for the most part, fall into the disorders of which I have had the honor to inform you. I shall use all possible means to induce them to engage in regular commerce; but as our nobles and councillors are all very poor and weighed down with debt, they could not get credit for a single crown piece." "Two days ago," he writes in another letter, "Monsieur de Saint-Ours, a gentleman of Dauphiny, came to me to ask leave to go back to France in search of bread. He says that he will put his ten children into the charge of any who will give them a living, and that he himself will go into the army again. His wife and he are in despair; and yet they do what they can. I have seen two of his girls reaping grain and holding the plough. Other families are in the same condition. They come to me with tears in their eyes. All our married officers are beggars; and I entreat you to send them aid. There is need that the King should provide support for their children, or else they will be tempted to go over to the English." Again he writes that the sons of the councillor D'Amours have been arrested as *coureurs de bois*, or outlaws in the bush; and that if the minister does not do something to help them, there is danger that all the sons of the *noblesse*, real or pretended, will turn bandits, since they have no other means of living.

The King, dispenser of charity for all Canada, came promptly to the rescue. He granted an alms of 100 crowns to each family, coupled with a warning to the recipients of his bounty that "their misery proceeds from their ambition to live as persons of quality and without labor."

At the same time, the minister announced that no more letters of nobility would be granted in Canada; adding, "to relieve the country of some of the children of those who are really noble; I send you [the governor] six commissions of *Gardes de la Marine*, and recommend you to take care not to give them to any who are not actually *gentils-hommes*." The *Garde de la Marine* answered to the midshipman of the English or American service. As the six commissions could bring little relief to the crowd of needy youths, it was further ordained that sons of nobles or persons living as such should be enrolled into companies at eight sous a day for those who should best conduct themselves, and six sous a day for the others. Nobles in Canada were also permitted to trade, even at retail, without derogating from their rank.

They had already assumed this right, without waiting for the royal license; but thus far it had profited them little. The *gentilhomme* was not a good shopkeeper, nor, as a rule, was the shopkeeper's vocation very lucrative in Canada. The domestic trade of the colony was small; and all trade was exposed to such vicissitudes from the intervention of intendants, ministers, and councils, that at one time it was almost banished. At best, it was carried on under conditions auspicious to a favored few and withering to the rest. Even when most willing to work, the position of the *gentilhomme* was a painful one. Unless he could gain a post under the Crown, which was rarely the case, he was as complete a political cipher as the meanest *habitant*. His rents were practically nothing, and he had no capital to improve his seigneurial estate. By a peasant's work he could gain a peasant's living, and this was all. The prospect was not inspiring. His long initiation of misery was the natural result of his position and surroundings; and it is no matter of wonder that he threw himself into the only field of action which in time of peace was open to him. It was trade, but trade seasoned by adventure and ennobled by danger, defiant of edict and ordinance, outlawed, conducted in arms among forests and savages; in short, it was the Western fur-trade. The tyro was likely to fail in it at first, but time and experience formed him to the work. On the Great Lakes, in the wastes of the Northwest, on the Mississippi and the plains beyond, we find the roving *gentilhomme*, chief of a gang of bush-rangers, often his own *habitants*, — sometimes proscribed by the government, sometimes leagued in contraband traffic with its highest officials; a hardy vidette of civilization, tracing unknown streams, piercing unknown forests, trading, fighting, negotiating, and building forts. Again we find him on the shores of Acadia or Maine, surrounded by Indian retainers, a menace and a terror to the neighboring English colonist. Saint-Castin, Du Lhut, La Durantaye, La Salle, La Mothe-Cadillac, Iberville, Bienville, La Vérendrye, are names that stand conspicuous on the page of half-savage romance that refreshes the hard and practical annals of American colonization. But a more substantial debt is due to their memory. It was they, and such as they, who discovered the Ohio, explored the Mississippi to its mouth, discovered the Rocky Mountains, and founded Detroit, St. Louis, and New Orleans.

Even in his earliest day, the *gentilhomme* was not always in the evil plight where we have found him. There were a few exceptions to the general misery, and the chief among them is that of the Le Moynes of Montreal. Charles Le Moyne, son of an innkeeper of Dieppe and founder of a family the most truly eminent in Canada, was a man of sterling qualities who had been long enough in the colony to learn how to live there. Others learned the same lesson at a later day, adapted themselves to soil and situation, took root, grew, and became more Canadian than French. As population increased, their seigneuries began to yield appreciable returns, and their reserved domains became worth cultivating. A future dawned upon them; they saw in hope their names, their seigneurial estates, their manor-houses, their tenantry, passing to their children and their children's children. The beggared noble of the early time became a sturdy country gentleman, — poor, but not wretched; ignorant of books, except possibly a few scraps of rusty Latin picked up in a Jesuit school; hardy as the hardiest woodsman, yet never forgetting his quality of *gentilhomme;* scrupulously wearing its badge, the sword, and copying as well as he could the fashions of the court, which glowed on his vision across the sea in all the effulgence of Versailles, and beamed with reflected ray from the Château of Quebec. He was at home among his tenants, at home among the Indians, and never more at home than when, a gun in his hand and a crucifix on his breast, he took the war-path with a crew of painted savages and Frenchmen almost as wild, and pounced like a lynx from the forest on some lonely farm or outlying hamlet of New England. How New England hated him, let her records tell. The reddest blood-streaks on her old annals mark the trace of the Canadian *gentilhomme*.[5]

[5] [Since Parkman's death there have been several new studies on the feudal system in Canada, of which the best are W. B. Munro *The Seigniorial System in Canada* (1907) and Guy Frégault *La Civilisation de la Nouvelle France* (1944) chap. iv.]

CHAPTER XIII

The Rulers of Canada

1663–1673

[The Old Régime in Canada, CHAPTER XIX]

The government of Canada was formed in its chief features after the government of a French province. Throughout France the past and the present stood side by side. The kingdom had a double administration; or, rather, the shadow of the old administration and the substance of the new. The government of provinces had long been held by the high nobles, often kindred to the Crown; and hence, in former times, great perils had arisen, amounting during the civil wars to the danger of dismemberment. The high nobles were still governors of provinces; but here, as elsewhere, they had ceased to be dangerous. Titles, honors, and ceremonial they had in abundance; but they were deprived of real power. Close beside them was the royal intendant, an obscure figure, lost amid the vainglories of the feudal sunset, but in the name of the King holding the reins of government, — a check and a spy on his gorgeous colleague. He was the King's agent; of modest birth, springing from the legal class; owing his present to the King, and dependent on him for his future; learned in the law and trained to administration. It was by such instruments that the powerful centralization of the monarchy enforced itself throughout the kingdom, and, penetrating beneath the crust of old prescriptions, supplanted without seeming to supplant them. The courtier noble looked down in the pride of rank on the busy man in black at his side; but this man in black, with the troop of officials at his beck, controlled finance, the royal courts, public works, and all the administrative business of the province.

The governor-general and the intendant of Canada answered to those of a French province. The governor, excepting in the earliest period of the colony, was a military noble, — in most cases bearing a title and sometimes of high rank. The intendant, as in France, was usually drawn from the *gens de robe*, or legal class. The mutual relations of the two officers were modified by the circumstances about them. The governor was superior in rank to the intendant; he commanded the troops, conducted relations with foreign colonies and Indian tribes, and took precedence on all occasions of ceremony. Unlike a provincial governor in France, he had great and substantial power. The King and the minister, his sole masters, were a thousand leagues distant, and he controlled the whole military force. If he abused his position, there was no remedy but in appeal to the court, which alone could hold him in check. There were local governors at Montreal and Three Rivers; but their power was carefully curbed, and they were forbidden to fine or imprison any person without authority from Quebec.

The intendant was virtually a spy on the governor-general, of whose proceedings and of everything else that took place he was required to make report. Every year he wrote to the minister of state one, two, three, or four letters, often forty or fifty pages long, filled with the secrets of the colony, political and personal, great and small, set forth with a minuteness often interesting, often instructive, and often excessively tedious. The governor, too, wrote letters of pitiless length; and each of the colleagues was jealous of the letters of the other. In truth, their relations to each other were so critical, and perfect harmony so rare, that they might almost be described as natural enemies. The court, it is certain, did not desire their perfect accord; nor, on the other hand, did it wish them to quarrel: it aimed to keep them on such terms that, without deranging the machinery of administration, each should be a check on the other.

The governor, the intendant, and the supreme council or court were absolute masters of Canada under the pleasure of the King. Legislative, judicial, and executive power, all centred in them. We have seen already the very unpromising beginnings of the supreme council. It had consisted at first of the governor, the bishop, and five councillors chosen by them. The intendant was soon added, to form the ruling triumvirate; but the appointment of the councillors, the occasion of so many quarrels, was afterwards exercised by the King himself. Even the name of the council underwent a change in the interest of his autocracy, and he commanded that it should no longer be called the *Supreme*, but only the *Superior* Council. The same charge had just been imposed on all the high tribunals of France. Under the shadow of the *fleur-de-lis*, the King alone was to be supreme.

In 1675 the number of councillors was increased to seven, and in

1703 it was again increased to twelve; but the character of the council or court remained the same. It issued decrees for the civil, commercial, and financial government of the colony, and gave judgment in civil and criminal causes according to the royal ordinances and the *Coutume de Paris*. It exercised also the function of registration borrowed from the parlement de Paris. That body, it will be remembered, had no analogy whatever with the English parliament. Its ordinary functions were not legislative, but judicial; and it was composed of judges hereditary under certain conditions. Nevertheless, it had long acted as a check on the royal power through its right of registration. No royal edict had the force of law till entered upon its books, and this custom had so deep a root in the monarchical constitution of France, that even Louis XIV, in the flush of his power, did not attempt to abolish it. He did better; he ordered his decrees to be registered, and the humbled parlement submissively obeyed. In like manner all edicts, ordinances, or declarations relating to Canada were entered on the registers of the superior council at Quebec. The order of registration was commonly affixed to the edict or other mandate, and nobody dreamed of disobeying it.

The council or court had its attorney-general, who heard complaints, and brought them before the tribunal if he thought necessary; its secretary, who kept its registers, and its *huissiers* or attendant officers. It sat once a week; and, though it was the highest court of appeal, it exercised a first original jurisdiction in very trivial cases. It was empowered to establish subordinate courts or judges throughout the colony. Besides these, there was a judge appointed by the King for each of the three districts into which Canada was divided, — those of Quebec, Three Rivers, and Montreal. To each of the three royal judges were joined a clerk and an attorney-general, under the supervision and control of the attorney-general of the superior court, to which tribunal appeal lay from all the subordinate jurisdictions. The jurisdiction of the seigneurs within their own limits has already been mentioned. They were entitled by the terms of their grants to the exercise of "high, middle, and low justice;" but most of them were practically restricted to the last of the three, — that is, to petty disputes between the *habitants*, involving not more than sixty sous, or offences for which the fine did not exceed ten sous. Thus limited, their judgments were often useful in saving time, trouble, and money to the disputants. The corporate seigneurs of Montreal long continued to hold a feudal court in form, with attorney-general, clerk, and *huissier;* but very few other seigneurs were in a condition to imitate them. Added to all these tribunals was the bishop's court at Quebec, to try causes held to be within the province of the Church.

The office of judge in Canada was no sinecure. The people were of a litigious disposition, — partly from their Norman blood; partly, perhaps, from the idleness of the long and tedious winter, which gave full leisure for gossip and quarrel; and partly from the very imperfect manner in which titles had been drawn and the boundaries of grants worked out, whence ensued disputes without end between neighbor and neighbor.

"I will not say," writes the satirical La Hontan, "that Justice is more chaste and disinterested here than in France; but, at least, if she is sold, she is sold cheaper. We do not pass through the clutches of advocates, the talons of attorneys, and the claws of clerks. These vermin do not infest Canada yet. Everybody pleads his own cause. Our Themis is prompt, and she does not bristle with fees, costs, and charges. The judges have only four hundred francs a year, — a great temptation to look for law in the bottom of the suitor's purse. Four hundred francs! Not enough to buy a cap and gown; so these gentry never wear them."

Thus far La Hontan. Now let us hear the King himself. "The greatest disorder which has hitherto existed in Canada," writes Louis XIV to the intendant Meules, "has come from the small degree of liberty which the officers of justice have had in the discharge of their duties, by reason of the violence to which they have been subjected, and the part they have been obliged to take in the continual quarrels between the governor and the intendant; insomuch that justice having been administered by cabal and animosity, the inhabitants have hitherto been far from the tranquillity and repose which can not be found in a place where everybody is compelled to take side with one party or another."

Nevertheless, on ordinary local questions between the *habitants*, justice seems to have been administered on the whole fairly; and judges of all grades often interposed in their personal capacity to bring parties to an agreement without a trial. From head to foot, the government kept its attitude of paternity.

Beyond and above all the regular tribunals, beyond and above the council itself, was the independent jurisdiction lodged in the person of the King's man, the intendant. His commission empowered him, if he saw fit, to call any cause whatever before himself for judgment; and he judged exclusively the cases which concerned the King, and those involving the relations of seigneur and vassal. He appointed subordinate judges, from whom there was appeal to him; but from his decisions, as well as from those of the superior council, there was no appeal but to the King in his council of state.

On any Monday morning one would have found the superior council in session in the antechamber of the governor's apartment, at the Château St. Louis. The members sat at a round table. At the head was the governor, with the bishop on his right, and the intendant on his left. The Councillors sat in the order of their appointment, and the attorney-general also had his place at the board. As La Hontan says, they were not in judicial robes, but in their ordinary dress, and all but the bishop wore swords. The want of the cap and gown greatly disturbed the intendant Meules; and he begs the minister to consider how important it is that the councillors, in order to inspire respect, should appear in public in long black robes, which on occasions of ceremony they should exchange for robes of red. He thinks that the principal persons of the colony would thus be induced to train up their children to so enviable a dignity; "and," he concludes, "as none of the councillors can afford to buy red robes, I hope that the King will vouchsafe to send out nine such. As for the black robes, they can furnish those themselves." The King did not respond, and the nine robes never arrived.

The official dignity of the council was sometimes exposed to trials against which even red gowns might have proved an insufficient protection. The same intendant urges that the tribunal ought to be provided immediately with a house of its own. "It is not decent," he says, "that it should sit in the governor's antechamber any longer. His guards and valets make such a noise that we cannot hear one another speak. I have continually to tell them to keep quiet, which causes them to make a thousand jokes at the councillors as they pass in and out." As the governor and the council were often on ill terms, the official head of the colony could not always be trusted to keep his attendants on their good behavior. The minister listened to the complaint of Meules, and adopted his suggestion that the government should buy the old brewery of Talon, — a large structure of mingled timber and masonry on the banks of the St. Charles. It was at an easy distance from the château; passing the Hôtel Dieu and descending the rock, one reached it by a walk of a few minutes. It was accordingly repaired, partly rebuilt, and fitted up to serve the double purpose of a lodging for the intendant and a court-house. Henceforth the transformed brewery was known as the Palace of the Intendant, or the Palace of Justice; and here the council and inferior courts long continued to hold their sessions.

Some of these inferior courts appear to have needed a lodging quite as much as the council. The watchful Meules informs the minister that the royal judge for the district of Quebec was accustomed in winter, with a view to saving fuel, to hear causes and pronounce judgment by his own fireside, in the midst of his children, whose gambols disturbed the even distribution of justice.

The superior council was not a very harmonious body. As its three chiefs — the man of the sword, the man of the church, and the man of the law — were often at variance, the councillors attached themselves to one party or the other, and hot disputes sometimes ensued. The intendant, though but third in rank, presided at the sessions, took votes, pronounced judgment, signed papers, and called special meetings. This matter of the presidency was for some time a source of contention between him and the governor, till the question was set at rest by a decree of the King.

The intendants in their reports to the minister do not paint the council in flattering colors. One of them complains that the councillors, being busy with their farms, neglect their official duties. Another says that they are all more or less in trade. A third calls them uneducated persons of slight account, allied to the chief families and chief merchants in Canada, in whose interest they make laws; and he adds, that, as a year and a half or even two years usually elapse before the answer to a complaint is received from France, they take advantage of this long interval to the injury of the King's service. These and other similar charges betray the continual friction between the several branches of the government.

The councillors were rarely changed, and they usually held office for life. In a few cases the King granted to the son of a councillor yet living the right of succeeding his father when the charge should become vacant. It was a post of honor and not of profit, at least of direct profit. The salaries were very small, and coupled with a prohibition to receive fees.

Judging solely by the terms of his commission, the intendant was the ruling power in the colony. He controlled all expenditure of public money, and not only presided at the council, but was clothed in his own person with independent legislative as well as judicial power. He was authorized to issue ordinances having the force of law whenever he thought necessary, and, in the words of his commission, "to order everything as he shall see just and proper." He was directed to be present at councils of war, though war was the special province of his colleague, and to protect soldiers and all others from official extortion and abuse; that is, to protect them from the governor. Yet there were practical difficulties in the way of his apparent power. The King, his master, was far away; but official jealousy was busy around him, and his patience was sometimes put to the proof. Thus the royal judge of Quebec had fallen into irregularities. "I can do nothing with him," writes the intendant; "he keeps on good terms with the governor and council, and sets me at naught." The governor had, as he thought, treated him amiss. "You have told me," he writes to the minister, "to bear everything from him and report to you;" and he proceeds to re-count his grievances. Again, "the attorney-general is bold to insolence, and needs to be repressed. The King's interposition is necessary." He modestly adds that the intendant is the only man in Canada whom his Majesty can trust, and that he ought to have more power.

These were far from being his only troubles. The enormous powers with which his commission clothed him were sometimes retrenched by contradictory instructions from the King; for this government, not of laws but of arbitrary will, is marked by frequent inconsistencies. When he quarrelled with the governor, and the governor chanced to have strong friends at court, his position became truly pitiable. He was berated as an imperious master berates an offending servant. "Your last letter is full of nothing but complaints." "You have exceeded your authority." "Study to know yourself, and to understand clearly the difference there is between a governor and an intendant." "Since you failed to comprehend the difference between you and the officer who represents the King's person, you are in danger of being often con-demned, or rather of being recalled; for his Majesty cannot endure so many petty complaints, founded on nothing but a certain *quasi* equality between the governor and you, which you assume, but which does not exist." "Meddle with nothing beyond your functions." "Take good care to tell me nothing but the truth." "You ask too many favors for your adherents." "You must not spend more than you have authority to spend, or it will be taken out of your pay." In short, there are several letters from the minister Colbert to his colonial man-of-all-work, which, from beginning to end, are one continued scold.

The luckless intendant was liable to be held to account for the action of natural laws. "If the population does not increase in proportion to the pains I take," writes the King to Duchesneau, "you are to lay the blame on yourself for not having executed my principal order [to promote marriages], and for having failed in the principal object for which I sent you to Canada."

A great number of ordinances of intendants are preserved. They were usually read to the people at the doors of churches after mass, or sometimes by the curé from his pulpit. They relate to a great variety of subjects, — regulation of inns and markets, poaching, preservation of game, sale of brandy, rent of pews, stray hogs, mad dogs, tithes, matrimonial quarrels, fast driving, wards and guardians, weights and measures, nuisances, value of coinage, trespass on lands, building churches, observance of Sunday, preservation of timber, seigneur and vassal, settlement of boundaries, and many other matters. If a curé with some of his parishioners reported that his church or his house needed repair or rebuilding, the intendant issued an ordinance requiring all the inhabitants of the parish, "both those who have consented and those who have not consented," to contribute materials and labor, on pain of fine or other penalty. The militia captain of the *côte* was to direct the work and see that each parishioner did his due part, which was determined by the extent of his farm, so, too, if the *grand voyer*, an officer charged with the superintendence of highways, reported that a new road was wanted or that an old one needed mending, an ordinance of the intendant set the whole neighborhood at work upon it, directed, as in the other case, by the captain of militia. If children were left fatherless, the intendant ordered the curé of the parish to assemble their relations or friends for the choice of a guardian. If a *censitaire* did not clear his land and live on it, the intendant took it from him and gave it back to the seigneur.

Chimney-sweeping having been neglected at Quebec, the intendant commands all householders promptly to do their duty in this respect, and at the same time fixes the pay of the sweep at six sous a chimney. Another order forbids quarrelling in church. Another assigns pews in due order of precedence to the seigneur, the captain of militia, and the wardens. The intendant Raudot, who seems to have been inspired even more than the others with the spirit of paternal intervention, issued a mandate to the effect, that, whereas the people of Montreal raise too many horses, which prevents them from raising cattle and sheep, "being therein ignorant of their true interest. . . . Now, therefore, we command that each inhabitant of the *côtes* of this government shall hereafter own no more than two horses, or mares, and one foal, — the same to take effect after the sowing-season of the ensuing year, 1710, giving them time to rid themselves of their horses in excess of said number, after which they will be required to kill any of such excess that may remain in their possession." Many other ordinances, if not equally preposterous, are equally stringent; such, for example, as that of the intendant Bigot, in which, with a view of promoting agriculture, and protecting the morals of the farmers by saving them from the temptations of cities, he proclaims to them: "We prohibit and forbid you to remove to this town [Quebec] under any pretext whatever, without our permission in writing, on pain of being expelled and sent back to your farms, your furniture and goods confiscated, and a fine of fifty livres laid on you for the benefit of the hospitals. And, furthermore, we forbid all inhabitants of the city to let houses or rooms to persons coming from the country, on pain of a fine of a hundred livres, also applicable to the hospitals." At about the same time a royal edict, designed to prevent the undue subdivision of farms, forbade the country people, except such as were authorized to live in villages, to build a house or barn on any piece of land less than one and a half arpents wide and thirty arpents long; while a subsequent ordinance of the intendant commands the immediate demolition of certain houses built in contravention of the edict.

The spirit of absolutism is everywhere apparent. "It is of very great consequence," writes the intendant Meules, "that the people should not be left at liberty to speak their minds." Hence public meetings were jealously restricted. Even those held by parishioners under the eye of the curé to estimate the cost of a new church seem to have required a special license from the intendant. During a number of years a meeting of the principal inhabitants of Quebec was called in spring and autumn by the council to discuss the price and quality of bread, the supply of firewood, and other similar matters. The council commissioned two of its members to preside at these meetings, and on hearing their report took what action it thought best. Thus, after the meeting held in February, 1686, it issued a decree, in which, after a long and formal preamble, it solemnly ordained "that besides white-bread and light brown-bread, all bakers shall hereafter make dark brown-bread whenever the same shall be required." Such assemblies, so controlled, could scarcely, one would think, wound the tenderest susceptibilities of authority; yet there was evident distrust of them, and after a few years this modest shred of self-government is seen no more. The syndic, too, that functionary whom the people of the towns were at first allowed to choose, under the eye of the authorities, was conjured out of existence by a word from the King. Seigneur, *censitaire*, and citizen were prostrate alike in flat subjection to the royal will. They were not free even to go home to France. No inhabitant of Canada, man or woman, could do so without leave; and several intendants express their belief that without this precaution there would soon be a falling off in the population.

In 1671 the council issued a curious decree. One Paul Dupuy had been heard to say that there is nothing like righting one's self, and that when the English cut off the head of Charles I. they did a good thing, with other discourse to the like effect. The council declared him guilty of speaking ill of royalty in the person of the King of England, and uttering words tending to sedition. He was condemned to be dragged from prison by the public executioner, and led in his shirt, with a rope about his neck and a torch in his hand, to the gate of the Château St. Louis, there to beg pardon of the King; thence to the pillory of the Lower Town to be branded with a *fleur-de-lis* on the cheek, and set in the stocks for half an hour; then to be led back to prison, and put in irons "till the information against him shall be completed."

If irreverence to royalty was thus rigorously chastised, irreverence to God was threatened with still sharper penalties. Louis XIV, ever haunted with the fear of the Devil, sought protection against him by his famous edict against swearing, duly registered on the books of the council at Quebec. "It is our will and pleasure," says this pious mandate, "that all persons convicted of profane swearing or blaspheming the name of God, the most Holy Virgin his mother, or the saints, be condemned for the first offence to a pecuniary fine according to their possessions and the greatness and enormity of the oath and blasphemy; and if those thus punished repeat the said oaths, then for the second, third, and fourth time they shall be condemned to a double, triple, and quadruple fine; and for the fifth time, they shall be set in the pillory on Sunday or other festival days, there to remain from eight in the morning till one in the afternoon, exposed to all sorts of opprobrium and abuse, and be condemned besides to a heavy fine; and for the sixth time, they shall be led to the pillory, and there have the upper lip cut with a hot iron; and for the seventh time, they shall be led to the pillory and have the lower lip cut; and if, by reason of obstinacy and inveterate bad habit, they continue after all these punishments to utter the said oaths and blasphemies, it is our will and command that they have the tongue completely cut out, so that thereafter they cannot utter them again." All those who should hear anybody swear were further required to report the fact to the nearest judge within twenty-four hours, on pain of fine.

This is far from being the only instance in which the temporal power lends aid to the spiritual. Among other cases, the following is worth mentioning: Louis Gaboury, an inhabitant of the island of Orleans, charged with eating meat in Lent without asking leave of the priest, was condemned by the local judge to be tied three hours to a stake in public, and then led to the door of the chapel, there on his knees, with head bare and hands clasped, to ask pardon of God and the King. The culprit appealed to the council, which revoked the sentence and imposed only a fine.

The due subordination of households had its share of attention. Servants who deserted their masters were to be set in the pillory for the first offence, and whipped and branded for the second; while any person harboring them was to pay a fine of twenty francs. On the other hand, nobody was allowed to employ a servant without a license.

In case of heinous charges, torture of the accused was permitted under the French law; and it was sometimes practised in Canada. Condemned murderers and felons were occasionally tortured before being strangled; and the dead body, enclosed in a kind of iron cage, was left hanging for months at the top of Cape Diamond, a terror to children and a warning to evil-doers. Yet, on the whole, Canadian justice, tried by the standard of the time, was neither vindictive nor cruel.

In reading the voluminous correspondence of governors and intendants, the minister and the King, nothing is more apparent than the interest with which, in the early part of his reign, Louis XIV regarded his colony. One of the faults of his rule is the excess of his benevolence; for not only did he give money to support parish priests, build churches, and aid the seminary, the Ursulines, the missions, and the hospitals; but he established a fund destined, among other objects, to relieve indigent persons, subsidized nearly every branch of trade and industry, and in other instances did for the colonists what they would far better have learned to do for themselves.

Meanwhile, the officers of government were far from suffering from an excess of royal beneficence. La Hontan says that the local governor of Three Rivers would die of hunger if, besides his pay, he did not gain something by trade with the Indians; and that Perrot, local governor of Montreal, with 1000 crowns of salary, traded to such purpose that in a few years he made 50,000 crowns. This trade, it may be observed, was in violation of the royal edicts. The pay of the governor-general varied from time to time. When La Potherie wrote, it was 12,000 francs a year, besides 3000 which he received in his capacity of local governor of Quebec.[1] This would hardly tempt a Frenchman of rank to expatriate himself; and yet some at least of the governors came out to the colony for the express purpose of mending their fortunes. Indeed, the higher nobility could scarcely, in time of peace, have other motives for going there; the court and the army were their element, and to be elsewhere was banishment. We shall see hereafter by what means they sought compensation for their exile in Canadian forests.

Loud complaints sometimes found their way to Versailles. A memorial addressed to the regent duke of Orleans, immediately after the King's death, declares that the ministers of state, who have been the real managers of the colony, have made their creatures and relations governors and intendants, and set them free from all responsibility. High colonial officers, pursues the writer, come home rich, while the colony languishes almost to perishing. As for lesser offices, they were multiplied to satisfy needy retainers, till lean and starving Canada was covered with official leeches, sucking, in famished desperation, at her bloodless veins.

The whole system of administration centred in the King, who, to borrow the formula of his edicts, "in the fulness of our power and our certain knowledge," was supposed to direct the whole machine, from its highest functions to its pettiest intervention in private affairs. That this theory, like all extreme theories of government, was an illusion, is no fault of Louis XIV. Hard-working monarch as he was, he spared no pains to guide his distant colony in the paths of prosperity. The prolix letters of governors and intendants were carefully studied; and many of the replies, signed by the royal hand, enter into details of surprising minuteness. That the King himself wrote these letters is incredible; but in the early part of his reign he certainly directed and controlled them. At a later time, when more absorbing interests engrossed him, he could no longer study in person the long-winded despatches of his Canadian officers. They were usually addressed to the minister of state, who caused abstracts to be made from them for the King's use, and perhaps for his own. The minister, or the minister's secretary, could suppress or color as he or those who influenced him saw fit.

In the latter half of his too long reign, when cares, calamities, and humiliations were thickening around the King, another influence was

[1] In 1674 the governor-general received 20,718 francs, out of which he was to pay 8718 to his guard of 20 men and officers.

added to make the theoretical supremacy of his royal will more than ever a mockery. That prince of annalists, Saint-Simon, has painted Louis XIV ruling his realm from the bedchamber of Madame de Maintenon, — seated with his minister at a small table beside the fire, the King in an arm-chair, the minister on a stool, with his bag of papers on a second stool near him. In another arm-chair, at another table on the other side of the fire, sat the sedate favorite, busy to all appearance with a book or a piece of tapestry, but listening to everything that passed. "She rarely spoke," says Saint-Simon, "except when the King asked her opinion, which he often did; and then she answered with great deliberation and gravity. She never, or very rarely, showed a partiality for any measure, still less for any person; but she had an understanding with the minister, who never dared do otherwise than she wished. Whenever any favor or appointment was in question, the business was settled between them beforehand. She would send to the minister that she wanted to speak to him, and he did not dare bring the matter on the carpet till he had received her orders." Saint-Simon next recounts the subtle methods by which Maintenon and the minister, her tool, beguiled the King to do their will, while never doubting that he was doing his own. "He thought," concludes the annalist, "that it was he alone who disposed of all appointments; while in reality he disposed of very few indeed, except on the rare occasions when he had taken a fancy to somebody, or when somebody whom he wanted to favor had spoken to him in behalf of somebody else."

Add to all this the rarity of communication with the distant colony. The ships from France arrived at Quebec in July, August or September, and returned in November. The machine of Canadian government, wound up once a year, was expected to run unaided at least a twelve-month. Indeed, it was often left to itself for two years, such was sometimes the tardiness of the overburdened government in answering the despatches of its colonial agents. It is no matter of surprise that a writer well versed in its affairs calls Canada the "country of abuses." [2]

2 *État présent du Canada*, 1758.

CHAPTER XIV

Trade and Industry

1663–1763

[*The Old Régime in Canada*, CHAPTER XX]

We have seen the head of the colony, its guiding intellect and will: it remains to observe its organs of nutrition. Whatever they might have been under a different treatment, they were perverted and enfeebled by the regimen to which they were subjected.

The spirit of restriction and monopoly had ruled from the beginning. The old governor Lauson, seigneur for a while of a great part of the colony, held that Montreal had no right to trade directly with France, but must draw all her supplies from Quebec; and this preposterous claim was revived in the time of Mézy. The successive companies to whose hands the colony was consigned had a baneful effect on individual enterprise. In 1674 the charter of the West India Company was revoked, and trade was declared open to all subjects of the King; yet commerce was still condemned to wear the ball and chain. New restrictions were imposed, meant for good, but resulting in evil. Merchants not resident in the colony were forbidden all trade, direct or indirect, with the Indians. They were also forbidden to sell any goods at retail except in August, September, and October; to trade anywhere in Canada above Quebec, and to sell clothing or domestic articles ready made. This last restriction was designed to develop colonial industry. No person, resident or not, could trade with the English colonies, or go thither without a special passport, and rigid examination by the military authorities. Foreign trade of any kind was stiffly prohibited. In 1719, after a new company had engrossed the beaver-trade, its agents were empowered to enter all houses in Canada, whether ecclesiastical or secular, and search them for foreign goods, which when found were publicly burned. In the next year the royal council ordered that vessels engaged in foreign trade should be captured by force of arms, like pirates, and confiscated along with their cargoes; while anybody having an article of foreign manufacture in his possession was subjected to a heavy fine.

Attempts were made to fix the exact amount of profit which merchants from France should be allowed to make in the colony; one of the first acts of the superior council was to order them to bring their invoices immediately before that body, which thereupon affixed prices to each article. The merchants who sold and the purchaser who bought above this tariff were alike condemned to heavy penalties; and so, too, was the merchant who chose to keep his goods rather than sell them at the price ordained. Resident merchants, on the other hand, were favored to the utmost: they could sell at what price they saw fit; and, according to La Hontan, they made great profit by the sale of laces, ribbons, watches, jewels, and similar superfluities to the poor but extravagant colonists.

A considerable number of the non-resident merchants were Huguenots, for most of the importations were from the old Huguenot city of Rochelle. No favor was shown them; they were held under rigid restraint, and forbidden to exercise their religion, or to remain in the colony during winter without special license. This sometimes bore very hard upon them. The governor, Denonville, an ardent Catholic, states the case of one Bernon, who had done great service to the colony, and whom La Hontan mentions as the principal French merchant in the Canadian trade. "It is a pity," says Denonville, "that he cannot be converted. As he is a Huguenot, the bishop wants me to order him home this autumn, — which I have done, though he carries on a large business, and a great deal of money remains due to him here."

For a long time the ships from France went home empty, except a favored few which carried furs, or occasionally a load of dried pease or of timber. Payment was made in money when there was any in Canada, or in bills of exchange. The colony, drawing everything from France and returning little besides beaver-skins, remained under a load of debt. French merchants were discouraged, and shipments from France languished. As for the trade with the West Indies, which Talon had tried by precept and example to build up, the intendant reports in 1680 that it had nearly ceased; though six years later it grew again to the modest proportions of three vessels loaded with wheat.

The besetting evil of trade and industry in Canada was the habit they contracted, and were encouraged to contract, of depending on the direct aid of government. Not a new enterprise was set on foot without a petition to the King to lend a helping hand. Sometimes the petition was sent through the governor, sometimes through the intendant; and it was rarely refused. Denonville writes that the merchants of Quebec, by a combined effort, had sent a vessel of sixty tons to France with colonial produce; and he asks that the royal commissaries at Rochefort be instructed to buy the whole cargo, in order to encourage so deserving an enterprise. One Hazeur set up a saw-mill at Mal Bay. Finding a large stock of planks and timber on his hands, he begs the King to send two vessels to carry them to France; and the King accordingly did so. A similar request was made in behalf of another saw-mill at St. Paul's Bay. Denonville announces that one Riverin wishes to embark in the whale and cod fishery, and that though strong in zeal he is weak in resources. The minister replies that he is to be encouraged, and that his Majesty will favorably consider his enterprise. Various gifts were soon after made him. He now took to himself a partner, the Sieur Chalons; whereupon the governor writes to ask the minister's protection for them. "The Basques," he says, "formerly carried on this fishery, but some monopoly or other put a stop to it." The remedy he proposes is homœopathic. He asks another monopoly for the two partners. Louis Joliet, the discoverer of the Mississippi, made a fishing-station on the island of Anticosti; and he begs help from the King, on the ground that his fishery will furnish a good and useful employment to young men. The Sieur Vitry wished to begin a fishery of white porpoises, and he begs the King to give him 2000 pounds of cod-line and 2000 pounds of one- and two-inch rope. His request was granted, on which he asked for 500 livres. The money was given him; and the next year he asked to have the gift renewed.[1]

The King was very anxious to develop the fisheries of the colony. "His Majesty," writes the minister, "wishes you to induce the inhabitants to unite with the merchants for this object, and to incite them by all sorts of means to overcome their natural laziness since there is no other way of saving them from the misery in which they now are." "I wish," says the zealous Denonville, "that fisheries could be well established to give employment to our young men, and prevent them from running wild in the woods;" and he adds mournfully, "they [the

[1] Vitry's porpoise-fishing appears to have ended in failure. In 1707 the intendant Raudot granted the porpoise fishery of the seigneury of Rivière Ouelle to six of the *habitants*. This fishery is carried on here successfully at the present day. A very interesting account of it was published in *L'Opinion Publique*, 1873, by my friend Abbé Casgrain, whose family residence is the seigneurial mansion of Rivière Ouelle.

fisheries] are enriching Boston at our expense." "They are our true mines," urges the intendant Meules; "but the English of Boston have got possession of those of Acadia, which belong to us, and we ought to prevent it." It was not prevented; and the Canadian fisheries, like other branches of Canadian industry, remained in a state of almost hopeless languor.[2]

The government applied various stimulants. One of these, proposed by the intendant Duchesneau, is characteristic. He advises the formation of a company which should have the exclusive right of exporting fish; but which on its part should be required to take, at a fixed price, all that the inhabitants should bring them. This notable plan did not find favor with the King. It was practised, however, in the case of beaver-skins, and also in that of wood-ashes. The farmers of the revenue were required to take this last commodity at a fixed price, on their own risk, and in any quantity offered. They remonstrated, saying that it was unsalable, — adding, that, if the inhabitants would but take the trouble to turn it into potash, it might be possible to find a market for it. The King released them entirely, coupling his order to that effect with a eulogy of free-trade.

In all departments of industry the appeals for help are endless. Governors and intendants are so many sturdy beggars for the languishing colony. "Send us money to build storehouses, to which the *habitants* can bring their produce and receive goods from the government in exchange." "Send us a teacher to make sailors of our young men: it is a pity the colony should remain in such a state for want of instruction for youth." "We want a surgeon: there is none in Canada who can set a bone." "Send us some tilers, brick-makers, and potters." "Send us iron-workers to work our mines." "It is to be wished that his Majesty would send us all sorts of artisans, especially potters and glass-workers." "Our Canadians need aid and instruction in their fisheries; they need pilots."

In 1688 the intendant reported that Canada was entirely without either pilots or sailors; and as late as 1712 the engineer Catalogne informed the government, that, though the St. Lawrence was dangerous, a pilot was rarely to be had. "There ought to be trade with the West Indies and other places," urges another writer. "Everybody says it is best, but nobody will undertake it. Our merchants are too poor, or else are engrossed by the fur-trade."

---

[2] The Canadian fisheries must not be confounded with the French fisheries of Newfoundland, which were prosperous but were carried on wholly from French ports.

The languor of commerce made agriculture languish. "It is of no use now," writes Meules, in 1682, "to raise any crops except what each family wants for itself." In vain the government sent out seeds for distribution; in vain intendants lectured the farmers, and lavished well-meant advice. Tillage remained careless and slovenly. "If," says the all-observing Catalogne, "the soil were not better cultivated in Europe than here, three-fourths of the people would starve." He complains that the festivals of the Church are so numerous that not ninety working-days are left during the whole working season. The people, he says, ought to be compelled to build granaries to store their crops, instead of selling them in autumn for almost nothing, and every *habitant* should be required to keep two or three sheep. The intendant Champigny calls for seed of hemp and flax, and promises to visit the farms, and show the people the lands best suited for their culture. He thinks that favors should be granted to those who raise hemp and flax as well as to those who marry. Denonville is of opinion that each *habitant* should be compelled to raise a little hemp every year, and that the King should then buy it of him at a high price. It will be well, he says, to make use of severity, while at the same time holding out a hope of gain; and he begs that weavers be sent out to teach the women and girls, who spend the winter in idleness, how to weave and spin. Weaving and spinning, however, as well as the culture of hemp and flax, were neglected till 1705, when the loss of a ship laden with goods for the colony gave the spur to home industry; and Madame de Repentigny set the example of making a kind of coarse blanket of nettle and linden bark.

The jealousy of colonial manufacturers shown by England appears but rarely in the relations of France with Canada. According to its light, the French government usually did its best to stimulate Canadian industry, with what results we have just seen. There was afterwards some improvement. In 1714 the intendant Bégon reported that coarse fabrics of wool and linen were made; that the sisters of the congregation wove cloth for their own habits as good as the same stuffs in France; that black cloth was made for priests, and blue cloth for the pupils of the colleges. The inhabitants, he says, have been taught these arts by necessity. They were naturally adroit at handiwork of all kinds; and during the last half-century of the French rule, when the population had settled into comparative stability, many of the mechanic arts were practised with success, notwithstanding the assertion of the Abbé La Tour that everything but bread and meat had still to be brought from France. This change may be said to date from the peace of Utrecht, or a few years before it. At that time one Duplessis had a new vessel on the stocks. Catalogne, who states the fact, calls it the beginning of ship-building in Canada, — evidently ignorant that Talon had made a fruitless beginning more than forty years before.

Of the arts of ornament not much could have been expected; but, strangely enough, they were in somewhat better condition than the useful arts. The nuns of the Hôtel-Dieu made artificial flowers for altars and shrines, under the direction of Mother Juchereau; and the boys of the seminary were taught to make carvings in wood for the decoration of churches. Pierre, son of the merchant Le Ber, had a turn for painting, and made religious pictures, described as very indifferent. His sister Jeanne, an enthusiastic devotee, made embroideries for vestments and altars, and her work was much admired.

The colonial finances were not prosperous. In the absence of coin, beaver-skins long served as currency. In 1669 the council declared wheat a legal tender, at four francs the *minot* or three French bushels; and, five years later, all creditors were ordered to receive moose-skins in payment at the market rate. Coin would not remain in the colony: if the company or the King sent any thither, it went back in the returning ships. The government devised a remedy. A coinage was ordered for Canada one-fourth less in value than that of France. Thus the Canadian livre or franc was worth, in reality, fifteen sous instead of twenty.[3] This shallow expedient produced only a nominal rise of prices, and coin fled the colony as before. Trade was carried on for a time by means of negotiable notes, payable in furs, goods, or farm produce. In 1685 the intendant Meules issued a card currency. He had no money to pay the soldiers, "and not knowing," he informs the minister, "to what saint to make my vows, the idea occurred to me of putting in circulation notes made of cards, each cut into four pieces; and I have issued an ordinance commanding the inhabitants to receive them in payment." The cards were common playing-cards and each piece was stamped with a *fleur-de-lis* and a crown, and signed by the governor, the intendant, and the clerk of the treasury at Quebec. The example of Meules found ready imitation. Governors and intendants made card-money whenever they saw fit; and, being worthless everywhere but in Canada, it showed no disposition to escape the colony. It was declared convertible not into coin, but into bills of exchange; and this conversion

[3] This device was of very early date. [It was also adopted in the English colonies, for the same reason, and with similar lack of success.]

could only take place at brief specified periods. "The currency used in Canada," says a writer in the last years of the French rule, "has no value as a representative of money. It is the sign of a sign." It was card representing paper, and this paper was very often dishonored. In 1714 the amount of card rubbish had risen to two million livres. Confidence was lost, and trade was half dead. The minister Ponchartrain came to the rescue, and promised to redeem it at half its nominal value. The holders preferred to lose half rather than the whole, and accepted the terms. A few of the cards were redeemed at the rate named; then the government broke faith, and payment ceased. "The afflicting news," says a writer of the time, "was brought out by the vessel which sailed from France last July."

In 1717 the government made another proposal, and the cards were converted into bills of exchange. At the same time a new issue was made, which it was declared should be the last. This issue was promptly redeemed; but twelve years later another followed it. In the interval, a certain quantity of coin circulated in the colony; but it underwent fluctuations through the intervention of government, and within eight years at least four edicts were issued affecting its value. Then came more promises to pay, till, in the last bitter years of its existence, the colony floundered in drifts of worthless paper.

One characteristic grievance was added to the countless woes of Canadian commerce. The government was so jealous of popular meetings of all kinds, that for a long time it forbade merchants to meet together for discussing their affairs; and it was not till 1717 that the establishment of a *bourse*, or exchange, was permitted at Quebec and Montreal.

In respect of taxation, Canada, as compared with France, had no reason to complain. If the King permitted governors and intendants to make card-money, he permitted nobody to impose taxes but himself. The Canadians paid no direct civil tax, except in a few instances where temporary and local assessments were ordered for special objects. It was the fur-trade on which the chief burden fell. One-fourth of the beaver-skins, and one-tenth of the moose-hides belonged to the King; and wine, brandy, and tobacco contributed a duty of ten per cent. During a long course of years these were the only imposts. The King also retained the exclusive right of the fur-trade at Tadoussac. A vast tract of wilderness extending from St. Paul's Bay to a point eighty leagues down the St. Lawrence, and stretching indefinitely northward towards Hudson's Bay, formed a sort of royal preserve, whence every settler was rigidly excluded. The farmers of the revenue had their trading-houses at Tadoussac, whither the northern tribes, until war, pestilence, and brandy consumed them, brought every summer a large quantity of furs.

When, in 1674, the West India Company, to whom these imposts had been granted, was extinguished, the King resumed possession of them. The various duties, along with the trade of Tadoussac, were now farmed out to one Oudiette and his associates, who paid the Crown 350,000 livres for their privilege.

We come now to a trade far more important than all the others together, one which absorbed the enterprise of the colony, drained the life-sap from other branches of commerce, and, even more than a vicious system of government, kept them in a state of chronic debility, — the hardy, adventurous, lawless, fascinating fur-trade. In the eighteenth century, Canada exported a moderate quantity of timber, wheat, the herb called ginseng, and a few other commodities; but from first to last she lived chiefly on beaver-skins. The government tried without ceasing to control and regulate this traffic; but it never succeeded. It aimed, above all things, to bring the trade home to the colonists; to prevent them from going to the Indians, and induce the Indians to come to them. To this end a great annual fair was established by order of the King at Montreal. Thither every summer a host of savages came down from the lakes in their bark canoes. A place was assigned them at a little distance from the town. They landed, drew up their canoes in a line on the bank, took out their packs of beaver-skins, set up their wigwams, slung their kettles, and encamped for the night. On the next day there was a grand council on the common, between St. Paul Street and the river. Speeches of compliment were made amid a solemn smoking of pipes. The governor-general was usually present, seated in an arm-chair, while the visitors formed a ring about him, ranged in the order of their tribes. On the next day the trade began in the same place. Merchants of high and low degree brought up their goods from Quebec, and every inhabitant of Montreal, of any substance, sought a share in the profit. Their booths were set along the palisades of the town, and each had an interpreter, to whom he usually promised a certain portion of his gains.

The scene abounded in those contrasts — not always edifying, but always picturesque — which mark the whole course of French-Canadian history. Here was a throng of Indians armed with bows and arrows, war-clubs, or the cheap guns of the trade, — some of them being completely naked, except for the feathers on their heads and the paint on their faces; French bush-rangers tricked out with savage finery; merchants and *habitants* in their coarse and plain attire, and the grave priests of St. Sulpice robed in black. Order and sobriety were their watchwords; but the wild gathering was beyond their control. The prohibition to sell brandy could rarely be enforced; and the fair ended at times in a pandemonium of drunken frenzy. The rapacity of trade, and the license of savages and *coureurs de bois*, had completely transformed the pious settlement.

A similar fair was established at Three Rivers, for the Algonquin tribes north of that place. These yearly markets did not fully answer the desired object. There was a constant tendency among the inhabitants of Canada to form settlements above Montreal, in order to intercept the Indians on their way down, drench them with brandy, and get their furs from them at low rates in advance of the fair. Such settlements were forbidden, but not prevented. The audacious "squatter" defied edict and ordinance and the fury of drunken savages, and boldly planted himself in the path of the descending trade. Nor is this a matter of surprise; for he was usually the secret agent of some high colonial officer, — an intendant, the local governor, or the governor-general, who often used his power to enforce the law against others, and to violate it himself.

This was not all; for the more youthful and vigorous part of the male population soon began to escape into the woods, and trade with the Indians far beyond the limits of the remotest settlements. Here, too, many of them were in league with the authorities, who denounced the abuse while secretly favoring the portion of it in which they themselves were interested. The home government, unable to prevent the evil, tried to regulate it. Licenses were issued for the forest-trade. Their number was limited to twenty-five, and the privileges which they conferred varied at different periods. In La Hontan's time, each license authorized the departure of two canoes loaded with goods. One canoe only was afterwards allowed, bearing three men with about four hundred pounds of freight. The licenses were sometimes sold for the profit of government; but many were given to widows of officers and other needy persons, to the hospitals, or to favorites and retainers of the governor. Those who could not themselves use them sold them to merchants or *voyageurs*, at a price varying from a thousand to eighteen hundred francs. They were valid for a year and a half; and each canoe-man had a share in the profits, which, if no accident happened, were

very large. The license system was several times suppressed and renewed again; but, like the fair at Montreal, it failed completely to
answer its purpose, and restrain the young men of Canada from a general exodus into the wilderness.

The most characteristic features of the Canadian fur-trade still remain to be seen. Oudiette and his associates were not only charged with
collecting the revenue, but were also vested with an exclusive right
of transporting all the beaver-skins of the colony to France. On their
part they were compelled to receive all beaver-skins brought to their
magazines, and, after deducting the fourth belonging to the King, to
pay for the rest at a fixed price. This price was graduated to the different qualities of the fur; but the average cost to the collectors was a
little more than three francs a pound. The inhabitants could barter their
furs with merchants; but the merchants must bring them all to the
magazines of Oudiette, who paid in receipts convertible into bills of
exchange. He soon found himself burdened with such a mass of beaver-
skins that the market was completely glutted. The French hatters refused to take them all; and for the part which they consented to take
they paid chiefly in hats, which Oudiette was not allowed to sell in
France, but only in the French West Indies, where few people wanted
them. An unlucky fashion of small hats diminished the consumption
of fur and increased his embarrassments, as did also a practice common
among the hatters of mixing rabbit fur with the beaver. In his extremity
he bethought him of setting up a hat factory for himself, under the
name of a certain licensed hatter, thinking thereby to alarm his customers into buying his stock. The other hatters rose in wrath, and petitioned the minister. The new factory was suppressed, and Oudiette soon
became bankrupt. Another company of farmers of the revenue took
his place with similar results. The action of the law of supply and
demand was completely arrested by the peremptory edict which, with
a view to the prosperity of the colony and the profit of the King,
required the company to take every beaver-skin offered.

All Canada, thinking itself sure of its price, rushed into the beaver-
trade, and the accumulation of unsalable furs became more and more
suffocating. The farmers of the revenue could not meet their engage-
ments. Their bills of exchange were unpaid, and Canada was filled with
distress and consternation. In 1700 a change of system was ordered.
The monopoly of exporting beaver was placed in the hands of a company formed of the chief inhabitants of Canada. Some of them hesitated to take the risk; but the government was not to be trifled with, and

the minister, Ponchartrain, wrote in terms so peremptory, and so menacing to the recusants, that, in the words of a writer of the time, he "shut everybody's mouth." About 150 merchants accordingly subscribed to the stock of the new company, and immediately petitioned the King for a ship and a loan of 700,000 francs. They were required to take off the hands of the farmers of the revenue an accumulation of more than 600,000 pounds of beaver, for which, however, they were to pay but half its usual price. The market of France absolutely refused it, and the directors of the new company saw no better course than to burn three-fourths of the troublesome and perishable commodity; nor was this the first resort to this strange expedient. One cannot repress a feeling of indignation at the fate of the interesting and unfortunate animals uselessly sacrificed to a false economic system. In order to rid themselves of what remained, the directors begged the King to issue a decree, requiring all hatters to put at least three ounces of genuine beaver-fur into each hat.

All was in vain. The affairs of the company fell into a confusion which was aggravated by the bad faith of some of its chief members. In 1707 it was succeeded by another company, to whose magazines every *habitant* or merchant was ordered to bring every beaver-skin in his possession within forty-eight hours; and the company, like its predecessors, was required to receive it, and pay for it in written promises. Again the market was overwhelmed with a surfeit of beaver. Again the bills of exchange were unpaid, and all was confusion and distress. Among the memorials and petitions to which this state of things gave birth, there is one conspicuous by the presence of good sense and the absence of self-interest. The writer proposes that there should be no more monopoly, but that everybody should be free to buy beaver-skins and send them to France, subject only to a moderate duty of entry. The proposal was not accepted. In 1721 the monopoly of exporting beaver-skins was given to the new West India Company; but this time it was provided that the government should direct from time to time, according to the capacities of the market, the quantity of furs which the company should be forced to receive.

Out of the beaver-trade rose a huge evil, baneful to the growth and the morals of Canada. All that was most active and vigorous in the colony took to the woods, and escaped from the control of intendants, councils, and priests, to the savage freedom of the wilderness. Not only were the possible profits great; but, in the pursuit of them, there was a fascinating element of adventure and danger. The bush-rangers, or *coureurs de bois*, were to the King an object of horror. They defeated his plans for the increase of the population, and shocked his native instinct of discipline and order. Edict after edict was directed against them; and more than once the colony presented the extraordinary spectacle of the greater part of its young men turned into forest outlaws. But severity was dangerous. The offenders might be driven over to the English, or converted into a lawless banditti, — renegades of civilization and the faith. Therefore, clemency alternated with rigor, and declarations of amnesty with edicts of proscription. Neither threats nor blandishments were of much avail. We hear of seigneuries abandoned; farms turning again into forests; wives and children left in destitution. The exodus of the *coureurs de bois* would take, at times, the character of an organized movement. The famous Du Lhut is said to have made a general combination of the young men of Canada to follow him into the woods. Their plan was to be absent four years, in order that the edicts against them might have time to relent. The intendant Duchesneau reported that 800 men out of a population of less than 10,000 souls had vanished from sight in the immensity of a boundless wilderness. Whereupon the King ordered that any person going into the woods without a license should be whipped and branded for the first offence, and sent for life to the galleys for the second.[4]

The order was more easily given than enforced. "I must not conceal from you, Monseigneur," again writes Duchesneau, "that the disobedience of the *coureurs de bois* has reached such a point that everybody boldly contravenes the King's interdictions; that there is no longer any concealment; and that parties are collected with astonishing insolence to go and trade in the Indian country. I have done all in my power to prevent this evil, which may cause the ruin of the colony. I have enacted ordinances against the *coureurs de bois;* against the merchants who furnish them with goods; against the gentlemen and others who harbor them; and even against those who have any knowledge of them, and will not inform the local judges. All has been in vain; inasmuch as some of the most considerable families are interested with them, and the governor lets them go on and even shares their profits." "You are aware, Monseigneur," writes Denonville, some years later, "that the *coureurs de bois* are a great evil, but you are not aware how great this evil is. It deprives the country of its effective men; makes them indocile, debauched, and incapable of discipline, and turns them into pretended

---

[4] Le Roy à Frontenac, 30 April 1681. On another occasion, it was ordered that any person thus offending should suffer death.

nobles, — wearing the sword and decked out with lace, both they and their relations, who all affect to be gentlemen and ladies. As for cultivating the soil, they will not hear of it. This, along with the scattered condition of the settlements, causes their children to be as unruly as Indians, being brought up in the same manner. Not that there are not some very good people here, but they are in a minority." In another despatch he enlarges on their vagabond and lawless ways, their indifference to marriage, and the mischief caused by their example; describes how, on their return from the woods, they swagger like lords, spend all their gains in dress and drunken revelry, and despise the peasants, whose daughters they will not deign to marry, though they are peasants themselves.

It was a curious scene when a party of *coureurs de bois* returned from their rovings. Montreal was their harboring place, and they conducted themselves much like the crew of a man-of-war paid off after a long voyage. As long as their beaver-skins lasted, they set no bounds to their riot. Every house in the place, we are told, was turned into a drinking-shop. The new-comers were bedizened with a strange mixture of French and Indian finery; while some of them, with instincts more thoroughly savage, stalked about the streets as naked as a Pottawattamie or a Sioux. The clamor of tongues was prodigious, and gambling and drinking filled the day and the night. When at last they were sober again, they sought absolution for their sins; nor could the priests venture to bear too hard on their unruly penitents, lest they should break wholly with the Church and dispense thenceforth with her sacraments.

Under such leaders as Du Lhut, the *coureurs de bois* built forts of palisades at various points throughout the West and Northwest. They had a post of this sort at Detroit some time before its permanent settlement, as well as others on Lake Superior and in the valley of the Mississippi. They occupied them as long as it suited their purposes, and then abandoned them to the next comer. Michilimackinac was, however, their chief resort; and thence they would set out, two or three together, to roam for hundreds of miles through the endless mesh-work of interlocking lakes and rivers which seams the northern wilderness.

No wonder that a year or two of bush-ranging spoiled them for civilization. Though not a very valuable member of society, and though a thorn in the side of princes and rulers, the *coureur de bois* had his uses, at least from an artistic point of view; and his strange figure, sometimes brutally savage, but oftener marked with the lines of a dare-devil courage, and a reckless, thoughtless gayety, will always be joined to the memories of that grand world of woods which the nineteenth century is fast civilizing out of existence. At least, he is picturesque, and with his red-skin companion serves to animate forest scenery. Perhaps he could sometimes feel, without knowing that he felt them, the charms of the savage nature that had adopted him. Rude as he was, her voice may not always have been meaningless for one who knew her haunts so well, — deep recesses where, veiled in foliage, some wild shy rivulet steals with timid music through breathless caves of verdure; gulfs where feathered crags rise like castle walls, where the noonday sun pierces with keen rays athwart the torrent, and the mossed arms of fallen pines cast wavering shadows on the illumined foam; pools of liquid crystal turned emerald in the reflected green of impending woods; rocks on whose rugged front the gleam of sunlit waters dances in quivering light; ancient trees hurled headlong by the storm, to dam the raging stream with their forlorn and savage ruin; or the stern depths of immemorial forests, dim and silent as a cavern, columned with innumerable trunks, each like an Atlas upholding its world of leaves, and sweating perpetual moisture down its dark and channelled rind, — some strong in youth, some grisly with decrepit age, nightmares of strange distortion, gnarled and knotted with wens and goitres; roots intertwined beneath like serpents petrified in an agony of contorted strife; green and glistening mosses carpeting the rough ground, mantling the rocks, turning pulpy stumps to mounds of verdure, and swathing fallen trunks as, bent in the impotence of rottenness, they lie outstretched over knoll and hollow, like mouldering reptiles of the primeval world, while around, and on and through them, springs the young growth that battens on their decay, — the forest devouring its own dead; or, to turn from its funereal shade to the light and life of the open woodland, the sheen of sparkling lakes, and mountains basking in the glory of the summer noon, flecked by the shadows of passing clouds that sail on snowy wings across the transparent azure.[5]

Yet it would be false coloring to paint the half-savage *coureur de bois* as a romantic lover of Nature. He liked the woods because they

[5] An adverse French critic gives as his opinion that the sketch of the primeval wilderness on the preceding page is drawn from fancy, and not from observation. It is, however, copied in every particular, without exception, from a virgin forest in a deep moist valley by the upper waters of the little river Pemigewasset in northern New Hampshire, where I spent a summer afternoon a few days before the passage was written.

emancipated him from restraint. He liked the lounging ease of the camp-fire, and the license of Indian villages. His life has a dark and ugly side, which is nowhere drawn more strongly than in a letter written by the Jesuit Carheil to the intendant Champigny. It was at a time when some of the outlying forest posts, originally either missions or transient stations of *coureurs de bois,* had received regular garrisons. Carheil writes from Michilimackinac, and describes the state of things around him like one whom long familiarity with them had stripped of every illusion.

But here, for the present, we pause; for the father touches on other matters than the *coureurs de bois,* and we reserve him and his letter for the next chapter.

CHAPTER XV

Priests and People
1663–1763

[The Old Régime in Canada, CHAPTER XXII, in part]

While Louis XIV tried to confine the priests to their ecclesiastical functions, he was at the same time, whether from religion, policy, or both combined, very liberal to the Canadian Church, of which, indeed, he was the main-stay. In the yearly estimate of "ordinary charges" of the colony, the Church holds the most prominent place; and the appropriations for religious purposes often exceed all the rest together. Thus, in 1667, out of a total of 36,360 francs, 28,000 are assigned to Church uses. The amount fluctuated, but was always relatively large. The Canadian curés were paid in great part by the King, who for many years gave 8000 francs annually towards their support. Such was the poverty of the country that, though in 1685 there were only twenty-five curés, each costing about 500 francs a year, the tithes utterly failed to meet the expense. As late as 1700, the intendant declared that Canada without the King's help could not maintain more than eight or nine curés. Louis XIV winced under these steady demands, and reminded the bishop that more than 4000 curés in France lived on less than 200 francs a year. "You say," he wrote to the intendant, "that it is impossible for a Canadian curé to live on five hundred francs. Then you must do the impossible to accomplish my intentions, which are always that the curés should live on the tithes alone." Yet the head of the Church still begged for money, and the King still paid it. "We are in the midst of a costly war," wrote the minister to the bishop, "yet in consequence of your urgency the gifts to ecclesiastics will be continued as before." And they did continue. More than half a century later, the King was still making them, and during the last years of the colony he gave 20,000 francs annually to support Canadian curés.

The maintenance of curés was but a part of his bounty. He endowed the bishopric with the revenues of two French abbeys, to which he afterwards added a third. The vast tracts of land which Laval had acquired were freed from feudal burdens, and emigrants were sent to them by the government in such numbers that, in 1667, the bishop's seigneury of Beaupré and Orleans contained more than a fourth of the entire population of Canada.[1] He had emerged from his condition of apostolic poverty to find himself the richest land-owner in the colony.

If by favors like these the King expected to lead the ecclesiastics into compliance with his wishes, he was doomed to disappointment. The system of movable curés, by which the bishop like a military chief could compel each member of his clerical army to come and go at his bidding, was from the first repugnant to Louis XIV. On the other hand, the bishop clung to it with his usual tenacity. Colbert denounced it as contrary to the laws of the kingdom. "His Majesty has reason to believe," he writes, "that the chief source of the difficulty which the bishop makes on this point is his wish to preserve a greater authority over the curés." The inflexible prelate, whose heart was bound up in the system he had established, opposed evasion and delay to each expression of the royal will; and even a royal edict failed to produce the desired effect. In the height of the dispute, Laval went to court, and, on the ground of failing health, asked for a successor in the bishopric. The King readily granted his prayer. The successor was appointed; but when Laval prepared to embark again for Canada, he was given to understand that he was to remain in France. In vain he promised to make no trouble; and it was not till after an absence of four years that he was permitted to return, no longer as its chief, to his beloved Canadian Church.

Meanwhile Saint-Vallier, the new bishop, had raised a new tempest. He attacked that organization of the seminary of Quebec by which Laval had endeavored to unite the secular priests of Canada into an attached and obedient family, with the bishop as its head and the seminary as its home, — a plan of which the system of movable curés was an essential part. The Canadian priests, devoted to Laval, met the innovations of Saint-Vallier with an opposition which seemed only to confirm his purpose. Laval, old and worn with toil and asceticism, was driven almost to despair. The seminary of Quebec was the cherished work of his life, and, to his thinking, the citadel of the Canadian

[1] Entire population, 4312; Beaupré and Orleans, 1185. (*Recensement de 1667*). Laval afterwards gave his lands to the seminary of Quebec.

Church; and now he beheld it battered and breached before his eyes. His successor, in fact, was trying to place the Church of Canada on the footing of the Church of France. The conflict lasted for years, with the rancor that marks the quarrels of non-combatants of both sexes. "He" [Saint-Vallier], says one of his opponents, "has made himself contemptible to almost everybody, and particularly odious to the priests born in Canada; for there is between them and him a mutual antipathy difficult to overcome." He is described by the same writer as a person "without reflection and judgment, extreme in all things, secret and artful, passionate when opposed, and a flatterer when he wishes to gain his point." This amiable critic adds that Saint-Vallier believes a bishop to be inspired, in virtue of his office, with a wisdom that needs no human aid; and that whatever thought comes to him in prayer is a divine inspiration to be carried into effect at all costs and in spite of all opposition.

The new bishop, notwithstanding the tempest he had raised, did not fully accomplish that establishment of the curés in their respective parishes which the King and the minister so much desired. The Canadian curé was more a missionary than a parish priest; and Nature as well as Bishop Laval threw difficulties in the way of settling him quietly over his charge.

On the Lower St. Lawrence, where it widens to an estuary, six leagues across, a ship from France, the last of the season, holds her way for Quebec, laden with stores and clothing, household utensils, goods for Indian trade, the newest court fashions, wine, brandy, tobacco, and the King's orders from Versailles. Swelling her patched and dingy sails, she glides through the wildness and the solitude where there is nothing but her to remind you of the great troubled world behind and the little troubled world before. On the far verge of the ocean-like river, clouds and mountains mingle in dim confusion; fresh gusts from the north dash waves against the ledges, sweep through the quivering spires of stiff and stunted fir-trees, and ruffle the feathers of the crow, perched on the dead bough after his feast of mussels among the sea-weed. You are not so solitary as you think. A small birch-canoe rounds the point of rocks, and it bears two men, — one in an old black cassock, and the other in a buckskin coat, — both working hard at the paddle to keep their slender craft off the shingle and the breakers. The man in the cassock is Father Morel, aged forty-eight, — the oldest country curé in Canada, most of his brethren being in the vigor of youth, as they had need to be. His parochial charge embraces a string of incipient parishes extending along the south shore from Rivière du Loup to Rivière du Sud, a distance reckoned at twenty-seven leagues, and his parishioners number in all 328 souls. He has administered spiritual consolation to the one inhabitant of Kamouraska; visited the eight families of La Bouteillerie and the five families of La Combe; and now he is on his way to the seigneury of St. Denis with its two houses and eleven souls.

The father lands where a shattered eel-pot high and dry on the pebbles betrays the neighborhood of man. His servant shoulders his portable chapel, and follows him through the belt of firs and the taller woods beyond, till the sunlight of a desolate clearing shines upon them. Charred trunks and limbs encumber the ground; dead trees, branchless, barkless, pierced by the woodpeckers, in part black with fire, in part bleached by sun and frost, tower ghastly and weird above the labyrinth of forest ruins, through which the priest and his follower wind their way, the cat-bird mewing, and the blue-jay screaming as they pass. Now the golden-rod and the aster, harbingers of autumn, fringe with yellow and purple the edge of the older clearing, where wheat and maize, the settler's meagre harvest, are growing among the stumps.

Wild-looking women, with sunburnt faces and neglected hair, run from their work to meet the curé; a man or two follow with soberer steps and less exuberant zeal; while half-savage children, the *coureurs de bois* of the future, bareheaded, barefooted, and half-clad, come to wonder and stare. To set up his altar in a room of the rugged log-cabin; say mass, hear confessions, impose penance, grant absolution; repeat the office of the dead over a grave made weeks before; baptize, perhaps, the last infant; marry, possibly, some pair who may or may not have waited for his coming; catechise as well as time and circumstance would allow the shy but turbulent brood of some former wedlock, — such was the work of the parish priest in the remoter districts. It was seldom that his charge was quite so scattered and so far extended as that of Father Morel; but there were fifteen or twenty others whose labors were like in kind, and in some cases no less arduous. All summer they paddled their canoes from settlement to settlement; and in winter they toiled on snow-shoes over the drifts, while the servant carried the portable chapel on his back, or dragged it on a sledge. Once, at least, in the year the curé paid his visit to Quebec, where, under the maternal roof of the seminary, he made his retreat of meditation and prayer, and then returned to his work. He rarely had a house of his own, but boarded in that of the seigneur or one of the *habitants*.

Many parishes or aggregations of parishes had no other church than a room fitted up for the purpose in the house of some pious settler. In the larger settlements there were churches and chapels of wood, thatched with straw, often ruinous, poor to the last degree, without ornaments, and sometimes without the sacred vessels necessary for the service. In 1683 there were but seven stone churches in all the colony. The population was so thin and scattered that many of the settlers heard mass only three or four times a year, and some of them not so often. The sick frequently died without absolution, and infants without baptism.

The splendid self-devotion of the early Jesuit missions has its record; so, too, have the unseemly bickerings of bishops and governors. But the patient toils of the missionary curé rest in the obscurity where the best of human virtues are buried from age to age. What we find set down concerning him is, that Louis XIV was unable to see why he should not live on two hundred francs a year as well as a village curé by the banks of the Garonne. The King did not know that his cassock and all his clothing cost him twice as much and lasted half as long; that he must have a canoe and a man to paddle it; and that when on his annual visit the seminary paid him five or six hundred francs, partly in clothes, partly in stores, and partly in money, the end of the year found him as poor as before except only in his conscience.

The Canadian priests held the manners of the colony under a rule as rigid as that of the Puritan churches of New England, — but with the difference that in Canada a large part of the population was restive under their control, while some of the civil authorities, often with the governor at their head, supported the opposition. This was due partly to an excess of clerical severity, and partly to the continued friction between the secular and ecclesiastical powers. It sometimes happened, however, that a new governor arrived, who was so pious that the clerical party felt that they could rely on him. Of these rare instances the principal is that of Denonville, who, with a wife as pious as himself, and a young daughter, landed at Quebec in 1685. On this, Bishop Saint-Vallier, anxious to turn his good dispositions to the best account, addressed to him a series of suggestions or rather directions for the guidance of his conduct, with a view to the spiritual profit of those over whom he was appointed to rule. The document was put on file, and the following are some of the points in it. It is divided into five different heads, — "Touching feasts," "touching balls and dances," "touching comedies and other declamations," "touching dress," "touching irreverence in church." The governor and madame his wife are desired to accept no invitations to suppers, — that is to say, late dinners, — as tending to nocturnal hours and dangerous pastimes; and they are further enjoined to express dissatisfaction, and refuse to come again, should any entertainment offered them be too sumptuous. "Although," continues the bishop under the second head of his address, "balls and dances are not sinful in their nature, nevertheless they are so dangerous by reason of the circumstances that attend them and the evil results that almost inevitably follow, that, in the opinion of Saint Francis of Sales, it should be said of them as physicians say of mushrooms, that at best they are good for nothing;" and, after enlarging on their perils, he declares it to be of great importance to the glory of God and the sanctification of the colony, that the governor and his wife neither give such entertainments nor countenance them by their presence. "Nevertheless," adds the mentor, "since the youth and vivacity of mademoiselle their daughter requires some diversion, it is permitted to relent somewhat, and indulge her in a little moderate and proper dancing, provided that it be solely with persons of her own sex, and in the presence of madame her mother; but by no means in the presence of men or youths, since it is this mingling of sexes which causes the disorders that spring from balls and dances."

Private theatricals in any form are next interdicted to the young lady. The bishop then passes to the subject of her dress, and exposes the abuses against which she is to be guarded. "The luxury of dress," he says, "appears in the rich and dazzling fabrics wherein the women and girls of Canada attire themselves, and which are far beyond their condition and their means; in the excess of ornaments which they put on; in the extraordinary head-dresses which they affect, their heads being uncovered and full of strange trinkets; and in the immodest curls so expressly forbidden in the epistles of Saint Peter and Saint Paul, as well as by all the fathers and doctors of the Church, and which God has often severely punished, — as may be seen by the example of the unhappy Pretextata, a lady of high quality, who, as we learn from Saint Jerome, who knew her, had her hands withered, and died suddenly five months after, and was precipitated into hell, as God had threatened her by an angel; because, by order of her husband, she had curled the hair of her niece, and attired her after a worldly fashion."

Whether the Marquis and Marchioness Denonville profited by so apt and terrible a warning, or whether their patience and good-nature survived the episcopal onslaught, does not appear on record. The subject of feminine apparel received great attention, both from Saint-Vallier and his predecessor, each of whom issued a number of pastoral mandates concerning it. Their severest denunciations were aimed at low-necked dresses, which they regarded as favorite devices of the enemy for the snaring of souls; and they also used strong language against certain knots of ribbons called *fontanges*, with which the belles of Quebec adorned their heads. Laval launches strenuous invectives against "the luxury and vanity of women and girls, who, forgetting the promises of their baptism, decorate themselves with the pomp of Satan, whom they have so solemnly renounced; and, in their wish to please the eyes of men, make themselves the instruments and the captives of the fiend."

In the journal of the superior of the Jesuits we find, under date of February 4, 1667, a record of the first ball in Canada, along with the pious wish, "God grant that nothing further come of it." Nevertheless more balls were not long in following; and, worse yet, sundry comedies were enacted under no less distinguished patronage than that of Frontenac, the governor. Laval denounced them vigorously, the Jesuit Dablon attacked them in a violent sermon; and such excitement followed that the affair was brought before the royal council, which declined to interfere. This flurry, however, was nothing to the storm raised ten or twelve years later by other dramatic aggressions. . . .

The morals of families were watched with unrelenting vigilance. Frontenac writes in a mood unusually temperate, "They [the priests] are full of virtue and piety, and if their zeal were less vehement and more moderate, they would perhaps succeed better in their efforts for the conversion of souls; but they often use means so extraordinary, and in France so unusual, that they repel most people instead of persuading them. I sometimes tell them my views frankly and as gently as I can, as I know the murmurs that their conduct excites, and often receive complaints of the constraint under which they place consciences. This is above all the case with the ecclesiastics at Montreal, where there is a curé from Franche Comté who wants to establish a sort of inquisition worse than that of Spain, and all out of an excess of zeal."

It was this curé, no doubt, of whom La Hontan complains. That unsanctified young officer was quartered at Montreal, in the house of one of the inhabitants. "During a part of the winter I was hunting with the Algonquins; the rest of it I spent here very disagreeably. One can neither go on a pleasure party, nor play a game of cards, nor visit the ladies, without the curé knowing it and preaching about it publicly from his pulpit. The priests excommunicate masqueraders, and even go in search of them to pull off their masks and overwhelm them with abuse. They watch more closely over the women and girls than their husbands and fathers. They prohibit and burn all books but books of devotion. I cannot think of this tyranny without cursing the indiscreet zeal of the curé of this town. He came to the house where I lived, and, finding some books on my table, presently pounced on the romance of Petronius, which I valued more than my life because it was not mutilated. He tore out almost all the leaves, so that if my host had not restrained me when I came in and saw the miserable wreck, I should have run after this rampant shepherd and torn out every hair of his beard." . . .

While the Sulpitians were thus rigorous at Montreal, the bishop and his Jesuit allies were scarcely less so at Quebec. There was little good-will between them and the Sulpitians, and some of the sharpest charges against the followers of Loyola are brought by their brother priests at Montreal. The Sulpitian Allet writes: "The Jesuits hold such domination over the people of this country that they go into the houses and see everything that passes there. They then tell what they have learned to each other at their meetings, and on this information they govern their policy. The Jesuit, Father Ragueneau, used to go every day down to the Lower Town, where the merchants live, to find out all that was going on in their families; and he often made people get up from table to confess to him." . . .

The Jesuits derived great power from the confessional; and, if their accusers are to be believed, they employed unusual means to make it effective. Cavelier de la Salle says: "They will confess nobody till he tells his name, and no servant till he tells the name of his master. When a crime is confessed, they insist on knowing the name of the accomplice, as well as all the circumstances, with the greatest particularity. Father Châtelain especially never fails to do this. They enter as it were by force into the secrets of families, and thus make themselves formidable; for what cannot be done by a clever man devoted to his work, who knows all the secrets of every family; above all, when he permits himself to tell them when it is for his interest to do so?" . . .

The Jesuits had long exercised solely the function of confessors in the colony, and a number of curious anecdotes are on record showing the reluctance with which they admitted the secular priests, and above all the Récollets, to share in it. The Récollets, of whom a considerable number had arrived from time to time, were on excellent terms with the civil powers, and were popular with the colonists; but with the bishop and the Jesuits they were not in favor, and one or two sharp collisions took place. The bishop was naturally annoyed when, while he was trying to persuade the King that a curé needed at least 600 francs a year, these mendicant friars came forward with an offer to serve the parishes for nothing; nor was he, it is likely, better pleased when, having asked the hospital nuns 800 francs annually for two masses a day in their chapel, the Récollets underbid him, and offered to say the masses for three hundred. They, on their part, complain bitterly of the bishop, who, they say, would gladly have ordered them out of the colony, but, being unable to do this, tried to shut them up in their convent, and prevent them from officiating as priests among the people. "We have as little liberty," says the Récollet writer, "as if we were in a country of heretics." He adds that the inhabitants ask earnestly for the ministrations of the friars, but that the bishop replies with invectives and calumnies against the Order; and that when the Récollets absolve a penitent, he often annuls the absolution.

In one respect this Canadian Church militant achieved a complete success. Heresy was scoured out of the colony. When Maintenon and her ghostly prompters overcame the better nature of the King, and wrought on his bigotry and his vanity to launch him into the dragonnades; when violence and lust bore the crucifix into thousands of Huguenot homes, and the land reeked with nameless infamies; when churches rang with *Te Deums*, and the heart of France withered in anguish, — when, in short, this hideous triumph of the faith was won, the royal tool of priestly ferocity sent orders that heresy should be treated in Canada as it had been treated in France. The orders were needless. The pious Denonville replies, "Praised be God! there is not a heretic here." He adds that a few abjured last year, and that he should be very glad if the King would make them a present. The Jesuits, he further says, go every day on board the ships in the harbor to look after the new converts from France. Now and then at a later day a real or suspected Jansenist found his way to Canada, and sometimes an *esprit fort*, like La Hontan, came over with the troops; but on the whole a community more free from positive heterodoxy perhaps never existed on earth. This exemption cost no bloodshed. What it did cost we may better judge hereafter.

If Canada escaped the dragonnades, so also she escaped another infliction from which a neighboring colony suffered deplorably. Her peace was never much troubled by witches. They were held to exist, it is true; but they wrought no panic. Mother Mary of the Incarnation reports on one occasion the discovery of a magician in the person of a converted Huguenot miller, who, being refused in marriage by a girl of Quebec, bewitched her, and filled the house where she lived with demons, which the bishop tried in vain to exorcise. The miller was thrown into prison, and the girl sent to the Hôtel-Dieu, where not a demon dared enter. The infernal crew took their revenge by creating a severe influenza among the citizens.

If there are no Canadian names on the calendar of saints, it is not because in byways and obscure places Canada had not virtues worthy of canonization.[2] Not alone her male martyrs and female devotees, whose merits have found a chronicle and a recognition; not the fantastic devotion of Madame d'Ailleboust, who, lest she should not suffer enough, took to herself a vicious and refractory servant girl, as an exercise of patience: and not certainly the mediæval pietism of Jeanne Le Ber, the venerated recluse of Montreal, — there are others quite as worthy of honor, whose names have died from memory. It is difficult to conceive a self-abnegation more complete than that of the hospital nuns of Quebec and Montreal. In the almost total absence of trained and skilled physicians, the burden of the sick and wounded fell upon them. Of the two communities, that of Montreal was the more wretchedly destitute, while that of Quebec was exposed, perhaps, to greater dangers. Nearly every ship from France brought some form of infection, and all infection found its way to the Hôtel-Dieu of Quebec. The nuns died, but they never complained. Removed from the arena of ecclesiastical strife, too busy for the morbidness of the cloister, too much absorbed in practical benevolence to become the prey of illusions, they and their sister community were models of that benign and tender charity of which the Roman Catholic Church is so rich in examples. Nor should the Ursulines and the nuns of the Congregation be forgotten among those who, in another field of labor, have toiled patiently according to their light.

Mademoiselle Jeanne Le Ber belonged to none of these sisterhoods. She was the favorite daughter of the chief merchant of Montreal, —

[2] [Since Parkman wrote, the following eight Jesuits who worked in the Canadian mission field have been canonized: Jean de Brébeuf, Gabriel Lalemant, Isaac Jogues, Charles Garnier, Noël Chabanal, Antoine Daniel, René Goupil and Jean de la Lande; and Sister Marguérite Bourgeoys has been beatified.]

the same who, with the help of his money, got himself ennobled. She seems to have been a girl of a fine and sensitive nature; ardent, affectionate, and extremely susceptible to religious impressions. Religion at last gained absolute sway over her. Nothing could appease her longings or content the demands of her excited conscience but an entire consecration of herself to Heaven. Constituted as she was, the resolution must have cost her an agony of mental conflict. Her story is a strange, and, as many will think, a very sad one. She renounced her suitors, and wished to renounce her inheritance; but her spiritual directors, too far-sighted to permit such a sacrifice, persuaded her to hold fast to her claims, and content herself with what they called "poverty of heart." Her mother died, and her father, left with a family of young children, greatly needed her help; but she refused to leave her chamber where she had immured herself. Here she remained ten years, seeing nobody but her confessor and the girl who brought her food. Once only she emerged, and this was when her brother lay dead in the adjacent room, killed in a fight with the English. She suddenly appeared before her astonished sisters, stood for a moment in silent prayer by the body, and then vanished without uttering a word. "Such," says her modern biographer, "was the sublimity of her virtue and the grandeur of her soul." Not content with this domestic seclusion, she caused a cell to be made behind the altar in the newly built church of the Congregation, and here we will permit ourselves to cast a stolen glance at her through the narrow opening through which food was passed in to her. Her bed, a pile of straw which she never moved, lest it should become too soft, was so placed that her head could touch the partition which alone separated it from the Host on the altar. Here she lay wrapped in a garment of coarse gray serge, worn, tattered, and unwashed. An old blanket, a stool, a spinning-wheel, a belt and shirt of haircloth, a scourge, and a pair of shoes made by herself of the husks of Indian-corn, appear to have formed the sum of her furniture and her wardrobe. Her employments were spinning and working embroidery for churches. She remained in this voluntary prison about twenty years; and the nun who brought her food testifies that she never omitted a mortification or a prayer, though commonly in a state of profound depression, and what her biographer calls "complete spiritual aridity." When her mother died, she had refused to see her; and, long after, no prayer of her dying father could draw her from her cell. "In the person of this modest virgin," writes her reverend eulogist, "we see, with astonishment, the love of God triumphant over earthly affection for parents, and a complete victory of faith over reason and of grace over nature."

In 1711, Canada was threatened with an attack by the English; and Mademoiselle Le Ber gave the nuns of the Congregation an image of the Virgin on which she had written a prayer to protect their granary from the invaders. Other persons, anxious for a similar protection, sent her images to write upon; but she declined the request. One of the disappointed applicants then stole the inscribed image from the granary of the Congregation, intending to place it on his own when the danger drew near. The English, however, did not come, their fleet having suffered a ruinous shipwreck ascribed to the prayers of Jeanne Le Ber. "It was," writes the Sulpitian Belmont, "the greatest miracle that ever happened since the days of Moses." Nor was this the only miracle of which she was the occasion. She herself declared that once when she had broken her spinning-wheel, an angel came and mended it for her. Angels also assisted in her embroidery, "no doubt," says Mother Juchereau, "taking great pleasure in the society of this angelic creature." In the church where she had secluded herself, an image of the Virgin continued after her death to heal the lame and cure the sick.

Though Jeanne rarely permitted herself to speak, yet some oracular utterance of the sainted recluse would now and then escape to the outer world. One of these was to the effect that teaching poor girls to read, unless they wanted to be nuns, was robbing them of their time. Nor was she far wrong, for in Canada there was very little to read except formulas of devotion and lives of saints. The dangerous innovation of a printing-press had not invaded the colony, and the first Canadian newspaper dates from the British conquest.

All education was controlled by priests or nuns. The ablest teachers in Canada were the Jesuits. Their college of Quebec was three years older than Harvard. We hear at an early date of public disputations by the pupils, after the pattern of those tournaments of barren logic which preceded the reign of inductive reason in Europe, and of which the archetype is to be found in the scholastic duels of the Sorbonne. The boys were sometimes permitted to act certain approved dramatic pieces of a religious character, like the *Sage Visionnaire*. On one occasion they were allowed to play the *Cid* of Corneille, which, though remarkable as a literary work, contained nothing threatening to orthodoxy. They were taught a little Latin, a little rhetoric, and a little logic; but against all that might rouse the faculties to independent action, the

Canadian schools prudently closed their doors. There was then no rival population, of a different origin and a different faith, to compel competition in the race of intelligence and knowledge. The Church stood sole mistress of the field. Under the old régime the real object of education in Canada was a religious and, in far less degree, a political one. The true purpose of the schools was: first, to make priests; and, secondly, to make obedient servants of the Church and the King. All the rest was extraneous and of slight account. In regard to this matter, the King and the bishop were of one mind. "As I have been informed," Louis XIV writes to Laval, "of your continued care to hold the people in their duty towards God and towards me by the good education you give or cause to be given to the young, I write this letter to express my satisfaction with conduct so salutary, and to exhort you to persevere in it."

The bishop did not fail to persevere. The school for boys attached to his seminary became the most important educational institution in Canada. It was regulated by thirty-four rules, "in honor of the thirty-four years which Jesus lived on earth." The qualities commended to the boys as those which they should labor diligently to acquire were "humility, obedience, purity, meekness, modesty, simplicity, chastity, charity, and an ardent love of Jesus and his Holy Mother." Here is a goodly roll of Christian virtues. What is chiefly noticeable in it is, that truth is allowed no place. That manly but unaccommodating virtue was not, it seems, thought important in forming the mind of youth. Humility and obedience lead the list; for in unquestioning submission to the spiritual director lay the guaranty of all other merits.

We have seen already, that, besides this seminary for boys, Laval established another for educating the humbler colonists. It was a sort of farm-school; though besides farming, various mechanical trades were also taught in it. It was well adapted to the wants of a great majority of Canadians, whose tendencies were anything but bookish; but here, as elsewhere, the real object was religious. It enabled the Church to extend her influence over classes which the ordinary schools could not reach. Besides manual training, the pupils were taught to read and write; and for a time a certain number of them received some instruction in Latin. When, in 1686, Saint-Vallier visited the school, he found in all thirty-one boys under the charge of two priests; but the number was afterwards greatly reduced, and the place served, as it still serves, chiefly as a retreat during vacations for the priests and pupils of the seminary of Quebec. A spot better suited for such a purpose cannot be conceived.

From the vast meadows of the parish of St. Joachim, which here border the St. Lawrence, there rises like an island a low flat hill, hedged round with forests like the tonsured head of a monk. It was here that Laval planted his school. Across the meadows, a mile or more distant, towers the mountain promontory of Cape Tourmente. You may climb its woody steeps, and from the top, waist-deep in blueberry-bushes, survey, from Kamouraska to Quebec, the grand Canadian world out-stretched below; or mount the neighboring heights of St. Anne, where, athwart the gaunt arms of ancient pines, the river lies shimmering in summer haze, the cottages of the *habitants* are strung like beads of a rosary along the meadows of Beaupré, the shores of Orleans bask in warm light, and far on the horizon the rock of Quebec rests like a faint gray cloud; or traverse the forest till the roar of the torrent guides you to the rocky solitude where it holds its savage revels. High on the cliffs above, young birch-trees stand smiling in the morning sun; while in the abyss beneath the snowy waters plunge from depth to depth, and, halfway down, the slender harebell hangs from its mossy nook, quivering in the steady thunder of the cataract. Game on the river; trout in lakes, brooks, and pools; wild fruits and flowers on meadows and mountains, — a thousand resources of honest and wholesome re-creation here wait the student emancipated from books, but not parted for a moment from the pious influence which hangs about the old walls embosomed in the woods of St. Joachim. Around on plains and hills stand the dwellings of a peaceful peasantry, as different from the restless population of the neighboring States as the denizens of some Norman or Breton village.

Above all, do not fail to make your pilgrimage to the shrine of St. Anne. You may see her chapel four or five miles away, nestled under the heights of the Petit Cap. Here, when Ailleboust was governor, he began with his own hands the pious work, and a *habitant* of Beaupré, Louis Guimont, sorely afflicted with rheumatism, came grinning with pain to lay three stones in the foundation, in honor probably of Saint Anne, Saint Joachim, and their daughter the Virgin. Instantly he was cured. It was but the beginning of a long course of miracles continued more than two centuries, and continuing still. Their fame spread far and wide. The devotion to Saint Anne became a distinguishing feature of Canadian Catholicity, till at the present day at least thirteen parishes bear her name. But of all her shrines, none can match the fame of St.

Anne du Petit Cap. Crowds flocked thither on the week of her festival, and marvellous cures were wrought unceasingly, as the sticks and crutches hanging on the walls and columns still attest. Sometimes the whole shore was covered with the wigwams of Indian converts who had paddled their birch canoes from the farthest wilds of Canada. The more fervent among them would crawl on their knees from the shore to the altar. And, in our own day, every summer a far greater concourse of pilgrims — not in paint and feathers, but in cloth and millinery, and not in canoes, but in steamboats — bring their offerings and their vows to the "Bonne Sainte Anne."

To return to Laval's industrial school. Judging from repeated complaints of governors and intendants of the dearth of skilled workmen, the priests in charge of it were more successful in making good Catholics than in making good masons, carpenters, blacksmiths, and weavers; and the number of pupils, even if well trained, was at no time sufficient to meet the wants of the colony, for, though the Canadians showed an aptitude for mechanical trades, they preferred above all things the savage liberty of the backwoods.

The education of girls was in the hands of the Ursulines and the nuns of the Congregation, of whom the former, besides careful instruction in religious duties, taught their pupils "all that a girl ought to know." This meant exceedingly little besides the manual arts suited to their sex; and, in the case of the nuns of the Congregation, who taught girls of the poorer class, it meant still less. It was on nuns as well as on priests that the charge fell, not only of spiritual and mental, but also of industrial training. Thus we find the King giving a sisterhood of Montreal 1000 francs to buy wool, and 1000 more for teaching girls to knit. The King also maintained a teacher of navigation and surveying at Quebec on the modest salary of 400 francs.

During the eighteenth century, some improvement is perceptible in the mental state of the population. As it became more numerous and more stable, it also became less ignorant; and the Canadian *habitant*, towards the end of the French rule, was probably better taught, so far as concerned religion, than the mass of French peasants. Yet secular instruction was still extremely meager, even in the *noblesse*.

"In spite of this defective education," says the famous navigator Bougainville, who knew the colony well in its last years, "the Canadians are naturally intelligent. They do not know how to write, but they speak with ease, and with an accent as good as the Parisian." He means, of course, the better class. "Even the children of officers and gentlemen," says another writer, "scarcely know how to read and write; they are ignorant of the first elements of geography and history." And evidence like this might be extended.

When France was heaving with the throes that prepared the Revolution; when new hopes, new dreams, new thoughts — good and evil, false and true — tossed the troubled waters of French society, Canada caught something of its social corruption but not the faintest impulsion of its roused mental life. The torrent surged on its way; while, in the deep nook beside it, the sticks and dry leaves floated their usual round and the unruffled pool slept in the placidity of intellectual torpor.

CHAPTER XVI

Morals and Manners

1640–1763

[*The Old Régime in Canada,* CHAPTER XXIII in part]

The mission period of Canada, or the period anterior to the year 1663, when the King took the colony in charge, has a character of its own. The whole population did not exceed that of a large French village. Its extreme poverty, the constant danger that surrounded it, and, above all, the contagious zeal of the missionaries, saved it from many vices, and inspired it with an extraordinary religious fervor. Without doubt an ideal picture has been drawn of this early epoch. Trade as well as propagandism was the business of the colony, and the colonists were far from being all in a state of grace; yet it is certain that zeal was higher, devotion more constant, and popular morals more pure, than at any later period of the French rule.

The intervention of the King wrought a change. The annual shipments of emigrants made by him were, in the most favorable view, of a very mixed character, and the portion which Mother Mary calls *canaille* was but too conspicuous. Along with them came a regiment of soldiers fresh from the license of camps and the excitements of Turkish wars, accustomed to obey their officers and to obey nothing else, and more ready to wear the scapulary of the Virgin in campaigns against the Mohawks than to square their lives by the rules of Christian ethics. "Our good King," writes Sister Morin, of Montreal, "has sent troops to defend us from the Iroquois, and the soldiers and officers have ruined the Lord's vineyard, and planted wickedness and sin and crime in our soil of Canada." Few, indeed, among the officers followed the example of one of their number, — Paul Dupuy, who, in his settlement of Isle aux Oies, below Quebec, lived, it is said, like a saint, and on Sundays and fête days exhorted his servants and *habitants* with such unction that their eyes filled with tears. Nor, let us hope, were there many imitators of Major La Fredière, who, with a company of the regiment, was sent to garrison Montreal, where he ruled with absolute sway over settlers and soldiers alike. His countenance naturally repulsive was made more so by the loss of an eye; yet he was irrepressible in gallantry, and women and girls fled in terror from the military Polyphemus. The men, too, feared and hated him, not without reason. One morning a settler named Demers was hoeing his field, when he saw a sportsman gun in hand striding through his half-grown wheat. "Steady there, steady!" he shouted in a tone of remonstrance; but the sportsman gave no heed. "Why do you spoil a poor man's wheat?" cried the outraged cultivator. "If I knew who you were, I would go and complain of you." "Whom would you complain to?" demanded the sportsman, who then proceeded to walk back into the middle of the wheat, and called out to Demers, "You are a rascal, and I'll thrash you." "Look at home for rascals," retorted Demers, "and keep your thrashing for your dogs." The sportsman came towards him in a rage to execute his threat. Demers picked up his gun, which, after the custom of the time, he had brought to the field with him, and, advancing to meet his adversary, recognized La Fredière, the commandant. On this he ran off. La Fredière sent soldiers to arrest him, threw him into prison, put him in irons, and the next day mounted him on the wooden horse, with a weight of sixty pounds tied to each foot. He repeated the torture a day or two after, and then let his victim go, saying, "If I could have caught you when I was in your wheat, I would have beaten you well."

The commandant next turned his quarters into a dram-shop for Indians, to whom he sold brandy in large quantities, but so diluted that his customers, finding themselves partially defrauded of their right of intoxication, complained grievously. About this time the intendant Talon made one of his domiciliary visits to Montreal, and when, in his character of father of the people, he inquired if they had any complaints to make, every tongue was loud in accusation against La Fredière. Talon caused full depositions to be made out from the statements of Demers and other witnesses. Copies were deposited in the hands of the notary, and it is from these that the above story is drawn. The tyrant was removed, and ordered home to France.

Many other officers embarked in the profitable trade of selling brandy to Indians, and several garrison posts became centres of disorder. Others of the regiment became notorious brawlers. . . .

Montreal, a frontier town at the head of the colony, was the natural resort of desperadoes, offering, as we have seen, a singular contrast between the rigor of its clerical seigneurs and the riotous license of the lawless crew which infested it. Dollier de Casson tells the story of an outlaw who broke prison ten or twelve times, and whom no walls, locks, or fetters could hold. "A few months ago," he says, "he was caught again, and put into the keeping of six or seven men, each with a good gun. They stacked their arms to play a game of cards, which their prisoner saw fit to interrupt to play a game of his own. He made a jump at the guns, took them under his arm like so many feathers, aimed at these fellows with one of them, swearing that he would kill the first who came near him, and so, falling back step by step, at last bade them good-by, and carried off all their guns. Since then he has not been caught, and is roaming the woods. Very likely he will become chief of our banditti, and make great trouble in the country when it pleases him to come back from the Dutch settlements, whither they say he is gone along with another rascal, and a French woman so depraved that she is said to have given or sold two of her children to the Indians."

When the governor, La Barre, visited Montreal, he found there some two hundred reprobates gambling, drinking, and stealing. If hard pressed by justice, they had only to cross the river and place themselves beyond the seigneurial jurisdiction. The military settlements of the Richelieu were in a condition somewhat similar, and La Barre complains of a prevailing spirit of disobedience and lawlessness. The most orderly and thrifty part of Canada appears to have been at this time the *côte* of Beaupré, belonging to the seminary of Quebec. Here the settlers had religious instruction from their curés, and industrial instruction also if they wanted it. Domestic spinning and weaving were practised at Beaupré sooner than in any other part of the colony.

When it is remembered that a population which in La Barre's time did not exceed ten thousand, and which forty years later did not much exceed twice that number, was scattered along both sides of a great river for 300 miles or more; that a large part of this population was in isolated groups of two, three, five, ten, or twenty houses at the edge of a savage wilderness; that between them there was little communication except by canoes; that the settlers were disbanded soldiers, or others whose lives had been equally adverse to habits of reflection or self-control; that they rarely saw a priest, and that a government omnipotent in name had not arms long enough to reach them, — we may listen without surprise to the lamentations of order-loving officials over the unruly condition of a great part of the colony. One accuses the seigneurs, who, he says, being often of low extraction, cannot keep their vassals in order. Another dwells sorrowfully on the "terrible dispersion" of the settlements where the inhabitants "live in a savage independence." But it is better that each should speak for himself, and among the rest let us hear the pious Denonville.

"This, Monseigneur," he says, "seems to me the place for rendering you an account of the disorders which prevail not only in the woods, but also in the settlements. They arise from the idleness of young persons, and the great liberty which fathers, mothers, and guardians have for a long time given them, or allowed them to assume, of going into the forest under pretence of hunting or trading. This has come to such a pass, that, from the moment a boy can carry a gun, the father cannot restrain him and dares not offend him. You can judge the mischief that follows. These disorders are always greatest in the families of those who are *gentilshommes*, or who through laziness or vanity pass themselves off as such. Having no resource but hunting, they must spend their lives in the woods, where they have no curés to trouble them, and no fathers or guardians to constrain them. I think, Monseigneur, that martial law would suit their case better than any judicial sentence. Monsieur de la Barre suppressed a certain order of knighthood which had sprung up here, but he did not abolish the usages belonging to it. It was thought a fine thing and a good joke to go about naked and tricked out like Indians, not only on carnival days, but on all other days of feasting and debauchery. These practices tend to encourage the disposition of our young men to live like savages, frequent their company, and be forever unruly and lawless like them. I cannot tell you, Monseigneur, how attractive this Indian life is to all our youth. It consists in doing nothing, caring for nothing, following every inclination, and getting out of the way of all correction."

He goes on to say that the mission villages governed by the Jesuits and Sulpitians are models of good order, and that drunkards are never seen there except when they come from the neighboring French settlements; but that the other Indians, who roam at large about the colony, do prodigious mischief, because the children of the seigneurs not only copy their way of life, but also run off with their women into the woods. "Nothing," he continues, "can be finer or better conceived than the regulations framed for the government of this country; but nothing, I assure you, is so ill observed as regards both the fur-trade and the general discipline of the colony. One great evil is the infinite number of drinking-shops, which makes it almost impossible to remedy the disorders resulting from them. All the rascals and idlers of the country are attracted into this business of tavern-keeping. They never dream of tilling the soil; but, on the contrary, they deter the other inhabitants from it, and end with ruining them. I know seigneuries where there are but twenty houses, and more than half of them dram-shops. At Three Rivers there are twenty-five houses, and liquor may be had at eighteen or twenty of them. Villemarie [Montreal] and Quebec are on the same footing."

The governor next dwells on the necessity of finding occupation for children and youths, — a matter which he regards as of the last importance. "It is sad to see the ignorance of the population at a distance from the abodes of the curés, who are put to the greatest trouble to remedy the evil by travelling from place to place through the parishes in their charge."

Drunkenness was at this time the most destructive vice in the colony. One writer declares that most of the Canadians drink so much brandy in the morning that they are unfit for work all day. Another says that a canoe-man when he is tired will lift a keg of brandy to his lips and drink the raw liquor from the bung-hole, after which, having spoiled his appetite, he goes to bed supperless; and that, what with drink and hardship, he is an old man at forty. Nevertheless the race did not deteriorate. The prevalence of early marriages, and the birth of numerous offspring before the vigor of the father had been wasted, insured the strength and hardihood which characterized the Canadians. As Denonville describes them, so they long remained. "The Canadians are tall, well-made, and well set on their legs, robust, vigorous, and accustomed in time of need to live on little. They have intelligence and vivacity, but are wayward, light-minded, and inclined to debauchery."

As the population increased, as the rage for bush-ranging began to abate, and, above all, as the curés multiplied, a change took place for the better. More churches were built, the charge of each priest was reduced within reasonable bounds, and a greater proportion of the inhabitants remained on their farms. They were better watched, controlled, and taught by the Church. The ecclesiastical power, wherever it had a hold, was exercised, as we have seen, with an undue rigor, yet it was the chief guardian of good morals; and the colony grew more orderly and more temperate as the Church gathered more and more of its wild and wandering flock fairly within its fold. In this, however, its success was but relative. It is true that in 1715 a well-informed writer says that the people were "perfectly instructed in religion;" but at that time the statement was only partially true.

During the seventeenth century, and some time after its close, Canada swarmed with beggars, — a singular feature in a new country where a good farm could be had for the asking. In countries intensely Roman Catholic begging is not regarded as an unmixed evil, being supposed to promote two cardinal virtues, — charity in the giver, and humility in the receiver. The Canadian officials nevertheless tried to restrain it. Vagabonds of both sexes were ordered to leave Quebec, and nobody was allowed to beg without a certificate of poverty from the curé or the local judge. These orders were not always observed. Bishop Saint-Vallier writes that he is overwhelmed by beggars, and the intendant echoes his complaint. Almshouses were established at Montreal, Three Rivers, and Quebec; and when Saint-Vallier founded the General Hospital, its chief purpose was to serve, not as a hospital in the ordinary sense of the word, but as a house of refuge, after the plan of the General Hospital of Paris. Appeal, as usual, was made to the King. Denonville asks his aid for two destitute families, and says that many others need it. Louis XIV did not fail to respond, and from time to time he sent considerable sums for the relief of the Canadian poor.

All the writers lament the extravagant habits of the people; and even La Hontan joins hands with the priests in wishing that the supply of ribbons, laces, brocades, jewelry, and the like might be cut off by act of law. Mother Juchereau tells us, that, when the English invasion was impending, the belles of Canada were scared for a while into modesty in order to gain the favor of Heaven; but, as may be imagined, the effect was short, and Father La Tour declares that in his time all the fashions except rouge came over regularly in the annual ships. . . .

One gets glimpses of the pristine state of Quebec through the early police regulations. Each inhabitant was required to make a gutter along the middle of the street before his house, and also to remove refuse and throw it into the river. All dogs, without exception, were ordered home at nine o'clock. On Tuesdays and Fridays there was a market in the public square, whither the neighboring *habitants*, male and female, brought their produce for sale, as they still continue to do. Smoking in the street was forbidden, as a precaution against fire; householders were required to provide themselves with ladders, and when the fire alarm was rung all able-bodied persons were obliged to run to the scene of danger with buckets or kettles full of water. This did not prevent the Lower Town from burning to the ground in 1682. It was soon rebuilt, but a repetition of the catastrophe seemed very likely. "This place," says Denonville, "is in a fearful state as regards fire; for the houses are crowded together out of all reason, and so surrounded with piles of cord-wood that it is pitiful to see." Add to this the stores of hay for the cows kept by many of the inhabitants for the benefit of their swarming progeny. The houses were at this time low, compact buildings, with gables of masonry, as required by law; but many had wooden fronts, and all had roofs covered with cedar shingles. The anxious governor begs, that, as the town has not a *sou* of revenue, his Majesty will be pleased to make it the gift of 200 crowns' worth of leather fire-buckets. Six or seven years after, certain citizens were authorized by the council to import from France, at their own cost, "a pump after the Dutch fashion, for throwing water on houses in case of fire." . . .

August, September, and October were the busy months at Quebec. Then the ships from France discharged their lading, the shops and warehouses of the Lower Town were filled with goods, and the *habitants* came to town to make their purchases. When the frosts began, the vessels sailed away, the harbor was deserted, the streets were silent again, and like ants or squirrels the people set at work to lay in their winter stores. Fathers of families packed their cellars with beets, carrots, potatoes, and cabbages; and, at the end of autumn, with meat, fowls, game, fish, and eels, all frozen to stony hardness. Most of the shops closed, and the long season of leisure and amusement began. New Year's day brought visits and mutual gifts. Thence till Lent dinner-parties were frequent, sometimes familiar and sometimes ceremonious. The governor's little court at the château was a standing example to all the aspiring spirits of Quebec, and forms and orders of precedence were in some houses punctiliously observed. There were dinners to the military and civic, dignitaries and their wives, and others, quite distinct to prominent citizens. The wives and daughters of the burghers of Quebec are said to have been superior in manners to women of the corresponding class in France. "They have wit," says La Potherie, "delicacy, good voices, and a great fondness for dancing. They are discreet, and not much given to flirting; but when they undertake to catch a lover, it is not easy for him to escape the bands of Hymen."

So much for the town. In the country parishes, there was the same autumnal stowing away of frozen vegetables, meat, fish, and eels, and unfortunately the same surfeit of leisure through five months of the year. During the seventeenth century, many of the people were so poor that women were forced to keep at home from sheer want of winter clothing. Nothing, however, could prevent their running from house to house to exchange gossip with the neighbors, who all knew one another, and, having nothing else to do, discussed each other's affairs with an industry which often bred bitter quarrels. At a later period, a more general introduction of family weaving and spinning served at once to furnish clothing and to promote domestic peace.

The most important persons in a parish were the curé, the seigneur, and the militia captain. The seigneur had his bench of honor in the church. Immediately behind it was the bench of the militia captain, whose duty it was to drill the able-bodied men of the neighborhood, direct roadmaking and other public works, and serve as deputy to the intendant, whose ordinances he was required to enforce. Next in honor came the local judge, if any there was, and the church-wardens.

The existence of slavery in Canada dates from the end of the seventeenth century. In 1688 the attorney-general made a visit to Paris, and urged upon the King the expediency of importing negroes from the West Indies as a remedy for the scarcity and dearness of labor. The King consented, but advised caution, on the ground that the rigor of the climate would make the venture a critical one. A number of slaves were brought into the colony; but the system never flourished, the climate and other circumstances being hostile to it. Many of the colonists, especially at Detroit and other outlying posts, owned slaves of a remote Indian tribe, the Pawnees. The fact is remarkable, since it would be difficult to find another of the wild tribes of the continent capable of subjection to domestic servitude. The Pawnee slaves were captives taken in war and sold at low prices to the Canadians. Their market value was much impaired by their propensity to run off.

It is curious to observe the views of the Canadians taken at different times by different writers. La Hontan says: "They are vigorous, enterprising, and indefatigable, and need nothing but education. They are presumptuous and full of self-conceit, regard themselves as above all the nations of the earth, and, unfortunately, have not the veneration for their parents that they ought to have. The women are generally pretty; few of them are brunettes; many of them are discreet, and a good number are lazy. They are fond to the last degree of dress and show, and each tries to outdo the rest in the art of catching a husband."

Fifty years later, the intendant Hocquart writes: "The Canadians are fond of distinctions and attentions, plume themselves on their courage, and are extremely sensitive to slights or the smallest corrections. They are self-interested, vindictive, prone to drunkenness, use a great deal of brandy, and pass for not being at all truthful. This portrait is true of many of them, particularly the country people: those of the towns are less vicious. They are all attached to religion, and criminals are rare. They are volatile, and think too well of themselves, which prevents their succeeding as they might in farming and trade. They have not the rude and rustic air of our French peasants. If they are put on their honor and governed with justice, they are tractable enough; but their natural disposition is indocile."

The navigator Bougainville, in the last years of the French rule, describes the Canadian *habitant* as essentially superior to the French peasant, and adds, "He is loud, boastful, mendacious, obliging, civil, and honest; indefatigable in hunting, travelling, and bush-ranging, but lazy in tilling the soil."

The Swedish botanist, Kalm, an excellent observer, was in Canada a few years before Bougainville, and sketches from life the following traits of Canadian manners. The language is that of the old English translation: "The men here [at Montreal] are extremely civil, and take their hats off to every person indifferently whom they meet in the streets. The women in general are handsome; they are well bred and virtuous, with an innocent and becoming freedom. They dress out very fine on Sundays, and though on the other days they do not take much pains with the other parts of their dress, yet they are very fond of adorning their heads, the hair of which is always curled and powdered and ornamented with glittering bodkins and aigrettes. They are not averse to taking part in all the business of housekeeping; and I have with pleasure seen the daughters of the better sort of people, and of the governor [of Montreal] himself, not too finely dressed, and going into kitchens and cellars to look that everything be done as it ought. What I have mentioned above of their dressing their heads too assiduously is the case with all the ladies throughout Canada. Their hair is always curled, even when they are at home in a dirty jacket and short coarse petticoat that does not reach to the middle of their legs. On those days when they pay or receive visits, they dress so gayly that one is almost induced to think their parents possess the greatest honors in the state. They are no less attentive to have the newest fashions, and they laugh at one another when they are not dressed to one another's fancy. One of the first questions they propose to a stranger is, whether he is married; the next, how he likes the ladies of the country, and whether he thinks them handsomer than those of his own country; and the third, whether he will take one home with him. The behavior of the ladies seemed to me somewhat too free at Quebec, and of a more becoming modesty at Montreal. Those of Quebec are not very industrious. The young ladies, especially those of a higher rank, get up at seven and dress till nine, drinking their coffee at the same time. When they are dressed, they place themselves near a window that opens into the street, take up some needlework and sew a stitch now and then, but turn their eyes into the street most of the time. When a young fellow comes in, whether they are acquainted with him or not, they immediately lay aside their work, sit down by him, and begin to chat, laugh, joke, and invent *double-entendres;* and this is reckoned being very witty. In this manner they frequently pass the whole day, leaving their mothers to do the business of the house. They are likewise cheerful and content, and nobody can say that they want either wit or charms. Their fault is that they think too well of themselves. However, the daughters of people of all ranks without exception go to market and carry home what they have bought. The girls at Montreal are very much displeased that those at Quebec get husbands sooner than they. The reason of this is that many young gentlemen who come over from France with the ships are captivated by the ladies at Quebec and marry them; but as these gentlemen seldom go up to Montreal, the girls there are not often so happy as those of the former place."

Long before Kalm's visit, the Jesuit Charlevoix, a traveller and a man of the world, wrote thus of Quebec in a letter to the Duchesse de Lesdiguières: "There is a select little society here which wants nothing to make it agreeable. In the *salons* of the wives of the governor and of the intendant, one finds circles as brilliant as in other countries." These circles were formed partly of the principal inhabitants, but chiefly of military officers and government officials, with their families. Charlevoix continues: "Everybody does his part to make the time pass pleasantly, with games and parties of pleasure, — drives and canoe excursions in summer, sleighing and skating in winter. There is a great deal of hunting and shooting, for many Canadian gentlemen are almost destitute of any other means of living at their ease. The news of the day amounts to very little indeed, as the country furnishes scarcely any, while that from Europe comes all at once. Science and the fine arts have their turn, and conversation does not fail. The Canadians breathe from their birth an air of liberty, which makes them very pleasant in the intercourse of life, and our language is nowhere more purely spoken. One finds here no rich persons whatever, and this is a great pity; for the Canadians like to get the credit of their money, and scarcely anybody amuses himself with hoarding it. They say it is very different with our neighbors the English; and one who knew the two colonies only by the way of living, acting, and speaking of the colonists would not hesitate to judge ours the more flourishing. In New England and the other British colonies there reigns an opulence by which the people seem not to know how to profit; while in New France poverty is hidden under an air of ease which appears entirely natural. The English colonist keeps as much and spends as little as possible; the French colonist enjoys what he has got, and often makes a display of what he has not got. The one labors for his heirs; the other leaves them to get on as they can, like himself. I could push the comparison further, but I must close here; the King's ship is about to sail, and the merchant vessels are getting ready to follow. In three days, perhaps, not one will be left in the harbor."

And now we, too, will leave Canada. Winter draws near, and the first patch of snow lies gleaming on the distant mountain of Cape Tourmente. The sun has set in chill autumnal beauty, and the sharp spires of fir-trees on the heights of Sillery stand stiff and black against the pure cold amber of the fading west. The ship sails in the morning; and before the old towers of Rochelle rise in sight there will be time to smoke many a pipe, and ponder what we have seen on the banks of the St. Lawrence.

CHAPTER XVII

Canadian Absolutism

1663–1763

[The Old Régime in Canada, CHAPTER XXIV]

Not institutions alone, but geographical position, climate, and many other conditions unite to form the educational influences that, acting through successive generations, shape the character of nations and communities.

It is easy to see the nature of the education, past and present, which wrought on the Canadians and made them what they were. An ignorant population, sprung from a brave and active race, but trained to subjection and dependence through centuries of feudal and monarchical despotism, was planted in the wilderness by the hand of authority, and told to grow and flourish. Artificial stimulants were applied, but freedom was withheld. Perpetual intervention of government, — regulations, restrictions, encouragements sometimes more mischievous than restrictions, a constant uncertainty what the authorities would do next, the fate of each man resting less with himself than with another, volition enfeebled, self-reliance paralyzed, — the condition, in short, of a child held always under the rule of a father, in the main well-meaning and kind, sometimes generous, sometimes neglectful, often capricious, and rarely very wise, — such were the influences under which Canada grew up. If she had prospered, it would have been sheer miracle. A man, to be a man, must feel that he holds his fate, in some good measure, in his own hands.

But this was not all. Against absolute authority there was a counter influence, rudely and wildly antagonistic. Canada was at the very portal of the great interior wilderness. The St. Lawrence and the Lakes were the highway to that domain of savage freedom; and thither the disfranchised, half-starved seigneur, and the discouraged *habitant* who could find no market for his produce naturally enough betook themselves. Their lesson of savagery was well learned, and for many a year a boundless license and a stiff-handed authority battled for the control of Canada. Nor, to the last, were Church and State fairly masters of the field. The French rule was drawing towards its close when the intendant complained that though twenty-eight companies of regular troops were quartered in the colony, there were not soldiers enough to keep the people in order. One cannot but remember that in a neighboring colony, far more populous, perfect order prevailed, with no other guardians than a few constables chosen by the people themselves.

Whence arose this difference, and other differences equally striking, between the rival colonies? It is easy to ascribe them to a difference of political and religious institutions; but the explanation does not cover the ground. The institutions of New England were utterly inapplicable to the population of New France, and the attempt to apply them would have wrought nothing but mischief. There are no political panaceas, except in the imagination of political quacks. To each degree and each variety of public development there are corresponding institutions, best answering the public needs; and what is meat to one is poison to another. Freedom is for those who are fit for it; the rest will lose it, or turn it to corruption. Church and State were right in exercising authority over a people which had not learned the first rudiments of self-government. Their fault was not that they exercised authority, but that they exercised too much of it, and, instead of weaning the child to go alone, kept him in perpetual leading-strings, making him, if possible, more and more dependent, and less and less fit for freedom.

In the building up of colonies, England succeeded and France failed. The cause lies chiefly in the vast advantage drawn by England from the historical training of her people in habits of reflection, forecast, industry, and self-reliance, — a training which enabled them to adopt and maintain an invigorating system of self-rule, totally inapplicable to their rivals.

The New England colonists were far less fugitives from oppression than voluntary exiles seeking the realization of an idea. They were neither peasants nor soldiers, but a substantial Puritan yeomanry, led by Puritan gentlemen and divines in thorough sympathy with them. They were neither sent out by the King, governed by him, nor helped by him. They grew up in utter neglect, and continued neglect was the only boon they asked. Till their increasing strength roused the jealousy of the Crown, they were virtually independent, — a republic, but by no means a democracy. They chose their governor and all their rulers from among themselves, made their own government and paid for it, supported their own clergy, defended themselves, and educated themselves. Under the hard and repellent surface of New England society lay the true foundations of a stable freedom, — conscience, reflection, faith, patience, and public spirit. The cement of common interests, hopes, and duties compacted the whole people like a rock of conglomerate; while the people of New France remained in a state of political segregation, like a basket of pebbles held together by the enclosure that surrounds them.

It may be that the difference of historical antecedents would alone explain the difference of character between the rival colonies; but there are deeper causes, the influence of which went far to determine the antecedents themselves. The Germanic race, and especially the Anglo-Saxon branch of it, is peculiarly masculine, and, therefore, peculiarly fitted for self-government. It submits its action habitually to the guidance of reason, and has the judicial faculty of seeing both sides of a question. The French Celt is cast in a different mould. He sees the end distinctly, and reasons about it with an admirable clearness; but his own impulses and passions continually turn him away from it. Opposition excites him; he is impatient of delay, is impelled always to extremes, and does not readily sacrifice a present inclination to an ultimate good. He delights in abstractions and generalizations, cuts loose from unpleasing facts, and roams through an ocean of desires and theories.

While New England prospered and Canada did not prosper, the French system had at least one great advantage. It favored military efficiency. The Canadian population sprang in great part from soldiers, and was to the last systematically reinforced by disbanded soldiers. Its chief occupation was a continual training for forest war; it had little or nothing to lose, and little to do but fight and range the woods. This was not all. The Canadian government was essentially military. At its head was a soldier nobleman, often an old and able commander; and those beneath him caught his spirit and emulated his example. In spite of its political nothingness, in spite of poverty and hardship, and in spite even of trade, the upper stratum of Canadian society was animated by the pride and fire of that gallant *noblesse* which held war as its only worthy calling, and prized honor more than life. As for the *habitant*, the forest, lake, and river were his true school; and here, at least, he was an apt scholar. A skillful woodsman, a bold and adroit canoe-man, a willing fighter in time of need, often serving without pay, and receiving from government only his provisions and his canoe, he was more than ready at any time for any hardy enterprise; and in the forest warfare of skirmish and surprise there were few to match him. An absolute government used him at will, and experienced leaders guided his rugged valor to the best account.

The New England man was precisely the same material with that of which Cromwell formed his invincible "Ironsides;" but he had very little forest experience. His geographical position cut him off completely from the great wilderness of the interior. The sea was his field of action. Without the aid of government, and in spite of its restrictions, he built up a prosperous commerce, and enriched himself by distant fisheries, neglected by the rivals before whose doors they lay. He knew every ocean from Greenland to Cape Horn, and the whales of the north and of the south had no more dangerous foe. But he was too busy to fight without good cause; and when he turned his hand to soldiering, it was only to meet some pressing need of the hour. The New England troops in the early wars were bands of raw fishermen and farmers, led by civilians, decorated with military titles, and subject to the slow and uncertain action of legislative bodies. The officers had not learned to command, nor the men to obey. The remarkable exploit of the capture of Louisburg, the strongest fortress in America, was the result of mere audacity and hardihood, backed by the rarest good luck.

One great fact stands out conspicuous in Canadian history, — the Church of Rome. More even than the royal power, she shaped the character and the destinies of the colony. She was its nurse and almost its mother; and, wayward and headstrong as it was, it never broke the ties of faith that held it to her. It was these ties which, in the absence of political franchises, formed under the old régime the only vital coherence in the population. The royal government was transient; the Church was permanent. The English conquest shattered the whole apparatus of civil administration at a blow, but it left her untouched. Governors, intendants, councils, and commandants, all were gone; the principal seigneurs fled the colony; and a people who had never learned to control themselves or help themselves were suddenly left to their own devices. Confusion, if not anarchy, would have followed but for the parish priests, who, in a character of double paternity, half spiritual and half temporal, became more than ever the guardians of order throughout Canada.

This English conquest was the grand crisis of Canadian history. It was the beginning of a new life. With England came Protestantism, and the Canadian Church grew purer and better in the presence of an adverse faith. Material growth; an increased mental activity; an education, real though fenced and guarded; a warm and genuine patriotism, — all date from the peace of 1763. England imposed by the sword on reluctant Canada the boon of rational and ordered liberty. Through centuries of striving she had advanced from stage to stage of progress, deliberate and calm, — never breaking with her past, but making each fresh gain the base of a new success, — enlarging popular liberties while bating nothing of that height and force of individual development which is the brain and heart of civilization; and now, through a hard-earned victory, she taught the conquered colony to share the blessings she had won. A happier calamity never befell a people than the conquest of Canada by the British arms.[1]

[1] [For a good-tempered French Canadian critique of this chapter, see Guy Frégault *La Civilisation de la Nouvelle France* (1944) chap. iii.]

CHAPTER XVIII

The Success of La Salle
1681–1682

[*La Salle and the Discovery of the Great West,* CHAPTER XX]

[THIS VOLUME describes the opening scene of the North American drama, the Westward Movement, and so is of peculiar interest. At the same time it is the best biography of him whom Parkman regarded as the greatest of all French explorers. The character of La Salle, his indefatigable pursuit of a seemingly unattainable object through natural obstacles, depressing accidents and personal intrigues, fascinated Parkman. The historian devoted his best energies to perfecting this volume, the first edition of which, called *The Discovery of the Great West,* appeared in 1869. The tenth edition, heavily revised after the publication of the Margry documents, came out in 1878. All later biographies of La Salle have drawn freely from Parkman, but none have approached him for dramatic vigor of style, vivid first-hand descriptions of the Western lands traversed by his hero, and knowledge of the many tribes of Indians with which both subject and author came in contact.

The exigencies of space have compelled the editor to select only seven of the twenty-nine chapters in this great book; but as the life of La Salle, to be understood, cannot be picked up in mid-career, a synopsis of the earlier chapters follows:

Robert Cavelier de la Salle was born in Rouen, to a well-to-do mercantile family, in November 1643. Educated in a Jesuit college, he entered the novitiate, and for a short time taught in a Jesuit school, but parted from the Order before taking his final vows. In the spring of 1666 he went to Montreal, where a brother was a priest of the Order of St. Sulpice, to seek his fortune. La Salle was always a devout Catholic, but he disliked the Jesuits and believed that they entertained an implacable enmity against him for leaving their fold.

The Sulpitians, eager to settle hardy men near Montreal to protect the settlement from the Iroquois, were granting lands on easy terms. La Salle obtained a seigneury at La Chine on the edge of Lac Saint-Louis, about eight miles from Montreal. He at once began to study the Indian languages and to make himself solid with such Indians as came to him for trade. In both he was very successful. From a band of Senecas he heard of the Ohio and Mississippi Rivers. Believing that the latter must flow into the Gulf of California, he conceived the idea of descending it and establishing a trading post at its mouth, with the object not only of profit but of discovering a short all-water route to the Pacific.

Both the governor of Canada and the Sulpitians favored the enterprise, and La Salle raised the necessary funds by selling his seigneury. On 6 July 1669 he started forth with a party of twenty-three Frenchmen in nine canoes, with Seneca guides. At the site of Hamilton, Ontario, they encountered the Canadian-born Louis Joliet returning from a fruitless attempt to discover the copper mines of Lake Superior. The Sulpitian members of La Salle's party, hoping to convert the tribes of the Upper Lakes about whom they were told by Joliet, insisted on pressing on to Lake Superior, and parted from La Salle. His movements from that point, and until 1673, are still a matter of controversy. It is probable that, with a few Frenchmen and an Onondaga guide, he marched overland to a tributary of the Ohio, reached that river and descended it as far as the Louisville rapids.[1]

The Jesuits already had two missions on the Upper Lakes — Sainte Marie du Sault (the present "Soo" or Sault Ste. Marie) at the outlet of Lake Superior, a favorite fishing place for the Ojibwas; and at Saint-Esprit near the western extremity of the same lake, where fugitive Hurons, Ottawas and many other tribes came yearly to trade. The missionary here was a young Jesuit father, Jacques Marquette, who like La Salle and Joliet was to leave his name on American geography. Père Marquette, too, had heard stories of the Great River and hoped to discover it; but unfortunately the Sioux made war on his converts, who fled to Michilimackinac, whither he had to follow them. In the fall of 1669 Père Claude Allouez was sent to found a mission at the head of Green Bay of Lake Michigan, another favorite Indian fishing place.

---

[1] [A recent attempt to solve these problems is Jean Delanglez S.J. *Some La Salle Journeys* (Chicago: Inst. of Jesuit History, 1938). Isaac J. Cox ed. *The Journeys of La Salle* (2 vols. New York: 1922) gives translations of the original narratives used by Parkman.]

Jean Talon, intendant of Canada, now appointed Daumont de Saint-Lusson to search for the copper mines. While on his way west, he sent messages ahead by Indians as far as Green Bay, inviting the tribes to send delegates to meet him at the Ste. Marie mission for an important ceremony. The invitation was accepted by no less than fourteen tribes; and at the Sault, on 14 June 1671, Saint-Lusson in their presence solemnly took possession of the entire American West, both what had been discovered and what would be discovered, for Louis XIV, King of France and of Navarre.

Talon now returned to France, but at his suggestion the new governor of Canada, Count Frontenac, sent Louis Joliet on a journey of discovery westward. At Michilimackinac he was joined by Père Marquette. With five other men in two canoes they coasted the northern shore of Lake Michigan, paddled to the mission at the head of Green Bay, up the Fox River, crossed Lake Winnebago, and with Indian guides reached the portage to the Wisconsin River. On 17 June 1673 they reached the site of Prairie du Chien, Wisconsin, entered the main stream of the mighty Mississippi, and floated down it past the mouth of the Missouri, the site of St. Louis and the mouth of the Ohio. They were entertained by the Arkansas Indians where the river of that name enters the Missisippi, and thence returned upstream to Canada. Joliet and Marquette ascertained that the Mississippi flowed into the Gulf of Mexico, not the Gulf of California.

Under the orders of Count Frontenac, La Salle built a sailing vessel, the *Griffin*, on the Niagara River near Buffalo in 1679 and sailed in her through the Lakes all the way to Green Bay on Lake Michigan. There the *Griffin* was loaded with furs collected by La Salle's agents at Green Bay, and started on her voyage back to Canada, but she was never heard of again. La Salle, four Frenchmen and one Indian in March 1680 pursued their voyage by canoe along the shores of Lake Michigan. Passing the site of Chicago, they reached the mouth of the St. Joseph River and paddled upstream to a point near the present city of South Bend, Indiana, and opposite the campus of St. Mary's College, Notre Dame University.[2] Thence they made a short and easy portage to the headwaters of the Kankakee, which the French called the Theakiki. The party paddled down the Illinois to Starved Rock,

[2] [C. H. Bartlett and R. H. Lyon *La Salle in the Valley of the St. Joseph* (South Bend, Ind.: 1899). Unfortunately it appears that La Salle's monument has been placed at the wrong spot, on the edge of the city of South Bend, where began a later portage used by wagons in the decades just before the coming of the railroad.]

between Utica and Ottawa, Illinois, which La Salle decided to hold and fortify as a fulcrum of defense of the West by the Indians of that region against the obstreperous Iroquois. Naming it Fort St. Louis, and leaving Tonty and a few others to defend it, La Salle with three followers made a thousand-mile journey in 65 days to Fort Frontenac in order to make arrangements for his supply line. Either on this or his next journey, he built Fort Miami on the site of the present St. Joseph, Michigan. During his absence, Fort St. Louis was captured and destroyed by a raiding party of Iroquois.

In November 1680, La Salle returned via the same St. Joseph-Kankakee portage and on the banks of the Illinois ran into a large herd of buffalo, from which he and his few companions shot a dozen bulls. Passing the site of the deserted fort, where grisly vestiges of Iroquois cruelty told the story of what had happened, they reached the Mississippi in early December, paddled back up the Illinois past the mouth of the Kankakee, and walked overland through nineteen days of continuous snowfall to Fort Miami on Lake Michigan, where he spent the winter of 1680–81. In the spring he again paddled up to the Kankakee portage, and there, not far from the present Notre Dame campus, harangued an assembly of the Miami Indians and secured their support for his next and final attempt to descend the Mississippi. This attempt began in December 1681 at Fort Miami, after La Salle had made another trip to Fort Frontenac and back. His facility at traveling through the western wilderness under all sorts of conditions is one of his remarkable accomplishments.

Now we may let Parkman take up the story.]

The season was far advanced. On the bare limbs of the forest hung a few withered remnants of its gay autumnal livery; and the smoke crept upward through the sullen November air from the squalid wigwams of La Salle's Abenaki and Mohegan allies. These, his new friends, were savages whose midnight yells had startled the border hamlets of New England; who had danced around Puritan scalps, and whom Puritan imaginations painted as incarnate fiends. La Salle chose eighteen of them, whom he added to the twenty-three Frenchmen who remained with him, some of the rest having deserted and others lagged behind. The Indians insisted on taking their squaws with them. These were ten in number, besides three children; and thus the expedition included fifty-four persons, of whom some were useless, and others a burden.

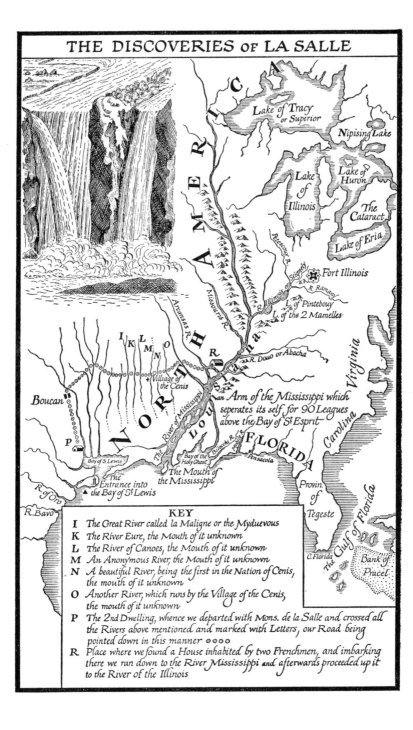

THE DISCOVERIES OF LA SALLE

KEY

I The Great River called la Maligne or the Myduevous

K The River Eure, the Mouth of it unknown

L The River of Canoes, the Mouth of it unknown

M An Anonymous River, the Mouth of it unknown

N A beautiful River, being the first in the Nation of Cenis, the mouth of it unknown

O Another River, which runs by the Village of the Cenis, the mouth of it unknown

P The 2nd Dwelling, whence we departed with Mons. de la Salle and crossed all the Rivers above mentioned and marked with Letters, our Road being pointed down in this manner ◦◦◦◦

R Place where we found a House inhabited by two Frenchmen, and imbarking there we ran down to the River Mississippi and afterwards proceeded up it to the River of the Illinois

On the 21st of December, Tonty and Membré set out from Fort Miami with some of the party in six canoes, and crossed to the little river Chicago. La Salle, with the rest of the men, joined them a few days later. It was the dead of winter, and the streams were frozen. They made sledges, placed on them the canoes, the baggage, and a disabled Frenchman; crossed from the Chicago to the northern branch of the Illinois, and filed in a long procession down its frozen course. They reached the site of the great Illinois village, found it tenantless, and continued their journey, still dragging their canoes, till at length they reached open water below Lake Peoria.

La Salle had abandoned for a time his original plan of building a vessel for the navigation of the Mississippi. Bitter experience had taught him the difficulty of the attempt, and he resolved to trust to his canoes alone. They embarked again, floating prosperously down between the leafless forests that flanked the tranquil river; till, on the sixth of February, they issued upon the majestic bosom of the Mississippi. Here, for the time, their progress was stopped; for the river was full of floating ice. La Salle's Indians, too, had lagged behind; but within a week all had arrived, the navigation was once more free, and they resumed their course. Towards evening they saw on their right the mouth of a great river; and the clear current was invaded by the headlong torrent of the Missouri, opaque with mud. They built their camp-fires in the neighboring forest; and at daylight, embarking anew on the dark and mighty stream, drifted swiftly down towards unknown destinies. They passed a deserted town of the Tamaroas; saw, three days after, the mouth of the Ohio; and, gliding by the wastes of bordering swamp, landed on the 24th of February near the Third Chickasaw Bluffs. They encamped, and the hunters went out for game. All returned, excepting Pierre Prudhomme; and as the others had seen fresh tracks of Indians, La Salle feared that he was killed. While some of his followers built a small stockade fort on a high bluff by the river, others ranged the woods in pursuit of the missing hunter. After six days of ceaseless and fruitless search, they met two Chickasaw Indians in the forest; and through them La Salle sent presents and peace-messages to that warlike people, whose villages were a few days' journey distant. Several days later Prudhomme was found, and brought into the camp, half-dead. He had lost his way while hunting; and to console him for his woes La Salle christened the newly built fort with his name, and left him, with a few others, in charge of it.

Again they embarked; and with every stage of their adventurous progress the mystery of this vast New World was more and more unveiled. More and more they entered the realms of spring. The hazy sunlight, the warm and drowsy air, the tender foliage, the opening flowers, betokened the reviving life of Nature. For several days more they followed the writhings of the great river on its tortuous course through wastes of swamp and canebrake, till on the thirteenth of March they found themselves wrapped in a thick fog. Neither shore was visible; but they heard on the right the booming of an Indian drum and the shrill outcries of the war-dance. La Salle at once crossed to the opposite side, where, in less than an hour, his men threw up a rude fort of felled trees. Meanwhile the fog cleared; and from the farther bank the astonished Indians saw the strange visitors at their work. Some of the French advanced to the edge of the water, and beckoned them to come over. Several of them approached, in a wooden canoe, to within the distance of a gun-shot. La Salle displayed the calumet, and sent a Frenchman to meet them. He was well received; and the friendly mood of the Indians being now apparent, the whole party crossed the river.

On landing, they found themselves at a town of the Kappa band of the Arkansas, a people dwelling near the mouth of the river which bears their name. "The whole village," writes Membré to his superior, "came down to the shore to meet us, except the women, who had run off. I cannot tell you the civility and kindness we received from these barbarians, who brought us poles to make huts, supplied us with firewood during the three days we were among them, and took turns in feasting us. But, my Reverend Father, this gives no idea of the good qualities of these savages, who are gay, civil, and free-hearted. The young men, though the most alert and spirited we had seen, are nevertheless so modest that not one of them would take the liberty to enter our hut, but all stood quietly at the door. They are so well formed that we were in admiration at their beauty. We did not lose the value of a pin while we were among them."

Various were the dances and ceremonies with which they entertained the strangers, who, on their part, responded with a solemnity which their hosts would have liked less if they had understood it better. La Salle and Tonty, at the head of their followers, marched to the open area in the midst of the village. Here, to the admiration of the gazing crowd of warriors, women, and children, a cross was raised bearing the arms of France. Membré, in canonicals, sang a hymn; the men shouted *Vive le Roi;* and La Salle, in the King's name, took formal possession of the country. The friar, not, he flatters himself, without success, labored to expound by signs the mysteries of the Faith; while La Salle, by methods equally satisfactory, drew from the chief an acknowledgment of fealty to Louis XIV.[3]

After touching at several other towns of this people, the voyagers resumed their course, guided by two of the Arkansas; passed the sites, since becoming historic, of Vicksburg and Grand Gulf; and, about three hundred miles below the Arkansas, stopped by the edge of a swamp on the western side of the river.[4] Here, as their two guides told them, was the path to the great town of the Taensas. Tonty and Membré were sent to visit it. They and their men shouldered their birch canoe through the swamp, and launched it on a lake which had once formed a portion of the channel of the river. In two hours, they reached the town; and Tonty gazed at it with astonishment. He had seen nothing like it in America, — large square dwellings, built of sun-baked mud mixed with straw, arched over with a dome-shaped roof of canes, and placed in regular order around an open area. Two of them were larger and better than the rest. One was the lodge of the chief; the other was the temple, or house of the Sun. They entered the former, and found a single room, forty feet square, where, in the dim light, — for there was no opening but the door, — the chief sat awaiting them on a sort of bedstead, three of his wives at his side; while sixty old men, wrapped in white cloaks woven of mulberry-bark, formed his divan. When he spoke, his wives howled to do him honor; and the assembled councillors listened with the reverence due to a potentate for whom, at his death, a hundred victims were to be sacrificed. He received the visitors graciously, and joyfully accepted the gifts which Tonty laid before him. This interview over, the Frenchmen repaired to the temple, wherein were kept the bones of the departed chiefs. In construction, it was much like the royal dwelling. Over it were rude wooden figures, representing three eagles turned towards the east. A strong mud wall surrounded it, planted with stakes, on which were stuck the skulls of enemies sacrificed to the Sun; while before the door was a block of wood, on which lay a large shell surrounded with the braided hair of the victims. The interior was rude

[3] The nation of the Arkansas dwelt on the west bank of the Mississippi, near the mouth of the Arkansas. They were divided into four tribes, living for the most part in separate villages. Those first visited by La Salle were the Kappas, or Quapaws, a remnant of whom still subsists.

[4] In Tensas County, Louisiana. It may interest sportsmen to know that the party killed several large alligators on their way.

as a barn, dimly lighted from the doorway, and full of smoke. There was a structure in the middle which Membré thinks was a kind of altar; and before it burned a perpetual fire, fed with three logs laid end to end, and watched by two old men devoted to this sacred office. There was a mysterious recess, too, which the strangers were forbidden to explore, but which, as Tonty was told, contained the riches of the nation, consisting of pearls from the Gulf, and trinkets obtained, probably through other tribes, from the Spaniards and other Europeans.

The chief condescended to visit La Salle at his camp, — a favor which he would by no means have granted, had the visitors been Indians. A master of ceremonies and six attendants preceded him, to clear the path and prepare the place of meeting. When all was ready, he was seen advancing, clothed in a white robe and preceded by two men bearing white fans, while a third displayed a disk of burnished copper, — doubtless to represent the Sun, his ancestor, or, as others will have it, his elder brother. His aspect was marvellously grave, and he and La Salle met with gestures of ceremonious courtesy. The interview was very friendly; and the chief returned well pleased with the gifts which his entertainer bestowed on him, and which, indeed, had been the principal motive of his visit.

On the next morning, as they descended the river, they saw a wooden canoe full of Indians; and Tonty gave chase. He had nearly overtaken it, when more than a hundred men appeared suddenly on the shore, with bows to defend their countrymen. La Salle called out to Tonty to withdraw. He obeyed; and the whole party encamped on the opposite bank. Tonty offered to cross the river with a peace pipe, and set out accordingly with a small party of men. When he landed, the Indians made signs of friendship by joining their hands, — a proceeding by which Tonty, having but one hand, was somewhat embarrassed; but he directed his men to respond in his stead. La Salle and Membré now joined him, and went with the Indians to their village, three leagues distant. Here they spent the night. "The Sieur de la Salle," writes Membré, "whose very air, engaging manners, tact, and address attract love and respect alike, produced such an effect on the hearts of these people that they did not know how to treat us well enough."

The Indians of this village were the Natchez; and their chief was brother of the great chief, or Sun, of the whole nation. His town was several leagues distant, near the site of the city of Natchez; and thither the French repaired to visit him. They saw what they had already seen among the Taensas, — a religious and political despotism, a privileged caste descended from the sun, a temple, and a sacred fire.[5] La Salle planted a large cross, with the arms of France attached, in the midst of the town; while the inhabitants looked on with a satisfaction which they would hardly have displayed had they understood the meaning of the act.

The French next visited the Coroas, at their village two leagues below; and here they found a reception no less auspicious. On the 31st of March, as they approached Red River, they passed in the fog a town of the Oumas, and three days later discovered a party of fishermen, in wooden canoes, among the canes along the margin of the water. They fled at sight of the Frenchmen. La Salle sent men to reconnoitre, who, as they struggled through the marsh, were greeted with a shower of arrows; while from the neighboring village of the Quinipissas,[6] invisible behind the canebrake, they heard the sound of an Indian drum and the whoops of the mustering warriors. La Salle, anxious to keep the peace with all the tribes along the river, recalled his men, and pursued his voyage. A few leagues below they saw a cluster of Indian lodges on the left bank, apparently void of inhabitants. They landed, and found three of them filled with corpses. It was a village of the Tangibao, sacked by their enemies only a few days before.

And now they neared their journey's end. On the 6th of April the river divided itself into three broad channels. La Salle followed that of the west, and Dautray that of the east; while Tonty took the middle passage. As he drifted down the turbid current, between the low and marshy shores, the brackish water changed to brine, and the breeze grew fresh with the salt breath of the sea. Then the broad bosom of the great Gulf opened on his sight, tossing its restless billows, limitless, voiceless, lonely as when born of chaos, without a sail, without a sign of life.

La Salle, in a canoe, coasted the marshy borders of the sea; and then the reunited parties assembled on a spot of dry ground, a short distance above the mouth of the river. Here a column was made ready, bearing the arms of France, and inscribed with the words, "Louis Le Grand, Roy de France et de Navarre, règne Neuvième Avril, 1682."

The Frenchmen were mustered under arms; and while the New

---

[5] By 1721 the Taensas were extinct. In 1729 the Natchez, enraged by the arbitrary conduct of a French commandant, massacred the neighboring settlers, and were in consequence expelled from their country and nearly destroyed.

[6] In St. Charles County, on the left bank, not far above New Orleans.

England Indians and their squaws looked on in wondering silence, they chanted the *Te Deum*, the *Exaudiat*, and the *Domine salvum fac Regem*. Then, amid volleys of musketry and shouts of *Vive le Roi*, La Salle planted the column in its place, and, standing near it, proclaimed in a loud voice, —

"In the name of the most high, mighty, invincible, and victorious Prince, Louis the Great, by the grace of God King of France and of Navarre, Fourteenth of that name, I, this ninth day of April, one thousand six hundred and eighty-two, in virtue of the commission of his Majesty, which I hold in my hand, and which may be seen by all whom it may concern, have taken, and do now take, in the name of his Majesty and of his successors to the crown, possession of this country of Louisiana, the seas, harbors, ports, bays, adjacent straits, and all the nations, peoples, provinces, cities, towns, villages, mines, minerals, fisheries, streams, and rivers, within the extent of the said Louisiana, from the mouth of the great river St. Louis, otherwise called the Ohio, . . . as also along the river Colbert, or Mississippi, and the rivers which discharge themselves thereinto, from its source beyond the country of the Sioux . . . as far as its mouth at the sea, or Gulf of Mexico, and also to the mouth of the River of Palms, upon the assurance we have had from the natives of these countries that we are the first Europeans who have descended or ascended the said river Colbert; hereby protesting against all who may hereafter undertake to invade any or all of these aforesaid countries, peoples, or lands, to the prejudice of the rights of his Majesty, acquired by the consent of the nations dwelling herein. Of which, and of all else that is needful, I hereby take to witness those who hear me, and demand an act of the notary here present."

Shouts of *Vive le Roi* and volleys of musketry responded to his words. Then a cross was planted beside the column, and a leaden plate buried near it, bearing the arms of France, with a Latin inscription, *Ludovicus Magnus regnat*. The weather-beaten voyagers joined their voices in the grand hymn of the *Vexilla Regis:* —

> "The banners of Heaven's King advance,
> The mystery of the Cross shines forth . . . "

and renewed shouts of *Vive le Roi* closed the ceremony.

On that day, the realm of France received on parchment a stupendous accession. The fertile plains of Texas; the vast basin of the Mississippi, from its frozen northern springs to the sultry borders of the Gulf; from the woody ridge of the Alleghanies to the bare peaks of the Rocky

Mountains, — a region of savannas and forests, sun-cracked deserts, and grassy prairies, watered by a thousand rivers, ranged by a thousand warlike tribes, passed beneath the sceptre of the Sultan of Versailles; and all by virtue of a feeble human voice, inaudible at half a mile.

CHAPTER XIX

St. Louis of the Illinois

1682–1683

[La Salle and the Discovery of the Great West, CHAPTER XXI]

Louisiana was the name bestowed by La Salle on the new domain of the French crown. The rule of the Bourbons in the West is a memory of the past, but the name of the Great King still survives in a narrow corner of their lost empire. The Louisiana of to-day is but a single State of the American republic. The Louisiana of La Salle stretched from the Alleghanies to the Rocky Mountains; from the Rio Grande and the Gulf to the farthest springs of the Missouri.

La Salle had written his name in history; but his hard-earned success was but the prelude of a harder task. Herculean labors lay before him, if he would realize the schemes with which his brain was pregnant. Bent on accomplishing them, he retraced his course, and urged his canoes upward against the muddy current. The party were famished. They had little to subsist on but the flesh of alligators. When they reached the Quinipissas, who had proved hostile on their way down, they resolved to risk an interview with them, in the hope of obtaining food. The treacherous savages dissembled, brought them corn, and on the following night made an attack upon them, but met with a bloody repulse. The party next revisited the Coroas, and found an unfavorable change in their disposition towards them. They feasted them, indeed, but during the repast surrounded them with an overwhelming force of warriors. The French, however, kept so well on their guard, that their entertainers dared not make an attack, and suffered them to depart unmolested.

And now, in a career of unwonted success and anticipated triumph, La Salle was arrested by a foe against which the boldest heart avails nothing. As he ascended the Mississippi, he was seized by a dangerous illness. Unable to proceed, he sent forward Tonty to Michilimackinac, whence, after despatching news of their discovery to Canada, he was to return to the Illinois. La Salle himself lay helpless at Fort Prudhomme, the palisade work which his men had built at the Chickasaw Bluffs on their way down. Father Zenobe Membré attended him; and at the end of July he was once more in a condition to advance by slow movements towards Fort Miami, which he reached in about a month.

In September he rejoined Tonty at Michilimackinac, and in the following month wrote to a friend in France: "Though my discovery is made, and I have descended the Mississippi to the Gulf of Mexico, I cannot send you this year either an account of my journey or a map. On the way back I was attacked by a deadly disease, which kept me in danger of my life for forty days, and left me so weak that I could think of nothing for four months after. I have hardly strength enough now to write my letters, and the season is so far advanced that I cannot detain a single day this canoe which I send expressly to carry them. If I had not feared being forced to winter on the way, I should have tried to get to Quebec to meet the new governor, if it is true that we are to have one; but in my present condition this would be an act of suicide, on account of the bad nourishment I should have all winter in case the snow and ice stopped me on the way. Besides, my presence is absolutely necessary in the place to which I am going. I pray you, my dear sir, to give me once more all the help you can. I have great enemies, who have succeeded in all they have undertaken. I do not pretend to resist them, but only to justify myself, so that I can pursue by sea the plans I have begun here by land."

This was what he had proposed to himself from the first; that is, to abandon the difficult access through Canada, beset with enemies, and open a way to his western domain through the Gulf and the Mississippi. This was the aim of all his toilsome explorations. Could he have accomplished his first intention of building a vessel on the Illinois and descending in her to the Gulf, he would have been able to defray in good measure the costs of the enterprise by means of the furs and buffalo-hides collected on the way and carried in her to France. With a fleet of canoes, this was impossible; and there was nothing to offset the enormous outlay which he and his associates had made. He meant, as we have seen, to found on the banks of the Illinois a colony of French and Indians to answer the double purpose of a bulwark against the Iroquois and a place of storage for the furs of all the western tribes; and he hoped in the following year to secure an outlet for this colony and for all the trade of the valley of the Mississippi, by occupying the mouth of that river with a fort and another colony. This, too, was an essential part of his original design.

But for his illness, he would have gone to France to provide for its execution. Meanwhile, he ordered Tonty to collect as many men as possible, and begin the projected colony on the banks of the Illinois. A report soon after reached him that those pests of the wilderness the Iroquois were about to renew their attacks on the western tribes. This would be fatal to his plans; and, following Tonty to the Illinois, he rejoined him near the site of the great town.

The cliff called "Starved Rock," now pointed out to travellers as the chief natural curiosity of the region, rises, steep on three sides as a castle wall, to the height of 125 feet above the river. In front, it overhangs the water that washes its base; its western brow looks down on the tops of the forest trees below; and on the east lies a wide gorge or ravine, choked with the mingled foliage of oaks, walnuts, and elms; while in its rocky depths a little brook creeps down to mingle with the river. From the trunk of the stunted cedar that leans forward from the brink, you may drop a plummet into the river below, where the cat-fish and the turtles may plainly be seen gliding over the wrinkled sands of the clear and shallow current. The cliff is accessible only from behind, where a man may climb up, not without difficulty, by a steep and narrow passage. The top is about an acre in extent. Here, in the month of December, La Salle and Tonty began to intrench themselves. They cut away the forest that crowned the rock, built storehouses and dwellings of its remains, dragged timber up the rugged pathway, and encircled the summit with a palisade.[1]

Thus the winter passed, and meanwhile the work of negotiation went prosperously on. The minds of the Indians had been already prepared. In La Salle they saw their champion against the Iroquois, the standing

[1] "Starved Rock" perfectly answers in every respect to the indications of the contemporary maps and documents concerning "Le Rocher," the site of La Salle's fort of St. Louis. It is laid down on several contemporary maps, besides the great map of La Salle's discoveries, made in 1684 [by Franquelin. Parkman's copy of this map, the original of which has disappeared, is in the Harvard College Library]. They all place it on the south side of the river. A traditional interest also attaches to this rock. It is said that, in the Indian wars that followed the assassination of Pontiac, a few years after the cession of Canada, a party of Illinois, assailed by the Pottawattamies, here took refuge, defying attack. At length they were all destroyed by starvation, and hence the name of "Starved Rock." [Parkman himself, with the aid of local inhabitants, located Starved Rock and the site of the Great Town of the Illinois Indians, in 1867. It is on the south side of the Illinois River, between Utica and Ottawa, in La Salle County, Illinois. He describes the search for it in a note to the end of Chapter XVI of his La Salle.]

terror of all this region. They gathered round his stronghold like the timorous peasantry of the middle ages around the rock-built castle of their feudal lord. From the wooden ramparts of St. Louis, — for so he named his fort, — high and inaccessible as an eagle's nest, a strange scene lay before his eye. The broad, flat valley of the Illinois was spread beneath him like a map, bounded in the distance by its low wall of woody hills. The river wound at his feet in devious channels among islands bordered with lofty trees; then, far on the left, flowed calmly westward through the vast meadows, till its glimmering blue ribbon was lost in hazy distance.

There had been a time, and that not remote, when these fair meadows were a waste of death and desolation, scathed with fire, and strewn with the ghastly relics of an Iroquois victory. Now all was changed. La Salle looked down from his rock on a concourse of wild human life. Lodges of bark and rushes, or cabins of logs, were clustered on the open plain or along the edges of the bordering forests. Squaws labored, warriors lounged in the sun, naked children whooped and gambolled on the grass. Beyond the river, a mile and a half on the left, the banks were studded once more with the lodges of the Illinois, who, to the number of six thousand, had returned, since their defeat, to this their favorite dwelling-place. Scattered along the valley, among the adjacent hills, or over the neighboring prairie, were the cantonments of a half-score of other tribes and fragments of tribes, gathered under the protecting ægis of the French, — Shawnees from the Ohio, Abenakis from Maine, Miamis from the sources of the Kankakee, with others whose barbarous names are hardly worth the record. Nor were these La Salle's only dependants. By the terms of his patent, he held seigneurial rights over this wild domain; and he now began to grant it out in parcels to his followers. These, however, were as yet but a score, — a lawless band, trained in forest license, and marrying, as their detractors affirm, a new squaw every day in the week. This was after their lord's departure, for his presence imposed a check on these eccentricities.

La Salle, in a memoir addressed to the Minister of the Marine, reports the total number of the Indians around Fort St. Louis at about four thousand warriors, or twenty thousand souls. His diplomacy had been crowned with a marvellous success, — for which his thanks were due, first to the Iroquois, and the universal terror they inspired; next, to his own address and unwearied energy. His colony had sprung up, as it were, in a night; but might not a night suffice to disperse it?

The conditions of maintaining it were twofold: first, he must give efficient aid to his savage colonists against the Iroquois; secondly, he must supply them with French goods in exchange for their furs. The men, arms, and ammunition for their defence, and the goods for trading with them, must be brought from Canada, until a better and surer avenue of supply could be provided through the entrepôt which he meant to establish at the mouth of the Mississippi. Canada was full of his enemies; but as long as Count Frontenac was in power, he was sure of support. Count Frontenac was in power no longer. He had been recalled to France through the intrigues of the party adverse to La Salle; and Le Febvre de la Barre reigned in his stead.

La Barre was an old naval officer of rank, advanced to a post for which he proved himself notably unfit. If he was without the arbitrary passions which had been the chief occasion of the recall of his predecessor, he was no less without his energies and his talents. He showed a weakness and an avarice for which his age may have been in some measure answerable. He was no whit less unscrupulous than his predecessor in his secret violation of the royal ordinances regulating the fur-trade, which it was his duty to enforce. Like Frontenac, he took advantage of his position to carry on an illicit traffic with the Indians; but it was with different associates. The late governor's friends were the new governor's enemies; and La Salle, armed with his monopolies, was the object of his especial jealousy.[2]

Meanwhile, La Salle, buried in the western wilderness, remained for the time ignorant of La Barre's disposition towards him, and made an effort to secure his good-will and countenance. He wrote to him from his rock of St. Louis, early in the spring of 1683, expressing the hope that he should have from him the same support as from Count Frontenac; "although," he says, "my enemies will try to influence you against me." His attachment to Frontenac, he pursues, has been the cause of all the late governor's enemies turning against him. He then recounts his voyage down the Mississippi; says that, with twenty-two Frenchmen, he caused all the tribes along the river to ask for peace; and speaks of his right under the royal patent to build forts anywhere along his route, and grant out lands around them, as at Fort Frontenac.

"My losses in my enterprise," he continues, "have exceeded forty thousand crowns. I am now going four hundred leagues south-south-

[2] The royal instructions to La Barre, on his assuming the government, dated at Versailles 10 May 1682, require him to give no further permission to make journeys of discovery towards the Sioux and the Mississippi, as his Majesty thinks his subjects better employed in cultivating the land. The letter adds, however, that La Salle is to be allowed to continue his discoveries, if they appear to be useful.

west of this place, to induce the Chickasaws to follow the Shawanoes and other tribes, and settle, like them, at St. Louis. It remained only to settle French colonists here, and this I have already done. I hope you will not detain them as *coureurs de bois*, when they come down to Montreal to make necessary purchases. I am aware that I have no right to trade with the tribes who descend to Montreal, and I shall not permit such trade to my men; nor have I ever issued licenses to that effect, as my enemies say that I have done."

Again, on the 4th of June following, he writes to La Barre, from the Chicago portage, complaining that some of his colonists, going to Montreal for necessary supplies, have been detained by his enemies, and begging that they may be allowed to return, that his enterprise may not be ruined. "The Iroquois," he pursues, "are again invading the country. Last year, the Miamis were so alarmed by them that they abandoned their town and fled; but at my return they came back, and have been induced to settle with the Illinois at my fort of St. Louis. The Iroquois have lately murdered some families of their nation, and they are all in terror again. I am afraid they will take flight, and so prevent the Missouris and neighboring tribes from coming to settle at St. Louis, as they are about to do.

"Some of the Hurons and French tell the Miamis that I am keeping them here for the Iroquois to destroy. I pray that you will let me hear from you, that I may give these people some assurances of protection before they are destroyed in my sight. Do not suffer my men who have come down to the settlements to be longer prevented from returning. There is great need here of reinforcements. The Iroquois, as I have said, have lately entered the country; and a great terror prevails. I have postponed going to Michilimackinac, because, if the Iroquois strike any blow in my absence, the Miamis will think that I am in league with them; whereas, if I and the French stay among them, they will regard us as protectors. But, Monsieur, it is in vain that we risk our lives here, and that I exhaust my means in order to fulfil the intentions of his Majesty, if all my measures are crossed in the settlements below, and if those who go down to bring munitions, without which we cannot defend ourselves, are detained under pretexts trumped up for the occasion. If I am prevented from bringing up men and supplies, as I am allowed to do by the permit of Count Frontenac, then my patent from the King is useless. It would be very hard for us, after having done what was required, even before the time prescribed, and after suffering severe losses, to have our efforts frustrated by obstacles got up designedly.

"I trust that, as it lies with you alone to prevent or to permit the return of the men whom I have sent down, you will not so act as to thwart my plans. A part of the goods which I have sent by them belong not to me, but to the Sieur de Tonty, and are a part of his pay. Others are to buy munitions indispensable for our defence. Do not let my creditors seize them. It is for their advantage that my fort, full as it is of goods, should be held against the enemy. I have only twenty men, with scarcely a hundred pounds of powder; and I cannot long hold the country without more. The Illinois are very capricious and uncertain. . . . If I had men enough to send out to reconnoitre the enemy, I would have done so before this; but I have not enough. I trust you will put it in my power to obtain more, that this important colony may be saved."

While La Salle was thus writing to La Barre, La Barre was writing to Seignelay, the Marine and Colonial Minister, decrying his correspondent's discoveries, and pretending to doubt their reality. "The Iroquois," he adds, "have sworn his [La Salle's] death. The imprudence of this man is about to involve the colony in war." And again he writes, in the following spring, to say that La Salle was with a score of vagabonds at Green Bay, where he set himself up as a king, pillaged his countrymen, and put them to ransom, exposed the tribes of the West to the incursions of the Iroquois, and all under pretence of a patent from his Majesty, the provisions of which he grossly abused; but, as his privileges would expire on the 12th of May ensuing, he would then be forced to come to Quebec, where his creditors, to whom he owed more than thirty thousand crowns, were anxiously awaiting him.[3]

Finally, when La Barre received the two letters from La Salle, of which the substance is given above, he sent copies of them to the Minister Seignelay, with the following comment: "By the copies of the Sieur de la Salle's letters, you will perceive that his head is turned, and that he has been bold enough to give you intelligence of a false discovery, and that, instead of returning to the colony to learn what the King wishes him to do, he does not come near me, but keeps in the backwoods, five hundred leagues off, with the idea of attracting the inhabitants to him, and building up an imaginary kingdom for himself, by debauching all the bankrupts and idlers of this country. If you will look at the two letters I had from him, you can judge the character of this personage better than I can. Affairs with the Iroquois are in such a state that I cannot allow him to muster all their enemies together and

---

[3] La Salle had spent the winter, not at Green Bay as this slanderous letter declares, but in the Illinois country.

put himself at their head. All the men who brought me news from him have abandoned him, and say not a word about returning, but sell the furs they have brought as if they were their own; so that he cannot hold his ground much longer." Such calumnies had their effect. The enemies of La Salle had already gained the ear of the King; and he had written in August, from Fontainebleau, to his new governor of Canada: "I am convinced, like you, that the discovery of the Sieur de la Salle is very useless, and that such enterprises ought to be prevented in future, as they tend only to debauch the inhabitants by the hope of gain, and to diminish the revenue from beaver-skins."

In order to understand the posture of affairs at this time, it must be remembered that Dutch and English traders of New York were urging on the Iroquois to attack the western tribes, with the object of gaining, through their conquest, the control of the fur-trade of the interior, and diverting it from Montreal to Albany. The scheme was full of danger to Canada, which the loss of the trade would have ruined. La Barre and his associates were greatly alarmed at it. Its complete success would have been fatal to their hopes of profit; but they nevertheless wished it such a measure of success as would ruin their rival, La Salle. Hence, no little satisfaction mingled with their anxiety when they heard that the Iroquois were again threatening to invade the Miamis and the Illinois; and thus La Barre, whose duty it was strenuously to oppose the intrigue of the English, and use every effort to quiet the ferocious bands whom they were hounding against the Indian allies of the French, was, in fact, but half-hearted in the work. He cut off La Salle from all supplies; detained the men whom he sent for succor; and, at a conference with the Iroquois, told them that they were welcome to plunder and kill him.

The old governor, and the unscrupulous ring with which he was associated, now took a step to which he was doubtless emboldened by the tone of the King's letter, in condemnation of La Salle's enterprise. He resolved to seize Fort Frontenac, the property of La Salle, under the pretext that the latter had not fulfilled the conditions of the grant, and had not maintained a sufficient garrison. Two of his associates, La Chesnaye and Le Ber, armed with an order from him, went up and took possession, despite the remonstrances of La Salle's creditors and mortgagees; lived on La Salle's stores, sold for their own profit, and (it is said) that of La Barre, the provisions sent by the King, and turned in the cattle to pasture on the growing crops. La Forest, La Salle's lieutenant, was told that he might retain the command of the fort if he would join the associates; but he refused, and sailed in the autumn for France.

Meanwhile La Salle remained at the Illinois in extreme embarrassment, cut off from supplies, robbed of his men who had gone to seek them, and disabled from fulfilling the pledges he had given to the surrounding Indians. Such was his position, when reports came to Fort St. Louis that the Iroquois were at hand. The Indian hamlets were wild with terror, beseeching him for succor which he had no power to give. Happily, the report proved false. No Iroquois appeared; the threatened attack was postponed, and the summer passed away in peace. But La Salle's position, with the governor his declared enemy, was intolerable and untenable; and there was no resource but in the protection of the court. Early in the autumn, he left Tonty in command of the rock, bade farewell to his savage retainers, and descended to Quebec, intending to sail for France.

On his way, he met the Chevalier de Baugis, an officer of the King's dragoons, commissioned by La Barre to take possession of Fort St. Louis, and bearing letters from the governor ordering La Salle to come to Quebec, — a superfluous command, as he was then on his way thither. He smothered his wrath and wrote to Tonty to receive De Baugis well. The chevalier and his party proceeded to the Illinois and took possession of the fort, — De Baugis commanding for the governor, while Tonty remained as representative of La Salle. The two officers could not live in harmony; but, with the return of spring, each found himself in sore need of aid from the other. Towards the end of March the Iroquois attacked their citadel, and besieged it for six days, but at length withdrew discomfited, carrying with them a number of Indian prisoners, most of whom escaped from their clutches.

Meanwhile, La Salle had sailed for France.

CHAPTER XX

La Salle Painted by Himself

[La Salle and the Discovery of the Great West, CHAPTER XXII]

We have seen La Salle in his acts. While he crosses the sea, let us look at him in himself. Few men knew him, even of those who saw him most. Reserved and self-contained as he was, with little vivacity or gayety or love of pleasure, he was a sealed book to those about him. His daring energy and endurance were patent to all; but the motive forces that urged him, and the influences that wrought beneath the surface of his character, were hidden where few eyes could pierce. His enemies were free to make their own interpretations, and they did not fail to use the opportunity.

The interests arrayed against him were incessantly at work. His men were persuaded to desert and rob him; the Iroquois were told that he was arming the western tribes against them; the western tribes were told that he was betraying them to the Iroquois; his proceedings were denounced to the court; and continual efforts were made to alienate his associates. They, on their part, sore as they were from disappointment and loss, were in a mood to listen to the aspersions cast upon him; and they pestered him with letters, asking questions, demanding explanations, and dunning him for money. It is through his answers that we are best able to judge him; and at times, by those touches of nature which make the whole world kin, they teach us to know him and to feel for him.

The main charges against him were that he was a crack-brained schemer, that he was harsh to his men, that he traded where he had no right to trade, and that his discoveries were nothing but a pretence for making money. No accusations appear that touch his integrity or his honor.

It was hard to convince those who were always losing by him. A remittance of good dividends would have been his best answer, and would have made any other answer needless; but, instead of bills of exchange, he had nothing to give but excuses and explanations. In the autumn of 1680, he wrote to an associate who had demanded the long-deferred profits: "I have had many misfortunes in the last two years. In the autumn of '78, I lost a vessel by the fault of the pilot; in the next summer, the deserters I told you about robbed me of eight or ten thousand livres' worth of goods. In the autumn of '79, I lost a vessel worth more than ten thousand crowns; in the next spring, five or six rascals stole the value of five or six thousand livres in goods and beaver-skins, at the Illinois, when I was absent. Two other men of mine, carrying furs worth four or five thousand livres, were killed or drowned in the St. Lawrence, and the furs were lost. Another robbed me of three thousand livres in beaver-skins stored at Michili-mackinac. This last spring, I lost about seventeen hundred livres' worth of goods by the upsetting of a canoe. Last winter, the fort and buildings at Niagara were burned by the fault of the commander; and in the spring the deserters, who passed that way, seized a part of the property that remained, and escaped to New York. All this does not discourage me in the least, and will only defer for a year or two the returns of profit which you ask for this year. These losses are no more my fault than the loss of the ship *St. Joseph* was yours. I cannot be everywhere, and cannot help making use of the people of the country."

He begs his correspondent to send out an agent of his own. "He need not be very *savant*, but he must be faithful, patient of labor, and fond neither of gambling, women, nor good cheer; for he will find none of these with me. Trusting in what he will write you, you may close your ears to what priests and Jesuits tell you.

"After having put matters in good trim for trade I mean to withdraw, though I think it will be very profitable; for I am disgusted to find that I must always be making excuses, which is a part I cannot play successfully. I am utterly tired of this business; for I see that it is not enough to put property and life in constant peril, but that it requires more pains to answer envy and detraction than to overcome the difficulties inseparable from my undertaking."

And he makes a variety of proposals, by which he hopes to get rid of a part of his responsibility to his correspondent. He begs him again to send out a confidential agent, saying that for his part he does not want to have any account to render, except that which he owes to the court, of his discoveries. He adds, strangely enough for a man burdened with such liabilities, "I have neither the habit nor the inclination to keep books, nor have I anybody with me who knows how." He says to another correspondent, "I think, like you, that partnerships in business are dangerous, on account of the little practice I have in these matters." It is not surprising that he wanted to leave his associates to manage business for themselves: "You know that this trade is good; and with a trusty agent to conduct it for you, you run no risk. As for me, I will keep the charge of the forts, the command of posts and of men, the management of Indians and Frenchmen, and the establishment of the colony, which will remain my property, leaving your agent and mine to look after our interests, and drawing my half without having any hand in what belongs to you."

La Salle was a very indifferent trader; and his heart was not in the commercial part of his enterprise. He aimed at achievement, and thirsted after greatness. His ambition was to found another France in the West; and if he meant to govern it also, — as without doubt he did, — it is not a matter of wonder or of blame. His misfortune was, that, in the pursuit of a great design, he was drawn into complications of business with which he was ill fitted to grapple. He had not the instinct of the successful merchant. He dared too much, and often dared unwisely; attempted more than he could grasp, and forgot, in his sanguine anticipations, to reckon with enormous and incalculable risks.

Except in the narrative parts, his letters are rambling and unconnected, — which is natural enough, written, as they were, at odd moments, by camp-fires and among Indians. The style is crude; and being well aware of this, he disliked writing, especially as the risk was extreme that his letters would miss their destination. "There is too little good faith in this country, and too many people on the watch, for me to trust anybody with what I wish to send you. Even sealed letters are not too safe. Not only are they liable to be lost or stopped by the way, but even such as escape the curiosity of spies lie at Montreal, waiting a long time to be forwarded."

Again, he writes: "I cannot pardon myself for the stoppage of my letters, though I made every effort to make them reach you. I wrote to you in '79 (in August), and sent my letters to M. de la Forest, who gave them in good faith to my brother. I don't know what he has done with them. I wrote you another, by the vessel that was lost last year. I sent two canoes, by two different routes; but the wind and the rain were so furious that they wintered on the way, and I found my letters at the fort on my return. I now send you one of them, which I wrote last year to M. Thouret, in which you will find a full account of what passed, from the time when we left the outlet of Lake Erie down to the sixteenth of August, 1680. What preceded was told at full length in the letters my brother has seen fit to intercept."

This brother was the Sulpitian priest, Jean Cavelier, who had been persuaded that La Salle's enterprise would be ruinous, and therefore set himself sometimes to stop it altogether, and sometimes to manage it in his own way. "His conduct towards me," says La Salle, "has always been so strange, through the small love he bears me, that it was clear gain for me when he went away; since while he stayed he did nothing but cross all my plans, which I was forced to change every moment to suit his caprice."

There was one point on which the interference of his brother and of his correspondents was peculiarly annoying. They thought it for their interest that he should remain a single man; whereas, it seems that his devotion to his purpose was not so engrossing as to exclude more tender subjects. He writes: —

"I am told that you have been uneasy about my pretended marriage. I had not thought about it at that time; and I shall not make any engagement of the sort till I have given you reason to be satisfied with me. It is a little extraordinary that I must render account of a matter which is free to all the world.

"In fine, Monsieur, it is only as an earnest of something more substantial that I write to you so much at length. I do not doubt that you will hereafter change the ideas about me which some persons wish to give you, and that you will be relieved of the anxiety which all that has happened reasonably causes you. I have written this letter at more than twenty different times; and I am more than a hundred and fifty leagues from where I began it. I have still two hundred more to get over, before reaching the Illinois. I am taking with me twenty-five men to the relief of the six or seven who remain with the Sieur de Tonty."

This was the journey which ended in that scene of horror at the ruined town of the Illinois.

To the same correspondent, pressing him for dividends, he says: "You repeat continually that you will not be satisfied unless I make you large returns of profit. Though I have reason to thank you for what you have done for this enterprise, it seems to me that I have done still more, since I have put everything at stake; and it would be hard to reproach me either with foolish outlays or with the ostentation which is falsely imputed to me. Let my accusers explain what they mean. Since I have been in this country, I have had neither servants nor clothes nor fare which did not savor more of meanness than of ostentation; and the moment I see that there is anything with which either you or the court find fault, I assure you that I will give it up, — for the life I am leading has no other attraction for me than that of honor; and the more danger and difficulty there is in undertakings of this sort, the more worthy of honor I think they are."

His career attests the sincerity of these words. They are a momentary betrayal of the deep enthusiasm of character which may be read in his life, but to which he rarely allowed the faintest expression.

"Above all," he continues, "if you want me to keep on, do not compel me to reply to all the questions and fancies of priests and Jesuits. They have more leisure than I; and I am not subtle enough to anticipate all their empty stories. I could easily give you the information you ask; but I have a right to expect that you will not believe all you hear, nor require me to prove to you that I am not a madman. That is the first point to which you should have attended, before having business with me; and in our long acquaintance, either you must have found me out, or else I must have had long intervals of sanity."

To another correspondent he defends himself against the charge of harshness to his men: "The facility I am said to want is out of place with this sort of people, who are libertines for the most part; and to indulge them means to tolerate blasphemy, drunkenness, lewdness, and a license incompatible with any kind of order. It will not be found that I have in any case whatever treated any man harshly, except for blasphemies and other such crimes openly committed. These I cannot tolerate: first, because such compliance would give grounds for another accusation, much more just; secondly, because, if I allowed such disorders to become habitual, it would be hard to keep the men in subordination and obedience, as regards executing the work I am commissioned to do; thirdly, because the debaucheries, too common with this rabble, are the source of endless delays and frequent thieving; and, finally, because I am a Christian, and do not want to bear the burden of their crimes.

"What is said about my servants has not even a show of truth; for I use no servants here, and all my men are on the same footing. I grant that as those who have lived with me are steadier and give me no reason to complain of their behavior, I treat them as gently as I should treat the others if they resembled them; and as those who were formerly my servants are the only ones I can trust, I speak more openly to them than to the rest, who are generally spies of my enemies. The twenty-two men who deserted and robbed me are not to be believed on their word, deserters and thieves as they are. They are ready enough to find some pretext for their crime; and it needs as unjust a judge as the intendant to prompt such rascals to enter complaints against a person to whom he had given a warrant to arrest them. But, to show the falsity of these charges, Martin Chartier, who was one of those who excited the rest to do as they did, was never with me at all; and the rest had made their plot before seeing me." And he proceeds to relate, in great detail, a variety of circumstances to prove that his men had been instigated first to desert, and then to slander him; adding, "Those who remain with me are the first I had, and they have not left me for six years."

"I have a hundred other proofs of the bad counsel given to these deserters, and will produce them when wanted; but as they themselves are the only witnesses of the severity they complain of, while the witnesses of their crimes are unimpeachable, why am I refused the justice I demand, and why is their secret escape connived at?

"I do not know what you mean by having popular manners. There is nothing special in my food, clothing, or lodging, which are all the same for me as for my men. How can it be that I do not talk with them? I have no other company. M. de Tonty has often found fault with me because I stopped too often to talk with them. You do not know the men one must employ here, when you exhort me to make merry with them. They are incapable of that; for they are never pleased, unless one gives free rein to their drunkenness and other vices. If that is what you call having popular manners, neither honor nor inclination would let me stoop to gain their favor in a way so disreputable; and, besides, the consequences would be dangerous, and they would have the same contempt for me that they have for all who treat them in this fashion.

"You write me that even my friends say that I am not a man of popular manners. I do not know what friends they are. I know of none in this country. To all appearance they are enemies, more subtle and secret than the rest. I make no exceptions; for I know that those who seem to give me support do not do it out of love for me, but because they are in some sort bound in honor, and that in their hearts they think I have dealt ill with them. M. Plet will tell you what he has heard about it himself, and the reasons they have to give.[1] I have seen it

---

[1] His cousin, François Plet, was in Canada in 1680 where, with La Salle's approval, he carried on the trade of Fort Frontenac, in order to indemnify himself for money advanced. La Salle always speaks of him with esteem and gratitude.

for a long time; and these secret stabs they give me show it very plainly. After that, it is not surprising that I open my mind to nobody, and distrust everybody. I have reasons that I cannot write.

"For the rest, Monsieur, pray be well assured that the information you are so good as to give me is received with a gratitude equal to the genuine friendship from which it proceeds; and, however unjust are the charges made against me, I should be much more unjust myself if I did not feel that I have as much reason to thank you for telling me of them as I have to complain of others for inventing them.

"As for what you say about my look and manner, I myself confess that you are not far from right. But *naturam expellas;* and if I am wanting in expansiveness and show of feeling towards those with whom I associate, *it is only through a timidity which is natural to me, and which has made me leave various employments, where without it I could have succeeded.* But as I judged myself ill-fitted for them on account of this defect, I have chosen a life more suited to my solitary disposition; which, nevertheless, does not make me harsh to my people, though, joined to a life among savages, it makes me, perhaps, less polished and complaisant than the atmosphere of Paris requires. I well believe that there is self-love in this; and that, knowing how little I am accustomed to a more polite life, the fear of making mistakes makes me more reserved than I like to be. So I rarely expose myself to conversation with those in whose company I am afraid of making blunders, and can hardly help making them. Abbé Renaudot knows with what repugnance I had the honor to appear before Monseigneur de Conti; and sometimes it took me a week to make up my mind to go to the audience, — that is, when I had time to think about myself, and was not driven by pressing business. It is much the same with letters, which I never write except when pushed to it, and for the same reason. It is a defect of which I shall never rid myself as long as I live, often as it spites me against myself, and often as I quarrel with myself about it." [2]

Here is a strange confession for a man like La Salle. Without doubt, the timidity of which he accuses himself had some of its roots in pride; but not the less was his pride vexed and humbled by it. It is surprising that, being what he was, he could have brought himself to such

[2] These extracts are from La Salle's long letters of 29 Sept. 1680 and 22 Aug. 1682 or 1681. Both are printed in the second volume of the Margry collection, and the originals of both are in the Bibliothèque Nationale. The latter seems to have been written to La Salle's friend Abbé Bernou; and the former, to a certain M. Thouret.

touch at Madeira, to replenish his water-casks. La Salle refused, lest by doing so the secret of the enterprise might reach the Spaniards. One Paget, a Huguenot, took up the word in support of Beaujeu. La Salle told him that the affair was none of his; and as Paget persisted with increased warmth and freedom, he demanded of Beaujeu if it was with his consent that a man of no rank spoke to him in that manner. Beaujeu sustained the Huguenot. "That is enough," returned La Salle, and withdrew into his cabin.

This was not the first misunderstanding; nor was it the last. There was incessant chafing between the two commanders; and the sailors of the *Joly* were soon of one mind with their captain. When the ship crossed the tropic, they made ready a tub on deck to baptize the passengers, after the villanous practice of the time; but La Salle refused to permit it, at which they were highly exasperated, having promised themselves a bountiful ransom, in money or liquor, from their victims. "Assuredly," says Joutel, "they would gladly have killed us all."

When, after a wretched voyage of two months the ships reached St. Domingo, a fresh dispute occurred. It had been resolved at a council of officers to stop at Port de Paix; but Beaujeu, on pretext of a fair wind, ran by that place in the night, and cast anchor at Petit Goave, on the other side of the island. La Salle was extremely vexed; for he expected to meet at Port de Paix the Marquis de Saint-Laurent, lieutenant-general of the islands, Bégon the intendant, and De Cussy, governor of Tortuga, who had orders to supply him with provisions and give him all possible aid.

The *Joly* was alone: the other vessels had lagged behind. She had more than fifty sick men on board, and La Salle was of the number. He sent a messenger to Saint-Laurent, Bégon, and Cussy, begging them to come to him; ordered Joutel to get the sick ashore, suffocating as they were in the hot and crowded ship; and caused the soldiers to be landed on a small island in the harbor. Scarcely had the voyagers sung *Te Deum* for their safe arrival, when two of the lagging vessels appeared, bringing tidings that the third, the ketch *St. François*, had been taken by Spanish buccaneers. She was laden with provisions, tools, and other necessaries for the colony; and the loss was irreparable. Beaujeu was answerable for it; for had he anchored at Port de Paix, it would not have occurred. The lieutenant-general, with Bégon and Cussy, who presently arrived, plainly spoke their minds to him.

La Salle's illness increased. "I was walking with him one day," writes Joutel, "when he was seized of a sudden with such a weakness that he could not stand, and was obliged to lie down on the ground. When he was a little better, I led him to a chamber of a house that the brothers Duhaut had hired. Here we put him to bed, and in the morning he was attacked by a violent fever." "It was so violent that," says another of his shipmates, "his imagination pictured to him things equally terrible and amazing." He lay delirious in the wretched garret, attended by his brother, and one or two others who stood faithful to him. A goldsmith of the neighborhood, moved at his deplorable condition, offered the use of his house and Abbé Cavelier had him removed thither. But there was a tavern hard by, and the patient was tormented with daily and nightly riot. At the height of the fever, a party of Beaujeu's sailors spent a night in singing and dancing before the house; and, says Cavelier, "The more we begged them to be quiet, the more noise they made." La Salle lost reason and well-nigh life; but at length his mind resumed its balance, and the violence of the disease abated. A friendly Capuchin friar offered him the shelter of his roof; and two of his men supported him thither on foot, giddy with exhaustion and hot with fever. Here he found repose, and was slowly recovering, when some of his attendants rashly told him the loss of the ketch *St. François;* and the consequence was a critical return of the disease.

There was no one to fill his place. Beaujeu would not; Cavelier could not. Joutel, the gardener's son, was apparently the most trusty man of the company; but the expedition was virtually without a head. The men roamed on shore, and plunged into every excess of debauchery, contracting diseases which eventually killed them.

Beaujeu, in the extremity of ill-humor, resumed his correspondence with Seignelay.[1] "But for the illness of the Sieur de la Salle," he writes, "I could not venture to report to you the progress of our voyage, as I am charged only with the navigation, and he with the secrets; but as his malady has deprived him of the use of his faculties, both of body and mind, I have thought myself obliged to acquaint you with what is passing, and of the condition in which we are."

He then declares that the ships freighted by La Salle were so slow that the *Joly* had continually been forced to wait for them, thus doubling the length of the voyage; that he had not had water enough for the passengers, as La Salle had not told him that there were to be any such till the day they came on board; that great numbers were sick, and that he had told La Salle there would be trouble if he filled

[1] [The French Minister of Marine.]

all the space between decks with his goods, and forced the soldiers and sailors to sleep on deck; that he had told him he would get no provisions at St. Domingo, but that he insisted on stopping; that it had always been so, — that whatever he proposed La Salle would refuse, alleging orders from the King; "and now," pursues the ruffled commander, "everybody is ill; and he himself has a violent fever, as dangerous, the surgeon tells me, to the mind as to the body."

The rest of the letter is in the same strain. He says that a day or two after La Salle's illness began, his brother Cavelier came to ask him to take charge of his affairs; but that he did not wish to meddle with them, especially as nobody knows anything about them, and as La Salle has sold some of the ammunition and provisions; that Cavelier tells him that he thinks his brother keeps no accounts, wishing to hide his affairs from everybody; that he learns from buccaneers that the entrance of the Mississippi is very shallow and difficult, and that this is the worst season for navigating the Gulf; that the Spaniards have in these seas six vessels of from thirty to sixty guns each, besides rowgalleys; but that he is not afraid, and will perish, or bring back an account of the Mississippi. "Nevertheless," he adds, "if the Sieur de la Salle dies, I shall pursue a course different from that which he has marked out; for I do not approve his plans."

"If," he continues, "you permit me to speak my mind, M. de la Salle ought to have been satisfied with discovering his river, without undertaking to conduct three vessels with troops two thousand leagues through so many different climates, and across seas entirely unknown to him. I grant that he is a man of knowledge, that he has reading, and even some tincture of navigation; but there is so much difference between theory and practice, that a man who has only the former will always be at fault. There is also a great difference between conducting canoes on lakes and along a river, and navigating ships with troops on distant oceans."

While Beaujeu was complaining of La Salle, his followers were deserting him. It was necessary to send them on board ship, and keep them there; for there were French buccaneers at Petit Goave, who painted the promised land in such dismal colors that many of the adventurers completely lost heart. Some, too, were dying. "The air of this place is bad," says Joutel: "so are the fruits; and there are plenty of women worse than either."

It was near the end of November before La Salle could resume the voyage. He was told that Beaujeu had said that he would not wait longer for the storeship *Aimable,* and that she might follow as she could. Moreover, La Salle was on ill terms with Aigron, her captain, who had declared that he would have nothing more to do with him. Fearing, therefore, that some mishap might befall her, he resolved to embark in her himself, with his brother Cavelier, Membré, Douay, and others, the trustiest of his followers. On the 25th they set sail; the *Joly* and the little frigate *Belle* following. They coasted the shore of Cuba, and landed at the Isle of Pines, where La Salle shot an alligator, which the soldiers ate; and the hunter brought in a wild pig, half of which he sent to Beaujeu. Then they advanced to Cape St. Antonio, where bad weather and contrary winds long detained them. A load of cares oppressed the mind of La Salle, pale and haggard with recent illness, wrapped within his own thoughts, and seeking sympathy from none.

At length they entered the Gulf of Mexico, that forbidden sea whence by a Spanish decree, dating from the reign of Philip II, all foreigners were excluded on pain of extermination. Not a man on board knew the secrets of its perilous navigation. Cautiously feeling their way, they held a northwesterly course, till on the 28th of December a sailor at the mast-head of the *Aimable* saw land. La Salle and all the pilots had been led to form an exaggerated idea of the force of the easterly currents; and they therefore supposed themselves near the Bay of Appalache, when, in fact, they were much farther westward.

On New Year's Day they anchored three leagues from the shore. La Salle, with the engineer Minet, went to explore it, and found nothing but a vast marshy plain, studded with clumps of rushes. Two days after there was a thick fog, and when at length it cleared, the *Joly* was nowhere to be seen. La Salle in the *Aimable,* followed closely by the little frigate *Belle,* stood westward along the coast. When at the mouth of the Mississippi in 1682, he had taken its latitude, but unhappily could not determine its longitude; and now every eye on board was strained to detect in the monotonous lines of the low shore some tokens of the great river. In fact, they had already passed it. On the 6th of January, a wide opening was descried between two low points of land; and the adjacent sea was discolored with mud. "La Salle," writes his brother Cavelier, "has always thought that this was the Mississippi." To all appearance, it was the entrance of Galveston Bay. But why did he not examine it? Joutel says that his attempts to do so were frustrated by the objections of the pilot of the *Aimable,* to which, with a facility very unusual with him, he suffered himself to yield. Cavelier declares, on the other hand, that he would not enter the opening because he was afraid of missing the *Joly*. But he might have entered with one of his two vessels, while the other watched outside for the absent ship. From whatever cause, he lay here five or six days, waiting in vain for Beaujeu; till, at last, thinking that he must have passed westward, he resolved to follow. The *Aimable* and the *Belle* again spread their sails, and coasted the shores of Texas. Joutel, with a boat's crew, tried to land; but the sand-bars and breakers repelled him. A party of Indians swam out through the surf, and were taken on board; but La Salle could learn nothing from them, as their language was unknown to him. Again Joutel tried to land, and again the breakers repelled him. He approached as near as he dared, and saw vast plains and a dim expanse of forest, buffalo running with their heavy gallop along the shore, and deer grazing on the marshy meadows.

Soon after, he succeeded in landing at a point somewhere between Matagorda Island and Corpus Christi Bay.[2] The aspect of the country was not cheering, with its barren plains, its reedy marshes, its interminable oyster-beds, and broad flats of mud bare at low tide. Joutel and his men sought in vain for fresh water, and after shooting some geese and ducks returned to the *Aimable*. Nothing had been seen of Beaujeu and the *Joly;* the coast was trending southward; and La Salle, convinced that he must have passed the missing ship, turned to retrace his course. He had sailed but a few miles when the wind failed, a fog covered the sea, and he was forced to anchor opposite one of the openings into the lagoons north of Mustang Island. At length, on the 19th, there came a faint breeze; the mists rolled away before it, and to his great joy he saw the *Joly* approaching.

"His joy," says Joutel, "was short." Beaujeu's lieutenant, Aire, came on board to charge him with having caused the separation, and La Salle retorted by throwing the blame on Beaujeu. Then came a debate as to their position. The priest Esmanville was present, and reports that La Salle seemed greatly perplexed. He had more cause for perplexity than he knew; for in his ignorance of the longitude of the Mississippi, he had sailed more than 400 miles beyond it.

Of this he had not the faintest suspicion. In full sight from his ship lay a reach of those vast lagoons which, separated from the sea by narrow strips of land, line this coast with little interruption from Galveston Bay to the Rio Grande. The idea took possession of him

[2] [Identified by Margry as Pass Cavallo on Matagorda Bay. This is concurred in by H. E. Bolton "Location of La Salle's Colony," *Mississippi Valley Historical Review* II (1915) 166.]

that the Mississippi discharged itself into these lagoons, and thence made its way to the sea through the various openings he had seen along the coast, chief among which was that he had discovered on the sixth, about fifty leagues from the place where he now was.

Yet he was full of doubt as to what he should do. Four days after rejoining Beaujeu, he wrote him the strange request to land the troops, that he "might fulfil his commission;" that is, that he might set out against the Spaniards. More than a week passed, a gale had set in, and nothing was done. Then La Salle wrote again, intimating some doubt as to whether he was really at one of the mouths of the Mississippi, and saying that, being sure that he had passed the principal mouth, he was determined to go back to look for it. Meanwhile, Beaujeu was in a state of great irritation. The weather was stormy, and the coast was dangerous. Supplies were scanty; and La Salle's soldiers, still crowded in the *Joly*, were consuming the provisions of the ship. Beaujeu gave vent to his annoyance, and La Salle retorted in the same strain.

According to Joutel, he urged the naval commander to sail back in search of the river; and Beaujeu refused, unless La Salle should give the soldiers provisions. La Salle, he adds, offered to supply them with rations for fifteen days; and Beaujeu declared this insufficient. There is reason, however, to believe that the request was neither made by the one nor refused by the other so positively as here appears.

2. *Ashore and Abandoned*

Impatience to rid himself of his colleague and to command alone no doubt had its influence on the judgment of La Salle. He presently declared that he would land the soldiers, and send them along the shore till they came to the principal outlet of the river. On this, the engineer Minet took up the word, — expressed his doubts as to whether the Mississippi discharged itself into the lagoons at all; represented that even if it did, the soldiers would be exposed to great risks; and gave as his opinion that all should reimbark and continue the search in company. The advice was good, but La Salle resented it as coming from one in whom he recognized no right to give it. "He treated me," complains the engineer, "as if I were the meanest of mankind."

He persisted in his purpose, and sent Joutel and Moranget with a party of soldiers to explore the coast. They made their way northeastward along the shore of Matagorda Island, till they were stopped on the third day by what Joutel calls a river, but which was in fact the entrance of Matagorda Bay. Here they encamped, and tried to make a raft of driftwood. "The difficulty was," says Joutel, "our great number of men, and the few of them who were fit for anything except eating. As I said before, they had all been caught by force or surprise, so that our company was like Noah's ark, which contained animals of all sorts." Before their raft was finished, they descried to their great joy the ships which had followed them along the coast.

La Salle landed, and announced that here was the western mouth of the Mississippi, and the place to which the King had sent him. He said further that he would land all his men, and bring the *Aimable* and the *Belle* to the safe harborage within. Beaujeu remonstrated, alleging the shallowness of the water and the force of the currents; but his remonstrance was vain.

The Bay of St. Louis, now Matagorda Bay, forms a broad and sheltered harbor, accessible from the sea by a narrow passage, obstructed by sand-bars and by the small island now called Pelican Island. Boats were sent to sound and buoy out the channel, and this was successfully accomplished on the 16th of February. The *Aimable* was ordered to enter; and, on the twentieth, she weighed anchor. La Salle was on shore watching her. A party of men, at a little distance, were cutting down a tree to make a canoe. Suddenly some of them ran towards him with terrified faces, crying out that they had been set upon by a troop of Indians, who had seized their companions and carried them off. La Salle ordered those about him to take their arms, and at once set out in pursuit. He overtook the Indians, and opened a parley with them; but when he wished to reclaim his men, he discovered that they had been led away during the conference to the Indian camp, a league and a half distant. Among them was one of his lieutenants, the young Marquis de la Sablonnière. He was deeply vexed, for the moment was critical; but the men must be recovered, and he led his followers in haste towards the camp. Yet he could not refrain from turning a moment to watch the *Aimable*, as she neared the shoals; and he remarked with deep anxiety to Joutel, who was with him, that if she held that course she would soon be aground.

They hurried on till they saw the Indian huts. About fifty of them, oven-shaped, and covered with mats and hides, were clustered on a rising ground, with their inmates gathered among and around them. As the French entered the camp, there was the report of a cannon from the seaward. The startled savages dropped flat with terror. A different fear seized La Salle, for he knew that the shot was a signal of disaster. Looking back, he saw the *Aimable* furling her sails, and his heart sank with the conviction that she had struck upon the reef. Smothering his distress, — she was laden with all the stores of the colony, — he pressed forward among the filthy wigwams, whose astonished inmates swarmed about the band of armed strangers, staring between curiosity and fear. La Salle knew those with whom he was dealing, and, without ceremony, entered the chief's lodge with his followers. The crowd closed around them, naked men and half-naked women, described by Joutel as of singular ugliness. They gave buffalo meat and dried porpoise to the unexpected guests, but La Salle, racked with anxiety, hastened to close the interview; and having without difficulty recovered the kidnapped men, he returned to the beach, leaving with the Indians, as usual, an impression of good-will and respect.

When he reached the shore, he saw his worst fears realized. The *Aimable* lay careened over on the reef, hopelessly aground. Little remained but to endure the calamity with firmness, and to save, as far as might be, the vessel's cargo. This was no easy task. The boat which hung at her stern had been stove in, — it is said, by design. Beaujeu sent a boat from the *Joly*, and one or more Indian pirogues were procured. La Salle urged on his men with stern and patient energy, and a quantity of gunpowder and flour was safely landed. But now the wind blew fresh from the sea; the waves began to rise; a storm came on; the vessel, rocking to and fro on the sand-bar, opened along her side, and the ravenous waves were strewn with her treasures. When the confusion was at its height, a troop of Indians came down to the shore, greedy for plunder. The drum was beat; the men were called to arms; La Salle set his trustiest followers to guard the gunpowder, in fear, not of the Indians alone, but of his own countrymen. On that lamentable night, the sentinels walked their rounds through the dreary bivouac among the casks, bales, and boxes which the sea had yielded up; and here, too, their fate-hunted chief held his drearier vigil, encompassed with treachery, darkness, and the storm.

Not only La Salle, but Joutel and others of his party, believed that the wreck of the *Aimable* was intentional. Aigron, who commanded her, had disobeyed orders and disregarded signals. Though he had been directed to tow the vessel through the channel, he went in under sail; and though little else was saved from the wreck, his personal property, including even some preserved fruits, was all landed safely. He had long been on ill terms with La Salle.

All La Salle's company were now encamped on the sands at the left side of the inlet where the *Aimable* was wrecked. "They were all," says the engineer Minet, "sick with nausea and dysentery. Five or six died every day, in consequence of brackish water and bad food. There was no grass, but plenty of rushes and plenty of oysters. There was nothing to make ovens, so that they had to eat flour saved from the wreck, boiled into messes of porridge with this brackish water. Along the shore were quantities of uprooted trees and rotten logs, thrown up by the sea and the lagoon." Of these, and fragments of the wreck, they made a sort of rampart to protect their camp; and here, among tents and hovels, bales, boxes, casks, spars, dismounted cannon, and pens for fowls and swine, were gathered the dejected men and homesick women who were to seize Nueva Viscaya and hold for France a region large as half Europe. The Spaniards, whom they were to conquer, were they knew not where. They knew not where they were themselves; and for 15,000 Indian allies who were to have joined them, they found 200 squalid savages, more like enemies than friends.

In fact, it was soon made plain that these their neighbors wished them no good. A few days after the wreck, the prairie was seen on fire. As the smoke and flame rolled towards them before the wind, La Salle caused all the grass about the camp to be cut and carried away, and especially around the spot where the powder was placed. The danger was averted; but it soon became known that the Indians had stolen a number of blankets and other articles, and carried them to their wigwams. Unwilling to leave his camp, La Salle sent his nephew Moranget and several other volunteers, with a party of men, to reclaim them. They went up the bay in a boat, landed at the Indian camp, and, with more mettle than discretion, marched into it, sword in hand. The Indians ran off, and the rash adventurers seized upon several canoes as an equivalent for the stolen goods. Not knowing how to manage them, they made slow progress on their way back, and were overtaken by night before reaching the French camp. They landed, made a fire, placed a sentinel, and lay down on the dry grass to sleep. The sentinel followed their example, when suddenly they were awakened by the war-whoop and a shower of arrows. Two volunteers, Oris and Desloges, were killed on the spot; a third, named Gayen, was severely wounded; and young Moranget received an arrow through the arm. He leaped up and fired his gun at the vociferous but invisible foe. Others of the party did the same, and the Indians fled.

It was about this time that Beaujeu prepared to return to France. He had accomplished his mission, and landed his passengers at what La Salle assured him to be one of the mouths of the Mississippi. His ship was in danger on this exposed and perilous coast, and he was anxious to find shelter. For some time past, his relations with La Salle had been amicable, and it was agreed between them that Beaujeu should stop at Galveston Bay, the supposed chief mouth of the Mississippi; or, failing to find harborage here, that he should proceed to Mobile Bay, and wait there till April, to hear from his colleague. Beaujeu remained a fortnight longer on the coast [after the *Aimable* was wrecked] and then told La Salle that being out of wood, water, and other necessaries, he must go to Mobile Bay to get them. Nevertheless, he lingered a week more, repeated his offer to bring supplies from Martinique, which La Salle again refused, and at last set sail on the 12th of March, after a leavetaking which was courteous on both sides.

La Salle and his colonists were left alone. Several of them had lost heart, and embarked for home with Beaujeu. Among these was Minet the engineer, who had fallen out with La Salle, and who when he reached France was imprisoned for deserting him. Even his brother, the priest Jean Cavelier, had a mind to abandon the enterprise, but was persuaded at last to remain, along with his nephew the hot-headed Moranget, and the younger Cavelier, a mere school-boy. The two Récollet friars, Zenobe Membré and Anastase Douay, the trusty Joutel, a man of sense and observation, and the Marquis de la Sablonnière, a debauched noble whose patrimony was his sword, were now the chief persons of the forlorn company. The rest were soldiers, raw and undisciplined, and artisans, most of whom knew nothing of their vocation. Add to these the miserable families and the infatuated young women who had come to tempt fortune in the swamps and cane-brakes of the Mississippi.

La Salle set out to explore the neighborhood. Joutel remained in command of the so-called fort. He was beset with wily enemies, and often at night the Indians would crawl in the grass around his feeble stockade, howling like wolves; but a few shots would put them to flight. A strict guard was kept; and a wooden horse was set in the enclosure, to punish the sentinel who should sleep at his post. They stood in daily fear of a more formidable foe, and once they saw a sail, which they doubted not was Spanish; but she happily passed without discovering them. They hunted on the prairies, and speared fish in the neighboring pools. On Easter Day, the Sieur le Gros, one of the chief men of the company, went out after the service to shoot snipes; but as he walked barefoot through the marsh, a snake bit him, and he soon after died. Two men deserted, to starve on the prairie, or to become savages among savages. Others tried to escape, but were caught; and one of them was hung. A knot of desperadoes conspired to kill Joutel; but one of them betrayed the secret, and the plot was crushed.

La Salle returned from his exploration, but his return brought no cheer. He had been forced to renounce the illusion to which he had clung so long, and was convinced at last that he was not at the mouth of the Mississippi. The wreck of the *Aimable* itself was not pregnant with consequences so disastrous.

CHAPTER XXII

St. Louis of Texas

1685–1687

[La Salle and the Discovery of the Great West, CHAPTER XXVI]

Of what avail to plant a colony by the mouth of a petty Texan river? The Mississippi was the life of the enterprise, the condition of its growth and of its existence. Without it, all was futile and meaningless, — a folly and a ruin. Cost what it might, the Mississippi must be found.

But the demands of the hour were imperative. The hapless colony, cast ashore like a wreck on the sands of Matagorda Bay, must gather up its shattered resources and recruit its exhausted strength, before it essayed anew its pilgrimage to the "fatal river." La Salle during his explorations had found a spot which he thought well fitted a temporary establishment. It was on the river which he named the La Vache, now the Lavaca, which enters the head of Matagorda Bay; and thither he ordered all the women and children, and most of the men, to remove; while the rest, thirty in number, remained with Joutel at the fort near the mouth of the bay. Here they spent their time in hunting, fishing, and squaring the logs of drift-wood which the sea washed up in abundance, and which La Salle proposed to use in building his new station on the Lavaca.[1] Thus the time passed till midsummer, when Joutel received orders to abandon his post, and rejoin the main body of the colonists. To this end, the little frigate *Belle* was sent down the bay. She was a gift from the King to La Salle, who had brought her safely over the bar, and regarded her as a mainstay of his hopes. She

---

[1] [Bolton in *Miss. Val. Hist. Rev.* II 177–81 tells how, with documents and maps from the Spanish archives telling of a Spanish expedition to this spot in 1690, he identified in 1914 the site of St. Louis of Texas on the Garcitas River, not far from the Lavaca. The actual spot, known locally as "The Old Mission," is on a ranch which then belonged to Claude Keeran. In 1722 a Spanish fort, Nuestra Señora de Loveto, was erected on the site.]

now took on board the stores and some of the men, while Joutel with the rest followed along shore to the post on the Lavaca. Here he found a state of things that was far from cheering. Crops had been sown, but the drought and the cattle had nearly destroyed them. The colonists were lodged under tents and hovels; and the only solid structure was a small square enclosure of pickets, in which the gunpowder and the brandy were stored. The site was good, a rising ground by the river; but there was no wood within the distance of a league, and no horses or oxen to drag it. Their work must be done by men. Some felled and squared the timber; and others dragged it by main force over the matted grass of the prairie, under the scorching Texas sun. The gun-carriages served to make the task somewhat easier; yet the strongest men soon gave out under it. Joutel went down to the first fort, made a raft and brought up the timber collected there, which proved a most seasonable and useful supply. Palisades and buildings began to rise. The men labored without spirit, yet strenuously; for they labored under the eye of La Salle. The carpenters brought from Rochelle proved worthless; and he himself made the plans of the work, marked out tenons and mortises, and directed the whole.

Death, meanwhile, made withering havoc among his followers; and under the sheds and hovels that shielded them from the sun lay a score of wretches slowly wasting away with the diseases contracted at St. Domingo. Of the soldiers enlisted for the expedition by La Salle's agents, many are affirmed to have spent their lives in begging at the church doors of Rochefort, and were consequently incapable of discipline. It was impossible to prevent either them or the sailors from devouring persimmons and other wild fruits to a destructive excess. Nearly all fell ill; and before the summer had passed, the graveyard had more than thirty tenants. The bearing of La Salle did not aid to raise the drooping spirits of his followers. The results of the enterprise had been far different from his hopes; and, after a season of flattering promise, he had entered again on those dark and obstructed paths which seemed his destined way of life. The present was beset with trouble; the future, thick with storms. The consciousness quickened his energies; but it made him stern, harsh, and often unjust to those beneath him.

Joutel was returning to camp one afternoon with the master-carpenter, when they saw game; and the carpenter went after it. He was never seen again. Perhaps he was lost on the prairie, perhaps killed by Indians. He knew little of his trade, but they nevertheless had need of him. Le Gros, a man of character and intelligence, suffered more and more from the bite of the snake received in the marsh on Easter Day. The injured limb was amputated, and he died. La Salle's brother, the priest, lay ill; and several others among the chief persons of the colony were in the same condition.

Meanwhile, the work was urged on. A large building was finished, constructed of timber, roofed with boards and raw hides, and divided into apartments for lodging and other uses. La Salle gave the new establishment his favorite name of Fort St. Louis, and the neighboring bay was also christened after the royal saint. The scene was not without its charms. Towards the southeast stretched the bay with its bordering meadows; and on the northeast the Lavaca ran along the base of green declivities. Around, far and near, rolled a sea of prairie, with distant forests, dim in the summer haze. At times, it was dotted with the browsing buffalo, not yet scared from their wonted pastures; and the grassy swells were spangled with the flowers for which Texas is renowned, and which now form the gay ornaments of our gardens.

And now, the needful work accomplished, and the colony in some measure housed and fortified, its indefatigable chief prepared to renew his quest of the "fatal river," as Joutel repeatedly calls it. Before his departure he made some preliminary explorations, in the course of which, according to the report of his brother the priest, he found evidence that the Spaniards had long before had a transient establishment at a spot about fifteen leagues from Fort St. Louis.

It was the last day of October when La Salle set out on his great journey of exploration. His brother Cavelier, who had now recovered, accompanied him with fifty men; and five cannon-shot from the fort saluted them as they departed. They were lightly equipped; but some of them wore corselets made of staves, to ward off arrows. Descending the Lavaca, they pursued their course eastward on foot along the margin of the bay, while Joutel remained in command of the fort. It was two leagues above the mouth of the river; and in it were thirty-four persons, including three Récollet friars, a number of women and girls from Paris, and two young orphan daughters of one Talon, a Canadian, who had lately died. Their live-stock consisted of some hogs and a litter of eight pigs, which, as Joutel does not forget to inform us, passed their time in wallowing in the ditch of the palisade; a cock and hen, with a young family; and a pair of goats, which, in a temporary dearth of fresh meat, were sacrificed to the needs of the invalid Abbé Cavelier. Joutel suffered no man to lie idle. The blacksmith, having no anvil, was supplied with a cannon as a substitute. Lodgings were built for the women and girls, and separate lodgings for the men. A small chapel was afterwards added, and the whole was fenced with a palisade. At the four corners of the house were mounted eight pieces of cannon, which, in the absence of balls, were loaded with bags of bullets. Between the palisades and the stream lay a narrow strip of marsh, the haunt of countless birds; and at a little distance it deepened into pools full of fish. All the surrounding prairies swarmed with game, — buffalo, deer, hares, turkeys, ducks, geese, swans, plover, snipe and grouse. The river supplied the colonists with turtles, and the bay with oysters. Of these last, they often found more than they wanted; for when in their excursions they shoved their log canoes into the water, wading shoeless through the deep, tenacious mud, the sharp shells would cut their feet like knives; "and what was worse," says Joutel, "the salt water came into the gashes, and made them smart atrociously."

He sometimes amused himself with shooting alligators. "I never spared them when I met them near the house. One day I killed an extremely large one, which was nearly four feet and a half in girth, and about twenty feet long." He describes with accuracy that curious native of the southwestern plains, the "horned frog," which, deceived by its uninviting appearance, he erroneously supposed to be venomous. "We had some of our animals bitten by snakes; among the others, a bitch that had belonged to the deceased Sieur le Gros. She was bitten in the jaw when she was with me, as I was fishing by the shore of the bay. I gave her a little theriac [an antidote then in vogue], which cured her, as it did one of our sows, which came home one day with her head so swelled that she could hardly hold it up. Thinking it must be some snake that had bitten her, I gave her a dose of the theriac mixed with meal and water." The patient began to mend at once. "I killed a good many rattle-snakes by means of the aforesaid bitch, for when she saw one she would bark around him, sometimes for a half hour together, till I took my gun and shot him. I often found them in the bushes, making a noise with their tails. When I had killed them, our hogs ate them." He devotes many pages to the plants and animals of the neighborhood, most of which may easily be recognized from his description.

With the buffalo, which he calls "our daily bread," his experiences were many and strange. Being, like the rest of the party, a novice in the art of shooting them, he met with many disappointments. Once having mounted to the roof of the large house in the fort, he saw a dark moving object on a swell of the prairie three miles off; and rightly thinking it was a herd of buffalo, he set out with six or seven men to try to kill some of them. After a while, he discovered two bulls lying in a hollow; and signing to the rest of his party to keep quiet, he made his approach, gun in hand. The bulls presently jumped up, and stared through their manes at the intruder. Joutel fired. It was a close shot; but the bulls merely shook their shaggy heads, wheeled about, and galloped heavily away. The same luck attended him the next day. "We saw plenty of buffalo. I approached several bands of them, and fired again and again, but could not make one of them fall." He had not yet learned that a buffalo rarely falls at once, unless hit in the spine. He continues: "I was not discouraged; and after approaching several more bands, — which was hard work, because I had to crawl on the ground, so as not to be seen, — I found myself in a herd of five or six thousand, but, to my great vexation, I could not bring one of them down. They all ran off to the right and left. It was near night, and I had killed nothing. Though I was very tired, I tried again, approached another band, and fired a number of shots; but not a buffalo would fall. The skin was off my knees with crawling. At last, as I was going back to rejoin our men, I saw a buffalo lying on the ground. I went towards it, and saw that it was dead. I examined it, and found that the bullet had gone in near the shoulder. Then I found others dead like the first. I beckoned the men to come on, and we set to work to cut up the meat, — a task which was new to us all." It would be impossible to write a more true and characteristic sketch of the experience of a novice in shooting buffalo on foot. A few days after, he went out again, with Father Anastase Douay; approached a bull, fired, and broke his shoulder. The bull hobbled off on three legs. Douay ran in his cassock to head him back, while Joutel reloaded his gun; upon which the enraged beast butted at the missionary, and knocked him down. He very narrowly escaped with his life. "There was another missionary," pursues Joutel, "named Father Maxime Le Clerc, who was very well fitted for such an undertaking as ours, because he was equal to anything, even to butchering a buffalo; and as I said before that every one of us must lend a hand, because we were too few for anybody to be waited upon, I made the women, girls, and children do their part, as well as him; for as they all wanted to eat, it was fair that they all should work." He had a scaffolding built near the fort, and set them to smoking buffalo meat, against a day of scarcity.

Thus the time passed till the middle of January; when late one evening, as all were gathered in the principal building, conversing perhaps, or smoking, or playing at cards, or dozing by the fire in homesick dreams of France, a man on guard came in to report that he had heard a voice from the river. They all went down to the bank, and descried a man in a canoe, who called out, "Dominic!" This was the name of the younger of the two brothers Duhaut, who was one of Joutel's followers. As the canoe approached, they recognized the elder, who had gone with La Salle on his journey of discovery, and who was perhaps the greatest villain of the company. Joutel was much perplexed. La Salle had ordered him to admit nobody into the fort without a pass and a watchword. Duhaut, when questioned, said that he had none, but told at the same time so plausible a story that Joutel no longer hesitated to receive him. As La Salle and his men were pursuing their march along the prairie, Duhaut, who was in the rear, had stopped to mend his moccasins, and when he tried to overtake the party, had lost his way, mistaking a buffalo-path for the trail of his companions. At night he fired his gun as a signal, but there was no answering shot. Seeing no hope of rejoining them, he turned back for the fort, found one of the canoes which La Salle had hidden at the shore, paddled by night and lay close by day, shot turkeys, deer, and buffalo for food, and, having no knife, cut the meat with a sharp flint, till after a month of excessive hardship he reached his destination. As the inmates of Fort St. Louis gathered about the weather-beaten wanderer, he told them dreary tidings. The pilot of the *Belle*, such was his story, had gone with five men to sound along the shore, by order of La Salle, who was then encamped in the neighborhood with his party of explorers. The boat's crew, being overtaken by the night, had rashly bivouacked on the beach without setting a guard; and as they slept, a band of Indians had rushed in upon them, and butchered them all. La Salle, alarmed by their long absence, had searched along the shore, and at length found their bodies scattered about the sands and half-devoured by wolves. Well would it have been, if Duhaut had shared their fate.

Weeks and months dragged on, when, at the end of March, Joutel, chancing to mount the roof of one of the buildings, saw seven or eight men approaching over the prairie. He went out to meet them with an equal number, well armed; and as he drew near recognized, with mixed joy and anxiety, La Salle and some of those who had gone with him. His brother Cavelier was at his side, with his cassock so tattered that, says Joutel, "there was hardly a piece left large enough to wrap a farthing's worth of salt. He had an old cap on his head, having lost his hat by the way. The rest were in no better plight, for their shirts were all in rags. Some of them carried loads of meat, because M. de la Salle was afraid that we might not have killed any buffalo. We met with great joy and many embraces. After our greetings were over, M. de la Salle, seeing Duhaut, asked me in an angry tone how it was that I had received this man who had abandoned him. I told him how it had happened, and repeated Duhaut's story. Duhaut defended himself, and M. de la Salle's anger was soon over. We went into the house, and refreshed ourselves with some bread and brandy, as there was no wine left."

La Salle and his companions told their story. They had wandered on through various savage tribes, with whom they had more than one encounter, scattering them like chaff by the terror of their firearms. At length they found a more friendly band, and learned much touching the Spaniards, who, they were told, were universally hated by the tribes of that country. It would be easy, said their informants, to gather a host of warriors and lead them over the Rio Grande; but La Salle was in no condition for attempting conquests, and the tribes in whose alliance he had trusted had, a few days before, been at blows with him. The invasion of Nueva Viscaya must be postponed to a more propitious day. Still advancing, he came to a large river, which he at first mistook for the Mississippi; and building a fort of palisades, he left several of his men. The fate of these unfortunates does not appear. He now retraced his steps towards Fort St. Louis, and, as he approached it, detached some of his men to look for his vessel, the *Belle*, for whose safety, since the loss of her pilot, he had become very anxious.

On the next day these men appeared at the fort, with downcast looks. They had not found the *Belle* at the place where she had been ordered to remain, nor were any tidings to be heard of her. From that hour, the conviction that she was lost possessed the mind of La Salle. Surrounded as he was, and had always been, with traitors, the belief now possessed him that her crew had abandoned the colony, and made sail for the West Indies or for France. The loss was incalculable. He had relied on this vessel to transport the colonists to the Mississippi, as soon as its exact position could be ascertained; and thinking her a safer place of deposit than the fort, he had put on board of her all his papers and personal baggage, besides a great quantity of stores, ammunition, and tools. In truth, she was of the last necessity to the unhappy exiles, and their only resource for escape from a position which was fast becoming desperate.

La Salle, as his brother tells us, now fell dangerously ill, — the fatigues of his journey, joined to the effects upon his mind of this last disaster, having overcome his strength, though not his fortitude. "In truth," writes the priest, "after the loss of the vessel which deprived us of our only means of returning to France, we had no resource but in the firm guidance of my brother, whose death each of us would have regarded as his own."

La Salle no sooner recovered than he embraced a resolution which could be the offspring only of a desperate necessity. He determined to make his way by the Mississippi and the Illinois to Canada, whence he might bring succor to the colonists, and send a report of their condition to France. The attempt was beset with uncertainties and dangers. The Mississippi was first to be found, then followed through all the perilous monotony of its interminable windings to a goal which was to be but the starting-point of a new and not less arduous journey. Cavelier his brother, Moranget his nephew, the friar Anastase Douay, and others to the number of twenty, were chosen to accompany him. Every corner of the magazine was ransacked for an outfit. Joutel generously gave up the better part of his wardrobe to La Salle and his two relatives. Duhaut, who had saved his baggage from the wreck of the *Aimable*, was required to contribute to the necessities of the party; and the scantily-furnished chests of those who had died were used to supply the wants of the living. Each man labored with needle and awl to patch his failing garments, or supply their place with buffalo or deer skins. On the 22nd of April, after mass and prayers in the chapel, they issued from the gate, each bearing his pack and his weapons, some with kettles slung at their backs, some with axes, some with gifts for Indians. In this guise, they held their way in silence across the prairie; while anxious eyes followed them from the palisades of St. Louis, whose inmates, not excepting Joutel himself, seem to have been ignorant of the extent and difficulty of the undertaking.

"On May Day," he writes, "at about two in the afternoon, as I was walking near the house, I heard a voice from the river below, crying out several times, *Qui vive?* Knowing that the Sieur Barbier had gone that way with two canoes to hunt buffalo, I thought that it might be one of these canoes coming back with meat, and did not think much of the matter till I heard the same voice again. I answered, *Versailles*, which was the password I had given the Sieur Barbier, in case he should come back in the night. But, as I was going towards the bank, I heard other voices which I had not heard for a long time. I recognized among the rest that of C. Chefdeville, which made me fear that some disaster had happened. I ran down to the bank, and my first greeting was to ask what had become of the *Belle*. They answered that she was wrecked on the other side of the bay, and that all on board were drowned except the six who were in the canoe; namely Sieur Chefdeville, the Marquis de la Sablonnière, the man named Teissier, a soldier, a girl, and a little boy."

From the young priest Chefdeville, Joutel learned the particulars of the disaster. Water had failed on board the *Belle;* a boat's crew of five men had gone in quest of it; the wind rose, their boat was swamped, and they were all drowned. Those who remained had now no means of going ashore; but if they had no water, they had wine and brandy in abundance, and Teissier, the master of the vessel, was drunk every day. After a while they left their moorings, and tried to reach the fort; but they were few, weak, and unskilful. A violent north wind drove them on a sand-bar. Some of them were drowned in trying to reach land on a raft. Others were more successful; and, after a long delay, they found a stranded canoe, in which they made their way to St. Louis, bringing with them some of La Salle's papers and baggage saved from the wreck.

These multiplied disasters bore hard on the spirits of the colonists; and Joutel, like a good commander as he was, spared no pains to cheer them. "We did what we could to amuse ourselves and drive away care. I encouraged our people to dance and sing in the evenings; for when M. de la Salle was among us, pleasure was often banished. Now, there is no use in being melancholy on such occasions. It is true M. de la Salle had no great cause for merry-making, after all his losses and disappointments; but his troubles made others suffer also. Though he had ordered me to allow to each person only a certain quantity of meat at every meal, I observed this rule only when meat was rare. The air here is very keen, and one has a great appetite. One must eat and act, if he wants good health and spirits. I speak from experience; for once, when I had ague chills, and was obliged to keep the house with nothing to do, I was dreary and down-hearted. On the contrary, if I was busy with hunting or anything else, I was not so dull by half. So I tried to keep the people as busy as possible. I set them to making a small cellar to keep meat fresh in hot weather; but when M. de la Salle came back, he said it was too small. As he always wanted to do everything on a grand scale, he prepared to make a large one, and marked out the plan." This plan of the large cellar, like more important undertakings of its unhappy projector, proved too extensive for execution, the colonists being engrossed by the daily care of keeping themselves alive.

A gleam of hilarity shot for an instant out of the clouds. The young Canadian, Barbier, usually conducted the hunting-parties; and some of the women and girls often went out with them, to aid in cutting up the meat. Barbier became enamoured of one of the girls; and as his devotion to her was the subject of comment, he asked Joutel for leave to marry her. The commandant, after due counsel with the priests and friars, vouchsafed his consent, and the rite was duly solemnized; whereupon, fired by the example, the Marquis de la Sablonnière begged leave to marry another of the girls. Joutel, the gardener's son, concerned that a marquis should so abase himself, and anxious at the same time for the morals of the fort, which La Salle had especially commended to his care, not only flatly refused, but, in the plenitude of his authority, forbade the lovers all further intercourse.

Father Zenobe Membré, superior of the mission, gave unwilling occasion for further merriment. These worthy friars were singularly unhappy in their dealings with the buffalo, one of which, it may be remembered, had already knocked down Father Anastase. Undeterred by his example, Father Zenobe one day went out with the hunters, carrying a gun like the rest. Joutel shot a buffalo, which was making off, badly wounded, when a second shot stopped it, and it presently lay down. The father superior thought it was dead; and, without heeding the warning shout of Joutel, he approached, and pushed it with the butt of his gun. The bull sprang up with an effort of expiring fury, and, in the words of Joutel, "trampled on the father, took the skin off his face in several places, and broke his gun, so that he could hardly manage to get away, and remained in an almost helpless state for more than three months. Bad as the accident was, he was laughed at nevertheless for his rashness."

The mishaps of the friars did not end here. Father Maxime Le Clerc was set upon by a boar belonging to the colony. "I do not know," says Joutel, "what spite the beast had against him, whether for a beating or some other offence; but, however, this may be, I saw the father running and crying for help, and the boar running after him. I went to the rescue, but could not come up in time. The father stooped as he ran, to gather up his cassock from his legs; and the boar, which ran faster than he, struck him in the arm with his tusks, so that some of the nerves were torn. Thus, all three of our good Récollet fathers were near being the victims of animals."

In spite of his efforts to encourage them, the followers of Joutel were fast losing heart. Father Maxime Le Clerc kept a journal, in which he set down various charges against La Salle. Joutel got possession of the paper, and burned it on the urgent entreaty of the friars, who dreaded what might ensue, should the absent commander become aware of the aspersions cast upon him. The elder Duhaut fomented the rising discontent of the colonists, played the demagogue, told them that La Salle would never return, and tried to make himself their leader. Joutel detected the mischief, and, with a lenity which he afterwards deeply regretted, contented himself with a rebuke to the offender, and words of reproof and encouragement to the dejected band.

He had caused the grass to be cut near the fort, so as to form a sort of playground; and here, one evening, he and some of the party were trying to amuse themselves, when they heard shouts from beyond the river, and Joutel recognized the voice of La Salle. Hastening to meet him in a wooden canoe, he brought him and his party to the fort. Twenty men had gone out with him, and eight had returned. Of the rest, four had deserted, one had been lost, one had been devoured by an alligator; and the others, giving out on the march, had probably perished in attempting to regain the fort. The travellers told of a rich country, a wild and beautiful landscape, — woods, rivers, groves, and prairies; but all availed nothing, and the acquisition of five horses was but an indifferent return for the loss of twelve men.

After leaving the fort, they had journeyed towards the northeast, over plains green as an emerald with the young verdure of April, till at length they saw, far as the eye could reach, the boundless prairie alive with herds of buffalo. The animals were in one of their tame or stupid moods; and they killed nine or ten of them without the least difficulty, drying the best parts of the meat. They crossed the Colorado on a raft, and reached the banks of another river, where one of the party, named Hiens, a German of Würtemberg, and an old buccaneer, was mired and nearly suffocated in a mud-hole. Unfortunately, as will soon appear, he managed to crawl out; and, to console him, the river was christened with his name. The party made a bridge of felled trees, on which they crossed in safety. La Salle now changed their course, and journeyed eastward, when the travellers soon found themselves in the midst of a numerous Indian population, where they were feasted and caressed without measure. At another village they were less fortunate. The inhabitants were friendly by day and hostile by night. They came to attack the French in their camp, but withdrew, daunted by the menacing voice of La Salle, who had heard them approaching through the cane-brake.

La Salle's favorite Shawnee hunter, Nika, who had followed him from Canada to France, and from France to Texas, was bitten by a rattlesnake; and, though he recovered, the accident detained the party for several days. At length they resumed their journey, but were stopped by a river, called by Douay, "La Rivière des Malheurs." La Salle and Cavelier, with a few others, tried to cross on a raft, which, as it reached the channel, was caught by a current of marvellous swiftness. Douay and Moranget, watching the transit from the edge of the cane-brake, beheld their commander swept down the stream, and vanishing, as it were, in an instant. All that day they remained with their companions on the bank, lamenting in despair for the loss of their guardian angel, for so Douay calls La Salle. It was fast growing dark, when, to their unspeakable relief, they saw him advancing with his party along the opposite bank, having succeeded, after great exertion, in guiding the raft to land. How to rejoin him was now the question. Douay and his companions, who had tasted no food that day, broke their fast on two young eagles which they knocked out of their nest, and then spent the night in rueful consultation as to the means of crossing the river. In the morning they waded into the marsh, the friar with his breviary in his hood to keep it dry, and hacked among the canes till they gathered enough to make another raft; on which, profiting by La Salle's experience, they safely crossed, and rejoined him.

Next, they became entangled in a cane-brake, where La Salle, as usual with him in such cases, took the lead, a hatchet in each hand, and hewed out a path for his followers. They soon reached the villages of the Cenis Indians, on and near the river Trinity, — a tribe then powerful, but long since extinct. Nothing could surpass the friendliness of their welcome. The chiefs came to meet them, bearing the calumet, and followed by warriors in shirts of embroidered deerskin. Then the whole village swarmed out like bees, gathering around the visitors with offerings of food and all that was precious in their eyes. La Salle was lodged with the great chief; but he compelled his men to encamp at a distance, lest the ardor of their gallantry might give occasion of offence. The lodges of the Cenis, forty or fifty feet high, and covered with a thatch of meadow-grass, looked like huge bee-hives. Each held several families, whose fire was in the middle, and their beds around the circumference. The spoil of the Spaniards was to be seen on all sides, — silver lamps and spoons, swords, old muskets, money, clothing, and a bull of the Pope dispensing the Spanish colonists of New Mexico from fasting during summer. These treasures, as well as their numerous horses, were obtained by the Cenis from their neighbors and allies the Comanches, that fierce prairie banditti who then, as now, scourged the Mexican border with their bloody forays. A party of these wild horsemen was in the village. Douay was edified at seeing them make the sign of the cross in imitation of the neophytes of one of the Spanish missions. They enacted, too, the ceremony of the mass; and one of them, in his rude way, drew a sketch of a picture he had seen in some church which he had pillaged, wherein the friar plainly recognized the Virgin weeping at the foot of the cross. They invited the French to join them on a raid into New Mexico; and they spoke with contempt, as their tribesmen will speak to this day, of the Spanish creoles, saying that it would be easy to conquer a nation of cowards who make people walk before them with fans to cool them in hot weather.

Soon after leaving the Cenis villages, both La Salle and his nephew Moranget were attacked by fever. This caused a delay of more than two months, during which the party seem to have remained encamped on the Neches, or possibly the Sabine. When at length the invalids had recovered sufficient strength to travel, the stock of ammunition was nearly spent, some of the men had deserted, and the condition of the travellers was such that there seemed no alternative but to return to Fort St. Louis. This they accordingly did, greatly aided in their march by the horses bought from the Cenis, and suffering no very serious accident by the way, — excepting the loss of La Salle's servant, Dumesnil, who was seized by an alligator while attempting to cross the Colorado.

The temporary excitement caused among the colonists by their return soon gave place to a dejection bordering on despair. "This pleasant land," writes Cavelier, "seemed to us an abode of weariness and a perpetual prison." Flattering themselves with the delusion, common to exiles of every kind, that they were objects of solicitude at home, they watched daily, with straining eyes, for an approaching sail. Ships, indeed, had ranged the coast to seek them, but with no friendly intent. Their thoughts dwelt, with unspeakable yearning, on the France they had left behind, which, to their longing fancy, was pictured as an unattainable Eden. Well might they despond; for of 180 colonists, besides the crew of the *Belle*, less than forty-five remained. The weary precincts of Fort St. Louis, with its fence of rigid palisades, its area of trampled earth, its buildings of weather-stained timber, and its well-peopled graveyard without, were hateful to their sight. La Salle had a heavy task to save them from despair. His composure, his unfailing equanimity, his words of encouragement and cheer, were the breath of life to this forlorn company; for though he could not impart to minds of less adamantine temper the audacity of hope with which he still clung to the final accomplishment of his purposes, the contagion of his hardihood touched, nevertheless, the drooping spirits of his followers.

The journey to Canada was clearly their only hope; and, after a brief rest, La Salle prepared to renew the attempt. He proposed that Joutel should this time be of the party; and should proceed from Quebec to France, with his brother Cavelier, to solicit succors for the colony, while he himself returned to Texas. A new obstacle was presently interposed. La Salle, whose constitution seems to have suffered from his long course of hardships, was attacked in November with hernia. Joutel offered to conduct the party in his stead; but La Salle replied that his own presence was indispensable at the Illinois. He had the good fortune to recover, within four or five weeks, sufficiently to undertake the journey; and all in the fort busied themselves in preparing an outfit. In such straits were they for clothing, that the sails of the *Belle* were cut up to make coats for the adventurers. Christmas came, and was solemnly observed. There was a midnight mass in the chapel, where Membré, Cavelier, Douay, and their priestly brethren stood before the altar, in vestments strangely contrasting with the rude temple and the ruder garb of the worshippers. And as Membré elevated the consecrated wafer, and the lamps burned dim through the clouds of incense, the kneeling group drew from the daily miracle such consolation as true Catholics alone can know. When Twelfth Night came, all gathered in the hall, and cried, after the jovial old custom, "The King drinks," with hearts, perhaps, as cheerless as their cups, which were filled with cold water.

On the morrow, the band of adventurers mustered for the fatal journey. The five horses, bought by La Salle of the Indians, stood in the area of the fort, packed for the march; and here was gathered the wretched remnant of the colony, — those who were to go, and those who were to stay behind. These latter were about twenty in all, — Barbier, who was to command in the place of Joutel; Sablonnière, who, despite his title of marquis, was held in great contempt; the friars, Membré and Le Clerc, and the priest Chefdeville, besides a surgeon, soldiers, laborers, seven women and girls, and several children, doomed, in this deadly exile, to wait the issues of the journey, and the possible arrival of a tardy succor. La Salle had made them a last address, delivered, we are told, with that winning air which, though alien from his usual bearing, seems to have been at times a natural expression of this unhappy man. It was a bitter parting, one of sighs, tears, and embracings, — the farewell of those on whose souls had sunk a heavy boding that they would never meet again. Equipped and weaponed for the journey, the adventurers filed from the gate, crossed the river, and held their slow march over the prairies beyond, till intervening woods and hills shut Fort St. Louis forever from their sight.

CHAPTER XXIII

Death of La Salle, End of the Colony

1687

[*La Salle and the Discovery of the Great West*, CHAPTER XXVII and part of XXIX]

The travellers were crossing a marshy prairie towards a distant belt of woods, that followed the course of a little river. They led with them their five horses, laden with their scanty baggage, and, with what was of no less importance, their stock of presents for Indians. Some wore the remains of the clothing they had worn from France, eked out with deer-skins, dressed in the Indian manner; and some had coats of old sail-cloth. Here was La Salle, in whom one would have known, at a glance, the chief of the party; and the priest, Cavelier, who seems to have shared not one of the high traits of his younger brother. Here, too, were their nephews, Moranget and the boy Cavelier, now about seventeen years old; the trusty soldier Joutel; and the friar Anastase Douay. Duhaut followed, a man of respectable birth and education; and Liotot, the surgeon of the party. At home, they might perhaps have lived and died with a fair repute; but the wilderness is a rude touch-stone, which often reveals traits that would have lain buried and unsuspected in civilized life. The German Hiens, the ex-buccaneer, was also of the number. He had probably sailed with an English crew; for he was sometimes known as *Gemme Anglais*, or "English Jem." The Sieur de Marle; Teissier, a pilot; L'Archevêque, a servant of Duhaut; and others, to the number in all of seventeen, — made up the party; to which is to be added Nika, La Salle's Shawnee hunter, who, as well as another Indian, had twice crossed the ocean with him, and still followed his fortunes with an admiring though undemonstrative fidelity.

They passed the prairie, and neared the forest. Here they saw buffalo; and the hunters approached, and killed several of them. Then they traversed the woods; found and forded the shallow and rushy stream, and pushed through the forest beyond, till they again reached the open prairie. Heavy clouds gathered over them, and it rained all night; but they sheltered themselves under the fresh hides of the buffalo they had killed.

It is impossible, as it would be needless, to follow the detail of their daily march. It was such an one, though with unwonted hardship, as is familiar to the memory of many a prairie traveller of our own time. They suffered greatly from the want of shoes, and found for a while no better substitute than a casing of raw buffalo-hide, which they were forced to keep always wet, as, when dry, it hardened about the foot like iron. At length they bought dressed deer-skin from the Indians, of which they made tolerable moccasins. The rivers, streams, and gullies filled with water were without number; and to cross them they made a boat of bull-hide, like the "bull boat" still used on the Upper Missouri. This did good service, as, with the help of their horses, they could carry it with them. Two or three men could cross in it at once, and the horses swam after them like dogs. Sometimes they traversed the sunny prairie; sometimes dived into the dark recesses of the forest, where the buffalo, descending daily from their pastures in long files to drink at the river, often made a broad and easy path for the travellers. When foul weather arrested them, they built huts of bark and long meadow-grass; and safely sheltered lounged away the day, while their horses, picketed near by, stood steaming in the rain. At night, they usually set a rude stockade about their camp; and here, by the grassy border of a brook, or at the edge of a grove where a spring bubbled up through the sands, they lay asleep around the embers of their fire, while the man on guard listened to the deep breathing of the slumbering horses, and the howling of the wolves that saluted the rising moon as it flooded the waste of prairie with pale mystic radiance.

They met Indians almost daily, — sometimes a band of hunters, mounted or on foot, chasing buffalo on the plains; sometimes a party of fishermen; sometimes a winter camp, on the slope of a hill or under the sheltering border of a forest. They held intercourse with them in the distance by signs; often they disarmed their distrust, and attracted them into their camp; and often they visited them in their lodges, where, seated on buffalo-robes, they smoked with their entertainers, passing the pipe from hand to hand, after the custom still in use among the prairie tribes. Cavelier says that they once saw a band of 150 mounted Indians attacking a herd of buffalo with lances pointed with sharpened bone. The old priest was delighted with the sport, which he pronounces "the most diverting thing in the world." On another occasion, when the party were encamped near the village of a tribe which

Cavelier calls Sassory, he saw them catch an alligator about twelve feet long, which they proceeded to torture as if he were a human enemy, — first putting out his eyes, and then leading him to the neighboring prairie, where, having confined him by a number of stakes, they spent the entire day in tormenting him.

Holding a northerly course, the travellers crossed the Brazos, and reached the waters of the Trinity. The weather was unfavorable, and on one occasion they encamped in the rain during four or five days together. It was not an harmonious company. La Salle's cold and haughty reserve had returned, at least for those of his followers to whom he was not partial. Duhaut and the surgeon Liotot, both of whom were men of some property, had a large pecuniary stake in the enterprise, and were disappointed and incensed at its ruinous result. They had a quarrel with young Moranget, whose hot and hasty temper was as little fitted to conciliate as was the harsh reserve of his uncle. Already at Fort St. Louis, Duhaut had intrigued among the men; and the mild admonition of Joutel had not, it seems, sufficed to divert him from his sinister purposes. Liotot, it is said, had secretly sworn vengeance against La Salle, whom he charged with having caused the death of his brother, or, as some will have it, his nephew. On one of the former journeys this young man's strength had failed; and, La Salle having ordered him to return to the fort, he had been killed by Indians on the way.

The party moved again as the weather improved, and on the 15th of March encamped within a few miles of a spot which La Salle had passed on his preceding journey, and where he had left a quantity of Indian corn and beans in *cache;* that is to say, hidden in the ground or in a hollow tree. As provisions were falling short, he sent a party from the camp to find it. These men were Duhaut, Liotot, Hiens the buccaneer, Teissier, L'Archevêque, Nika the hunter, and La Salle's servant Saget. They opened the *cache*, and found the contents spoiled; but as they returned from their bootless errand they saw buffalo, and Nika shot two of them. They now encamped on the spot, and sent the servant to inform La Salle, in order that he might send horses to bring in the meat. Accordingly, on the next day, he directed Moranget and De Marle, with the necessary horses, to go with Saget to the hunters' camp. When they arrived, they found that Duhaut and his companions had already cut up the meat, and laid it upon scaffolds for smoking, though it was not yet so dry as, it seems, this process required. Duhaut and the others had also put by, for themselves, the marrow-bones and certain portions of the meat, to which, by woodland custom, they had a perfect right. Moranget, whose rashness and violence had once before caused a fatal catastrophe, fell into a most unreasonable fit of rage, berated and menaced Duhaut and his party, and ended by seizing upon the whole of the meat, including the reserved portions. This added fuel to the fire of Duhaut's old grudge against Moranget and his uncle. There is reason to think that he had harbored deadly designs, the execution of which was only hastened by the present outbreak. The surgeon also bore hatred against Moranget, whom he had nursed with constant attention when wounded by an Indian arrow, and who had since repaid him with abuse. These two now took counsel apart with Hiens, Teissier, and L'Archevêque; and it was resolved to kill Moranget that night. Nika, La Salle's devoted follower, and Saget, his faithful servant, must die with him. All of the five were of one mind except the pilot Teissier, who neither aided nor opposed the plot.

Night came; the woods grew dark; the evening meal was finished, and the evening pipes were smoked. The order of the guard was arranged; and, doubtless by design, the first hour of the night was assigned to Moranget, the second to Saget, and the third to Nika. Gun in hand, each stood watch in turn over the silent but not sleeping forms around him, till, his time expiring, he called the man who was to relieve him, wrapped himself in his blanket, and was soon buried in a slumber that was to be his last. Now the assassins rose. Duhaut and Hiens stood with their guns cocked, ready to shoot down any one of the destined victims who should resist or fly. The surgeon, with an axe, stole towards the three sleepers, and struck a rapid blow at each in turn. Saget and Nika died with little movement; but Moranget started spasmodically into a sitting posture, gasping and unable to speak; and the murderers compelled De Marle, who was not in their plot, to compromise himself by despatching him.

The floodgates of murder were open, and the torrent must have its way. Vengeance and safety alike demanded the death of La Salle. Hiens, or "English Jem," alone seems to have hesitated; for he was one of those to whom that stern commander had always been partial. Meanwhile, the intended victim was still at his camp, about six miles distant. It is easy to picture, with sufficient accuracy, the features of the scene, — the sheds of bark and branches, beneath which, among blankets and buffalo-robes, camp-utensils, pack-saddles, rude harness, guns, powder-horns, and bullet-pouches, the men lounged away the hour, sleeping or smoking, or talking among themselves; the blackened kettles that hung from tripods of poles over the fires; the Indians strolling about the place or lying, like dogs in the sun, with eyes half-shut, yet all observant; and, in the neighboring meadow, the horses grazing under the eye of a watchman.

It was the 18th of March. Moranget and his companions had been expected to return the night before; but the whole day passed, and they did not appear. La Salle became very anxious. He resolved to go and look for them; but not well knowing the way, he told the Indians who were about the camp that he would give them a hatchet if they would guide him. One of them accepted the offer; and La Salle prepared to set out in the morning, at the same time directing Joutel to be ready to go with him. Joutel says: "That evening, while we were talking about what could have happened to the absent men, he seemed to have a presentiment of what was to take place. He asked me if I had heard of any machinations against them, or if I had noticed any bad design on the part of Duhaut and the rest. I answered that I had heard nothing, except that they sometimes complained of being found fault with so often; and that this was all I knew; besides which, as they were persuaded that I was in his interest, they would not have told me of any bad design they might have. We were very uneasy all the rest of the evening."

In the morning, La Salle set out with his Indian guide. He had changed his mind with regard to Joutel, whom he now directed to remain in charge of the camp and to keep a careful watch. He told the friar Anastase Douay to come with him instead of Joutel, whose gun, which was the best in the party, he borrowed for the occasion, as well as his pistol. The three proceeded on their way, — La Salle, the friar, and the Indian. "All the way," writes the friar, "he spoke to me of nothing but matters of piety, grace, and predestination; enlarging on the debt he owed to God, who had saved him from so many perils during more than twenty years of travel in America. Suddenly, I saw him overwhelmed with a profound sadness, for which he himself could not account. He was so much moved that I scarcely knew him." He soon recovered his usual calmness; and they walked on till they approached the camp of Duhaut, which was on the farther side of a small river. Looking about him with the eye of a woodsman, La Salle saw two eagles circling in the air nearly over him, as if attracted by carcasses of beasts or men. He fired his gun and his pistol, as a summons to any of his followers who might be within hearing. The shots reached the ears of the conspirators. Rightly conjecturing by whom they were fired, several of them, led by Duhaut, crossed the river at a little distance above, where trees or other intervening objects hid them from sight. Duhaut and the surgeon crouched like Indians in the long, dry, reed-like grass of the last summer's growth, while L'Archevêque stood in sight near the bank. La Salle, continuing to advance, soon saw him, and, calling to him, demanded where was Moranget. The man, without lifting his hat, or any show of respect, replied in an agitated and broken voice, but with a tone of studied insolence, that Moranget was strolling about somewhere. La Salle rebuked and menaced him. He rejoined with increased insolence, drawing back, as he spoke, towards the ambuscade, while the incensed commander advanced to chastise him. At that moment a shot was fired from the grass, instantly followed by another; and, pierced through the brain, La Salle dropped dead.

The friar at his side stood terror-stricken, unable to advance or to fly; when Duhaut, rising from the ambuscade, called out to him to take courage, for he had nothing to fear. The murderers now came forward, and with wild looks gathered about their victim. "There thou liest, great Bashaw! There thou liest!" exclaimed the surgeon Liotot, in base exultation over the unconscious corpse. With mockery and insult, they stripped it naked, dragged it into the bushes, and left it there, a prey to the buzzards and the wolves.

Thus in the vigor of his manhood, at the age of forty-three, died Robert Cavelier de la Salle, "one of the greatest men," writes Tonty, "of this age;" without question one of the most remarkable explorers whose names live in history. His faithful officer Joutel thus sketches his portrait: "His firmness, his courage, his great knowledge of the arts and sciences, which made him equal to every undertaking, and his un-tiring energy, which enabled him to surmount every obstacle, would have won at last a glorious success for his grand enterprise, had not all his fine qualities been counterbalanced by a haughtiness of manner which often made him insupportable, and by a harshness towards those under his command which drew upon him an implacable hatred, and was at last the cause of his death."

The enthusiasm of the disinterested and chivalrous Champlain was not the enthusiasm of La Salle; nor had he any part in the self-devoted zeal of the early Jesuit explorers. He belonged not to the age of the knight-errant and the saint, but to the modern world of practical study and practical action. He was the hero not of a principle nor of a faith, but simply of a fixed idea and a determined purpose. As often happens with concentred and energetic natures, his purpose was to him a passion and an inspiration; and he clung to it with a certain fanaticism of devotion. It was the offspring of an ambition vast and comprehensive, yet acting in the interest both of France and of civilization.

Serious in all things, incapable of the lighter pleasures, incapable of repose, finding no joy but in the pursuit of great designs, too shy for society and too reserved for popularity, often unsympathetic and always seeming so, smothering emotions which he could not utter, schooled to universal distrust, stern to his followers and pitiless to himself, bearing the brunt of every hardship and every danger, demanding of others an equal constancy joined to an implicit deference, heeding no counsel but his own, attempting the impossible and grasping at what was too vast to hold, — he contained in his own complex and painful nature the chief springs of his triumphs, his failures, and his death.

It is easy to reckon up his defects, but it is not easy to hide from sight the Roman virtues that redeemed them. Beset by a throng of enemies, he stands, like the King of Israel, head and shoulders above them all. He was a tower of adamant, against whose impregnable front hardship and danger, the rage of man and of the elements, the southern sun, the northern blast, fatigue, famine, disease, delay, disappointment, and deferred hope emptied their quivers in vain. That very pride which, Coriolanus-like, declared itself most sternly in the thickest press of foes, has in it something to challenge admiration. Never, under the impenetrable mail of paladin or crusader, beat a heart of more intrepid mettle than within the stoic panoply that armed the breast of La Salle. To estimate aright the marvels of his patient fortitude, one must follow on his track through the vast scene of his interminable journeyings, — those thousands of weary miles of forest, marsh, and river, where, again and again, in the bitterness of baffled striving, the untiring pilgrim pushed onward towards the goal which he was never to attain. America owes him an enduring memory; for in this masculine figure she sees the pioneer who guided her to the possession of her richest heritage.[1]

*   *   *

[1] [According to the researches of Bolton, *loc. cit.* p. 168, the murder took place near the present city of Navasota, Texas, between the Brazos and Navasota Rivers. The survivors of La Salle's party made their way across the Red River to the mouth of the Arkansas and finally reached Canada. Tonty attempted to reach St. Louis of Texas in 1689 but failed. That year, most of the survivors at the Texas fort were killed by the Karaukawa Indians. In the meantime the Viceroy of Mexico had sent out more than one expedition to find out where the French were and to capture or destroy them. The experiences of the De Leon expedition of 1689 on arriving at the site of the fort are told by Parkman in Chapter XXIX of *La Salle.*]

End of the Colony

As they [the Spanish search party] drew near, no banner was displayed, no sentry challenged; and the silence of death reigned over the shattered palisades and neglected dwellings. The Spaniards spurred their reluctant horses through the gateway, and a scene of desolation met their sight. No living thing was stirring. Doors were torn from their hinges; broken boxes, staved barrels, and rusty kettles, mingled with a great number of stocks of arquebuses and muskets, were scattered about in confusion. Here, too, trampled in mud and soaked with rain, they saw more than two hundred books, many of which still retained the traces of costly bindings. On the adjacent prairie lay three dead bodies, one of which, from fragments of dress still clinging to the wasted remains, they saw to be that of a woman. It was in vain to question the imperturbable savages, who, wrapped to the throat in their buffalo-robes, stood gazing on the scene with looks of wooden immobility. Two strangers, however, at length arrived.[2] Their faces were smeared with paint, and they were wrapped in buffalo-robes like the rest; yet these seeming Indians were L'Archevêque, the tool of La Salle's murderer Duhaut, and Grollet, the companion of the white savage Ruter. The Spanish commander, learning that these two men were in the district of the tribe called Texas,[3] had sent to invite them to his camp under a pledge of good treatment; and they had resolved to trust Spanish clemency rather than endure longer a life that had become intolerable. From them the Spaniards learned nearly all that is known of the fate of Barbier, Zenobe Membré, and their companions. Three months before, a large band of Indians had approached the fort, the inmates of which had suffered severely from the ravages of the small-pox. From fear of treachery, they refused to admit their visitors, but received them at a cabin without the palisades. Here the French began a trade with them; when suddenly a band of warriors, yelling the war-whoop, rushed from an ambuscade under the bank of the river, and butchered the greater number. The children of one Talon, together with an Italian and a young man from Paris named Breman, were saved by the Indian women, who carried them off on their backs. L'Archevêque and Grollet, who with others of their stamp were domesticated in

[2] May 1st. The Spaniards reached the fort April 22, 1689.

[3] The first instance in which the name occurs. In a letter written by a member of De Leon's party, the Texan Indians are mentioned several times. The name Tejas, or Texas, was first applied as a local designation to a spot on the river Neches, in the Cenis territory, whence it extended to the whole country.

the Indian villages, came to the scene of slaughter, and, as they affirmed, buried fourteen dead bodies.

L'Archevêque and Grollet were sent to Spain, where, in spite of the pledge given them, they were thrown into prison, with the intention of sending them back to labor in the mines.[4] The Indians, some time after De Leon's expedition, gave up their captives to the Spaniards. The Italian was imprisoned at Vera Cruz. Breman's fate is unknown. Pierre and Jean Baptiste Talon, who were now old enough to bear arms, were enrolled in the Spanish navy, and, being captured in 1696 by a French ship of war, regained their liberty; while their younger brothers and their sister were carried to Spain by the Viceroy. With respect to the ruffian companions of Hiens, the conviction of Tonty that they had been put to death by the Indians may have been well founded; but the buccaneer himself is said to have been killed in a quarrel with his accomplice Ruter, the white savage; and thus in ignominy and darkness died the last embers of the doomed colony of La Salle.

Here ends the wild and mournful story of the explorers of the Mississippi. Of all their toil and sacrifice, no fruit remained but a great geographical discovery, and a grand type of incarnate energy and will. Where La Salle had ploughed, others were to sow the seed; and on the path which the undespairing Norman had hewn out, the Canadian D'Iberville was to win for France a vast though a transient dominion.[5]

[4] [According to Bolton, *loc. cit.* p. 168, L'Archevêque eventually settled in New Mexico and in 1720 was killed by Indians when taking part in a Spanish expedition to Kansas.]

[5] [The best recent account of La Salle and his significance is Bernard DeVoto *The Course of Empire* (1952) chapter iv.]

CHAPTER XXIV

King William's War on the New England Frontier
1690–1697

[*Count Frontenac and New France Under Louis XIV*, CHAPTER XVII]

"This stroke," says Villebon, speaking of the success at Oyster River, "is of great advantage, because it breaks off all the talk of peace between our Indians and the English. The English are in despair, for not even infants in the cradle were spared."

I have given the story in detail, as showing the origin and character of the destructive raids, of which New England annalists show only the results.[1] The borders of New England were peculiarly vulnerable. In Canada the settlers built their houses in lines, within supporting distance of one another, along the margin of a river which supplied easy transportation for troops; and in time of danger they all took refuge in forts under command of the local seigneurs, or of officers with detachments of soldiers. The exposed part of the French colony extended along the St. Lawrence about ninety miles. The exposed frontier of New England was between two and three hundred miles long, and consisted of farms and hamlets loosely scattered through an almost impervious forest. Mutual support was difficult or impossible. A body of Indians and Canadians, approaching secretly and swiftly, dividing into small bands, and falling at once upon the isolated houses of an extensive district, could commit prodigious havoc in a short time, and with little danger. Even in so-called villages the houses were far apart, because, except on the seashore, the people lived by farming. Such as

---

[1] [The attack on Oyster River, now Durham, N.H., by Lieut. Villieu and Fr. Pierre Thury, with 105 Abenaki Indians in June 1694, is told by Parkman in the previous chapter. Twenty houses were burned, 27 prisoners taken and 104 persons, mostly women and children, killed.]

were able to do so fenced their dwellings with palisades, or built them of solid timber, with loopholes, a projecting upper story like a block-house, and sometimes a flanker at one or more of the corners. In the more considerable settlements the largest of these fortified houses was occupied, in time of danger, by armed men, and served as a place of refuge for the neighbors. The palisaded house defended by Convers at Wells was of this sort, and so also was the Woodman house at Oyster River. These were "garrison houses," properly so called, though the name was often given to fortified dwellings occupied only by the family. The French and Indian war-parties commonly avoided the true garrison houses, and very rarely captured them, except unawares; for their tactics were essentially Iroquois, and consisted, for the most part, in pouncing upon peaceful settlers by surprise, and generally in the night. Combatants and non-combatants were slaughtered together. By parading the number of slain, without mentioning that most of them were women and children, and by counting as forts mere private houses surrounded with palisades, Charlevoix and later writers have given the air of gallant exploits to acts which deserve a very different name. To attack military posts, like Casco and Pemaquid, was a legitimate act of war; but systematically to butcher helpless farmers and their families can hardly pass as such, except from the Iroquois point of view.

The chief alleged motive for this ruthless warfare was to prevent the people of New England from invading Canada, by giving them employment at home; though, in fact, they had never thought of invading Canada till after these attacks began. But for the intrigues of Denonville, the Bigots, Thury, and Saint-Castin, before war was declared, and the destruction of Salmon Falls after it, Phips's expedition would never have taken place. By successful raids against the borders of New England, Frontenac roused the Canadians from their dejection, and prevented his red allies from deserting him; but in so doing he brought upon himself an enemy who, as Charlevoix himself says, asked only to be let alone. If there was a political necessity for butchering women and children on the frontier of New England, it was a necessity created by the French themselves.

There was no such necessity. Massachusetts was the only one of the New England colonies which took an aggressive part in the contest. Connecticut did little or nothing. Rhode Island was non-combatant through Quaker influence; and New Hampshire was too weak for offensive war. Massachusetts was in no condition to fight, nor was she impelled to do so by the home government. Canada was organized for war, and must fight at the bidding of the King, who made the war and paid for it. Massachusetts was organized for peace; and if she chose an aggressive part, it was at her own risk and her own cost. She had had fighting enough already against infuriated savages far more numerous than the Iroquois, and poverty and political revolution made peace a necessity to her. If there was danger of another attack on Quebec, it was not from New England, but from Old; and no amount of frontier butchery could avert it.

Nor, except their inveterate habit of poaching on Acadian fisheries, had the people of New England provoked these barbarous attacks. They never even attempted to retaliate them, though the settlements of Acadia offered a safe and easy revenge. Once, it is true, they pillaged Beaubassin; but they killed nobody, though countless butcheries in settlements yet more defenceless were fresh in their memory.

With New York, a colony separate in government and widely sundered in local position, the case was different. Its rulers had instigated the Iroquois to attack Canada, possibly before the declaration of war, and certainly after it; and they had no right to complain of reprisal. Yet the frontier of New York was less frequently assailed, because it was less exposed; while that of New England was drenched in blood because it was open to attack, because the Abenakis were convenient instruments for attacking it, because the adhesion of these tribes was necessary to the maintenance of French power in Acadia, and because this adhesion could best be secured by inciting them to constant hostility against the English. They were not only needed as the barrier of Canada against New England, but the French commanders hoped, by means of their tomahawks, to drive the English beyond the Piscataqua, and secure the whole of Maine to the French crown.

Who were answerable for these offences against Christianity and civilization? First, the King; and, next, the governors and military officers who were charged with executing his orders, and who often executed them with needless barbarity. But a far different responsibility rests on the missionary priests, who hounded their converts on the track of innocent blood. The Acadian priests are not all open to this charge. Some of them are even accused of being too favorable to the English; while others gave themselves to their proper work, and neither abused their influence, nor perverted their teaching to political ends. The most prominent among the apostles of carnage, at this time, are the Jesuit Bigot on the Kennebec, and the seminary priest Thury on the Penobscot. There is little doubt that the latter instigated attacks on the

English frontier before the war, and there is conclusive evidence that he had a hand in repeated forays after it began. Whether acting from fanaticism, policy, or an odious compound of both, he was found so useful that the minister Ponchartrain twice wrote him letters of commendation, praising him in the same breath for his care of the souls of the Indians and his zeal in exciting them to war. "There is no better man," says an Acadian official, "to prompt the savages to any enterprise." The King was begged to reward him with money; and Ponchartrain wrote to the bishop of Quebec to increase his pay out of the allowance furnished by the government to the Acadian clergy, because he, Thury, had persuaded the Abenakis to begin the war anew.

The French missionaries are said to have made use of singular methods to excite their flocks against the heretics. The Abenaki chief Bomazeen, when a prisoner at Boston in 1696, declared that they told the Indian that Jesus Christ was a Frenchman, and his mother, the Virgin, a French lady; that the English had murdered him, and that the best way to gain his favor was to revenge his death.

Whether or not these articles of faith formed a part of the teachings of Thury and his fellow-apostles, there is no doubt that it was a recognized part of their functions to keep their converts in hostility to the English, and that their credit with the civil powers depended on their success in doing so. The same holds true of the priests of the mission villages in Canada. They avoided all that might impair the warlike spirit of the neophyte, and they were well aware that in savages the warlike spirit is mainly dependent on native ferocity. They taught temperance, conjugal fidelity, devotion to the rites of their religion, and submission to the priest; but they left the savage a savage still. In spite of the remonstrances of the civil authorities, the mission Indian was separated as far as possible from intercourse with the French, and discouraged from learning the French tongue. He wore a crucifix, hung wampum on the shrine of the Virgin, told his beads, prayed three times a day, knelt for hours before the Host, invoked the saints, and confessed to the priest; but, with rare exceptions, he murdered, scalped, and tortured like his heathen countrymen.

The picture has another side, which must not pass unnoticed. Early in the war, the French of Canada began the merciful practice of buying English prisoners, and especially children, from their Indian allies. After the first fury of attack, many lives were spared for the sake of this ransom. Sometimes, but not always, the redeemed captives were made to work for their benefactors. They were uniformly treated well, and often with such kindness that they would not be exchanged, and became Canadians by adoption.

Villebon was still full of anxiety as to the adhesion of the Abenakis. Thury saw the danger still more clearly, and told Frontenac that their late attack at Oyster River was due more to levity than to any other cause; that they were greatly alarmed, wavering, half stupefied, afraid of the English, and distrustful of the French, whom they accused of using them as tools. It was clear that something must be done; and nothing could answer the purpose so well as the capture of Pemaquid, — that English stronghold which held them in constant menace, and at the same time tempted them by offers of goods at a low rate. To the capture of Pemaquid, therefore, the French government turned its thoughts.

One Pascho Chubb, of Andover, commanded the post, with a garrison of ninety-five militia-men. Stoughton, governor of Massachusetts, had written to the Abenakis, upbraiding them for breaking the peace, and ordering them to bring in their prisoners without delay. The Indians of Bigot's mission, that is to say, Bigot in their name, retorted by a letter to the last degree haughty and abusive. Those of Thury's mission, however, were so anxious to recover their friends held in prison at Boston that they came to Pemaquid, and opened a conference with Chubb. The French say that they meant only to deceive him. This does not justify the Massachusetts officer, who, by an act of odious treachery, killed several of them, and captured the chief, Egeremet. Nor was this the only occasion on which the English had acted in bad faith. It was but playing into the hands of the French, who saw with delight that the folly of their enemies had aided their own intrigues.

Early in 1696 two ships of war, the *Envieux* and the *Profond*, one commanded by Iberville and the other by Bonaventure, sailed from Rochefort to Quebec, where they took on board eighty troops and Canadians; then proceeded to Cape Breton, embarked thirty Micmac Indians, and steered for the St. John. Here they met two British frigates and a provincial tender belonging to Massachusetts. A fight ensued. The forces were very unequal. The *Newport*, of twenty-four guns, was dismasted and taken; but her companion frigate along with the tender escaped in the fog. The French then anchored at the mouth of the St. John, where Villebon and the priest Simon were waiting for them, with fifty more Micmacs. Simon and the Indians went on board; and they all sailed for Pentegoet, where Villieu, with twenty-five soldiers, and Thury and Saint-Castin, with some three hundred Abenakis, were ready to join them. After the usual feasting, these new allies paddled for Pemaquid; the ships followed; and on the next day, the 14th of August, they all reached their destination.

The fort of Pemaquid stood at the west side of the promontory of the same name, on a rocky point at the mouth of Pemaquid River. It was a quadrangle, with ramparts of rough stone, built at great pains and cost, but exposed to artillery, and incapable of resisting heavy shot. The government of Massachusetts, with its usual military fatuity, had placed it in the keeping of an unfit commander, and permitted some of the yeoman garrison to bring their wives and children to this dangerous and important post.[2]

Saint-Castin and his Indians landed at New Harbor, half a league from the fort. Troops and cannon were sent ashore; and at five o'clock in the afternoon Chubb was summoned to surrender. He replied that he would fight, "even if the sea were covered with French ships and the land with Indians." The firing then began; and the Indian marksmen, favored by the nature of the ground, ensconced themselves near the fort, well covered from its cannon. During the night, mortars and heavy ships' guns were landed, and by great exertion were got into position, the two priests working lustily with the rest. They opened fire at three o'clock on the next day. Saint-Castin had just before sent Chubb a letter, telling him that if the garrison were obstinate they would get no quarter, and would be butchered by the Indians. Close upon this message followed four or five bombshells. Chubb succumbed immediately, sounded a parley, and gave up the fort, on condition that he and his men should be protected from the Indians, sent to Boston, and exchanged for French and Abenaki prisoners. They all marched out without arms; and Iberville, true to his pledge, sent them to an island in the bay, beyond the reach of his red allies. Villieu took possession of the fort, where an Indian prisoner was found in irons, half dead from long confinement. This so enraged his countrymen that a massacre would infallibly have taken place but for the precaution of Iberville.

The cannon of Pemaquid were carried on board the ships, and the small arms and ammunition given to the Indians. Two days were spent in destroying the works, and then the victors withdrew in triumph. Disgraceful as was the prompt surrender of the fort, it may be doubted

[2] [The site of the fort has been excavated in the present century, one of the stone bastions restored, and fitted up as a local museum. It lies directly across Pemaquid Point from the head of New Harbor.]

if, even with the best defence, it could have held out many days; for it had no casemates, and its occupants were defenceless against the explosion of shells. Chubb was arrested for cowardice on his return, and remained some months in prison. After his release he returned to his family at Andover, twenty miles from Boston; and here, in the year following, he and his wife were killed by Indians, who seem to have pursued him to this apparently safe asylum to take revenge for his treachery toward their countrymen.

The people of Massachusetts, compelled by a royal order to build and maintain Pemaquid, had no love for it, and underrated its importance. Having been accustomed to spend their money as they themselves saw fit, they revolted at compulsion, though exercised for their good. Pemaquid was nevertheless of the utmost value for the preservation of their hold on Maine, and its conquest was a crowning triumph to the French.

The conquerors now projected a greater exploit. The Marquis de Nesmond, with a powerful squadron of fifteen ships, including some of the best in the royal navy, sailed for Newfoundland, with orders to defeat an English squadron supposed to be there, and then to proceed to the mouth of the Penobscot, where he was to be joined by the Abenaki warriors and 1500 troops from Canada. The whole united force was then to fall upon Boston. The French had an exact knowledge of the place. Meneval, when a prisoner there, lodged in the house of John Nelson, had carefully examined it; and so also had the Chevalier d'Aux; while La Mothe-Cadillac had reconnoitred the town and harbor before the war began. An accurate map of them was made for the use of the expedition, and the plan of operations was arranged with great care. Twelve hundred troops and Canadians were to land with artillery at Dorchester, and march at once to force the barricade across the neck of the peninsula on which the town stood. At the same time Saint-Castin was to land at Noddle's Island,[3] with a troop of Canadians and all the Indians; pass over in canoes to Charlestown; and, after mastering it, cross to the north point of Boston, which would thus be attacked at both ends. During these movements 200 soldiers were to seize the battery on Castle Island,[4] and then land in front of the town near Long Wharf, under the guns of the fleet.

Boston had about 7000 inhabitants; but owing to the seafaring habits of the people many of its best men were generally absent, and in the belief of the French its available force did not much exceed 800. "There

---

[3] [The present East Boston.]   [4] [The present Fort Independence.]

are no soldiers in the place," say the directions for attack, "at least there were none last September, except the garrison from Pemaquid, who do not deserve the name." An easy victory was expected. After Boston was taken, the land forces, French and Indian, were to march on Salem, and thence northward to Portsmouth, conquering as they went; while the ships followed along the coast to lend aid, when necessary. All captured places were to be completely destroyed after removing all valuable property. A portion of this plunder was to be abandoned to the officers and men, in order to encourage them, and the rest stowed in the ships for transportation to France.

Notice of the proposed expedition had reached Frontenac in the spring; and he began at once to collect men, canoes, and supplies for the long and arduous march to the rendezvous. He saw clearly the uncertainties of the attempt; but, in spite of his seventy-seven years, he resolved to command the land force in person. He was ready in June, and waited only to hear from Nesmond. The summer passed; and it was not till September that a ship reached Quebec with a letter from the marquis, telling him that head-winds had detained the fleet till only fifty days' provision remained, and it was too late for action. The enterprise had completely failed, and even at Newfoundland nothing was accomplished. It proved a positive advantage to New England, since a host of Indians, who would otherwise have been turned loose upon the borders, were gathered by Saint-Castin at the Penobscot to wait for the fleet, and kept there idle all summer.

It is needless to dwell further on the war in Acadia. There were petty combats by land and sea; Villieu was captured and carried to Boston; a band of New England rustics made a futile attempt to dislodge Villebon from his fort at Naxouat; while throughout the contest rivalry and jealousy rankled among the French officials, who continually maligned one another in telltale letters to the court. Their hope that the Abenakis would force back the English boundary to the Piscataqua was never fulfilled. At Kittery, at Wells, and even among the ashes of York, the stubborn settlers held their ground, while war-parties prowled along the whole frontier, from the Kennebec to the Connecticut. A single incident will show the nature of the situation, and the qualities which it sometimes called forth.

Early in the spring that followed the capture of Pemaquid a band of Indians fell, after daybreak, on a number of farmhouses near the village of Haverhill. One of them belonged to a settler named Dustan, whose wife Hannah had borne a child a week before, and lay in the house, nursed by Mary Neff, one of her neighbors. Dustan had gone to his work in a neighboring field, taking with him his seven children, of whom the youngest was two years old. Hearing the noise of the attack, he told them to run to the nearest fortified house, a mile or more distant, and, snatching up his gun, threw himself on one of his horses and galloped towards his own house to save his wife. It was too late: the Indians were already there. He now thought only of saving his children; and, keeping behind them as they ran, he fired on the pursuing savages, and held them at bay till he and his flock reached a place of safety. Meanwhile, the house was set on fire, and his wife and the nurse carried off. Her husband, no doubt, had given her up as lost, when weeks after, she reappeared, accompanied by Mary Neff and a boy, and bringing ten Indian scalps. Her story was to the following effect.

The Indians had killed the new-born child by dashing it against a tree, after which the mother and the nurse were dragged into the forest, where they found a number of friends and neighbors, their fellows in misery. Some of these were presently tomahawked, and the rest divided among their captors. Hannah Dustan and the nurse fell to the share of a family consisting of two warriors, three squaws, and seven children, who separated from the rest, and, hunting as they went, moved northward towards an Abenaki village, 250 miles distant, probably that of the mission on the Chaudière. Every morning, noon, and evening they told their beads, and repeated their prayers. An English boy, captured at Worcester, was also of the party. After a while, the Indians began to amuse themselves by telling the women that when they reached the village they would be stripped, made to run the gantlet, and severely beaten, according to custom.

Hannah Dustan now resolved on a desperate effort to escape, and Mary Neff and the boy agreed to join in it. They were in the depths of the forest, halfway on their journey, and the Indians, who had no distrust of them, were all asleep about their campfire, when, late in the night, the two women and the boy took each a hatchet, and crouched silently by the bare heads of the unconscious savages. Then they all struck at once, with blows so rapid and true that ten of the twelve were killed before they were well awake. One old squaw sprang up wounded, and ran screeching into the forest, followed by a small boy whom they had purposely left unharmed. Hannah Dustan and her companions watched by the corpses till daylight; then the Amazon scalped them all, and the three made their way back to the settlements, with the trophies of their exploit.

CHAPTER XXV

The Death of Frontenac

1698

[*Count Frontenac and New France Under Louis XIV*, CHAPTER XX]

In November, when the last ship had gone, and Canada was sealed from the world for half a year, a mortal illness fell upon the governor. On the 22nd he had strength enough to dictate his will, seated in an easy chair in his chamber at the château. His colleague and adversary, Champigny, often came to visit him, and did all in his power to soothe his last moments. The reconciliation between them was complete. One of his Récollet friends, Father Olivier Goyer, administered extreme unction; and on the afternoon of the 28th he died, in perfect composure and full possession of his faculties. He was in his seventy-eighth year.

He was greatly beloved by the humbler classes, who, days before his death, beset the château, praising and lamenting him. Many of higher station shared the popular grief. "He was the love and delight of New France," says one of them; "churchmen honored him for his piety, nobles esteemed him for his valor, merchants respected him for his equity, and the people loved him for his kindness." "He was the father of the poor," says another, "the protector of the oppressed, and a perfect model of virtue and piety." An Ursuline nun regrets him as the friend and patron of her sisterhood, and so also does the superior of the Hôtel-Dieu. His most conspicuous though not his bitterest opponent, the intendant Champigny, thus announced his death to the court: "I venture to send this letter by way of New England to tell you that Monsieur le Comte de Frontenac died on the twenty-eighth of last month, with the sentiments of a true Christian. After all the disputes we have had together, you will hardly believe, Monseigneur, how truly and deeply I am touched by his death. He treated me during his illness in a manner so obliging that I should be utterly void of gratitude if I did not feel thankful to him."

As a mark of kind feeling, Frontenac had bequeathed to the intendant a valuable crucifix, and to Madame de Champigny a reliquary which he had long been accustomed to wear. For the rest, he gave fifteen hundred livres to the Récollets, to be expended in masses for his soul, and that of his wife after her death. To her he bequeathed all the remainder of his small property, and he also directed that his heart should be sent her in a case of lead or silver. His enemies reported that she refused to accept it, saying that she had never had it when he was living, and did not want it when he was dead.

On the Friday after his death he was buried as he had directed, not in the cathedral, but in the church of the Récollets, — a preference deeply offensive to many of the clergy. The bishop officiated; and then the Récollet, Father Goyer, who had attended his death-bed, and seems to have been his confessor, mounted the pulpit, and delivered his funeral oration. "This funeral pageantry," exclaimed the orator, "this temple draped in mourning, these dim lights, this sad and solemn music, this great assembly bowed in sorrow, and all this pomp and circumstance of death may well penetrate your hearts. I will not seek to dry your tears, for I cannot contain my own. After all, this is a time to weep, and never did people weep for a better governor."

A copy of this eulogy fell into the hands of an enemy of Frontenac, who wrote a running commentary upon it. The copy thus annotated is still preserved at Quebec. A few passages from the orator and his critic will show the violent conflict of opinion concerning the governor, and illustrate in some sort, though with more force than fairness, the contradictions of his character: —

THE ORATOR: This wise man, to whom the Senate of Venice listened with respectful attention, because he spoke before them with all the force of that eloquence which you, Messieurs, have so often admired —

> THE CRITIC: It was not his eloquence that they admired, but his extravagant pretensions, his bursts of rage, and his unworthy treatment of those who did not agree with him.

THE ORATOR: This disinterested man, more busied with duty than with gain —

> THE CRITIC: The less said about that the better.

THE ORATOR: Who made the fortune of others, but did not increase his own —

THE CRITIC: Not for want of trying, and that very often in spite of his conscience and the King's orders.

THE ORATOR: Devoted to the service of his King, whose majesty he represented, and whose person he loved —

THE CRITIC: Not at all. How often has he opposed his orders, even with force and violence, to the great scandal of everybody!

THE ORATOR: Great in the midst of difficulties, by that consummate prudence, that solid judgment, that presence of mind, that breadth and elevation of thought, which he retained to the last moment of his life —

THE CRITIC: He had in fact a great capacity for political manœuvres and tricks; but as for the solid judgment ascribed to him, his conduct gives it the lie, or else, if he had it, the vehemence of his passions often unsettled it. It is much to be feared that his presence of mind was the effect of an obstinate and hardened self-confidence by which he put himself above everybody and everything, since he never used it to repair, so far as in him lay, the public and private wrongs he caused. What ought he not to have done here, in this temple, to ask pardon for the obstinate and furious heat with which he so long persecuted the Church; upheld and even instigated rebellion against her; protected libertines, scandal-mongers, and creatures of evil life against the ministers of Heaven; molested, persecuted, vexed persons most eminent in virtue, nay, even the priests and magistrates, who defended the cause of God; sustained in all sorts of ways the wrongful and scandalous traffic in brandy with the Indians; permitted, approved, and supported the license and abuse of taverns; authorized and even introduced, in spite of the remonstrances of the servants of God, criminal and dangerous diversions; tried to decry the bishop and the clergy, the missionaries, and other persons of virtue, and to injure them, both here and in France, by libels and calumnies; caused, in fine, either by himself or through others, a multitude of disorders, under which this infant church has groaned for many years? What, I say, ought he not to have done before dying to atone for these scandals, and give proof of sincere penitence and compunction? God gave him full time to recognize his errors, and yet to the last he showed a great indifference in all these matters. When, in presence of the Holy Sacrament, he was asked according to the ritual, 'Do you not beg pardon for all the ill examples you may have given?' he answered, 'Yes,' but did not confess that he had ever given any. In a word, he behaved during the few days before his death like one who had led an irreproachable life, and had nothing to fear. And this is the presence of mind that he retained to his last moment!

THE ORATOR: Great in dangers by his courage, he always came off with honor, and never was reproached with rashness —

THE CRITIC: True; he was not rash, as was seen when the Bostonnais besieged Quebec.

THE ORATOR: Great in religion by his piety, he practised its good works in spirit and in truth —

THE CRITIC: Say rather that he practised its forms with parade and ostentation: witness the inordinate ambition with which he always claimed honors in the Church, to which he had no right; outrageously affronted intendants, who opposed his pretensions; required priests to address him when preaching, and in their intercourse with him demanded from them humiliations which he did not exact from the meanest military officer. This was his way of making himself great in *religion and piety*, or, more truly, in vanity and hypocrisy. How can a man be called *great in religion*, when he openly holds opinions entirely opposed to the True Faith, such as, that *all men are predestined*, that *Hell will not last forever*, and the like?

THE ORATOR: His very look inspired esteem and confidence —

THE CRITIC: Then one must have taken him at exactly the right moment, and not when he was foaming at the mouth with rage.

THE ORATOR: A mingled air of nobility and gentleness; a countenance that bespoke the probity that appeared in all his acts, and a sincerity that could not dissimulate —

THE CRITIC: The eulogist did not know the old fox.

THE ORATOR: An inviolable fidelity to friends —

THE CRITIC: What friends? Was it persons of the other sex? Of these he was always fond, and too much for the honor of some of them.

THE ORATOR: Disinterested for himself, ardent for others, he used his credit at court only to recommend their services, excuse their faults, and obtain favors for them —

THE CRITIC: True; but it was for his creatures, and for nobody else.

THE ORATOR: I pass in silence that reading of spiritual books which he practised as an indispensable duty more than forty years; that holy avidity with which he listened to the word of God —

THE CRITIC: Only if the preacher addressed the sermon to him, and called him *Monseigneur.* As for his reading, it was often Jansenist books, of which he had a great many, and which he greatly praised and lent freely to others.

THE ORATOR: He prepared for the sacraments by meditation and retreat —

THE CRITIC: And generally came out of his retreat more excited than ever against the Church.

THE ORATOR: Let us not recall his ancient and noble descent, his family connected with all that is greatest in the army, the magistracy, and the government, — Knights, Marshals of France, Governors of Provinces, Judges, Councillors, and Ministers of State: let us not, I say, recall all these without remembering that their examples roused this generous heart to noble emulation; and, as an expiring flame grows brighter as it dies, so did all the virtues of his race unite at last in him to end with glory a long line of great men, that shall be no more except in history.

THE CRITIC: Well laid on, and too well for his hearers to believe him. Far from agreeing that all these virtues were collected in the person of his pretended *hero*, they would find it very hard to admit that he had even one of them.

It is clear enough from what quiver these arrows came. From the first, Frontenac had set himself in opposition to the most influential of the Canadian clergy. When he came to the colony, their power in the government was still enormous, and even the most devout of his predecessors had been forced into conflict with them to defend the civil authority; but when Frontenac entered the strife, he brought into it an irritability, a jealous and exacting vanity, a love of rule, and a passion for having his own way, even in trifles, which made him the most exasperating of adversaries. Hence it was that many of the clerical party felt towards him a bitterness that was far from ending with his life.

The sentiment of a religion often survives its convictions. However heterodox in doctrine, he was still wedded to the observances of the Church, and practised them, under the ministration of the Récollets, with an assiduity that made full amends to his conscience for the vivacity with which he opposed the rest of the clergy. To the Récollets their patron was the most devout of men; to his ultramontane adversaries, he was an impious persecutor.

Frontenac's own acts and words best paint his character, and it is needless to enlarge upon it. What perhaps may be least forgiven him is the barbarity of the warfare that he waged, and the cruelties that he permitted. He had seen too many towns sacked to be much subject to the scruples of modern humanitarianism; yet he was no whit more ruthless than his times and his surroundings, and some of his contemporaries find fault with him for not allowing more Indian captives to be tortured. Many surpassed him in cruelty, none equalled him in capacity and vigor. When civilized enemies were once within his power, he treated them, according to their degree, with a chivalrous courtesy, or a generous kindness. If he was a hot and pertinacious foe, he was also a fast friend; and he excited love and hatred in about equal measure. His attitude towards public enemies was always proud and peremptory, yet his courage was guided by so clear a sagacity that he never was forced to recede from the position he had taken. Towards Indians, he was an admirable compound of sternness and conciliation. Of the immensity of his services to the colony there can be no doubt. He found it, under Denonville, in humiliation and terror; and he left it in honor, and almost in triumph.

In spite of Father Goyer, greatness must be denied him; but a more remarkable figure, in its bold and salient individuality and sharply marked light and shadow, is nowhere seen in American history.

CHAPTER XXVI

The Founding of Detroit
1694–1704

[A Half-Century of Conflict, CHAPTER II]

In the few years of doubtful peace that preceded Queen Anne's War, an enterprise was begun, which, nowise in accord with the wishes and expectations of those engaged in it, was destined to produce as its last result an American city.

Antoine de La Mothe-Cadillac commanded at Michilimackinac, whither Frontenac had sent him in 1694. This old mission of the Jesuits, where they had gathered the remnants of the lake tribes dispersed by the Iroquois at the middle of the seventeenth century, now savored little of its apostolic beginnings. It was the centre of the western fur-trade and the favorite haunt of the *coureurs de bois*. Brandy and squaws abounded, and according to the Jesuit Carheil, the spot where Marquette had labored was now a witness of scenes the most unedifying.

At Michilimackinac was seen a curious survival of Huron-Iroquois customs. The villages of the Hurons and Ottawas, which were side by side, separated only by a fence, were surrounded by a common enclosure of triple palisades, which, with the addition of loopholes for musketry, were precisely like those seen by Cartier at Hochelaga, and by Champlain in the Onondaga country. The dwellings which these defences enclosed were also after the old Huron-Iroquois pattern, — those long arched structures covered with bark which Brébeuf found by the shores of Matchedash Bay, and Jogues on the banks of the Mohawk. Besides the Indians, there was a French colony at the place, chiefly of fur-traders, lodged in log-cabins, roofed with cedar bark, and forming a street along the shore close to the palisaded villages of the Hurons and Ottawas. The fort, known as Fort Buade, stood at the head of the little bay.

The Hurons and Ottawas were thorough savages, though the Hurons retained the forms of Roman Catholic Christianity. This tribe, writes Cadillac, "are reduced to a very small number; and it is well for us that they are, for they are ill-disposed and mischievous, with a turn for intrigue and a capacity for large undertakings. Luckily, their power is not great; but as they cannot play the lion, they play the fox, and do their best to make trouble between us and our allies."

La Mothe-Cadillac [1] was a captain in the colony troops, and an admirer of the late governor, Frontenac, to whose policy he adhered, and whose prejudices he shared. He was amply gifted with the kind of intelligence that consists in quick observation, sharpened by an inveterate spirit of sarcasm, was energetic, enterprising, well instructed, and a bold and sometimes a visionary schemer, with a restless spirit, a nimble and biting wit, a Gascon impetuosity of temperament, and as much devotion as an officer of the King was forced to profess, coupled with small love of priests and an aversion to Jesuits. Carheil and Marest, missionaries of that order at Michilimackinac, were objects of his especial antipathy, which they fully returned. The two priests were impatient of a military commandant to whose authority they were in some small measure subjected; and they imputed to him the disorders which he did not, and perhaps could not, prevent. They were opposed also to the traffic in brandy, which was favored by Cadillac on the usual ground that it attracted the Indians, and so prevented the English from getting control of the fur-trade, — an argument which he reinforced by sanitary considerations based on the supposed unwholesomeness of the fish and smoked meat which formed the chief diet of Michilimackinac. "A little brandy after the meal," he says, with the solemnity of the learned Purgon, "seems necessary to cook the bilious meats and the crudities they leave in the stomach."

Cadillac calls Carheil, superior of the mission, the most passionate and domineering man he ever knew, and further declares that the Jesuit tried to provoke him to acts of violence, in order to make matter of accusation against him. If this was Carheil's aim, he was near succeeding. Once, in a dispute with the commandant on the brandy-

[1] He wrote his name as above. La Mothe-Cadillac came of a good family of Languedoc. His father, Jean de La Mothe, seigneur de Cadillac et de Launay, or Laumet, was a counsellor in the Parliament of Toulouse. After serving as lieutenant in the regiment of Clairembault, he went to Canada about the year 1683. He became skilled in managing Indians, made himself well acquainted with the coasts of New England, and strongly urged an attack by sea on New York and Boston as the only sure means of securing French ascendancy. He was always in opposition to the clerical party.

trade, he upbraided him sharply for permitting it; to which Cadillac replied that he only obeyed the orders of the court. The Jesuit rejoined that he ought to obey God, and not man, — "on which," says the commandant, "I told him that his talk smelt of sedition a hundred yards off, and begged that he would amend it. He told me that I gave myself airs that did not belong to me, holding his fist before my nose at the same time. I confess I almost forgot that he was a priest, and felt for a moment like knocking his jaw out of joint; but, thank God, I contented myself with taking him by the arm, pushing him out, and ordering him not to come back."

Such being the relations of the commandant and the Father Superior, it is not surprising to find the one complaining that he cannot get absolved from his sins, and the other painting the morals and manners of Michilimackinac in the blackest colors.

I have spoken elsewhere of the two opposing policies that divided Canada, — the policies of concentration and of expansion, on the one hand leaving the west to the keeping of the Jesuits, and confining the population to the borders of the St. Lawrence; on the other, the occupation of the interior of the continent by posts of war and trade. Through the force of events the latter view had prevailed; yet while the military chiefs of Canada could not but favor it, the Jesuits were unwilling to accept it, and various interests in the colony still opposed it openly or secretly. Frontenac had been its strongest champion, and Cadillac followed in his steps. It seemed to him that the time had come for securing the west for France.

The strait — *détroit* — which connects Lake Huron with Lake Erie was the most important of all the western passes. It was the key of the three upper lakes, with the vast countries watered by their tributaries, and it gave Canada her readiest access to the valley of the Mississippi. If the French held it, the English would be shut out from the northwest; if, as seemed likely, the English should seize it, the Canadian fur-trade would be ruined. The possession of it by the French would be a constant curb and menace to the Five Nations, as well as a barrier between those still formidable tribes and the western Indians, allies of Canada; and when the intended French establishment at the mouth of the Mississippi should be made, Detroit would be an indispensable link of communication between Canada and Louisiana.

Denonville had recognized the importance of the position, and it was by his orders that Greysolon Du Lhut, in 1686, had occupied it for a time, and built a picket fort near the site of Fort Gratiot.

It would be idle to imagine that the motives of Cadillac were wholly patriotic. Fur-trading interests were deeply involved in his plans, and bitter opposition was certain. The fur-trade, in its nature, was a constant breeder of discord. The people of Montreal would have the tribes come down every summer from the west and northwest and hold a fair under the palisades of their town. It is said that more than 400 French families lived wholly or in part by this home trade, and therefore regarded with deep jealousy the establishment of interior posts, which would forestall it. Again, every new western post would draw away trade from those already established, and every trading license granted to a company or an individual would rouse the animosity of those who had been licensed before. The prosperity of Detroit would be the ruin of Michilimackinac, and those whose interests centred at the latter post angrily opposed the scheme of Cadillac.

He laid his plans before Count de Maurepas by a characteristic memorial, apparently written in 1699. In this he proposed to gather all the tribes of the lakes at Detroit, civilize them and teach them French, "insomuch that from pagans they would become children of the Church, and therefore good subjects of the King." They will form, he continues, a considerable settlement, "strong enough to bring the English and the Iroquois to reason, or, with help from Montreal, to destroy both of them." Detroit, he adds, should be the seat of trade, which should not be permitted in the countries beyond it. By this regulation the intolerable glut of beaver-skins, which spoils the market, may be prevented. This proposed restriction of the beaver-trade to Detroit was enough in itself to raise a tempest against the whole scheme. "Cadillac well knows that he has enemies," pursues the memorial, "but he keeps on his way without turning or stopping for the noise of the puppies who bark after him."

Among the essential features of his plan was a well-garrisoned fort, and a church, served not by Jesuits alone, but also by Récollet friars and priests of the Missions Étrangères. The idea of this ecclesiastical partnership was odious to the Jesuits, who felt that the west was their proper field, and that only they had a right there. Another part of Cadillac's proposal pleased them no better. This was his plan of civilizing the Indians and teaching them to speak French; for it was the reproach of the Jesuit missions that they left the savage a savage still, and asked little of him but the practice of certain rites and the passive acceptance of dogmas to him incomprehensible.

"It is essential," says the memorial, "that in this matter of teaching the Indians our language the missionaries should act in good faith, and that his Majesty should have the goodness to impose his strictest orders upon them; for which there are several good reasons. The first and most stringent is that when members of religious orders or other ecclesiastics undertake anything, they never let it go. The second is that by not teaching French to the Indians they make themselves necessary [as interpreters] to the King and the governor. The third is that if all Indians spoke French, all kinds of ecclesiastics would be able to instruct them. This might cause them [the Jesuits] to lose some of the presents they get; for though these Reverend Fathers come here only for the glory of God, yet the one thing does not prevent the other," — meaning that God and Mammon may be served at once. "Nobody can deny that the priests own three quarters of Canada. From St. Paul's Bay to Quebec, there is nothing but the seigneury of Beauport that belongs to a private person. All the rest, which is the best part, belongs to the Jesuits or other ecclesiastics. The Upper Town of Quebec is composed of six or seven superb palaces belonging to Hospital Nuns, Ursulines, Jesuits, Récollets, Seminary priests, and the bishop. There may be some forty private houses, and even these pay rent to the ecclesiastics, which shows that *the one thing does not prevent the other.*" From this it will be seen that, in the words of one of his enemies, Cadillac "was not quite in the odor of sanctity."

"One may as well knock one's head against a wall," concludes the memorial, "as hope to convert the Indians in any other way [than that of civilizing them]; for thus far all the fruits of the missions consist in the baptism of infants who die before reaching the age of reason." This was not literally true, though the results of the Jesuit missions in the west had been meager and transient to a surprising degree.

Cadillac's plan of a settlement at Detroit was not at first received with favor by Callières, the governor; while the intendant Champigny, a fast friend of the Jesuits, strongly opposed it. By their order the chief inhabitants of Quebec met at the Château St. Louis, — Callières, Champigny, and Cadillac himself being present. There was a heated debate on the beaver-trade, after which the intendant commanded silence, explained the projects of Cadillac, and proceeded to oppose them. His first point was that the natives should not be taught French, because the Indian girls brought up at the Ursuline Convent led looser lives than the young squaws who had received no instruction, while it was much the same with the boys brought up at the Seminary.

"M. de Champigny," returned the sarcastic Cadillac, "does great honor to the Ursulines and the Seminary. It is true that some Indian women who have learned our language have lived viciously; but that is because their teachers were too stiff with them, and tried to make them nuns."

Champigny's position, as stated by his adversary, was that "all intimacy of the Indians with the French is dangerous and corrupting to their morals," and that their only safety lies in keeping them at a distance from the settlements. This was the view of the Jesuits, and there is much to be said in its favor; but it remains not the less true that conversion must go hand in hand with civilization, or it is a failure and a fraud.

Cadillac was not satisfied with the results of the meeting at the Château St. Louis, and he wrote to the minister: "You can never hope that this business will succeed if it is discussed here on the spot. Canada is a country of cabals and intrigues, and it is impossible to reconcile so many different interests." He sailed for France, apparently in the autumn of 1699, to urge his scheme at court. Here he had an interview with the colonial minister, Ponchartrain, to whom he represented the military and political expediency of his proposed establishment; and in a letter which seems to be addressed to La Touche, chief clerk in the Department of Marine and Colonies, he promised that the execution of his plan would insure the safety of Canada and the ruin of the British colonies. He asked for fifty soldiers and fifty Canadians to begin the work, to be followed in the next year by twenty or thirty families and by 200 picked men of various trades, sent out at the King's charge, along with priests of several communities, and nuns to attend the sick and teach the Indian girls. "I cannot tell you," continues Cadillac, "the efforts my enemies have made to deprive me of the honor of executing my project; but so soon as M. de Ponchartrain decides in its favor, the whole country will applaud it."

Ponchartrain accepted the plan, and Cadillac returned to Canada commissioned to execute it. Early in June, 1701, he left La Chine with 100 men in twenty-five canoes loaded with provisions, goods, munitions, and tools. He was accompanied by Alphonse de Tonty, brother of Henri de Tonty, the companion of La Salle, and by two half-pay lieutenants, Dugué and Chacornacle, together with a Jesuit and a Récollet. Following the difficult route of the Ottawa and Lake Huron, they reached their destination on the 24th of July, and built a picket fort sixty yards square, which by order of the governor they named Fort Ponchartrain. It stood near the west bank of the strait, about forty paces from the water. Thus was planted the germ of the city of Detroit.

Cadillac sent back Chacornacle with the report of what he had done, and a description of the country written in a strain of swelling and gushing rhetoric in singular contrast with his usual sarcastic utterances. "None but enemies of the truth," his letter concludes, "are enemies of this establishment, so necessary to the glory of the King, the progress of religion, and the destruction of the throne of Baal."

What he had, perhaps, still more at heart was making money out of it by the fur-trade. By command of the King a radical change had lately been made in this chief commerce of Canada, and the entire control of it had been placed in the hands of a company in which all Canadians might take shares. But as the risks were great and the conditions ill-defined, the number of subscribers was not much above 150; and the rest of the colony found themselves shut out from the trade, — to the ruin of some, and the injury of all.

All trade in furs was restricted to Detroit and Fort Frontenac, both of which were granted to the company, subject to be resumed by the King at his pleasure. The company was to repay the 80,000 francs which the expedition to Detroit had cost; and to this were added various other burdens. The King, however, was to maintain the garrison.

All the affairs of the company were placed in the hands of seven directors, who began immediately to compain that their burdens were too heavy, and to beg for more privileges; while an outcry against the privileges already granted rose from those who had not taken shares in the enterprise. Both in the company and out of it there was nothing but discontent. None were worse pleased than the two Jesuits Carheil and Marest, who saw their flocks at Michilimackinac, both Hurons and Ottawas, lured away to a new home at Detroit. Cadillac took a peculiar satisfaction in depriving Carheil of his converts, and in 1703 we find him writing to the minister Ponchartrain, that only twenty-five Hurons are left at Michilimackinac; and "I hope," he adds, "that in the autumn I shall pluck this last feather from his wing; and I am convinced that this obstinate priest will die in his parish without one parishioner to bury him."

If the Indians came to Detroit, the French would not come. Cadillac had asked for five or six families as the modest beginning of a settlement; but not one had appeared. The Indians, too, were angry because the company asked too much for its goods; while the company complained that a forbidden trade, fatal to its interests, went on through all the region of the upper lakes. It was easy to ordain a monopoly, but impossible to enforce it. The prospects of the new establishment were deplorable; and Cadillac lost no time in presenting his views of the situation to the court. "Detroit is good, or it is bad," he writes to Ponchartrain. "If it is good, it ought to be sustained, without allowing the people of Canada to deliberate any more about it. If it is bad, the court ought to make up its mind concerning it as soon as may be. I have said what I think. I have explained the situation. You have felt the need of Detroit, and its utility for the glory of God, the progress of religion, and the good of the colony. Nothing is left me to do but to imitate the governor of the Holy City, — take water, and wash my hands of it." His aim now appears. He says that if Detroit were made a separate government, and he were put at the head of it, its prospects would improve. "You may well believe that the company cares for nothing but to make a profit out of it. It only wants to have a storehouse and clerks; no officers, no troops, no inhabitants. Take this business in hand, Monseigneur, and I promise that in two years your Detroit shall be established of itself." He then informs the minister that as the company complain of losing money, he has told them that if they will make over their rights to him, he will pay them back all their past outlays. "I promise you," he informs Ponchartrain, "that if they accept my proposal and you approve it, I will make our Detroit flourish. Judge if it is agreeable to me to have to answer for my actions to five or six merchants [the directors of the company], who not long ago were blacking their masters' boots." He is scarcely more reserved as to the Jesuits. "I do what I can to make them my friends, but, impiety apart, one had better sin against God than against them; for in that case one gets one's pardon, whereas in the other the offence is never forgiven in this world, and perhaps never would be in the other, if their credit were as great there as it is here."

The letters of Cadillac to the court are unique. No governor of New France, not even the audacious Frontenac, ever wrote to a minister of Louis XIV with such off-hand freedom of language as this singular personage, — a mere captain in the colony troops; and to a more stable and balanced character it would have been impossible.

Cadillac's proposal was accepted. The company was required to abandon Detroit to him on his paying them the expenses they had incurred. Their monopoly was transferred to him; but as far as concerned beaver-skins, his trade was limited to 20,000 francs a year. The governor was ordered to give him as many soldiers as he might want, permit as many persons to settle at Detroit as might choose to do so, and provide missionaries. The minister exhorted him to quarrel no more with the Jesuits, or anybody else, to banish blasphemy and bad morals from the post, and not to offend the Five Nations.

The promised era of prosperity did not come. Detroit lingered on in a weak and troubled infancy, disturbed, as we shall see, by startling incidents. Its occupation by the French produced a noteworthy result. The Five Nations, filled with jealousy and alarm, appealed to the King of England for protection, and, the better to insure it, conveyed the whole country from Lake Ontario northward to Lake Superior, and westward as far as Chicago, "unto our souveraigne Lord King William the Third" and his heirs and successors forever. This territory is described in the deed as being about 800 miles long and 400 wide, and was claimed by the Five Nations as theirs by right of conquest. It of course included Detroit itself. The conveyance was drawn by the English authorities at Albany in a form to suit their purposes, and included terms of subjection and sovereignty which the signers could understand but imperfectly, if at all. The Five Nations gave away their land to no purpose. The French remained in undisturbed possession of Detroit. The English made no attempt to enforce their title, but they put the deed on file and used it long after, as the base of their claim to the region of the Lakes.

CHAPTER XXVII

Queen Anne's War
1703–1713

[*A Half-Century of Conflict*, CHAPTER III]

For untold ages Maine had been one unbroken forest, and it was so still. Only along the rocky seaboard or on the lower waters of one or two great rivers a few rough settlements had gnawed slight indentations into this wilderness of woods; and a little farther inland some dismal clearing around a blockhouse or stockade let in the sunlight to a soil that had lain in shadow time out of mind. This waste of savage vegetation survives, in some part, to this day, with the same prodigality of vital force, the same struggle for existence and mutual havoc that mark all organized beings, from men to mushrooms. Young seedlings in millions spring every summer from the black mould, rich with the decay of those that had preceded them, crowding, choking, and killing one another, perishing by their very abundance, — all but a scattered few, stronger than the rest, or more fortunate in position, which survive by blighting those about them. They in turn, as they grow, interlock their boughs, and repeat in a season or two the same process of mutual suffocation. The forest is full of lean saplings dead or dying with vainly stretching towards the light. Not one infant tree in a thousand lives to maturity; yet these survivors form an innumerable host, pressed together in struggling confusion, squeezed out of symmetry and robbed of normal development, as men are said to be in the level sameness of democratic society. Seen from above, their mingled tops spread in a sea of verdure basking in light; seen from below, all is shadow, through which spots of timid sunshine steal down among legions of lank, mossy trunks, toadstools and rank ferns, protruding roots, matted bushes, and rotting carcasses of fallen trees. A generation ago one might find here and there the rugged trunk of some great pine lifting its verdant spire above the undistinguished myriads of the forest. The woods of Maine had their aristocracy; but the axe of the woodman has laid them low, and these lords of the wilderness are seen no more.

The life and light of this grim solitude were in its countless streams and lakes, from little brooks stealing clear and cold under the alders, full of the small fry of trout, to the mighty arteries of the Penobscot and the Kennebec; from the great reservoir of Moosehead to a thousand nameless ponds shining in the hollow places of the forest.

It had and still has its beast of prey, — wolves, savage, cowardly, and mean; bears, gentle and mild compared to their grisly relatives of the Far West, vegetarians when they can do no better, and not without something grotesque and quaint in manners and behavior; sometimes, though rarely, the strong and sullen wolverine; frequently the lynx; and now and then the fierce and agile cougar.

The human denizens of this wilderness were no less fierce, and far more dangerous. These were the various tribes and sub-tribes of the Abenakis, whose villages were on the Saco, the Kennebec, the Penobscot, and the other great watercourses. Most of them had been converted by the Jesuits, and, as we have seen already, some had been persuaded to remove to Canada, like the converted Iroquois of Caughnawaga. The rest remained in their native haunts, where, under the direction of their missionaries, they could be used to keep the English settlements in check.

We know how busily they plied their tomahawks in William and Mary's War, and what havoc they made among the scattered settlements of the border. Another war with France was declared on the 4th of May, 1702, on which the Abenakis again assumed a threatening attitude. In June of the next year Dudley, governor of Massachusetts, called the chiefs of the various bands to a council at Casco. Here presently appeared the Norridgewocks from the Kennebec, the Penobscots and Androscoggins from the rivers that bear their names, the Penacooks from the Merrimac, and the Pequawkets from the Saco, all well armed, and daubed with ceremonial paint. The principal among them, gathered under a large tent, were addressed by Dudley in a conciliatory speech. Their orator replied that they wanted nothing but peace, and that their thoughts were as far from war as the sun was from the earth, — words which they duly confirmed by a belt of wampum. Presents were distributed among them and received with apparent satisfaction, while two of their principal chiefs, known as Captain Samuel and Captain Bomazeen, declared that several French missionaries had lately come among them to excite them against the English, but that they were "firm as mountains," and would remain so "as long as the sun and moon endured." They ended the meeting with dancing, singing, and whoops of joy, followed by a volley of musketry, answered by another from the English. It was discovered, however, that the Indians had loaded their guns with ball, intending, as the English believed, to murder Dudley and his attendants if they could have done so without danger to their chiefs, whom the governor had prudently kept about him. It was afterwards found, if we may believe a highly respectable member of the party, that 200 French and Indians were on their way, "resolved to seize the governor, council, and gentlemen, and then to sacrifice the inhabitants at pleasure;" but when they arrived, the English officials had been gone three days.

The French governor, Vaudreuil, says that about this time some of the Abenakis were killed or maltreated by Englishmen. It may have been so: desperadoes, drunk or sober, were not rare along the frontier; but Vaudreuil gives no particulars, and the only English outrage that appears on record at the time was the act of a gang of vagabonds who plundered the house of the younger Saint-Castin, where the town of Castine now stands. He was Abenaki by his mother; but he was absent when the attack took place, and the marauders seem to have shed no blood. Nevertheless, within six weeks after the Treaty of Casco, every unprotected farmhouse in Maine was in a blaze.

The settlements of Maine, confined to the southwestern corner of what is now the State of Maine, extended along the coast in a feeble and broken line from Kittery to Casco. Ten years of murderous warfare had almost ruined them. East of the village of Wells little was left except one or two forts and the so-called "garrisons," which were private houses pierced with loopholes and having an upper story projecting over the lower, so that the defenders could fire down on assailants battering the door or piling fagots against the walls. A few were fenced with palisades, as was the case with the house of Joseph Storer at the east end of Wells, where an overwhelming force of French and Indians had been gallantly repulsed in the summer of 1692. These fortified houses were, however, very rarely attacked, except by surprise and treachery. In case of alarm such of the inhabitants as found time took refuge in them with their families, and left their dwellings to the flames; for the first thought of the settler was to put his women and children beyond reach of the scalping-knife. There were several of these asylums in different parts of Wells; and without them the place must have been abandoned. In the little settlement of York, farther westward, there were five of them, which had saved a part of the inhabitants when the rest were surprised and massacred.

Wells was a long, straggling settlement, consisting at the beginning of William and Mary's War of about eighty houses and log-cabins,[1] strung at intervals along the north side of the rough track, known as the King's Road, which ran parallel to the sea. Behind the houses were rude, half-cleared pastures, and behind these again, the primeval forest. The cultivated land was on the south side of the road; in front of the houses, and beyond it, spread great salt-marshes, bordering the sea and haunted by innumerable game-birds.

The settlements of Maine were a dependency of Massachusetts, — a position that did not please their inhabitants, but which they accepted because they needed the help of their Puritan neighbors, from whom they differed widely both in their qualities and in their faults. The Indian wars that checked their growth had kept them in a condition more than half barbarous. They were a hard-working and hard-drinking race; for though tea and coffee were scarcely known, the land flowed with New England rum, which was ranked among the necessaries of life. The better sort could read and write in a bungling way; but many were wholly illiterate, and it was not till long after Queen Anne's War that the remoter settlements established schools, taught by poor students from Harvard or less competent instructors, and held at first in private houses or under sheds. The church at Wells had been burned by the Indians; and though the settlers were beggared by the war, they voted in town-meeting to build another. The new temple, begun in 1699, was a plain wooden structure thirty feet square. For want of money the windows long remained unglazed, the walls without plaster, and the floor without seats; yet services were duly held here under direction of the minister, Samuel Emery, to whom they paid £45 a year, half in provincial currency, and half in farm-produce and fire-wood.

In spite of these efforts to maintain public worship, they were far from being a religious community; nor were they a peaceful one. Gossip and scandal ran riot; social jealousies abounded; and under what seemed entire democratic equality, the lazy, drunken, and shiftless envied the industrious and thrifty. Wells was infested, moreover, by several "frightfully turbulent women," as the chronicle styles them, from

[1] Bourne *History of Wells and Kennebunk*. [There were, however, few if any log cabins on the Maine frontier this early.]

whose rabid tongues the minister himself did not always escape; and once, in its earlier days, the town had been indicted for not providing a ducking-stool to correct these breeders of discord.

Judicial officers were sometimes informally chosen by popular vote, and sometimes appointed by the governor of Massachusetts from among the inhabitants. As they knew no law, they gave judgment according to their own ideas of justice, and their sentences were oftener wanting in wisdom than in severity. Until after 1700 the county courts met by beat of drum at some of the primitive inns or taverns with which the frontier abounded.

At Wells and other outlying and endangered hamlets life was still exceedingly rude. The log-cabins of the least thrifty were no better furnished than Indian wigwams. The house of Edmond Littlefield, reputed the richest man in Wells, consisted of two bedrooms and a kitchen, which last served a great variety of uses, and was supplied with a table, a pewter pot, a frying-pan, and a skillet; but no chairs, cups, saucers, knives, forks, or spoons. In each of the two bedrooms there was a bed, a blanket, and a chest. Another village notable — Ensign John Barrett — was better provided, being the possessor of two beds, two chests and a box, four pewter dishes, four earthen pots, two iron pots, seven trays, two buckets, some pieces of wooden-ware, a skillet, and a frying-pan. In the inventory of the patriarchal Francis Littlefield, who died in 1712, we find the exceptional items of one looking-glass, two old chairs, and two old books. Such of the family as had no bed slept on hay or straw, and no provision for the toilet is recorded.

On the 10th of August, 1703, these rugged borderers were about their usual callings, unconscious of danger, — the women at their household work, the men in the fields or on the more distant salt-marshes. The wife of Thomas Wells had reached the time of her confinement, and her husband had gone for a nurse. Some miles east of Wells's cabin lived Stephen Harding, — hunter, blacksmith, and tavern-keeper, a sturdy, good-natured man, who loved the woods, and whose frequent hunting trips sometimes led him nearly to the White Mountains. Distant gunshots were heard from the westward, and his quick eye presently discovered Indians approaching, on which he told his frightened wife to go with their infant to a certain oak-tree beyond the creek while he waited to learn whether the strangers were friends or foes.

That morning several parties of Indians had stolen out of the dismal woods behind the houses and farms of Wells, and approached different dwellings of the far-extended settlement at about the same time. They entered the cabin of Thomas Wells, where his wife lay in the pains of childbirth, and murdered her and her two small children. At the same time they killed Joseph Sayer, a neighbor of Wells, with all his family.

Meanwhile Stephen Harding, having sent his wife and child to a safe distance, returned to his blacksmith's shop, and, seeing nobody, gave a defiant whoop; on which four Indians sprang at him from the bushes. He escaped through a back-door of the shop, eluded his pursuers, and found his wife and child in a cornfield, where the woman had fainted with fright. They spent the night in the woods, and on the next day, after a circuit of nine miles, reached the palisaded house of Joseph Storer.

They found the inmates in distress and agitation. Storer's daughter Mary, a girl of eighteen, was missing. The Indians had caught her, and afterwards carried her prisoner to Canada. Samuel Hill and his family were captured, and the younger children butchered. But it is useless to record the names and fate of the sufferers. Thirty-nine in all, chiefly women and children, were killed or carried off, and then the Indians disappeared as quickly and silently as they had come, leaving many of the houses in flames.

This raid upon Wells was only part of a combined attack on all the settlements from that place to Casco. Those eastward of Wells had been, as we have seen, abandoned in the last war, excepting the forts and fortified houses; but the inhabitants, reassured, no doubt, by the Treaty of Casco, had begun to return. On this same day, the 10th of August, they were startled from their security. A band of Indians mixed with Frenchmen fell upon the settlements about the stone fort near the Falls of the Saco, killed eleven persons, captured twenty-four, and vainly attacked the fort itself. Others surprised the settlers at a place called Spurwink, and killed or captured twenty-two. Others, again, destroyed the huts of the fishermen at Cape Porpoise, and attacked the fortified house at Winter Harbor, the inmates of which, after a brave resistance, were forced to capitulate. The settlers at Scarborough were also in a fortified house, where they made a long and obstinate defence till help at last arrived. Nine families were settled at Purpooduck Point, near the present city of Portland. They had no place of refuge, and the men being, no doubt, fishermen, were all absent, when the Indians burst into the hamlet, butchered twenty-five women and children, and carried off eight.

The fort at Casco, or Falmouth, was held by Major March with thirty-six men. He had no thought of danger, when three well-known chiefs from Norridgewock appeared with a white flag, and asked for an interview. As they seemed to be alone and unarmed, he went to meet them, followed by two or three soldiers and accompanied by two old men named Phippeny and Kent, inhabitants of the place. They had hardly reached the spot when the three chiefs drew hatchets from under a kind of mantle which they wore and sprang upon them, while other Indians, ambushed near by, leaped up and joined in the attack. The two old men were killed at once; but March, who was noted for strength and agility, wrenched a hatchet from one of his assailants, and kept them all at bay till Sergeant Hook came to his aid with a file of men and drove them off.

They soon reappeared, burned the deserted cabins in the neighborhood, and beset the garrison in numbers that continually increased, till in a few days the entire force that had been busied in ravaging the scattered settlements was gathered around the place. It consisted of about 500 Indians of several tribes, and a few Frenchmen under an officer named Beaubassin. Being elated with past successes, they laid siege to the fort, sheltering themselves under a steep bank by the waterside and burrowing their way towards the rampart. March could not dislodge them, and they continued their approaches till the third day, when Captain Southack, with the Massachusetts armed vessel known as the *Province Galley*, sailed into the harbor, recaptured three small vessels that the Indians had taken along the coast, and destroyed a great number of their canoes, on which they gave up their enterprise and disappeared.

Such was the beginning of Queen Anne's War. These attacks were due less to the Abenakis than to the French who set them on. "Monsieur de Vaudreuil," writes the Jesuit historian Charlevoix, "formed a party of these savages, to whom he joined some Frenchmen under the direction of the Sieur de Beaubassin, when they effected some ravages of no great consequence; they killed, however, about three hundred men." This last statement is doubly incorrect. The whole number of persons killed and carried off during the August attacks did not much exceed 160; and these were of both sexes and all ages, from octogenarians to newborn infants. The able-bodied men among them were few, as most of the attacks were made upon unprotected houses in the absence of the head of the family; and the only fortified place captured was the garrison-house at Winter Harbor, which surrendered on terms of capitulation. The instruments of this ignoble warfare and the revolting atrocities that accompanied it were all, or nearly all, converted Indians of the missions. Charlevoix has no word of disapproval for it, and seems to regard its partial success as a gratifying one so far as it went.

One of the objects was, no doubt, to check the progress of the English settlements; but, pursues Charlevoix, "the essential point was to commit the Abenakis in such a manner that they could not draw back." This object was constantly kept in view. The French claimed at this time that the territory of Acadia reached as far westward as the Kennebec, which therefore formed, in their view, the boundary between the rival nations, and they trusted in the Abenakis to defend this assumed line of demarcation. But the Abenakis sorely needed English guns, knives, hatchets, and kettles, and nothing but the utmost vigilance could prevent them from coming to terms with those who could supply their necessities. Hence the policy of the French authorities on the frontier of New England was the opposite of their policy on the frontier of New York. They left the latter undisturbed, lest by attacking the Dutch and English settlers they should stir up the Five Nations to attack Canada; while, on the other hand, they constantly spurred the Abenakis against New England, in order to avert the dreaded event of their making peace with her.

The attack on Wells, Casco, and the intervening settlements was followed by murders and depredations that lasted through the autumn and extended along 200 miles of frontier. Thirty Indians attacked the village of Hampton, killed the Widow Mussey, a famous Quakeress, and then fled to escape pursuit. At Black Point nineteen men going to their work in the meadows were ambushed by 200 Indians, and all but one were shot or captured. The fort was next attacked. It was garrisoned by eight men under Lieutenant Wyatt, who stood their ground for some time, and then escaped by means of a sloop in the harbor. At York the wife and children of Arthur Brandon were killed, and the Widow Parsons and her daughter carried off. At Berwick the Indians attacked the fortified house of Andrew Neal, but were repulsed with the loss of nine killed and many wounded, for which they revenged themselves by burning alive Joseph Ring, a prisoner whom they had taken. Early in February a small party of them hovered about the fortified house of Joseph Bradley at Haverhill, till, seeing the gate open and nobody on the watch, they rushed in. The woman of the house was boiling soap, and in her desperation she snatched up the kettle and threw the contents over them with such effect that one of them, it is said, was scalded to death. The man who should have been on the watch was killed, and several persons were captured, including the woman. It was the second time that she had been a prisoner in Indian hands. Half starved and bearing a heavy load, she followed her captors in their hasty retreat towards Canada. After a time she was safely delivered of an infant in the midst of the winter forest; but the child pined for want of sustenance, and the Indians hastened its death by throwing hot coals into its mouth when it cried. The astonishing vitality of the woman carried her to the end of the frightful journey. A Frenchman bought her from the Indians, and she was finally ransomed by her husband.

By far the most dangerous and harassing attacks were those of small parties skulking under the edge of the forest, or lying hidden for days together, watching their opportunity to murder unawares, and vanishing when they had done so. Against such an enemy there was no defence. The Massachusetts government sent a troop of horse to Portsmouth, and another to Wells. These had the advantage of rapid movement in case of alarm along the roads and forest-paths from settlement to settlement; but once in the woods, their horses were worse than useless, and they could only fight on foot. Fighting, however, was rarely possible; for on reaching the scene of action they found nothing but mangled corpses and burning houses.

The best defence was to take the offensive. In September Governor Dudley sent 360 men to the upper Saco, the haunt of the Pequawket tribe; but the place was deserted. Major, now Colonel, March soon after repeated the attempt, killing six Indians, and capturing as many more. The General Court offered £40 for every Indian scalp, and one Captain Tyng, in consequence, surprised an Indian village in midwinter and brought back five of these disgusting trophies. In the spring of 1704 word came from Albany that a band of French Indians had built a fort and planted corn at Coos meadows, high up the river Connecticut. On this, one Caleb Lyman with five friendly Indians, probably Mohegans, set out from Northampton, and after a long march through the forest, surprised, under cover of a thunderstorm, a wigwam containing nine warriors, — bound, no doubt, against the frontier. They killed seven of them; and this was all that was done at present in the way of reprisal or prevention.

The murders and burnings along the borders were destined to continue with little variety and little interruption during ten years. It was a repetition of what the pedantic Cotton Mather calls *Decennium luctuosum*, or the "woeful decade" of William and Mary's War. The wonder is that the outlying settlements were not abandoned. These ghastly, insidious, and ever-present dangers demanded a more obstinate courage than the hottest battle in the open field.

One curious frontier incident may be mentioned here, though it did not happen till towards the end of the war. In spite of poverty, danger, and tribulation, marrying and giving in marriage did not cease among the sturdy borderers; and on a day in September there was a notable wedding feast at the palisaded house of John Wheelwright, one of the chief men of Wells. Elisha Plaisted was to espouse Wheelwright's daughter Hannah, and many guests were assembled, some from Portsmouth, and even beyond it. Probably most of them came in sailboats; for the way by land was full of peril, especially on the road from York, which ran through dense woods, where Indians often waylaid the traveller. The bridegroom's father was present with the rest. It was a concourse of men in homespun, and women and girls in such improvised finery as their poor resources could supply; possibly, in default of better, some wore nightgowns, more or less disguised, over their daily dress, as happened on similar occasions half a century later among the frontiersmen of West Virginia. After an evening of rough merriment and gymnastic dancing, the guests lay down to sleep under the roof of their host or in adjacent barns and sheds. When morning came, and they were preparing to depart, it was found that two horses were missing; and not doubting that they had strayed away, three young men — Sergeant Tucker, Joshua Downing, and Isaac Cole — went to find them. In a few minutes several gunshots were heard. The three young men did not return. Downing and Cole were killed, and Tucker was wounded and made prisoner.

Believing that, as usual, the attack came from some small scalping-party, Elisha Plaisted and eight or ten more threw themselves on the horses that stood saddled before the house, and galloped across the fields in the direction of the firing; while others ran to cut off the enemy's retreat. A volley was presently heard, and several of the party were seen running back towards the house. Elisha Plaisted and his companions had fallen into an ambuscade of two hundred Indians. One or more of them were shot, and the unfortunate bridegroom was captured. The distress of his young wife, who was but eighteen, may be imagined.

Two companies of armed men in the pay of Massachusetts were then in Wells, and some of them had come to the wedding. Seventy marksmen went to meet the Indians, who ensconced themselves in the edge of the forest, whence they could not be dislodged. There was some desultory firing, and one of the combatants was killed on each side, after which the whites gave up the attack, and Lieutenant Banks went forward with a flag of truce, in the hope of ransoming the prisoners. He was met by six chiefs, among whom were two noted Indians of his acquaintance, Bomazeen and Captain Nathaniel. They well knew that the living Plaisted was worth more than his scalp; and though they would not come to terms at once, they promised to meet the English at Richmond's Island in a few days and give up both him and Tucker on payment of a sufficient ransom. The flag of truce was respected, and Banks came back safe, bringing a hasty note to the elder Plaisted from his captive son. This note now lies before me, and it runs thus, in the dutiful formality of the olden time:—

> SIR, — I am in the hands of a great many Indians, with which there is six captains. They say that what they will have for me is 50 pounds, and thirty pounds for Tucker, my fellow prisoner, in good goods, as broadcloth, some provisions, some tobacco pipes, Pomisstone [pumice-stone], stockings, and a little of all things. If you will, come to Richmond's Island in 5 days at farthest, for here is 200 Indians, and they belong to Canada.
>
> If you do not come in 5 days, you will not see me, for Captain Nathaniel the Indian will not stay no longer, for the Canada Indians is not willing for to sell me. Pray, Sir, don't fail, for they have given me one day, for the days were but 4 at first. Give my kind love to my dear wife. This from your dutiful son till death,
>
> ELISHA PLAISTED

The alarm being spread and a sufficient number of men mustered, they set out to attack the enemy and recover the prisoners by force; but not an Indian could be found.

Bomazeen and Captain Nathaniel were true to the rendezvous; in due time Elisha Plaisted was ransomed and restored to his bride.

CHAPTER XXVIII

The Sack of Deerfield

1704

[A Half-Century of Conflict, CHAPTER IV]

About midwinter the governor of Canada sent another large war-party against the New England border. The object of attack was an unoffending hamlet, that from its position could never be a menace to the French, and the destruction of which could profit them nothing. The aim of the enterprise was not military, but political. "I have sent no war-party towards Albany," writes Vaudreuil, "because we must do nothing that might cause a rupture between us and the Iroquois; but we must keep things astir in the direction of Boston, or else the Abenakis will declare for the English." In short, the object was fully to commit these savages to hostility against New England, and convince them at the same time that the French would back their quarrel.[1]

The party consisted, according to French accounts, of fifty Canadians and 200 Abenakis and Caughnawagas, — the latter of whom, while trading constantly with Albany, were rarely averse to a raid against Massachusetts or New Hampshire. The command was given to the younger Hertel de Rouville, who was accompanied by four of his brothers. They began their march in the depth of winter, journeyed nearly 300 miles on snow-shoes through the forest, and approached their destination on the afternoon of 28 February, 1704. It was the village of Deerfield, which then formed the extreme northwestern frontier of Massachusetts, — its feeble neighbor, the infant settlement of Northfield, a little higher up the Connecticut, having been abandoned during the last war. Rouville halted his followers at a place now called Petty's Plain, two miles from the village; and here, under the shelter of a pine forest, they all lay hidden, shivering with cold, — for they dared not make fires, — and hungry as wolves, for their provisions were spent. Though

[1] Vaudreuil au Ministre, 14 Nov. 1703, 3 Apr., 17 Nov. 1704.

their numbers, by the lowest account, were nearly equal to the whole population of Deerfield, — men, women, and children, — they had no thought of an open attack, but trusted to darkness and surprise for an easy victory.

Deerfield stood on a plateau above the river meadows, and the houses — forty-one in all — were chiefly along the road towards the villages of Hadley and Hatfield, a few miles distant. In the middle of the place, on a rising ground called Meeting-house Hill, was a small square wooden meeting-house. This, with about fifteen private houses, besides barns and sheds, was enclosed by a fence of palisades eight feet high, flanked by "mounts," or blockhouses, at two or more of the corners. The four sides of this palisaded enclosure, which was called the fort, measured in all no less than 202 rods, and within it lived some of the principal inhabitants of the village, of which it formed the centre or citadel. Chief among its inmates was John Williams, the minister, a man of character and education, who, after graduating at Harvard, had come to Deerfield when it was still suffering under the ruinous effects of King Philip's War, and entered on his ministry with a salary of sixty pounds in depreciated New England currency, payable, not in money, but in wheat, Indian-corn, and pork. His parishioners built him a house, he married, and had now eight children, one of whom was absent with friends at Hadley. His next neighbor was Benoni Stebbins, sergeant in the county militia, who lived a few rods from the meeting-house. About fifty yards distant, and near the northwest angle of the enclosure, stood the house of Ensign John Sheldon, a framed building, one of the largest in the village, and, like that of Stebbins, made bullet-proof by a layer of bricks between the outer and inner sheathing, while its small windows and its projecting upper story also helped to make it defensible.

The space enclosed by the palisade, though much too large for effective defence, served in time of alarm as an asylum for the inhabitants outside, whose houses were scattered, — some on the north towards the hidden enemy, and some on the south towards Hadley and Hatfield. Among those on the south side was that of the militia captain, Jonathan Wells, which had a palisade of its own, and, like the so-called fort, served as an asylum for the neighbors.

These private fortified houses were sometimes built by the owners alone, though more often they were the joint work of the owners and of the inhabitants, to whose safety they contributed. The palisade fence that enclosed the central part of the village was made under a vote of the town, each inhabitant being required to do his share; and as they were greatly impoverished by the last war, the General Court of the province remitted for a time a part of their taxes in consideration of a work which aided the general defence.

Down to the Peace of Ryswick the neighborhood had been constantly infested by scalping-parties, and once the village had been attacked by a considerable force of French and Indians, who were beaten off. Of late there had been warnings of fresh disturbance. Lord Cornbury, governor of New York, wrote that he had heard through spies that Deerfield was again to be attacked, and a message to the same effect came from Peter Schuyler, who had received intimations of the danger from Mohawks lately on a visit to their Caughnawaga relatives. During the autumn the alarm was so great that the people took refuge within the palisades, and the houses of the enclosure were crowded with them; but the panic had now subsided, and many, though not all, had returned to their homes. They were reassured by the presence of twenty volunteers from the villages below, whom, on application from the minister, Williams, the General Court had sent as a garrison to Deerfield, where they were lodged in the houses of the villagers. On the night when Hertel de Rouville and his band lay hidden among the pines there were in all the settlement a little less than 300 souls, of whom 268 were inhabitants, twenty were yeomen soldiers of the garrison, two were visitors from Hatfield, and three were negro slaves. They were of all ages, — from the Widow Allison, in her eighty-fifth year, to the infant son of Deacon French, aged four weeks.

Heavy snows had lately fallen and buried the clearings, the meadow, and the frozen river to the depth of full three feet. On the northwestern side the drifts were piled nearly to the top of the palisade fence, so that it was no longer an obstruction to an active enemy.

As the afternoon waned, the sights and sounds of the little border hamlet were, no doubt, like those of any other rustic New England village at the end of a winter day, — an ox sledge creaking on the frosty snow as it brought in the last load of firewood, boys in homespun snowballing one another in the village street, farmers feeding their horses and cattle in the barns, a matron drawing a pail of water with the help of one of those long well-sweeps still used in some remote districts, or a girl bringing a pail of milk from the cow-shed. In the houses, where one room served as kitchen, dining-room, and parlor, the housewife cooked the evening meal, children sat at their bowls of mush and milk, and the men of the family, their day's work over, gathered about the fire, while perhaps some village coquette sat in the corner with fingers busy at the spinning-wheel, and ears intent on the stammered wooings of her rustic lover. Deerfield kept early hours, and it is likely that by nine o'clock all were in their beds. There was a patrol inside the palisade, but there was little discipline among these extemporized soldiers; the watchers grew careless as the frosty night went on; and it is said that towards morning they, like the villagers, betook themselves to their beds.

Rouville and his men, savage with hunger, lay shivering under the pines till about two hours before dawn; then, leaving their packs and their snow-shoes behind, they moved cautiously towards their prey. There was a crust on the snow strong enough to bear their weight, though not to prevent a rustling noise as it crunched under the feet of so many men. It is said that from time to time Rouville commanded a halt, in order that the sentinels, if such there were, might mistake the distant sound for rising and falling gusts of wind. In any case, no alarm was given till they had mounted the palisade and dropped silently into the unconscious village. Then with one accord they screeched the war-whoop, and assailed the doors of the houses with axes and hatchets.

The hideous din startled the minister, Williams, from his sleep. Half-wakened, he sprang out of bed, and saw dimly a crowd of savages bursting through the shattered door. He shouted to two soldiers who were lodged in the house; and then, with more valor than discretion, snatched a pistol that hung at the head of the bed, cocked it, and snapped it at the breast of the foremost Indian, who proved to be a Caughnawaga chief. It missed fire, or Williams would, no doubt, have been killed on the spot. Amid the screams of his terrified children, three of the party seized him and bound him fast; for they came well provided with cords, since prisoners had a market value. Nevertheless, in the first fury of their attack they dragged to the door and murdered two of the children and a negro woman called Parthena, who was probably their nurse. In an upper room lodged a young man named Stoddard, who had time to snatch a cloak, throw himself out of the window, climb the palisade, and escape in the darkness. Half-naked as he was, he made his way over the snow to Hatfield, binding his bare feet with strips torn from the cloak.

They kept Williams shivering in his shirt for an hour while a frightful uproar of yells, shrieks, and gunshots sounded from without. At length they permitted him, his wife, and five remaining children to dress themselves. Meanwhile the Indians and their allies burst into most of the houses, killed such of the men as resisted, butchered some of the women and children, and seized and bound the rest. Some of the villagers escaped in the confusion, like Stoddard, and either fled half dead with cold towards Hatfield, or sought refuge in the fortified house of Jonathan Wells.

The house of Stebbins, the minister's next neighbor, had not been attacked so soon as the rest, and the inmates had a little time for preparation. They consisted of Stebbins himself, with his wife and five children, David Hoyt, Joseph Catlin, Benjamin Church, a namesake of the old Indian fighter of Philip's War, and three other men, — probably refugees who had brought their wives and families within the palisaded enclosure for safety. Thus the house contained seven men, four or five women, and a considerable number of children. Though the walls were bullet-proof, it was not built for defence. The men, however, were well supplied with guns, powder, and lead, and they seem to have found some means of barricading the windows. When the enemy tried to break in, they drove them back with loss. On this, the French and Indians gathered in great numbers before the house, showered bullets upon it, and tried to set it on fire. They were again repulsed, with the loss of several killed and wounded; among the former a Caughnawaga chief, and among the latter a French officer. Still the firing continued. If the assailants had made a resolute assault, the defenders must have been overpowered; but to risk lives in open attack was contrary to every maxim of forest warfare. The women in the house behaved with great courage, and moulded bullets, which the men shot at the enemy. Stebbins was killed outright, and Church was wounded, as was also the wife of David Hoyt. At length most of the French and Indians, disgusted with the obstinacy of the defence, turned their attention to other quarters; though some kept up their fire under cover of the meeting-house and another building within easy range of gunshot.

This building was the house of Ensign John Sheldon, already mentioned. The Indians had had some difficulty in mastering it; for the door being of thick oak plank, studded with nails of wrought iron and well barred, they could not break it open. After a time, however, they hacked a hole in it, through which they fired and killed Mrs. Sheldon as she sat on the edge of a bed in a lower room. Her husband, a man of great resolution, seems to have been absent. Their son John, with Hannah his wife, jumped from an upper chamber window. The young woman sprained her ankle in the fall, and lay helpless, but begged her husband to run to Hatfield for aid, which he did, while she remained a prisoner. The Indians soon got in at a back door, seized Mercy Sheldon, a little girl of two years, and dashed out her brains on the door-stone.

Her two brothers and her sister Mary, a girl of sixteen, were captured. The house was used for a short time as a depot for prisoners, and here also was brought the French officer wounded in the attack on the Stebbins house. A family tradition relates that as he lay in great torment he begged for water, and that it was brought him by one of the prisoners, Mrs. John Catlin, whose husband, son, and infant grandson had been killed, and who, nevertheless, did all in her power to relieve the sufferings of the wounded man. Probably it was in recognition of this charity that when the other prisoners were led away, Mrs. Catlin was left behind. She died of grief a few weeks later.

The sun was scarcely an hour high when the miserable drove of captives was conducted across the river to the foot of a mountain or high hill. Williams and his family were soon compelled to follow, and his house was set on fire. As they led him off he saw that other houses within the palisade were burning, and that all were in the power of the enemy except that of his neighbor Stebbins, where the gallant defenders still kept their assailants at bay. Having collected all their prisoners, the main body of the French and Indians began to withdraw towards the pine forest, where they had left their packs and snow-shoes, and to prepare for a retreat before the country should be roused, first murdering in cold blood Marah Carter, a little girl of five years, whom they probably thought unequal to the march. Several parties, however, still lingered in the village, firing on the Stebbins house, killing cattle, hogs, and sheep, and gathering such plunder as the place afforded.

Early in the attack, and while it was yet dark, the light of burning houses, reflected from the fields of snow, had been seen at Hatfield, Hadley, and Northampton. The alarm was sounded through the slumbering hamlets, and parties of men mounted on farm-horses, with saddles or without, hastened to the rescue, not doubting that the fires were kindled by Indians. When the sun was about two hours high, between thirty and forty of them were gathered at the fortified house of Jonathan Wells, at the southern end of the village. The houses of this neighborhood were still standing, and seem not to have been attacked, — the stubborn defence of the Stebbins house having apparently prevented the enemy from pushing much beyond the palisaded enclosure. The house of Wells was full of refugee families. A few Deerfield men here joined the horsemen from the lower towns, as also did four or five of the yeoman soldiers who had escaped the fate of most of their comrades. The horsemen left their horses within Wells's fence; he himself took the lead, and the whole party rushed in together at the southern gate of the palisaded enclosure, drove out the plunderers, and retook a part of their plunder. The assailants of the Stebbins house, after firing at it for three hours, were put to flight, and those of its male occupants who were still alive joined their countrymen, while the women and children ran back for harborage to the house of Wells.

Wells and his men, now upwards of fifty, drove the flying enemy more than a mile across the river meadows, and ran in headlong pursuit over the crusted snow, killing a considerable number. In the eagerness of the chase many threw off their overcoats, and even their jackets. Wells saw the danger, and vainly called on them to stop. Their blood was up, and most of them were young and inexperienced.

Meanwhile the firing at the village had been heard by Rouville's main body, who had already begun their retreat northward. They turned back to support their comrades, and hid themselves under the bank of the river till the pursuers drew near, when they gave them a close volley and rushed upon them with the war-whoop. Some of the English were shot down, and the rest driven back. There was no panic. "We retreated," says Wells, "facing about and firing." When they reached the palisade they made a final stand, covering by their fire such of their comrades as had fallen within range of musket-shot, and thus saving them from the scalping-knife. The French did not try to dislodge them. Nine of them had been killed, several were wounded, and one was captured.

The number of English carried off prisoners was 111, and the number killed was according to one list forty-seven, and according to another fifty-three, the latter including some who were smothered in the cellars of their burning houses. The names, and in most cases the ages, of both captives and slain are preserved. Those who escaped with life and freedom were, by the best account, 137. An official tabular statement, drawn up on the spot, sets the number of houses burned at seventeen. The house of the town clerk, Thomas French, escaped, as before mentioned, and the town records, with other papers in his charge, were saved. The meeting-house also was left standing. The house of Sheldon was hastily set on fire by the French and Indians when their rear was driven out of the village by Wells and his men; but the fire was extinguished, and "the Old Indian House," as it was called, stood till the year 1849. Its door, deeply scarred with hatchets, and with a hole cut near the middle, is still preserved in the Memorial Hall at Deerfield.

Vaudreuil wrote to the minister, Ponchartrain, that the French lost two or three killed, and twenty or twenty-one wounded, Rouville himself being among the latter. This cannot include the Indians, since there is proof that the enemy left behind a considerable number of their dead. Wherever resistance was possible, it had been of the most prompt and determined character.

Long before noon the French and Indians were on their northward march with their train of captives. More armed men came up from the settlements below, and by midnight about eighty were gathered at the ruined village. Couriers had been set to rouse the country, and before evening of the next day (the first of March) the force at Deerfield was increased to two hundred and fifty; but a thaw and a warm rain had set in, and as few of the men had snow-shoes, pursuit was out of the question. Even could the agile savages and their allies have been overtaken, the probable consequence would have been the murdering of the captives to prevent their escape.

In spite of the foul blow dealt upon it, Deerfield was not abandoned. Such of its men as were left were taken as soldiers into the pay of the province, while the women and children were sent to the villages below. A small garrison was also stationed at the spot, under command of Captain Jonathan Wells, and thus the village held its ground till the storm of war should pass over.

We have seen that the minister, Williams, with his wife and family, were led from their burning house across the river to the foot of the mountain, where the crowd of terrified and disconsolate captives — friends, neighbors, and relatives — were already gathered. Here they presently saw the fight in the meadow, and were told that if their countrymen attempted a rescue, they should all be put to death. "After this," writes Williams, "we went up the mountain, and saw the smoke of the fires in town, and beheld the awful desolation of Deerfield; and before we marched any farther they killed a sucking child of the English."

The French and Indians marched that afternoon only four or five miles, — to Greenfield meadows, — where they stopped to encamp, dug away the snow, laid spruce-boughs on the ground for beds, and bound fast such of the prisoners as seemed able to escape. The Indians then held a carousal on some liquor they had found in the village, and in their drunken rage murdered a negro man belonging to Williams. In spite of their precautions, Joseph Alexander, one of the prisoners, escaped during the night, at which they were greatly incensed; and

Rouville ordered Williams to tell his companions in misfortune that if any more of them ran off, the rest should be burned alive.[2]

The prisoners were the property of those who had taken them. Williams had two masters, one of the three who had seized him having been shot in the attack on the house of Stebbins. His principal owner was a surly fellow who would not let him speak to the other prisoners; but as he was presently chosen to guard the rear, the minister was left in the hands of his other master, who allowed him to walk beside his wife and help her on the way. Having borne a child a few weeks before, she was in no condition for such a march, and felt that her hour was near. Williams speaks of her in the strongest terms of affection. She made no complaint, and accepted her fate with resignation. "We discoursed," he says, "of the happiness of those who had God for a father and friend, as also that it was our reasonable duty quietly to submit to his will." Her thoughts were for her remaining children, whom she commended to her husband's care. Their intercourse was short. The Indian who had gone to the rear of the train soon returned, separated them, ordered Williams to the front, "and so made me take a last farewell of my dear wife, the desire of my eyes and companion in many mercies and afflictions." They came soon after to Green River, a stream then about knee-deep, and so swift that the water had not frozen. After wading it with difficulty, they climbed a snow-covered hill beyond. The minister, with strength almost spent, was permitted to rest a few moments at the top; and as the other prisoners passed by in turn, he questioned each for news of his wife. He was not left long in suspense. She had fallen from weakness in fording the stream, but gained her feet again, and, drenched in the icy current, struggled to the farther bank, when the savage who owned her, finding that she could not climb the hill, killed her with one stroke of his hatchet. Her body was left on the snow till a few of her townsmen, who had followed the trail, found it a day or two after, carried it back to Deerfield, and buried it in the churchyard.

On the next day the Indians killed an infant and a little girl of eleven years; on the day following, Friday, they tomahawked a woman, and on Saturday four others. This apparent cruelty was in fact a kind of mercy. The victims could not keep up with the party, and the death-blow saved them from a lonely and lingering death from cold and starvation. Some of the children, when spent with the march, were carried on the backs of their owners, — partly, perhaps, through kindness, and partly because every child had its price.

[2] John Williams *The Redeemed Captive*.

On the fourth day of the march they came to the mouth of West River, which enters the Connecticut a little above the present town of Brattleboro. Some of the Indians were discontented with the distribution of the captives, alleging that others had got more than their share, on which the whole troop were mustered together, and some changes of ownership were agreed upon. At this place dog-trains and sledges had been left, and these served to carry their wounded, as well as some of the captive children. Williams was stripped of the better part of his clothes, and others given him instead, so full of vermin that they were a torment to him through all the journey. The march now continued with pitiless speed up the frozen Connecticut, where the recent thaw had covered the ice with slush and water ankle-deep.

On Sunday they made a halt, and the minister was permitted to preach a sermon from the text, "Hear, all people, and behold my sorrow: my virgins and my young men are gone into captivity." Then amid the ice, the snow, the forest, and the savages, his forlorn flock joined their voices in a psalm.[3] On Monday guns were heard from the rear, and the Indians and their allies, in great alarm, bound their prisoners fast, and prepared for battle. It proved, however, that the guns had been fired at wild geese by some of their own number; on which they recovered their spirits, fired a volley for joy, and boasted that the English could not overtake them. More women fainted by the way and died under the hatchet, — some with pious resignation, some with despairing apathy, some with a desperate joy.

Two hundred miles of wilderness still lay between them and the Canadian settlements. It was a waste without a house or even a wigwam, except here and there the bark shed of some savage hunter. At the mouth of White River, the party divided into small bands, — no doubt in order to subsist by hunting, for provisions were fast failing. The Williams family were separated. Stephen was carried up the Connecticut; Samuel and Eunice, with two younger children, were carried off in various directions; while the wretched father, along with two small children of one of his parishioners, was compelled to follow his Indian masters up the valley of White River. One of the children — a little girl — was killed on the next morning by her Caughnawaga owner, who was unable to carry her. On the next Sunday the minister was left in camp with one Indian and the surviving child, — a boy of nine, — while the rest of the party were hunting. "My spirit," he says, "was

---

[3] The small stream at the mouth of which Williams is supposed to have preached is still called Williams River.

almost overwhelmed within me." But he found comfort in the text, "Leave thy fatherless children, I will preserve them alive." Nor was his hope deceived. His youngest surviving child, — a boy of four, — though harshly treated by his owners, was carried on their shoulders or dragged on a sledge to the end of the journey. His youngest daughter — seven years old — was treated with great kindness throughout. Samuel and Eunice suffered much from hunger, but were dragged on sledges when too faint to walk. Stephen nearly starved to death; but after eight months in the forest, he safely reached Chambly with his Indian masters.

Of the whole band of captives, only about half ever again saw friends and home. Seventeen broke down on the way and were killed; while David Hoyt and Jacob Hix died of starvation at Coos Meadows, on the upper Connecticut. During the entire march, no woman seems to have been subjected to violence; and this holds true, with rare exceptions, in all the Indian wars of New England. This remarkable forbearance towards female prisoners, so different from the practice of many western tribes, was probably due to a form of superstition, aided perhaps by the influence of the missionaries. It is to be observed, however, that the heathen savages of King Philip's War, who had never seen a Jesuit, were no less forbearing in this respect.

The hunters of Williams's party killed five moose, the flesh of which, smoked and dried, was carried on their backs and that of the prisoner whom they had provided with snow-shoes. Thus burdened, the minister toiled on, following his masters along the frozen current of White River till, crossing the snowy backs of the Green Mountains, they struck the headwaters of the stream then called French River, now the Winooski, or Onion. Being in great fear of a thaw, they pushed on with double speed. Williams was not used to snow-shoes, and they gave him those painful cramps of the legs and ankles called in Canada *mal à la raquette*. One morning at dawn he was waked by his chief master and ordered to get up, say his prayers, and eat his breakfast, for they must make a long march that day. The minister was in despair. "After prayers," he says, "I arose from my knees; but my feet were so tender, swollen, bruised, and full of pain that I could scarce stand upon them without holding on the wigwam. And when the Indians said, 'You must run to-day,' I answered I could not run. My master, pointing to his hatchet, said to me, 'Then I must dash out your brains and take your scalp.'" The Indian proved better than his word, and Williams was suffered to struggle on as he could. "God wonderfully supported me," he writes, "and my strength was restored and renewed to admiration." He thinks that he walked that day forty miles on the snow. Following the Winooski to its mouth, the party reached Lake Champlain a little north of the present city of Burlington. Here the swollen feet of the prisoner were tortured by the rough ice, till snow began to fall and cover it with a soft carpet. Bending under his load, and powdered by the falling flakes, he toiled on till, at noon of a Saturday, lean, tired, and ragged, he and his masters reached the French outpost of Chambly, twelve or fifteen miles from Montreal.

Here the unhappy wayfarer was treated with great kindness both by the officers of the fort and by the inhabitants, one of the chief among whom lodged him in his house and welcomed him to his table. After a short stay at Chambly, Williams and his masters set out in a canoe for Sorel. On the way a Frenchwoman came down to the bank of the river and invited the party to her house, telling the minister that she herself had once been a prisoner among the Indians, and knew how to feel for him. She seated him at a table, spread a table-cloth, and placed food before him, while the Indians, to their great indignation, were supplied with a meal in the chimney-corner. Similar kindness was shown by the inhabitants along the way till the party reached their destination, the Abenaki village of St. Francis, to which his masters belonged. Here there was a fort, in which lived two Jesuits, directors of the mission, and here Williams found several English children, captured the summer before during the raid on the settlements of Maine, and already transformed into little Indians both in dress and behavior. At the gate of the fort one of the Jesuits met him, and asked him to go into the church and give thanks to God for sparing his life, to which he replied that he would give thanks in some other place. The priest then commanded him to go, which he refused to do. When on the next day the bell rang for mass, one of his Indian masters seized him and dragged him into the church, where he got behind the door, and watched the service from his retreat with extreme disapprobation. One of the Jesuits telling him that he would go to hell for not accepting the apostolic traditions, and trusting only in the Bible, he replied that he was glad to know that Christ was to be his judge, and not they. His chief master, who was a zealot in his way, and as much bound to the rites and forms of the Church as he had been before his conversion to his "medicines," or practices of heathen superstition, one day ordered him to make the sign of the cross, and on his refusal, tried to force him. But as the minister was tough and muscular, the Indian could not guide his hand.

Then, pulling out a crucifix that hung at his neck, he told Williams in broken English to kiss it; and being again refused, he brandished his hatchet over him and threatened to knock out his brains. This failing of the desired effect, he threw down the hatchet and said he would first bite out the minister's finger-nails, — a form of torture then in vogue among the northern Indians, both converts and heathen. Williams offered him a hand and invited him to begin; on which he gave the thumbnail a gripe with his teeth, and then let it go, saying, "No good minister, bad as the devil." The failure seems to have discouraged him, for he made no further attempt to convert the intractable heretic.

The direct and simple narrative of Williams is plainly the work of an honest and courageous man. He was the most important capture of the year; and the governor, hearing that he was at St. Francis, despatched a canoe to request the Jesuits of the mission to send him to Montreal. Thither, therefore, his masters carried him, expecting, no doubt, a good price for their prisoner. Vaudreuil, in fact, bought him, exchanged his tattered clothes for good ones, lodged him in his house, and, in the words of Williams, "was in all respects relating to my outward man courteous and charitable to admiration." He sent for two of the minister's children who were in the town, bought his eldest daughter from the Indians, and promised to do what he could to get the others out of their hands. His youngest son was bought by a lady of the place, and his eldest by a merchant. His youngest daughter, Eunice, then seven or eight years old, was at the mission of St. Louis, or Caughnawaga. Vaudreuil sent a priest to conduct Williams thither and try to ransom the child. But the Jesuits of the mission flatly refused to let him speak to or see her. Williams says that Vaudreuil was very angry at hearing of this; and a few days after, he went himself to Caughnawaga with the minister. This time the Jesuits, whose authority within their mission seemed almost to override that of the governor himself, yielded so far as to permit the father to see his child, on condition that he spoke to no other English prisoner. He talked with her for an hour, exhorting her never to forget her catechism, which she had learned by rote. Vaudreuil and his wife afterwards did all in their power to procure her ransom; but the Indians, or the missionaries in their name, would not let her go. "She is there still," writes Williams two years later, "and has forgotten to speak English." What grieved him still more, Eunice had forgotten her catechism.

While he was at Montreal, his movements were continually watched, lest he should speak to other prisoners and prevent their conversion. He thinks these precautions were due to the priests, whose constant endeavor it was to turn the captives, or at least the younger and more manageable among them, into Catholics and Canadians. The governor's kindness towards him never failed, though he told him that he should not be set free till the English gave up one Captain Baptiste, a noted sea-rover whom they had captured some time before.

He was soon after sent down the river to Quebec along with the superior of the Jesuits. Here he lodged seven weeks with a member of the council, who treated him kindly, but told him that if he did not avoid intercourse with the other English prisoners he would be sent farther away. He saw much of the Jesuits, who courteously asked him to dine; though he says that one of them afterwards made some Latin verses about him, in which he was likened to a captive wolf. Another Jesuit told him that when the mission Indians set out on their raid against Deerfield, he charged them to baptize all children before killing them, — such, he said, was his desire for the salvation even of his enemies. To murdering the children after they were baptized, he appears to have made no objection. Williams says that in their dread lest he should prevent the conversion of the other prisoners, the missionaries promised him a pension from the King and free intercourse with his children and neighbors if he would embrace the Catholic faith and remain in Canada; to which he answered that he would do so without reward if he thought their religion was true, but as he believed the contrary, "the offer of the whole world would tempt him no more than a blackberry."

To prevent him more effectually from perverting the minds of his captive countrymen, and fortifying them in their heresy, he was sent to Château Richer, a little below Quebec, and lodged with the parish priest, who was very kind to him. "I am persuaded," he writes, "that he abhorred their sending down the heathen to commit outrages against the English, saying it is more like committing murders than carrying on war."

He was sorely tried by the incessant efforts to convert the prisoners. "Sometimes they would tell me my children, sometimes my neighbors, were turned to be of their religion. Some made it their work to allure poor souls by flatteries and great promises; some threatened, some offered abuse to such as refused to go to church and be present at mass; and some they industriously contrived to get married among them. I understood they would tell the English that I was turned, that they might gain them to change their religion. These their endeavors to seduce to popery were very exercising to me."

After a time he was permitted to return to Quebec, where he met an English Franciscan, who, he says, had been sent from France to aid in converting the prisoners. Lest the minister should counteract the efforts of the friar, the priests had him sent back to Château Richer; "but," he observes, "God showed his dislike of such a persecuting spirit; for the very next day the Seminary, a very famous building, was most of it burnt down, by a joiner letting a coal of fire drop among the shavings."

The heaviest of all his tribulations now fell upon him. His son Samuel, about sixteen years old, had been kept at Montreal under the tutelage of Father Meriel, a priest of St. Sulpice. The boy afterwards declared that he was promised great rewards if he would make the sign of the cross, and severe punishment if he would not. Proving obstinate, he was whipped till at last he made the sign; after which he was told to go to mass, and on his refusal, four stout boys of the school were ordered to drag him in. Williams presently received a letter in Samuel's hand-writing, though dictated, as the father believed, by his priestly tutors. In this was recounted, with many edifying particulars, the deathbed conversion of two New England women; and to the minister's unspeakable grief and horror, the messenger who brought the letter told him that the boy himself had turned Catholic. "I have heard the news," he wrote to his recreant son, "with the most distressing, afflicting, sorrowful spirit. Oh, I pity you, I mourn over you day and night. Oh, I pity your weakness that, through the craftiness of man, you are turned from the simplicity of the gospel." Though his correspondence was strictly watched, he managed to convey to the boy a long exposition, from his own pen, of the infallible truth of Calvinistic orthodoxy, and the damnable errors of Rome. This, or something else, had its effect. Samuel returned to the creed of his fathers; and being at last exchanged, went home to Deerfield, where he was chosen town-clerk in 1713, and where he soon after died.

Williams gives many particulars of the efforts of the priests to convert the prisoners, and his account, like the rest of his story, bears the marks of truth. There was a treble motive for conversion: it recruited the Church, weakened the enemy, and strengthened Canada, since few of the converts would peril their souls by returning to their heretic relatives. The means of conversion varied. They were gentle when gentleness seemed likely to answer the purpose. Little girls and young women were placed in convents, where it is safe to assume that they were treated with the most tender kindness by the sisterhood, who fully believed that to gain them to the faith was to snatch them from perdition. But when they or their brothers proved obdurate, different means were used. Threats of hell were varied by threats of a whipping, which, according to Williams, were often put into execution. Parents were rigorously severed from their families; though one Lalande, who had been sent to watch the elder prisoners, reported that they would persist in trying to see their children, till some of them were killed in the attempt. "Here," writes Williams, "might be a history in itself of the trials and sufferings of many of our children, who, after separation from grown persons, have been made to do as they would have them. I mourned when I thought with myself that I had one child with the Maquas [Caughnawagas], a second turned papist, and a little child of six years of age in danger to be instructed in popery, and knew full well that all endeavors would be used to prevent my seeing or speaking with them." He also says that he and others were told that if they would turn Catholic their children should be restored to them; and among other devices, some of his parishioners were assured that their pastor himself had seen the error of his ways and bowed in submission to Holy Church.

In midwinter, not quite a year after their capture, the prisoners were visited by a gleam of hope. John Sheldon, accompanied by young John Wells, of Deerfield, and Captain Livingston, of Albany, came to Montreal with letters from Governor Dudley, proposing an exchange. Sheldon's wife and infant child, his brother-in-law, and his son-in-law had been killed. Four of his children, with his daughter-in-law, Hannah, the same who had sprained her ankle in leaping from her chamber window, — besides others of his near relatives and connections, were prisoners in Canada; and so also was the mother of young Wells. In the last December, Sheldon and Wells had gone to Boston and begged to be sent as envoys to the French governor. The petition was readily granted, and Livingston, who chanced to be in the town, was engaged to accompany them. After a snow-shoe journey of extreme hardship they reached their destination, and were received with courtesy by Vaudreuil. But difficulties arose. The French, and above all the clergy, were unwilling to part with captives, many of whom they hoped to transform into Canadians by conversion and adoption. Many also were in the hands of the Indians, who demanded payment for them, — which Dudley had always refused, declaring that he would not "set up an Algiers trade" by buying them from their pretended owners; and he wrote to Vaudreuil that for his own part he "would never permit a savage to tell him that any Christian prisoner was at his disposal." Vaudreuil had insisted that his Indians could not be compelled to give up their captives, since they were not subjects of France, but only allies, — which, so far as concerned the mission Indians within the colony, was but a pretext. It is true, however, that the French authorities were in such fear of offending even these that they rarely ventured to cross their interests or their passions. Other difficulties were raised, and though the envoys remained in Canada till late in spring, they accomplished little. At last, probably to get rid of their importunities, five prisoners were given up to them, — Sheldon's daughter-in-law, Hannah; Esther Williams, eldest daughter of the minister; a certain Ebenezer Carter; and two others unknown. With these, Sheldon and his companions set out in May on their return; and soon after they were gone, four young men, — Baker, Nims, Kellogg, and Petty, — desperate at being left in captivity, made their escape from Montreal, and reached Deerfield before the end of June, half dead with hunger.

Sheldon and his party were escorted homeward by eight soldiers under Courtemanche, an officer of distinction, whose orders were to "make himself acquainted with the country." He fell ill at Boston, where he was treated with much kindness, and on his recovery was sent home by sea, along with Captain Vetch and Samuel Hill, charged to open a fresh negotiation. With these, at the request of Courtemanche, went young William Dudley, son of the governor.

They were received at Quebec with a courtesy qualified by extreme caution, lest they should spy out the secrets of the land. The mission was not very successful, though the elder Dudley had now a good number of French prisoners in his hands, captured in Acadia or on the adjacent seas. A few only of the English were released, including the boy, Stephen Williams, whom Vaudreuil had bought for forty crowns from his Indian master.

In the following winter John Sheldon made another journey on foot to Canada, with larger powers than before. He arrived in March, 1706, and returned with forty-four of his released countrymen, who, says Williams, were chiefly adults permitted to go because there was no hope of converting them. The English governor had by this time seen the necessity of greater concessions, and had even consented to release the noted Captain Baptiste, whom the Boston merchants regarded as a pirate. In the same summer Samuel Appleton and John Bonner, in the brigantine "Hope," brought a considerable number of French prisoners to Quebec, and returned to Boston at the end of October with fifty-seven English, of all ages. For three, at least, of this number money was paid by the English, probably on account of prisoners bought by Frenchmen from the Indians. The minister, Williams, was exchanged for Baptiste, the so-called pirate, and two of his children were also redeemed, though the Caughnawagas, or their missionaries, refused to part with his daughter Eunice. Williams says that the priests made great efforts to induce the prisoners to remain in Canada, tempting some with the prospect of pensions from the King, and frightening others with promises of damnation, joined with predictions of shipwreck on the way home. He thinks that about one hundred were left in Canada, many of whom were children in the hands of the Indians, who could easily hide them in the woods, and who were known in some cases to have done so. Seven more were redeemed in the following year by the indefatigable Sheldon, on a third visit to Canada.

The exchanged prisoners had been captured at various times and places. Those from Deerfield amounted in all to about sixty, or a little more than half the whole number carried off. Most of the others were dead or converted. Some married Canadians, and others their fellow-captives. The history of some of them can be traced with certainty. Thus, Thomas French, blacksmith and town clerk of Deerfield, and deacon of the church, was captured, with his wife and six children. His wife and infant child were killed on the way to Canada. He and his two eldest children were exchanged and brought home. His daughter Freedom was converted, baptized under the name of Marie Françoise, and married to Jean Daulnay, a Canadian. His daughter Martha was baptized as Marguerite, and married to Jacques Roy, on whose death she married Jean Louis Ménard, by whom she became ancestress of Joseph Plessis, eleventh bishop of Quebec. Elizabeth Corse, eight years old when captured, was baptized under her own name, and married to Jean Dumontel. Abigail Stebbins, baptized as Marguerite, lived many years at Boucherville, wife of Jacques de Noyon, a sergeant in the colony troops. The widow, Sarah Hurst, whose youngest child, Benjamin, had been murdered on the Deerfield meadows, was baptized as Marie Jeanne. Joanna Kellogg, eleven years old when taken, married a Caughnawaga chief, and became, at all points, an Indian squaw.

She was not alone in this strange transformation. Eunice Williams, the namesake of her slaughtered mother, remained in the wigwams of the Caughnawagas, forgot, as we have seen, her English and her catechism, was baptized, and in due time married to an Indian of the tribe, who thenceforward called himself Williams. Thus her hybrid children bore her family name. Her father, who returned to his parish at Deerfield, and her brother Stephen, who became a minister like his parent, never ceased to pray for her return to her country and her faith. Many years after, in 1740, she came with her husband to visit her relatives in Deerfield, dressed as a squaw and wrapped in an Indian blanket. Nothing would induce her to stay, though she was persuaded on one occasion to put on a civilized dress and go to church; after which she impatiently discarded her gown and resumed her blanket. As she was kindly treated by her relatives, and as no attempt was made to detain her against her will, she came again in the next year, bringing two of her half-breed children, and twice afterwards repeated the visit. She and her husband were offered a tract of land if they would settle in New England; but she positively refused, saying that it would endanger her soul. She lived to a great age, a squaw to the last.

One of her grandsons, Eleazer Williams, turned Protestant, was educated at Dartmouth College at the charge of friends in New England, and was for a time missionary to the Indians of Green Bay, in Wisconsin. His character for veracity was not of the best. He deceived the excellent antiquarian, Hoyt, by various inventions touching the attack on Deerfield, and in the latter part of his life tried to pass himself off as the lost Dauphin, son of Louis XVI.[4]

[4] I remember to have seen Eleazer Williams at my father's house in Boston, when a boy. My impression of him is that of a goodlooking and somewhat portly man, showing little trace of Indian blood, and whose features, I was told, resembled those of the Bourbons. Probably this likeness, real or imagined, suggested the imposition he was practising at the time. The story of the "Bell of St. Regis" is probably another of his inventions. It is to the effect that the bell of the church at Deerfield was carried by the Indians to the mission of St. Regis, and that it is there still. But there is reason to believe that there was no church bell at Deerfield, and it is certain that St. Regis did not exist till more than a half-century after Deerfield was attacked. It has been said that the story is true, except that the name of Caughnawaga should be substituted for that of St. Regis; but the evidence for this conjecture is weak. [The full-blown story states that the bell, originally cast in France for the Indian church at St. Regis, was part of the booty taken by a Yankee privateer from a French ship en route to Canada, and was then purchased by the Deerfield church; that the Indians, hearing of this, persuaded the Governor to authorize the raid, in order to recover their rightful bell. This legend, a favorite in French Canada because it gives a sentimental and religious motive to the sack of Deerfield, has recently been revived by Dr. Marius Barbeau in *Proceedings* American Philosophical Society XCIV (1950) 522–48, an article which includes a valuable bibliography on Indian Captivities. Dr. Barbeau's source is "a ms. of several foolscap pages, apparently published in 1827 and copied by the Rev. Joseph Marcout, missionary at Caughnawaga. . . . " This editor examined said manuscript at the Archives of the Grand Séminaire, Quebec, and found it to be a

Here it may be observed that the descendants of young captives brought into Canada by the mission Indians during the various wars with the English colonies became a considerable element in the Canadian population. Perhaps the most prominent example is that of the Gill family. In June, 1697, a boy named Samuel Gill, then in his tenth year, was captured by the Abenakis at Salisbury in Massachusetts, carried to St. Francis, and converted. Some years later he married a young English girl, said to have been named James, and to have been captured at Kennebunk. In 1866 the late Abbé Maurault, missionary at St. Francis, computed their descendants at 952, in whose veins French, English, and Abenaki blood were mixed in every conceivable proportion. He gives the tables of genealogy in full, and says that 213 of this prolific race still bear the surname of Gill. "If," concludes the worthy priest, "one should trace out all the English families brought into Canada by the Abenakis, one would be astonished at the number of persons who to-day are indebted to these savages for the blessing of being Catholics and the advantage of being Canadians," — an advantage for which French-Canadians are so ungrateful that they migrate to the United States by myriads.[5]

---

transcription of an article by John Galt, a Canadian novelist, in *Fraser's Magazine for Town and Country* I (1830) 268–70. It was built on a story that had already appeared in Epaphras Hoyt *Antiquarian Researches* (Greenfield, Mass., 1824), Hoyt having obtained it from Eleazer Williams; but the novelist added many embellishments. There is no record of Deerfield having had a bell in 1704; and in the numerous accounts of the raid, French and English, and in Williams's account of his captivity, there is no reference to a bell being captured and dragged through the snow to Quebec, as the legend relates.]

[5] [Theodore Roosevelt, after receiving a copy of *Half-Century of Conflict* from Parkman, wrote to him prophetically on 22 May 1892:

"Looking over the recent census figures for New England it is curious, and rather melancholy, to see the strange revenge which time is bringing to the French of Canada. They are swarming into New England with ominous rapidity. Of course they will conform to and keep our laws, and in most places our language, though I should not be surprised to see French become the tongue of occasional counties in the north, and possibly even of one or two manufacturing towns. But their race will in many places supplant the old American stock; and I am inclined to believe that in a generation or two more, Catholicism, though in a liberalized form, will become the dominant creed in several of the Puritan commonwealths. Yet I am a firm believer that the future will somehow bring things right in the end for our land." E. E. Morison ed. *Letters of Theodore Roosevelt*, I 282–3.]

CHAPTER XXIX

A Mad Scheme

1744–1745

[*A Half-Century of Conflict*, CHAPTER XVIII]

[SUBSEQUENT to the Peace of Utrecht (1712) which ended Queen Anne's War, New France and New England enjoyed peace for thirty years, interrupted only by the brief frontier struggle known as Governor Dummer's War, in which Father Sebastien Rale was killed under circumstances which appear to have aroused a perpetual controversy. In 1745 began the War of the Austrian Succession, the American phase of which is known as King George's War. The great event of that war was the siege and capture of Louisbourg on Cape Breton Island.]

Louisbourg was a standing menace to all the northern British colonies. It was the only French naval station on the continent, and was such a haunt of privateers that it was called the American Dunkirk. It commanded the chief entrance of Canada, and threatened to ruin the fisheries, which were nearly as vital to New England as was the fur-trade to New France. The French government had spent twenty-five years in fortifying it, and the cost of its powerful defences — constructed after the system of Vauban — was reckoned at thirty million livres.

This was the fortress which William Vaughan of Damariscotta advised Governor Shirley to attack with 1500 raw New England militia. Vaughan was born at Portsmouth in 1703, and graduated at Harvard College nineteen years later. His father, also a graduate of Harvard, was for a time lieutenant-governor of New Hampshire. Soon after leaving college, the younger Vaughan — a youth of restless and impetuous activity — established a fishing-station on the island of Matinicus, off the coast of Maine, and afterwards became the owner of most of the land on both sides of the little river Damariscotta, where he built a garrison-house, or wooden fort, established a considerable settlement, and carried on an extensive trade in fish and timber. He passed for a man of ability and force, but was accused of a headstrong rashness, a self-confidence that hesitated at nothing, and a harebrained contempt of every obstacle in his way. Once, having fitted out a number of small vessels at Portsmouth for his fishing at Matinicus, he named a time for sailing. It was a gusty and boisterous March day, the sea was rough, and old sailors told him that such craft could not carry sail. Vaughan would not listen, but went on board and ordered his men to follow. One vessel was wrecked at the mouth of the river; the rest, after severe buffeting, came safe, with their owner, to Matinicus.

Being interested in the fisheries, Vaughan was doubly hostile to Louisbourg, — their worst enemy. He found a willing listener in the governor, William Shirley. Shirley was an English barrister who had come to Massachusetts in 1731 to practise his profession and seek his fortune. After filling various offices with credit, he was made governor of the province in 1741, and had discharged his duties with both tact and talent. He was able, sanguine, and a sincere well-wisher to the province, though gnawed by an insatiable hunger for distinction. He thought himself a born strategist, and was possessed by a propensity for contriving military operations, which finally cost him dear. Vaughan, who knew something of Louisbourg, told him that in winter the snow-drifts were often banked so high against the rampart that it could be mounted readily, if the assailants could but time their arrival at the right moment. This was not easy, as that rocky and tempestuous coast was often made inaccessible by fogs and surf; Shirley therefore preferred a plan of his own contriving. But nothing could be done without first persuading his Assembly to consent.

On the 9th of January the General Court of Massachusetts — a convention of grave city merchants and solemn rustics from the country villages — was astonished by a message from the governor to the effect that he had a communication to make, so critical that he wished the whole body to swear secrecy. The request was novel, but being then on good terms with Shirley, the representatives consented, and took the oath. Then, to their amazement, the governor invited them to undertake forthwith the reduction of Louisbourg. The idea of an attack on that redoubtable fortress was not new. Since the autumn, proposals had been heard to petition the British ministry to make the attempt, under a promise that the colonies would give their best aid. But that Massachusetts should venture it alone, or with such doubtful help as her neighbors might give, at her own charge and risk, though already insolvent, without the approval or consent of the ministry, and without experienced officers or trained soldiers, was a startling suggestion to the sober-minded legislators of the General Court. They listened, however, with respect to the governor's reasons, and appointed a committee of the two houses to consider them. The committee deliberated for several days, and then made a report adverse to the plan, as was also the vote of the Court.

Meanwhile, in spite of the oath, the secret had escaped. It is said that a country member, more pious than discreet, prayed so loud and fervently, at his lodgings, for light to guide him on the momentous question, that his words were overheard, and the mystery of the closed doors was revealed. The news flew through the town, and soon spread through all the province.

After his defeat in the Assembly, Shirley returned, vexed and disappointed, to his house in Roxbury. A few days later, James Gibson, a Boston merchant, says that he saw him "walking slowly down King Street, with his head bowed down, as if in a deep study." "He entered my counting-room," pursues the merchant, "and abruptly said, 'Gibson, do you feel like giving up the expedition to Louisbourg?'" Gibson replied that he wished the House would reconsider their vote. "You are the very man I want!" exclaimed the governor. They then drew up a petition for reconsideration, which Gibson signed, promising to get also the signatures of merchants, not only of Boston, but of Salem, Marblehead, and other towns along the coast. In this he was completely successful, as all New England merchants looked on Louisbourg as an arch-enemy.

The petition was presented, and the question came again before the Assembly. There had been much intercourse between Boston and Louisbourg, which had largely depended on New England for provisions. The captured militiamen of Canseau, who, after some delay, had been sent to Boston, according to the terms of the surrender, had used their opportunities to the utmost, and could give Shirley much information concerning the fortress. It was reported that the garrison was mutinous, and that provisions were fallen short, so that the place could not hold out without supplies from France. These, however, could be cut off only by blockading the harbor with a stronger naval force than all the colonies together could supply. The Assembly had before reached the reasonable conclusion that the capture of Louisbourg was beyond the strength of Massachusetts, and that the only course was to ask the help of the mother-country.

The reports of mutiny, it was urged, could not be depended on; raw militia in the open field were no match for disciplined troops behind ramparts; the expense would be enormous, and the credit of the province, already sunk low, would collapse under it; we should fail, and instead of sympathy, get nothing but ridicule. Such were the arguments of the opposition, to which there was little to answer, except that if Massachusetts waited for help from England, Louisbourg would be reinforced and the golden opportunity lost. The impetuous and irrepressible Vaughan put forth all his energy; the plan was carried by a single vote. And even this result was said to be due to the accident of a member in opposition falling and breaking a leg as he was hastening to the House.

The die was cast, and now doubt and hesitation vanished. All alike set themselves to push on the work. Shirley wrote to all the colonies, as far south as Pennsylvania, to ask for co-operation. All excused themselves except Connecticut, New Hampshire, and Rhode Island, and the whole burden fell on the four New England colonies. These, and Massachusetts above all, blazed with pious zeal; for as the enterprise was directed against Roman Catholics, it was supposed in a peculiar manner to commend itself to Heaven. There were prayers without ceasing in churches and families, and all was ardor, energy, and confidence; while the other colonies looked on with distrust, dashed with derision. When Benjamin Franklin, in Philadelphia, heard what was afoot, he wrote to his brother in Boston, "Fortified towns are hard nuts to crack, and your teeth are not accustomed to it; but some seem to think that forts are as easy taken as snuff." It has been said of Franklin that while he represented some of the New England qualities, he had no part in that enthusiasm of which our own time saw a crowning example when the cannon opened at Fort Sumter, and which pushes to its end without reckoning chances, counting costs, or heeding the scoffs of ill-wishers.

The prevailing hope and faith were, it is true, born largely of ignorance, aided by the contagious zeal of those who first broached the project; for as usual in such cases, a few individuals supplied the initiate force of the enterprise. Vaughan the indefatigable rode express to Portsmouth with a letter from Shirley to Benning Wentworth, governor of New Hampshire. That pompous and self-important personage admired the Massachusetts governor, who far surpassed him in talents and acquirements, and who at the same time knew how to soothe his vanity. Wentworth was ready to do his part, but his province had no money, and the King had ordered him to permit the issue of no more paper currency. The same prohibition had been laid upon Shirley; but he, with sagacious forecast, had persuaded his masters to relent so far as to permit the issue of £50,000 in what were called bills of credit to meet any pressing exigency of war. He told this to Wentworth, and succeeded in convincing him that his province might stretch her credit like Massachusetts, in case of similar military need. New Hampshire was thus enabled to raise a regiment of 500 men out of her scanty population, with the condition that 150 of them should be paid and fed by Massachusetts.

Shirley was less fortunate in Rhode Island. The governor of that little colony called Massachusetts "our avowed enemy, always trying to defame us." There was a grudge between the neighbors, due partly to notorious ill-treatment by the Massachusetts Puritans of Roger Williams, founder of Rhode Island, and partly to one of those boundary disputes which often produced ill-blood among the colonies. The representatives of Rhode Island, forgetting past differences, voted to raise 150 men for the expedition, till, learning that the project was neither ordered nor approved by the Home Government, they prudently reconsidered their action. They voted, however, that the colony sloop *Tartar*, carrying fourteen cannon and twelve swivels, should be equipped and manned for the service, and that the governor should be instructed to find and commission a captain and a lieutenant to command her.

Connecticut promised 516 men and officers, on condition that Roger Wolcott, their commander, should have the second rank in the expedition. Shirley accordingly commissioned him as major-general. As Massachusetts was to supply above 3000 men, or more than three quarters of the whole force, she had a natural right to name a commander-in-chief.

It was not easy to choose one. The colony had been at peace for twenty years, and except some grizzled Indian fighters of the last war, and some survivors of the Carthagena expedition, nobody had seen service. Few knew well what a fortress was, and nobody knew how to attack one. Courage, energy, good sense, and popularity were the best qualities to be hoped for in the leader. Popularity was indispensable, for the soldiers were all to be volunteers, and they would not enlist under a commander whom they did not like. Shirley's choice was William Pepperrell, a merchant of Kittery. Knowing that Benning

Wentworth thought himself the man for the place, he made an effort to placate him, and wrote that he would gladly have given him the chief command, but for his gouty legs. Wentworth took fire at the suggestion, forgot his gout, and declared himself ready to serve his country and assume the burden of command. The position was awkward, and Shirley was forced to reply, "On communicating your offer to two or three gentlemen in whose judgment I most confide, I found them clearly of opinion that any alteration of the present command would be attended with great risk, both with respect to our Assembly and the soldiers being entirely disgusted."

The painter Smibert has left us a portrait of Pepperrell, — a good bourgeois face, not without dignity, though with no suggestion of the soldier. His spacious house at Kittery Point still stands, sound and firm, though curtailed in some of its proportions. Not far distant is another noted relic of colonial times, the not less spacious mansion built by the disappointed Wentworth at Little Harbor.[1] I write these lines at a window of this curious old house, and before me spreads the scene familiar to Pepperrell from childhood. Here the river Piscataqua widens to join the sea, holding in its gaping mouth the large island of Newcastle, with attendant groups of islets and island rocks, battered with the rack of ages, studded with dwarf savins, or half clad with patches of whortleberry bushes, sumach, and the shining wax-myrtle, green in summer, red with the touch of October. The flood tide pours strong and full around them, only to ebb away and lay bare a desolation of rocks and stones buried in a shock of brown drenched seaweed, broad tracts of glistening mud, sand-banks black with mussel-beds, and half-submerged meadows of eel-grass, with myriads of minute shell-fish clinging to its long lank tresses. Beyond all these lies the main, or northern channel, more than deep enough, even when the tide is out, to float a line-of-battle-ship. On its farther bank stands the old house of the Pepperrells, wearing even now an air of dingy respectability. Looking through its small, quaint window-panes, one could see across the water the rude dwellings of fishermen along the shore of New-

---

[1] [This is the house belonging to Parkman's son-in-law, J. Templeman Coolidge, jr., where the historian spent a part of every summer after 1886. It was originally a 17th-century farmhouse to which Governor Wentworth built many additions, including a spacious drawing room where he often held his council meetings. As the road thence to Portsmouth was long and rough, the Governor maintained a rowing barge big enough to float his coach, when he wished to visit his capital. The Little Harbor estate is still one of the most beautiful in New England, with a view that extends to the Isles of Shoals.]

castle, and the neglected earthwork called Fort William and Mary, that feebly guarded the river's mouth. In front, the Piscataqua, curving southward, widened to meet the Atlantic between rocky headlands and foaming reefs, and in dim distance the Isles of Shoals seemed floating on the pale gray sea.

Behind the Pepperrell house was a garden, probably more useful than ornamental, and at the foot of it were the owner's wharves, with storehouses for salt-fish, naval stores, and imported goods for the country trade.

Pepperrell was the son of a Welshman who migrated in early life to the Isles of Shoals, and thence to Kittery, where, by trade, ship-building, and the fisheries, he made a fortune, most of which he left to his son William. The young Pepperrell learned what little was taught at the village school, supplemented by a private tutor, whose instructions, however, did not perfect him in English grammar. In the eyes of his self-made father, education was valuable only so far as it could make a successful trader; and on this point he had reason to be satisfied, as his son passed for many years as the chief merchant in New England. He dealt in ships, timber, naval stores, fish, and miscellaneous goods brought from England; and he also greatly prospered by successful land purchases, becoming owner of the greater part of the growing towns of Saco and Scarborough. When scarcely twenty-one, he was made justice of the peace, on which he ordered from London what his biographer calls a law library, consisting of a law dictionary, Danvers' "Abridgment of the Common Law," the "Complete Solicitor," and several other books. In law as in war, his best qualities were good sense and good-will. About the time when he was made a justice, he was commissioned captain of militia, then major, then lieutenant-colonel, and at last colonel, commanding all the militia of Maine. The town of Kittery chose him to represent her in the General Court, Maine being then a part of Massachusetts. Finally, he was made a member of the Governor's Council, — a post which he held for thirty-two years, during eighteen of which he was president of the board.

These civil dignities served him as educators better than tutor or village school; for they brought him into close contact with the chief men of the province; and in the Massachusetts of that time, so different from our own, the best education and breeding were found in the official class. At once a provincial magnate and the great man of a small rustic village, his manners are said to have answered to both positions, — certainly they were such as to make him popular. But whatever he became as a man, he learned nothing to fit him to command an army and lay siege to Louisbourg. Perhaps he felt this, and thought, with the governor of Rhode Island, that "the attempt to reduce that prodigiously strong town was too much for New England, which had not one officer of experience, nor even an engineer." Moreover, he was unwilling to leave his wife, children, and business. He was of a religious turn of mind, and partial to the clergy, who, on their part, held him in high favor. One of them, the famous preacher, George Whitefield, was a guest at his house when he heard that Shirley had appointed him to command the expedition against Louisbourg. Whitefield had been the leading spirit in the recent religious fermentation called the Great Awakening, which, though it produced bitter quarrels among the ministers, besides other undesirable results, was imagined by many to make for righteousness. So thought the Rev. Thomas Prince, who mourned over the subsiding delirium of his flock as a sign of backsliding. "The heavenly shower was over," he sadly exclaims; "from fighting the devil they must turn to fighting the French." Pepperrell, always inclined to the clergy, and now in great perplexity and doubt, asked his guest Whitefield whether or not he had better accept the command. Whitefield gave him cold comfort, told him that the enterprise was not very promising, and that if he undertook it, he must do so "with a single eye," prepared for obloquy if he failed, and envy if he succeeded.

Henry Sherburn, commissary of the New Hampshire regiment, begged Whitefield to furnish a motto for the flag. The preacher, who, zealot as he was, seemed unwilling to mix himself with so madcap a business, hesitated at first, but at length consented, and suggested the words, *Nil desperandum Christo duce*, which, being adopted, gave the enterprise the air of a crusade. It had, in fact, something of the character of one. The cause was imagined to be the cause of Heaven, crowned with celestial benediction. It had the fervent support of the ministers, not only by prayers and sermons, but, in one case, by counsels wholly temporal. A certain pastor, much esteemed for benevolence, proposed to Pepperrell, who had at last accepted the command, a plan, unknown to Vauban, for confounding the devices of the enemy. He advised that two trustworthy persons should cautiously walk together along the front of the French ramparts under cover of night, one of them carrying a mallet, with which he was to hammer the ground at short intervals. The French sentinels, it seems to have been supposed, on hearing this mysterious thumping, would be so bewildered as to give no alarm. While one of the two partners was thus employed, the other was to lay his ear to the ground, which, as the adviser thought, would return a hollow sound if the artful foe had dug a mine under it; and whenever such secret danger was detected, a mark was to be set on the spot, to warn off the soldiers.

Equally zealous, after another fashion, was the Rev. Samuel Moody, popularly known as Father Moody, or Parson Moody, minister of York and senior chaplain of the expedition. Though about seventy years old, he was amazingly tough and sturdy. He still lives in the traditions of York as the spiritual despot of the settlement and the uncompromising guardian of its manners and doctrine, predominating over it like a rough little village pope. The comparison would have kindled his burning wrath, for he abhorred the Holy Father as an embodied Antichrist. Many are the stories told of him by the descendants of those who lived under his rod, and sometimes felt its weight; for he was known to have corrected offending parishioners with his cane. When some one of his flock, nettled by his strictures from the pulpit, walked in dudgeon towards the church door, Moody would shout after him, "Come back, you graceless sinner, come back!" or if any ventured to the alehouse of a Saturday night, the strenuous pastor would go in after them, collar them, drag them out, and send them home with rousing admonition. Few dared gainsay him, by reason both of his irritable temper and of the thick-skinned insensibility that encased him like armor of proof. And while his pachydermatous nature made him invulnerable as a rhinoceros, he had at the same time a rough and ready humor that supplied keen weapons for the warfare of words and made him a formidable antagonist. This commended him to the rude borderers, who also relished the sulphurous theology of their spiritual dictator, just as they liked the raw and fiery liquors that would have scorched more susceptible stomachs. What they did not like was the pitiless length of his prayers, which sometimes kept them afoot above two hours shivering in the polar cold of the unheated meetinghouse, and which were followed by sermons of equal endurance; for the old man's lungs were of brass, and his nerves of hammered iron. Some of the sufferers ventured to remonstrate; but this only exasperated him, till one parishioner, more worldly wise than the rest, accompanied his modest petition for mercy with the gift of a barrel of cider, after which the parson's ministrations were perceptibly less exhausting than before. He had an irrepressible conscience and a highly aggressive sense of duty, which made him an intolerable meddler in the affairs of other people, and which, joined to an underlying kindness of heart, made him so indiscreet in his charities that his wife and children were often driven to vain protest against the excesses of his almsgiving. The old Puritan fanaticism was rampant in him; and when he sailed for Louisbourg, he took with him an axe, intended, as he said, to hew down the altars of Antichrist and demolish his idols.[2]

Shirley's choice of a commander was perhaps the best that could have been made; for Pepperrell joined to an unusual popularity as little military incompetency as anybody else who could be had. Popularity, we have seen, was indispensable, and even company officers were appointed with an eye to it. Many of these were well-known men in rustic neighborhoods, who had raised companies in the hope of being commissioned to command them. Others were militia officers recruiting under orders of the governor. Thus, John Storer, major in the Maine militia, raised in a single day, it is said, a company of sixty-one, the oldest being sixty years old, and the youngest sixteen. They formed about a quarter of the fencible population of the town of Wells, one of the most exposed places on the border. Volunteers offered themselves readily everywhere; though the pay was meagre, especially in Maine and Massachusetts, where in the new provincial currency it was twenty-five shillings a month, — then equal to fourteen shillings sterling, or less than sixpence a day, the soldier furnishing his own clothing and bringing his own gun. A full third of the Massachusetts contingent, or more than a thousand men, are reported to have come from the hardy population of Maine, whose entire fighting force, as shown by the muster-rolls, was then but 2855. Perhaps there was not one officer among them whose experience of war extended beyond a drill on muster day and the sham fight that closed the performance, when it generally happened that the rustic warriors were treated with rum at the charge of their captain, to put them in good humor, and so induce them to obey the word of command.

As the three provinces contributing soldiers recognized no common authority nearer than the King, Pepperrell received three several commissions as lieutenant-general, — one from the governor of Massachusetts, and the others from the governors of Connecticut and New

---

[2] Moody found sympathizers in his iconoclastic zeal. Deacon John Gray of Biddeford wrote to Pepperrell: "Oh that I could be with you and dear Parson Moody in that church [at Louisbourg] to destroy the images there set up, and hear the true Gospel of our Lord and Saviour there preached!"

Hampshire; while Wolcott, commander of the Connecticut forces, was commissioned as major-general by both the governor of his own province and that of Massachusetts. When the levies were complete, it was found that Massachusetts had contributed about 3300 men, Connecticut 516, and New Hampshire 304 in her own pay, besides 150 paid by her wealthier neighbor. Rhode Island had lost faith and disbanded her 150 men; but afterwards raised them again, though too late to take part in the siege.

Each of the four New England colonies had a little navy of its own, consisting of from one to three or four small armed vessels; and as privateering — which was sometimes a euphemism for piracy where Frenchmen and Spaniards were concerned — was a favorite occupation, it was possible to extemporize an additional force in case of need. For a naval commander, Shirley chose Captain Edward Tyng, who had signalized himself in the past summer by capturing a French privateer of greater strength than his own. Shirley authorized him to buy for the province the best ship he could find, equip her for fighting, and take command of her. Tyng soon found a brig to his mind, on the stocks nearly ready for launching. She was rapidly fitted for her new destination, converted into a frigate, mounted with 24 guns, and named the *Massachusetts*. The rest of the naval force consisted of the ship *Cæsar*, of 20 guns; a vessel called the *Shirley*, commanded by Captain Rous, and also carrying 20 guns; another of the kind called a snow, carrying 16 guns; one sloop of 12 guns, and two of 8 guns each; the *Boston Packet*, of 16 guns; two sloops from Connecticut of 16 guns each; a privateer hired in Rhode Island, of 20 guns; the government sloop *Tartar*, of the same colony, carrying 14 carriage guns and 12 swivels; and, finally, the sloop of 14 guns which formed the navy of New Hampshire.

It was said, with apparent reason, that one or two heavy French ships-of-war — and a number of such was expected in the spring — would outmatch the whole colonial squadron, and, after mastering it, would hold all the transport at mercy; so that the troops on shore, having no means of return and no hope of succor, would be forced to surrender or starve. The danger was real and serious, and Shirley felt the necessity of help from a few British ships-of-war. Commodore Peter Warren was then with a small squadron at Antigua. Shirley sent an express boat to him with a letter stating the situation and asking his aid. Warren, who had married an American woman and who owned large tracts of land on the Mohawk, was known to be a warm friend to the provinces. It is clear that he would gladly have complied with Shirley's request; but when he laid the question before a council of officers, they were of one mind that without orders from the Admiralty he would not be justified in supporting any attempt made without the approval of the King. He therefore saw no choice but to decline. Shirley, fearing that his refusal would be too discouraging, kept it secret from all but Pepperrell and General Wolcott, or, as others say, Brigadier Waldo. He had written to the Duke of Newcastle in the preceding autumn that Acadia and the fisheries were in great danger, and that ships-of-war were needed for their protection. On this, the duke had written to Warren, ordering him to sail for Boston and concert measures with Shirley "for the annoyance of the enemy, and his Majesty's service in North America." Newcastle's letter reached Warren only two or three days after he had sent back his refusal of Shirley's request. Thinking himself now sufficiently authorized to give the desired aid, he made all sail for Boston with his three ships, the *Superbe*, *Mermaid*, and *Launceston*. On the way he met a schooner from Boston, and learned from its officers that the expedition had already sailed; on which, detaining the master as a pilot, he changed his course and made directly for Canseau, — the place of rendezvous of the expedition, — and at the same time sent orders by the schooner that any king's ships that might arrive at Boston should immediately join him.

Within seven weeks after Shirley issued his proclamation for volunteers, the preparations were all made, and the unique armament was afloat. Transports, such as they were, could be had in abundance; for the harbors of Salem and Marblehead were full of fishing-vessels thrown out of employment by the war. These were hired and insured by the province for the security of the owners. There was a great dearth of cannon. The few that could be had were too light, the heaviest being of twenty-two-pound calibre. New York lent ten eighteen-pounders to the expedition. But the adventurers looked to the French for their chief supply. A detached work near Louisbourg, called the Grand, or Royal, Battery, was known to be armed with thirty heavy pieces; and these it was proposed to capture and turn against the town, — which, as Hutchinson remarks, was "like selling the skin of the bear before catching him."

It was clear that the expedition must run for luck against risks of all kinds. Those whose hopes were highest, based them on a belief in the special and direct interposition of Providence; others were sanguine through ignorance and provincial self-conceit. As soon as the troops were embarked, Shirley wrote to the ministers of what was going on, telling them that, accidents apart, 4000 New England men would land on Cape Breton in April, and that, even should they fail to capture Louisbourg, he would answer for it that they would lay the town in ruins, retake Canseau, do other good service to his Majesty, and then come safe home. On receiving this communication, the government resolved to aid the enterprise if there should yet be time, and accordingly ordered several ships-of-war to sail for Louisbourg.

The sarcastic Dr. Douglas, then living at Boston, writes that the expedition had a lawyer for contriver, a merchant for general, and farmers, fishermen, and mechanics for soldiers. In fact, it had something of the character of broad farce, to which Shirley himself, with all his ability and general good sense, was a chief contributor. He wrote to the Duke of Newcastle that though the officers had no experience and the men no discipline, he would take care to provide against these defects, — meaning that he would give exact directions how to take Louisbourg. Accordingly, he drew up copious instructions to that effect. These seem to have undergone a process of evolution, for several distinct drafts of them are preserved. The complete and final one is among the Pepperrell Papers, copied entire in the neat, commercial hand of the general himself. It seems to assume that Providence would work a continued miracle, and on every occasion supply the expedition with weather precisely suited to its wants. "It is thought," says this singular document, "that Louisbourg may be surprised if they [the French] have no advice of your coming. To effect it you must time your arrival about nine of the clock in the evening, taking care that the fleet be far enough in the offing to prevent their being seen from the town in the daytime." He then goes on to prescribe how the troops are to land, after dark, at a place called Flat Point Cove, in four divisions, three of which are to march to the back of certain hills a mile and a half west of the town, where two of the three "are to halt and keep a profound silence;" the third continuing its march "under cover of the said hills," till it comes opposite the Grand Battery, which it will attack at a concerted signal; while one of the two divisions behind the hills assaults the west gate, and the other moves up to support the attack.

While this is going on, the soldiers of the fourth division are to march with all speed along the shore till they come to a certain part of the town wall, which they are to scale; then proceed "as fast as can

be" to the citadel and "secure the windows of the governor's apartments." After this follow page after page of complicated details which
must have stricken the general with stupefaction. The rocks, surf, fogs,
and gales of that tempestuous coast are all left out of the account;
and so, too, is the nature of the country, which consists of deep
marshes, rocky hills, and hollows choked with evergreen thickets.
Yet a series of complex and mutually dependent operations, involving
long marches through this rugged and pathless region, was to be accomplished, in the darkness of one April night, by raw soldiers who
knew nothing of the country. This rare specimen of amateur soldiering
is redeemed in some measure by a postscript in which the governor sets
free the hands of the general, thus: "Notwithstanding the instructions
you have received from me, I must leave you to act, upon unforeseen
emergencies, according to your best discretion."

On the 24th of March, the fleet, consisting of about ninety transports,
escorted by the provincial cruisers, sailed from Nantasket Roads, followed by prayers and benedictions, and also by toasts drunk with
cheers, in bumpers of rum punch.[3]

---

[3] The following letter of 24 April 1745 is from John Payne of Boston to
Colonel Robert Hale of the Essex regiment: "SIR, — I hope this will find you at
Louisbourg with a Bowl of Punch a Pipe and a P——k of C——ds in your hand
and whatever else you desire (I had forgot to mention a Pretty French Madam-
moselle). We are very Impatiently expecting to hear from you, your Friend Luke
has lost several Beaver Hatts already concerning the Expedition, he is so very
zealous about it that he has turned Poor Boutier out of his House for saying he
believed you would not Take the Place. — Damn his Blood says Luke, let him be
an Englishman or a Frenchman and not pretend to be an Englishman when he is
a Frenchman in his Heart. If drinking to your success would Take Cape Briton,
you must be in Possession of it now, for it's a standing Toast. I think the least
thing you Military Gentlemen can do is to send us some arrack when you take
the Place to celebrate your Victory and not to force us to do it in Rum Punch
or Luke's bad wine or sour cyder."

CHAPTER XXX

Louisbourg Besieged

1745

[*A Half-Century of Conflict*, CHAPTER XIX]

On board one of the transports was Seth Pomeroy, gunsmith at Northampton, and now major of Willard's Massachusetts regiment. He had a turn for soldiering, and fought, ten years later, in the battle of Lake George. Again, twenty years later still, when Northampton was astir with rumors of war from Boston, he borrowed a neighbor's horse, rode a hundred miles, reached Cambridge on the morning of the battle of Bunker Hill, left his borrowed horse out of the way of harm, walked over Charlestown Neck, then swept by the fire of the ships-of-war, and reached the scene of action as the British were forming for the attack. When Israel Putnam, his comrade in the last war, saw from the rebel breastwork the old man striding, gun in hand, up the hill, he shouted, "By God, Pomeroy, you here! A cannon-shot would waken you out of your grave!"

But Pomeroy, with other landsmen, crowded in the small and malodorous fishing-vessels that were made to serve as transports, was now in the gripe of the most unheroic of maladies. "A terrible northeast storm" had fallen upon them, and, he says, "we lay rolling in the seas, with our sails furled, among prodigious waves." "Sick, day and night," writes the miserable gunsmith, "so bad that I have not words to set it forth." The gale increased and the fleet was scattered, there being, as a Massachusetts private soldier writes in his diary, " a very fierse Storm of Snow, som Rain and very Dangerous weather to be so nigh ye Shore as we was; but we escaped the Rocks, and that was all."

On Friday, April 5, Pomeroy's vessel entered the harbor of Canseau, about fifty miles from Louisbourg. Here was the English fishing-hamlet, the seizure of which by the French had first provoked the expedition. The place now quietly changed hands again. Sixty-eight of the transports lay here at anchor, and the rest came dropping in from day to day, sorely buffeted, but all safe. On Sunday there was a great concourse to hear Parson Moody preach an open-air sermon from the text, "Thy people shall be willing in the day of thy power," concerning which occasion the soldier diarist observes, — "Several sorts of Busnesses was Going on, Som a Exercising, Som a Hearing Preaching." The attention of Parson Moody's listeners was, in fact, distracted by shouts of command and the awkward drill of squads of homespun soldiers on the adjacent pasture.

Captain Ammi Cutter, with two companies, was ordered to remain at Canseau and defend it from farther vicissitudes; to which end a blockhouse was also built, and mounted with eight small cannon. Some of the armed vessels had been set to cruise off Louisbourg, which they did to good purpose, and presently brought in six French prizes, with supplies for the fortress. On the other hand, they brought the ominous news that Louisbourg and the adjoining bay were so blocked with ice that landing was impossible. This was a serious misfortune, involving long delay, and perhaps ruin to the expedition, as the expected ships-of-war might arrive meanwhile from France. Indeed, they had already begun to appear. On Thursday, the 18th, heavy cannonading was heard far out at sea, and again on Friday "the cannon," says Pomeroy, "fired at a great rate till about 2 of the clock." It was the provincial cruisers attacking a French frigate, the *Renommée*, of thirty-six guns. As their united force was too much for her, she kept up a running fight, outsailed them, and escaped after a chase of more than thirty hours, being, as Pomeroy quaintly observes, "a smart ship." She carried despatches to the governor of Louisbourg, and being unable to deliver them, sailed back for France to report what she had seen.

On Monday, the 22nd, a clear, cold, windy day, a large ship, under British colors, sailed into the harbor, and proved to be the frigate *Eltham*, escort to the annual mast fleet from New England. On orders from Commander Warren she had left her charge in waiting, and sailed for Canseau to join the expedition, bringing the unexpected and welcome news that Warren himself would soon follow. On the next day, to the delight of all, he appeared in the ship *Superbe*, of sixty guns, accompanied by the *Launceston* and the *Mermaid*, of forty guns each. Here was force enough to oppose any ships likely to come to the aid of Louisbourg; and Warren, after communicating with Pepperrell, sailed to blockade the port, along with the provincial cruisers, which, by order of Shirley, were placed under his command.

The transports lay at Canseau nearly three weeks, waiting for the ice to break up. The time was passed in drilling the raw soldiers and forming them into divisions of four and six hundred each, according to the directions of Shirley. At length, on Friday, the 27th, they heard that Gabarus Bay was free from ice, and on the morning of the 29th, with the first fair wind, they sailed out of Canseau harbor, expecting to reach Louisbourg at nine in the evening, as prescribed in the governor's receipt for taking Louisbourg "while the enemy were asleep." But a lull in the wind defeated this plan; and after sailing all day, they found themselves becalmed towards night. It was not till the next morning that they could see the town, — no very imposing spectacle, for the buildings, with a few exceptions, were small, and the massive ramparts that belted them round rose to no conspicuous height.

Louisbourg stood on a tongue of land which lay between its harbor and the sea, and the end of which was prolonged eastward by reefs and shoals that partly barred the entrance to the port, leaving a navigable passage not half a mile wide. This passage was commanded by a powerful battery called the "Island Battery," being upon a small rocky island at the west side of the channel, and was also secured by another detached work called the "Grand," or "Royal Battery," which stood on the shore of the harbor, opposite the entrance, and more than a mile from the town. Thus a hostile squadron trying to force its way in would receive a flank fire from the one battery, and a front fire from the other. The strongest line of defence of the fortress was drawn across the base of the tongue of land from the harbor on one side to the sea on the other, — a distance of about twelve hundred yards. The ditch was eighty feet wide and from thirty to thirty-six feet deep; and the rampart of earth faced with masonry, was about sixty feet thick. The glacis sloped down to a vast marsh, which formed one of the best defences of the place. The fortress, without counting its outworks, had embrasures for 148 cannon; but the number in position was much less, and is variously stated. Pomeroy says that at the end of the siege a little above ninety were found, with "a great number of swivels;" others say seventy-six. In the Grand and Island batteries there were sixty heavy pieces more. Against this formidable armament the asasailants had brought thirty-four cannon and mortars, of much inferior weight, to be used in bombarding the fortress, should they chance to fail of carrying it by surprise, "while the enemy were asleep." Apparently they distrusted the efficacy of their siege-train, though it was far stronger than Shirley had at first thought sufficient; for they brought with them good store of balls of forty-two pounds, to be used in French cannon of that calibre which they expected to capture, their own largest pieces being but twenty-two pounders.

According to the *Habitant de Louisbourg*, the garrison consisted of 560 regular troops, of whom several companies were Swiss, beside some 1300 or 1400 militia, inhabitants partly of the town, and partly of neighboring settlements. The regulars were in bad condition. About the preceding Christmas they had broken into mutiny, being discontented with their rations and exasperated with getting no extra pay for work on the fortifications. The affair was so serious that though order was restored, some of the officers lost all confidence in the soldiers; and this distrust proved most unfortunate during the siege. The governor, Chevalier Duchambon, successor of Duquesnel, who had died in the autumn, was not a man to grapple with a crisis, being deficient in decision of character, if not in capacity.

He expected an attack. "We were informed of the preparations from the first," says the *Habitant de Louisbourg*. Some Indians, who had been to Boston, carried to Canada the news of what was going on there; but it was not believed, and excited no alarm. It was not so at Louisbourg, where, says the French writer just quoted, "we lost precious moments in useless deliberations and resolutions no sooner made than broken. Nothing to the purpose was done, so that we were as much taken by surprise as if the enemy had pounced upon us unawares."

It was about the 25th of March when the garrison first saw the provincial cruisers hovering off the mouth of the harbor. They continued to do so at intervals till daybreak of the 30th of April, when the whole fleet of transports appeared standing towards Flat Point, which projects into Gabarus Bay, three miles west of the town. On this, Duchambon sent Morpain, captain of a privateer, or "corsair," to oppose the landing. He had with him eighty men, and was to be joined by forty more, already on the watch near the supposed point of disembarkation. At the same time cannon were fired and alarm bells rung in Louisbourg, to call in the militia of the neighborhood.

Pepperrell managed the critical work of landing with creditable skill. The rocks and the surf were more dangerous than the enemy. Several boats, filled with men, rowed towards Flat Point; but on a signal from the flagship *Shirley* rowed back again, Morpain flattering himself that his appearance had frightened them off. Being joined by several other boats, the united party, 100 men in all, pulled for another landing-place called Fresh-water Cove, or Anse de la Cormorandière, two miles farther up Gabarus Bay. Morpain and his party ran to meet them; but

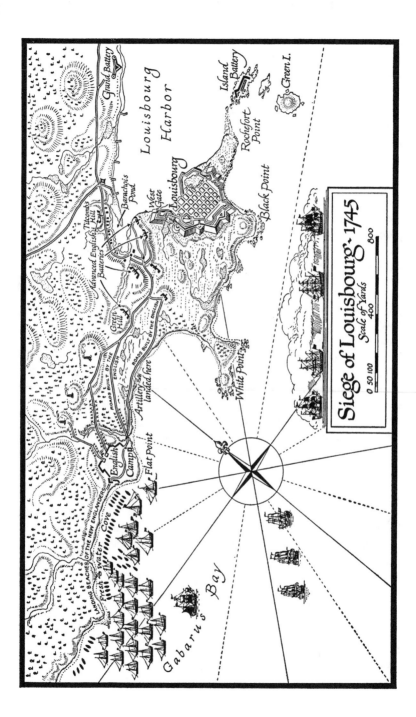

Siege of Louisbourg · 1745

Scale of Yards

0 50 100   400   800

the boats were first in the race, and as soon as the New England men got ashore, they rushed upon the French, killed six of them, captured as many more, including an officer named Boularderie, and put the rest to flight, with the loss, on their own side, of two men slightly wounded. Further resistance to the landing was impossible, for a swarm of boats pushed against the rough and stony beach, the men dashing through the surf, till before night about 2000 were on shore. The rest, or about 2000 more, landed at their leisure on the next day.

On the 2nd of May Vaughan led 400 men to the hills near the town, and saluted it with three cheers, — somewhat to the discomposure of the French, though they described the unwelcome visitors as a disorderly crowd. Vaughan's next proceeding pleased them still less. He marched behind the hills, in rear of the Grand Battery, to the northeast arm of the harbor, where there were extensive magazines of naval stores. These his men set on fire, and the pitch, tar, and other combustibles made a prodigious smoke. He was returning, in the morning, with a small party of followers behind the hills, when coming opposite the Grand Battery, and observing it from the ridge, he saw neither flag on the flagstaff, nor smoke from the barrack chimneys. One of his party was a Cape Cod Indian. Vaughan bribed him with a flask of brandy which he had in his pocket, — though, as the clerical historian takes pains to assure us, he never used it himself, — and the Indian, pretending to be drunk, or, as some say, mad, staggered towards the battery to reconnoitre. All was quiet. He clambered in at an embrasure, and found the place empty. The rest of the party followed, and one of them, William Tufts, of Medford, a boy of eighteen, climbed the flagstaff, holding in his teeth his red coat, which he made fast at the top, as a substitute for the British flag, — a proceeding that drew upon him a volley of unsuccessful cannon-shot from the town batteries.

Vaughan then sent this hasty note to Pepperrell: "May it please your Honour to be informed that by the grace of God and the courage of 13 men, I entered the Royal Battery about 9 o'clock, and am waiting for a reinforcement and a flag." Soon after, four boats, filled with men, approached from the town to reoccupy the battery, — no doubt in order to save the munitions and stores, and complete the destruction of the cannon. Vaughan and his thirteen men, standing on the open beach, under the fire of the town and the Island Battery, plied the boats with musketry, and kept them from landing, till Lieutenant-Colonel Bradstreet appeared with a reinforcement, on which the French pulled back to Louisbourg.

The English supposed that the French in the battery, when the clouds of smoke drifted over them from the burning storehouses, thought that they were to be attacked in force, and abandoned their post in a panic. This was not the case. "A detachment of the enemy," writes the *Habitant de Louisbourg*, "advanced to the neighborhood of the Royal Battery." This was Vaughan's four hundred on their way to burn the storehouses. "At once we were all seized with fright," pursues this candid writer, "and on the instant it was proposed to abandon this magnificent battery, which would have been our best defence, if one had known how to use it. Various councils were held, in a tumultuous way. It would be hard to tell the reasons for such a strange proceeding. Not one shot had yet been fired at the battery, which the enemy could not take, except by making regular approaches, as if against the town itself, and by besieging it, so to speak, in form. Some persons remonstrated, but in vain; and so a battery of thirty cannon, which had cost the King immense sums, was abandoned before it was attacked."

Duchambon says that soon after the English landed, he got a letter from Thierry, the captain in command of the Royal Battery, advising that the cannon should be spiked and the works blown up. It was then, according to the governor, that the council was called, and a unanimous vote passed to follow Thierry's advice, on the ground that the defences of the battery were in bad condition, and that the 400 men posted there could not stand against three or four thousand. The engineer, Verrier, opposed the blowing up of the works, and they were therefore left untouched. Thierry and his garrison came off in boats, after spiking the cannon in a hasty way, without stopping to knock off the trunnions or burn the carriages. They threw their loose gunpowder into the well, but left behind a good number of cannon cartridges, 280 large bombshells, and other ordinance stores, invaluable both to the enemy and to themselves. Brigadier Waldo was sent to occupy the battery with his regiment, and Major Seth Pomeroy, the gunsmith, with twenty soldier-mechanics, was set at drilling out the spiked touch-holes of the cannon. There were twenty-eight forty-two-pounders, and two eighteen-pounders. Several were ready for use the next morning, and immediately opened on the town, — which, writes a soldier in his diary, "damaged the houses and made the women cry." "The enemy," says the *Habitant de Louisbourg*, "saluted us with our own cannon, and made a terrific fire, smashing everything within range."

The English occupation of the Grand Battery may be called the decisive event of the siege. There seems no doubt that the French could have averted the disaster long enough to make it of little help to the invaders. The water-front of the battery was impregnable. The rear defences consisted of a loop-holed wall of masonry, with a ditch ten feet deep and twelve feet wide, and also a covered way and glacis, which General Wolcott describes as unfinished. In this he mistook. They were not unfinished, but had been partly demolished, with a view to reconstruction. The rear wall was flanked by two towers, which, says Duchambon, were demolished; but General Wolcott declares that swivels were still mounted on them, and he adds that "two hundred men might hold the battery against five thousand without cannon." The English landed their cannon near Flat Point; and before they could be turned against the Grand Battery, they must be dragged four miles over hills and rocks, through spongy marshes and jungles of matted evergreens. This would have required a week or more. The alternative was an escalade, in which the undisciplined assailants would no doubt have met a bloody rebuff. Thus this Grand Battery, which, says Wolcott, "is in fact a fort," might at least have been held long enough to save the munitions and stores, and effectually disable the cannon, which supplied the English with the only artillery they had, competent to the work before them. The hasty abandonment of this important post was not Duchambon's only blunder, but it was the worst of them all.

On the night after their landing, the New England men slept in the woods, wet or dry, with or without blankets, as the case might be, and in the morning set themselves to encamping with as much order as they were capable of. A brook ran down from the hills and entered the sea two miles or more from the town. The ground on each side, though rough, was high and dry, and here most of the regiments made their quarters, — Willard's, Moulton's, and Moore's on the east side, and Burr's and Pepperrell's on the west. Those on the east, in some cases, saw fit to extend themselves towards Louisbourg as far as the edge of the intervening marsh, but were soon forced back to a safer position by the cannon-balls of the fortress, which came bowling amongst them. This marsh was that green, flat sponge of mud and moss that stretched from this point to the glacis of Louisbourg.

There was great want of tents, for material to make them was scarce in New England. Old sails were often used instead, being stretched over poles, — perhaps after the fashion of a Sioux teepee. When these could not be had, the men built huts of sods, with roofs of spruce-boughs overlapping like a thatch; for at that early season, bark would not peel from the trees. The landing of guns, munitions, and stores was a formidable task, consuming many days and destroying many boats, as happened again when Amherst landed his cannon at this same place. Large flat boats, brought from Boston, were used for the purpose, and the loads were carried ashore on the heads of the men, wading through ice-cold surf to the waist, after which, having no change of clothing, they slept on the ground through the chill and foggy nights, reckless of future rheumatisms.

A worse task was before them. The cannon were to be dragged over the marsh to Green Hill, a spur of the line of rough heights that half encircled the town and harbor. Here the first battery was to be planted; and from this point other guns were to be dragged onward to more advanced stations, — a distance in all of more than two miles, thought by the French to be impassable. So, in fact, it seemed; for at the first attempt, the wheels of the cannon sank to the hubs in mud and moss, then the carriage, and finally the piece itself slowly disappeared. Lieutenant-Colonel Meserve, of the New Hampshire regiment, a shipbuilder by trade, presently overcame the difficulty. By his direction sledges of timber were made, sixteen feet long and five feet wide; a cannon was placed on each of these, and it was then dragged over the marsh by a team of 200 men, harnessed with rope-traces and breast-straps, and wading to the knees. Horses or oxen would have foundered in the mire. The way had often to be changed, as the mossy surface was soon churned into a hopeless slough along the line of march. The work could be done only at night or in thick fog, the men being completely exposed to the cannon of the town. Thirteen years after, when General Amherst besieged Louisbourg again, he dragged his cannon to the same hill over the same marsh; but having at his command, instead of 4000 militiamen, 11,000 British regulars, with all appliances and means to boot, he made a road, with prodigious labor, through the mire, and protected it from the French shot by an epaulement, or lateral earthwork.

Pepperrell writes in ardent words of the cheerfulness of his men "under almost incredible hardships." Shoes and clothing failed, till many were in tatters and many barefooted; yet they toiled on with unconquerable spirit, and within four days had planted a battery of six guns on Green Hill, which was about a mile from the King's Bastion of Louisbourg. In another week they had dragged four twenty-two-pound cannon and ten coehorns — gravely called "cowhorns" by the bucolic Pomeroy — six or seven hundred yards farther, and planted them within easy range of the citadel. Two of the cannon burst, and were replaced by four more and a large mortar, which burst in its turn, and Shirley was begged to send another. Meanwhile a battery, chiefly of coehorns, had been planted on a hillock 440 yards from the West Gate, where it greatly annoyed the French; and on the next night an advanced battery was placed just opposite the same gate, and scarcely two hundred and fifty yards from it. This West Gate, the principal gate of Louisbourg, opened upon the tract of high, firm ground that lay on the left of the besiegers, between the marsh and the harbor, an arm of which here extended westward beyond the town, into what was called the Barachois, a salt pond formed by a projecting spit of sand. On the side of the Barachois farthest from the town was a hillock on which stood the house of an *habitant* named Martissan. Here, on the 20th of May, a fifth battery was planted, consisting of two of the French forty-two-pounders taken in the Grand Battery, to which three others were afterwards added. Each of these heavy pieces was dragged to its destination by a team of 300 men over rough and rocky ground swept by the French artillery. This fifth battery, called the Northwest, or Titcomb's, proved most destructive to the fortress.

All these operations were accomplished with the utmost ardor and energy, but with a scorn of rule and precedent that astonished and bewildered the French. The raw New England men went their own way, laughed at trenches and zigzags, and persisted in trusting their lives to the night and the fog. Several writers say that the English engineer Bastide tried to teach them discretion; but this could hardly be, for Bastide, whose station was Annapolis, did not reach Louisbourg till the 5th of June, when the batteries were finished, and the siege was nearly ended. A recent French writer makes the curious assertion that it was one of the ministers, or army chaplains, who took upon him the vain task of instruction in the art of war on this occasion.

This ignorant and self-satisfied recklessness might have cost the besiegers dear if the French, instead of being perplexed and startled at the novelty of their proceedings, had taken advantage of it; but Duchambon and some of his officers, remembering the mutiny of the past winter, feared to make sorties, lest the soldiers might desert or take part with the enemy. The danger of this appears to have been small. Warren speaks with wonder in his letters of the rarity of desertions, of which there appear to have been but three during the siege, — one being that of a half-idiot, from whom no information could be got. A bolder commander would not have stood idle while his own cannon were planted by the enemy to batter down his walls; and whatever the risks of a sortie, the risks of not making one were greater. "Both troops and militia eagerly demanded it, and I believe it would have succeeded," writes the intendant, Bigot. The attempt was actually made more than once in a half-hearted way, — notably on the eighth of May, when the French attacked the most advanced battery, and were repulsed, with little loss on either side.

The *Habitant de Louisbourg* says: "The enemy did not attack us with any regularity, and made no intrenchments to cover themselves." This last is not exact. Not being wholly demented, they made intrenchments, such as they were, — at least, at the advanced battery; as they would otherwise have been swept out of existence, being under the concentrated fire of several French batteries, two of which were within range of a musket-shot.

The scarcity of good gunners was one of the chief difficulties of the besiegers. As privateering, and piracy also, against Frenchmen and Spaniards was a favorite pursuit in New England, there were men in Pepperrell's army who knew how to handle cannon; but their number was insufficient, and the general sent a note to Warren, begging that he would lend him a few experienced gunners to teach their trade to the raw hands at the batteries. Three or four were sent, and they found apt pupils.

Pepperrell placed the advanced battery in charge of Captain Joseph Sherburn, telling him to enlist as many gunners as he could. On the next day Sherburn reported that he had found six, one of whom seems to have been sent by Warren. With these and a number of raw men he repaired to his perilous station, where "I found," he says, "a very poor intrenchment. Our best shelter from the French fire, which was very hot, was hogsheads filled with earth." He and his men made the West Gate their chief mark; but before they could get a fair sight of it, they were forced to shoot down the fish-flakes, or stages for drying cod, that obstructed the view. Some of their party were soon killed, — Captain Pierce by a cannon-ball, Thomas Ash by a "bumb," and others by musketry. In the night they improved their defences, and mounted on them three more guns, one of eighteen-pound calibre, and the others of forty-two, — French pieces dragged from the Grand Battery, a mile and three quarters round the Barachois.

The cannon could be loaded only under a constant fire of musketry, which the enemy briskly returned. The French practice was excellent. A soldier who in bravado mounted the rampart and stood there for a moment was shot dead with five bullets. The men on both sides called to each other in scraps of bad French or broken English; while the French drank ironical healths to the New England men, and gave them bantering invitations to breakfast.

Sherburn continues his diary. "Sunday morning. Began our fire with as much fury as possible, and the French returned it as warmly from the Citidale [citadel], West Gate, and North East Battery with Cannon, Mortars, and continual showers of musket balls; but by 11 o'clock we had beat them all from their guns." He goes on to say that at noon his men were forced to stop firing from want of powder, that he went with his gunners to get some, and that while they were gone, some-body, said to be Mr. Vaughan, brought a supply, on which the men loaded the forty-two pounders in a bungling way, and fired them. One was dismounted, and the other burst; a barrel and a half-barrel of powder blew up, killed two men, and injured two more. Again: "Wed-nesday. Hot fire on both sides, till the French were beat from all their guns. May 29th went to 2 Gun [Titcomb's] Battery to give the gunners some directions; then returned to my own station, where I spent the rest of the day with pleasure, seeing our Shott Tumble down their walls and Flagg Staff."

The following is the intendant Bigot's account of the effect of the New England fire: "The enemy established their batteries to such effect that they soon destroyed the greater part of the town, broke the right flank of the King's Bastion, ruined the Dauphin Battery with its spur, and made a breach at the Porte Dauphine [West Gate], the neighbor-ing wall, and the sort of redan adjacent." Duchambon says in addition that the cannon of the right flank of the King's Bastion could not be served, by reason of the continual fire of the enemy, which broke the embrasures to pieces; that when he had them repaired, they were broken to pieces (*démantibulés*) again, — and nobody could keep his ground behind the wall of the quay, which was shot through and through and completely riddled. The town was ploughed with cannon-balls, the streets were raked from end to end, nearly all the houses damaged, and the people driven for refuge into the stifling casemates. The results were creditable to novices in gunnery.

The repeated accidents from the bursting of cannon were no doubt largely due to unskilful loading and the practice of double-shotting, to which the overzealous artillerists are said to have often resorted.

It is said, in proof of the orderly conduct of the men, that not one of them was punished during all the siege; but this shows the mild and conciliating character of the general quite as much as any peculiar merit of the soldiers. The state of things in and about the camp was compared by the caustic Dr. Douglas to "a Cambridge Commencement," which academic festival was then attended by much rough frolic and boisterous horseplay among the disorderly crowds, white and black, bond and free, who swarmed among the booths on Cambridge Common. The careful and scrupulous Belknap, who knew many who took part in the siege, says: "Those who were on the spot have frequently, in my hearing, laughed at the recital of their own irregularities, and expressed their admiration when they reflected on the almost miraculous preservation of the army from destruction." While the cannon bellowed in the front, frolic and confusion reigned at the camp, where the men raced, wrestled, pitched quoits, fired at marks, — though there was no ammunition to spare, — and ran after the French cannon-balls, which were carried to the batteries, to be returned to those who sent them. Nor were calmer recreations wanting. "Some of our men went a fishing, about 2 miles off," writes Lieutenant Benjamin Cleaves in his diary: "caught 6 Troutts." And, on the same day, "Our men went to catch Lobsters: caught 30." In view of this truant disposition, it is not surprising that the besiegers now and then lost their scalps at the hands of prowling Indians who infested the neighborhood. Yet through all these gambols ran an undertow of enthusiasm, born in brains still fevered from the "Great Awakening." The New England soldier, a growth of sectarian hotbeds, fancied that he was doing the work of God. The army was Israel, and the French were Canaanitish idolaters. Red-hot Calvinism, acting through generations, had modified the transplanted Englishman; and the descendant of the Puritans was never so well pleased as when teaching their duty to other people, whether by pen, voice, or bombshells. The ragged artillerymen, battering the walls of papistical Louisbourg, flattered themselves with the notion that they were champions of gospel truth.

Barefoot and tattered, they toiled on with indomitable pluck and cheerfulness, doing the work which oxen could not do, with no comfort but their daily dram of New England rum, as they plodded through the marsh and over rocks, dragging the ponderous guns through fog and darkness. Their spirit could not save them from the effects of excessive fatigue and exposure. They were ravaged with diarrhœa and fever, till fifteen hundred men were at one time on the sick-list, and at another, Pepperrell reported that of the 4000 only about 2100 were fit for duty. Nearly all at last recovered, for the weather was unusually good; yet the number fit for service was absurdly small. Pepperrell begged for reinforcements, but got none till the siege was ended.

It was not his nature to rule with a stiff hand, — and this, perhaps, was fortunate. Order and discipline, the sinews of an army, were out of the question; and it remained to do as well as might be without them, keep men and officers in good-humor, and avoid all that could dash their ardor. For this, at least, the merchant-general was well fitted. His popularity had helped to raise the army, and perhaps it helped now to make it efficient. His position was no bed of roses. Worries, small and great, pursued him without end. He made friends of his officers, kept a bountiful table at his tent, and labored to soothe their disputes and jealousies, and satisfy their complaints. So generous were his contributions to the common cause that according to a British officer who speaks highly of his services, he gave to it, in one form or another, £10,000 out of his own pocket.

His letter-books reveal a swarm of petty annoyances, which may have tried his strength and patience as much as more serious cares. The soldiers complained that they were left without clothing, shoes, or rum; and when he implored the Committee of War to send them, Osborne, the chairman, replied with explanations why it could not be done. Letters came from wives and fathers entreating that husbands and sons who had gone to the war should be sent back. At the end of the siege a captain "humble begs leave for to go home," because he lives in a very dangerous country, and his wife and children are "in a declining way" without him. Then two entire companies raised on the frontier offered the same petition on similar grounds. Sometimes Pepperrell was beset with prayers for favors and promotion; sometimes with complaints from one corps or another that an undue share of work had been imposed on it. One Morris, of Cambridge, writes a moving petition that his slave "Cuffee," who had joined the army, should be restored to him, his lawful master. One John Alford sends the general a number of copies of the Rev. Mr. Prentice's late sermon; for distribution, assuring him that "it will please your whole army of volunteers, as he has shown them the way to gain by their gallantry the hearts and affections of the Ladys." The end of the siege brought countless letters of congratulation, which, whether lay or clerical, never failed to remind him, in set phrases, that he was but an instrument in the hands of Providence.

One of his most persistent correspondents was his son-in-law,

Nathaniel Sparhawk, a thrifty merchant, with a constant eye to business, who generally began his long-winded epistles with a bulletin concerning the health of "Mother Pepperrell," and rarely ended them without charging his father-in-law with some commission, such as buying for him the cargo of a French prize, if he could get it cheap. Or thus: "If you would procure for me a hogshead of the best Clarett, and a hogshead of the best white wine, at a reasonable rate, it would be very grateful to me." After pestering him with a few other commissions, he tells him that "Andrew and Betty [children of Pepperrell] send their proper compliments," and signs himself, with the starched flourish of provincial breeding, "With all possible Respect, Honoured Sir, Your Obedient Son and Servant." Pepperrell was much annoyed by the conduct of the masters of the transports, of whom he wrote: "The unaccountable irregular behaviour of these fellows is the greatest fatigue I meet with;" but it may be doubted whether his son-in-law did not prove an equally efficient persecutor.

CHAPTER XXXI

Louisbourg Taken

1745

[A Half-Century of Conflict, CHAPTER XX]

Frequent councils of war were held in solemn form at headquarters. On the 7th of May a summons to surrender was sent to Duchambon, who replied that he would answer with his cannon. Two days after, we find in the record of the council the following startling entry: "Advised unanimously that the Town of Louisbourg be attacked by storm this Night." Vaughan was a member of the board, and perhaps his impetuous rashness had turned the heads of his colleagues. To storm the fortress at that time would have been a desperate attempt for the best-trained and best-led troops. There was as yet no breach in the walls, nor the beginning of one; and the French were so confident in the strength of their fortifications that they boasted that women alone could defend them. Nine in ten of the men had no bayonets, many had no shoes, and it is said that the scaling-ladders they had brought from Boston were ten feet too short. Perhaps it was unfortunate for the French that the army was more prudent than its leaders; and another council being called on the same day, it was "Advised, That, inasmuch as there appears a great Dissatisfaction in many of the officers and Soldiers at the designed attack of the Town by Storm this Night, the said Attack be deferred for the present."

Another plan was adopted, hardly less critical, though it found favor with the army. This was the assault of the Island Battery, which closed the entrance of the harbor to the British squadron, and kept it open to ships from France. Nobody knew precisely how to find the two landing-places of this formidable work, which were narrow gaps between rocks lashed with almost constant surf; but Vaughan would see no difficulties, and wrote to Pepperrell that if he would give him the command and leave him to manage the attack in his own way, he would engage to send the French flag to headquarters within forty-eight hours. On the next day he seems to have thought the command assured to him, and writes from the Grand Battery that the carpenters are at work mending whale-boats and making paddles, asking at the same time for plenty of pistols and 100 hand grenades, with men who know how to use them. The weather proved bad, and the attempt was deferred. This happened several times, till Warren grew impatient and offered to support the attack with 200 sailors.

At length, on the 23rd, the volunteers for the perilous enterprise mustered at the Grand Battery, whence the boats were to set out. Brigadier Waldo, who still commanded there, saw them with concern and anxiety, as they came dropping in, in small squads, without officers, noisy, disorderly, and, in some cases, more or less drunk. "I doubt," he told the general, "whether straggling fellows, three, four, or seven out of a company, ought to go on such a service." A bright moon and northern lights again put off the attack. The volunteers remained at the Grand Battery, waiting for better luck. "They seem to be impatient for action," writes Waldo. "If there were a more regular appearance, it would give me greater sattysfaction." On the 26th their wish for action was fully gratified. The night was still and dark, and the boats put out from the battery towards twelve o'clock, with about 300 men on board. These were to be joined by 100 or 150 more from Gorham's regiment, then stationed at Lighthouse Point. The commander was not Vaughan, but one Brooks, — the choice of the men themselves, as were also his subordinates. They moved slowly, the boats being propelled, not by oars, but by paddles, which, if skilfully used, would make no noise. The wind presently rose; and when they found a landing-place, the surf was lashing the rocks with even more than usual fury. There was room for but three boats at once between the breakers on each hand. They pushed in, and the men scrambled ashore with what speed they might.

The Island Battery was a strong work, walled in on all sides, garrisoned by 180 men, and armed with thirty cannon, seven swivels, and two mortars. It was now a little after midnight. Captain d'Aillebout, the commandant, was on the watch, pacing the battery platform; but he seems to have seen nothing unusual till about 150 men had got on shore, when they had the folly to announce their presence by three cheers. Then, in the words of General Wolcott, the battery "blazed with cannon, swivels, and small-arms." The crowd of boats, dimly visible through the darkness, as they lay just off the landing, waiting their turn to go in, were at once the target for volleys of grape-shot, langrage-shot, and musket-balls; of which the men on shore had also their share. These succeeded, however, in planting twelve scaling-ladders against the wall. It is said that some of them climbed into the place, and the improbable story is told that Brooks, their commander, was hauling down the French flag when a Swiss grenadier cut him down with a cutlass. Many of the boats were shattered or sunk, while those in the rear, seeing the state of things, appear to have sheered off. The affair was soon reduced to an exchange of shots between the garrison and the men who had landed, and who, standing on the open ground without the walls, were not wholly invisible, while the French, behind their ramparts, were completely hidden. "The fire of the English," says Bigot, "was extremely obstinate, but without effect, as they could not see to take aim." They kept it up till daybreak, or about two hours and a half; and then, seeing themselves at the mercy of the French, surrendered to the number of 119, including the wounded, three or more of whom died almost immediately. By the most trustworthy accounts the English loss in killed, drowned, and captured was 189; or, in the words of Pepperrell, "nearly half our party." Disorder, precipitation, and weak leadership ruined what hopes the attempt ever had.

As this was the only French success during the siege, Duchambon makes the most of it. He reports that the battery was attacked by 1000 men, supported by 800 more, who were afraid to show themselves; and, farther, that there were thirty-five boats, all of which were destroyed or sunk, — though he afterwards says that two of them got away with thirty men, being all that were left of the thousand. Bigot, more moderate, puts the number of assailants at 500, of whom he says that all perished, except 119 who were captured.

At daybreak Louisbourg rang with shouts of triumph. It was plain that a disorderly militia could not capture the Island Battery. Yet captured or silenced it must be; and orders were given to plant a battery against it at Lighthouse Point, on the eastern side of the harbor's mouth, at the distance of a short half-mile. The neighboring shore was rocky and almost inaccessible. Cannon and mortars were carried in boats to the nearest landing-place, hauled up a steep cliff, and dragged a mile and a quarter to the chosen spot, where they were planted under the orders of Colonel Gridley, who thirty years after directed the earthworks on Bunker Hill. The new battery soon opened fire with deadly effect.

The French, much encouraged by their late success, were plunged again into despondency by a disaster which had happened a week before the affair of the Island Battery, but did not come to their knowledge till some time after. On the 19th of May a fierce cannonade was heard from the harbor, and a large French ship-of-war was seen hotly engaged with several vessels of the squadron. She was the *Vigilant*, carrying 64 guns and 560 men, and commanded by the Marquis de la Maisonfort. She had come from France with munitions and stores, when on approaching Louisbourg she met one of the English cruisers, — some say the *Mermaid* of 40 guns, and others the *Shirley* of 20. Being no match for her, the British or provincial frigate kept up a running fight and led her towards the English fleet. The *Vigilant* soon found herself beset by several other vessels, and after a gallant resistance and the loss of eighty men, struck her colors. Nothing could be more timely for the New England army, whose ammunition and provisions had sunk perilously low. The French prize now supplied their needs, and drew from the *Habitant de Louisbourg* the mournful comment, "We were victims devoted to appease the wrath of Heaven, which turned our own arms into weapons for our enemies."

Nor was this the last time when the defenders of Louisbourg supplied the instruments of their own destruction; for ten cannon were presently unearthed at low tide from the flats near the careening wharf in the northeast arm of the harbor, where they had been hidden by the French some time before. Most of them proved sound; and being mounted at Lighthouse Point, they were turned against their late owners at the Island Battery.

When Gorham's regiment first took post at Lighthouse Point, Duchambon thought the movement so threatening that he forgot his former doubts, and ordered a sortie against it, under the Sieur de Beaubassin. Beaubassin landed, with 100 men, at a place called Lorembec, and advanced to surprise the English detachment; but was discovered by an outpost of forty men, who attacked and routed his party. Being then joined by eighty Indians, Beaubassin had several other skirmishes with English scouting-parties, till, pushed by superior numbers, and their leader severely wounded, his men regained Louisbourg by sea, escaping with difficulty from the guard-boats of the squadron. The Sieur de la Vallière, with a considerable party of men, tried to burn Pepperrell's storehouses, near Flat Point Cove; but ten or twelve of his followers were captured, and nearly all the rest wounded. Various other petty encounters took place between English scouting-parties and roving bands of French and Indians, always ending, according to Pepperrell, in the discomfiture of the latter. To this, however, there was at least one exception. Twenty English were waylaid and surrounded near Petit Lorembec by forty or fifty Indians, accompanied by two or three Frenchmen. Most of the English were shot down, several escaped, and the rest surrendered on promise of life; upon which the Indians, in cold blood, shot or speared some of them, and atrociously tortured others.

This suggested to Warren a device which had two objects, — to prevent such outrages in future, and to make known to the French that the ship *Vigilant*, the mainstay of their hopes, was in English hands. The treatment of the captives was told to the Marquis de la Maisonfort, late captain of the *Vigilant*, now a prisoner on board the ship he had commanded, and he was requested to lay the facts before Duchambon. This he did with great readiness, in a letter containing these words: "It is well that you should be informed that the captains and officers of this squadron treat us, not as their prisoners, but as their good friends, and take particular pains that my officers and crew should want for nothing; therefore it seems to me just to treat them in like manner, and to punish those who do otherwise and offer any insult to the prisoners who may fall into your hands."

Captain M'Donald, of the marines, carried this letter to Duchambon under a flag-of-truce. Though familiar with the French language, he spoke to the governor through an interpreter, so that the French officers present, who hitherto had only known that a large ship had been taken, expressed to each other without reserve their discouragement and dismay when they learned that the prize was no other than the *Vigilant*. Duchambon replied to La Maisonfort's letter that the Indians alone were answerable for the cruelties in question, and that he would forbid such conduct for the future.

The besiegers were now threatened by a new danger. We have seen that in the last summer the Sieur Duvivier had attacked Annapolis. Undaunted by ill-luck, he had gone to France to beg for help to attack it again; 2000 men were promised him, and in anticipation of their arrival the governor of Canada sent a body of French and Indians, under the noted partisan Marin, to meet and co-operate with them. Marin was ordered to wait at Les Mines till he heard of the arrival of the troops from France; but he grew impatient, and resolved to attack Annapolis without them. Accordingly, he laid siege to it with the six or seven hundred whites and Indians of his party, aided by the so-called Acadian neutrals. Mascarene, the governor, kept them at bay till the 24th of May, when, to his surprise, they all disappeared. Duchambon had sent them an order to make all haste to the aid of Louisbourg. As the report of this reached the besiegers, multiplying Marin's force fourfold, they expected to be attacked by numbers more than equal to those of their own effective men. This wrought a wholesome reform. Order was established in the camp, which was now fenced with palisades and watched by sentinels and scouting-parties.

Another tribulation fell upon the general. Shirley had enjoined it upon him to keep in perfect harmony with the naval commander, and the injunction was in accord with Pepperrell's conciliating temper. Warren was no less earnest than he for the success of the enterprise, lent him ammunition in time of need, and offered every aid in his power, while Pepperrell in letters to Shirley and Newcastle praised his colleague without stint. But in habits and character the two men differed widely. Warren was in the prime of life, and the ardor of youth still burned in him. He was impatient at the slow movement of the siege. Prisoners told him of a squadron expected from Brest, of which the *Vigilant* was the forerunner; and he feared that even if it could not defeat him, it might elude the blockade, and with the help of the continual fogs, get into Louisbourg in spite of him, thus making its capture impossible. Therefore he called a council of his captains on board his flagship, the *Superbe*, and proposed a plan for taking the place without further delay. On the same day he laid it before Pepperrell. It was to the effect that all the King's ships and provincial cruisers should enter the harbor, after taking on board 1600 of Pepperrell's men, and attack the town from the water side, while what was left of the army should assault it by land. To accept the proposal would have been to pass over the command to Warren, only about 2100 of the New England men being fit for service at the time, while of these the general informs Warren that "six hundred are gone in quest of two bodies of French and Indians, who, we are informed, are gathering, one to the eastward, and the other to the westward."

To this Warren replies, with some appearance of pique, "I am very sorry that no one plan of mine, though approved by all my captains, has been so fortunate as to meet your approbation or have any weight with you." And to show his title to consideration, he gives an extract from a letter written to him by Shirley, in which that inveterate flatterer hints his regret that, by reason of other employments, Warren could not take command of the whole expedition, — "which I doubt not," says the governor, "would be a most happy event for his Majesty's service."

Pepperrell kept his temper under this thrust, and wrote to the commodore with invincible courtesy: "Am extremely sorry the fogs prevent me from the pleasure of waiting on you on board your ship," adding that six hundred men should be furnished from the army and the transports to man the *Vigilant*, which was now the most powerful ship in the squadron. In short, he showed every disposition to meet Warren halfway. But the commodore was beginning to feel some doubts as to the expediency of the bold action he had proposed, and informed Pepperrell that his pilots thought it impossible to go into the harbor until the Island Battery was silenced. In fact, there was danger that if the ships got in while that battery was still alive and active, they would never get out again, but be kept there as in a trap, under the fire from the town ramparts.

Gridley's artillery at Lighthouse Point had been doing its best, dropping bombshells with such precision into the Island Battery that the French soldiers were sometimes seen running into the sea to escape the explosions. Many of the Island guns were dismounted, and the place was fast becoming untenable. At the same time the English batteries on the land side were pushing their work of destruction with relentless industry, and walls and bastions crumbled under their fire. The French labored with energy under cover of night to repair the mischief; closed the shattered West Gate with a wall of stone and earth twenty feet thick, made an epaulement to protect what was left of the formidable Circular Battery, — all but three of whose sixteen guns had been dismounted, — stopped the throat of the Dauphin's Bastion with a barricade of stone, and built a cavalier, or raised battery, on the King's Bastion, — where, however, the English fire soon ruined it. Against that near and peculiarly dangerous neighbor, the advanced battery, or, as they called it, the *Batterie de Francœur*, they planted three heavy cannon to take it in flank. "These," says Duchambon, "produced a marvellous effect, dismounted one of the cannon of the Bastonnais, and damaged all their embrasures, — which," concludes the governor, "did not prevent them from keeping up a constant fire; and they repaired by night the mischief we did them by day."

Pepperrell and Warren at length came to an understanding as to a joint attack by land and water. The Island Battery was by this time crippled, and the town batteries that commanded the interior of the harbor were nearly destroyed. It was agreed that Warren, whose squadron was now increased by recent arrivals to eleven ships, besides the provincial cruisers, should enter the harbor with the first fair wind, cannonade the town and attack it in boats, while Pepperrell stormed it from the land side. Warren was to hoist a Dutch flag under his pennant, at his main-top-gallant mast-head, as a signal that he was about to sail in; and Pepperrell was to answer by three columns of smoke, marching at the same time towards the walls with drums beating and colors flying.

The French saw with dismay a large quantity of fascines carried to the foot of the glacis, ready to fill the ditch, and their scouts came in with reports that more than a thousand scaling-ladders were lying behind the ridge of the nearest hill. Toil, loss of sleep, and the stifling air of the casemates, in which they were forced to take refuge, had sapped the strength of the besieged. The town was a ruin; only one house was untouched by shot or shell. "We could have borne all this," writes the intendant Bigot; "but the scarcity of powder, the loss of the *Vigilant*, the presence of the squadron, and the absence of any news from Marin, who had been ordered to join us with his Canadians and Indians, spread terror among troops and inhabitants. The townspeople said that they did not want to be put to the sword, and were not strong enough to resist a general assault." On the 15th of June they brought a petition to Duchambon, begging him to capitulate.

On that day Captain Sherburn, at the advanced battery, wrote in his diary: "By 12 o'clock we had got all our platforms laid, embrazures mended, guns in order, shot in place, cartridges ready, dined, gunners quartered, matches lighted to return their last favours, when we heard their drums beat a parley; and soon appeared a flag of truce, which I received midway between our battery and their walls, conducted the officer to Green Hill, and delivered him to Colonel Richmond."

La Perelle, the French officer, delivered a note from Duchambon, directed to both Pepperrell and Warren, and asking for a suspension of arms to enable him to draw up proposals for capitulation. Warren chanced to be on shore when the note came; and the two commanders answered jointly that it had come in good time, as they had just resolved on a general attack, and that they would give the governor till eight o'clock of the next morning to make his proposals.

They came in due time, but were of such a nature that Pepperrell refused to listen to them, and sent back Bonaventure, the officer who brought them, with counter-proposals. These were the terms which Duchambon had rejected on the 7th of May, with added conditions; as, among others, that no officer, soldier, or inhabitant of Louisbourg should bear arms against the King of England or any of his allies for the space of a year. Duchambon stipulated, as the condition of his acceptance, that his troops should march out of the fortress with their arms and colors. To this both the English commanders consented, Warren observing to Pepperrell "the uncertainty of our affairs, that depend so much on wind and weather, makes it necessary not to stickle at trifles." The articles were signed on both sides, and on the 17th the ships sailed peacefully into the harbor, while Pepperrell with a part of his ragged army entered the south gate of the town. "Never was a place more mal'd with cannon and shells," he writes to Shirley; "neither have I red in History of any troops behaving with greater courage. We gave them about nine thousand cannon-balls and six hundred bombs." Thus this unique military performance ended in complete and astonishing success.

According to English accounts, the French had lost about 300 men during the siege; but their real loss seems to have been not much above a third of that number. On the side of the besiegers, the deaths from all causes were only 130, about thirty of which were from disease. The French used their muskets to good purpose; but their mortar practice was bad, and close as was the advanced battery to their walls, they often failed to hit it, while the ground on both sides of it looked like a ploughed field, from the bursting of their shells. Their surrender was largely determined by want of ammunition, as, according to one account, the French had but thirty-seven barrels of gunpowder left, — in which particular the besiegers fared little better.

The New England men had been full of confidence in the result of the proposed assault, and a French writer says that the timely capitulation saved Louisbourg from a terrible catastrophe; yet, ill-armed and disorderly as the besiegers were, it may be doubted whether the quiet ending of the siege was not as fortunate for them as for their foes. The discouragement of the French was increased by greatly exaggerated ideas of the force of the "Bastonnais." The *Habitant de Louisbourg* ⚑aces the land-force alone at eight or nine thousand men, and Duchambon reports to the minister D'Argenson that he was attacked in all by 13,000. His mortifying position was a sharp temptation to exaggerate; but his conduct can only be explained by a belief that the force of his enemy was far greater than it was in fact.

Warren thought that the proposed assault would succeed, and wrote to Pepperrell that he hoped they would "soon keep a good house together, and give the Ladys of Louisbourg a Gallant Ball." During his visit to the camp on the day when the flag of truce came out, he made a speech to the New England soldiers, exhorting them to behave like true Englishmen; at which they cheered lustily. Making a visit to the Grand Battery on the same day, he won high favor with the regiment stationed there by the gift of a hogshead of rum to drink his health.

Whether Warren's "gallant ball" ever took place in Louisbourg does not clearly appear. Pepperrell, on his part, celebrated the victory by a dinner to the commodore and his officers. As the redoubtable Parson Moody was the general's chaplain and the oldest man in the army, he expected to ask a blessing at the board, and was, in fact, invited to do so, — to the great concern of those who knew his habitual prolixity, and dreaded its effect on the guests. At the same time, not one of them dared rasp his irritable temper by any suggestion of brevity; and hence they came in terror to the feast, expecting an invocation of a good half-hour, ended by open revolt of the hungry Britons; when, to their surprise and relief, Moody said: "Good Lord, we have so much to thank thee for, that time will be too short, and we must leave it for eternity. Bless our food and fellowship upon this joyful occasion, for the sake of Christ our Lord, Amen." And with that he sat down.

It is said that he had been seen in the French church hewing at the altar and images with the axe that he had brought for that purpose; and perhaps this iconoclastic performance had eased the high pressure of his zeal.

Amazing as their triumph was, Pepperrell's soldiers were not satisfied with the capitulation, and one of them utters his disapproval in his diary thus: "Sabbath Day, ye 16th June. They came to Termes for us to enter ye Sitty to morrow, and Poore Termes they Bee too."

The occasion of discontent was the security of property assured to the inhabitants, "by which means," says that dull chronicler, Niles, "the poor soldiers lost all their hopes and just demerit [desert] of plunder promised them." In the meagreness of their pay they thought themselves entitled to the plunder of Louisbourg, which they imagined to be a seat of wealth and luxury. Nathaniel Sparhawk, Pepperrell's thrifty son-in-law, shared this illusion, and begged the general to get for him (at a low price) a handsome service of silver plate. When the volunteers exchanged their wet and dreary camp for what they expected to be the comfortable quarters of the town, they were disgusted to see the houses still occupied by the owners, and to find themselves forced to stand guard at the doors, to protect them. "A great Noys and hubbub a mongst ye Solders a bout ye Plunder; Som Cursing, som a Swarein," writes one of the disgusted victors.

They were not, and perhaps could not be, long kept in order; and when, in accordance with the capitulation, the inhabitants had been sent on board vessels for transportation to France, discipline gave way, and General Wolcott records that, while Moody was preaching on a Sunday in the garrison-chapel, there was "excessive stealing in every part of the town." Little, however, was left to steal.

But if the army found but meagre gleanings, the navy reaped a rich harvest. French ships, instead of being barred out of the harbor, were now lured to enter it. The French flag was kept flying over the town, and in this way prizes were entrapped to the estimated value of a million sterling, half of which went to the Crown, and the rest to the British officers and crews, the army getting no share whatever.

Now rose the vexed question of the relative part borne by the colonies and the Crown, the army and the navy, in the capture of Louisbourg; and here it may be well to observe the impressions of a French witness of the siege. "It was an enterprise less of the English nation and its King than of the inhabitants of New England alone. This singular people have their own laws and administration, and their governor plays the sovereign. Admiral Warren had no authority over the troops sent by the Governor of Boston, and he was only a spectator. . . . Nobody would have said that their sea and land forces were of the same nation and under the same prince. No nation but the English is capable of such eccentricities (*bizarreries*), — which, nevertheless, are a part of the precious liberty of which they show themselves so jealous."

The French writer is correct when he says that the land and sea forces were under separate commands, and it is equally true that but for the conciliating temper of Pepperrell, harmony could not have been preserved between the two chiefs; but when he calls Warren a mere spectator, he does glaring injustice to that gallant officer, whose activity and that of his captains was incessant, and whose services were invaluable. They maintained, with slight lapses, an almost impossible blockade, without which the siege must have failed. Two or three small vessels got into the harbor; but the capture of the *Vigilant*, more than any other event of the siege, discouraged the French and prepared them for surrender.

Several English writers speak of Warren and the navy as the captors of Louisbourg, and all New England writers give the chief honor to Pepperrell and the army. Neither army nor navy would have been successful without the other. Warren and his officers, in a council of war, had determined that so long as the Island Battery and the water batteries of the town remained in an efficient state, the ships could not enter the harbor; and Warren had personally expressed the same opinion. He did not mean to enter till all the batteries which had made the attempt impracticable, including the Circular Battery, which was the most formidable of all, had been silenced or crippled by the army, and by the army alone. The whole work of the siege fell upon the land forces; and though it had been proposed to send a body of marines on shore, this was not done. Three or four gunners, "to put your men in the way of loading cannon," was Warren's contribution to the operations of the siege; though the fear of attack by the ships, jointly with the land force, no doubt hastened the surrender. Beauharnois, governor of Canada, ascribes the defeat to the extreme activity with which the New England men pushed their attacks.

The *Habitant de Louisbourg* says that each of the two commanders was eager that the keys of the fortress should be delivered to him, and not to his colleague; that before the surrender, Warren sent an officer to persuade the French that it would be for their advantage to make their submission to him rather than to Pepperrell; and that it was in fact so made. Wolcott, on the other hand, with the best means of learning the truth, says in his diary that Pepperrell received the keys at the South Gate. The report that it was the British commodore, and not their own general, to whom Louisbourg surrendered, made a prodigious stir among the inhabitants of New England, who had the touchiness common to small and ambitious peoples; and as they had begun the enterprise and borne most of its burdens and dangers, they thought themselves entitled to the chief credit of it. Pepperrell was blamed as lukewarm for the honor of his country because he did not demand the keys and reject the capitulation if they were refused. After all this ebullition it appeared that the keys were in his hands, for when, soon after the siege, Shirley came to Louisbourg, Pepperrell formally presented them to him, in presence of the soldiers.

Warren no doubt thought that he had a right to precedence, as being an officer of the King in regular standing, while Pepperrell was but a civilian, clothed with temporary rank by the appointment of a provincial governor. Warren was an impetuous sailor accustomed to command, and Pepperrell was a merchant accustomed to manage and persuade. The difference appears in their correspondence during the siege. Warren is sometimes brusque and almost peremptory; Pepperrell is forbearing and considerate to the last degree. He liked Warren, and, to the last, continued to praise him highly in letters to Shirley and other provincial governors; while Warren, on occasion of Shirley's arrival at Louisbourg, made a speech highly complimentary to both the general and his soldiers.

The news that Louisbourg was taken, reached Boston at one o'clock in the morning of the 3rd of July by a vessel sent express. A din of bells and cannon proclaimed it to the slumbering townsmen, and before the sun rose, the streets were filled with shouting crowds. At night every window shone with lamps, and the town was ablaze with fireworks and bonfires. The next Thursday was appointed a day of general thanksgiving for a victory believed to be the direct work of Providence. New York and Philadelphia also hailed the great news with illuminations, ringing of bells, and firing of cannon.

In England the tidings were received with astonishment and a joy that was dashed with reflections on the strength and mettle of colonists supposed already to aspire to independence. Pepperrell was made a baronet, and Warren an admiral. The merchant soldier was commissioned colonel in the British army; a regiment was given him, to be raised in America and maintained by the King, while a similar recognition was granted to the lawyer Shirley.

A question vital to Massachusetts worried her in the midst of her triumph. She had been bankrupt for many years, and of the large volume of her outstanding obligations, a part was not worth eight pence in the pound. Added to her load of debt, she had spent £183,649 sterling on the Louisbourg expedition. That which Smollett calls "the most important achievement of the war" would never have taken place but for her, and Old England, and not New, was to reap the profit; for Louisbourg, conquered by arms, was to be restored by diplomacy. If the money she had spent for the mother country were not repaid, her ruin was certain. William Bollan, English by birth and a son-in-law of Shirley, was sent out to urge the just claim of the province, and after long and vigorous solicitation, he succeeded. The full amount, in sterling value, was paid to Massachusetts, and the expenditures of New Hampshire, Connecticut, and Rhode Island were also reimbursed. The people of Boston saw twenty-seven of those long unwieldy trucks which many elders of the place still remember as used in their youth, rumbling up King Street to the treasury, loaded with 217 chests of Spanish dollars, and 100 barrels of copper coin. A pound sterling was worth eleven pounds of the old-tenor currency of Massachusetts, and thirty shillings of the new-tenor. Those beneficent trucks carried enough to buy in at a stroke nine-tenths of the old-tenor notes of the province, — nominally worth above two millions. A stringent tax, laid on by the Assembly, paid the remaining tenth, and Massachusetts was restored to financial health.[1]

[1] The English documents on the siege of Louisbourg are many and voluminous. The Pepperrell Papers and the Belknap Papers, both in the library of the Massachusetts Historical Society, afford a vast number of contemporary letters and documents on the subject. The large volume entitled *Siege of Louisbourg*, in the same repository, contains many more, including a number of autograph diaries of soldiers and others. [Some of these have since been printed in L. A. de Forest ed. *Louisbourg Journals 1745* (Society of Colonial Wars, New York, 1932). The rare *Lettre d'un habitant de Louisbourg* (1745) from which Parkman frequently quotes, is printed by him, with other French and English sources, in an Appendix to *Half-Century of Conflict*, Vol. II. J. S. McLennan *Louisbourg from its Foundation to its Fall 1713–1758* (London 1918), the best account of the first siege to appear since Parkman's, is amply illustrated with maps and colored prints. Around 1928 the Canadian government acquired the site of the fort, created the Louisbourg National Historic Park, and has since done considerable excavation and restoration, which have made Louisbourg a most interesting historic site. With Parkman's account in hand, one can trace almost every incident of the siege.]

CHAPTER XXXII

Ticonderoga

1758

[*Montcalm and Wolfe*, CHAPTER XX]

[THIS WORK, perhaps the most famous of all by Parkman, gives the story of the Seven Years' War (the Old French and Indian War as it used to be called) in North America, from the preliminary mission of Celeron de Bienville down the Ohio, to the Peace of Paris. The first of Parkman's volumes to be planned, in 1841, it was finished over forty years later, and "affectionately inscribed" to "Harvard College, the Alma Mater under whose influence the purpose of writing it was conceived." In order to leave room for Parkman's grand finale, the Battle of the Plains of Abraham and the Conquest of Quebec, the editor has had to leave out all of the earlier chapters except this. The chapter opens with details on the financial contribution of Massachusetts to the war, in order to answer the charge of a British writer that the Bay Province "would never move hand or foot in her own defense."]

In June the combined British and provincial force which Abercrombie was to lead against Ticonderoga was gathered at the head of Lake George; while Montcalm lay at its outlet around the walls of the French stronghold, with an army not one-fourth so numerous. Vaudreuil [1] had devised a plan for saving Ticonderoga by a diversion into the valley of the Mohawk under Lévis, Rigaud, and Longueuil, with 1600 men, who were to be joined by as many Indians. The English forts of that region were to be attacked, Schenectady threatened, and the Five Nations compelled to declare for France. Thus, as the governor gave out, the English would be forced to cease from aggression, leave Montcalm in peace, and think only of defending themselves. "This,"

[1] [The Marquis de Vaudreuil, Governor of New France.]

writes Bougainville [2] on the 15th of June, "is what M. de Vaudreuil thinks will happen, because he never doubts anything. Ticonderoga, which is the point really threatened, is abandoned without support to the troops of the line and their general. It would even be wished that they might meet a reverse, if the consequences to the colony would not be too disastrous."

The proposed movement promised, no doubt, great advantages; but it was not destined to take effect. Some rangers taken on Lake George by a partisan officer named Langy declared with pardonable exaggeration that twenty-five or thirty thousand men would attack Ticonderoga in less than a fortnight. Vaudreuil saw himself forced to abandon his Mohawk expedition, and to order Lévis and his followers, who had not yet left Montreal, to reinforce Montcalm. Why they did not go at once is not clear. The governor declares that there were not boats enough. From whatever cause, there was a long delay, and Montcalm was left to defend himself as he could.

He hesitated whether he should not fall back to Crown Point. The engineer, Lotbinière, opposed the plan, as did also Le Mercier. It was but a choice of difficulties, and he stayed at Ticonderoga. His troops were disposed as they had been in the summer before; one battalion, that of Berry, being left near the fort, while the main body, under Montcalm himself, was encamped by the saw-mill at the Falls, and the rest, under Bourlamaque, occupied the head of the portage, with a small advanced force at the landing-place on Lake George. It remained to determine at which of these points he should concentrate them and make his stand against the English. Ruin threatened him in any case; each position had its fatal weakness or its peculiar danger, and his best hope was in the ignorance or blundering of his enemy. He seems to have been several days in a state of indecision.

In the afternoon of the 5th of July the partisan Langy, who had again gone out to reconnoitre towards the head of Lake George, came back in haste with the report that the English were embarked in great force. Montcalm sent a canoe down Lake Champlain to hasten Lévis to his aid, and ordered the battalion of Berry to begin a breastwork and abattis on the high ground in front of the fort. That they were not

[2] [The Comte de Bougainville, Montcalm's aide-de-camp. Subsequent to the war he conducted an exploring expedition to the Pacific, where he rediscovered the Solomon Islands, naming one after himself, and brought back from Tahiti samples of the flowering vine now known as the bougainvillea. In the War of American Independence he commanded a squadron of De Grasse's fleet in the Battle off the Capes of the Chesapeake.]

begun before shows that he was in doubt as to his plan of defence; and that his whole army was not now set to work at them shows that his doubt was still unsolved.

It was nearly a month since Abercrombie had begun his camp at the head of Lake George. Here, on the ground where Johnson had beaten Dieskau, where Montcalm had planted his batteries, and Munro vainly defended the wooden ramparts of Fort William Henry, were now assembled more than 15,000 men; and the shores, the foot of the mountains, and the broken plains between them were studded thick with tents. Of regulars there were 6,367, officers and soldiers, and of provincials 9,034. To the New England levies, or at least to their chaplains, the expedition seemed a crusade against the abomination of Babylon; and they discoursed in their sermons of Moses sending forth Joshua against Amalek. Abercrombie, raised to his place by political influence, was little but the nominal commander. "A heavy man," said Wolfe in a letter to his father; "an aged gentleman, infirm in body and mind," wrote William Parkman, a boy of seventeen, who carried a musket in a Massachusetts regiment, and kept in his knapsack a dingy little note-book, in which he jotted down what passed each day.[3] The age of the aged gentleman was fifty-two.

Pitt meant that the actual command of the army should be in the hands of Brigadier Lord Howe, and he was in fact its real chief; "the noblest Englishman that has appeared in my time, and the best soldier in the British army," says Wolfe. And he elsewhere speaks of him as "that great man." Abercrombie testifies to the universal respect and love with which officers and men regarded him, and Pitt calls him "a character of ancient times; a complete model of military virtue." High as this praise is, it seems to have been deserved. The young nobleman, who was then in his thirty-fourth year, had the qualities of a leader of men. The army felt him, from general to drummer-boy. He was its soul; and while breathing into it his own energy and ardor, and bracing it by stringent discipline, he broke through the traditions of the service and gave it new shapes to suit the time and place. During the past year he had studied the art of forest warfare, and joined Rogers and his rangers in their scouting-parties, sharing all their hardships and making himself one of them. Perhaps the reforms that he introduced were fruits of this rough self-imposed schooling. He made officers and men throw off all useless encumbrances, cut their hair

[3] Great-uncle of the writer and son of the Rev. Ebenezer Parkman, graduate of Harvard and minister of Westborough, Mass.

close, wear leggings to protect them from briers, brown the barrels of their muskets, and carry in their knapsacks thirty pounds of meal, which they cooked for themselves; so that, according to an admiring Frenchman, they could live a month without their supply-trains. "You would laugh to see the droll figure we all make," writes an officer. "Regulars as well as provincials have cut their coats so as scarcely to reach their waists. No officer or private is allowed to carry more than one blanket and a bearskin. A small portmanteau is allowed each officer. No women follow the camp to wash our linen. Lord Howe has already shown an example by going to the brook and washing his own."

Here, as in all things, he shared the lot of the soldier, and required his officers to share it. A story is told of him that before the army embarked he invited some of them to dinner in his tent, where they found no seats but logs, and no carpet but bearskins. A servant presently placed on the ground a large dish of pork and peas, on which his lordship took from his pocket a sheath containing a knife and fork and began to cut the meat. The guests looked on in some embarrassment; upon which he said: "Is it possible, gentlemen, that you have come on this campaign without providing yourselves with what is necessary?" And he gave each of them a sheath, with a knife and fork, like his own.

Yet this Lycurgus of the camp, as a contemporary calls him, is described as a man of social accomplishments rare even in his rank. He made himself greatly beloved by the provincial officers, with many of whom he was on terms of intimacy, and he did what he could to break down the barriers between the colonial soldiers and the British regulars. When he was at Albany, sharing with other high officers the kindly hospitalities of Mrs. Schuyler, he so won the heart of that excellent matron that she loved him like a son; and, though not given to such effusion, embraced him with tears on the morning when he left her to lead his division to the lake. In Westminster Abbey may be seen the tablet on which Massachusetts pays grateful tribute to his virtues, and commemorates "the affection her officers and soldiers bore to his command."

On the evening of the 4th of July, baggage, stores, and ammunition were all on board the boats, and the whole army embarked on the morning of the 5th. The arrangements were perfect. Each corps marched without confusion to its appointed station on the beach, and the sun was scarcely above the ridge of French Mountain when all were afloat. A spectator watching them from the shore says that when the fleet was three miles on its way, the surface of the lake at that distance was completely hidden from sight. There were 900 bateaux, 135 whaleboats, and a large number of heavy flatboats carrying the artillery. The whole advanced in three divisions, the regulars in the centre, and the provincials on the flanks. Each corps had its flags and its music. The day was fair and men and officers were in the highest spirits.

Before ten o'clock they began to enter the Narrows; and the boats of the three divisions extended themselves into long files as the mountains closed on either hand upon the contracted lake. From front to rear the line was six miles long. The spectacle was superb: the brightness of the summer day; the romantic beauty of the scenery; the sheen and sparkle of those crystal waters; the countless islets, tufted with pine, birch, and fir; the bordering mountains, with their green summits and sunny crags; the flash of oars and glitter of weapons; the banners, the varied uniforms, and the notes of bugle, trumpet, bagpipe, and drum, answered and prolonged by a hundred woodland echoes. "I never beheld so delightful a prospect," wrote a wounded officer at Albany a fortnight after.

Rogers with the rangers, and Gage with the light infantry, led the way in whaleboats, followed by Bradstreet with his corps of boatmen, armed and drilled as soldiers. Then came the main body. The central column of regulars was commanded by Lord Howe, his own regiment, the 55th, in the van, followed by the Royal Americans, the 27th, 44th, 46th, and 80th Infantry, and the Highlanders of the 42nd, with their major, Duncan Campbell of Inverawe, silent and gloomy amid the general cheer, for his soul was dark with foreshadowings of death. With this central column came what are described as two floating castles, which were no doubt batteries to cover the landing of the troops. On the right hand and the left were the provincials, uniformed in blue, regiment after regiment, from Massachusetts, Connecticut, New York, New Jersey, and Rhode Island. Behind them all came the bateaux, loaded with stores and baggage, and the heavy flatboats that carried the artillery, while a rear-guard of provincials and regulars closed the long procession.

At five in the afternoon they reached Sabbath-Day Point, twenty-five miles down the lake, where they stopped till late in the evening, waiting for the baggage and artillery, which had lagged behind; and here Lord Howe, lying on a bearskin by the side of the ranger, John

Stark, questioned him as to the position of Ticonderoga and its best points of approach. At about eleven o'clock they set out again, and at daybreak entered what was then called the Second Narrows; that is to say, the contraction of the lake where it approaches its outlet. Close on their left, ruddy in the warm sunrise, rose the vast bare face of Rogers Rock, whence a French advance party, under Langy and an officer named Trepezec, was watching their movements. Lord Howe, with Rogers and Bradstreet, went in whaleboats to reconnoitre the landing. At the place which the French called the Burned Camp, where Montcalm had embarked the summer before, they saw a detachment of the enemy too weak to oppose them. Their men landed and drove them off. At noon the whole army was on shore. Rogers, with a party of rangers, was ordered forward to reconnoitre, and the troops were formed for the march.

From this part of the shore a plain covered with forest stretched northwestward half a mile or more to the mountains behind which lay the valley of Trout Brook. On this plain the army began its march in four columns, with the intention of passing round the western bank of the river of the outlet, since the bridge over it had been destroyed. Rogers, with the provincial regiments of Fitch and Lyman, led the way, at some distance before the rest. The forest was extremely dense and heavy, and so obstructed with undergrowth that it was impossible to see more than a few yards in any direction, while the ground was encumbered with fallen trees in every stage of decay. The ranks were broken, and the men struggled on as they could in dampness and shade, under a canopy of boughs that the sun could scarcely pierce. The difficulty increased when, after advancing about a mile, they came upon undulating and broken ground. They were now not far from the upper rapids of the outlet. The guides became bewildered in the maze of trunks and boughs; the marching columns were confused, and fell in one upon the other. They were in the strange situation of an army lost in the woods.

The advanced party of French under Langy and Trepezec, about 350 in all, regulars and Canadians, had tried to retreat; but before they could do so, the whole English army had passed them, landed, and placed itself between them and their countrymen. They had no resource but to take to the woods. They seem to have climbed the steep gorge at the side of Rogers Rock and followed the Indian path that led to the valley of Trout Brook, thinking to descend it, and, by circling along the outskirts of the valley of Ticonderoga, reach

Montcalm's camp at the sawmill. Langy was used to bush-ranging; but he too became perplexed in the blind intricacies of the forest. Towards the close of the day he and his men had come out from the valley of Trout Brook, and were near the junction of that stream with the river of the outlet, in a state of some anxiety, for they could see nothing but brown trunks and green boughs. Could any of them have climbed one of the great pines that here and there reared their shaggy spires high above the surrounding forest, they would have discovered where they were, but would have gained not the faintest knowledge of the enemy. Out of the woods on the right they would have seen a smoke rising from the burning huts of the French camp at the head of the portage, which Bourlamaque had set on fire and abandoned. At a mile or more in front, the saw-mill at the Falls might perhaps have been descried, and, by glimpses between the trees, the tents of the neighboring camp where Montcalm still lay with his main force. All the rest seemed lonely as the grave; mountain and valley lay wrapped in primeval woods, and none could have dreamed that, not far distant, an army was groping its way, buried in foliage; no rumbling of wagons and artillery trains, for none were there; all silent but the cawing of some crow flapping his black wings over the sea of tree-tops.

Lord Howe, with Major Israel Putnam and 200 rangers, was at the head of the principal column, which was a little in advance of the three others. Suddenly the challenge, *Qui vive!* rang sharply from the thickets in front. *Français!* was the reply. Langy's men were not deceived: they fired out of the bushes. The shots were returned; a hot skirmish followed; and Lord Howe dropped dead, shot through the breast. All was confusion. The dull, vicious reports of musketry in thick woods, at first few and scattering, then in fierce and rapid volleys, reached the troops behind. They could hear, but see nothing. Already harassed and perplexed, they became perturbed. For all they knew, Montcalm's whole army was upon them. Nothing prevented a panic but the steadiness of the rangers, who maintained the fight alone till the rest came back to their senses. Rogers, with his reconnoitring party, and the regiments of Fitch and Lyman, were at no great distance in front. They all turned on hearing the musketry, and thus the French were caught between two fires. They fought with desperation. About fifty of them at length escaped; 148 were captured, and the rest killed or drowned in trying to cross the rapids. The loss of the English was small in numbers, but immeasurable in the death of Howe. "The fall of this noble and brave officer," says Rogers, "seemed to produce an almost general languor and consternation through the whole army." "In Lord Howe," writes another contemporary, Major Thomas Mante, "the soul of General Abercrombie's army seemed to expire. From the unhappy moment the General was deprived of his advice, neither order nor discipline was observed, and a strange kind of infatuation usurped the place of resolution." The death of one man was the ruin of fifteen thousand.[4]

The evil news was despatched to Albany, and in two or three days the messenger who bore it passed the house of Mrs. Schuyler on the meadows above the town. "In the afternoon," says her biographer, "a man was seen coming from the north galloping violently without his hat. Pedrom, as he was familiarly called, Colonel Schuyler's only surviving brother, was with her, and ran instantly to inquire, well knowing that he rode express. The man galloped on, crying out that Lord Howe was killed. The mind of our good aunt had been so engrossed by her anxiety and fears for the event impending, and so impressed with the merit and magnanimity of her favorite hero, that her wonted firmness sank under the stroke, and she broke out into bitter lamentations. This had such an effect on her friends and domestics that shrieks and sobs of anguish echoed through every part of the house."

The effect of the loss was seen at once. The army was needlessly kept under arms all night in the forest, and in the morning was ordered back to the landing whence it came. Towards noon, however, Bradstreet was sent with a detachment of regulars and provincials to take possession of the sawmill at the Falls, which Montcalm had abandoned the evening before. Bradstreet rebuilt the bridges destroyed by the retiring enemy, and sent word to his commander that the way was open; on which Abercrombie again put his army in motion, reached the Falls late in the afternoon, and occupied the deserted encampment of the French.

Montcalm with his main force had held this position at the Falls through most of the preceding day, doubtful, it seems, to the last whether he should not make his final stand there. Bourlamaque was for doing so; but two old officers, Bernès and Montguy, pointed out the danger that the English would occupy the neighboring heights;

---

[4] [Brigadier Lord Howe was one of the most beloved British officers who ever led provincial troops in America. Massachusetts-Bay put up a monument to him in Westminster Abbey, where it may still be seen. He was a brother to Admiral Lord Howe and General "Billy" Howe of the War of Independence.]

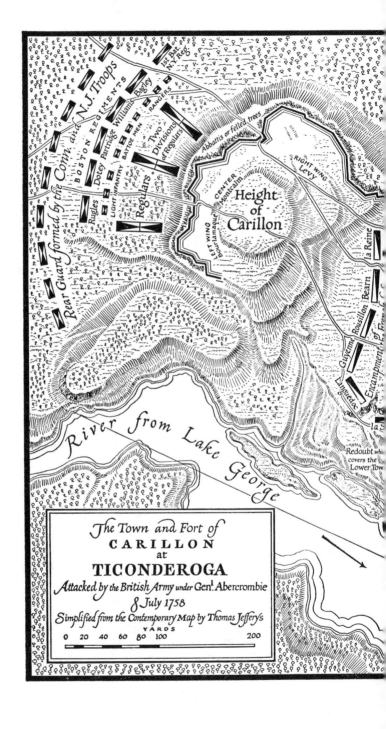

The Town and Fort of
CARILLON
at
TICONDEROGA
Attacked by the British Army under Gen.ˡ Abercrombie
8 July 1758
Simplified from the Contemporary Map by Thomas Jefferys

YARDS

0   20   40   60   80   100   200

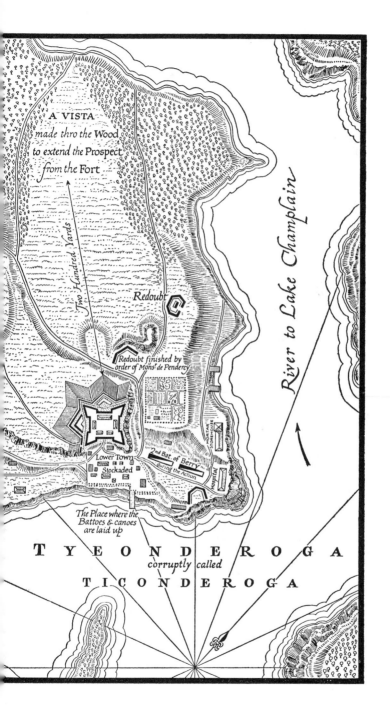

A VISTA
made thro the Wood
to extend the Prospect
from the Fort

Two Hundred Yards

River to Lake Champlain

Redoubt

Redoubt finished by
order of Monsr de Pendercy

MORTAR STOREHOUSE

Lower Town
Stockaded

2nd Batt. of Berry
during the Action

Hospital

The Place where the
Battoes & canoes
are laid up

T Y E O N D E R O G A
corruptly called
T I C O N D E R O G A

whereupon Montcalm at length resolved to fall back. The camp was broken up at five o'clock. Some of the troops embarked in bateaux, while others marched a mile and a half along the forest road, passed the place where the battalion of Berry was still at work on the breastwork begun in the morning, and made their bivouac a little farther on, upon the cleared ground that surrounded the fort.

The peninsula of Ticonderoga consists of a rocky plateau, with low grounds on each side, bordering Lake Champlain on the one hand, and the outlet of Lake George on the other. The fort stood near the end of the peninsula, which points towards the southeast. Thence, as one goes westward, the ground declines a little, and then slowly rises, till, about half a mile from the fort, it reaches its greatest elevation, and begins still more gradually to decline again. Thus a ridge is formed across the plateau between the steep declivities that sink to the low grounds on right and left. Some weeks before, a French officer named Hugues had suggested the defence of this ridge by means of an abattis. Montcalm approved his plan; and now, at the eleventh hour, he resolved to make his stand here. The two engineers, Pontleroy and Desandrouin, had already traced the outline of the works, and the soldiers of the battalion of Berry had made some progress in constructing them. At dawn of the seventh, while Abercrombie, fortunately for his enemy, was drawing his troops back to the landing-place, the whole French army fell to their task. The regimental colors were planted along the line, and the officers, stripped to the shirt, took axe in hand and labored with their men. The trees that covered the ground were hewn down by thousands, the tops lopped off, and the trunks piled one upon another to form a massive breastwork. The line followed the top of the ridge, along which it zigzagged in such a manner that the whole front could be swept by flank-fires of musketry and grape. Abercrombie describes the wall of logs as between eight and nine feet high; in which case there must have been a rude *banquette*, or platform to fire from, on the inner side. It was certainly so high that nothing could be seen over it but the crowns of the soldiers' hats. The upper tier was formed of single logs, in which notches were cut to serve as loopholes; and in some places sods and bags of sand were piled along the top, with narrow spaces to fire through. From the central part of the line the ground sloped away like a natural glacis; while at the sides, and especially on the left, it was undulating and broken. Over this whole space, to the distance of a musket-shot from the works, the forest was cut down, and the trees left lying where they fell among the stumps, with tops turned outwards, forming one vast abattis, which, as a Massachusetts officer says, looked like a forest laid flat by a hurricane. But the most formidable obstruction was immediately along the front of the breastwork, where the ground was covered with heavy boughs, overlapping and interlaced, with sharpened points bristling into the face of the assailant like the quills of a porcupine. As these works were all of wood, no vestige of them remains. The earthworks now shown to tourists as the lines of Montcalm are of later construction; and though on the same ground, are not on the same plan.[5]

Here, then, was a position which, if attacked in front with musketry alone, might be called impregnable. But would Abercrombie so attack it? He had several alternatives. He might attempt the flank and rear of his enemy by way of the low grounds on the right and left of the plateau, a movement which the precautions of Montcalm had made difficult, but not impossible. Or, instead of leaving his artillery idle on the strand of Lake George, he might bring it to the front and batter the breastwork, which, though impervious to musketry, was worthless against heavy cannon. Or he might do what Burgoyne did with success a score of years later, and plant a battery on the heights of Rattlesnake Hill, now called Mount Defiance, which commanded the position of the French, and whence the inside of their breastwork could be scoured with round-shot from end to end. Or, while threatening the French front with a part of his army, he could march the rest a short distance through the woods on his left to the road which led from Ticonderoga to Crown Point, and which would soon have brought him to the place called Five-Mile Point, where Lake Champlain narrows to the width of an easy rifle-shot, and where a battery of field-pieces would have cut off all Montcalm's supplies and closed his only way of retreat. As the French were provisioned for but eight days, their position would thus have been desperate. They plainly saw the danger;

[5] [Parkman was wrong here; the "French lines" now shown are the originals. In the present century an immense amount of archaelogical and historical research has been expended on Fort Ticonderoga — largely by the Pell family, who own the site; and Fort Carillon, as rebuilt by the British according to the original plans by Vauban, after being blown up by Hebecourt in 1759, has been completely restored. One of the buildings houses a museum which contains relics of the different sieges sustained by the fort, examples of colonial uniforms, and historical paintings. It is now one of the most beautiful and interesting as well as the most accessible historical sites in the northern United States. See S. H. P. Pell *Fort Ticonderoga, a Short History,* published by the Fort Ticonderoga Museum 1954, and the quarterly *Bulletin* published by the Museum.

and Doreil declares that had the movement been made, their whole army must have surrendered. Montcalm had done what he could; but the danger of his position was inevitable and extreme. His hope lay in Abercrombie; and it was a hope well founded. The action of the English general answered the utmost wishes of his enemy.

Abercrombie had been told by his prisoners that Montcalm had 6000 men, and that 3000 more were expected every hour. Therefore he was in haste to attack before these succors could arrive. As was the general, so was the army. "I believe," writes an officer, "we were one and all infatuated by a notion of carrying every obstacle by a mere *coup de mousqueterie*." Leadership perished with Lord Howe, and nothing was left but blind, headlong valor.

Clerk, chief engineer, was sent to reconnoitre the French works from Mount Defiance; and came back with the report that, to judge from what he could see, they might be carried by assault. Then, without waiting to bring up his cannon, Abercrombie prepared to storm the lines.

The French finished their breastwork and abattis on the evening of the seventh, encamped behind them, slung their kettles, and rested after their heavy toil. Lévis had not yet appeared; but at twilight one of his officers, Captain Pouchot, arrived with 300 regulars, and announced that his commander would come before morning with 100 more. The reinforcement, though small, was welcome, and Lévis was a host in himself. Pouchot was told that the army was half a mile off. Thither he repaired, made his report to Montcalm, and looked with amazement at the prodigious amount of work accomplished in one day. Lévis himself arrived in the course of the night, and approved the arrangement of the troops. They lay behind their lines till daybreak; then the drums beat, and they formed in order of battle. The battalions of La Sarre and Languedoc were posted on the left, under Bourlamaque, the first battalion of Berry with that of Royal Roussillon in the centre, under Montcalm, and those of La Reine, Béarn, and Guienne on the right, under Lévis. A detachment of volunteers occupied the low grounds between the breastwork and the outlet of Lake George; while, at the foot of the declivity on the side towards Lake Champlain, were stationed 450 colony regulars and Canadians, behind an abattis which they had made for themselves; and as they were covered by the cannon of the fort, there was some hope that they would check any flank movement which the English might attempt on that side. Their posts being thus assigned, the men fell to work again to strengthen their defences. Including those who came with Lévis, the total force of effective soldiers was now 3600.

Soon after nine o'clock a distant and harmless fire of small-arms began on the slopes of Mount Defiance. It came from a party of Indians who had just arrived with Sir William Johnson, and who, after amusing themselves in this manner for a time, remained for the rest of the day safe spectators of the fight. The soldiers worked undisturbed till noon, when volleys of musketry were heard from the forest in front. It was the English light troops driving in the French pickets. A cannon was fired as a signal to drop tools and form for battle. The white uniforms lined the breastwork in a triple row, with the grenadiers behind them as a reserve, and the second battalion of Berry watching the flanks and rear.

Meanwhile the English army had moved forward from its camp by the sawmill. First came the rangers, the light infantry, and Bradstreet's armed boatmen, who, emerging into the open space, began a spattering fire. Some of the provincial troops followed, extending from left to right, and opening fire in turn; then the regulars, who had formed in columns of attack under cover of the forest, advanced their solid red masses into the sunlight, and passing through the intervals between the provincial regiments, pushed forward to the assault. Across the rough ground, with its maze of fallen trees whose leaves hung withering in the July sun, they could see the top of the breastwork, but not the men behind it; when, in an instant, all the line was obscured by a gush of smoke, a crash of exploding fire-arms tore the air, and grapeshot and musket-balls swept the whole space like a tempest; "a damnable fire," says an officer who heard them screaming about his ears. The English had been ordered to carry the works with the bayonet; but their ranks were broken by the obstructions through which they struggled in vain to force their way, and they soon began to fire in turn. The storm raged in full fury for an hour. The assailants pushed close to the breastwork; but there they were stopped by the bristling mass of sharpened branches, which they could not pass under the murderous cross-fires that swept them from front and flank. At length they fell back, exclaiming that the works were impregnable. Abercrombie, who was at the sawmill, a mile and a half in the rear, sent orders to attack again, and again they came on as before.

The scene was frightful: masses of infuriated men who could not go forward and would not go back; straining for an enemy they could not reach, and firing on an enemy they could not see; caught in the entanglement of fallen trees; tripped by briers, stumbling over logs, tearing through boughs; shouting, yelling, cursing, and pelted all the while with bullets that killed them by scores, stretched them on the ground, or hung them on jagged branches in strange attitudes of death. The provincials supported the regulars with spirit, and some of them forced their way to the foot of the wooden wall.

The French fought with the intrepid gaiety of their nation, and shouts of *Vive le Roi!* and *Vive notre Général!* mingled with the din of musketry. Montcalm, with his coat off, for the day was hot, directed the defence of the centre, and repaired to any part of the line where the danger for the time seemed greatest. He is warm in praise of his enemy, and declares that between one and seven o'clock they attacked him six successive times. Early in the action Abercrombie tried to turn the French left by sending twenty bateaux, filled with troops, down the outlet of Lake George. They were met by the fire of the volunteers stationed to defend the low grounds on that side, and, still advancing, came within range of the cannon of the fort, which sank two of them and drove back the rest.

A curious incident happened during one of the attacks. De Bassignac, a captain in the battalion of Royal Roussillon, tied his handkerchief to the end of a musket and waved it over the breastwork in defiance. The English mistook it for a sign of surrender, and came forward with all possible speed, holding their muskets crossed over their heads in both hands, and crying *Quarter*. The French made the same mistake; and thinking that their enemies were giving themselves up as prisoners, ceased firing, and mounted on the top of the breastwork to receive them. Captain Pouchot, astonished, as he says, to see them perched there, looked out to learn the cause, and saw that the enemy meant anything but surrender. Whereupon he shouted with all his might: "*Tirez! Tirez! Ne voyez-vous pas que ces gens-là vont vous enlever?*"[6] The soldiers, still standing on the breastwork, instantly gave the English a volley, which killed some of them, and sent back the rest discomfited.

This was set to the account of Gallic treachery. "Another deceit the enemy put upon us," says a military letter-writer: "they raised their hats above the breastwork, which our people fired at; they, having loopholes to fire through, and being covered by the sods, we did them little damage, except shooting their hats to pieces." In one of the last assaults a soldier of the Rhode Island regiment, William Smith, man-

[6] ["Fire! Fire! Don't you see that those guys are going to take you?"]

aged to get through all obstructions and ensconce himself close under the breastwork, where in the confusion he remained for a time unnoticed, improving his advantages meanwhile by shooting several Frenchmen. Being at length observed, a soldier fired vertically down upon him and wounded him severely, but not enough to prevent his springing up, striking at one of his enemies over the top of the wall, and braining him with his hatchet. A British officer who saw the feat, and was struck by the reckless daring of the man, ordered two regulars to bring him off; which, covered by a brisk fire of musketry, they succeeded in doing. A letter from the camp two or three weeks later reports him as in a fair way to recover, being, says the writer, much braced and invigorated by his anger against the French, on whom he was swearing to have his revenge.

Towards five o'clock two English columns joined in a most determined assault on the extreme right of the French, defended by the battalions of Guienne and Béarn. The danger for a time was imminent. Montcalm hastened to the spot with the reserves. The assailants hewed their way to the foot of the breastwork; and though again and again repulsed, they again and again renewed the attack. The Highlanders fought with stubborn and unconquerable fury. "Even those who were mortally wounded," writes one of their lieutenants, "cried to their companions not to lose a thought upon them, but to follow their officers and mind the honor of their country. Their ardor was such that it was difficult to bring them off." Their major, Campbell of Inverawe, found his foreboding true. He received a mortal shot, and his clansmen bore him from the field. Twenty-five of their officers were killed or wounded, and half the men fell under the deadly fire that poured from the loopholes. Captain John Campbell and a few followers tore their way through the abattis, climbed the breastwork, leaped down among the French, and were bayoneted there.

As the colony troops and Canadians on the low ground were left undisturbed, Lévis sent them an order to make a sortie and attack the left flank of the charging columns. They accordingly posted themselves among the trees along the declivity, and fired upwards at the enemy, who presently shifted their position to the right, out of the line of shot. The assault still continued, but in vain; and at six there was another effort, equally fruitless. From this time till half-past seven a lingering fight was kept up by the rangers and other provincials, firing from the edge of the woods and from behind the stumps, bushes, and fallen trees in front of the lines. Its only objects were to cover their comrades, who were collecting and bringing off the wounded, and to protect the retreat of the regulars, who fell back in disorder to the Falls. As twilight came on, the last combatant withdrew, and none were left but the dead. Abercrombie had lost in killed, wounded, and missing, 1944 officers and men. The loss of the French, not counting that of Langy's detachment, was 327. Bourlamaque was dangerously wounded; Bougainville slightly; and the hat of Lévis was twice shot through.

Montcalm, with a mighty load lifted from his soul, passed along the lines, and gave the tired soldiers the thanks they nobly deserved. Beer, wine, and food were served out to them, and they bivouacked for the night on the level ground between the breastwork and the fort. The enemy had met a terrible rebuff; yet the danger was not over. Abercrombie still had more than 13,000 men, and he might renew the attack with cannon. But, on the morning of the ninth, a band of volunteers who had gone out to watch him brought back the report that he was in full retreat. The sawmill at the Falls was on fire, and the last English soldier was gone. On the morning of the tenth, Lévis, with a strong detachment, followed the road to the landing-place, and found signs that a panic had overtaken the defeated troops. They had left behind several hundred barrels of provisions and a large quantity of baggage; while in a marshy place that they had crossed was found a considerable number of their shoes, which had stuck in the mud, and which they had not stopped to recover. They had embarked on the morning after the battle, and retreated to the head of the lake in a disorder and dejection wofully contrasted with the pomp of their advance. A gallant army was sacrificed by the blunders of its chief.

Montcalm announced his victory to his wife in a strain of exaggeration that marks the exaltation of his mind. "Without Indians, almost without Canadians or colony troops, — I had only four hundred, — alone with Lévis and Bourlamaque and the troops of the line, thirty-one hundred fighting men, I have beaten an army of twenty-five thousand. They repassed the lake precipitately, with a loss of at least five thousand. This glorious day does infinite honor to the valor of our battalions. I have no time to write more. I am well, my dearest, and I embrace you." And he wrote to his friend Doreil: "The army, the too-small army of the King, has beaten the enemy. What a day for France! If I had had two hundred Indians to send out at the head of a thousand picked men under the Chevalier de Lévis, not many would have escaped. Ah, my dear Doreil, what soldiers are ours! I never saw the like. Why were they not at Louisbourg?"

On the morrow of his victory he caused a great cross to be planted on the battle-field, inscribed with these lines, composed by the soldier-scholar himself, —

Quid dux? quid miles? quid strata ingentia ligna?
En signum! en victor! Deus hîc, Deus ipse triumphat.

Soldier and chief and rampart's strength are nought;
Behold the conquering Cross! 'Tis God the triumph wrought.

CHAPTER XXXIII

James Wolfe
1758–1759

[*Montcalm and Wolfe*, CHAPTER XXIV, in part]

Knox [1] does not record his impressions of his new commander, which must have been disappointing. He called him afterwards a British Achilles; but in person at least Wolfe bore no likeness to the son of Peleus, for never was the soul of a hero cased in a frame so incongruous. His face, when seen in profile, was singular as that of the Great Condé. The forehead and chin receded; the nose, slightly upturned, formed with the other features the point of an obtuse triangle; the mouth was by no means shaped to express resolution; and nothing but the clear, bright, and piercing eye bespoke the spirit within. On his head he wore a black three-cornered hat; his red hair was tied in a queue behind; his narrow shoulders, slender body, and long, thin limbs were cased in a scarlet frock, with broad cuffs and ample skirts that reached the knee; while on his left arm he wore a band of crape in mourning for his father, of whose death he had heard a few days before.

James Wolfe was in his thirty-third year. His father was an officer of distinction, Major-General Edward Wolfe, and he himself, a delicate and sensitive child, but an impetuous and somewhat headstrong youth,

[1] Captain John Knox of the 43rd Regiment, who left an interesting journal of this campaign, published at London in 1769 as *An Historical Journal of the Campaigns in North America*. The latest and best edition, A. G. Doughty ed., was published by the Champlain Society in 3 vols. in 1914–16. Parkman wrote before the standard Beckles Willson *Life and Letters of James Wolfe* (1909) appeared, but he used many letters of Wolfe in the British archives that have since been published. The most exhaustive account of this campaign is A. G. Doughty *The Siege of Quebec* (6 vols., Quebec, 1901). G. M. Wrong *The Fall of Canada 1759–60* (1914) is largely a digest of Doughty and Parkman. There are two good short recent accounts: the chapter by C. T. Atkinson in *The Cambridge History of the British Empire* VI (1930), and L. H. Gipson *The Great War for the Empire* VII (1949): *The Victorious Years, 1758–1760*.

had served the King since the age of fifteen. From childhood he had dreamed of the army and the wars. At sixteen he was in Flanders, adjutant of his regiment, discharging the duties of the post in a way that gained him early promotion and, along with a painstaking assiduity, showing a precocious faculty for commanding men. He passed with credit through several campaigns, took part in the victory of Dettingen, and then went to Scotland to fight at Culloden. Next we find him at Stirling, Perth, and Glasgow, always ardent and always diligent, constant in military duty, and giving his spare hours to mathematics and Latin. He presently fell in love; and being disappointed, plunged into a variety of dissipations, contrary to his usual habits, which were far above the standard of that profligate time.

At twenty-three he was a lieutenant-colonel, commanding his regiment in the then dirty and barbarous town of Inverness, amid a disaffected and turbulent population whom it was his duty to keep in order: a difficult task, which he accomplished so well as to gain the special commendation of the King, and even the goodwill of the Highlanders themselves. He was five years among these northern hills, battling with ill-health, and restless under the intellectual barrenness of his surroundings. He felt his position to be in no way salutary, and wrote to his mother: "The fear of becoming a mere ruffian and of imbibing the tyrannical principles of an absolute commander, or giving way insensibly to the temptations of power till I become proud, insolent, and intolerable, — these considerations will make me wish to leave the regiment before next winter; that by frequenting men above myself I may know my true condition, and by discoursing with the other sex may learn some civility and mildness of carriage." He got leave of absence, and spent six months in Paris, where he was presented at court and saw much of the best society. That did not prevent him from working hard to perfect himself in French, as well as in horsemanship, fencing, dancing, and other accomplishments, and from earnestly seeking an opportunity to study the various armies of Europe. In this he was thwarted by the stupidity and prejudice of the commander-in-chief; and he made what amends he could by extensive reading in all that bore on military matters.

His martial instincts were balanced by strong domestic inclinations. He was fond of children; and after his disappointment in love used to say that they were the only true inducement to marriage. He was a most dutiful son, and wrote continually to both his parents. Sometimes he would philosophize on the good and ill of life; sometimes he held questionings with his conscience; and once he wrote to his mother in a strain of self-accusation not to be expected from a bold and determined soldier. His nature was a compound of tenderness and fire, which last sometimes showed itself in sharp and unpleasant flashes. His excitable temper was capable almost of fierceness, and he could now and then be needlessly stern; but towards his father, mother, and friends he was a model of steady affection. He made friends readily, and kept them, and was usually a pleasant companion, though subject to sallies of imperious irritability which occasionally broke through his strong sense of good breeding. For this his susceptible constitution was largely answerable, for he was a living barometer, and his spirits rose and fell with every change of weather. In spite of his impatient outbursts, the officers whom he had commanded remained attached to him for life; and, in spite of his rigorous discipline, he was beloved by his soldiers, to whose comfort he was always attentive. Frankness, directness, essential good feeling, and a high integrity atoned for all his faults.

In his own view, as expressed to his mother, he was a person of very moderate abilities, aided by more than usual diligence; but this modest judgment of himself by no means deprived him of self-confidence, nor, in time of need, of self-assertion. He delighted in every kind of hardihood; and, in his contempt for effeminacy, once said to his mother: "Better be a savage of some use than a gentle, amorous puppy, obnoxious to all the world." He was far from despising fame; but the controlling principles of his life were duty to his country and his profession, loyalty to the King, and fidelity to his own ideal of the perfect soldier. To the parent who was the confidant of his most intimate thoughts he said: "All that I wish for myself is that I may at all times be ready and firm to meet that fate we cannot shun, and to die gracefully and properly when the hour comes." Never was wish more signally fulfilled. Again he tells her: "My utmost desire and ambition is to look steadily upon danger;" and his desire was accomplished. His intrepidity was complete. No form of death had power to daunt him. Once and again, when bound on some deadly enterprise of war, he calmly counts the chances whether or not he can compel his feeble body to bear him on till the work is done. A frame so delicately strung could not have been insensible to danger; but forgetfulness of self, and the absorption of every faculty in the object before him, shut out the sense of fear. He seems always to have been at his best in the thick of battle; most complete in his mastery over himself and over others. . . .

When about to sail on the expedition against Louisbourg, he was anxious for his parents, and wrote to his uncle, Major Wolfe, at Dublin: "I trust you will give the best advice to my mother, and such assistance, if it should be wanted, as the distance between you will permit. I mention this because the General seems to decline apace, and narrowly escaped being carried off in the spring. She, poor woman, is in a bad state of health, and needs the care of some friendly hand. She has long and painful fits of illness, which by succession and inheritance are likely to devolve on me, since I feel the early symptoms of them." Of his friends Guy Carleton, afterwards Lord Dorchester, and George Warde, the companion of his boyhood, he also asks help for his mother in his absence.

His part in the taking of Louisbourg greatly increased his reputation. After his return he went to Bath to recruit his health; and it seems to have been here that he wooed and won Miss Katherine Lowther, daughter of an ex-governor of Barbadoes, and sister of the future Lord Lonsdale. A betrothal took place, and Wolfe wore her portrait till the night before his death. It was a little before this engagement that he wrote to his friend Lieutenant-Colonel Rickson: "I have this day signified to Mr. Pitt that he may dispose of my slight carcass as he pleases, and that I am ready for any undertaking within the compass of my skill and cunning. I am in a very bad condition both with the gravel and rheumatism; but I had much rather die than decline any kind of service that offers. If I followed my own taste it would lead me into Germany. However, it is not our part to choose, but to obey. My opinion is that I shall join the army in America."

Pitt chose him to command the expedition then fitting out against Quebec; made him a major-general, though, to avoid giving offence to older officers, he was to hold that rank in America alone; and permitted him to choose his own staff. Appointments made for merit, and not through routine and patronage, shocked the Duke of Newcastle, to whom a man like Wolfe was a hopeless enigma; and he told George II that Pitt's new general was mad. "Mad is he?" returned the old King; "then I hope he will bite some others of my generals."

At the end of January the fleet was almost ready, and Wolfe wrote to his uncle Walter: "I am to act a greater part in this business than I wished. The backwardness of some of the older officers has in some measure forced the Government to come down so low. I shall do my best, and leave the rest to fortune, as perforce we must when there are not the most commanding abilities. We expect to sail in about three weeks. A London life and little exercise disagrees entirely with me, but the sea still more. If I have health and constitution enough for the campaign, I shall think myself a lucky man; what happens afterwards is of no great consequence." [2] He sent to his mother an affectionate letter of farewell, went to Spithead, embarked with Admiral Saunders in the ship *Neptune*, and set sail on the seventeenth of February. In a few hours the whole squadron was at sea, the transports, the frigates, and the great line-of-battle ships, with their ponderous armament and their freight of rude humanity armed and trained for destruction; while on the heaving deck of the *Neptune*, wretched with seasickness and racked with pain, stood the gallant invalid who was master of it all.

The fleet consisted of twenty-two ships-of-the-line, with frigates, sloops-of-war, and a great number of transports. When Admiral Saunders arrived with his squadron off Louisbourg, he found the entrance blocked by ice, and was forced to seek harborage at Halifax. The squadron of Admiral Holmes, which had sailed a few days earlier, proceeded to New York to take on board troops destined for the expedition, while the squadron of Admiral Durell steered for the St. Lawrence to intercept the expected ships from France.

In May the whole fleet, except the ten ships with Durell, was united in the harbor of Louisbourg. Twelve thousand troops were to have been employed for the expedition; but several regiments expected from the West Indies were for some reason countermanded, while the accessions from New York and the Nova Scotia garrisons fell far short of the looked-for numbers. Three weeks before leaving Louisbourg, Wolfe writes to his uncle Walter that he has an army of 9000 men. The actual number seems to have been somewhat less. "Our troops are good," he informs Pitt; "and if valor can make amends for the want of numbers, we shall probably succeed."

Three brigadiers, all in the early prime of life, held command under him: Monckton, Townshend, and Murray. They were all his superiors in birth, and one of them, Townshend, never forgot that he was so. "George Townshend," says Walpole, "has thrust himself again into the service; and, as far as wrongheadedness will go, is very proper for a hero." The same caustic writer says further that he was of "a proud, sullen, and contemptuous temper," and that he "saw everything in an ill-natured and ridiculous light." Though his perverse and envious disposition made him a difficult colleague, Townshend had both talents

---

[2] [Wolfe really wanted to serve on the continent of Europe, and in the cavalry; he complained to a friend that it was his "fortune to be cursed with American service." Gipson p. 372, quoting Beckles Willson p. 404.]

and energy; as also had Monckton, the same officers who commanded at the capture of Beauséjour in 1775. Murray, too, was well matched to the work in hand, in spite of some lingering remains of youthful rashness.

On the 6th of June the last ship of the fleet sailed out of Louisbourg harbor, the troops cheering and the officers drinking to the toast, "British colors on every French fort, port, and garrison in America." The ships that had gone before lay to till the whole fleet was reunited, and then all steered together for the St. Lawrence. From the headland of Cape Egmont, the Micmac hunter, gazing far out over the shimmering sea, saw the horizon flecked with their canvas wings, as they bore northward on their errand of havoc.[3]

[3] [According to Gipson p. 378 the Fleet now numbered 9 ships of the line, 13 frigates, sloops and other men of war, and 119 transports, supply and ordnance vessels, carrying about 9000 troops. Thirteen more ships of the line under Rear Admiral Philip Durell joined them at the Ile d'Orléans.]

CHAPTER XXXIV

Wolfe at Quebec

1759

[Montcalm and Wolfe, CHAPTER XXV]

In early spring the chiefs of Canada met at Montreal to settle a plan of defence. What at first they most dreaded was an advance of the enemy by way of Lake Champlain. Bourlamaque, with three battalions, was ordered to take post at Ticonderoga, hold it if he could, or, if overborne by numbers, fall back to Isle-aux-Noix, at the outlet of the lake. La Corne was sent with a strong detachment to intrench himself at the head of the rapids of the St. Lawrence, and oppose any hostile movement from Lake Ontario. Every able-bodied man in the colony, and every boy who could fire a gun, was to be called to the field. Vaudreuil sent a circular letter to the militia captains of all the parishes, with orders to read it to the parishioners. It exhorted them to defend their religion, their wives, their children, and their goods from the fury of the heretics; declared that he, the governor, would never yield up Canada on any terms whatever; and ordered them to join the army at once, leaving none behind but the old, the sick, the women, and the children. The bishop issued a pastoral mandate: "On every side, dearest brethren, the enemy is making immense preparations. His forces, at least six times more numerous than ours, are already in motion. Never was Canada in a state so critical and full of peril. Never were we so destitute, or threatened with an attack so fierce, so general, and so obstinate. Now, in truth, we may say, more than ever before, that our only resource is in the powerful succor of our Lord. Then, dearest brethren, make every effort to deserve it. 'Seek first the kingdom of God; and all these things shall be added unto you.'" And he reproves their sins, exhorts them to repentance, and ordains processions, masses, and prayers.

Vaudreuil bustled and boasted. In May he wrote to the minister: "The zeal with which I am animated for the service of the King will always make me surmount the greatest obstacles. I am taking the most proper measures to give the enemy a good reception whenever he may attack us. I keep in view the defence of Quebec. I have given orders in the parishes below to muster the inhabitants who are able to bear arms, and place women, children, cattle, and even hay and grain, in places of safety. Permit me, Monseigneur, to beg you to have the goodness to assure His Majesty that, to whatever hard extremity I may be reduced, my zeal will be equally ardent and indefatigable, and that I shall do the impossible to prevent our enemies from making progress in any direction, or, at least, to make them pay extremely dear for it." Then he writes again to say that Amherst with a great army will, as he learns, attack Ticonderoga; that Bradstreet, with 6000 men, will advance to Lake Ontario; and that 6000 more will march to the Ohio. "Whatever progress they may make," he adds, "I am resolved to yield them nothing, but hold my ground even to annihilation." He promises to do his best to keep on good terms with Montcalm, and ends with a warm eulogy of Bigot.

It was in the midst of all these preparations that Bougainville arrived from France with news that a great fleet was on its way to attack Quebec. The town was filled with consternation mixed with surprise, for the Canadians had believed that the dangerous navigation of the St. Lawrence would deter their enemies from the attempt. "Everybody," writes one of them, "was stupefied at an enterprise that seemed so bold." In a few days a crowd of sails was seen approaching. They were not enemies but friends. It was the fleet of the contractor Cadet, commanded by an officer named Kanon, and loaded with supplies for the colony. They anchored in the harbor, eighteen sail in all, and their arrival spread universal joy. Admiral Durell had come too late to intercept them, catching but three stragglers that had lagged behind the rest. Still others succeeded in eluding him, and before the 1st of June five more ships had come safely into port.

When the news brought by Bougainville reached Montreal, nearly the whole force of the colony, except the detachments of Bourlamaque and La Corne, was ordered to Quebec. Montcalm hastened thither, and Vaudreuil followed. The governor-general wrote to the minister in his usual strain, as if all the hope of Canada rested in him. Such, he says, was his activity, that, though very busy, he reached Quebec only a day and a half after Montcalm; and, on arriving, learned from his scouts that English ships-of-war had already appeared at Isle-aux-Coudres. These were the squadron of Durell. "I expect," Vaudreuil goes on, "to be sharply attacked, and that our enemies will make their most powerful efforts to conquer this colony; but there is no ruse, no resource, no means which my zeal does not suggest to lay snares for them, and finally, when the exigency demands it, to fight them with an ardor, and even a fury, which exceeds the range of their ambitious designs. The troops, the Canadians, and the Indians are not ignorant of the resolution I have taken, and from which I shall not recoil under any circumstance whatever. The burghers of this city have already put their goods and furniture in places of safety. The old men, women, and children hold themselves ready to leave town. My firmness is generally applauded. It has penetrated every heart; and each man says aloud: 'Canada, our native land, shall bury us under its ruins before we surrender to the English!' This is decidedly my own determination, and I shall hold to it inviolably." He launches into high praise of the contractor Cadet, whose zeal for the service of the King and the defence of the colony he declares to be triumphant over every difficulty. It is necessary, he adds, that ample supplies of all kinds should be sent out in the autumn, with the distribution of which Cadet offers to charge himself, and to account for them at their first cost; but he does not say what prices his disinterested friend will compel the destitute Canadians to pay for them.

Five battalions from France, nearly all the colony troops, and the militia from every part of Canada poured into Quebec, along with 1000 or more Indians, who, at the call of Vaudreuil, came to lend their scalping-knives to the defence. Such was the ardor of the people that boys of fifteen and men of eighty were to be seen in the camp. Isle-aux-Coudres and Isle d'Orléans were ordered to be evacuated, and an excited crowd on the rock of Quebec watched hourly for the approaching fleet. Days passed and weeks passed, yet it did not appear. Meanwhile Vaudreuil held council after council to settle a plan of defence. They were strange scenes: a crowd of officers of every rank, mixed pell-mell in a small room, pushing, shouting, elbowing each other, interrupting each other; till Montcalm, in despair, took each aside after the meeting was over, and made him give his opinion in writing.

He himself had at first proposed to encamp the army on the Plains of Abraham and the meadows of the St. Charles, making that river his line of defence; but he changed his plan, and, with the concurrence of Vaudreuil, resolved to post his whole force on the St. Lawrence below the city, with his right resting on the St. Charles, and his left on the Montmorenci. Here, accordingly, the troops and militia were stationed as they arrived. Early in June, standing at the northeastern brink of the rock of Quebec, one could have seen the whole position at a glance. On the curving shore from the St. Charles to the rocky gorge of the Montmorenci, a distance of seven or eight miles, the whitewashed dwellings of the parish of Beauport stretched down the road in a double chain, and the fields on both sides were studded with tents, huts, and Indian wigwams. Along the borders of the St. Lawrence, as far as the eye could distinguish them, gangs of men were throwing up redoubts, batteries, and lines of intrenchment. About midway between the two extremities of the encampment ran the little river of Beauport; and on the rising ground just beyond it stood a large stone house, round which the tents were thickly clustered; for here Montcalm had made his headquarters.

A boom of logs chained together was drawn across the mouth of the St. Charles, which was further guarded by two hulks mounted with cannon. The bridge of boats that crossed the stream nearly a mile above formed the chief communication between the city and the camp. Its head towards Beauport was protected by a strong and extensive earthwork; and the banks of the stream on the Quebec side were also intrenched, to form a second line of defence in case the position at Beauport should be forced.

In the city itself every gate, except the Palace Gate, which gave access to the bridge, was closed and barricaded. A hundred and six cannon were mounted on the walls. A floating battery of twelve heavy pieces, a number of gunboats, eight fireships, and several firerafts formed the river defences. The largest merchantmen of Kanon's fleet were sacrificed to make the fireships; and the rest, along with the frigates that came with them, were sent for safety up the St. Lawrence beyond the river Richelieu, whence about 1000 of their sailors returned to man the batteries and gunboats.

In the camps along the Beauport shore were about 14,000 men, besides Indians. The regulars held the centre; the militia of Quebec and Three Rivers were on the right, and those of Montreal on the left. In Quebec itself there was a garrison of between one and two thousand men under the Chevalier de Ramesay. Thus the whole number, including Indians, amounted to more than 16,000; and though the Canadians who formed the greater part of it were of little use in the open field, they could be trusted to fight well behind intrenchments. Against this force, posted behind defensive works, on positions almost impregnable by nature, Wolfe brought less than 9000 men available for operations on land.

The steep and lofty heights that lined the river made the cannon of the ships for the most part useless, while the exigencies of the naval service forbade employing the sailors on shore. In two or three instances only, throughout the siege, small squads of them landed to aid in moving and working cannon; and the actual fighting fell to the troops alone.

Vaudreuil and Bigot took up their quarters with the army. The governor-general had delegated the command of the land-forces to Montcalm, whom, in his own words, he authorized "to give orders everywhere, provisionally." His relations with him were more than ever anomalous and critical; for while Vaudreuil, in virtue of his office, had a right to supreme command, Montcalm, now a lieutenant-general, held a military grade far above him; and the governor, while always writing himself down in his despatches as the head and front of every movement, had too little self-confidence not to leave the actual command in the hands of his rival.

Days and weeks wore on, and the first excitement gave way to restless impatience. Why did not the English come? Many of the Canadians thought that Heaven would interpose and wreck the English fleet, as it had wrecked that of Admiral Walker half a century before. There were processions, prayers, and vows toward this happy consummation. Food was scarce. Bigot and Cadet lived in luxury; fowls by thousands were fattened with wheat for their tables, while the people were put on rations of two ounces of bread a day. Durell and his ships were reported to be still at Isle-aux-Coudres. Vaudreuil sent thither a party of Canadians, and they captured three midshipmen, who, says Montcalm, had gone ashore *pour polissonner*, that is, on a lark. These youths were brought to Quebec, where they increased the general anxiety by grossly exaggerating the English force.

At length it became known that eight English vessels were anchored in the north channel of Orleans, and on the 21st of June the masts of three of them could plainly be seen. One of the fireships was consumed in a vain attempt to burn them, and several firerafts and a sort of infernal machine were tried with no better success; the unwelcome visitors still held their posts.

Meanwhile the whole English fleet had slowly advanced, piloted by Denis de Vitré, a Canadian of good birth, captured at sea some time before, and now compelled to serve, under a threat of being hanged if he refused. Nor was he alone; for when Durell reached the place where the river pilots were usually taken on board, he raised a French flag to his mast-head, causing great rejoicings among the Canadians on shore, who thought that a fleet was come to their rescue, and that their country was saved. The pilots launched their canoes and came out to the ships, where they were all made prisoners; then the French flag was lowered, and the red cross displayed in its stead. The spectators on shore turned from joy to despair; and a priest who stood watching the squadron with a telescope is said to have dropped dead with the revulsion of feeling.

Towards the end of June the main fleet was near the mountain of Cape Tourmente. The passage called the Traverse, between the Cape and the lower end of the Island of Orleans, was reputed one of the most dangerous parts of the St. Lawrence; and as the ships successively came up, the captive pilots were put on board to carry them safely through, on pain of death. One of these men was assigned to the transport *Goodwill*, in which was Captain Knox, who spoke French, and who reports thus in his Diary, "He gasconaded at a most extravagant rate, and gave us to understand that it was much against his will that he was become an English pilot. The poor fellow assumed great latitude in his conversation, and said 'he made no doubt that some of the fleet would return to England, but they should have a dismal tale to carry with them; for Canada should be the grave of the whole army, and he expected in a short time to see the walls of Quebec ornamented with English scalps.' Had it not been in obedience to the Admiral, who gave orders that he should not be ill used, he would certainly have been thrown overboard." The master of the transport was an old sailor named Killick, who despised the whole Gallic race, and had no mind to see his ship in charge of a Frenchman. "He would not let the pilot speak," continues Knox, "but fixed his mate at the helm, charged him not to take orders from any person but himself, and going forward with his trumpet to the forecastle, gave the necessary instructions. All that could be said by the commanding officer and the other gentlemen on board was to no purpose; the pilot declared we should be lost, for that no French ship ever presumed to pass there without a pilot. 'Ay, ay, my dear,' replied our son of Neptune, 'but damn me, I'll convince you that an Englishman shall go where a Frenchman dare not show his nose.' The *Richmond* frigate being close astern of us, the commanding officer called out to the captain and told him our case; he inquired who the master was, and was answered from the forecastle by the man himself, who told him 'he was old Killick, and that was enough.' I went forward with this experienced mariner, who pointed out the channel to me as we passed; showing me by the ripple and color of the water where there was any danger, and distinguishing the places where there were ledges of rock (to me invisible) from banks of sand, mud, or gravel. He gave his orders with great unconcern, joked with the sounding-boats which lay off on each side with different colored flags for our guidance; and when any of them called to him and pointed to the deepest water, he answered: 'Ay, ay, my dear, chalk it down, a damned dangerous navigation, eh! If you don't make a sputter about it you'll get no credit in England.' After we had cleared this remarkable place, where the channel forms a complete zigzag, the master called to his mate to give the helm to somebody else, saying, 'Damn me if there are not a thousand places in the Thames fifty times more hazardous than this; I am ashamed that Englishmen should make such a rout about it.' The Frenchman asked me if the captain had not been there before. I assured him in the negative; upon which he viewed him with great attention, lifting at the same time his hands and eyes to heaven with astonishment and fervency."

Vaudreuil was blamed for not planting cannon at a certain plateau on the side of the mountain of Cape Tourmente, where the gunners would have been inaccessible, and whence they could have battered every passing ship with a plunging fire. As it was, the whole fleet sailed safely through. On the 26th of June they were all anchored off the south shore of the Island of Orleans, a few miles from Quebec; and, writes Knox, "here we are entertained with a most agreeable prospect of a delightful country on every side; windmills, watermills, churches, chapels, and compact farmhouses, all built with stone, and covered, some with wood, and others with straw. The lands appear to be everywhere well cultivated; and with the help of my glass I can discern that they are sowed with flax, wheat, barley, peas, etc., and the grounds are enclosed with wooden pales. The weather to-day is agreeably warm. A light fog sometimes hangs over the highlands, but in the river we have a fine clear air. In the curve of the river, while we were under sail, we had a transient view of a stupendous natural curiosity called the waterfall of Montmorenci."

That night Lieutenant Meech, with forty New England rangers, landed on the Island of Orleans, and found a body of armed inhabitants, who tried to surround him. He beat them off, and took possession of a neighboring farmhouse, where he remained till daylight; then pursued the enemy, and found that they had crossed to the north shore. The whole army now landed, and were drawn up on the beach. As they were kept there for some time, Knox and several brother officers went to visit the neighboring church of St. Laurent, where they found a letter from the parish priest, directed to "The Worthy Officers of the British Army," praying that they would protect the sacred edifice, and also his own adjoining house, and adding, with somewhat needless civility, that he wished they had come sooner, that they might have enjoyed the asparagus and radishes of his garden, now unhappily going to seed. The letter concluded with many compliments and good wishes, in which the Britons to whom they were addressed saw only "the frothy politeness so peculiar to the French." The army marched westward and encamped. Wolfe, with his chief engineer, Major Mackellar, and an escort of light infantry, advanced to the extreme point of the island.

Here he could see, in part, the desperate nature of the task he had undertaken. Before him, three or four miles away, Quebec sat perched upon her rock, a congregation of stone houses, churches, palaces, convents, and hospitals; the green trees of the Seminary garden and the spires of the Cathedral, the Ursulines, the Récollets, and the Jesuits. Beyond rose the loftier height of Cape Diamond, edged with palisades and capped with redoubt and parapet. Batteries frowned everywhere; the Château battery, the Clergy battery, the Hospital battery, on the rock above, and the Royal, Dauphin's, and Queen's batteries on the strand, where the dwellings and warehouses of the lower town clustered beneath the cliff.

Full in sight lay the far-extended camp of Montcalm, stretching from the St. Charles, beneath the city walls, to the chasm and cataract of the Montmorenci. From the cataract to the river of Beauport, its front was covered by earthworks along the brink of abrupt and lofty heights; and from the river of Beauport to the St. Charles, by broad flats of mud swept by the fire of redoubts, intrenchments, a floating battery, and the city itself. Above the city, Cape Diamond hid the view; but could Wolfe have looked beyond it, he would have beheld a prospect still more disheartening. Here, mile after mile, the St. Lawrence was walled by a range of steeps, often inaccessible, and always so difficult that a few men at the top could hold an army in check; while at Cap-Rouge, about eight miles distant, the high plateau was cleft by the channel of a stream which formed a line of defence as strong as that of the Montmorenci. Quebec was a natural fortress. Bougainville had long before examined the position, and reported that "by the help of intrenchments, easily and quickly made, and defended by three or four thousand men, I think the city would be safe. I do not believe that the English will make any attempt against it; but they may have the madness to do so, and it is well to be prepared against surprise."

Not 4000 men, but four times 4000, now stood in its defence; and their chiefs wisely resolved not to throw away the advantages of their position. Nothing more was heard of Vaudreuil's bold plan of attacking the invaders at their landing; and Montcalm had declared that he would play the part, not of Hannibal, but of Fabius. His plan was to avoid a general battle, run no risks, and protract the defence till the resources of the enemy were exhausted, or till approaching winter forced them to withdraw. Success was almost certain but for one contingency. Amherst, with a force larger than that of Wolfe, was moving against Ticonderoga. If he should capture it, and advance into the colony, Montcalm would be forced to weaken his army by sending strong detachments to oppose him. Here was Wolfe's best hope. This failing, his only chance was in audacity. The game was desperate; but, intrepid gamester as he was in war, he was a man, in the last resort, to stake everything on the cast of the dice.

The elements declared for France. On the afternoon of the day when Wolfe's army landed, a violent squall swept over the St. Lawrence, dashed the ships together, drove several ashore, and destroyed many of the flat-boats from which the troops had just disembarked. "I never saw so much distress among shipping in my whole life," writes an officer to a friend in Boston. Fortunately the storm subsided as quickly as it rose. Vaudreuil saw that the hoped-for deliverance had failed; and as the tempest had not destroyed the British fleet, he resolved to try the virtue of his fireships. "I am afraid," says Montcalm, "that they have cost us a million, and will be good for nothing after all." This remained to be seen. Vaudreuil gave the chief command of them to a naval officer named Delouche; and on the evening of the 28th, after long consultation and much debate among their respective captains, they set sail together at ten o'clock. The night was moonless and dark. In less than an hour they were at the entrance of the north channel. Delouche had been all enthusiasm; but as he neared the danger his nerves failed, and he set fire to his ship half an hour too soon, the rest following his example.

There was an English outpost at the Point of Orleans; and, about eleven o'clock, the sentries descried through the gloom the ghostly outlines of the approaching ships. As they gazed, these mysterious strangers began to dart tongues of flame; fire ran like lightning up their masts and sails, and then they burst out like volcanoes. Filled as they were with pitch, tar, and every manner of combustible, mixed with fireworks, bombs, grenades, and old cannon, swivels, and muskets loaded to the throat, the effect was terrific. The troops at the Point, amazed at the sudden eruption, the din of the explosions, and the showers of grapeshot that rattled among the trees, lost their wits and fled. The blazing dragons hissed and roared, spouted sheets of fire, vomited smoke in black, pitchy volumes and vast illumined clouds, and shed their infernal glare on the distant city, the tents of Montcalm, and the long red lines of the British army, drawn up in array of battle, lest the French should cross from their encampments to attack them in the confusion. Knox calls the display "the grandest fireworks that can possibly be conceived." Yet the fireships did no other harm than burning alive one of their own captains and six or seven of his sailors who failed to escape in their boats. Some of them ran ashore before reaching the fleet; the others were seized by the intrepid English sailors, who, approaching in their boats, threw grappling-irons upon them and towed them towards land, till they swung round and stranded. Here, after venting their fury for a while they subsided into quiet conflagration, which lasted till morning. Vaudreuil watched the result of his experiment from the steeple of the church at Beauport; then returned, dejected, to Quebec.

Wolfe longed to fight his enemy; but his sagacious enemy would not gratify him. From the heights of Beauport, the rock of Quebec, or the summit of Cape Diamond, Montcalm could look down on the river and its shores as on a map, and watch each movement of the invaders. He was hopeful, perhaps confident; and for a month or more he wrote almost daily to Bourlamaque at Ticonderoga, in a cheerful, and often a jocose vein, mingling orders and instructions with pleasantries and bits of news. Yet his vigilance was unceasing. "We pass every night in bivouac, or else sleep in our clothes. Perhaps you are doing as much, my dear Bourlamaque."

Of the two commanders, Vaudreuil was the more sanguine, and professed full faith that all would go well. He too corresponded with Bourlamaque, to whom he gave his opinion, founded on the reports of deserters, that Wolfe had no chance of success unless Amherst should come to his aid. This he pronounced impossible; and he expressed a strong desire that the English would attack him, "so that we may rid ourselves of them at once." He was courageous, except in the immediate presence of danger, and failed only when the crisis came.

Wolfe, held in check at every other point, had one movement in his power. He could seize the heights of Point Levi, opposite the city; and this, along with his occupation of the Island of Orleans, would give him command of the Basin of Quebec. Thence also he could fire on the place across the St. Lawrence, which is here less than a mile wide. The movement was begun on the afternoon of the 29th, when, shivering in a north wind and a sharp frost, a part of Monckton's brigade was ferried over to Beaumont, on the south shore, and the rest followed in the morning. The rangers had a brush with a party of Canadians, whom they drove off, and the regulars then landed unopposed. Monckton ordered a proclamation, signed by Wolfe, to be posted on the door of the parish church. It called on the Canadians, in peremptory terms, to stand neutral in the contest, promised them, if they did so, full protection in property and religion, and threatened that, if they presumed to resist the invaders, their houses, goods, and harvests should be destroyed, and their churches despoiled. As soon as the troops were out of sight the inhabitants took down the placard and carried it to Vaudreuil.

The brigade marched along the river road to Point Levi, drove off a body of French and Indians posted in the church, and took possession of the houses and the surrounding heights. In the morning they were intrenching themselves, when they were greeted by a brisk fire from the edge of the woods. It came from a party of Indians, whom the rangers presently put to flight, and, imitating their own ferocity, scalped nine of them. Wolfe came over to the camp on the next day, went with an escort to the heights opposite Quebec, examined it with a spy-glass, and chose a position from which to bombard it. Cannon and mortars were brought ashore, fascines and gabions made, intrenchments thrown up, and batteries planted. Knox came over from the main camp, and says that he had "a most agreeable view of the city of Quebec. It is a very fair object for our artillery, particularly the lower town." But why did Wolfe wish to bombard it? Its fortifications were but little exposed to his fire, and to knock its houses, convents, and churches to pieces would bring him no nearer to his object. His guns at Point Levi could destroy the city, but could not capture it; yet doubtless they would have good moral effect, discourage the French, and cheer his own soldiers with the flattering belief that they were achieving something.

The guns of Quebec showered balls and bombs upon his workmen; but they still toiled on, and the French saw the fatal batteries fast growing to completion. The citizens, alarmed at the threatened destruction, begged the governor for leave to cross the river and dislodge their assailants. At length he consented. A party of twelve or fifteen hundred was made up of armed burghers, Canadians from the camp, a few Indians, some pupils of the Seminary, and about 100 volunteers from the regulars. Dumas, an experienced officer, took command of them; and, going up to Sillery, they crossed the river on the night of the 12th of July. They had hardly climbed the heights of the south shore when they grew exceedingly nervous, though the enemy was still three miles off. The Seminary scholars fired on some of their own party, whom they mistook for English; and the same mishap was repeated a second and a third time. A panic seized the whole body, and Dumas could not control them. They turned and made for their canoes, rolling over each other as they rushed down the heights, and reappeared at Quebec at six in the morning, overwhelmed with despair and shame.

The presentiment of the unhappy burghers proved too true. The English batteries fell to their work, and the families of the town fled to the country for safety. In a single day eighteen houses and the cathedral were burned by exploding shells; and fiercer and fiercer the storm of fire and iron hailed upon Quebec.

Wolfe did not rest content with distressing his enemy. With an ardor and a daring that no difficulties could cool, he sought means to strike an effective blow. It was nothing to lay Quebec in ruins if he could not defeat the army that protected it. To land from boats and attack Montcalm in front, through the mud of the Beauport flats or up the heights along the neighboring shore, was an enterprise too rash even for his temerity. It might, however, be possible to land below the cataract of Montmorenci, cross the stream higher up, and strike the French army in flank or rear; and he had no sooner secured his positions at the points of Levi and Orleans, than he addressed himself to this attempt.

On the 8th of July several frigates and a bomb-ketch took their stations before the camp of the Chevalier de Lévis, who, with his division of Canadian militia, occupied the heights along the St. Lawrence just above the cataract. Here they shelled and cannonaded him all day; though, from his elevated position, with very little effect. Towards evening the troops on the Point of Orleans broke up their camp. Major Hardy, with a detachment of marines, was left to hold that post, while the rest embarked at night in the boats of the fleet. They were the brigades of Townshend and Murray, consisting of five battalions, with a body of grenadiers, light infantry, and rangers, — in all 3000 men. They landed before daybreak in front of the parish of L'Ange Gardien, a little below the cataract. The only opposition was from a troop of Canadians and Indians, whom they routed, after some loss, climbed the heights, gained the plateau above, and began to intrench themselves. A company of rangers, supported by detachments of regulars, was sent into the neighboring forest to protect the parties who were cutting fascines, and apparently, also, to look for a fording-place.

Lévis, with his Scotch-Jacobite aide-de-camp, Johnstone, had watched the movements of Wolfe from the heights across the cataract. Johnstone says that he asked his commander if he was sure there was no ford higher up on the Montmorenci, by which the English could cross. Lévis averred that there was none, and that he himself had examined the stream to its source; on which a Canadian who stood by whispered to the aide-de-camp: "The general is mistaken; there is a ford." Johnstone told this to Lévis, who would not believe it, and so browbeat the Canadian that he dared not repeat what he had said. Johnstone, taking him aside, told him to go and find somebody who had lately crossed the ford, and bring him at once to the general's quarters; whereupon he soon reappeared with a man who affirmed that he had crossed it the night before with a sack of wheat on his back. A detachment was immediately sent to the place, with orders to intrench itself, and Repentigny, lieutenant of Lévis, was posted not far off with 1100 Canadians.

Four hundred Indians passed the ford under the partisan Langlade, discovered Wolfe's detachment, hid themselves, and sent their commander to tell Repentigny that there was a body of English in the forest, who might all be destroyed if he would come over at once with his Canadians. Repentigny sent for orders to Lévis, and Lévis sent for orders to Vaudreuil, whose quarters were three or four miles distant. Vaudreuil answered that no risk should be run, and that he would come and see to the matter himself. It was about two hours before he arrived; and meanwhile the Indians grew impatient, rose from their hiding-place, fired on the rangers, and drove them back with heavy loss upon the regulars, who stood their ground, and at last repulsed the assailants. The Indians recrossed the ford with thirty-six scalps. If Repentigny had advanced, and Lévis had followed with his main body, the consequences to the English might have been serious; for, as Johnstone remarks, "a Canadian in the woods is worth three disciplined soldiers, as a soldier in a plain is worth three Canadians." Vaudreuil called a council of war. The question was whether an effort should be made to dislodge Wolfe's main force. Montcalm and the governor were this time of one mind, and both thought it inexpedient to attack, with militia, a body of regular troops whose numbers and position were imperfectly known. Bigot gave his voice for the attack. He was overruled, and Wolfe was left to fortify himself in peace.

His occupation of the heights of Montmorenci exposed him to great risks. The left wing of his army at Point Levi was six miles from its right wing at the cataract, and Major Hardy's detachment on the Point of Orleans was between them, separated from each by a wide arm of the St. Lawrence. Any one of the three camps might be overpowered before the others could support it; and Hardy with his small force was above all in danger of being cut to pieces. But the French kept persistently on the defensive; and after the failure of Dumas to dislodge the English from Point Levi, Vaudreuil would not hear of another such attempt. Wolfe was soon well intrenched; but it was easier to defend himself than to strike at his enemy. Montcalm, when urged to attack him, is said to have answered: "Let him amuse himself where he is. If we drive him off, he may go to some place where he can do us harm." His late movement, however, had a discouraging effect on the Canadians, who now for the first time began to desert. His batteries, too, played across the chasm of Montmorenci upon the left wing of the French army with an effect extremely annoying.

The position of the hostile forces was a remarkable one. They were separated by the vast gorge that opens upon the St. Lawrence; an amphitheatre of lofty precipices, their brows crested with forests, and their steep brown sides scantily feathered with stunted birch and fir. Into this abyss leaps the Montmorenci with one headlong plunge of nearly 250 feet, a living column of snowy white, with its spray, its foam, its mists, and its rainbows; then spreads itself in broad, thin sheets over a floor of rock and gravel, and creeps tamely to the St. Lawrence. It was but a gunshot across the gulf, and the sentinels on each side watched each other over the roar and turmoil of the cataract. Captain Knox, coming one day from Point Levi to receive orders from Wolfe, improved a spare hour to visit this marvel of nature. "I had very nigh paid dear for my inquisitiveness; for while I stood on the eminence I was hastily called to by one of our sentinels, when, throwing my eyes about, I saw a Frenchman creeping under the eastern extremity of their breastwork to fire at me. This obliged me to retire as fast as I could out of his reach, and, making up to the sentry to thank him for his attention, he told me the fellow had snapped his piece twice, and the second time it flashed in the pan at the instant I turned away from the Fall." Another officer, less fortunate, had a leg broken by a shot from the opposite cliffs.

Day after day went by, and the invaders made no progress. Flags of truce passed often between the hostile camps. "You will demolish the town, no doubt," said the bearer of one of them, "but you shall never get inside of it." To which Wolfe replied: "I will have Quebec if I stay here till the end of November." Sometimes the heat was intense, and sometimes there were floods of summer rain that inundated the tents. Along the river, from the Montmorenci to Point Levi, there were ceaseless artillery fights between gunboats, frigates, and batteries on shore. Bands of Indians infested the outskirts of the camps, killing sentries and patrols. The rangers chased them through the woods; there were brisk skirmishes, and scalps lost and won. Sometimes the regulars took part in these forest battles; and once it was announced, in orders of the day, that "the General has ordered two sheep and some rum to Captain Cosnan's company of grenadiers for the spirit they showed this morning in pushing those scoundrels of Indians." The Indians complained that the British soldiers were learning how to fight, and no longer stood still in a mass to be shot at, as in Braddock's time. The Canadian *coureurs de bois* mixed with their red allies and wore their livery. One of them was caught on 18 July. He was naked, daubed red and blue, and adorned with a bunch of painted feathers dangling from the top of his head. He and his companions used the scalping-knife as freely as the Indians themselves; nor were the New England rangers much behind them in this respect, till an order came from Wolfe forbidding "the inhuman practice of scalping, except when the enemy are Indians, or Canadians dressed like Indians."

A part of the fleet worked up into the Basin, beyond the Point of Orleans; and here, on the warm summer nights, officers and men watched the cannon flashing and thundering from the heights of Montmorenci on one side, and those of Point Levi on the other, and the bombs sailing through the air in fiery semi-circles. Often the gloom was lighted up by the blaze of the burning houses of Quebec, kindled by incendiary shells. Both the lower and the upper town were nearly deserted by the inhabitants, some retreating into the country, and some into the suburb of St. Roch; while the Ursulines and Hospital nuns abandoned their convents to seek harborage beyond the range of shot. The city was a prey to robbers, who pillaged the empty houses, till an order came from headquarters promising the gallows to all who should be caught. News reached the French that Niagara was attacked,

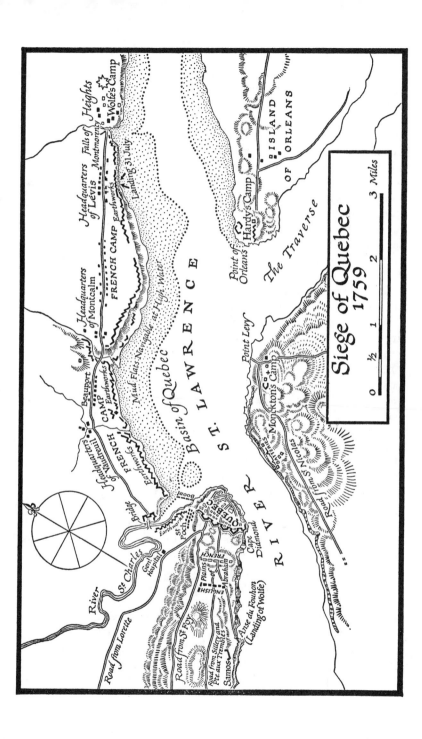

Siege of Quebec
1759

0 ½ 1 2 3 Miles

Wolfe's Camp

Heights
Falls of
Montmorency
Headquarters of Lévis
Landing 31 July
FRENCH CAMP Earthworks

Headquarters of Montcalm

Beauport
CAMP
Earthworks

FRENCH CAMP

Mud Flat. Navigable at High Water

Headquarters of Vaudreuil

FRENCH
Earthworks

Bridge

St. Charles River

River

Road from Lorette

General Hospital

St. Roch
Earthworks
QUEBEC

Plains
of
FRENCH
Abraham
ENGLISH

Cape Diamond

Anse du Foulon
(Landing of Wolfe)

Samos
Road from Sillery and Pte. aux Trembles
Road from St. Foy

BATTERIES
Point from St. Nicolas
Monckton's Camp

Point Levy

Road from St. Nicolas

S T.   L A W R E N C E

Basin of Quebec

R I V E R

Point of Orleans
Hardy's Camp

ISLAND

OF ORLEANS

The Traverse

and that the army of Amherst was moving against Ticonderoga. The Canadians deserted more and more. They were disheartened by the defensive attitude in which both Vaudreuil and Montcalm steadily persisted; and accustomed as they were to rapid raids, sudden strokes, and a quick return to their homes, they tired of long weeks of inaction. The English patrols caught one of them as he was passing the time in fishing. "He seemed to be a subtle old rogue," says Knox, "of seventy years of age, as he told us. We plied him well with port wine, and then his heart was more open; and seeing that we laughed at the exaggerated accounts he had given us, he said he 'wished the affair was well over, one way or the other; that his countrymen were all discontented, and would either surrender, or disperse and act a neutral part, if it were not for the persuasions of their priests and the fear of being maltreated by the savages, with whom they are threatened on all occasions.' " A deserter reported on the 19th of July that nothing but dread of the Indians kept the Canadians in the camp.

Wolfe's proclamation, at first unavailing, was now taking effect. A large number of Canadian prisoners, brought in on the 25th, declared that their countrymen would gladly accept his offers but for the threats of their commanders that if they did so the Indians should be set upon them. The prisoners said further that "they had been under apprehension for several days past of having a body of 400 barbarians sent to rifle their parish and habitations." Such threats were not wholly effectual. A French chronicler of the time says: "The Canadians showed their disgust every day, and deserted at every opportunity, in spite of the means taken to prevent them." "The people were intimidated, seeing all our army kept in one body and solely on the defensive; while the English, though far less numerous, divided their forces, and undertook various bold enterprises without meeting resistance."

On the 18th the English accomplished a feat which promised important results. The French commanders had thought it impossible for any hostile ship to pass the batteries of Quebec; but about eleven o'clock at night, favored by the wind, and covered by a furious cannonade from Point Levi, the ship *Sutherland*, with a frigate and several small vessels, sailed safely by and reached the river above the town. Here they at once attacked and destroyed a fireship and some small craft that they found there. Now, for the first time, it became necessary for Montcalm to weaken his army at Beauport by sending 600 men, under Dumas, to defend the accessible points in the line of precipices between Quebec and Cap-Rouge. Several hundred more were sent on the next day, when it became known that the English had dragged a fleet of boats over Point Levi, launched them above the town, and despatched troops to embark in them. Thus a new feature was introduced into the siege operations, and danger had risen on a side where the French thought themselves safe. On the other hand, Wolfe had become more vulnerable than ever. His army was now divided, not into three parts, but into four, each so far from the rest that, in case of sudden attack, it must defend itself alone. That Montcalm did not improve his opportunity was apparently due to want of confidence in his militia.

The force above the town did not lie idle. On the night of the 20th of July, Colonel Carleton, with 600 men, rowed eighteen miles up the river, and landed at Pointe-aux-Trembles, on the north shore. Here some of the families of Quebec had sought asylum; and Wolfe had been told by prisoners that not only were stores in great quantity to be found he.e, but also letters and papers throwing light on the French plans. Carleton and his men drove off a band of Indians who fired on them, and spent a quiet day around the parish church; but found few papers, and still fewer stores. They withdrew towards evening, carrying with them nearly 100 women, children, and old men; and they were no sooner gone than the Indians returned to plunder the empty houses of their unfortunate allies. The prisoners were treated with great kindness. The ladies among them were entertained at supper by Wolfe, who jested with them on the caution of the French generals, saying: "I have given good chances to attack me, and am surprised that they have not profited by them." On the next day the prisoners were all sent to Quebec under a flag of truce.

Thus far Wolfe had refrained from executing the threats he had affixed the month before to the church of Beaumont. But now he issued another proclamation. It declared that the Canadians had shown themselves unworthy of the offers he had made them, and that he had therefore ordered his light troops to ravage their country and bring them prisoners to his camp. Such of the Canadian militia as belonged to the parishes near Quebec were now in a sad dilemma; for Montcalm threatened them on one side, and Wolfe on the other. They might desert to their homes, or they might stand by their colors; in the one case their houses were to be burned by French savages, and in the other by British light infantry.

Wolfe at once gave orders in accord with his late proclamation; but he commanded that no church should be profaned, and no woman or child injured. The first effects of his stern policy are thus recorded by

Knox: "Major Dalling's light infantry brought in this afternoon to our camp two hundred and fifty male and female prisoners. Among this number was a very respectable looking priest, and about forty men fit to bear arms. There was almost an equal number of black cattle, with about seventy sheep and lambs, and a few horses. Brigadier Monckton entertained the reverend father and some other fashionable personages in his tent, and most humanely ordered refreshments to all the rest of the captives; which noble example was followed by the soldiery, who generously crowded about those unhappy people, sharing their provisions, rum, and tobacco with them. They were sent in the evening on board of transports in the river." Again, two days later: "Colonel Fraser's detachment returned this morning, and presented us with more scenes of distress and the dismal consequences of war, by a great number of wretched families, whom they brought in prisoners, with some of their effects, and near three hundred black cattle, sheep, hogs, and horses."

On the next night the attention of the excellent journalist was otherwise engaged. Vaudreuil tried again to burn the English fleet. "Late last night," writes Knox, under date of the 28th, "the enemy sent down a most formidable fireraft, which consisted of a parcel of schooners, shallops, and stages chained together. It could not be less than a hundred fathoms in length, and was covered with grenades, old swivels, gun and pistol barrels loaded up to their muzzles, and various other inventions and combustible matters. This seemed to be their last attempt against our fleet, which happily miscarried, as before; for our gallant seamen, with their usual expertness, grappled them before they got down above a third part of the Basin, towed them safe to shore, and left them at anchor, continually repeating, *All's well*. A remarkable expression from some of these intrepid souls to their comrades on this occasion I must not omit, on account of its singular uncouthness; namely: 'Damme, Jack, didst thee ever take hell in tow before?' "

According to a French account, this aquatic infernal machine consisted of seventy rafts, boats, and schooners. Its failure was due to no shortcoming on the part of its conductors; who, under a brave Canadian named Courval, acted with coolness and resolution. Nothing saved the fleet but the courage of the sailors, swarming out in their boats to fight the approaching conflagration.

It was now the end of July. More than half the summer was gone, and Quebec seemed as far as ever beyond the grasp of Wolfe. Its buildings were in ruins, and the neighboring parishes were burned and ravaged; but its living rampart, the army of Montcalm, still lay in patient defiance along the shores of Beauport, while above the city every point where a wildcat could climb the precipices was watched and guarded, and Dumas with 1000 men held the impregnable heights of Cap-Rouge. Montcalm persisted in doing nothing that his enemy wished him to do. He would not fight on Wolfe's terms, and Wolfe resolved at last to fight him on his own; that is, to attack his camp in front.

The plan was desperate; for, after leaving troops enough to hold Point Levi and the heights of Montmorenci, less than 5000 men would be left to attack a position of commanding strength, where Montcalm at an hour's notice could collect twice as many to oppose them. But Wolfe had a boundless trust in the disciplined valor of his soldiers, and an utter scorn of the militia who made the greater part of his enemy's force.

Towards the Montmorenci the borders of the St. Lawrence are, as we have seen, extremely steep. At a mile from the gorge of the cataract there is, at high tide, a strand, about the eighth of a mile wide, between the foot of these heights and the river; and beyond this strand the receding tide lays bare a tract of mud nearly half a mile wide. At the edge of the dry ground the French had built a redoubt mounted with cannon, and there were other similar works on the strand a quarter of a mile nearer the cataract. Wolfe could not see from the river that these redoubts were commanded by the musketry of the intrenchments along the brink of the heights above. These intrenchments were so constructed that they swept with cross-fires the whole face of the declivity, which was covered with grass, and was very steep. Wolfe hoped that, if he attacked one of the redoubts, the French would come down to defend it, and so bring on a general engagement; or, if they did not, that he should gain an opportunity of reconnoitring the heights to find some point where they could be stormed with a chance of success.

In front of the gorge of the Montmorenci there was a ford during several hours of low tide, so that troops from the adjoining English camp might cross to co-operate with their comrades landing in boats from Point Levi and the Island of Orleans. On the morning of the 31st of July, the tide then being at the flood, the French saw the ship *Centurion*, of 64 guns, anchor near the Montmorenci and open fire on the redoubts. Then two armed transports, each of 14 guns, stood in as close as possible to the first redoubt and fired upon it, stranding as the tide went out, till in the afternoon they lay bare upon the mud. At the same time a battery of more than 40 heavy pieces, planted on the lofty promontory beyond the Montmorenci, began a furious cannonade upon the flank of the French intrenchments. It did no great harm, however, for the works were protected by a great number of traverses, which stopped the shot; and the Canadians, who manned this part of the lines, held their ground with excellent steadiness.

About eleven o'clock a fleet of boats filled with troops, chiefly from Point Levi, appeared in the river and hovered off the shore west of the parish church of Beauport, as if meaning to land there. Montcalm was perplexed, doubting whether the real attack was to be made here, or toward the Montmorenci. Hour after hour the boats moved to and fro, to increase his doubts and hide the real design; but he soon became convinced that the camp of Lévis at the Montmorenci was the true object of his enemy; and about two o'clock he went thither, greeted as he rode along the lines by shouts of *Vive notre Général!* Lévis had already made preparations for defence with his usual skill. His Canadians were reinforced by the battalions of Béarn, Guienne, and Royal Roussillon; and, as the intentions of Wolfe became certain, the right of the camp was nearly abandoned, the main strength of the army being gathered between the river of Beauport and the Montmorenci, where, according to a French writer, there were, towards the end of the afternoon, about 12,000 men.

At half-past five o'clock the tide was out, and the crisis came. The batteries across the Montmorenci, the distant batteries of Point Levi, the cannon of the *Centurion*, and those of the two stranded ships, all opened together with redoubled fury. The French batteries replied; and, amid this deafening roar of artillery, the English boats set their troops ashore at the edge of the broad tract of sedgy mud that the receding river had left bare. At the same time a column of 2000 men was seen, a mile away, moving in perfect order across the Montmorenci ford. The first troops that landed from the boats were thirteen companies of grenadiers and a detachment of Royal Americans. They dashed swiftly forward; while at some distance behind came Monckton's brigade, composed of the 15th, or Amherst's regiment, and the 78th, or Fraser's Highlanders. The day had been fair and warm; but the sky was now thick with clouds, and large raindrops began to fall, the precursors of a summer storm.

With the utmost precipitation, without orders, and without waiting for Monckton's brigade to come up, the grenadiers in front made a rush for the redoubt near the foot of the hill. The French abandoned it;

but the assailants had no sooner gained their prize than the thronged heights above blazed with musketry, and a tempest of bullets fell among them. Nothing daunted, they dashed forward again, reserving their fire, and struggling to climb the steep ascent; while, with yells and shouts of *Vive le Roi!* the troops and Canadians at the top poured upon them a hailstorm of musket-balls and buck-shot, and dead and wounded in numbers rolled together down the slope. At that instant the clouds burst, and the rain fell in torrents. "We could not see halfway down the hill," says the Chevalier Johnstone, who was at this part of the line. Ammunition was wet on both sides, and the grassy steeps became so slippery that it was impossible to climb them. The English say that the storm saved the French; the French, with as much reason, that it saved the English.

The baffled grenadiers drew back into the redoubt. Wolfe saw the madness of persisting, and ordered a retreat. The rain ceased, and troops of Indians came down the heights to scalp the fallen. Some of them ran towards Lieutenant Peyton, of the Royal Americans, as he lay disabled by a musket-shot. With his double-barrelled gun he brought down two of his assailants, when a Highland sergeant snatched him in his arms, dragged him half a mile over the mud-flats, and placed him in one of the boats. A friend of Peyton, Captain Ochterlony, had received a mortal wound, and an Indian would have scalped him but for the generous intrepidity of a soldier of the battalion of Guienne; who, seizing the enraged savage, held him back till several French officers interposed, and had the dying man carried to a place of safety.

The English retreated in good order, after setting fire to the two stranded vessels. Those of the grenadiers and Royal Americans who were left alive rowed for the Point of Orleans; the 15th regiment rowed for Point Levi; and the Highlanders, led by Wolfe himself, joined the column from beyond the Montmorenci, placing themselves in its rear as it slowly retired along the flats and across the ford, the Indians yelling and the French shouting from the heights, while the British waved their hats, daring them to come down and fight.

The grenadiers and the Royal Americans, who had borne the brunt of the fray, bore also nearly all the loss; which, in proportion to their numbers, was enormous. Knox reports it at 443, killed, wounded, and missing, including one colonel, eight captains, twenty-one lieutenants, and three ensigns.[1]

---

[1] Among the killed in this affair was Edward Botwood, sergeant in the grenadiers of the 47th or Lascelles' Regiment. "Ned" Botwood was well known among

Vaudreuil, delighted, wrote to Bourlamaque an account of the affair. "I have no more anxiety about Quebec. M. Wolfe, I can assure you, will make no progress. Luckily for him, his prudence saved him from the consequences of his mad enterprise, and he contented himself with losing about five hundred of his best soldiers. Deserters say that he will try us again in a few days. That is what we want; he'll find somebody to talk to (*il trouvera à qui parler*)."

---

his comrades as a poet; and the following lines of his, written on the eve of the expedition to Quebec, continued to be favorites with the British troops during the War of the Revolution:

HOT STUFF
Air: *Lilies of France*

Come, each death-doing dog who dares venture his neck,
Come, follow the hero that goes to Quebec;
Jump aboard of the transports, and loose every sail,
Pay your debts at the tavern by giving leg-bail;
And ye that love fighting shall soon have enough:
Wolfe commands us, my boys; we shall give them Hot Stuff.

Up the River St. Lawrence our troops shall advance,
To the Grenadiers' March we shall teach them to dance.
Cape Breton we have taken, and next we will try
At their capital to give them another black eye.
Vaudreuil, 'tis in vain you pretend to look gruff —
Those are coming who know how to give you Hot Stuff.

With powder in his periwig and snuff in his nose,
Monsieur will run down our descent to oppose;
And the Indians will come: but the light infantry
Will soon oblige *them* to betake to a tree.
From such rascals as these may we fear a rebuff?
Advance, grenadiers, and let fly your Hot Stuff!

CHAPTER XXXV

The Heights of Abraham

1759

[*Montcalm and Wolfe*, CHAPTER XXVII]

Wolfe was deeply moved by the disaster at the heights of Montmorenci, and in a General Order on the next day he rebuked the grenadiers for their precipitation. "Such impetuous, irregular, and unsoldierlike proceedings destroy all order, make it impossible for the commanders to form any disposition for an attack, and put it out of the general's power to execute his plans. The grenadiers could not suppose that they could beat the French alone."

The French were elated by their success. "Everybody," says the commissary Berniers, "thought that the campaign was as good as ended, gloriously for us." They had been sufficiently confident even before their victory; and the bearer of a flag of truce told the English officers that he had never imagined they were such fools as to attack Quebec with so small a force. Wolfe, on the other hand, had every reason to despond. At the outset, before he had seen Quebec and learned the nature of the ground, he had meant to begin the campaign by taking post on the Plains of Abraham, and thence laying siege to the town; but he soon discovered that the Plains of Abraham were hardly more within his reach than was Quebec itself. Such hope as was left him lay in the composition of Montcalm's army. He respected the French commander, and thought his disciplined soldiers not unworthy of the British steel; but he held his militia in high scorn, and could he but face them in the open field, he never doubted the result. But Montcalm also distrusted them, and persisted in refusing the coveted battle.

Wolfe, therefore, was forced to the conviction that his chances were of the smallest. It is said that, despairing of any decisive stroke, he conceived the idea of fortifying Isle-aux-Coudres, and leaving a part of his troops there when he sailed for home, against another attempt in the spring. The more to weaken the enemy and prepare his future conquest, he began at the same time a course of action which for his credit one would gladly wipe from the record; for, though far from inhuman, he threw himself with extraordinary intensity into whatever work he had in hand, and, to accomplish it, spared others scarcely more than he spared himself. About the middle of August he issued a third proclamation to the Canadians, declaring that as they had refused his offers of protection and "had made such ungrateful returns in practising the most unchristian barbarities against his troops on all occasions, he could no longer refrain in justice to himself and his army from chastising them as they deserved." The barbarities in question consisted in the frequent scalping and mutilating of sentinels and men on outpost duty, perpetrated no less by Canadians than by Indians. Wolfe's object was twofold: first, to cause the militia to desert, and, secondly, to exhaust the colony. Rangers, light infantry, and Highlanders were sent to waste the settlements far and wide. Wherever resistance was offered, farmhouses and villages were laid in ashes, though churches were generally spared. St. Paul, far below Quebec, was sacked and burned, and the settlements of the opposite shore were partially destroyed. The parishes of L'Ange Gardien, Château Richer, and St. Joachim were wasted with fire and sword. Night after night the garrison of Quebec could see the light of burning houses as far down as the mountain of Cape Tourmente. Near St. Joachim there was a severe skirmish, followed by atrocious cruelties. Captain Alexander Montgomery, of the 43rd regiment, who commanded the detachment, and who has been most unjustly confounded with the revolutionary general, Richard Montgomery, ordered the prisoners to be shot in cold blood, to the indignation of his own officers. Robineau de Portneuf, curé of St. Joachim, placed himself at the head of thirty parishioners and took possession of a large stone house in the adjacent parish of Château Richer, where for a time he held the English at bay. At length he and his followers were drawn out into an ambush, where they were surrounded and killed; and, being disguised as Indians, the rangers scalped them all.

Most of the French writers of the time mention these barbarities without much comment, while Vaudreuil loudly denounces them. Yet he himself was answerable for atrocities incomparably worse, and on a far larger scale. He had turned loose his savages, red and white, along a frontier of 600 miles, to waste, burn, and murder at will.

"Women and children," such were the orders of Wolfe, "are to be treated with humanity; if any violence is offered to a woman, the offender shall be punished with death." These orders were generally obeyed. The English, with the single exception of Montgomery, killed none but armed men in the act of resistance or attack; Vaudreuil's war-parties spared neither age nor sex.

Montcalm let the parishes burn, and still lay fast intrenched in his lines of Beauport. He would not imperil all Canada to save a few hundred farmhouses; and Wolfe was as far as ever from the battle that he coveted. Hitherto, his attacks had been made chiefly below the town; but, these having failed, he now changed his plan and renewed on a larger scale the movements begun above it in July. With every fair wind, ships and transports passed the batteries of Quebec, favored by a hot fire from Point Levi, and generally succeeded, with more or less damage, in gaining the upper river. A fleet of flatboats was also sent thither, and 1200 troops marched overland to embark in them, under Brigadier Murray. Admiral Holmes took command of the little fleet now gathered above the town, and operations in that quarter were systematically resumed.

To oppose them, Bougainville was sent from the camp at Beauport with 1500 men. His was a most arduous and exhausting duty. He must watch the shores for fifteen or twenty miles, divide his force into detachments, and subject himself and his followers to the strain of incessant vigilance and incessant marching. Murray made a descent at Pointe-aux-Trembles, and was repulsed with loss. He tried a second time at another place, was met before landing by a body of ambushed Canadians, and was again driven back, his foremost boats full of dead and wounded. A third time he succeeded, landed at Deschambault, and burned a large building filled with stores and all the spare baggage of the French regular officers. The blow was so alarming that Montcalm hastened from Beauport to take command in person; but when he arrived the English were gone.[1]

Vaudreuil now saw his mistake in sending the French frigates up the river out of harm's way, and withdrawing their crews to serve the batteries of Quebec. Had these ships been there, they might have overpowered those of the English in detail as they passed the town. An attempt was made to retrieve the blunder. The sailors were sent to man the frigates anew and attack the squadron of Holmes. It was too late. Holmes was already too strong for them, and they were

[1] [These actions took place on 8 and 17 Aug. respectively.]

recalled. Yet the difficulties of the English still seemed insurmountable. Dysentery and fever broke out in their camps, the number of their effective men was greatly reduced, and the advancing season told them that their work must be done quickly, or not done at all.

On the other side, the distress of the French grew greater every day. Their army was on short rations. The operations of the English above the town filled the camp of Beauport with dismay, for troops and Canadians alike dreaded the cutting off of their supplies. These were all drawn from the districts of Three Rivers and Montreal; and, at best, they were in great danger, since when brought down in boats at night they were apt to be intercepted, while the difficulty of bringing them by land was extreme, through the scarcity of cattle and horses. Discipline was relaxed, disorder and pillage were rife, and the Canadians deserted so fast, that towards the end of August 200 of them, it is said, would sometimes go off in one night. Early in the month the disheartening news came of the loss of Ticonderoga and Crown Point, the retreat of Bourlamaque, the fall of Niagara, and the expected advance of Amherst on Montreal. It was then that Lévis was despatched to the scene of danger; and Quebec was deplorably weakened by his absence. About this time the Lower Town was again set on fire by the English batteries, and 167 houses were burned in a night. In the front of the Upper Town nearly every building was a ruin. At the General Hospital, which was remote enough to be safe from the bombardment, every barn, shed, and garret, and even the chapel itself, were crowded with sick and wounded, with women and children from the town, and the nuns of the Ursulines and the Hôtel-Dieu, driven thither for refuge. Bishop Pontbriand, though suffering from a mortal disease, came almost daily to visit and console them from his lodging in the house of the curé at Charlesbourg.

Towards the end of August the sky brightened again. It became known that Amherst was not moving on Montreal, and Bourlamaque wrote that his position at Isle-aux-Noix was impregnable. On the 27th a deserter from Wolfe's army brought the welcome assurance that the invaders despaired of success, and would soon sail for home; while there were movements in the English camps and fleet that seemed to confirm what he said. Vaudreuil breathed more freely, and renewed hope and confidence visited the army of Beauport.

Meanwhile a deep cloud fell on the English. Since the siege began, Wolfe had passed with ceaseless energy from camp to camp, animating the troops, observing everything, and directing everything; but now the pale face and tall lean form were seen no more, and the rumor spread that the general was dangerously ill. He had in fact been seized by an access of the disease that had tortured him for some time past; and fever had followed. His quarters were at a French farmhouse in the camp at Montmorenci; and here, as he lay in an upper chamber, helpless in bed, his singular and most unmilitary features haggard with disease and drawn with pain, no man could less have looked the hero. But as the needle, though quivering, points always to the pole, so, through torment and languor and the heats of fever, the mind of Wolfe dwelt on the capture of Quebec. His illness, which began before the 20th of August, had so far subsided on the 25th that Knox wrote in his Diary of that day: "His Excellency General Wolfe is on the recovery, to the inconceivable joy of the whole army." On the 29th he was able to write or dictate a letter to the three brigadiers, Monckton, Townshend, and Murray: "That the public service may not suffer by the General's indisposition, he begs the brigadiers will meet and consult together for the public utility and advantage, and consider of the best method to attack the enemy." The letter then proposes three plans, all bold to audacity. The first was to send a part of the army to ford the Montmorenci eight or nine miles above its mouth, march through the forest, and fall on the rear of the French at Beauport, while the rest landed and attacked them in front. The second was to cross the ford at the mouth of the Montmorenci and march along the strand, under the French intrenchments, till a place could be found where the troops might climb the heights. The third was to make a general attack from boats at the Beauport flats. Wolfe had before entertained two other plans, one of which was to scale the heights at St. Michel, about a league above Quebec; but this he had abandoned on learning that the French were there in force to receive him. The other was to storm the Lower Town; but this also he had abandoned, because the Upper Town, which commanded it, would still remain inaccessible.

The brigadiers met in consultation, rejected the three plans proposed in the letter, and advised that an attempt should be made to gain a footing on the north shore above the town, place the army between Montcalm and his base of supply, and so force him to fight or surrender. The scheme was similar to that of the heights of St. Michel. It seemed desperate, but so did all the rest; and if by chance it should succeed, the gain was far greater than could follow any success below the town. Wolfe embraced it at once.

Not that he saw much hope in it. He knew that every chance was against him. Disappointment in the past and gloom in the future, the pain and exhaustion of disease, toils, and anxieties "too great," in the words of Burke, "to be supported by a delicate constitution, and a body unequal to the vigorous and enterprising soul that it lodged," threw him at times into deep dejection. By those intimate with him he was heard to say that he would not go back defeated, "to be exposed to the censure and reproach of an ignorant populace." In other moods he felt that he ought not to sacrifice what was left of his diminished army in vain conflict with hopeless obstacles. But his final resolve once taken, he would not swerve from it. His fear was that he might not be able to lead his troops in person. "I know perfectly well you cannot cure me," he said to his physician; "but pray make me up so that I may be without pain for a few days, and able to do any duty: that is all I want."

In a despatch which Wolfe had written to Pitt, Admiral Saunders conceived that he had ascribed to the fleet more than its just share in the disaster at Montmorenci; and he sent him a letter on the subject. Major Barré kept it from the invalid till the fever had abated. Wolfe then wrote a long answer, which reveals his mixed dejection and resolve. He affirms the justice of what Saunders had said, but adds: "I shall leave out that part of my letter to Mr. Pitt which you object to. I am sensible of my own errors in the course of the campaign, see clearly wherein I have been deficient, and think a little more or less blame to a man that must necessarily be ruined, of little or no consequence. I take the blame of that unlucky day entirely upon my own shoulders, and I expect to suffer for it." Then, speaking of the new project of an attack above Quebec, he says despondingly: "My ill state of health prevents me from executing my own plan; it is of too desperate a nature to order others to execute." [2] He proceeds, however, to give directions for it. "It will be necessary to run as many small craft as possible above the town, with provisions for six weeks, for about five thousand, which is all I intend to take. My letters, I hope, will be ready to-morrow, and I hope I shall have strength to lead these men to wherever we can find the enemy."

On the next day, the last of August, he was able for the first time to leave the house. It was on this same day that he wrote his last letter

---

[2] [Wolfe to Saunders, 30 Aug. 1759. Gipson p. 407 points out that this sentence, if read in its context, does not refer to the plan of attack above Quebec, which was what his three brigadiers advised, but to his own plan for a renewed frontal attack on the Beauport heights.]

to his mother: "My writing to you will convince you that no personal evils worse than defeats and disappointments have fallen upon me. The enemy puts nothing to risk, and I can't in conscience put the whole army to risk. My antagonist has wisely shut himself up in inaccessible intrenchments, so that I can't get at him without spilling a torrent of blood, and that perhaps to little purpose. The Marquis de Montcalm is at the head of a great number of bad soldiers, and I am at the head of a small number of good ones, that wish for nothing so much as to fight him; but the wary old fellow avoids an action, doubtful of the behavior of his army. People must be of the profession to understand the disadvantages and difficulties we labor under, arising from the uncommon natural strength of the country."

On the 2nd of September a vessel was sent to England with his last despatch to Pitt. It begins thus: "The obstacles we have met with in the operations of the campaign are much greater than we had reason to expect or could foresee; not so much from the number of the enemy (though superior to us) as from the natural strength of the country, which the Marquis of Montcalm seems wisely to depend upon. When I learned that succors of all kinds had been thrown into Quebec; that five battalions of regular troops, completed from the best inhabitants of the country, some of the troops of the colony, and every Canadian that was able to bear arms, besides several nations of savages, had taken the field in a very advantageous situation, — I could not flatter myself that I should be able to reduce the place. I sought, however, an occasion to attack their army, knowing well that with these troops I was able to fight, and hoping that a victory might disperse them." Then, after recounting the events of the campaign with admirable clearness, he continues: "I found myself so ill, and am still so weak, that I begged the general officers to consult together for the general utility. They are all of opinion that, as more ships and provisions are now got above the town, they should try, by conveying up a corps of four or five thousand men (which is nearly the whole strength of the army after the Points of Levi and Orleans are left in a proper state of defence), to draw the enemy from their present situation and bring them to an action. I have acquiesced in the proposal, and we are preparing to put it into execution." The letter ends thus: "By the list of disabled officers, many of whom are of rank, you may perceive that the army is much weakened. By the nature of the river, the most formidable part of this armament is deprived of the power of acting; yet we have almost the whole force of Canada to oppose. In this situation there is such a choice of difficulties that I own myself at a loss how to determine. The affairs of Great Britain, I know, require the most vigorous measures; but the courage of a handful of brave troops should be exerted only when there is some hope of a favorable event; however, you may be assured that the small part of the campaign which remains shall be employed, as far as I am able, for the honor of His Majesty and the interest of the nation, in which I am sure of being well seconded by the Admiral and by the generals; happy if our efforts here can contribute to the success of His Majesty's arms in any other parts of America."

Some days later, he wrote to the Earl of Holdernesse: "The Marquis of Montcalm has a numerous body of armed men (I cannot call it an army), and the strongest country perhaps in the world. Our fleet blocks up the river above and below the town, but can give no manner of aid in an attack upon the Canadian army. We are now here [*off Cap-Rouge*] with about thirty-six hundred men, waiting to attack them when and wherever they can best be got at. I am so far recovered as to do business; but my constitution is entirely ruined, without the consolation of doing any considerable service to the state, and without any prospect of it." He had just learned, through the letter brought from Amherst by Ensign Hutchins, that he could expect no help from that quarter.

Perhaps he was as near despair as his undaunted nature was capable of being. In his present state of body and mind he was a hero without the light and cheer of heroism. He flattered himself with no illusions, but saw the worst and faced it all. He seems to have been entirely without excitement. The languor of disease, the desperation of the chances, and the greatness of the stake may have wrought to tranquillize him. His energy was doubly tasked: to bear up his own sinking frame, and to achieve an almost hopeless feat of arms.

Audacious as it was, his plan cannot be called rash if we may accept the statement of two well-informed writers on the French side. They say that on the 10th of September the English naval commanders held a council on board the flagship, in which it was resolved that the lateness of the season required the fleet to leave Quebec without delay. They say further that Wolfe then went to the admiral, told him that he had found a place where the heights could be scaled, that he would send up 150 picked men to feel the way, and that if they gained a lodgement at the top, the other troops should follow; if, on the other hand, the French were there in force to oppose them, he would not sacrifice the army in a hopeless attempt, but embark them for home, consoled by the thought that all had been done that man could do. On this, concludes the story, the admiral and his officers consented to wait the result.[3]

As Wolfe had informed Pitt, his army was greatly weakened. Since the end of June his loss in killed and wounded was more than 850, including two colonels, two majors, nineteen captains, and thirty-four subalterns; and to these were to be added a greater number disabled by disease.

The squadron of Admiral Holmes above Quebec had now increased to twenty-two vessels, great and small. One of the last that went up was a diminutive schooner, armed with a few swivels, and jocosely named the *Terror of France*. She sailed by the town in broad daylight, the French, incensed at her impudence, blazing at her from all their batteries; but she passed unharmed, anchored by the admiral's ship, and saluted him triumphantly with her swivels.

Wolfe's first move towards executing his plan was the critical one of evacuating the camp at Montmorenci. This was accomplished on the third of September. Montcalm sent a strong force to fall on the rear of the retiring English. Monckton saw the movement from Point Levi, embarked two battalions in the boats of the fleet, and made a feint of landing at Beauport. Montcalm recalled his troops to repulse the threatened attack; and the English withdrew from Montmorenci unmolested, some to the Point of Orleans, others to Point Levi. On the night of the 4th a fleet of flatboats passed above the town with the baggage and stores. On the 5th, Murray, with four battalions, marched up the river Etechemin, and forded it under a hot fire from the French batteries at Sillery. Monckton and Townshend followed with three more battalions, and the united force, of about 3600 men, was embarked on board the ships of Holmes, where Wolfe joined them on the same evening.[4]

These movements of the English filled the French commanders with mingled perplexity, anxiety, and hope. A deserter told them that Admiral Saunders was impatient to be gone. Vaudreuil grew confident. "The breaking up of the camp at Montmorenci," he says, "and the abandonment of the intrenchments there, the re-embarkation on board the vessels above Quebec of the troops who had encamped on the

[3] [On this story, see Gipson pp. 415–6, notes. He believes it to be correct.]

[4] [Gipson p. 409 says, "Wolfe on the night of the 6th joined the troops and ships on the upper river, and the following day he issued his orders for his line of battle. . . . "]

south bank, the movements of these vessels, the removal of the heaviest pieces of artillery from the batteries of Point Levi, — these and the lateness of the season all combined to announce the speedy departure of the fleet, several vessels of which had even sailed down the river already. The prisoners and the deserters who daily came in told us that this was the common report in their army." He wrote to Bourlamaque on the 1st of September: "Everything proves that the grand design of the English has failed."

Yet he was ceaselessly watchful. So was Montcalm; and he, too, on the night of the second, snatched a moment to write to Bourlamaque from his headquarters in the stone house, by the river of Beauport: "The night is dark; it rains; our troops are in their tents, with clothes on, ready for an alarm; I in my boots; my horses saddled. In fact, this is my usual way. I wish you were here; for I cannot be everywhere, though I multiply myself, and have not taken off my clothes since the 23rd of June." On the eleventh of September he wrote his last letter to Bourlamaque, and probably the last that his pen ever traced. "I am overwhelmed with work, and should often lose temper, like you, if I did not remember that I am paid by Europe for not losing it. Nothing new since my last. I give the enemy another month, or something less, to stay here." The more sanguine Vaudreuil would hardly give them a week.

Meanwhile, no precaution was spared. The force under Bougainville above Quebec was raised to three thousand men. He was ordered to watch the shore as far as Jacques-Cartier, and follow with his main body every movement of Holmes's squadron. There was little fear for the heights near the town; they were thought inaccessible. Even Montcalm believed them safe, and had expressed himself to that effect some time before. "We need not suppose," he wrote to Vaudreuil, "that the enemy have wings;" and again, speaking of the very place where Wolfe afterwards landed, "I swear to you that a hundred men posted there would stop their whole army." He was right. A hundred watchful and determined men could have held the position long enough for reinforcements to come up.

The 100 men were there. Captain de Vergor, of the colony troops, commanded them, and reinforcements were within his call; for the battalion of Guienne had been ordered to encamp close at hand on the Plains of Abraham. Vergor's post, called Anse du Foulon, was a mile and a half from Quebec. A little beyond it, by the brink of the cliffs, was another post, called Samos, held by 70 men with four cannon; and, beyond this again, the heights of Sillery were guarded by 130 men, also with cannon. These were outposts of Bougainville, whose headquarters were at Cap-Rouge, six miles above Sillery, and whose troops were in continual movement along the intervening shore. Thus all was vigilance; for while the French were strong in the hope of speedy delivery, they felt that there was no safety till the tents of the invader had vanished from their shores and his ships from their river. "What we knew," says one of them, "of the character of M. Wolfe, that impetuous, bold, and intrepid warrior, prepared us for a last attack before he left us."

Wolfe had been very ill on the evening of the 4th of September. The troops knew it, and their spirits sank; but, after a night of torment, he grew better, and was soon among them again, rekindling their ardor, and imparting a cheer that he could not share. For himself he had no pity; but when he heard of the illness of two officers in one of the ships, he sent them a message of warm sympathy, advised them to return to Point Levi, and offered them his own barge and an escort. They thanked him, but replied that, come what might, they would see the enterprise to an end. Another officer remarked in his hearing that one of the invalids had a very delicate constitution. "Don't tell me of constitution," said Wolfe; "he has good spirit, and good spirit will carry a man through everything." An immense moral force bore up his own frail body and forced it to its work.

Major Robert Stobo, who, five years before, had been given as a hostage to the French at the capture of Fort Necessity, arrived about this time in a vessel from Halifax. He had long been a prisoner at Quebec, not always in close custody, and had used his opportunities to acquaint himself with the neighborhood. In the spring of this year he and an officer of rangers named Stevens had made their escape with extraordinary skill and daring; and he now returned to give his countrymen the benefit of his local knowledge. His biographer says that it was he who directed Wolfe in the choice of a landing-place. Be this as it may, Wolfe in person examined the river and the shores as far as Pointe-aux-Trembles; till at length, landing on the south side a little above Quebec, and looking across the water with a telescope, he descried a path that ran with a long slope up the face of the woody precipice, and saw at the top a cluster of tents. They were those of Vergor's guard at the Anse du Foulon, now called Wolfe's Cove. As he could see but ten or twelve of them, he thought that the guard could not be numerous, and might be overpowered. His hope would have been stronger if he had known that Vergor had once been tried for misconduct and cowardice in the surrender of Beauséjour, and saved from merited disgrace by the friendship of Bigot and the protection of Vaudreuil.

The morning of the 7th was fair and warm, and the vessels of Holmes, their crowded decks gay with scarlet uniforms, sailed up the river to Cap-Rouge. A lively scene awaited them; for here were the headquarters of Bougainville, and here lay his principal force, while the rest watched the banks above and below. The cove into which the little river runs was guarded by floating batteries; the surrounding shore was defended by breastworks; and a large body of regulars, militia, and mounted Canadians in blue uniforms moved to and fro, with restless activity, on the hills behind. When the vessels came to anchor, the horsemen dismounted and formed in line with the infantry; then, with loud shouts, the whole rushed down the heights to man their works at the shore. That true Briton, Captain Knox, looked on with a critical eye from the gangway of his ship, and wrote that night in his Diary that they had made a ridiculous noise. "How different!" he exclaims, "how nobly awful and expressive of true valor is the customary silence of the British troops!"

In the afternoon the ships opened fire, while the troops entered the boats and rowed up and down as if looking for a landing-place. It was but a feint of Wolfe to deceive Bougainville as to his real design. A heavy easterly rain set in on the next morning, and lasted two days without respite. All operations were suspended, and the men suffered greatly in the crowded transports. Half of them were therefore landed on the south shore, where they made their quarters in the village of St. Nicolas, refreshed themselves, and dried their wet clothing, knapsacks, and blankets.

For several successive days the squadron of Holmes was allowed to drift up the river with the flood tide and down with the ebb, thus passing and repassing incessantly between the neighborhood of Quebec on one hand, and a point high above Cap-Rouge on the other; while Bougainville, perplexed, and always expecting an attack, followed the ships to and fro along the shore, by day and by night, till his men were exhausted with ceaseless forced marches.

At last the time for action came. On Wednesday, 12 September the troops at St. Nicolas were embarked again, and all were told to hold themselves in readiness. Wolfe, from the flagship *Sutherland*, issued his last general orders. "The enemy's force is now divided, great scarcity of provisions in their camp, and universal discontent among the Canadians. Our troops below are in readiness to join us; all the light artillery and tools are embarked at the Point of Levi; and the troops will land where the French seem least to expect it. The first body that gets on shore is to march directly to the enemy and drive them from any little post they may occupy; the officers must be careful that the succeeding bodies do not by any mistake fire on those who go before them. The battalions must form on the upper ground with expedition, and be ready to charge whatever presents itself. When the artillery and troops are landed, a corps will be left to secure the landing-place, while the rest march on and endeavor to bring the Canadians and French to a battle. The officers and men will remember what their country expects from them, and what a determined body of soldiers inured to war is capable of doing against five weak French battalions mingled with a disorderly peasantry."

The spirit of the army answered to that of its chief. The troops loved and admired their general, trusted their officers, and were ready for any attempt. "Nay, how could it be otherwise," quaintly asks honest Sergeant John Johnson, of the 58th regiment, "being at the heels of gentlemen whose whole thirst, equal with their general, was for glory? We had seen them tried, and always found them sterling. We knew that they would stand by us to the last extremity." [5]

Wolfe had 3600 men and officers with him on board the vessels of Holmes; and he now sent orders to Colonel Burton at Point Levi to bring to his aid all who could be spared from that place and the Point of Orleans. They were to march along the south bank, after nightfall, and wait further orders at a designated spot convenient for embarkation. Their number was about 1200, so that the entire force destined for the enterprise was at the utmost 4800.[6] With these, Wolfe meant to

[5] [The brigadiers were not so enthusiastic. Wolfe issued oral orders for the Anse du Foulon landing, to Monckton only; Townshend and Murray, who had only the vague indication of the General Order to "land where the French seem least to expect it," begged Wolfe, before the end of the day, to be more precise. Instead, they received a mild rebuke for their presumption. The correspondence is printed in Doughty *Siege of Quebec* VI 59–61. The spectacular success of Wolfe's bold plan to steal up to the Plains of Abraham from the Anse du Foulon should not blind us to the fact that a landing further up the river at Point-aux-Trembles, which his brigadiers wanted, might have been equally effective with less risk; but, on the other hand, the complete surprise that Wolfe obtained was worth a great deal of risk.]

[6] The tabular return given by Knox shows the number of officers and men in each corps engaged. According to this, the battalions as they stood on the Plains of Abraham before the battle varied in strength from 322 (Monckton's) to 683

climb the heights of Abraham in the teeth of an enemy who, though much reduced, were still twice as numerous as their assailants.

Admiral Saunders lay with the main fleet in the Basin of Quebec. This excellent officer, whatever may have been his views as to the necessity of a speedy departure, aided Wolfe to the last with unfailing energy and zeal. It was agreed between them that while the general made the real attack, the admiral should engage Montcalm's attention by a pretended one. As night approached, the fleet ranged itself along the Beauport shore; the boats were lowered and filled with sailors, marines, and the few troops that had been left behind; while ship signalled to ship, cannon flashed and thundered, and shot ploughed the beach, as if to clear a way for assailants to land. In the gloom of the evening the effect was imposing. Montcalm, who thought that the movements of the English above the town were only a feint, that their main force was still below it, and that their real attack would be made there, was completely deceived, and massed his troops in front of Beauport to repel the expected landing. But while in the fleet of Saunders all was uproar and ostentatious menace, the danger was ten miles away, where the squadron of Holmes lay tranquil and silent at its anchorage off Cap-Rouge.

It was less tranquil than it seemed. All on board knew that a blow would be struck that night, though only a few high officers knew where. Colonel Howe,[7] of the light infantry, called for volunteers to lead the unknown and desperate venture, promising, in the words of one of them, "that if any of us survived we might depend on being recommended to the general." As many as were wanted — twenty-four in all — soon came forward. Thirty large bateaux and some boats be-

---

(Webb's), making a total of 4828, including officers. But another return, less specific, signed George Townshend, Brigadier, makes the entire number only 4441. Wolfe's front line, which alone met and turned the French attack, was made up as follows, the figures including officers and men:

35th Regiment	519	28th Regiment	421
58th "	335	47th "	360
78th "	662	43rd "	327
Louisbourg Grenadiers	241	Light Infantry	400

Making a total of 3265

[Doughty II 52 estimates the total number of troops under Montcalm at about 14,000, including militia and Indians. Parkman thinks that not more than 3500 French troops advanced to the attack, since some of the militia held back; that "at least as many French were out of the battle as were in it," and that "the numbers engaged on each side seem to have been about equal."]

[7] [William Howe, brother to Brigadier Lord Howe killed at Ticonderoga; later famous as Major General "Billy" Howe in the War of Independence.]

longing to the squadron lay moored alongside the vessels; and late in the evening the troops were ordered into them, the twenty-four volunteers taking their place in the foremost. They held in all about 1700 men. The rest remained on board.

Bougainville could discern the movement, and misjudged it, thinking that he himself was to be attacked. The tide was still flowing; and, the better to deceive him, the vessels and boats were allowed to drift upward with it for a little distance, as if to land above Cap-Rouge.

The day had been fortunate for Wolfe. Two deserters came from the camp of Bougainville with intelligence that, at ebb tide on the next night, he was to send down a convoy of provisions to Montcalm. The necessities of the camp at Beauport, and the difficulties of transportation by land, had before compelled the French to resort to this perilous means of conveying supplies; and their boats, drifting in darkness under the shadows of the northern shore, had commonly passed in safety. Wolfe saw at once that, if his own boats went down in advance of the convoy, he could turn the intelligence of the deserters to good account.

He was still on board the *Sutherland*. Every preparation was made, and every order given; it only remained to wait the turning of the tide. Seated with him in the cabin was the commander of the sloop-of-war *Porcupine*, his former school-fellow, John Jervis, afterwards Earl St. Vincent. Wolfe told him that he expected to die in the battle of the next day; and taking from his bosom a miniature of Miss Lowther, his betrothed, he gave it to him with a request that he would return it to her if the presentiment should prove true.

Towards two o'clock the tide began to ebb, and a fresh wind blew down the river. Two lanterns were raised into the maintop shrouds of the *Sutherland*. It was the appointed signal: the boats cast off and fell down with the current, those of the light infantry leading the way. The vessels with the rest of the troops had orders to follow a little later.

To look for a moment at the chances on which this bold adventure hung. First, the deserters told Wolfe that provision-boats were ordered to go down to Quebec that night; secondly, Bougainville countermanded them; thirdly, the sentries posted along the heights were told of the order, but not of the countermand; fourthly, Vergor at the Anse du Foulon had permitted most of his men, chiefly Canadians from Lorette, to go home for a time and work at their harvesting, on condition, it is said, that they should afterwards work in a neighboring field of his own; fifthly, he kept careless watch, and went quietly to bed;

sixthly, the battalion of Guienne, ordered to take post on the Plains of Abraham, had, for reasons unexplained, remained encamped by the St. Charles; and lastly, when Bougainville saw Holmes's vessels drift down the stream, he did not tax his weary troops to follow them, thinking that they would return as usual with the flood tide. But for these conspiring circumstances New France might have lived a little longer, and the fruitless heroism of Wolfe would have passed, with countless other heroisms, into oblivion.

For full two hours the procession of boats, borne on the current, steered silently down the St. Lawrence. The stars were visible, but the night was moonless and sufficiently dark. The general was in one of the foremost boats, and near him was a young midshipman, John Robison, afterwards professor of natural philosophy in the University of Edinburgh. He used to tell in his later life how Wolfe, with a low voice, repeated Gray's "Elegy in a Country Churchyard" to the officers about him. Probably it was to relieve the intense strain of his thoughts. Among the rest was the verse which his own fate was soon to illustrate, —

The paths of glory lead but to the grave.

"Gentlemen," he said, as his recital ended, "I would rather have written those lines than take Quebec." None were there to tell him that the hero is greater than the poet.

As they neared their destination, the tide bore them in towards the shore, and the mighty wall of rock and forest towered in darkness on their left. The dead stillness was suddenly broken by the sharp *Qui vive!* of a French sentry, invisible in the thick gloom. *France!* answered a Highland officer of Fraser's regiment from one of the boats of the light infantry. He had served in Holland, and spoke French fluently.

A quel régiment?

De la Reine, replied the Highlander. He knew that a part of that corps was with Bougainville. The sentry, expecting the convoy of provisions, was satisfied, and did not ask for the password.

Soon after, the foremost boats were passing the heights of Samos, when another sentry challenged them, and they could see him through the darkness running down to the edge of the water, within range of a pistol-shot. In answer to his questions, the same officer replied, in French: "Provision-boats. Don't make a noise; the English will hear us." In fact, the sloop-of-war *Hunter* was anchored in the stream not far off. This time, again, the sentry let them pass. In a few moments they rounded the headland above the Anse du Foulon. There was no sentry there. The strong current swept the boats of the light infantry a little below the intended landing-place. They disembarked on a narrow strand at the foot of heights as steep as a hill covered with trees can be. The twenty-four volunteers led the way, climbing with what silence they might, closely followed by a much larger body. When they reached the top they saw in the dim light a cluster of tents at a short distance, and immediately made a dash at them. Vergor leaped from bed and tried to run off, but was shot in the heel and captured. His men, taken by surprise, made little resistance. One or two were caught, and the rest fled.

The main body of troops waited in their boats by the edge of the strand. The heights near by were cleft by a great ravine choked with forest trees; and in its depths ran a little brook called Ruisseau St. Denis, which, swollen by the late rains, fell plashing in the stillness over a rock. Other than this no sound could reach the strained ear of Wolfe but the gurgle of the tide and the cautious climbing of his advance-parties as they mounted the steeps at some little distance from where he sat listening. At length from the top came a sound of musket-shots, followed by loud huzzas, and he knew that his men were masters of the position. The word was given; the troops leaped from the boats and scaled the heights, some here, some there, clutching at trees and bushes, their muskets slung at their backs. Tradition still points out the place, near the mouth of the ravine, where the foremost reached the top. Wolfe said to an officer near him: "You can try it, but I don't think you'll get up." He himself, however, found strength to drag himself up with the rest. The narrow slanting path on the face of the heights had been made impassable by trenches and abattis; but all obstructions were soon cleared away, and then the ascent was easy. In the gray of the morning the long file of red-coated soldiers moved quickly upward, and formed in order on the plateau above.[8]

Before many of them had reached the top, cannon were heard close on the left. It was the battery at Samos firing on the boats in the rear and the vessels descending from Cap-Rouge. A party was sent to silence it; this was soon effected, and the more distant battery at Sillery was

---

[8] [According to a letter of Brigadier Townshend written over 15 years after the event, Wolfe, when he heard the shots exchanged at the top of the cliff, thought that his plan had failed, and sent word to his aide, Adjutant General Isaac Barré, who was acting N.O.I.C. on the beach, to allow no more troops to land; but Barré disregarded his orders. Gipson p. 415.]

next attacked and taken. As fast as the boats were emptied they returned for the troops left on board the vessels and for those waiting on the southern shore under Colonel Burton.

The 13th day of September broke in clouds and threatening rain. Wolfe's battalions were drawn up along the crest of the heights. No enemy was in sight, though a body of Canadians had sallied from the town and moved along the strand towards the landing-place, whence they were quickly driven back. He had achieved the most critical part of his enterprise; yet the success that he coveted placed him in imminent danger. On one side was the garrison of Quebec and the army of Beauport, and Bougainville was on the other. Wolfe's alternative was victory or ruin; for if he should be overwhelmed by a combined attack, retreat would be hopeless. His feelings no man can know; but it would be safe to say that hesitation or doubt had no part in them.

He went to reconnoitre the ground, and soon came to the Plains of Abraham, so called from Abraham Martin, a pilot known as Maître Abraham, who had owned a piece of land here in the early times of the colony. The Plains were a tract of grass, tolerably level in most parts, patched here and there with cornfields, studded with clumps of bushes, and forming a part of the high plateau at the eastern end of which Quebec stood. On the south it was bounded by the declivities along the St. Lawrence; on the north, by those along the St. Charles, or rather along the meadows through which that lazy stream crawled like a writhing snake. At the place that Wolfe chose for his battle-field the plateau was less than a mile wide.

Thither the troops advanced, marched by files till they reached the ground, and then wheeled to form their line of battle, which stretched across the plateau and faced the city. It consisted of six battalions and the detached grenadiers from Louisbourg, all drawn up in ranks three deep. Its right wing was near the brink of the heights along the St. Lawrence; but the left could not reach those along the St. Charles. On this side a wide space was perforce left open, and there was danger of being outflanked. To prevent this, Brigadier Townshend was stationed here with two battalions, drawn up at right angles with the rest, and fronting the St. Charles. The battalion of Webb's regiment, under Colonel Burton, formed the reserve; the 3rd battalion of Royal Americans was left to guard the landing; and Howe's light infantry occupied a wood far in the rear. Wolfe, with Monckton and Murray, commanded the front line, on which the heavy fighting was to fall, and which, when all the troops had arrived, numbered less than 3500 men.

Quebec was not a mile distant, but they could not see it; for a ridge of broken ground intervened, called Buttes-à-Neveu, about 600 paces off. The first division of troops had scarcely come up when, about six o'clock, this ridge was suddenly thronged with white uniforms. It was the battalion of Guienne, arrived at the eleventh hour from its camp by the St. Charles. Some time after there was hot firing in the rear. It came from a detachment of Bougainville's command attacking a house where some of the light infantry were posted. The assailants were repulsed, and the firing ceased. Light showers fell at intervals, besprinkling the troops as they stood patiently waiting the event.

Montcalm had passed a troubled night. Through all the evening the cannon bellowed from the ships of Saunders, and the boats of the fleet hovered in the dusk off the Beauport shore, threatening every moment to land. Troops lined the intrenchments till day, while the general walked the field that adjoined his headquarters till one in the morning, accompanied by the Chevalier Johnstone and Colonel Poulariez. Johnstone says that he was in great agitation, and took no rest all night. At daybreak he heard the sound of cannon above the town. It was the battery at Samos firing on the English ships. He had sent an officer to the quarters of Vaudreuil, which were much nearer Quebec, with orders to bring him word at once should anything unusual happen. But no word came, and about six o'clock he mounted and rode thither with Johnstone. As they advanced, the country behind the town opened more and more upon their sight; till at length, when opposite Vaudreuil's house, they saw across the St. Charles, some two miles away, the red ranks of British soldiers on the heights beyond.

"This is a serious business," Montcalm said; and sent off Johnstone at full gallop to bring up the troops from the centre and left of the camp. Those of the right were in motion already, doubtless by the governor's order. Vaudreuil came out of the house. Montcalm stopped for a few words with him; then set spurs to his horse, and rode over the bridge of the St. Charles to the scene of danger. He rode with a fixed look, uttering not a word.

The army followed in such order as it might, crossed the bridge in hot haste, passed under the northern rampart of Quebec, entered at the Palace Gate, and pressed on in headlong march along the quaint narrow streets of the warlike town: troops of Indians in scalp-locks and war-paint, a savage glitter in their deep-set eyes; bands of Canadians whose all was at stake, — faith, country, and home; the colony regulars; the battalions of Old France, a torrent of white uniforms and gleaming bayonets, La Sarre, Languedoc, Roussillon, Béarn, — victors of Oswego, William Henry, and Ticonderoga. So they swept on, poured out upon the plain, some by the gate of St. Louis, and some by that of St. John, and hurried, breathless, to where the banners of Guienne still fluttered on the ridge.

Montcalm was amazed at what he saw. He had expected a detachment, and he found an army. Full in sight before him stretched the lines of Wolfe: the close ranks of the English infantry, a silent wall of red, and the wild array of the Highlanders, with their waving tartans, and bagpipes screaming defiance. Vaudreuil had not come; but not the less was felt the evil of a divided authority and the jealousy of the rival chiefs. Montcalm waited long for the forces he had ordered to join him from the left wing of the army. He waited in vain. It is said that the governor had detained them, lest the English should attack the Beauport shore. Even if they did so, and succeeded, the French might defy them, could they but put Wolfe to rout on the Plains of Abraham. Neither did the garrison of Quebec come to the aid of Montcalm. He sent to Ramesay, its commander, for twenty-five field-pieces which were on the Palace battery. Ramesay would give him only three, saying that he wanted them for his own defence. There were orders and counter-orders; misunderstanding, haste, delay, perplexity.

Montcalm and his chief officers held a council of war. It is said that he and they alike were for immediate attack. His enemies declare that he was afraid lest Vaudreuil should arrive and take command; but the governor was not a man to assume responsibility at such a crisis. Others say that his impetuosity overcame his better judgment; and of this charge it is hard to acquit him. Bougainville was but a few miles distant, and some of his troops were much nearer; a messenger sent by way of Old Lorette could have reached him in an hour and a half at most, and a combined attack in front and rear might have been concerted with him. If, moreover, Montcalm could have come to an understanding with Vaudreuil, his own force might have been strengthened by two or three thousand additional men from the town and the camp of Beauport; but he felt that there was no time to lose, for he imagined that Wolfe would soon be reinforced, which was impossible, and he believed that the English were fortifying themselves, which was no less an error. He has been blamed not only for fighting too soon, but for fighting at all. In this he could not choose. Fight he must, for Wolfe was now in a position to cut off all his supplies. His men were full of ardor, and he resolved to attack before their ardor cooled. He spoke a few words to them in his keen, vehement way. "I remember very well how he looked," one of the Canadians, then a boy of eighteen, used to say in his old age; "he rode a black or dark bay horse along the front of our lines, brandishing his sword, as if to excite us to do our duty. He wore a coat with wide sleeves, which fell back as he raised his arm, and showed the white linen of the wristband."

The English waited the result with a composure which, if not quite real, was at least well feigned. The three field-pieces sent by Ramesay plied them with canister-shot, and 1500 Canadians and Indians fusilladed them in front and flank. Over all the plain, from behind bushes and knolls and the edge of cornfields, puffs of smoke sprang incessantly from the guns of these hidden marksmen. Skirmishers were thrown out before the lines to hold them in check, and the soldiers were ordered to lie on the grass to avoid the shot. The firing was liveliest on the English left, where bands of sharpshooters got under the edge of the declivity, among thickets, and behind scattered houses, whence they killed and wounded a considerable number of Townshend's men. The light infantry were called up from the rear. The houses were taken and retaken, and one or more of them was burned.

Wolfe was everywhere. How cool he was, and why his followers loved him, is shown by an incident that happened in the course of the morning. One of his captains was shot through the lungs; and on recovering consciousness he saw the general standing at his side. Wolfe pressed his hand, told him not to despair, praised his services, promised him early promotion, and sent an aide-de-camp to Monckton to beg that officer to keep the promise if he himself should fall.

It was towards ten o'clock when, from the high ground on the right of the line, Wolfe saw that the crisis was near. The French on the ridge had formed themselves into three bodies, regulars in the centre, regulars and Canadians on right and left. Two field-pieces, which had been dragged up the heights at Anse du Foulon, fired on them with grape-shot, and the troops, rising from the ground, prepared to receive them. In a few moments more they were in motion. They came on rapidly, uttering loud shouts, and firing as soon as they were within range. Their ranks, ill ordered at the best, were further confused by a number of Canadians who had been mixed among the regulars, and who, after hastily firing, threw themselves on the ground to reload.[9] The British advanced a few rods; then halted and stood still. When the French were within forty paces the word of command rang out, and a crash of musketry answered all along the line. The volley was delivered with remarkable precision. In the battalions of the centre, which had suffered least from the enemy's bullets, the simultaneous explosion was afterwards said by French officers to have sounded like a cannon-shot. Another volley followed, and then a furious clattering fire that lasted but a minute or two. When the smoke rose, a miserable sight was revealed: the ground cumbered with dead and wounded, the advancing masses stopped short and turned into a frantic mob, shouting, cursing, gesticulating. The order was given to charge. Then over the field rose the British cheer, mixed with the fierce yell of the Highland slogan. Some of the corps pushed forward with the bayonet; some advanced firing. The clansmen drew their broadswords and dashed on, keen and swift as bloodhounds. At the English right, though the attacking column was broken to pieces, a fire was still kept up, chiefly, it seems, by sharpshooters from the bushes and cornfields, where they had lain for an hour or more. Here Wolfe himself led the charge, at the head of the Louisbourg grenadiers. A shot shattered his wrist. He wrapped his handkerchief about it and kept on. Another shot struck him, and he still advanced, when a third lodged in his breast. He staggered, and sat on the ground. Lieutenant Brown, of the grenadiers, one Henderson, a volunteer in the same company, and a private soldier, aided by an officer of artillery who ran to join them, carried him in their arms to the rear. He begged them to lay him down. They did so, and asked if he would have a surgeon. "There's no need," he answered; "it's all over with me." A moment after, one of them cried out: "They run; see how they run!" "Who run?" Wolfe demanded, like a man roused from sleep. "The enemy, sir. Egad, they give way everywhere!" "Go, one of you, to Colonel Burton," returned the dying man; "tell him to march Webb's regiment down to Charles River, to cut off their retreat from the bridge." Then, turning on his side, he murmured, "Now, God be

---

[9] [The Canadians, apparently, were accustomed to reload their muskets *ventre à terre*, but what happened was not entirely the fault of these tactics. The entire French line first fired at 140 yards, an ineffective range for muskets. After the reloading they fired a second and a third time, but the British held their fire until the French were within 40 yards. And the British musket (the "Brown Bess") was more effective than that of the French.]

praised, I will die in peace!" and in a few moments his gallant soul had fled.

Montcalm, still on horseback, was borne with the tide of fugitives towards the town. As he approached the walls a shot passed through his body. He kept his seat; two soldiers supported him, one on each side, and led his horse through the St. Louis Gate. On the open space within, among the excited crowd, were several women, drawn, no doubt, by eagerness to know the result of the fight. One of them recognized him, saw the streaming blood, and shrieked, "*O mon Dieu! mon Dieu! le Marquis est tué!*" "It's nothing, it's nothing," replied the death-stricken man; "don't be troubled for me, my good friends." ("*Ce n'est rien, ce n'est rien; ne vous affligez pas pour moi, mes bonnes amies.*")

CHAPTER XXXVI

The Fall of Quebec

1759

[*Montcalm and Wolfe*, CHAPTER XXVIII]

"Never was rout more complete than that of our army," says a French official. It was the more so because Montcalm held no troops in reserve, but launched his whole force at once against the English. Nevertheless there was some resistance to the pursuit. It came chiefly from the Canadians, many of whom had not advanced with the regulars to the attack. Those on the right wing, instead of doing so, threw themselves into an extensive tract of bushes that lay in front of the English left; and from this cover they opened a fire, too distant for much effect, till the victors advanced in their turn, when the shot of the hidden marksmen told severely upon them. Two battalions, therefore, deployed before the bushes, fired volleys into them, and drove their occupants out.

Again, those of the Canadians who, before the main battle began, attacked the English left from the brink of the plateau towards the St. Charles, withdrew when the rout took place, and ran along the edge of the declivity till, at the part of it called Côte Ste.-Geneviève, they came to a place where it was overgrown with thickets. Into these they threw themselves; and were no sooner under cover than they faced about to fire upon the Highlanders, who presently came up. As many of these mountaineers, according to their old custom, threw down their muskets when they charged, and had no weapons but their broadswords, they tried in vain to dislodge the marksmen, and suffered greatly in the attempt. Other troops came to their aid, cleared the thickets, after stout resistance, and drove their occupants across the meadow to the bridge of boats. The conduct of the Canadians at the Côte Ste.-Geneviève went far to atone for the shortcomings of some of them on the battlefield.

A part of the fugitives escaped into the town by the gates of St. Louis and St. John, while the greater number fled along the front of the ramparts, rushed down the declivity to the suburb of St. Roch, and ran over the meadows to the bridge, protected by the cannon of the town and the two armed hulks in the river. The rout had but just begun when Vaudreuil crossed the bridge from the camp of Beauport. It was four hours since he first heard the alarm, and his quarters were not much more than two miles from the battle-field. He does not explain why he did not come sooner; it is certain that his coming was well timed to throw the blame on Montcalm in case of defeat, or to claim some of the honor for himself in case of victory. "Monsieur the Marquis of Montcalm," he says, "unfortunately made his attack before I had joined him." His joining him could have done no good; for though he had at last brought with him the rest of the militia from the Beauport camp, they had come no farther than the bridge over the St. Charles, having, as he alleges, been kept there by an unauthorized order from the chief of staff, Montreuil. He declares that the regulars were in such a fright that he could not stop them; but that the Canadians listened to his voice, and that it was he who rallied them at the Côte Ste.-Geneviève. Of this the evidence is his own word. From other accounts it would appear that the Canadians rallied themselves. Vaudreuil lost no time in recrossing the bridge and joining the militia in the redoubt at the farther end, where a crowd of fugitives soon poured in after him.

The aide-de-camp Johnstone, mounted on horseback, had stopped for a moment in what is now the suburb of St. John to encourage some soldiers who were trying to save a cannon that had stuck fast in a marshy hollow; when, on spurring his horse to the higher ground, he saw within musket-shot a long line of British troops, who immediately fired upon him. The bullets whistled about his ears, tore his clothes, and wounded his horse; which, however, carried him along the edge of the declivity to a windmill, near which was a roadway to a bakehouse on the meadow below. He descended, crossed the meadow, reached the bridge, and rode over it to the great redoubt or hornwork that guarded its head.

The place was full of troops and Canadians in a wild panic. "It is impossible," says Johnstone, "to imagine the disorder and confusion I found in the hornwork. Consternation was general. M. de Vaudreuil listened to everybody, and was always of the opinion of him who spoke last. On the appearance of the English troops on the plain by the bakehouse, Montguet and La Motte, two old captains in the regiment of Béarn, cried out with vehemence to M. de Vaudreuil 'that the hornwork would be taken in an instant by assault, sword in hand; that we all should be cut to pieces without quarter; and that nothing would save us but an immediate and general capitulation of Canada, giving it up to the English.' " Yet the river was wide and deep, and the hornwork was protected on the water side by strong palisades, with cannon. Nevertheless there rose a general cry to cut the bridge of boats. By doing so more than half the army, who had not yet crossed, would have been sacrificed. The axemen were already at work, when they were stopped by some officers who had not lost their wits.

"M. de Vaudreuil," pursues Johnstone, "was closeted in a house in the inside of the hornwork with the Intendant and some other persons. I suspected they were busy drafting the articles for a general capitulation, and I entered the house, where I had only time to see the Intendant, with a pen in his hand, writing upon a sheet of paper, when M. de Vaudreuil told me I had no business there. Having answered him that what he had said was true, I retired immediately, in wrath to see them intent on giving up so scandalously a dependency for the preservation of which so much blood and treasure had been expended." On going out he met Lieutenant-Colonels Dalquier and Poulariez, whom he begged to prevent the apprehended disgrace; and, in fact, if Vaudreuil really meant to capitulate for the colony, he was presently dissuaded by firmer spirits than his own.

Johnstone, whose horse could carry him no farther, set out on foot for Beauport, and, in his own words, "continued sorrowfully jogging on, with a very heavy heart for the loss of my dear friend M. de Montcalm, sinking with weariness, and lost in reflection upon the changes which Providence had brought about in the space of three or four hours."

Great indeed were these changes. Montcalm was dying; his second in command, the Brigadier Senezergues, was mortally wounded; the army, routed and demoralized, was virtually without a head; and the colony, yesterday cheered as on the eve of deliverance, was plunged into sudden despair. "Ah, what a cruel day!" cries Bougainville; "how fatal to all that was dearest to us! My heart is torn in its most tender parts. We shall be fortunate if the approach of winter saves the country from total ruin."

The victors were fortifying themselves on the field of battle. Like the French, they had lost two generals; for Monckton, second in rank, was disabled by a musket-shot, and the command had fallen upon Townshend at the moment when the enemy were in full flight. He had recalled the pursuers, and formed them again in line of battle, knowing that another foe was at hand. Bougainville, in fact, appeared at noon from Cap-Rouge with about 2000 men; but withdrew on seeing double that force prepared to receive him. He had not heard till eight o'clock that the English were on the Plains of Abraham; and the delay of his arrival was no doubt due to his endeavors to collect as many as possible of his detachments posted along the St. Lawrence for many miles towards Jacques-Cartier.

Before midnight the English had made good progress in their redoubts and intrenchments, had brought cannon up the heights to defend them, planted a battery on the Côte Ste.-Geneviève, descended into the meadows of the St. Charles, and taken possession of the General Hospital, with its crowds of sick and wounded. Their victory had cost them 664 of all ranks, killed, wounded, and missing. The French loss is placed by Vaudreuil at about 640, and by the English official reports at about 1500. Measured by the numbers engaged, the battle of Quebec was but a heavy skirmish; measured by results, it was one of the great battles of the world.

Vaudreuil went from the hornwork to his quarters on the Beauport road and called a council of war. It was a tumultuous scene. A letter was despatched to Quebec to ask advice of Montcalm. The dying general sent a brief message to the effect that there was a threefold choice, — to fight again, retreat to Jacques-Cartier, or give up the colony. There was much in favor of fighting. When Bougainville had gathered all his force from the river above, he would have 3000 men; and these, joined to the garrison of Quebec, the sailors at the batteries, and the militia and artillerymen of the Beauport camp, would form a body of fresh soldiers more than equal to the English then on the Plains of Abraham. Add to these the defeated troops, and the victors would be greatly outnumbered. Bigot gave his voice for fighting. Vaudreuil expressed himself to the same effect; but he says that all the officers were against him. "In vain I remarked to these gentlemen that we were superior to the enemy, and should beat them if we managed well. I could not at all change their opinion, and my love for the service and for the colony made me subscribe to the views of the council. In fact, if I had attacked the English against the advice of all the principal officers, their ill-will would have exposed me to the risk of losing the battle and the colony also."

It was said at the time that the officers voted for retreat because they thought Vaudreuil unfit to command an army, and, still more, to fight a battle. There was no need, however, to fight at once. The object of the English was to take Quebec, and that of Vaudreuil should have been to keep it. By a march of a few miles he could have joined Bougainville; and by then intrenching himself at or near Ste.-Foy he would have placed a greatly superior force in the English rear, where his position might have been made impregnable. Here he might be easily furnished with provisions, and from hence he could readily throw men and supplies into Quebec, which the English were too few to invest. He could harass the besiegers, or attack them, should opportunity offer, and either raise the siege or so protract it that they would be forced by approaching winter to sail homeward, robbed of the fruit of their victory.

At least he might have taken a night for reflection. He was safe behind the St. Charles. The English, spent by fighting, toil and want of sleep, were in no condition to disturb him. A part of his own men were in deadly need of rest; the night would have brought refreshment, and the morning might have brought wise counsel. Vaudreuil would not wait, and orders were given at once for retreat. It began at nine o'clock that evening. Quebec was abandoned to its fate. The cannon were left in the lines of Beauport, the tents in the encampments, and provisions enough in the storehouses to supply the army for a week. "The loss of the Marquis de Montcalm," says a French officer then on the spot, "robbed his successors of their senses, and they thought of nothing but flight; such was their fear that the enemy would attack the intrenchments the next day. The army abandoned the camp in such disorder that the like was never known." "It was not a retreat," says Johnstone, who was himself a part of it, "but an abominable flight, with such disorder and confusion that, had the English known it, three hundred men sent after us would have been sufficient to cut all our army to pieces. The soldiers were all mixed, scattered, dispersed, and running as hard as they could, as if the English army were at their heels." They passed Charlesbourg, Lorette, and St. Augustin, till on the 15th, they found rest on the impregnable hill of Jacques-Cartier, by the brink of the St. Lawrence, thirty miles from danger.

In the night of humiliation when Vaudreuil abandoned Quebec, Montcalm was breathing his last within its walls. When he was brought wounded from the field, he was placed in the house of the Surgeon Arnoux, who was then with Bourlamaque at Isle-aux-Noix, but whose younger brother, also a surgeon, examined the wound and pronounced it mortal. "I am glad of it," Montcalm said quietly; and then asked how long he had to live. "Twelve hours, more or less," was the reply. "So much the better," he returned. "I am happy that I shall not live to see the surrender of Quebec." He is reported to have said that since he had lost the battle it consoled him to have been defeated by so brave an enemy; and some of his last words were in praise of his successor, Lévis, for whose talents and fitness for command he expressed high esteem. When Vaudreuil sent to ask his opinion, he gave it; but when Ramesay, commandant of the garrison, came to receive his orders, he replied: "I will neither give orders nor interfere any further. I have much business that must be attended to, of greater moment than your ruined garrison and this wretched country. My time is very short; therefore pray leave me. I wish you all comfort, and to be happily extricated from your present perplexities." Nevertheless he thought to the last of those who had been under his command, and sent the following note to Brigadier Townshend: "Monsieur, the humanity of the English sets my mind at peace concerning the fate of the French prisoners and the Canadians. Feel towards them as they have caused me to feel. Do not let them perceive that they have changed masters. Be their protector as I have been their father."

Bishop Pontbriand, himself fast sinking with mortal disease, attended his death-bed and administered the last sacraments. He died peacefully at four o'clock on the 14th of September. He was in his forty-eighth year.

In the confusion of the time no workman could be found to make a coffin, and an old servant of the Ursulines, known as Bonhomme Michel, gathered a few boards and nailed them together so as to form a rough box. In it was laid the body of the dead soldier; and late in the evening of the same day he was carried to his rest. There was no tolling of bells or firing of cannon. The officers of the garrison followed the bier, and some of the populace, including women and children, joined the procession as it moved in dreary silence along the dusky street, shattered with cannon-ball and bomb, to the chapel of the Ursuline convent. Here a shell, bursting under the floor, had made a cavity which had been hollowed into a grave. Three priests of the Cathedral, several nuns, Ramesay with his officers, and a throng of townspeople were present at the rite. After the service and the chant, the body was lowered into the grave by the light of torches; and then, says the chronicle, "the tears and sobs burst forth. It seemed as if the last hope of the colony were buried with the remains of the General." In truth, the funeral of Montcalm was the funeral of New France.

It was no time for grief. The demands of the hour were too exigent and stern. When, on the morning after the battle, the people of Quebec saw the tents standing in the camp of Beauport, they thought the army still there to defend them. Ramesay knew that the hope was vain. On the evening before, Vaudreuil had sent two hasty notes to tell him of his flight. "The position of the enemy," wrote the governor, "becomes stronger every instant; and this, with other reasons, obliges me to retreat." "I have received all your letters. As I set out this moment, I pray you not to write again. You shall hear from me to-morrow. I wish you good evening." With these notes came the following order: "M. de Ramesay is not to wait till the enemy carries the town by assault. As soon as provisions fail, he will raise the white flag." This order was accompanied by a memorandum of terms which Ramesay was to ask of the victors.

"What a blow for me," says the unfortunate commandant, "to find myself abandoned so soon by the army, which alone could defend the town!" His garrison consisted of between one and two hundred troops of the line, some four or five hundred colony troops, a considerable number of sailors, and the local militia. These last were in a state of despair. The inhabitants who, during the siege, had sought refuge in the suburb of St. Roch, had returned after the battle, and there were now 2600 women and children, with about a thousand invalids and other non-combatants to be supported, though the provisions in the town, even at half rations, would hardly last a week. Ramesay had not been informed that a good supply was left in the camps of Beauport; and when he heard at last that it was there, and sent out parties to get it, they found that the Indians and the famished country people had carried it off.

"Despondency," he says again, "was complete; discouragement extreme and universal. Murmurs and complaints against the army that had abandoned us rose to a general outcry. I could not prevent the merchants, all of whom were officers of the town militia, from meeting at the house of M. Daine, the mayor. There they declared for capitulating, and presented me a petition to that effect, signed by M. Daine and all the principal citizens."

Ramesay called a council of war. One officer alone, Fiedmont, captain of artillery, was for reducing the rations still more, and holding out to the last. All the others gave their voices for capitulation. Ramesay might have yielded without dishonor; but he still held out till an event fraught with new hope took place at Jacques-Cartier.

This event was the arrival of Lévis. On the afternoon of the battle Vaudreuil took one rational step; he sent a courier to Montreal to summon that able officer to his aid. Lévis set out at once, reached Jacques-Cartier, and found his worst fears realized. "The great number of fugitives that I began to meet at Three Rivers prepared me for the disorder in which I found the army. I never in my life knew the like of it. They left everything behind in the camp at Beauport; tents, baggage, and kettles."

He spoke his mind freely; loudly blamed the retreat, and urged Vaudreuil to march back with all speed to whence he came. The governor, stiff at ordinary times, but pliant at a crisis, welcomed the firmer mind that decided for him, consented that the troops should return, and wrote afterwards in his despatch to the minister: "I was much charmed to find M. de Lévis disposed to march with the army towards Quebec."

Lévis, on his part, wrote: "The condition in which I found the army, bereft of everything, did not discourage me, because M. de Vaudreuil told me that Quebec was not taken, and that he had left there a sufficiently numerous garrison; I therefore resolved, in order to repair the fault that had been committed, to engage M. de Vaudreuil to march the army back to the relief of the place. I represented to him that this was the only way to prevent the complete defection of the Canadians and Indians; that our knowledge of the country would enable us to approach very near the enemy, whom we knew to be intrenching themselves on the heights of Quebec and constructing batteries to breach the walls; that if we found their army ill posted, we could attack them, or, at any rate, could prolong the siege by throwing men and supplies into the town; and that if we could not save it, we could evacuate and burn it, so that the enemy could not possibly winter there."

Lévis quickly made his presence felt in the military chaos about him. Bigot bestirred himself with his usual vigor to collect provisions; and before the next morning all was ready. Bougainville had taken no part in the retreat, but sturdily held his ground at Cap-Rouge while the fugitive mob swept by him. A hundred of the mounted Canadians who formed part of his command were now sent to Quebec, each with a bag of biscuit across his saddle. They were to circle round to the Beauport side, where there was no enemy, and whence they could cross the St. Charles in canoes to the town. Bougainville followed close with a larger supply. Vaudreuil sent Ramesay a message, revoking his order to surrender if threatened with assault, telling him to hold out to the last, and assuring him that the whole army was coming to his relief. Lévis hastened to be gone; but first he found time to write a few lines to Bourlamaque. "We have had a very great loss, for we have lost M. de Montcalm. I regret him as my general and my friend. I found our army here. It is now on the march to retrieve our fortunes. I can trust you to hold your position; as I have not M. de Montcalm's talents, I look to you to second me and advise me. Put a good face on it. Hide this business as long as you can. I am mounting my horse this moment. Write me all the news."

The army marched that morning 18 September. In the evening it reached St. Augustin; and here it was stopped by the chilling news that Quebec had surrendered.

Utter confusion had reigned in the disheartened garrison. Men deserted hourly, some to the country, and some to the English camp; while Townshend pushed his trenches nearer and nearer to the walls, in spite of the cannonade with which Fiedmont and his artillerymen tried to check them. On the evening of the 17th, the English ships of war moved towards the Lower Town, and a column of troops was seen approaching over the meadows of the St. Charles, as if to storm the Palace Gate. The drums beat the alarm; but the militia refused to fight. Their officers came to Ramesay in a body; declared that they had no mind to sustain an assault; that they knew he had orders against it; that they would carry their guns back to the arsenal; that they were no longer soldiers, but citizens; that if the army had not abandoned them they would fight with as much spirit as ever; but that they would not get themselves killed to no purpose. The town-major Joannès, in a rage, beat two of them with the flat of his sword.

The white flag was raised; Joannès pulled it down, thinking, or pretending to think, that it was raised without authority; but Ramesay presently ordered him to go to the English camp and get what terms he could. He went, through driving rain, to the quarters of Townshend, and, in hope of the promised succor, spun out the negotiation to the utmost, pretended that he had no power to yield certain points demanded, and was at last sent back to confer with Ramesay, under a promise from the English commander that, if Quebec were not given up before eleven o'clock, he would take it by storm. On this Ramesay signed the articles, and Joannès carried them back within the time prescribed. Scarcely had he left the town, when the Canadian horsemen appeared with their sacks of biscuit and a renewed assurance that help was near; but it was too late. Ramesay had surrendered, and would not break his word. He dreaded an assault, which he knew he could not withstand, and he but half believed in the promised succor. "How could I trust it?" he asks. "The army had not dared to face the enemy before he had fortified himself; and could I hope that it would come to attack him in an intrenched camp, defended by a formidable artillery?" Whatever may be thought of his conduct, it was to Vaudreuil, and not to him, that the loss of Quebec was due.

The conditions granted were favorable, for Townshend knew the danger of his position, and was glad to have Quebec on any terms. The troops and sailors of the garrison were to march out of the place with the honors of war, and to be carried to France. The inhabitants were to have protection in person and property, and free exercise of religion.

In the afternoon a company of artillerymen with a field-piece entered the town, and marched to the place of arms, followed by a body of infantry. Detachments took post at all the gates. The British flag was raised on the heights near the top of Mountain Street, and the capital of New France passed into the hands of its hereditary foes. The question remained, should they keep, or destroy it? It was resolved to keep it at every risk. The marines, the grenadiers from Louisbourg, and some of the rangers were to re-embark in the fleet; while the ten battalions, with the artillery and one company of rangers, were to remain behind, bide the Canadian winter, and defend the ruins of Quebec against the efforts of Lévis. Monckton, the oldest brigadier, was disabled by his wound, and could not stay; while Townshend returned home, to parade his laurels and claim more than his share of the honors of victory. The command, therefore, rested with Murray.

The troops were not idle. Levelling their own field-works, repairing the defences of the town, storing provisions sent ashore from the fleet, making fascines, and cutting firewood, busied them through the autumn days bright with sunshine, or dark and chill with premonition of the bitter months to come. Admiral Saunders put off his departure longer than he had once thought possible; and it was past the middle of October when he fired a parting salute, and sailed down the river with his fleet. In it was the ship *Royal William*, carrying the embalmed remains of Wolfe.

Montcalm lay in his soldier's grave before the humble altar of the Ursulines, nevermore to see the home for which he yearned, the wife, mother, and children whom he loved, the olive-trees and chestnut-groves of his beloved Candiac. He slept in peace among triumphant enemies, who respected his memory, though they hardly knew his resting-place. It was left for a fellow-countryman — a colleague and brother-in-arms — to belittle his achievements and blacken his name. The jealous spite of Vaudreuil pursued him even in death. Leaving Lévis to command at Jacques-Cartier, whither the army had again withdrawn, the governor retired to Montreal, whence he wrote a series of despatches to justify himself at the expense of others, and above all of the slain general, against whom his accusations were never so bitter as now, when the lips were cold that could have answered them. First, he threw on Ramesay all the blame of the surrender of Quebec. Then he addressed himself to his chief task, the defamation of his unconscious rival. "The letter that you wrote in cipher, on the 10th of February, to Monsieur the Marquis of Montcalm and me, in common, flattered his self-love to such a degree that, far from seeking conciliation, he did nothing but try to persuade the public that his authority surpassed mine. From the moment of Monsieur de Montcalm's arrival in this colony down to that of his death, he did not cease to sacrifice everything to his boundless ambition. He sowed dissension among the troops, tolerated the most indecent talk against the government, attached to himself the most disreputable persons, used means to corrupt the most virtuous, and, when he could not succeed, became their cruel enemy. He wanted to be Governor-General. He privately flattered with favors and promises of patronage every officer of the colony troops who adopted his ideas. He spared no pains to gain over the people of whatever calling, and persuade them of his attachment; while, either by himself or by means of the troops of the line, he made them bear the most frightful yoke (*le joug le plus affreux*). He defamed honest people, encouraged insubordination, and closed his eyes to the rapine of his soldiers."

This letter was written to Vaudreuil's official superior and confidant, the minister of the marine and colonies. In another letter, written about the same time to the minister of war, who held similar relations to his rival, he declares that he "greatly regretted Monsieur de Montcalm."

His charges are strange ones from a man who was by turns the patron, advocate, and tool of the official villains who cheated the King and plundered the people. Bigot, Cadet, and the rest of the harpies that preyed on Canada looked to Vaudreuil for support, and found it. It was but three or four weeks since he had written to the court in high eulogy of Bigot and effusive praise of Cadet, coupled with the request that a patent of nobility should be given to that notorious public thief. The corruptions which disgraced his government were rife, not only in the civil administration, but also among the officers of the colony troops, over whom he had complete control. They did not, as has been seen already, extend to the officers of the line, who were outside the circle of peculation. It was these who were the habitual associates of Montcalm; and when Vaudreuil charges him with "attaching to himself the most disreputable persons, and using means to corrupt the most virtuous," the true interpretation of his words is that the former were disreputable because they disliked him (the governor), and the latter virtuous because they were his partisans.

Vaudreuil continues thus: "I am in despair, Monseigneur, to be under the necessity of painting you such a portrait after death of Monsieur the Marquis of Montcalm. Though it contains the exact truth, I would have deferred it if his personal hatred to me were alone to be considered; but I feel too deeply the loss of the colony to hide from you the cause of it. I can assure you that if I had been the sole master, Quebec would still belong to the King, and that nothing is so disadvantageous in a colony as a division of authority and the mingling of troops of the line with marine [colony] troops. Thoroughly knowing Monsieur de Montcalm, I did not doubt in the least that unless I condescended to all his wishes, he would succeed in ruining Canada and wrecking all my plans."

He then charges the dead man with losing the battle of Quebec by attacking before he, the governor, arrived to take command; and this, he says, was due to Montcalm's absolute determination to exercise independent authority, without caring whether the colony was saved or lost. "I cannot hide from you, Monseigneur, that if he had had his way in past years Oswego and Fort George [William Henry] would never have been attacked or taken; and he owed the success at Ticonderoga to the orders I had given him." Montcalm, on the other hand, declared at the time that Vaudreuil had ordered him not to risk a battle, and that it was only through his disobedience that Ticonderoga was saved.

Ten days later Vaudreuil wrote again: "I have already had the honor, by my letter written in cipher on the 30th of last month, to give you a sketch of the character of Monsieur the Marquis of Montcalm; but I have just been informed of a stroke so black that I think, Monseigneur, that I should fail in my duty to you if I did not tell you of it." He goes on to say that, a little before his death, and "no doubt in fear of the fate that befell him," Montcalm placed in the hands of Father Roubaud, missionary at St. Francis, two packets of papers containing remarks on the administration of the colony, and especially on the manner in which the military posts were furnished with supplies; that these observations were accompanied by certificates; and that they involved charges against him, the governor, of complicity in peculation. Roubaud, he continues, was to send these papers to France; "but now, Monseigneur, that you are informed about them, I feel no anxiety, and I am sure that the King will receive no impression from them without acquainting himself with their truth or falsity."

Vaudreuil's anxiety was natural; and so was the action of Montcalm in making known to the court the outrageous abuses that threatened the King's service with ruin. His doing so was necessary, both for his own justification and for the public good; and afterwards, when Vaudreuil and others were brought to trial at Paris, and when one of the counsel for the defence charged the late general with slanderously accusing his clients, the court ordered the charge to be struck from the record. The papers the existence of which, if they did exist, so terrified Vaudreuil, have thus far escaped research. But the correspondence of the two rivals with the chiefs of the departments on which they severally depended is in large measure preserved; and while that of the governor is filled with defamation of Montcalm and praise of himself, that of the general is neither egotistic nor abusive. The faults of Montcalm have sufficiently appeared. They were those of an impetuous, excitable, and impatient nature, by no means free from either ambition or vanity; but they were never inconsistent with the character of a man of honor. His impulsive utterances, reported by retainers and sycophants, kept Vaudreuil in a state of chronic rage; and, void as he was of all magnanimity, gnawed with undying jealousy, and mortally in dread of being compromised by the knaveries to which he had lent his countenance, he could not contain himself within the bounds of decency or sense. In another letter he had the baseness to say that Montcalm met his death in trying to escape from the English.

Among the governor's charges are some which cannot be flatly denied. When he accuses his rival of haste and precipitation in attacking the English army, he touches a fair subject of criticism; but, as a whole, he is as false in his detraction of Montcalm as in his praises of Bigot and Cadet.

The letter which Wolfe sent to Pitt a few days before his death, written in what may be called a spirit of resolute despair, and representing success as almost hopeless, filled England with a dejection that found utterance in loud grumblings against the ministry. Horace Walpole wrote the bad news to his friend Mann, ambassador at Florence: "Two days ago came letters from Wolfe, despairing as much as heroes can despair. Quebec is well victualled, Amherst is not arrived, and 15,000 men are encamped to defend it. We have lost many men by the enemy, and some by our friends; that is, we now call our 9000 only 7000. How this little army will get away from a much larger, and in this season, in that country, I don't guess: yes, I do."

Hardly were these lines written when tidings came that Montcalm was defeated, Quebec taken, and Wolfe killed. A flood of mixed emotion swept over England. Even Walpole grew half serious as he sent a packet of newspapers to his friend the ambassador. "You may now give yourself what airs you please. An ambassador is the only man in the world whom bullying becomes. All precedents are on your side: Persians, Greeks, Romans, always insulted their neighbors when they took Quebec. Think how pert the French would have been on such an occasion! What a scene! An army in the night dragging itself up a precipice by stumps of trees to assault a town and attack an enemy strongly intrenched and double in numbers! The King is overwhelmed with addresses on our victories; he will have enough to paper his palace."

When, in soberer mood, he wrote the annals of his time, and turned, not for the better, from the epistolary style to the historical, he thus described the impression made on the English public by the touching and inspiring story of Wolfe's heroism and death: "The incidents of dramatic fiction could not be conducted with more address to lead an audience from despondency to sudden exaltation than accident prepared to excite the passions of a whole people. They despaired, they triumphed, and they wept; for Wolfe had fallen in the hour of victory. Joy, curiosity, astonishment, was painted on every countenance. The more they inquired, the more their admiration rose. Not an incident but was heroic and affecting." England blazed with bonfires. In one spot alone all was dark and silent; for here a widowed mother mourned for a loving and devoted son, and the people forbore to profane her grief with the clamor of their rejoicings.

New England had still more cause of joy than Old, and she filled the land with jubilation. The pulpits resounded with sermons of thanksgiving, some of which were worthy of the occasion that called them forth. Among the rest, Jonathan Mayhew, a young but justly celebrated minister of Boston, pictured with enthusiasm the future greatness of the British-American colonies, with the continent thrown open before them, and foretold that, "with the continued blessing of Heaven, they will become, in another century or two, a mighty empire;" adding in cautious parenthesis, "*I do not mean an independent one.*" He read Wolfe's victory aright, and divined its far-reaching consequence.

Bibliography

Finally, a brief bibliography. First, Parkman's own historical works, apart from his magazine articles:

The California and Oregon Trail. New York: Putnam, 1849. The 3rd ed., 1852, is renamed *Prairie and Rocky Mountain Life; or, the California and Oregon Trail.* The 4th edition, 1872 (Boston, Little, Brown & Company), was renamed *The Oregon Trail,* under which title it has become a classic. Since then there have been dozens of editions in the United States and Great Britain; Parkman wrote a new preface for that of 1892.

The following works, mentioned in the order of publication, constitute the series *France and England in North America;* the Roman numerals indicate their order when the series was completed in 1892: —

VIII. *The History of the Conspiracy of Pontiac.* Boston: C. C. Little and James Brown, and London: Richard Bentley, 1851. In the 6th edition, revised and enlarged, Boston: Little, Brown & Company, 1870, it was renamed *The Conspiracy of Pontiac and the Indian War after the Conquest of Canada,* and enlarged to two volumes. The 10th edition, again revised, appeared in 1893.

I. *Pioneers of France in the New World.* Boston: Little, Brown & Co., 1865. Twenty years later the 23rd or 25th edition, enlarged and revised, with the section on Florida largely rewritten, was published both in Boston and in London.

II. *The Jesuits in North America in the Seventeenth Century.* Boston: Little, Brown & Co., 1867. This does not appear to have been substantially revised in later editions, of which the 33rd appeared in 1894.

III. *The Discovery of the Great West*. Boston: Little, Brown & Co., 1869. The 10th edition, Boston, 1878, revised after publication of the Margry documents, was renamed *La Salle and the Discovery of the Great West*. The 12th edition, 1893, was further revised.

IV. *The Old Régime in Canada*. Boston: Little, Brown & Co., 1874. The 29th edition, 1893; contained 50 additional pages on "The Feudal Chiefs of Acadia," and was the last history that Parkman wrote. The 25th edition was published by Macmillan, London.

V. *Count Frontenac and New France under Louis XIV*. Boston: Little, Brown & Co., 1877. This does not appear to have been substantially revised in later editions, the 28th of which appeared in 1893.

VII. *Montcalm and Wolfe*. Two volumes, Boston: Little, Brown & Co., 1884. The 20th edition appeared in 1893; the 17th, of 1892, was published in London by Macmillan & Co.

VI. *A Half-Century of Conflict*. Two volumes, Boston: Little, Brown & Co., 1892. The author had no opportunity to revise this, the last of his works to be published. The 5th edition, 1894, was published both in Boston and London (Macmillan & Co.).

Besides the editions mentioned above, there were newly dated "editions" too numerous to mention, which were mere reprintings with a few errors corrected.

These volumes include a considerable number of maps, but no illustrations except a frontispiece portrait of one of the principal protagonists. But the several editions of Parkman's complete works, all of which appeared after his death, are liberally illustrated with reproductions of contemporary portraits, and drawings by Howard Pyle, Frederick Remington and others, made expressly for them.

Of the *Complete Works*, Little, Brown and Company published five different editions, all from the same plates. (The "Parkman's Works" in 8 volumes, published in 1880, included only I–V, VIII and *Oregon*.)

1. Champlain Edition, 20 vols., 1897–98, with Introduction by John Fiske. *Jesuits*, *La Salle*, *Old Régime* and *Frontenac* are each in two volumes; *Montcalm* and *Pontiac* each in three.

2. DeLuxe or La Salle Edition, of same date; identical except for different title pages and a more expensive binding.

3. New Library Edition, 13 vols., 1901–02 (also 1909 and later), includes *The Oregon Trail* and the *Life of Parkman* by C. D. Farnham.

Usually bound in green cloth with gold stamping. The other titles return to the same number of volumes as in the original editions.

4. Frontenac Edition, 16 volumes, 1905–07, with the Farnham *Life* as an extra, unnumbered volume; *Montcalm and Wolfe* are again in three, *Jesuits* and *Old Régime* each in two volumes. Various bindings.

5. Centenary Edition, 12 volumes, 1923; the imprint of the latest printing is 1942. Arrangement of volumes is same as in the New Library edition, minus the Farnham *Life*. Bound in blue buckram with white labels.

Translations

By ULRICH BARTHE: —
  La prise de Québec et ses consequences; traduction d'une partie [chapters xxv, xxvii–xxxii] *de l'ouvrage Montcalm and Wolfe.* Quebec: 1908.
By the COUNTESS GÉDÉON DE CLERMONT-TONNÈRE: —
  Les pionniers français dans l'Amérique du Nord. Paris: 1874.
  Les jésuites dans l'Amérique de Nord au xviiᵉ siècle. Paris: 1874.
By FRIEDRICH KAPP: —
  Die Pioniere Frankreichs in der Neuen Welt. Stuttgart: 1875.
  Das Ancien Régime in Canada. Stuttgart: 1876.
  Die Jesuiten in Nord-Amerika in Siebzehnten Jahrhundert. Stuttgart: 1878.

Journals, Letters and Autobiography

HOWARD DOUGHTY, "Parkman's Dark Years: Letters to Mary Dwight Parkman," *Harvard Library Bulletin* IV (1950) 53–85.

ARTHUR MAHEUX, "Ving-huit ans de correspondance [de l'Abbé Casgrain] avec M. Parkman," *Le Canada français* XXIX (1942), 410–14, 493–501, 587–96, 693–700, 789–803, 897–904. Parkman's letters only; Casgrain's replies are still in ms., in the Massachusetts Historical Society.

MASON WADE, ed., *The Journals of Francis Parkman.* 2 vols., New York: Harpers, 1947. The one edition of the Journals, including much of the raw material for the histories and *The Oregon Trail;* almost as fascinating as the histories themselves.

Parkman left two autobiographical fragments. The one of 1868 is printed in 2nd series *Proceedings* Massachusetts Historical Society VIII (1894) 350–60; the other, written ten years or more later, is printed in an appendix to Sedgwick's biography (*see Biographies.*)

Personal Tributes and Memoirs

CHARLES H. FARNHAM, *A Life of Francis Parkman*. Boston: Little, Brown & Co., 1900; also in the New Library Edition of Parkman's *Works*. The author was Parkman's secretary for several years and accompanied him on his last camping trip to Canada. Valuable for details not found elsewhere and for the best bibliography hitherto published; but responsible for the misleading picture of Parkman as "a solitary, often a pathetic, figure, in the silence and shadow of his study."

TRIBUTES BY FRIENDS, and a formal Memoir by OCTAVIUS B. FROTH-INGHAM, are in 2nd Series *Proceedings* Massachusetts Historical Society VIII 362–9, 520–62.

TRIBUTES in *Parkman Centenary Celebration at Montreal, 13th November 1923. McGill University Publications* Series I No. 6, Montreal. Jules Jusserand, Bliss Perry, Ægidius Fauteux and others.

BARRETT WENDELL, "Francis Parkman," *Proceedings* American Academy of Arts and Sciences XXIX (1894) 435–77. The best analysis of his style, with some first-hand impressions of his personality.

EDWARD WHEELWRIGHT, "Memoir of Francis Parkman," *Publications* Colonial Society of Massachusetts I (1895) 304–50. By a friend and classmate.

Biographies and Critiques

VAN WYCK BROOKS, *New England: Indian Summer*. New York: E. P. Dutton & Co. 1940, pp. 169–83.

THE REVEREND HENRI-RAYMOND CASGRAIN, *Francis Parkman*. Québec: C. Darveau, 1872. Also in his *Oeuvres complètes* (Québec 1885).

OTIS A. PEASE, *Parkman's History; the Historian as Literary Artist.*

New Haven: Yale University Press, 1953. A brief but useful analysis of his style.

WILBUR L. SCHRAMM, *Francis Parkman, Representative Selections.* New York: American Book Co., 1938. The 100-page Introduction by the editor is a well-documented biography, and the bibliography supplements Farnham's.

HENRY D. SEDGWICK, *Francis Parkman* in American Men of Letters series. Boston: Houghton, Mifflin Co., 1904. The most detailed account of Parkman's preparation, and excellent on his personality, with long extracts from Journals and Letters.

RICHARD SONDEREGGER, *Francis Parkman.* 41 pp. Mexico, D. F., 1951. A pamphlet in the *Historiadores de América* series published by the Instituto Panaméricano de Geografía e Historia. A good analysis.

MASON WADE, *Francis Parkman, Heroic Historian.* New York: Viking Press, 1942. The best of the biographies.

The Sale of Parkman's Works

Some very erroneous figures have been quoted for the sale of Parkman's works. For instance, Van Wyck Brooks in *The Flowering of New England* p. 500 says that they appeared in "little editions of 700 copies. Only a handful of readers noticed them." That is correct only for the first year of the first edition of *Pontiac.*

The following figures have been supplied by Little, Brown and Company. They are divided into sales through 1893, the year of the author's death, and sales in the years 1894–1953 inclusive. Each title is counted as one copy, whether it is in one, two or three volumes. Sales of the eight-volume "Parkman's Works" of 1880, and of the Champlain and Centenary editions, have been added to those of each title included in that particular set. Sales of the other sets are as follows: —

DeLuxe or La Salle Edition of 20 volumes	144
Frontenac Edition, 16 volumes	5,517
New Library Edition, 13 volumes	1,888
TOTAL	7,549

This figure, therefore, may be added to the sales for each title subsequent to 1893.

Sales for *The Oregon Trail* were 13,514 copies for the years 1873–1893, and 103,279 since 1893, plus the 7,549 copies in the sets. There are no figures for sales prior to 1873, and there have been numerous editions by other publishers since the copyright expired.

Year of Publication		Through 1893	1894–1953	Total
1851	Conspiracy of Pontiac	10,804	31,371	42,175
1865	Pioneers of France	11,352	42,049	53,401
1867	Jesuits in North America	11,753	31,005	42,758
1869	Discovery of the Great West (La Salle)	11,967	49,865	61,832
1874	Old Régime in Canada	12,328	26,501	38,829
1877	Frontenac and New France	11,370	24,829	36,199
1884	Montcalm and Wolfe	9,755	34,458	44,213
1892	Half-Century of Conflict	5,861	25,359	31,220
	Total for France and England	85,190	265,437	350,617

INDEX

Index

ABENAKIS, 27, 120, 274, 286, 344; attacks on New England frontier, 336–339, 361–371
Abercrombie, General James, 434–436, 441, 444–448
Abraham, Heights of, 481–503
Absolutism, 219–220, 266–270
Acadia, 93; ruin of, 131–134; expulsion of French, 21
Agriculture, 228
Ailleboust, Madame d', 248
Aimable, 304–309
Albany. *See* Fort Orange
Algonquins, 25–28, 142–143, 175, 232; at Long Saut, 179–183
Amherst, Major General Jeffrey, 413, 466, 474, 484
Andrews, Charles M., 130*n.*
Annapolis, Nova Scotia, 95, 424
Anse du Foulon, 490–491, 497
Anticosti, 226
Architecture, 194, 243
Argall, Samuel, 128–134
Argenson, Vicomte d', 175, 184
Arkansas Indians, 273, 277–278
Armouchiquois, 99, 110, 120–121
Asticou, 127
Aubry, Nicolas, 95–96

BACCALAOS, 79–80
Barbeau, Dr. Marius, 389*n.*
Barré, Adjutant General Isaac, 497
Basques, 136–139
Beaujeu, Sieur de, 300–310
Beauport, 197, 461, 474, 483–485, 494
Beaupré, 197, 252, 257
Beaver. *See* Fur trade
Begging, 260

Belle, 304–307, 320
Berwick, Maine, 367
Biard, Pierre, 113–133
Bibliography, 519–524
Biencourt, 114–134
Bienville, Le Moyne de, 210
Biggar, H. P., 84*n.*, 91*n.*
Bigot, François, intendant, 462, 514
Bigot, Vincent, 337–340
Blasphemy, 220–221
Bolton, H. E., 305*n.*, 312*n.*, 333*n.*
Bomazeen, 339, 361, 370
Boston, Parkman's homes in, 4, 8; and fisheries, 227; threatened attack on, 342–343
Botwood, Edward, 479*n.*
Bougainville, Comte de, on education, 253–254; on the *habitant*, 263; in 1758–1759 campaigns, 435, 459, 483, 490–500, 506–507, 511
Bourlamaque, Chevalier de, in 1758–1759 campaigns, 435–450, 458–459, 467, 484, 490, 512
Bradstreet, Lieutenant Colonel John, 438·441
Brazos River, 329
Brébeuf, Jean de, 151, 248*n.*
Brew, J. Otis, 59*n.*
Buffalo, 274, 305, 315–316, 321, 327–329

CADILLAC, ANTOINE DE LA MOTHE-, 210, 342; founds Detroit, 351–359
Campbell, Major Duncan, 438, 449
Canada, name of, 72*n.*; government, 211–223; trade and industry, 224–238; character of people, 184–190, 255–265; attacks on New England, 336–344. *See* Population of Canada

Canoes, 32, 147–148
Canseau, Nova Scotia, 402, 405–407
Cap Rouge, 81–83, 198; in 1759 campaign, 492
Cape Ann, 99
Cape Breton Island, 65n., 340
Cape Cod, 99, 105
Cape Diamond, 221
Cape Porpoise, 365
Cape Tourmente, 197, 252
Card-money, 229–230
Carheil, Etienne, 238; and Cadillac, 351–353, 357
Carignan-Salières Regiment, 184–187, 193
Carleton, Colonel Guy, 455, 475
Cartier, Jacques, voyages of, 71–85
Casco Bay, and Treaty, 361–362, 365
Casgrain, Abbé H. R., 21, 226n.; relations with Parkman, 3–7, 9, 16, 521
Casson, Dollier de, 257
Catalogne, engineer, 227–229; report, 206n.
Catholic Church, and Parkman, 12, 20; organization and influence in Canada, 175, 228, 236–254, 259–260, 269
Caughnawaga, Quebec, 383, 389n.
Caughnawagas, 371, 380, 386–388
Cavelier, Abbé Jean, 302–304, 310, 314, 317–319
Cenis, 323–324
Censitaire, 203–205, 218–220
Chambly, Quebec, 382
Chambly, Sieur de, 194
Champigny, intendant, 345–346; on Canadian gentry, 207–208; on agriculture, 228; and Cadillac, 355–356
Champlain, Samuel de, 90–152; voyages: to West Indies, 90–91; of 1603, 92–93; of 1604–1605, 94–101; of 1606, 105–106; of 1608, 136–140; founds Quebec, 135–141; expedition against Iroquois, 142–150; death of, 151–152
Charles V, 78–80
Charlevoix, Father, 264, 337; on French strategy, 366–367
Chatillon, 15–16
Chicago and River, 273, 276
Chickasaws, 276, 288
Chubb, Pasco, 340–342
Churches, 195, 198, 259
Colbert, J. B., interest in Canada, 184–191; letters to intendants, 217

Colorado River, 322–324
Connecticut, in Louisbourg expedition, 395–404, 401, 432
Cortereal, Gaspar, 70
Côte, 195–196, 218
Coton, Father, 112–113, 118
Council, the Supreme, 212–219
Count Frontenac and New France, 19, 520, 524; selections from, 336–350
Couture, Guillaume, 155–159, 164, 169
Currency, 229–230

Dahcotahs, 63n.
Dale, Sir Thomas, 128, 131–133
Dancing, 244
Daulac, Adam, 177–182
De Baugis, Chevalier, 291
De Chastes, Aymer, 91–93
Deerfield, sack of, 371–390
De Monts, Pierre du Guast, 93–112
Denonville, Marquis, on Canadian gentry, 207–208; trade, 225–226; on agriculture, 228; instructions from the Bishop, 243–244; quoted, 207–208, 225–227, 247, 258–261; intrigues of, 337
Detroit, founding of, 351–359; name, 353
DeVoto, Bernard, 335n.
Diamonds of Canada, 82, 85n.
Diseases, 248
Dochet Island, 96n.
Donnaconna, 92–99
Doughty, A. G., 452n.
Douglas, Dr. William, 403, 417
Drinking, 248–249
Duchambon, Chevalier, 408–412, 420–424, 427–428
Dudley, Joseph, 361–368, 386
Duhaut, 329–334
Du Lhut, Greysolon, 210, 235–236, 353
Dupuy, Paul, 253
Durell, Admiral, 456
Durham, New Hampshire, 336n.
Duschesneau, intendant, 217, 235; on Canadian gentry, 207–208; and fisheries, 227
Dustin, Hannah, 343–344
Dutch, in St. Lawrence, 110
Du Thet, Gilbert, 124–125, 129
Duval, 139–140

Education, 251–254, 262–264
Etchemins, 27, 99

FALMOUTH, Maine, 365
Family life, 193, 100–110
Fauteux, Ægidius, on Parkman, x
Feudalism, 193
Fisheries, 66, 86, 226–227
Fiske, John, on Parkman, 24
Five Nations, 142, 150, 153, 353, 359, 367; names of, 41*n.*, 44
Fort on the Illinois, 274
Fort Carillon. *See* Ticonderoga
Fort Frontenac, 274, 287, 357; seized, 290
Fort Miami, 274–276
Fort Orange, 123*n.*, 153, 162–166, 170
Fort Prudhomme, 276, 284
Fort William Henry, 436, 515
Francis I, 67, 70–71, 78
Franklin, Benjamin, 394
Frenchman's Bay, 126
Frontenac, Comte de, 245, 273, 287, 343; death and character of, 345–350
Fur trade, 86–93, 209, 221–222, 230–238, 352–359

GASPÉ PENINSULA, 71
Gentry of Canada, 206–210
George II, 455
Gill family, 390
Gipson, L. H., 452*n.*, 486*n.*, 489*n.*
Gloucester, 105
Goupil, René, 155–160, 248*n.*
Governor-general, 211–212, 221–222
Green Bay, 272–273, 389
Griffin, 273, 289
Guercheville, Mme. de, 115–126, 132–134
Guion, Jean, 201–202

Habitants, 201–214, 228, 232–234, 253, 263, 268
Hale, Richard W., 130*n.*
Half-Century, 19, 23, 520, 524; selections from, 351–437
Hampton, New Hampshire, 367
Harding, Stephen, 364–365
Haverhill, 343–344, 367
Henry IV, 88–90, 112–115
Heresy, 247
Hiawatha, 57–58
Hochelaga, 72–76
Holmes, Rear Admiral Charles, 483, 489–490, 496
Honfleur, 92, 125, 136

Horse raising, 218–219
Horticulture, 5, 18, 22–23
"Hot Stuff," 480*n.*
Housing, 194
Howe, Brigadier Lord (George Augustus), 436–441
Howe, Colonel William, 494, 498
Hundred Associates, 150, 200
Huron-Iroquois Family, 38–44, 351
Hurons, 28–38, 42–44, 49, 59–61, 142–143, 150–154, 351, 357; mission, 154; at Long Saut, 179–183

IBERVILLE, PIERRE LE MOYNE D', 210, 340–341
Illinois River and country, 273, 276, 284–291
Indians, Parkman's general description of, 25–64; social and political organization, 41–44; religion, 52–64; defensive works, 145; in Quebec campaign, 470–475, 482, 499. *See* names of tribes
Indian captivities, 339–340, 366–368
Intendant, 211–219, 227
Iroquois, 26, 40–52, 142; fight with Champlain, 147–150; attacks on Hurons and French, 153–156, 175–183; at Long Saut, 180–183; invade Illinois country, 286–291; deed to England, 359

JAMAICA PLAIN, 4–5, 17–18, 22–24
Jervis, Commander John, 495
Jesuits, as observers of Indians, 59*n.*; and Poutrincourt, 112–134; and Port Royal colony, 119–125; theory of torture, 176; college, 250; and La Salle, 271; and Cadillac, 352–358; and Williams, 383–386
Jesuits in North America, 19, 519, 524; selections from, 25–64, 153–173
Jogues, Isaac, prisoner of Mohawks, 154–164; escape, 163–167; martyrdom, 169–173; canonized, 248*n.*
Johnstone, Chevalier, 470, 479, 505–506
Joliet, Louis, 226, 272–273
Joly, 300–310
Jonas, 103–105, 108–111, 125
Joutel, Henri, 301–335; map, 275; on La Salle, 332
Judicial system, 213–217

KALM, PETER, 263–264

Kankakee River, 273–274, 286
Kennebec River, 120, 361, 367
King, power of in Canada, 211–223.
    See Louis XIV
King William's War, 336–344
Kittery Point, Maine, 395–397
Knox, Captain John, 452; on Quebec
    campaign, 463–492

LA BARRE, LEFEBVRE DE, 257–258; and
    La Salle, 287–291
Labrador, 79n.
La Chine, 198, 272
La Forest, 290, 300
La Hêve, 94, 126
La Hontan, 221, 224; quoted, 187–189,
    214–215, 245–246, 260–262
Lake Champlain, 146–149, 153, 156, 382,
    435–451
Lake George, 147, 156; names of, 157n.,
    170; in Ticonderoga campaign, 434–
    436, 444–448
Lake Michigan, 272–274
Lake Peoria, 276
Lake St. Louis, 198
Lake of St. Peter, 143, 154–155
Lake Superior, 272
Lalande, Jean de, 171–173, 248n.
Land system, 193–199, 205
L'Archevêque, 327–329, 334–335
La Roche, Marquis de, 87–89
La Salle, Robert Cavelier de, 198, 210;
    on Jesuits, 246, 271; early career, 271–
    274, 292–298; voyage down Missis-
    sippi, 274–282; illness, 283, 301–303;
    object, 284; at Fort St. Louis, 285–
    291; character of, 292–299, 332–333;
    voyage to Gulf, 300–306; explores
    Texas, 314–329; murdered, 332
La Salle, 20, 520, 524; selections from,
    274–335
La Saussaye, 125–130
Lavaca River, 312–314
Laval, Bishop, 184–185, 240–241, 245,
    251–253
Le Ber, Jeanne, 248–250
Le Moyne family, 178, 210. See Bien-
    ville, Iberville
Léry, Baron de, 67, 88
Lescarbot, Marc, 101–112
Lévis, Chevalier de, 434–435, 446–450;
    in 1759 campaign, 469–470, 478, 484,
    511–513

Little Harbor, New Hampshire, 18, 22,
    396
Log cabins, 194n.
Long Saut, Heroes of the, 174–183
Louis XIV, 200, 213, 220, 223, 247; in-
    terest in Canada, 184–196, 208–209,
    214, 217–218, 221, 226–227, 235, 251,
    260, 287n., 290, 300; and Church, 239–
    253
Louisbourg, first siege and capture of,
    391–433; description and map, 407–
    409; 2nd siege of, 454–457
Louisiana, La Salle in, 278–283
Lyman, Caleb, 368

MAINE, EXPLORATION OF, 98; in 1702–
    1704, 360–369; in Louisbourg expedi-
    tion, 400
Maintenon, Madame de, 223, 247
Maisonneuve, Governor, 177–178
Mal (Murray) Bay, 196, 226
Mallebarre, 99
Manabozho, 55–58
Manhattan Island, 123n., 165–166
Manufacturing, 228
Margry, Pierre, 20, 23, 305n.
Marguerite, 82–83
Marie de l'Incarnation, 197; on emi-
    grants, 185–190; on housing, 194n.;
    on marriage and family life, 184–191,
    199; on witchcraft, 248
Marquette, Jacques, 272–273
Massachusetts, in King William's War,
    337–342; in Louisbourg expedition,
    392–433; Navy, 401
Massachusetts Indians, 99
Matagorda Bay and Island, 305–312
Mather, Cotton, 368
Matinicus Island, 391–392
Mayhew, Jonathan, 517
Megapolensis, Dominie, 162, 165
Membertou, 105, 108–110, 113–114, 121
Membré, Zenobe, 276–279, 284, 321
Merchants, 225, 230, 232–234
Mexico, Gulf of, 273, 280–281, 284; La
    Salle's voyage to, 304–309
Miamis, 286–290
Michilimackinac, 236–238, 272–273, 283–
    284, 288; supplanted by Detroit, 351–
    354, 357
Micmacs, 27, 99, 122, 340
Mills, 195

Mississippi River, Joliet on, 273; La Salle on, 274–282

Missouri River, 276

Mohawks, 198; attacks on Hurons and French, 153–156; towns, 158*n.*; and Jogues, 154–164, 169–173

Mohegans, 274

Monckton, Brigadier Robert, 456–476, 485, 489, 493–506, 513

Montagnais, 27, 137, 140, 143, 149, 196

Montcalm, Marquis de, and defense of Ticonderoga, 434–451; in 1759 campaign, 462–516; last letter of, 490; death, 509; character of, 516

Montcalm and Wolfe, 19, 21, 424, 520; selections from, 434–518

Montmorenci, Wolfe's landing at, 471, 477–480, 486, 489

Montreal, 74–76, 93; settlement of, 193; in 1670, 198; fair at, 231; life in, 256–257; Kalm on, 263

Moody, Samuel, 398–399, 406, 429

Morals and manners, 255–265

Moranget, 309–310, 319, 327–329; death of, 330–332

Morel, Father, 241–242

Morgan, L. H., 25, 44*n.*

Mount Desert Island, 98, 106; attempted colony, 125–132

Murray, Brigadier James, 456, 483–485, 489, 493, 498, 513

Natchez, 279–280

Nauset, 99–100

Neches River, 324

Negro slavery, 262

Nesmond, Marquis de, 342–343

Neutral Nation, 39, 60

Newcastle, Duke of, 455

New England, Indians of, 26; compared with Canada, 266–270; Canadian attacks on, 336–344

Newfoundland, discovery of, 65*n.*; fisheries, 66, 86

New Hampshire, in Louisbourg expedition, 394, 401, 432

New Harbor, 341

New York, relations with Canada, 338

Nipissings, 28

Noblesse, 190, 205–208, 253

Noël, Jean, 202

Norumbega, 79*n.*, 98

Ohio River, 272

Ojibwas, 154, 272

Old Régime, 19–20, 23, 520, 524; selections from, 174–270

Oregon Trail, 15, 519, 523

Orleans, Island of, 197, 464

Ottawas, 351, 357

Oudiette, 231–233

Oyster River, 336–337

Parish priest, life of a, 241–243

Parkman, Francis, life and character of, 3–24; autobiographies, 522; bibliography and sales, 519–524

Pass Cavallo, 305*n.*

Passamaquoddy, 93*n.*, 95

Paternalism, 218–220, 224–229, 266–270

Payne, John, 404

Pell, Stephen H. P., 445*n.*

Pemaquid, 337; capture of, 340–343

Pemigewasset River, 237*n.*

Pepperrell, William, 396–433

Pequawkets, 361, 368

Pioneers of France, 18, 519, 524; selections from, 65–152

Pitt, William, 455, 486–489

Plaisted, Elisha, 369–370

Plymouth, Champlain at, 99

Pocahontas, 128

Pointe aux Trembles, 198, 475, 483, 491, 493*n.*

Pomeroy, Seth, 405–407, 411–413

Pontchartrain, 230, 234, 339, 356–358

Pontgravé the elder, 89–95, 98, 136–140; voyage of 1609, 142

Pontgravé the son, 120

Pontiac, 13–14, 17, 519, 524

Population of Canada in 1617, 150; 1641, 153; 1640–1660, 174; 1666–1668, 185*n.*, 197*n.*; 1682, 257; eighteenth century, 191*n.*, 257

Port Mouton, 94

Port Royal, 95–97, 100–114; Jesuits at, 119–125; destroyed and rebuilt, 132–134

Portsmouth, New Hampshire, 394–396*n.*

Portuguese, 25*n.*, 79*n.*

Poutrincourt, Baron de, 94–97; at Port Royal, 102–111; and Jesuits, 112–134

Prairie du Chien, 273

Priests, and people, 239–254; instigate attacks, 338–339

Prout's Neck, 99

Public meetings, 219, 230
Punishments, 220–221, 235
Puritanism in Canada, 243–247
Putnam, Israel, 440

QUAPAWS, 278n.
Quebec, the name, 138n.; discovery and
founding, 73, 135–141, 195–198; capital, 212; education, 250–251; life in,
260–261, 264–265; siege and capture
of, 458–517; map, 473
Queen Anne's War, 360–389
Quentin, Father, 125, 132–133

RAMESAY, CHEVALIER DE, 461, 509–513
Récollets, 247, 310, 314, 321; and Fron-
tenac, 345–350; and Cadillac, 354–356
Rhode Island, in Louisbourg expedi-
tion, 394–395, 401, 432
Richelieu, Cardinal, 150–151, 200
Richelieu River, 143, 153, 156, 193–194
Roberval, Sieur de, 78–84
Rogers, Captain Robert, 438–440
Roosevelt, Theodore, compared with
Parkman, 10–11; letter from, 390n.
Rouville, Hertel de, 371–374, 378
Royal Americans, 479

SABLE ISLAND, 87–89
Saco Bay, 98–99
Saguenay, River and "Kingdom," 72,
85n.
St. Anne de Beaupré, 177, 252
Saint-Castin, 337–343, 362
St. Croix, winter at, 96–101; destroyed,
132
St. Domingo, 301–304
St. Joachim, 252; battle near, 482
St. John River, 95, 120–121
St. Joseph-Kankakee portage, 273–274
St. Lawrence River and Gulf, explora-
tion of, 72–85; Dutch at, 110; descrip-
tion of, in 1670, 196–199
St. Louis of the Illinois, 274, 285–291
St. Louis of Texas, 312–335
Saint-Lusson, Daumont de, 273
St. Malo, 71–72, 87
St. Mary's Bay, 95–96
St. Regis, Bell of, 389n.
St. Sauveur, 126–127
Saint-Villier, Bishop, 240–245
Saints, 248n.
Samos, 490, 496

Sault Ste. Marie, 154, 272–273
Saunders, Vice Admiral Charles, 456,
486, 489, 494, 513
Schoolcraft, H. R., Parkman's dim view
of, 59n.
Schuyler, Peter, 373
Scots Highlanders, at Ticonderoga, 438,
449; in 1759 campaign, 478, 496, 500
Seignelay, Marquis de, 289, 302
Seigneurial system, 193–210, 218–220,
262
Shawnees, 286–288
Sheldon, Ensign John, 372, 375–377,
386–388
Sherburn, Captain Joseph, 415–416
Shipbuilding, 229
Shirley, William, 391–402
Shopkeepers, 209
Sioux, 15, 236, 272
Sparhawk, Nathaniel, 419, 429
Stadaconé, 73, 77
Starved Rock, 273, 285–291
Stebbins, Benoni, 372, 375–376
Stobo, Major Robert, 491
Storer family, 365
Sulpitians, 184–186, 193, 198, 246, 258,
272

TADOUSSAC, 27, 89, 95, 136–139, 142, 150,
196, 231
Taensas, 278–280
Talon, Jean, 185, 189–196, 201, 225, 256,
273
Taxation, 230–231
Texas, the name, 335n.; La Salle in, 281,
305–333; Spain takes over, 334–335
Theatricals, 244, 250
Thevet, André, 66, 82–85
Three Rivers, 153–154, 198, 212–213,
232, 259
Thury, Pierre, 336–340
Ticonderoga, 147, 157; campaign, 434–
451; map and description, 442–445; in
1759 campaign, 466–467, 474; cap-
tured by Amherst, 484
Tionnontates, 38, 44
Tobacco Nation, 38, 154
Tonty, Alphonse de, 356
Tonty, Henri de, 274–291, 297, 332–333
Torture, among Indians, 36, 175–176;
French, 221, 256
Townshend, Brigadier George, 456,
485, 489, 493n., 507–512; criticizes

Wolfe, 497n.; Quebec surrendered to, 513
Tracy, Marquis de, 184, 198, 201, 206–207
Trade and industry, 224–238
Trout Brook, action at, 439–441
Tuscaroras, 51
Tyng, Captain Edward, 401

Vassal Morton, 17
Vaudreuil, Chevalier de, 362, 366; and Deerfield, 371, 378, 383, 386–387
Vaudreuil, Marquis de, 434–435; defense of Canada, 458–516; abandons Quebec, 508; jealous spite, 514–516
Vaughan, William, 391–420
Verrazano, Giovanni, 67–71
Vicksburg, 278
Villebon, Governor, 336–340
Virginia, 128, 131

Wade, Mason, Francis Parkman, 523
Waldo, Brigadier, 402, 411, 421
Walpole, Horace, 456, 517
Wampum, 32, 48
Warren, Commodore Peter, 401–432

Wells, John, 386
Wells, Jonathan, 372, 375–378
Wells, Maine, 362–365, 368–369, 400
Wendell, Barrett, quoted, 13
Wentworth, Benning, 394–396
West, exploration of the, 209–210, 272–335, 351–359
West India Company, 231, 234
West Indies, trade with the, 225, 233
Whitefield, George, 398
Williams, Eleazer, 389
Williams, Eunice, 388–389
Williams, John, 372–374; captivity, 378–389
Winooski River, 381–382
Winter Harbor, 365–366
Wisconsin River, 273
Witchcraft, 248
Wolcott, Roger, 395, 401–402, 412, 421
Wolf Indian, 175–176
Wolfe, General James, 436, 452–502; his brigadiers' plans, 485; final plan, 488–489, 492–493; feint on Cap-Rouge, 492; quotes Gray's "Elegy," 496; at Plains of Abraham, 501–502

York, Maine, 363, 367, 399

Other titles of interest

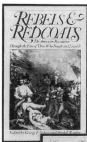
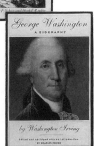